The Average Consumer in Confusion-based
Disputes in European Trademark Law and Similar
Fictions

Rasmus Dalgaard Laustsen

The Average Consumer in Confusion-based Disputes in European Trademark Law and Similar Fictions

Springer

Rasmus Dalgaard Laustsen (iD)
IPR & Compliance, Group Legal
Grundfos Holding A/S
Bjerringbro, Denmark

ISBN 978-3-030-26349-2   ISBN 978-3-030-26350-8   (eBook)
https://doi.org/10.1007/978-3-030-26350-8

This Springer imprint is published by the registered company Springer Nature Switzerland AG.
The registered company address is: Gewerbestrasse 11, 6330 Cham, Switzerland

Preface

A verse of a song by the Icelandic singer Björk goes: *"If you ever get close to a human, And human behavior, Be ready, be ready to get confused, And me and my hereafter, There's definitely, definitely, definitely no logic, To human behavior, But yet so, yet so irresistible".*[1] In many ways, this verse captures this project on the average consumer in European trademark law.

Some years back as a student, I first encountered trademark law as part of an inspiring trademark law course at the University of Manchester taught by Professor Andrew Griffiths. Back then, I was puzzled when I encountered the average consumer and its characteristics, "reasonably well-informed and reasonably observant and circumspect". I am still in some ways puzzled, but more profoundly.

At the early stage of this project in 2013/2014, my initial interest was the average consumer with a more narrow focus on the online environment. I soon realised, though, that there was much more to be gained from taking a more general approach to the analysis since the contemporary scholarly analysis of this area of law was surprisingly untouched.

It has been a fruitful and challenging experience to conduct this project. In a broader perspective, the average consumer is law's way of trying to fit its own logic to an at times illogical human behaviour. Due to centrality of the topic to European trademark law, this project has given me (and hopefully will give the reader) some valuable insight into the key infrastructure of trademark law and this area of law in a broader scientific perspective. The approach of this book is one among many ways to analyse the average consumer in European trademark law since this topic has threads into broader trademark law, law in general and into other areas of social science.

This book builds on my PhD thesis successfully defended 2 June 2017 at Aarhus University, the Department of Law. As part of turning the PhD thesis into a book, the content has been updated until 31 July 2018. Some more recent updates have been made though, most importantly on the implementation of the TM Directive into new

---

[1]Björk, *Human Behaviour*, no 1 on 'Debut' (Elektra Records, 1993).

national trademark acts in the UK, Sweden and Denmark. After the most recent updates of this book, it is surely possible to find relevant sources. That said, I will claim that the main points of this book remain unchanged for some time since they are rooted in legal theory, the nature of EU law, inherent differences between the included jurisdictions and the finding that the average consumer in EU law is rooted in historical EU case law and *Sabel, Gut Springenheide* and *Lloyd* from 1997 to 1999. I am naturally the sole responsible person for the structure and content of my book, but I owe many people my acknowledgement.

Bjerringbro, Denmark   Rasmus Dalgaard Laustsen

Acknowledgements

I am thankful to my PhD supervisor Tine Sommer (Professor at Aarhus University, Department of Law) for her encouragements and invaluable inputs. From Aarhus University, I am also grateful for the encouragements and assistance by many of my previous colleagues, in particular Cita Dyveke Kristensen (PhD Secretary) and Viktoria Obolevich (Research Assistant, PhD), and the AU Library staff. I want to thank the committee of my PhD defence for the challenges and assessment, i.e. chairman Palle Bo Madsen (Professor at Aarhus University, Department of Law), Jens Hemmingsen Schovsbo (Professor at Centre for Information and Innovation Law, University of Copenhagen) and Katja Lindroos (Weckström) (Professor at University of Eastern Finland Law School).

During my visiting research stay at William & Mary Law School in the US in the spring semester of 2016, I benefitted from the professional and personal hospitality of many researchers and staff members. I am especially grateful for my sparring with Laura Heyman (Chancellor Professor of Law). In the US, I also had the joy of discussing my project with James Gibson (Professor at the School of Law at the University of Richmond) and Olena Zhylinkova (Assistant Professor at Kharkiv National University).

I have been fortunate to participate in three network meetings held by the Nordic/German Intellectual Property Network. I presented my project at University of Lapland in April 2015. This network has given me feedback on my project and introduced me to a unique and thriving Nordic/German IP community.

I will like to thank Dreyers Fond for financially supporting the publication of this book.

On a private level, owing to this project, I have been nothing more than averagely attentive for a long time. I am grateful for my partner, Helle, and my family for their support in this project and that they continuously have tried to ensure my connection to "real life".

Bjerringbro, Denmark   Rasmus Dalgaard Laustsen
16 June 2019

Contents

Abbreviations

International and European (Non-EU)

DCFR	von Bar, Christian et al (eds.), 'Principles, Definitions and Model Rules of European Private Law - Draft Common Frame of Reference (DCFR) Outline Edition', (1st edn, Sellier European Law Publishers, 2009)
EEA	The European Economic Area
EEA Agreement	Agreement on the European Economic Area Final Act, of 3 March 1994, [1994], OJ L 1
EFTA	European Free Trade Association
EPC	European Patent Convention 16th edition of June 2016
EPC Protocol	Protocol on the Interpretation of Article 69 EPC of 5 October 1973 as revised by the Act revising the EPC of 29 November 2001
EPO	European Patent Office
EPO Case Law	Case Law of the Boards of Appeal of the European Patent Office 8th Edition of July 2016
EPO Case Law Supplement	Supplement to the EPO Case Law published in Supplementary publication 3, Official Journal EPO 2018
EPO Guidelines	Guidelines for Examination in the European Patent Office of November 2017
Nice Agreement	Nice Agreement Concerning the International Classification of Goods and Services for the Purposes of the Registration of Marks 11th edition, version 2019, entering into force 1 January 2019
Nice Classification	Classification system for goods and services set out in the Nice Agreement

Paris Convention	Paris Convention for the Protection of Industrial Property of March 20 1883, as most recently amended on 28 September 1979
PETL	European Group on Tort Law, Principles of European Tort Law, of May 2005
TRIPS	Trade-Related Aspects of Intellectual Property Rights
TRIPS Agreement	Agreement on Trade-Related Aspects of Intellectual Property Rights of 15 April 1994
WIPO	World Intellectual Property Organization
WIPO Recommendations	WIPO Joint Recommendation Concerning Provisions on the Protection of Well-Known Marks adopted by the Assembly of the Paris Union for the Protection of Industrial Property and the General Assembly of WIPO at the Thirty-Fourth Series of Meetings of the Assemblies of the Member States of WIPO September 20 to 29 1999
WTO	World Trade Organisation
WTO Agreement	The Agreement establishing the World Trade Organisation of 15 April 1994

European Union ("EU")

Agreement on the Patent Court	Council Agreement on a Unified Patent Court (2013/C 175/01) of 20 June 2013, [2013] OJ C 175/1
Amsterdam Treaty	Treaty of Amsterdam, [1997], OJ C340/01
CJEU	Court of Justice of the European Union
Design Directive	EP and Council Directive 98/71/EC of 13 October 1998 on the legal protection of designs, [1998] OJ L 289/28
Design Green Paper	Commission Green Paper on the legal protection of industrial design No 111/51311/91 of June 1991
Design Regulation	Council Regulation (EC) No 6/2002 of 12 December 2001 on Community designs, [2002] OJ L 3/1
Design Regulation Proposal	Commission Proposal for a European Parliament and Council Regulation on the Community Design COM(93) 342 final-COD 463 of 3 December 1993
EEC	European Economic Community
EEC Treaty	Treaty of Rome of 25 March 1957 establishing the European Economic Community

EESC	European Economic and Social Committee
EESC TM Opinion 2013	Opinion of the European Economic and Social Committee on the 'Proposal for a Directive of the European Parliament and of the Council to approximate the laws of the Member States relating to trade marks' of 12 November 2013, COM(2013) 162 final—2013/0089 (COD), [2013] OJ C 327/09
Egg Regulation	Council Regulation (EEC) No 1907/90 of 26 June 1990 on certain marketing standards for eggs, [1990] OJ L173
EU Charter	Charter of Fundamental Rights of the European Union, [2012] OJ C 326/391
EU Commission	European Commission
EU Constitutional Treaty	Treaty Establishing a Constitution for Europe [2004]
EU design legislation	Design Regulation and Design Directive
EUIPO	European Union Intellectual Property Office
EUIPO TM Guidelines	The EUIPO Guidelines for Examination of European Union Trade Marks, Final Version 1.0 of 1 October 2017
EU Parliament	European Parliament
EU Patent Package	Unitary Patent Regulation, Patent Translations Regulation and Agreement on the Patent Court
EU trademark legislation	Trademark Regulation and Trademark Directive
Lisbon Treaty	Treaty of Lisbon amending the Treaty on European Union and the Treaty Establishing the European Community of 13 December 2007, [2007] OJ C 306/01
Max Planck TM Report	Study on the Overall Functioning of the European Trade Mark System presented by Max Planck Institute for Intellectual Property and Competition Law Munich 15 February 2011
Medical Product Directive 1965	Council Directive of 26 January 1965 on the approximation of provisions laid down by law, regulation or administrative action relating to proprietary medicinal products (65/65/EEC), [1965] OJ 369/65
MEQR	Measures having equivalent effect as quantitative restrictions on imports
Nice Treaty	Treaty of Nice, [2002] OJ C 325/01
OHIM	Office for Harmonization in the Internal Market

Patent Translations Regulation	Council Regulation (EU) No 1260/2012 of 17 December 2012 implementing enhanced cooperation in the area of the creation of unitary patent protection with regard to the applicable translation arrangements, [2012] OJ L361/89
Service Directive	EP and Council directive (EC) No 2006/123 of 12 December 2006 on services of the Internal Market
Single European Act	Single European Act, of 28 February 1987, [1987] OJ L 169/1
Statute of the CJEU	TEU Protocol (No 3) on the Statute of the Court of Justice of the European Union
TEU	Treaty of European Union (consolidated version), [2012] OJ C 326/13
TEU Pre-Lisbon	Treaty on the European Union (consolidated version), [2006] OJ C 321 E/5
TFEU	Treaty on the Functioning of the European Union (consolidated version), [2012] OJ C 326/47
TFEU Pre-Lisbon	Treaty Establishing the European Community (consolidated version), [2006] OJ C 321 E/37
TM Amendment Regulation	EP and Council Regulation (EU) 2015/2424 of 16 December 2015 amending Council Regulation (EC) No 207/2009 on the Community trade mark and Commission Regulation (EC) No 2868/95 implementing Council Regulation (EC) No 40/94 on the Community trade mark, and repealing Commission Regulation (EC) No 2869/95 on the fees payable to the Office for Harmonization in the Internal Market (Trade Marks and Designs), [2015] OJ L 341/21
TM Directive	EP and Council Directive (EU) No 2015/2436 of 16 December 2015 to approximate the laws of the Member States relating to trade marks (Recast), [2015] OJ L 336/1
TM Directive 1989	First Council Directive of 21 December 1988 to approximate the laws of the Member States relating to trade marks (89/104/EEC), [1989] OJ L 40/1
TM Directive 2008	EP and Council Directive 2008/95/EC of 22 October 2008 to approximate the laws of the Member States relating to trade marks (Codified version), [2008] OJ L 299/25

TM Directive Proposal 1980

Commission Proposal for a first Council Directive to approximate the laws of the Member States relating to trade marks of 31 December 1980, [1980] OJ C 351/1

TM Memorandum 1976

Commission Memorandum on the creation of an EEC trade mark adopted by the Commission on 6 July 1976, [1976] Bulletin of the European Communities Supplement 8/76

TM Regulation

European Parliament and Council Regulation (EU) 2017/1001 of 14 June 2017 on the European Union trade mark (codification), OJ L 154/3

TM Regulation 1994

Council Regulation (EC) No 40/94 of 20 December 1993 on the Community trade Mark, [1994] OJ L 11 / 1

TM Regulation 2009

Council Regulation (EC) No 207/2009 of 26 February 2009 on the Community trade mark (codified version), [2009] OJ L 78/1

UCPD

EP and Council Directive 2005/29/EC of 11 May 2005 concerning unfair business-to-consumer commercial practices in the internal market and amending Council Directive 84/450/EEC, Directives 97/7/EC, 98/27/EC and 2002/65/EC of the European Parliament and of the Council and Regulation (EC) No 2006/2004 of the European Parliament and of the Council (Unfair Commercial Practices Directive'), [2005] OJ

UCPD Working Paper 2003

Commission Staff Working Paper Extended Impact Assessment on the EP and Council Directive concerning unfair business-to-consumer commercial practices in the Internal Market and amending directives 84/450/EEC, 97/7/EC and 98/27/EC (the Unfair Commercial Practices Directive) of 18 June 2003, COM (2003)356 final

UCPD Working Paper 2016

Commission Staff Working Document Guidance on the Implementation/Application of Directive 2005/29/EC on Unfair Commercial Practices Accompanying the document Communication From the Commission to the European Parliament, the Council, the European Economic and Social Committee and the Regions - A comprehensive approach to

Unitary Patent Regulation	stimulating cross-border e-Commerce for Europe's citizens and businesses (COM(2016) 320 final) of 25 May 2016 SWD(2016) 163 final EP and Council Regulation (EU) No 1257/2012 of 17 December 2012 implementing enhanced cooperation in the area of the creation of unitary patent protection, [2012] OJ L361/1

United Kingdom ("UK")

Interflora Court of Justice	Interflora v. Marks & Spencer, Case C-323/09, [2011] ECR I-8625
Interflora EWCA I	Interflora v. Marks & Spencer, [2012] EWCA Civ 1501
Interflora EWCA III	Interflora v. Marks & Spencer, [2014] EWCA Civ 1403
Interflora EWHC	Interflora v. Marks & Spencer, [2013] EWHC 1291 (Ch)
OFT	Office of Fair Trading
UK Court of Appeal ("EWCA")	Court of Appeal of England and Wales
UK High Court ("EWHC")	High Court of England and Wales
UKIPO	UK Intellectual Property Office
UKSC	UK Supreme Court
UK TM Act 1938	Trade Marks Act 1938 (C. 22)
UK TM Act 1994	Trade Marks Act 1994 (consolidated version) (C.26)
UK TM White Paper	Reform of Trade Marks Law, [1990] (Cm 1203)

Nordic

1882 Nordic TM Proposal	Motiver til det af de Svensk-Norsk-Dansk kommitterede Forslag til Lov om beskyttelse af Varemærker of 12 August 1882

Sweden ("SE")

SE Court of Appeal ("SECA")	Svea Hovrätt
SE District Court ("SEDC")	Stockholms Tingsrätt
SE Supreme Court ("SESC")	Högsta Domstolen
SE TM Act 1960	Varumärkeslagen, No 644 of 2 December 1960
SE TM Act 2010	Varumärkeslagen, SFS 2010:1877 of 9 December 2010

| SE TM Prop. 2009/10:225 | Regeringens proposition 2009/10:225 Ny varumärkeslag och ändringar i firmalagen, of 3 June 2010 |
| SE TM Prop. 2018/18:267 | Regeringens proposition 2017/18:267 Modernare regler om varumärken och en ny lag om företagsnamn, of 7 June 2018. The amendments are implemented into the consolidated Lag om ändring i varumärkeslagen (2010:1877), SFS 2018:1652 of 15 November 2018. |

Denmark ("DK")

DK Court of Appeal ("DKCA")	Vestre Landsret and Østre Landsret
DK Maritime and Commercial High Court ("DK MCH Court/DKMCHC")	Sø-og Handelsretten
DK Supreme Court ("DKSC")	Højesteret
DK TM Act 1890	Varemærkeloven, Act. No 52 of 17 April 1890
DK TM Act 1959	Varemærkelov, Act. No 211 of 11 June 1959
DK TM Act 1991	Varemærkelov, Act No 341 of 6 June 1991
DK TM Bet. 199/1958	Betænkning vedrørende en ny dansk varemærkelov, No 199 of 18 April 1958
UfR	Ugeskrift for Retsvæsen

Norway ("NO")

NO Court of Appeal ("NOCA")	Borgarting Lagmannsrett
NO District Court ("NODC")	Oslo Tingsrett
NO Supreme Court ("NOSC")	Høyesterett
NO TM Act 1961	Varemerkeloven, Act No 4 of 3 March 1961
NO TM Act 2010	Varemerkeloven, Act No 8 of 26 March 2010, as most recently changed by Act No 65 of 19 June 2015

Other

B2B	Business-to-business
B2C	Business-to-consumer
FMCG	Fast-moving consumer goods

Part I
The Average Consumer: A Consumer Fiction in European Trademark Law

Chapter 1
Background

1.1 Introduction

It is presumably rare to find that a part of a well-established legal protection system was, until recently, almost overlooked in the literature. It is presumably rarer to still find that such an underpinning is not mentioned at all in the relevant legislation. The "average consumer" in European trademark law is one such finding, and it provides the subject for this analysis. Essentially, the average consumer in European trademark law is a way for the law to single out a population group, for solving various issues. One issue is the determination of alleged confusion involving identical or similar trademarks for identical or similar products.

It emerges from the wording of the regulation (EU) 2017/1001 (the "TM Regulation")[1] and the directive (EU) 2015/2436 (the "TM Directive")[2] that to find infringement between two confusingly similar trademarks "a likelihood of confusion" must exist "on the part of the public." The EU legislature has left a gap for the European judiciaries to define, what is the relevant "part of the public"? The legislature has thus clarified that there is a difference between the public as a whole and different parts of the public. The (EU) Court of Justice has introduced the average consumer to fill this gap and as a key representative of the "part of the public."[3] Although the average consumer, according to the Court of Justice, is not the sole representative of the public, it is seemingly its main representative.

---

[1]European Parliament and Council Regulation (EU) 2017/1001 of 14 June 2017 on the European Union trade mark (codification), [2017] OJ L 154/3 (the "TM Regulation"). See also Chap. 9.

[2]EP and Council Directive (EU) No 2015/2436 of 16 December 2015 to approximate the laws of the Member States relating to trade marks (Recast), [2015] OJ L 336/1 (the "TM Directive"). Although the previous TM Directive will not be repealed until 15 January 2019 reference in this book is to the TM Directive. See also, Chap. 9.

[3]Laustsen, Rasmus D., 'An Economic Analysis of EU Trademark Law; the Role of the Average Consumer in Trademark Infringement between Two Confusingly Similar Trademarks', in Lyngsie,

© Springer Nature Switzerland AG 2020

R. D. Laustsen, *The Average Consumer in Confusion-based Disputes in European Trademark Law and Similar Fictions*, https://doi.org/10.1007/978-3-030-26350-8_1

In all areas of law, the legislature has drawn a line between what is acceptable and what is not. In intellectual property law there is according to Robin Jacob,[4] an "umbra" (a core) of intellectual property assets clearly legally protected and a broader "penumbra" of assets clearly not protected. Between the two reside the "woolly areas" where "there is room for divergent opinions as to the 'right' answer" on what is protectable subject matter."[5] The concept of "woolly areas" of intellectual property law does not include the case of a competitor making a one-to-one copy of an already protected intellectual property asset. In trademark law this may be seen in instances related to "double identity" issues where the junior trademark owner's mark is identical to that of the senior trademark owner[6] for identical products.[7]

Some of the main "woolly areas" of intellectual property law are infringement disputes decided to refer to a degree of similarity. Fromer and Lemley have stated that "[a] principle question in IP infringement disputes is whether the defendant's product (or work, or brand, or idea) is too similar in some respect to the plaintiff's."[8] In addition, that "[e]ach regime's choice of audience drives its definition of infringement, which in turn determines how well the IP regime achieves its goals."[9]

Deciding "confusion" as part of registration or infringement in European trademark law inherently involves a significant discretion. The Court of Justice has chosen the average consumer to be the key audience in registration and infringement disputes involving confusion. In its early case law, the Court of Justice stated that the average consumer is "reasonably well-informed and reasonably observant and circumspect."[10] The average consumer represents to some degree a proxy of purchasing behaviour involved in the judicial process of deciding confusion. Although the Court of Justice and the (EU) General Court (jointly the "CJEU"),[11] and in some

---

Jacob, Mortensen, Bent O. G. and Østergaard, Kim eds., Rets- og Kontraktøkonomi: Law & Economics an Anthology (Djøf Publishing, 2016), 37, p. 42.

[4]Former judge at the Court of Appeal of England and Wales.

[5]Jacob, Robin, 'IP and Other Things: A Collection of Essays and Speeches', (1st edn, Hart, 2015), p. 86.

[6]References to "trademark owner," unless referred to otherwise, also cover "trademark user" since the trademark owner has the right to bring proceedings for infringement of EU and national trademarks, except in a licensing arrangement where an exclusive license is given by the trademark owner (the licensor) to the trademark user (the licensee). "Senior trademark" is taken to be the same as "earlier trade mark." As defined in art. 8(2)(a)(i)-(iv) of the TM Regulation and art. 5(2)(a)(i)-(iii) of the TM Directive.

[7]That the main "woolly areas" are not found in these "double identity" instances is not the same as saying that these issues are not litigated upon.

[8]Fromer, Jeanne C., and Lemley, Mark A., 'The Audience in Intellectual Property Infringement', Michigan Law Review, vol. 112/no. 7, (2014), pp. 1251, p. 1252. Although Fromer and Lemley's article analyses US law, their overall considerations apply to a European context.

[9]*Ibid*, p. 1254.

[10]Gut Springenheide and Tusky, Case C-210/96, [1998] ECR I-4657, para 31.

[11]The "CJEU" is taken to include the Court of Justice, as assisted by the Advocates General and the General Court in line with use of the term in art. 19 (1) and (2) of the TEU.

form or another before that by the national judiciaries,[12] for almost two decades have referred to the average consumer it may be regarded as a paradox: well-established but ill-defined.

The recent scholarly[13] and judicial[14] grappling with the average consumer in European trademark law and more generally as part of "the Images of the EU Consumer"[15] illustrates the elusiveness, complexity and significance of the average consumer.

1.2 Who/What Is the Average Consumer?

Before moving to its substantial meaning and effects, part of the grappling with the average consumer is caused by the theoretical assumption of who/what is the average consumer and mere terminology. How is it possible to describe the average

---

[12]The historical backcloth of the average consumer is analysed in Chap. 8.

[13]Dinwoodie, Graeme, and Gangjee, Dev, 'The Image of the Consumer in EU Trade Mark Law', in Leczykiewicz, Dorota, and Weatherill, Stephen eds., The Images of the Consumer in EU Law: Legislation, Free Movement and Competition Law (1st edn, Hart, 2016), 339, Weatherall, Kimberlee, 'The Consumer as the Empirical Measure of Trade Mark Law', Modern Law Review, vol. 80/no. 1, (2017), pp. 57, Laustsen, Rasmus D., 'An Economic Analysis of EU Trademark Law; the Role of the Average Consumer in Trademark Infringement between Two Confusingly Similar Trademarks', in Lyngsie, Jacob, Mortensen, Bent O. G. and Østergaard, Kim eds., Rets- og Kontraktøkonomi: Law & Economics an Anthology (Djøf Publishing, 2016), 37, Jennifer, 'Revisiting the Average Consumer: An Uncertain Presence in European Trade Mark', Intellectual Property Quarterly, no. 1, (2015), pp. 15, Blythe, Alice, 'In Search of Mr. Average: Attempting to Identify the Average Consumer and His Role within Trade Mark Law', European Intellectual Property Review, vol. 37/no. 11, (2015), pp. 709 and Carboni, Anna. 'Confusion Surveys and Confused Judges', Jiplp, vol. 10/no. 1, (2015), pp. 1.

[14]Although mentioned by different national judiciaries, in particular the UK judiciaries have in recent years elaborated explicitly on the average consumer. Most notably in the UK High Court in Interflora v. Marks & Spencer, [2013] EWHC 1291 (Ch), paras 194-224, Enterprise v. Europcar, [2015] EWHC 17 (Ch), paras 130-143, Supreme Petfoods v. Henry Bell, [2015] EWHC 256 (Ch), paras 50-55, London Taxi Company v. Frazer-Nash Research and Ecotive, [2016] EWHC 52 (Ch), paras 159-163 and Walton International, Giordano v. Verweij Fashion, [2018] EWHC 1608 (Ch), para 106, and in the UK Court of Appeal in Interflora v. Marks & Spencer, [2014] EWCA Civ 1403, paras 107-130 and London Taxi Company v. Frazer-Nash Research and Ecotive, [2017] EWCA Civ 1729, paras 20-35. Arnold J giving the lead judgement in the mentioned UK High Court decisions is key to developing the UK precedence on the average consumer, and hence more broadly the European discussions on this.

[15]Leczykiewicz, Dorota and Weatherill, Stephen, eds., The Images of the Consumer in EU Law: Legislation, Free Movement and Competition Law (1st edn, Hart, 2016), also containing the article on the average consumer in European trademark law: Dinwoodie, Graeme, and Gangjee, Dev, 'The Image of the Consumer in EU Trade Mark Law', in Leczykiewicz, Dorota, and Weatherill, Stephen eds., The Images of the Consumer in EU Law: Legislation, Free Movement and Competition Law (1st edn, Hart, 2016), 339.

consumer in line with legal theory? Is it a legal concept, legal standard, a legal fiction, a one-to-one proxy for real consumers, or something else?

Analysing the average consumer in European trademark law must be seen in the legal context of various other versions of the "consumer" that co-exist across the domains of overarching EU law. These versions have different characteristics and yet all represent somehow a legal duplicate of the European "consumer" for the legislature and judiciaries in a given field of EU law. Collecting a series of such analyses, Leczykiewicz and Weatherill have recently argued that it is important to address which method is used for constructing a given consumer image, and how it is infused with empirical evidence, because this makes it possible to decide if the image is factual or fictional.[16] If the consumer is considered a legal fiction, "it reveals whether it is an expression of antecedent policy choices only masquerading (...) actual needs and characteristics of EU consumers, or the fictions are there merely as the necessary generalisations ensuring workability of the regulatory framework."[17] Legal fictions should not be confused with fictions used in hard sciences, where fictions are used to explain and predict the behaviour of an object. The criterion of success in hard sciences is that the fiction (a model) corresponds with the examined object.[18]

As it will be elaborated on, it is the stance of this analysis that the average consumer is a legal fiction consisting of normative and factual elements.[19] Therefore, the average consumer will be referred as such or "it"[20] hence; *it* is seen as "masquerading" factual matters and "necessary generalisations." A legal fiction is understood as "simply a form of creative lawmaking, a phenomenon of legal (primarily judicial) technique employed to resolve trouble in the legal environment."[21] The average consumer is thus not perceived as bipolar, either being a

---

[16]Leczykiewicz, Dorota and Weatherill, Stephen, 'The Images of the Consumer in EU Law', in Leczykiewicz, Dorota and Weatherill, Stephen eds., The Images of the Consumer in EU Law: Legislation, Free Movement and Competition Law (1st edn, Hart, 2016), 1.

[17]See *ibid*, p. 14. Two prominent trademark law scholars have been included in that book to discuss the image of the average consumer in EU trademark law. See Dinwoodie, Graeme, and Gangjee, Dev, 'The Image of the Consumer in EU Trade Mark Law', in Leczykiewicz, Dorota, and Weatherill, Stephen eds., The Images of the Consumer in EU Law: Legislation, Free Movement and Competition Law (1st edn, Hart, 2016), 339.

[18]Samuel, Geoffrey, 'Is Law a Fiction?', in Del Mar, Maksymilian and Twining, William eds., Legal Fictions in Theory and Practice (1st edn, Springer, 2015), 31, p. 33.

[19]See Chap. 5.

[20]And not "he/she" as used by other authors. See among others, Davis, Jennifer, 'Revisiting the Average Consumer: An Uncertain Presence in European Trade Mark', Intellectual Property Quarterly, no. 1, (2015), pp. 15, p. 15, Dinwoodie, Graeme, and Gangjee, Dev, 'The Image of the Consumer in EU Trade Mark Law', in Leczykiewicz, Dorota, and Weatherill, Stephen eds., The Images of the Consumer in EU Law: Legislation, Free Movement and Competition Law (1st edn, Hart, 2016), 339, p. 375 and Weatherall, Kimberlee, 'The Consumer as the Empirical Measure of Trade Mark Law', Modern Law Review, vol. 80/no. 1, (2017), pp. 57, p. 73.

[21]Lind, Douglas, 'The Pragmatic Value of Legal Fictions', in Del Mar, Maksymilian and Twining, William eds., Legal Fictions in Theory and Practice (1st edn, Springer, 2015), 83, p. 84.

legal fiction or descriptive since even if evidence is imbued with a high degree of normativity and uncertainty. In addition, the average consumer is ultimately framed *in law* by judiciaries. It also emerges from case law of the Court of Justice, that the average consumer is not purely descriptive.[22] Even if it is possible by way of factual findings to describe the average consumer, this description is imbued with many variables. For instance, what is the "correct" (quantitative or qualitative) method for doing marketing research,[23] what are the inputs from neoclassical and behavioural economics on consumer rationality,[24] and what is understood by *average* and *consumer* and even more so the two words combined into an *average consumer*? Although not part of the analysis, some of these variables are referred to throughout this book. In sum, it is the stance of this book that it is impossible to regard the average consumer fiction as a model akin to fictions in hard sciences that can be positively tested in real life.

It is the assumption that terminology matters in the sense it potentially feeds into the framing of the average consumer in substantial trademark law. If the average consumer is a legal fiction allows linkage between legal theory and practical trademark law. It allows the analysis to focus on its application *in law* and the balance between normative and descriptive elements vested in the average consumer—not the fiction description dichotomy as such. This theoretical account is followed up by mirroring the average consumer against fictions from other areas of law—the informed user of EU design law, the person skilled in the art of European Patent law and the reasonable person of European tort law—and outside of law against economics' rational actor model. These other legal models and the rational actor model are figuratively called more or less distant "cousins" of the average consumer. Essentially, this mirroring is done to get insight into what the average consumer *is* and *is not*.[25]

---

[22] Gut Springenheide and Tusky, Case C-210/96, [1998] ECR I-4657, para 14.

[23] It has thus been stated by Gummesson: "Marketing situations are not easy to grasp. It should be unnecessary to say that marketing decisions and actions are not just based on analyses of data, because data are mostly hard to find, hard to define, and they are incomplete. The reason I mention this is that there seems to be a scholarly dream that if we just do more research and collect more data ("get all the facts") we will eliminate uncertainty and risk and make rational decisions. However, the real world does not allow this." Gummesson, Evert, 'Qualitative Research in Marketing: Road-Map for a Wilderness of Complexity and Unpredictability', European Journal of Marketing, vol. 39/no. 3/4, (2005), pp. 309, p. 311. Also, Addis and Podestà have stated that marketing "approaches have been the object of a constant process of systematisation and refining. The activities that can be ascribed to the market domain have been evolving in the course of time, drawing frequently from other disciplines; let us think, for example, of the market segmentation which draws its technique from psychology and statistics, or of the study of purchaser and customer behaviour which availed itself on psychological, sociological, and economic principles and models, and so on." Addis, Michela, and Stefano Podestà, 'Long Life to Marketing Research: A Postmodern View', European Journal of Marketing, vol. 39/no. 3/4, (2005), pp. 386.

[24] Towfigh, Emanuel V. and Petersen, Niels, 'Economic Methods for Lawyers', (1st edn, Edward Elgar, 2015), p. 18 and p. 25.

[25] See Chap. 6.

The bald answer to the question in the heading is that the average consumer is a legal fiction.

1.3   Purpose of Trademarks and European Trademark Law

Part of the analysis is to determine how well the average consumer operates, given the purpose of European trademark law. This section addresses the purpose of the law according to how the EU legislature in the legislation and preparatory works has set out the purpose, and how Court of Justice has set out the purpose. This account inevitably involves setting out the purpose of *trademarks* and EU *trademark law.*[26]

1.3.1   The Legal Functions of Trademarks

Repeatedly the Court of Justice has stated that the "origin function" of trademarks is the "essential function."[27] From early stages of EU trademark legislation this was equally emphasised. In a memorandum from 1976 on the creation of a community wide trademark (the "TM Memorandum 1976") it was thus stated that consumers face an increasing number of goods of the same type "not distinguished, like raw materials and many agricultural products, by natural or technical features alone, but have numerous variations and differences in quality, special properties, taste and appearance."[28] For consumers to navigate between these goods, and services, they can use trademarks as product identifiers. Furthermore, that only identifying companies as such is generally insufficient since manufacturers often market different

---

[26]The Court of Justice stated in *Björnekulla* that national trademark law had to be interpreted by the national court in accordance with not only the wording but also the purpose of the TM Directive 1989. This applied, even if the purpose was contrary to the purpose of the national trademark law as set out in the preparatory works of the national trademark legislation. Björnekulla, Case C-371/02, [2004] ECR I-5791, para 13.

[27]See for instance, Mitsubishi v. Duma Forklifts, Case C-129/17, [2018], para 35, Canon Kabushiki Kaisha v. Metro-Goldwyn-Mayer. Case C-39/97, [1998] ECR I-5507, para 28 and Arsenal v. Reed, Case C-206/01, [2002] ECR I-10273, paras 48 and 50. *Canon* referred to CNL-SUCA v. HAG, Case C-10/89, [1990] ECR I-3711, para 14. *CNL-SUCA v. HAG and Arsenal v. Reed* both referred to Hoffmann-La Roche v. Centrafarm, Case 102/77, [1978] ECR 1139, para 7 and CNL-SUCA v. HAG also referred to Centrafarm v. American Home Products, Case 3/78, [1978] ECR 1823, paras 11-12. *Hoffmann-La Roche v. Centrafarm* was the first time the Court of Justice referred to the "essential function" of trademarks. On the background of the origin function Simon, Ilanah, 'How Does "Essential Function" Doctrine Drive European Trade Mark Law?', IIC, vol. 36/4, (2005), pp. 401, in particular p. 413-414.

[28]Commission Memorandum on the creation of an EEC trade mark adopted by the Commission on 6 July 1976, [1976] Bulletin of the European Communities Supplement 8/76, p. 8, para 11. The memorandum may be considered as part of the preparatory works preceding the TM Regulation 1994. The role of preparatory works as a legal source is discussed in Chap. 3.

types of products. Trademarks are thus used by consumers as assistance "in the first instance when consumer goods of the same kind are offered for sale, facilitate a further purchase of same article and enable the consumer to distinguish, according to his wishes, between the various goods offered for sale."[29]

It was already clear from the TM Memorandum 1976 that trademarks served functions other than the origin function in a narrow sense, including a "quality" and "advertising" function. It was thus stated in the memorandum that in preserving the origin function, "the consumer can count on a similarity of composition and *quality of goods bearing the trade mark*; and *the advertising value of the trade mark* requires that between the trade marked goods and the owner of the trade mark there is a definite legal relationship." Although the quality function was allocated to prevail "in the mind of the consumer" and the advertising function "in the mind of the producer," the reason for the being of those functions is still the origin function.[30] The quality and investment functions of trademarks were more recently emphasised by the European Economic and Social Committee ("EESC") in their opinion from 2013 on the proposal for the TM Directive (the "EESC TM Opinion 2013").[31]

The legislative emphasis on the origin function as essential is immediately apparent from the recitals of the most recent EU trademark legislation where it emerges that "[t]he protection afforded by the registered trade mark, the function of which is *in particular to guarantee the trade mark as an indication of origin*."[32] Cornish *et al*, have pointed out that this legislative reference to "origin" is "plainly here (. . .) used in a broad sense."[33] Further, the origin function is also stressed by the EU legislature in that for a mark to be registrable it must be "capable of distinguishing the goods or services of one undertaking from those of other undertakings,"[34] As a negative definition of the origin function, the EU legislature has set out that a trademark may be revoked if it becomes generic (and thus no longer can distinguish the products for which it is registered).[35]

---

[29]*Ibid*, p. 8, para 12.

[30]The TM Memorandum 1976, p. 20 (italics in the first quote are added). The guarantee and advertising functions are also mentioned in *ibid*, p. 8.

[31]Opinion of the European Economic and Social Committee on the 'Proposal for a Directive of the European Parliament and of the Council to approximate the laws of the Member States relating to trade marks' of 12 November 2013, COM(2013) 162 final - 2013/0089 (COD), [2013] OJ C 327/09, p. 44 para 3.1.2. The EESC is part of the legislative process cf. art. 114 of the TFEU.

[32]Recital 11 of the TM Regulation and recital 16 of the TM Directive.

[33]Cornish, William R., Llewelyn, David, and Alpin, Tanya, 'Intellectual Property: Patents, Copyright, Trademarks and Allied Rights', (8th edn, Sweet & Maxwell, 2013), p. 648.

[34]Cf. recital 13 of the TM Regulation and TM Directive and art. 4(a) of the TM Regulation and art. 3 (a) of the TM Directive. See also Björnekulla Fruktindustrier, Case C-371/02, [2004] ECR I-5791, para 21, Merz & Krell, Case C-517/99, [2001] ECR I-6959, paras 23-24 and Mendes SA v. EUIPO, Case T-419/17, [2018], para 24.

[35]Cf. art. 58(1)(b) of the TM Regulation and art. 20(a) of the TM Directive. See also Björnekulla Fruktindustrier, Case C-371/02, [2004] ECR I-5791, para 22 and Mendes SA v. EUIPO, Case T-419/17, para 25.

In some of its early decisions, the Court of Justice set out what is today understood by the origin function. Thus, in *Hoffmann-La Roche v. Centrafarm*, the court stated that trademarks serve to "guarantee to the proprietor of the trademark that he has the exclusive right to use that trade-mark for the purpose of putting a product into circulation." To reach this end, the "essential function" of trademarks "is to guarantee the identity of the origin of the trade-marked product to the consumer or ultimate user, by enabling him without any possibility of confusion to distinguish that product from products which have another origin."[36] In *CNL-SUCA v. HAG*, the Court of Justice stated that "trademark rights" is "an essential element in the system of undistorted competition" and that "an undertaking must be in a position to keep its customers *by virtue of the quality of its products and services*, something which is possible only *if there are distinctive marks which enable customers to identify those products and services*." Further, that "[f]or the trade mark to be able to fulfil this role, it must offer a guarantee that all goods bearing it have been produced under the control of a single undertaking which is accountable for their quality."[37] These findings by the Court of Justice clearly establish a link between likelihood of confusion and the origin function.

It appears that AG Jacobs aimed at telling coherent narrative on the function of European trademark in his two opinions given the same day in *Sabel* and *Parfums Christian Dior v. Evora*.[38] Whereas Jacobs in *Sabel* focused on the origin function in a narrow sense,[39] he gave his opinion in *Parfums Christian Dior v. Evora* on the overlap between the origin and quality function. Building on the just set out finding by the Court of Justice in *CNL-SUCA v. HAG*, Jacobs stated that the court "recognizes that marks deserve protection because they symbolize qualities associated by consumers with certain goods or services and guarantee that the goods or services measure up to expectations." Further, that "[i]t is apparent that the aspects of trade marks (sometimes referred to as the 'quality or guarantee function') can be regarded as part of the origin function."[40] More recently, the Court of Justice in *L'Oréal v. Bellure* stated that besides the origin function, trademarks also serve the functions other than the origin function, including "that of guaranteeing the quality of the

---

[36]Hoffmann-La Roche v. Centrafarm, Case 102/77, [1978] ECR 1139, para 7. See also Centrafarm v. American Home Products Corporation, Case 3/78, [1978] ECR 1823, paras 11-12, CNL-SUCA v. HAG, Case C-10/89, [1990] ECR I-371, para 14 and recently building on this, Schweppes v. Red Paralela, Case C-291/16, [2017], para 37. See further on the background of the origin function Simon, Ilanah, 'How Does "Essential Function" Doctrine Drive European Trade Mark Law?', IIC, vol. 36/4, (2005), pp. 401, in particular p. 401-408.

[37]CNL-SUCA v. HAG, Case C-10/89, [1990] ECR I-371, para 13 (italics added), and recently building on this, Schweppes v. Red Paralela, Case C-291/16, [2017], para 37.

[38]The former being on likelihood of confusion and the latter on protecting a trademarks' reputation.. Sabel v. Puma, Case C-251/95, [1997] ECR I-6191, (opinion of AG Jacobs) and Parfums Christian Dior v. Evora, Case C-337/95, [1997] ECR I-6013, (opinion of AG Jacobs).

[39]Sabel v. Puma, Case C-251/95, [1997] ECR I-6191, (opinion of AG Jacobs), para 32.

[40]Parfums Christian Dior v. Evora, Case C-337/95, [1997] ECR I-6013, (opinion of AG Jacobs), para 41.

goods or services in question."[41] The EFTA Court is aligned with the Court of Justice on the trademark functions.[42]

The Court of Justice recently stated in *Daimler v. Együd Garage* that despite functions other than the origin function, it is only possible to find confusion-based infringement, if use of the junior mark "affects, or is liable to affect, the origin function."[43] This finding by the court seems to mean the origin function in a narrow sense, not including the quality function.[44] However, the close connection between the origin function and the quality function was stressed by Advocate General Kokott in *Viking Gas v. Kosan Gas*. Kokott thus found that "[a]s a rule, the function of guaranteeing the quality of the goods goes hand in hand with the function of guaranteeing its origin. The trade mark indicates that the goods satisfy the quality standards of the recognisable proprietor of the trade mark."[45]

In *L'Oréal v. Bellure* the Court of Justice stated that besides the origin and quality functions, trademarks also have other functions, "in particular that of (. . .) communication, investment or advertising."[46] As for the functions other than the origin

---

[41]L'Oréal v. Bellure, Case C-487/07, [2009] ECR I-5185, para 58. See also *Google France cases*, Cases C-236/08 – C-238/08 [2010] ECR I-2417, para 77, Die BergSpechte Outdoor Reisen v. trekking.at Reisen, Case C-278/08, [2010] ECR I-2517, para 31, Portakabin v. Primakabin, Case C-558/08, [2010] ECR I-6963, para 30, Budějovický Budvar v. Anheuser-Busch, Case C-482/09, [2011] ECR I-8701, para 71, Interflora v. Marks & Spencer, Case C-323/09, [2011] ECR I-8625, para 38, Daimler v. Együd Garage, Case C-179/15, [2016], para 26 and Mitsubishi v. Duma Forklifts, Case C-129/17, [2018], para 34.

[42]Thus, based on the practice of the Court of Justice, the EFTA Court has ruled that the origin function is the main function of trademarks. See Paranova, Case E-3/02, [2003], para 36 and Vigeland, Case E-5/16, [2017], para 67. Also, the EFTA Court has emphasised the other functions of trademarks as reflected in L'Oréal v. Bellure. See Vigeland, Case E-5/16, [2017], para 71. On the influence of the decisions of the EFTA Court to the analyses of this book, see Chap. 3, Sect. 3.3.2.3.

[43]Daimler v. Együd Garage, Case C-179/15, [2016], para 27.

[44]The finding by the court was made immediately after it had stated referring to the functions of trademarks other than the origin function as set out in e.g. L'Oréal v. Bellure, Case C-487/07, [2009] ECR I-5185, para 58: "By application of Article 5(1)(a) of Directive 2008/95 [TM Directive 2008], the proprietor of a trade mark is entitled to prevent a third party from using, without his consent, a sign identical with that trade mark when that use is in the course of trade, is in relation to goods or services which are identical with those for which that trade mark is registered, and affects, or is liable to affect, the functions of the trade mark, including not only the essential function of the trade mark, which is to guarantee to consumers the origin of the goods or service ('the origin function'), but also its other functions such as, in particular, that of guaranteeing the quality of those goods or services or those of communication, investment or advertising." Daimler v. Együd Garage, Case C-179/15, [2016], para 26.

[45]The quote continues: "Therefore, as a rule, the function in relation to quality is adversely affected, if goods not attaining those quality requirements are commercialised under the trade mark, for example, by licensees or following impairment by the purchaser." Viking Gas v. Kosan Gas, Case C-46/10, [2011] ECR I-6161, (opinion of AG Kokott), para 45.

[46]L'Oréal v. Bellure, Case C-487/07, [2009] ECR I-5185, para 58. See also *Google France cases*, Cases C-236/08 – C-238/08 [2010] ECR I-2417, para 77, Die BergSpechte Outdoor Reisen v. trekking.at Reisen, Case C-278/08, [2010] ECR I-2517, para 31, Portakabin v. Primakabin, Case C-558/08, [2010] ECR I-6963, para 30, Budějovický Budvar v. Anheuser-Busch, Case C-482/

function, it has been found by Bently *et al* that "[t]he precise nature of the other functions remains extremely unclear."[47] In similar veins, Cornish *et al* have found that it is "apparent that there is no agreement what these "functions" are and that disagreement often reflect the underlying commitment of the proponent."[48] Recently in *Mitsubishi v. Duma Forklifts,* the Court of Justice could further explain these other functions and their differences, but did no more than sum up the findings in its previous decisions.[49] Due to the focus on confusion-based disputes, no reconciliation of functions other than the origin and quality functions is attempted here since they mainly reside in disputes about "double identity" marks and marks with a reputation.

From the above, at least the quality function is arguably within the origin function, and this has caused Gangjee to hold that "the 'guarantee of quality' function follows closely from the essential function and they are seen as two sides of the same coin."[50] To focus trademark law on the origin function as a standalone function or as also including the quality function has been criticised by different commentators. Thus, Tritton *et al* build an argument around a modern global corporation where changes in ownership structures and the supply chain make the origin function as a standalone function elusive. According to Tritton *et al*, it is maybe "better to say that a trade mark permits a *predictability of experience* for consumers."[51] Gielen airs an even stronger critique of the origin function, both as a standalone function, but also as including the quality function. Gielen advocates a

---

09, [2011] ECR I-8701, para 71, Interflora v. Marks & Spencer, Case C-323/09, [2011] ECR I-8625, para 38, Daimler v. Együd Garage, Case C-179/15, [2016], para 26 and Mitsubishi v. Duma Forklifts, Case C-129/17, [2018], para 34. More broadly, Advocate General Trstenjak stated in *Budějovický Budvar v. Anheuser-Busch* that "[t]he [legal and economic] functions inherent in or essential or ascribed to a trade mark are manifold. They include, according to legal writing on trade mark law, inter alia the coding, guarantee, origin, identification and individualisation, information and communication, monopolising, naming, quality, distinction, confidence, distribution and advertising functions, without the individual functions always having legal relevance in addition." Budějovický Budvar v. Anheuser-Busch, Case C-482/09, [2011] ECR I-8701, (opinion of AG Trstenjak), footnote 26 and main text at para 63 of the opinion, including the scholarly sources referred to here.

[47]Bently, Lionel, Sherman, Brad, Gangjee, Dev and Johnson, Phillip 'Intellectual Property Law', (5th edn, Oxford University Press, 2018), p. 1122.

[48]Cornish, William R., Llewelyn, David, and Alpin, Tanya, 'Intellectual Property: Patents, Copyright, Trademarks and Allied Rights', (8th edn, Sweet & Maxwell, 2013), p. 646. Similarly, when analysing these other functions of trademarks, Kur and Senftleben have stated that Court of Justice "judgements are notoriously tight-lipped, with information on the core considerations being dispensed in minimal dosage." Kur, Annette and Senftleben, Martin, 'European Trade Mark Law: A Commentary', (1st edn, Oxford University Press, 2017), p. 16, footnote 45.

[49]Mitsubishi v. Duma Forklifts, Case C-129/17, [2018], paras 34-37.

[50]Gangjee, Dev S., 'Property in brands. The commodification of conversation', in Howe, Helena and Griffiths, Jonathan ed., Concepts of Property in Intellectual Property Law (1st edn, Cambridge University Press, 2013), 29, p. 40.

[51]Davis, Richard, St Quintin, Thomas and Tritton, Guy, 'Tritton on Intellectual Property in Europe', (5th edn, Sweet & Maxwell, 2018), p. 281.

"modern approach" to trademark protection that recognises "trade mark functions as a means of identification and communication," and simply admitting that "[t]he origin of a product is of no importance to consumers." The explanation for this is "the increasing importance of retail trade, the decrease in quality discrepancies among products and services and the development of lifestyle marks together with the resultant shift in the character of the mark from the rational and physical to the emotional and psychological."[52]

It is correct that the roles of trademarks have changed Since the early decisions of the Court of Justice in late 1970'ies setting out the origin function. However, due to the nature of likelihood of confusion focusing on *confusion*, it makes sense to include the quality function. As found by Gielen, it is probably correct that there are fewer "discrepancies" in quality between products. That said, the corporate landscape is continuously becoming more globalised as global companies grow organically and through mergers and acquisitions. The globalisation entails a focus for companies to create a unified brand identity through fewer core global trademarks.[53] The globalisation means that quality issues of the products in for instance Asia may affect the sales of products (with no quality issues) sold in the USA under the same trademark. Quality issues could also manifest in issues in the production line and supply chain of non-compliance with corporate social responsibility standards.[54] For consumers to choose the relevant products with the relevant qualities of the products (be they qualities of the products as such or aspects of the production of the products), it is crucial that likelihood of confusion is prevented. Consequently, the likelihood of confusion standard in this book is assumed to pursue the origin function as including the quality function.

1.3.2   Economic Functions of Trademarks[55]

A key economic function of trademarks is lowering consumer search costs. That it is not farfetched to establish a connection between this economic function and

---

[52]Gielen, Charles, 'Harmonisation of trade mark law in Europe: the first trade mark harmonisation Directive of the European Council', European Intellectual Property Review, vol. 14/no. 8, (1992), pp. 262, p. 264.

[53]Lego is good example of this, when they already as a global company decided in 1973 to apply the same Lego trademark to all its products. See the history of Lego set out here: https://www.lego.com/en-us/aboutus/lego-group/the_lego_history/1970 (last visited 26 May 2019).

[54]Griffiths, Andrew, 'Brands, Business and Social Responsibility', in Faure, Michael and Stephen, Frank ed., Essays in the Law and Economics of Regulation in Honour of Anthony Ogus (1st edn, Intersentia, 2008), pp. 193, p. 210.

[55]This section is an adapted insertion from Laustsen, Rasmus D., 'An Economic Analysis of EU Trademark Law; the Role of the Average Consumer in Trademark Infringement between Two Confusingly Similar Trademarks', in Lyngsie, Jacob, Mortensen, Bent O. G. and Østergaard, Kim eds., Rets- og Kontraktøkonomi: Law & Economics an Anthology (Djøf Publishing, 2016), 37, pp. 45.

European trademark law was clarified by the EESC TM Opinion 2013 where it is stated that "the protection of trade marks reduces search costs for consumers."[56] After this opinion, Advocate General Szpunar in *Hauck v. Stokke* referred to scholarly literature on the economic function of trademarks. Szpunar stated that "the trade mark system enhances market transparency by redressing the imbalance between a complicated marketing background and the consumer's limited knowledge of that background."[57]

In economic sense, trademarks are generally considered information, and they function as a banner of origin because they guarantee the identity of the marked products to consumers, enabling them to distinguish the marked products from products having a different origin.[58] It is assumed that one of the key components in a competitive market is that consumers have full information of the marketed products and their characteristics.[59] Trademarks are significant in informing consumers on marketed products in that *"they provide a cipher linking information acquired by experience or from other sources to a product, thus aiding judgments about quality."*[60]

Trademarks as indicators of origin are said to lower consumers' costs in searching for products, in particular products with non-visible features.[61] Rather than investigating the features of the products upon placing purchases, consumers can search solely for products bearing a trademark known from own or other's past experiences. Consumers may equally use trademarks as *"a means of retaliation"* and choose not to buy products bearing the trademark due to negative past experiences.[62] Posner has described this situation as a hostage situation where the consumer as "the hostage-

---

[56]The EESC TM Opinion 2013, p. 44 para 3.1.2.

[57]Hauck v. Stokke, Case C-205/13, [2014], (opinion of AG Szpunar), para 30, including footnote 11 of the opinion. Reference was made by Szpunar to Griffiths, Landes and Posner. Landes and Posner are two of the pioneers describing the economic role trademarks play in lowering consumer search costs. See also and Laustsen, Rasmus D., 'An Economic Analysis of EU Trademark Law; the Role of the Average Consumer in Trademark Infringement between Two Confusingly Similar Trademarks', in Lyngsie, Jacob, Mortensen, Bent O. G. and Østergaard, Kim eds., Rets- og Kontraktøkonomi: Law & Economics an Anthology (Djøf Publishing, 2016), 37, p. 54-55.

[58]See, among others, Cornish, William, and Phillips, Jennifer, 'The Economic Function of Trade Marks: An Analysis with Special Reference to Developing Countries', IIC, vol. 13/1, (1982), pp. 41, p. 41 – 42 and Griffiths, Andrew, 'An Economic Perspective on Trade Mark Law', (1st edn, Edward Elgar, 2011), p. 61.

[59]Ozga, S. A., 'Imperfect Markets through Lack of Knowledge', the Quarterly Journal of Economics, vol. 74/no. 1, (1960), pp. 29, p. 29.

[60]Cornish, William, and Phillips, Jennifer, 'The Economic Function of Trade Marks: An Analysis with Special Reference to Developing Countries', IIC, vol. 13/1, (1982), pp. 41, p. 46 (italics added).

[61]Landes, William M., and Posner, Richard A., 'The Economic Structure of Intellectual Property Law', (1st edn, Harvard University Press, 2003), p. 168.

[62]Akerlof, George A., 'The Market for "Lemons": Quality Uncertainty and the Market Mechanism', the Quarterly Journal of Economics, vol. 84/no. 3, (1970), pp. 488, p. 500. Landes, William M., and Posner, Richard A., 'The Economic Structure of Intellectual Property Law', (1st edn, Harvard University Press, 2003), pp. 167.

taker (...) will "kill" the brand if the quality drops."[63] Essentially, the "hostage situation" creates an incentive for sellers to provide products with a consistent quality. This economic function of trademarks does not terminologically correspond to the *legal* origin function but is within the realm of the closely connected legal "quality function."

In that information by way of trademarks is less expensive than full product descriptions, consumer demand for this information will increase and at the end promote market competition.[64] Since trademarks solve the information asymmetry between sellers and consumers, it is assumed that consumers will pay more for the marked products and that the sellers consequently can reap higher profits.[65]

Trademark law ensures that the trademark owner obtains, with some limitations, an exclusive right to control which product bearing the trademark may be marketed.[66] With some limitations, this exclusive right translates into a property right.

1.3.3 Functions of European Trademark System

The above legal and economic functions of trademarks are not ends in their own right but should be seen, given the broader function of the European trademark system.

It was stated in the first trademark directive (the "TM Directive 1989")[67] that "the trade mark laws at present applicable in the Member States contain disparities which may impede the free movement of goods and freedom to provide services and may

---

[63]Posner, Richard A., 'Intellectual Property: The Law and Economics Approach', the Journal of Economic Perspectives, vol. 19/no. 2, (2005), pp. 57, p. 67. See also Davis, Richard, St Quintin, Thomas and Tritton, Guy, 'Tritton on Intellectual Property in Europe', (5th edn, Sweet & Maxwell, 2018), p. 287 and Kur, Annette and Senftleben, Martin, 'European Trade Mark Law: A Commentary', (1st edn, Oxford University Press, 2017), p. 8-9.

[64]Dogan, Stacey L., and Lemley, Mark A., 'Trademarks and Consumer Search Costs on the Internet', Houston Law Review, vol. 41/no. 3, (2004), pp. 777, p. 787.

[65]Landes, William M., and Posner, Richard A., 'The Economic Structure of Intellectual Property Law', (1st edn, Harvard University Press, 2003), p. 168. Today trademarks are not the only devices solving the information asymmetry. Possible solutions to the information asymmetry, and one solution to avoid selling "lemons" as new cars, are to define what pre-sale information on the products sellers have to disclose to the consumers. Hoffer, George E. and Michael D. Pratt, 'Used Vehicles, Lemons Markets, and used Car Rules: Some Empirical Evidence', Journal of Consumer Policy, vol. 10/no. 4, (1987), pp. 409, p. 411. Also, within EU a so-called information paradigm focusing consumer information transparency is said to be one of the main methods of consumer protection. Howells, Geraint, and Wilhelmsson, Thomas 'EC Consumer Law: Has it Come of Age?', European Law Review, vol. 28/no. 3, (2003), pp. 370, p. 380-381.

[66]Griffiths, Andrew, 'An Economic Perspective on Trade Mark Law', (1st edn, Edward Elgar, 2011), p. 2-3.

[67]First Council Directive of 21 December 1988 to approximate the laws of the Member States relating to trade marks (89/104/EEC), [1989] OJ L 40/1.

distort competition within the common market."[68] The directive is said to have paved "the way for the establishment of the single Community trade mark and register" by the first trademark regulation (EC) No 40/94 of 20 December 1993 (the "TM Regulation 1994").[69] In line with the TM Directive 1989, the TM Regulation 1994 stated that to create an internal market "and make it increasingly a single market, not only must barriers to free movement of goods and services be removed and arrangements be instituted which ensure that competition is not distorted, but, in addition, legal conditions must be created which enable undertakings to adapt their activities to the scale of the Community."[70] Hence, the initial EU trademark legislation was clearly linked to the "principles" of the Single European Act[71] as amended until the Lisbon Treaty.[72] The references to undistorted competition were maintained in the trademark directive (EC) No 2008/95 of 22 October 2008 (the "TM Directive 2008")[73] and regulation (EC) No 207/209 of 26 February 2009 (the "TM Regulation 2009").[74] The link between trademark law and the ensuring of undistorted competition has also been established by the Court of Justice

---

[68]Recital 1 of the TM Directive 1989.

[69]Council Regulation (EC) No 40/94 of 20 December 1993 on the Community trade mark, [1994] OJ L 11 / 1. Jaffey, Peter, 'The New European Trade Marks Regime', International Review of Industrial Property and Competition Law, vol. 28/no. 2, (1997), pp. 153, p. 188. Tritton *et al* have pointed out that it was intended that the TM Directive 1989 and the TM Regulation 1994 should have been introduced at the same time. One reason for this not happening according to the Tritton *et al* was the thorny road of agreeing on where to locate OHIM. Davis, Richard, St Quintin, Thomas and Tritton, Guy, 'Tritton on Intellectual Property in Europe', (5th edn, Sweet & Maxwell, 2018), , p. 296. The author of this book attended a summer school at Bucerius Law School Hamburg in 2014 where the first vice president of OHIM, von Mühlendahl, during a lecture mentioned the negotiations on where to locate the OHIM. In similar veins as Tritton *et al*, von Mühlendahl held that the negotiation process was a thorny road. Adding to this, von Mühlendahl held that Spain, although maybe not the dream scenario at the time of negotiation, today has to be content with the European Intellectual Property Office (as it is known today) ending up in Alicante since the institution has grown to become a significant player in the EU institutional landscape. This latter reference is merely anecdotal.

[70]Recital 1 of the TM Regulation 1994.

[71]The Single European Act, of 28 February 1987, [1987] OJ L 169/1 (the "Single European Act").

[72]Treaty of Lisbon amending the Treaty on European Union and the Treaty Establishing the European Community of 13 December 2007, [2007] OJ C 306/01 (the "Lisbon Treaty"). Hence, it was stated in art. 3(1)(f) of the Single European Act that "[f]or the purposes set out in Article 2, the activities of the Community shall include, as provided in this Treaty and in accordance with the timetable set out therein (f) the institution of a system ensuring that competition in the common market is not distorted." This was reiterated by art. 3(1)(g) of the TEU Pre-Lisbon (both treaties as further defined in Chap. 3, Sect. 3.2.1. The provisions are categorised under "principles."

[73]EP and Council Directive 2008/95/EC of 22 October 2008 to approximate the laws of the Member States relating to trade marks (Codified version), [2008] OJ L 299/25. Recital 2 of the TM Directive 2008.

[74]Council Regulation (EC) No 207/2009 of 26 February 2009 on the Community trade mark (codified version), [2009] OJ L 78/1. Recital 2 of the TM Regulation 2009 and recital 3 of the TM Regulation.

on many occasion starting with *CNL-SUCA v. HAG*,[75] and on the TM Directive 1989 *Canon*[76] and the TM Regulation 2009 *Alcon v. OHIM*.[77]

As argued by Weatherill, it may be questioned if the amendments of the Lisbon Treaty "'soften' the economic focus of free movement law under the treaty," one reason for this being the "the (Relegated?) Commitment to Undistorted Competition."[78] The reason for this finding is the removal from the "principles" of the Treaty on European Union post Lisbon (the "TEU")[79] of the obligation to ensure undistorted competition.[80] Also, Weatherill has argued, the softening is caused by the EU Charter of Fundamental Rights in the European Union (the "EU Charter")[81] that through the Lisbon Treaty was given treaty status.[82] Other functions have been ascribed to the European trademark system, such as consumer protection and protection of intellectual property.

The EU legislature has left no doubt that consumers are given no legal standing to enforce likelihood of confusion. However, as pointed out by Phillips, consumers

---

[75]CNL-SUCA v. HAG, Case C-10/89, [1990] ECR I-3711, para 13.

[76]Canon Kabushiki Kaisha v. Metro-Goldwyn-Mayer. Case C-39/97, [1998] ECR I-5507, para 28. See also Arsenal v. Reed, Case C-206/01, [2002] ECR I-10273, para 48, Céline SARL v. Céline SA, Case C-17/06, [2007] ECR I-7041, para 27 and recently Mitsubishi v. Duma Forklifts, Case C-129/17, [2018], para 30.

[77]Alcon v. OHIM, Case C-412/05 P, [2007] ECR I-3569, para 54 referring to Canon Kabushiki Kaisha v. Metro-Goldwyn-Mayer. Case C-39/97, [1998] ECR I-5507, para 28.

[78]Weatherill, Stephen, 'From Economic Rights to Fundamental Rights', in Vries, Sybe Alexander de, Bernitz, Ulf and Weatherill, Stephen eds., The Protection of Fundamental Rights in the EU After Lisbon (1st edn, Hart, 2013), 11, pp. 29. As Weatherill has pointed out, it is no longer a declared purpose of the EU to create "a system ensuring that competition in the internal market is not distorted." Art. 3(1)(g) of the TFEU Pre Lisbon. *Ibid*, p. 32-33.

[79]Treaty of European Union (consolidated version), [2012] OJ C 326/13 (the "TEU").

[80]It is now stated in art. 3(3) of the TEU that "[t]he Union shall establish an internal market. It shall work for the sustainable development of Europe based on balanced economic growth and price stability, a highly competitive social market economy, aiming at full employment and social progress, and a high level of protection and improvement of the quality of the environment. It shall promote scientific and technological advance" (italics added).

[81]The Charter of Fundamental Rights of the European Union, [2012] OJ C 326/391 (the "EU Charter"). Weatherill, Stephen, 'From Economic Rights to Fundamental Rights', in Vries, Sybe Alexander de, Bernitz, Ulf and Weatherill, Stephen eds., The Protection of Fundamental Rights in the EU After Lisbon (1st edn, Hart, 2013), 11, p. 30. Besides the two mentioned reasons for softening of the "economic focus," Weatherill has also referred to the importance of certain "horizontal clauses" and the "constitutional identity." *Ibid*, p. 30-32.

[82]Cf. art. 6(2) of the TEU. It is stated in art. 6(1) of the TEU, that "[t]he Union recognises the rights, freedoms and principles set out in the Charter of Fundamental Rights of the European Union of 7 December 2000, as adapted at Strasbourg, on 12 December 2007, which shall have the same legal value as the Treaties." According to Skouris, the Court of Justice took the approach that the principles of supremacy and direct effect, as touched upon above, "could not hold their ground without being coupled with a system of judicial review of violations of fundamental rights." Skouris, Vassilios, 'Preface', in Peers, Steve, *et al* eds., The EU Charter of Fundamental Rights: A Commentary (1st edn, Hart, 2014), i. Vassilios Skouris was president of the Court of Justice from 7 October 2003 – 6 October 2015.

may be "among the beneficiaries of trademark law and among its victims."[83] This means that, in terms of confusion and the average consumer, the below and above averagely inattentive consumers are thus not protected.[84] Sanders and Maniatis have stated that consumer protection under trademark law is "indirect" instead of "direct."[85] The authors have found that an increased focus on consumer protection "may lead to closer and more effective blending of trade mark and consumer protection laws."[86] The link to consumer protection has become more apparent than when this statement was made. Hence, art. 38 of the EU Charter requires that "Union policies shall ensure a high level of consumer protection." This is akin to the Treaty on the Functioning of the European Union (the "TFEU")[87] where the introductory policy statement in art. 12 and art. 169 specifically related to consumer protection.[88] These provisions may more broadly affect free movement law and actual legislation.[89]

Besides consumer protection, art. 17(2) of the EU Charter also stipulates that "[i]ntellectual property shall be protected" in line with the requirement of creating a uniform protection of "intellectual property rights" laid down in art. 118 of the TFEU.[90]

---

[83]Phillips, Jeremy, 'Trade Mark Law a Practical Anatomy', (1st edn, Oxford University Press, 2003), p. 20-21.

[84]See further on the "discounted" consumer from the average consumer model, Chap. 11, Sect. 11.2.

[85]As an example of *indirect* consumer protection, Sanders and Maniatis referred to the origin function as described by WIPO. As an example of *direct* consumer protection, the authors referred to Council Directive 85/374/EEC of 25 July 1985 on the approximation of the laws, regulations and administrative provisions of the Member States concerning liability for defective products, [1985] OJ L 210/29, but reference could have been made to any number of consumer protection directives, such as the UCPD offering general consumer protection against unfair commercial practices. Sanders, Anselm Kamperman and Maniatis, Spyros M., 'A Consumer Trade Mark: Protection Based on Origin and Quality', European Intellectual Property Review, vol. 15/no. 11, (1993), pp. 406, p. 410.

[86]*Ibid.* See also Skrzydło-Tefelska, Ewa, and Żuk, Mateusz, 'Article 9: Rights Conferred by a Community Trade Mark', in Hasselblatt, Gordian N. ed., Community Trade Mark Regulation (EC) no 207/2009: A Commentary (1st edn, Beck/Hart, 2015), 295, p. 303.

[87]Treaty on the Functioning of the European Union (consolidated version), [2012] OJ C 326/47 (the "TFEU"). The content of art. 12 was previously set out in art. 153(2) of the TFEU Pre-Lisbon where it was placed under the heading "Consumer Protection" to a broader section headed "Provisions Having General Application." This provision is an example of what Weatherill has denoted a "horizontal clause." See below in Sect. 1.3. Weatherill, Stephen, 'From Economic Rights to Fundamental Rights', in Vries, Sybe Alexander de, Bernitz, Ulf and Weatherill, Stephen eds., The Protection of Fundamental Rights in the EU After Lisbon (1st edn, Hart, 2013), 11, p. 30.

[88]This provision appears under Title XV "Consumer Protection" of the TFEU (art. 153 of the TFEU Pre-Lisbon).

[89]Weatherill, Stephen, 'Art. 38 - Consumer Protection', in Peers, Steve *et al* eds., The EU Charter of Fundamental Rights: A Commentary (1st edn, Hart, 2014), 1005, p. 1011-1012.

[90]As pointed out by Pila art. 17(2) of the EU Charter and art. 118 of the TFEU were the first articles to refer to "intellectual property." Pila, Justine, 'Intellectual Property as a Case Study in Europeanization: Methodological Themes and Context', in Ohly, Ansgar and Pila, Justine eds.,

It now appears in the recitals of the EU trademark legislation that "it should be applied in a way that ensures full respect for fundamental rights and freedoms, and in particular the freedom of expression."[91] The reference to these two fundamental rights are also found in the EESC TM Opinion 2013 referring to both the EU Charter[92] and more broadly to protecting intellectual property rights and consumer protection.[93]

1.4 Contextualisation

The average consumer nests in a market reality of different products being traded in different marketplaces by different persons. In *Lloyd*, the Court of Justice addressed the inevitable impact by the complex market realities on the judicial framing of the average consumer. This was the first time the court referred to the global appreciation test as part of the likelihood of confusion standard and as part of this repeated the characteristics of the average consumer as stated in *Gut Springenheide*, i.e. "reasonably well-informed and reasonably observant and circumspect." The court further stated that "[i]t should also be borne in mind that the average consumer's level of attention is likely to vary according to the category of goods or services in question."[94] Based on these findings, European judiciaries as a matter of law and fact have adapted the average consumer to these different market realities. In this book, this is referred to as "contextualisation." That the market realities that confront consumers are complex and ever changing begs for the contextualisation to somehow create order out of chaos.

In terms of the different market realities, it is possible to perceive many variables relevant for an analysis of how the average consumer is applied. In this book the main taxonomy used for contextualising the analysis is a division according to different (i) product markets (everyday consumer goods and more specialised goods) and (ii) market places (physical and online markets).

The Court of Justice has stated that "findings relating to the characteristics of the relevant public and to consumers' degree of attention, perception or attitude

---

The Europeanization of Intellectual Property Law: Towards a European Legal Methodology (1st edn, Oxford University Press, 2013), 3, p. 15. Consequences of this is further touched upon below in Sect. 1.3.3.

[91]Recital 21 of the TM Regulation and 27 of the TM Directive.

[92]Reference in the opinion was made to art. 17(2) of the EU Charter. *Ibid* p. 43 section 2.5.1.

[93]Reference in the opinion was made more generally to the (alleged) consumer underpinning of EU trademark law and to art. 169 of the TFEU. *Ibid* respectively p. 44 section 3.1.1 and p. 45 section 3.9.

[94]Lloyd Schuhfabrik Meyer v. Klijsen Handel BV, Case C-342/97, [1999] ECR I-3819, para 26. The Court of Justice referred to Gut Springenheide and Tusky, Case C-210/96, [1998] ECR I-4657, para 31.

represent appraisals of fact" be it in relation to so-called "everyday consumer goods"[95] or more specialised goods.[96] It is thus left for the General Court and national courts to determine the level of attention of the average consumer based on the facts in cases related to likelihood of confusion. The General Court has indicated that the relevant public for so-called "everyday consumer goods" is the average consumer, and that the level of attention of the average consumer may vary according to different types of goods within this category.[97] Outside of everyday consumer goods, the relevant public may be represented by a more specialised public with a higher degree of attention than the average consumer.[98]

As for contextualising, the average consumer to different market places, the Court of Justice has not explicitly stated if it is the average consumer known from physical market places that has to be used in the realm of online market places. In particular, use of trademarks in online communication challenges the underlying assumptions of the relevant public. Is it the average consumer known from the physical environment and if so, what is its level of attention? So far, the Court of Justice in the Google AdWords[99] disputes has held that the relevant public is the "average internet user"[100] who is assumed to be "reasonably well-informed and reasonably observant."[101] Contextualisation plays an important role in the analysis. Unless stated otherwise, reference throughout the book will be made to "products" as including "goods and services." The focal point of the contextualisation analysis though will be on goods, since consumers purchasing goods that are not distinguished by their own features was fundamental to developing trademark law and still is. Also, consumers are most often daily confronted with trademarks as part of everyday purchases of goods.[102] On an EU level, the European Commission (the "EU Commission") stressed the importance of goods in the Internal Market in 2013 stating that the free movement of goods "gives consumers a wide choice of products

---

[95]*Shoe Branding v. Adidas* relating to sports shoes and clothing (class 25 of the Nice Agreement). Shoe Branding v. Adidas, Case C-396/15 P, [2016], para 15.

[96]*Longevity Health Products v. OHIM* relating to certain pharmaceuticals and other preparations for medical or veterinary purposes (class 5 of the Nice Agreement). Longevity Health Products v. OHIM, Case C-81/11 P, [2012]. On the distinction between fact and law (the "fact/law divide") see Chap. 4, Sect. 4.3.1.

[97]Meica Ammerländische Fleischwarenfabrik v. OHIM, Case T-247/14, [2016], paras 37 and 39. See in more detail Chap. 11, Sect. 11.4.1.1.

[98]See e.g. LR Health & Beauty Systems v. OHIM, Case T-202/14, [2016], para 23.

[99]Google AdWords are now called "Google Ads."

[100]L'Oréal v. eBay International, Case C-324/09, [2011] ECR I-6011, para 94.

[101]Interflora v. Marks & Spencer, Case C-323/09, [2011] ECR I-8625, paras 44 and 50 and L'Oréal v. eBay International, Case C-324/09, [2011] ECR I-6011, para 94.

[102]See among others, Laustsen, Rasmus D., 'An Economic Analysis of EU Trademark Law; the Role of the Average Consumer in Trademark Infringement between Two Confusingly Similar Trademarks', in Lyngsie, Jacob, Mortensen, Bent O. G. and Østergaard, Kim eds., Rets- og Kontraktøkonomi: Law & Economics an Anthology (Djøf Publishing, 2016), 37, p. 40, including references, and below Chap. 11, Sect. 11.4.

and allows them to shop around for the best available offer." Furthermore, approximately "75% of intra-EU trade is in goods."[103]

The above picturing of the average consumer as nesting in a trademark law and market reality—both in flux—provide a basis for the analysis and structure of this book, that has to depict the overall lines and the details of the average consumer picture.

As part of some *de lege ferenda* and *de sententia ferenda* observations, the last chapter links law's contextualisation into product markets and markets places with contextualisation in light of economic theory.[104] As laid out above there is a connection between the essential *legal* function of trademarks, the origin function, and the *economic* function of trademarks as lowering consumers search costs. In economic theory, there is a division between different categories of goods, namely experience goods, search goods and credence goods. The point is that there are different levels of consumer search costs for different goods, and that trademarks used for goods with the highest level of search costs should be given the broadest protection.[105]

1.5 Delimitation

The average consumer in European trademark law has branches in all central areas of trademark law, into other areas of law and into other disciplines. The complexity of analysing the average consumer has recently been addressed by Weatherall who has conducted the analysis from within trademark law and with insight from other disciplines, for instance behavioural science.[106] The analyses of this book are legal though. That said, references are made to other disciplines where it adds to the legal analysis. Examples of these are found above with the "translation" of the legal function of European trademark law into the economic purpose of having trademarks and the addressing in Chap. 6 of the rational actor model from economics.

The below delimits this book according to its main parts. First, how is it delimited towards other areas of trademark law outside of likelihood of confusion also employing the average consumer? Second, how is it delimited temporally and third, geographically? Related to the geographical delimitation is fourth, how is the book delimited towards national procedural rules on evidence? Fifth, in a broader

---

[103]Commission, Free movement of goods: Guide to the Application of Treaty Provisions Governing the Free Movement of Goods, of 18 December 2013, p. 8.

[104]On the meaning of the terms *de lege ferenda* and *de sententia ferenda*, see Chap. 2, Sect. 2.1.

[105]See Chap. 12, Sect. 12.6 that builds on Laustsen, Rasmus D., 'An Economic Analysis of EU Trademark Law; the Role of the Average Consumer in Trademark Infringement between Two Confusingly Similar Trademarks', in Lyngsie, Jacob, Mortensen, Bent O. G. and Østergaard, Kim eds., Rets- og Kontraktøkonomi: Law & Economics an Anthology (Djøf Publishing, 2016), 37.

[106]Weatherall, Kimberlee, 'The Consumer as the Empirical Measure of Trade Mark Law', Modern Law Review, vol. 80/no. 1, (2017), p. 57-58.

perspective, how is the subject of the analysis delimited vis-à-vis other areas of law, in this book directive (EC) No 2005/29 of 11 May 2005 on unfair business-to-consumer commercial practices (the "UCPD")?[107]

1.5.1 Why Likelihood of Confusion?

The average consumer is important not only to disputes related to likelihood of confusion, so why substantially delimiting this book to the role the average consumer deciding likelihood of confusion? The everyday relevance of the average consumer in European trademark law for resolving possible and actual disputes outside of confusion disputes can hardly be underestimated. The average consumer features in case law related to the absolute grounds for refusal of registration,[108] the relative grounds for refusal of registration[109] and trademark infringement related to

---

[107]EP and Council Directive 2005/29/EC of 11 May 2005 concerning unfair business-to-consumer commercial practices in the internal market and amending Council Directive 84/450/EEC, Directives 97/7/EC, 98/27/EC and 2002/65/EC of the European Parliament and of the Council and Regulation (EC) No 2006/2004 of the European Parliament and of the Council (Unfair Commercial Practices Directive'), [2005] OJ L 149/22.

[108]As part of the absolute grounds for refusal of registration, it has to be decided if the sign to be registered is non-distinctive, descriptive or generic and hence bared from registration, cf. art. 7(1) (b)-(d) of the TM Regulation and art. 4(1)(b)-(d) of the TM Directive. The "predictive assessment" of the sign is conducted referring to the average consumer of the relevant category of products. Bently, Lionel, Sherman, Brad, Gangjee, Dev and Johnson, Phillip 'Intellectual Property Law', (5th edn, Oxford University Press, 2018), p. 979-980. See also Matratzen Concord v. Hukla, Case C-421/04, [2006] ECR I-2303, para and 24 Nestlé v. Cadbury, Case C-215/14, [2015], para 61, both including references. It is clear from these decisions, that the average consumer must be applied when deciding distinctiveness and descriptiveness. However, so far, the Court of Justice has not stated that the average consumer as such must be applied when deciding genericness. See Björnekulla Fruktindustrier, Case C-371/02, [2004] ECR I-5791, paras 23-25 and Kornspitz Company v. Pfahnl Backmittel, Case C-409/12, [2014], paras 29-30. Signs are barred from registration if they "consist exclusively of: (i) the shape, or another characteristic, which results from the nature of the goods themselves; (ii) the shape, or another characteristic, of goods which is necessary to obtain a technical result; (iii) the shape, or another characteristic, which gives substantial value to the goods.", cf. art. 7(1)(e)(i)-(iii) of the TM Regulation and art. 4(1)(i)-(iii) of the TM Directive. In assessing (iii) the Court of Justice has stated that the perception of the average consumer is not decisive, however, it is relevant for determining what are "the essential characteristics" of the sign. Lego Juris v. OHIM, Case C-48/09 P, [2010] ECR I-8403, para 76 and Hauck v. Stokke, Case C-205/13, [2014], para 34.

[109]For "double identity" disputes as part of the relative grounds for refusal of registration see below footnote 110 and for marks with a reputation see below footnote 111.

"double identity,"[110] and trademarks with reputation.[111] Thus, the average consumer features in crucial areas of substantive European trademark law.

One reason for narrowing the analysis of the average consumer is the significant extent to which it is applied in European trademark law. Also, a confusion standard has always been important to trademark law, and the judicial grappling with it has caused challenges. Analysing how different jurisdictions dealt with the confusion standard, Andreasen stated 70 years ago that a jurisdiction's dealing with the confusion standard "exposes the life nerve of trademark protection."[112] Maeyaert and Muyldermans have stated that "likelihood of confusion" is "probably one of the

---

[110]In the double identity disputes, the perception of the average consumer is used to determine if there is identity between the sign and the mark. LTJ Diffusion v. Sadas, Case C-291/00, [2003] ECR I- 2799, para 52. In art. 9(2)(a) of the TM Regulation: "Without prejudice to the rights of proprietors acquired before the filing date or the priority date of the EU trade mark, the proprietor of that EU trade mark shall be entitled to prevent all third parties not having his consent from using in the course of trade, in relation to goods or services, any sign where: (a) the sign is identical with the EU trade mark and is used in relation to goods or services which are identical with those for which the EU trade mark is registered" See the TM Directive art. 10(2)(a). As for registration, see art. 8(1) (a) of the TM Regulation and the TM Directive art. 5(1)(a).

[111]A later mark is not registrable under the TM Regulation and TM Directive if it (i) "is identical with, or similar to" an earlier mark, (ii) where the earlier mark "has a reputation in the Community" and (iii) "where the use of the later trade mark without due cause would take unfair advantage of, or be detrimental to, the distinctive character or the repute" of the earlier mark. The Court of Justice has stated that: Ad (i) For there to be a minimum of similarity between the marks there has to be a "link" between the two and that "[t]he fact that for the average consumer, who is reasonably well informed and reasonably observant and circumspect, the later mark calls the earlier mark with a reputation to mind is tantamount to the existence of such a link, within the meaning of Adidas-Salomon and Adidas Benelux, between the conflicting marks." Intel v. CPM, Case C-252/07, [2008] ECR I-8823, para 63 and also Adidas-Salomon and Adidas Benelux v. Fitnessworld, Case C-408/01, [2003] ECR I-12537, para 29 and El Corte Inglés v. OHIM, Case C-603/14 P, [2015], para 42. Ad (ii) "A trade mark's distinctiveness and its reputation must be assessed, first, by reference to the perception of the relevant public, which consists of average consumers." Intel v. CPM, Case C-252/07, [2008] ECR I-8823, para 34. Ad (iii) to show detriment "to the distinctive character of the earlier mark requires evidence of a change in the economic behaviour of the average consumer." Ibid, para 77. As for detriment to the reputation of the earlier mark "such detriment is caused when the goods or services for which the identical or similar sign is used by the third party may be perceived by the public in such a way that the trade mark's power of attraction is reduced." L'Oréal v. Bellure, Case C-487/07, [2009] ECR I-5185, para 40. "[A]s regards injury consisting of unfair advantage taken of the distinctive character or the repute of the earlier mark, in so far as what is prohibited is the drawing of benefit from that mark by the proprietor of the later mark, the existence of such injury must be assessed by reference to average consumers." Intel v. CPM, Case C-252/07, [2008] ECR I-8823, para 36. As for infringement see art. 9(2)(c) of the TM Regulation and the TM Directive art. 10(2)(c). As for registration see art. 8(5) of the TM Regulation and art. 5 (3) of the TM Directive.

[112]In Danish: "blotlægges Varemærkebeskyttelsens Livsnerve." Andreasen, Hardy, 'Varemærkeretten i Konkurrenceretlig Belysning. En Retssammenlignende Analyse Af Varemærkerettens Grundbegreber Og En Fremstilling Af Ejendomstetten Til Varemærker', (1st edn, Ejnar Munksgaard, 1948), p. 274.

most important concepts in [European] trademark law."[113] In similar veins, Fhima and Denvir state that "[t]he likelihood of confusion forms the basis of the most pervasive form of infringement, relative ground for the refusal of registration and ground for invalidity."[114]

The analysis focuses on the average consumer in the judicial determination of confusion-based infringement of registered trademark rights under European trademark law. This directs the attention to infringement disputes relying, at times significantly, on the average consumer to determine if the mark of the junior trademark owner is confusingly similar to that of the senior trademark owner as used in relation to the same or similar products. Naturally, since the rules on confusion-based infringement are substantially identical with those of registration, the solving of those registration disputes by European judiciaries is included in the analysis.[115] However, no focus will be on the potential influence of factual circumstance in the time gap between opposition to the registration of trademarks and the invalidation of already registered trademarks.[116] The central legal question in typical confusion cases can be framed as: is the average consumer likely to have been confused about a link between the claimant and defendant's businesses, due to the defendant's unauthorized use of the claimant's trademark, or that the average consumer may believe that the sets of products are from the same company?

In addition, the overall topic of confusion in European trademark law has regularly featured in several scholarly analyses that also focus on the average

---

[113]Maeyaert, Paul, and Muyldermans, Jeroen, 'Likelihood of Confusion in Trademark Law: A Practical Guide Based on the Case Law in Community Trade Mark Oppositions from 2002 to 2012', Trademark Reporter, vol. 103/no. 5, (2013), pp. 1032, p. 1038. Although the article focuses on the registration of trademarks in Europe, the importance of the likelihood of confusion query seems to be stressed in a broader light, i.e. also related to infringement.

[114]Fhima, Ilanah, and Denvir, Catrina, 'An Empirical Analysis of the Likelihood of Confusion Factors in European Trade Mark Law', IIC, vol. 46/no. 3, (2015), pp. 310, p. 311.

[115]In framing the average consumer, there are significant differences between the registration and infringement scenarios. One being that the former is more hypothetical given that the junior trademark is not in use whereas this is not the case in the latter. See for instance, Chap. 10, Sect. 10.2.2 for a further account of the different scenarios.

[116]The relative grounds for refusal or invalidity related to the likelihood confusion are found in art. 5 (1)(b) of the TM Directive and arts. 8(1)(b) and 60(1)(a) of the TM Regulation. As Bøggild and Staunstrup have pointed out, what has happened in the market between the registration of the junior trademark (and the opposition to this registration) and the invalidation claim by the senior trademark owner may influence the invalidation decision. For instance, it may influence an invalidation decision if it is possible for any of the parties to substantiate that the relevant public has changed or for the senior trademark owner to substantiate that actual confusion has occurred. Bøggild, Frank, and Staunstrup, Kolja, 'EU-Varemærkeret', (1st edn, Karnov Group, 2015), p. 430-431. See also, Davis, Richard, St Quintin, Thomas and Tritton, Guy, 'Tritton on Intellectual Property in Europe', (5th edn, Sweet & Maxwell, 2018), p. 365-366 and 375 and Mellor, James, David Llewelyn, Moody-Stuart, Thomas et al, 'Kerly's Law of Trade Marks and Trade Names', (16th edn, Sweet & Maxwell, 2018), p. 426-427.

consumer.[117] In one such analysis, it has been stated that "[t]he perception of the trademarks by the average consumer of the goods or services in question plays a decisive role in the global appreciation of the likelihood of confusion."[118] This introduces the "global appreciation test," a critical and connected part of the cumulative judicial process involving the average consumer in EU confusion-based infringement set out below.[119]

Outside of high-profile trademark infringement litigation before Europe's highest courts, the average consumer is of upmost importance. The European Union Intellectual Property Office (the "EUIPO")[120] and many national registries do not assess the relative grounds for refusal of registration *ex officio*, including the question on confusion referring to the perception of the average consumer.[121] Essentially, the EU legislature and national legislatures in these member state jurisdictions leave it for the "market to regulate itself and for applicants to 'have a go' at registering borderline or, possibly invalid marks."[122] The "market" is arguably represented by the senior trademark owner who may oppose to the registration of a mark (EU trademarks or national trademarks) of the junior trademark owner, which is confusingly similar to that of the senior trademark owner, or seeks to have such

---

[117]See among others, Maeyaert, Paul, and Muyldermans, Jeroen, 'Likelihood of Confusion in Trademark Law: A Practical Guide Based on the Case Law in Community Trade Mark Oppositions from 2002 to 2012', Trademark Reporter, vol. 103/no. 5, (2013), pp. 1032, p. 1041 and Dent focusing on the history for confusion in an Australian context in Dent, Chris, 'Confusion in a Legal Regime Built on Deception: The Case of Trade Marks', Queen Mary Journal of Intellectual Property, vol. 5/no. 1, (2015), pp. 2. Fhima, Ilanah, and Denvir, Catrina, 'An Empirical Analysis of the Likelihood of Confusion Factors in European Trade Mark Law', IIC, vol. 46/no. 3, (2015), pp. 310. and the forthcoming, Fhima, Ilanah S., and Gangjee, Dev S., 'The Confusion Test in European Trade Mark Law', (1st edn, Oxford University Press, 2019 (forthcoming)) to be published in March 2017. See also the sources referred by Maeyaert, Paul, and Muyldermans, Jeroen, 'Likelihood of Confusion in Trademark Law: A Practical Guide Based on the Case Law in Community Trade Mark Oppositions from 2002 to 2012', Trademark Reporter, vol. 103/no. 5, (2013), pp. 1032.

[118]See Maeyaert, Paul, and Muyldermans, Jeroen, 'Likelihood of Confusion in Trademark Law: A Practical Guide Based on the Case Law in Community Trade Mark Oppositions from 2002 to 2012', Trademark Reporter, vol. 103/no. 5, (2013), pp. 1032, p. 1041.

[119]As explained by Mellor *et al* "the term "global appreciation" is used in four different contexts in relation to the relative grounds (and infringement): (i) in the assessment as to whether marks are identical(...) (ii) whether there is a likelihood of confusion, (...) (iii) whether there is a link between the earlier and later mark, (...) and (iv) if so, whether the link gives rise to an unfair advantage or would be detrimental to the distinctive character of the earlier trade mark." Mellor, James, David Llewelyn, Moody-Stuart, Thomas, *et al*, 'Kerly's Law of Trade Marks and Trade Names', (16th edn, Sweet & Maxwell, 2018), p. 399.

[120]As per recital 2 of the TM Amendment Regulation the name of the Office for Harmonisation of the European Union (OHIM) has been changed into the EUIPO and the Community trade mark into the EU trademark.

[121]Davis, Richard, St Quintin, Thomas and Tritton, Guy, 'Tritton on Intellectual Property in Europe', (5th edn, Sweet & Maxwell, 2018), p. 515.

[122]Firth, Alison, Lea, Gary R. and Cornford, Peter, 'Trade Marks: Law and Practice', (4th edn, Jordans, 2016), p. 9.

marks invalidated after registration. Here, respectively EUIPO and the national trademark registries decide the opposition invalidation proceedings referring to the average consumer as it is laid out by the judiciaries.[123]

The long line of rulings in Europe on this specific area of European trademark law indicates its practical importance and relevance to the market. The large volume of cases on confusion-based disputes across Europe reflects that likelihood of confusion features both in assessing the relative grounds for refusal of registration as part of opposition and invalidity proceedings and as part of infringement proceedings. For example, in the "double-identity" cases the role of the average consumer is narrowed to deciding if the two marks are identical[124] and confusion is assumed.[125] In disputes related to whether trademarks enjoy a protectable reputation, the role of the average consumer is more fragmented compared to confusion-based disputes. This may reflect a debate on the functions of trademarks and the basis for protecting such reputable trademarks where there is no requirement of proving confusion. Such other functions are those "of guaranteeing the quality of the goods or services in question and those of communication, investment or advertising."[126] With all this said, comparisons to non-confusion-based disputes on trademark registration- and reputation-based areas of jurisprudence and practice are made on several occasions.

Partly, the aim of this book is to fasten the law and practice analysed to a theoretical content and perspective. As theoretical background, the basis of the legal protection afforded by registered trademarks under European trademark law to prevent confusion is set out in the preamble to the TM Directive: "The likelihood of confusion, the appreciation of which depends on many elements and, in particular, on the recognition of the trade mark on the market, the association which can be made with the used or registered sign, the degree of similarity between the trade mark and the sign and between the goods or services identified, should constitute the specific condition for such protection." This explanation is anchored to the preliminary legislative statement that: "the function of which [legal protection] is in particular to guarantee the trade mark as an indication of origin."[127]

---

[123]In 2017 the number of heard EUIPO opposition decisions on EU trademarks was 6,668 (an increase of 33% compared to 2016) and cancellation decisions on EU trademarks (i.e. including both revocations and invalidations of registered trademarks) was 727 (a decrease of approximately 36% compared to 2016). See the European Intellectual Property Office Annual Report 2017, available at: https://euipo.europa.eu/tunnel-web/secure/webdav/guest/document_library/contentPdfs/about_euipo/annual_report/annual_report_2017_en.pdf (last visited 26 May 2019), p. 20-421.

[124]See above footnote 110.

[125]Senftleben, Martin, 'Trade Mark Protection - A Black Hole in the Intellectual Property Galaxy?', IIC, vol. 42/no. 4, (2011), pp. 383, p. 383.

[126]The functions, other than the origin functions, were prominently set out in L'Oréal v. Bellure, Case C-487/07, [2009] ECR I-5185, para 58. Bently, Lionel, 'From communication to thing: historical aspects of the conceptualisation of trade marks as property', in Dinwoodie, Graeme B., and Janis, Mark D. eds., Trademark Law and Theory: A Handbook of Contemporary Research (1st edn, Edward Elgar, 2008), 41. See below Sect. 1.3.1.

[127]Recital 16 of the TM Directive. See also recital 11 of the TM Regulation.

The focus on the average consumer, while worthwhile in itself for the reasons cited above, connects closely to the perceived justificatory basis of European trademark law *per se* and registered senior rights specifically given the significance of confusion within European trademark law. This focus recognises that confusion-based disputes assessed referring to the average consumer accurately links to the core theoretical basis of legal protection for trademarks in the EU, i.e. the "essential function" of trademarks as interpreted under EU jurisprudence, namely the "origin function" and their corresponding ability to enhance competition.[128]

1.5.2 Temporal Delimitation

Since the focus of this analysis is the average consumer in *European* trademark law, it is natural to have as the temporal starting point when it was actually introduced in *Europe*. The temporal starting point for European trademark law is found in the first trademark directive, the TM Directive 1989 harmonising member state trademark law.[129] As is clear now though, the TM Directive 1989 or the subsequent EU regulation did not introduce the average consumer. To detect the average consumer, one approach could be looking at national decisions after implementing the directive into national law. However, this approach would not capture any inconsistency of the use of the average consumer in different member states. Although the decisions of one member state may have some relevance on the adjudication of other member states, it is not feasible to talk about a *European* average consumer, before the Court of Justice pushed it forward to the European stage. This was done 11 November 1997 where the Court of Justice made its decision in *Sabel*.[130] This date constitutes the temporal starting point for the main analysis. Also, *Sabel* is part of a "trinity" of decisions that include *Gut Springenheide* and *Lloyd*.[131] In this book, the three decisions have been deemed to be the main sources of the average consumer now known to European trademark law.

The cut-off date does by no means indicate that relevant decisions to the formation of the average consumer are not found in Court of Justice case law before that date. It is thus argued that the development can be traced back to *Cassis de Dijon* and the bulk of free movement case law developing in (almost) two decades after this decision.[132]

---

[128]For the purpose of European trademark law, see Sect. 1.3 below.

[129]The directive was to be implemented by the member states no later than 28 December 1991, cf. art. 16(1) of the TM Directive 1989.

[130]Sabel v. Puma, Case C-251/95, [1997] ECR I-6191

[131]Gut Springenheide and Tusky, Case C-210/96, [1998] ECR I-4657 and Lloyd Schuhfabrik Meyer v. Klijsen Handel BV, Case C-342/97, [1999] ECR I-3819. This "trinity" of decisions is analysed in Chap. 10.

[132]The early beginnings from *Cassis de Dijon to Sabel* is addressed in Chap. 8.

1.5.3   Geographical Delimitation

Since the average consumer is fleshed out by the national courts in EU when they decide on infringement and registration disputes of national trademarks and on infringement disputes of EU trademarks, this book not only focuses on CJEU case law but also on national case law. The national jurisdictions chosen are England and Wales (representing the UK), Sweden, Denmark and Norway. These countries give an insight into how the different national judiciaries use and develop the average consumer as set out by mainly the Court of Justice and they are the representatives of two legal families, the Common law legal family, and the Nordic law legal family. The book is thus geographical delimitated to the mentioned jurisdictions. In Chap. 2, this delimitation is further defined, and it is argued why and how Norway, as the only non-EU member, fits into the EU context.

Arguably, Germany could have been included as main representative of the Germanic legal family since it is often contrasted with Common Law.[133] The reason for not including German law is to avoid covering too much substantial ground. The aim is to ensure that the findings will have more research validity.

As it so often happens to researchers being part of longer research projects, reality outplays certain aspects of the research. Speculation on the significance of the so-called "Brexit" (the 2016 vote of the UK people to leave the EU) has been roaring since the result of the referendum was known.[134] It has recently been stated by the UK Intellectual Property Office (the "UK IPO"), that "[t]he existing UK system for protecting trade mark rights will remain largely unaffected by the UK's decision to leave the EU."[135] It must also be borne in mind that after Brexit, there are legal and commercial interests in maintaining the *status quo* of UK trademark law. Thus, as mentioned in a recent explanatory memorandum on the amendment of the

---

[133]See among others, Lundmark, Thomas, 'Charting the Divide between Common and Civil Law', (1st edn, Oxford University Press, 2012), Zweigert, Konrad, and Kötz, Hein, 'Introduction to Comparative Law', (3rd edn, Oxford University Press, 1998), p. 69, Husa, Jaakko, Nuotio, Kimmo and Pihlajamäki, Heikki, 'Nordic Law - between Tradition and Dynamism', in Jaakko, Husa, Nuotio, Kimmo and Pihlajamäki, Heikki eds., Nordic Law - between Tradition and Dynamism (1st edn, Intersentia, 2007), pp. 1, p. 9. See also Husa, Jaakko, and Tapani, Jussi, 'Germanic and Nordic Fraud - A Comparative Look Under the Surface of Commonalities', Global Jurist Advances, vol. 5/no. 2, (2005), pp. 1, p. 11-12 and p. 14, Husa, Jaakko, Nuotio, Kimmo and Pihlajamäki, Heikki, 'Nordic Law - between Tradition and Dynamism', in Jaakko, Husa, Nuotio, Kimmo and Pihlajamäki, Heikki eds., Nordic Law - between Tradition and Dynamism (1st edn, Intersentia, 2007), pp. 1, p. 9, Smiths, Jan M., 'Nordic Law in a European Context: Some Comparative Observations', in Husa, Jaakko, Nuotio, Kimmo and Pihlajamäki, Heikki eds., Nordic Law - between Tradition and Dynamism (1st edn, Intersentia, 2007), 55, p. 61.

[134]Finalising this book, the current state of the Brexit is that the UK is still a member of the EU, and that the withdrawal procedure under art. 50 of the TEU has been formally initiated, meaning that the UK is due to leave the EU 29 March 2019 with a likely transition period until 31 December 2020.

[135]See: https://www.gov.uk/government/publications/ip-and-brexit-the-facts (the website is last updated 1 March 2019) (last visited 26 May 2019). On this website, the UK IPO ongoingly informs about the consequences of Brexit to Intellectual Property law in the UK.

UK TM Act 1994, "stakeholders are keen for UK law to retain parity with EU trade mark systems for as long as possible post EU Exit."[136] One feasible way to reach this end could have been the EEA Agreement scenario (as it is known in a mature form in e.g. Norway),[137] where the UK with some limitations would have to follow future EU trademark directives and the decisions of the Court of Justice on this legislation. However, the EEA solution seems elusive since as of June 2018 it was not an objective for the UK Government when negotiating an exit agreement with the EU to stay in the EEA.[138]

No matter the future influence of Brexit on UK trademark legislation (when/if Brexit manifests), the UK case law is already highly influenced by EU trademark law, as it is based on the trademark directives or regulations, and therefore also the average consumer as set out by the Court of Justice.[139] Thus, a speculative conclusion on the influence on Brexit on the part of the UK trademark law relevant to this book is that substantially, the average consumer under UK law will remain the same. This is based on the many decisions of the UK courts, at least of the courts of England and Wales, providing detailed guidelines for applying the average consumer in trademark law. Some of these decisions are found in the series of decisions in Interflora v. M&S issued by the High Court and Court of Appeal of England and Wales.[140]

1.5.4 National Procedural Rules and Evidence

Drawing on national law, it has to be borne in mind, that trademark disputes decided by national courts are decided according to national procedural rules.[141] Thus, in a recital of the TM Directive it is stated that "[t]he ways in which a likelihood of

---

[136]Explanatory Memorandum to the Trade Marks Regulations 2018, No. 825, p. 5.

[137]Agreement on the European Economic Area Final Act, of 3 March 1994, [1994], OJ L 1 (the "EEA Agreement"). See Chap. 3, Sect. 3.3.2, in particular Sect. 3.3.2.3.

[138]The EU (Withdrawal) Act 2018 repeals from the date of the UK exit from the EU the European Communities Act of 1972 that gives force to EU law in the UK. Close to passing by Parliament of the Withdrawal Act on 26 June 2018, the House of Commons on 13 June 2018 rejected certain amendments to the act suggested by the House of Lord that would have made it a mandatory negotiating objective of the Government when negotiating the exit agreement to stay in the European Economic Area. See: https://www.parliament.uk/business/news/2017/september/com mons-european-union-withdrawal-bill/ (last visited 26 May 2019).

[139]Curtis, Lee, and Somers, Lauren, 'What a Brexit would Mean for UK and EU Trademark Law', World Trademark Review, vol. October/November (2015), p. 50.

[140]On these decisions, see mainly Chap. 11.

[141]In art. 129(3) of the TM Regulation it is stated: "Unless otherwise provided for in this Regulation, an EU trade mark court shall apply the rules of procedure governing the same type of action relating to a national trade mark in the Member State in which the court is located." See also Davis, Richard, St Quintin, Thomas and Tritton, Guy, 'Tritton on Intellectual Property in Europe', (5th edn, Sweet & Maxwell, 2018), p. 296-299 and 513-514.

confusion can be established, and in particular the onus of proof in that regard, should be a matter for national procedural rules which should not be prejudiced by this Directive."[142] As for the division between what is substantial trademark law interpreted ultimately by the Court of Justice and factual matters left to be decided by the national courts, the Court of Justice is not always clear.[143] The distinction actually matters for the framing of the average consumer in that "the Court [of Justice] will defer to national court application of its global appreciation test of confusion absent reliance on an incorrect principle of law, and national courts have begun to fleshing out the test in ways that are more practically helpful than the formulaic incantations emanating from the CJEU."[144] The national courts' application of the facts of a case of the global appreciation test involving the average consumer takes place under national procedural rules. National procedural rules include rules on what evidence may be presented on the perception of the average consumer. Examples of such evidence could be survey evidence and expert evidence. Referring to survey evidence Viken has held that "[i]n presenting such surveys as evidence of factual perceptions in the market, the division between legal interpretations on the one hand, and assessments based on procedural rules on the other, becomes readily apparent."[145]

As appeal court to the General Court, the Court of Justice in disputes on registration of EU trademarks on many occasions has stated that based on treaty law "[t]he General Court (…) has exclusive jurisdiction to find and appraise the relevant facts and to assess the evidence. The appraisal of those facts and the assessment of that evidence thus do not, save where the facts or evidence are

---

[142]Recital 16 of the TM Directive.

[143]See below in Chap. 11. As Tritton *et al* pointed out in the 2014 edition of their book, the starting point is that it is for the proprietor of the registered trademark to prove "that the use of the sign by a defendant will adversely affect the essential function (or other functions) of a trade mark." However, referring to *Interflora Court of Justice*, Tritton *et al* have seen a deviation from the starting point, since "if either it is difficult to ascertain whether the goods or services of the advertiser originate from the proprietor of the earlier trade mark or indeed, if the average consumer is unable to determine such a fact, then it should be assumed that there is an adverse effect on the function of the trade mark." In this context, reference was made to Interflora v. Marks & Spencer, Case C-323/09, [2011] ECR I-8625, paras 44-45. Tritton, Guy, Davis, Richard, Longstaff, Ben, *et al*, 'Tritton on Intellectual Property in Europe', (4th edn, Sweet & Maxwell, 2014), p. 406-408, and less elaborative in his recent version of the book. See Davis, Richard, St. Quintin, Thomas and Tritton, Guy, 'Tritton on Intellectual Property in Europe', (5th edn, Sweet & Maxwell, 2018), 286-287.

[144]Dinwoodie, Graeme B, 'The Europeanization of Trade Mark Law', in Ohly, Ansgar and Pila, Justine eds., The Europeanization of Intellectual Property Law: Towards a European Legal Methodology (1st edn, Oxford University Press, 2013), 72, p. 92.

[145]Viken, Monica, 'Legal Aspects regarding the use of Market Surveys as Evidence', NIR, vol. 3/(2012), pp. 220, p. 222. The article (in English) from which this quote is taken addresses the use of survey evidence in Nordic trademark and marketing law cases. The article is condensing some of the conclusions of Viken's preceding PhD project (in Norwegian) on the topic, i.e. Viken, Monica, 'Markedsundersøkelser som Bevis i Varemerke- og Markedsføringsrett', (1st edn, Oslo, Gyldendal, 2011).

distorted, constitute a point of law which, as such, is open to review by the Court of Justice on appeal."[146]

Procedural rules are not addressed as such in this book since focus is on substantive trademark law. However, the overall understanding of which facts are to be assessed by the national courts and which by the General Court under their procedural rules is relevant to better understand the factual and normative side of the average consumer fiction. In that capacity the distinction between procedural law and substantial law is addressed. This is referred to in this book as the fact/law divide.

1.5.5 Adjacent Areas of Law

The cousins of the average consumer are found in EU design law in European Patent law and in tort law. An average consumer as such is found in adjacent areas of law, including the UCPD. The cousins of the average consumer and the average consumer under the UCPD potentially influence the average consumer in European trademark law.

With *PepsiCo v. Grupo Promer* on EU design law the Court of Justice negatively defined the "informed user" in design law referring to the "average consumer" from trademark law and the "sectoral expert" from patent law.[147] With this decision, the court thus invited for an account of the differences and similarities between those fictions. Also, the reasonable person in tort law is relevant to this account since it resembles the other fictions.

The UCPD explicitly refers to an average consumer. At a glance, it is identical to that of European trademark law, but at a closer look, significant differences emerge within the legislative subtext and from case law on the UCPD. Since focus of this book is *European* trademark law, the analysis of the UCPD is kept at an *EU* level meaning an analysis of the UCPD as such and the case law of the Court of Justice interpreting the directive.[148] One reason for including the UCPD is its real and false friendship with European trademark law. As clarified below, the two areas of law may be treated as adjacent areas of law, though remembering that European trademark law is focused on business-to-business ("B2B") relationships whereas the UCPD protects consumers in business-to-consumer ("B2C") relationships. As part of the recently finalised EU trademark reform, it was stated that the UCPD forms part

---

[146]Arnoldi Mondadori v. OHIM, Case C-548/14 P, [2015], para 38 and the case law referred to here.

[147]PepsiCo v. Grupo Promer, Case C-281/10 P, [2011] ECR I-10153, paras 53 and 59. See Chap. 6.

[148]A flipside of this focus is found in Duivenvoorde's 2015 PhD thesis, "The Consumer Benchmarks in the Unfair Commercial Practices Directive" also considering the UCPD as implemented by the member states and national case law but only focusing on EU trademark law. Duivenvoorde, Bram B., 'The Consumer Benchmarks in the Unfair Commercial Practices Directive', (1st edn, Springer, 2015).

of an "overall legal framework" with European trademark law.[149] The UCPD is a "framework directive" that will step aside in case of sectoral regulation according to the principle *lex generalis derogat legi speciali*.[150] Hence, "[i]n the case of conflict between the provisions of this Directive [the UCPD] and other Community rules regulating specific aspects of unfair commercial practices, the latter shall prevail and apply to those specific aspects."[151]

After searching on EUR-Lex,[152] it emerges that the average consumer is not only referred to in the UCPD but also in other secondary EU legislation. It appears from the search, that the first time the average consumer was mentioned by the EU legislature was in a directive from 1990 on nutrition labelling for foodstuffs where it was stated that "[w]hereas, to appeal to the average consumer and to serve the purpose for which it [the directive] is introduced, and given the current low level of knowledge on the subject of nutrition, the information provided should be simple and easily understood."[153] Subsequently, the average consumer has, most notably been referred to in a regulation from 2011 on the provision of food information to consumers[154] repealing the just mentioned directive and amending a regulation from

---

[149]The Max Planck TM Report pk. 1.21, p. 50. See also below Chap. 7.

[150]For a recent mentioning of the principle, see e.g. Dinwoodie, Graeme B., 'Introduction', in Dinwoodie, Graeme B. ed., Intellectual Property and General Legal Principles: Is IP a Lex Specialis? (1st edn, Edward Elgar, 2015), 1. That the UCPD is considered a *lex generalis* stepping aside for *lex specialis* appears from art. 3(4) of the directive. See also Citroën Commerce v. ZLW, Case C-476/14, [2016], para 42.

[151]Cf. art. 3(4) of the UCPD. See also Garde, Amandine, 'Can the UCP Directive Really Be a Vector of Legal Certainty?' in van Boom, Willem, Garde, Amandine and Akseli, Orkun eds., The European Unfair Commercial Practices Directive: Impact, Enforcement Strategies and National Legal Systems (1st edn, Farnham, Ashgate, 2014), 109, p. 120-126.

[152]The EUR-Lex database provides access to documents such as i) the Official Journal of the European Union, ii) EU law, iii) preparatory acts and iv) EFTA documents.

[153]Council Directive of 24 September 1990 on nutrition labelling for foodstuffs (90/496/EEC), [1990] OJ L 276/40. Recital 9 of the directive.

[154]EP and Council Regulation (EU) No 1169/2011 of 25 October 2011 on the provision of food information to consumers, amending Regulations (EC) No 1924/2006 and (EC) No 1925/2006 of the European Parliament and of the Council, and repealing Commission Directive 87/250/EEC, Council Directive 90/496/EEC, Commission Directive 1999/10/EC, Directive 2000/13/EC of the European Parliament and of the Council, Commission Directives 2002/67/EC and 2008/5/EC and Commission Regulation (EC) No 608/2004, [2011] OJ L 304/18. In the regulation it is stated in recital 41, that "[t]o appeal to the average consumer and to serve the informative purpose for which it is introduced, and given the current level of knowledge on the subject of nutrition, the nutrition information provided should be simple and easily understood. To have the nutrition information partly in the principal field of vision, commonly known as the 'front of pack', and partly on another side on the pack, for instance the 'back of pack', might confuse consumers." (. . .) A free choice as to the information that could be repeated might confuse consumers. Therefore it is necessary to clarify which information may be repeated." Furthermore, in recital 43 that "[t]here have been recent developments in the expression of the nutrition declaration, other than per 100 g, per 100 ml or per portion, or in its presentation, through the use of graphical forms or symbols, by some Member States and organisations in the food sector. Such additional forms of expression and presentation may help consumers to better understand the nutrition declaration. *However, there is insufficient*

2006 on nutrition and health claims made on food also referring to the average consumer.[155] Besides in the regulation from 2011, the average consumer is referred to in a regulation from 2013 setting the rules for applications concerning the use of generic descriptors (denominations)[156] and a repealed directive from 2007 as regards labelling, advertising or presenting foods intended for energy-restricted diets for weight reduction.[157] Most recently, in a regulation from 2017 on energy labelling of

---

evidence across all the Union on how the average consumer understands and uses the alternative forms of expression or presentation of the information. Therefore, it is appropriate to allow for different forms of expression and presentation to be developed on the basis of criteria established in this Regulation and to invite the Commission to prepare a report regarding the use of those forms of expression and presentation, their effect on the internal market and the advisability of further harmonisation" (italics added).

In art. 35 of the regulation it is specified how certain nutrition information "may be given by other forms of expression and/or presented using graphical forms or symbols in addition to words or numbers (. . .)" one requirement for using these alternative forms of expression is that *"d) they are supported by scientifically valid evidence of understanding of such forms of expression or presentation by the average consumer"* (italics added).

[155]EP and Council Regulation (EC) No 1924/2006 of 20 December 2006 on nutrition and health claims made on foods, [2006] OJ L 404/9. Recital 16 of the regulation states that "[i]t is important that claims on foods can be understood by the consumer and it is appropriate to protect all consumers from misleading claims." This recital continues in a substantially identical way to set out the relevance of the average consumer akin to recital 18 of the UCPD analysed in Chap. 7. Furthermore, art. 5(2) of the regulation states that "[t]he use of nutrition and health claims shall only be permitted if the average consumer can be expected to understand the beneficial effects as expressed in the claim." Under art. 13 of the directive certain "health claims" with no reference "to the reduction of disease risk and to children's development and health" "may be made without undergoing the procedures laid down in Articles 15 to 19, if they are: (i) based on generally accepted scientific evidence; and (ii) *well understood by the average consumer"* (italics added).

[156]Commission Regulation (EU) No 907/2013 of 20 September 2013 setting the rules for applications concerning the use of generic descriptors (denominations), [2013] OJ L 251/7. Recital 5 of the regulation states that "[i]n order, inter alia, to ensure a high level of protection for consumers, the use of claims should not be false, ambiguous or misleading. The same principle should apply for the use of generic descriptors (denominations) which could imply an effect on health. In order to achieve such objective and in line with the principle of proportionality, national authorities will have to exercise their own faculty of judgment, having regard to the case law of the Court of Justice, to determine *the typical reaction of the average consumer in a given case."* Italics added. According to art. 1 of the directive, the "[a]pplications concerning the use of generic descriptors (denominations) within the meaning of Article 1(4) of Regulation (EC) No 1924/2006 shall be submitted and presented in accordance with the rules set out in the Annex" of the directive.

[157]Commission Directive 2007/29/EC of 30 May 2007 amending Directive 96/8/EC as regards labelling, advertising or presenting foods intended for use in energy-restricted diets for weight reduction, [2007] OJ L 139/22. Recital 4 of the directive states that "[a]llowing claims referring to a reduction in the sense of hunger or an increase in the sense of satiety under the condition that such claims are based on generally accepted scientific evidence and are well understood by the average consumer reflects the evolution in the range and properties of products." This directive was repealed by the following regulation where the reference to the average consumer does not appear: Commission Regulation (EU) No 609/2013 of 12 June 2013 on food intended for infants and young children, food for special medical purposes, and total diet replacement for weight control, [2013] OJ L 181/35.

energy-related products, it is stated that when given this labelling information among other aspects the "average consumer behaviour" should be considered.[158]

To get a broader understanding of the role of the average consumer at EU level, it would be relevant to address the areas of law categorised as *lex specialis* left solely to be regulated by sectoral EU legislation and which areas are not covered by *lex specialis* legislation but left to the UCPD as the fall-back *lex generalis* legislation.

In sum, EU design law, European patent law and European tort law are included as examples of areas of law where fictions similar to the average consumer are used. Only the UCPD is included as an example of a directive that explicitly refers to an average consumer whereas the specific EU legislation that also refers to an average consumer is not included. The legal principles of those adjacent areas of law are only addressed from overall EU/European perspectives and not from national perspectives. This is done to get an understanding of the law relevant to their respective fictions and a better understanding of the average consumer of European trademark law.

1.6   Purpose and Outline of the Analysis

It is the proposition of this book that the average consumer as applied in European trademark law is incoherent and inconsistent. The proposition is rooted in the finding already laid out, namely that the EU legislature has left the likelihood of confusion standard vaguely defined, and that the Court of Justice has only provided a broad legal frame reining in the standard referring to the average consumer as a key element. The proposition is also rooted in the complex and dynamic legal setting of the average consumer.[159] What is exactly contained within the legal fiction frame of the average consumer consisting of normative and factual aspects? If at all, how are the normative elements rooted in trademark policy, and how do the descriptive elements reflect actual purchasing behaviour? Overall, what impact does the average consumer have on European trademark law and the European trademark system, including the ability to achieve its policy goals? The aim of the analysis is to provide a surer platform to improve the academic and practical understanding of the role and effects of the average consumer as a matter of legal principle and as an integral part of the European trademark system.

The dynamics surrounding the average consumer derive from inside and outside of European trademark law and from the nature of the average consumer that plays a part in the fragmented marketplace.

The internal view of trademark law reflects a "silo" view, which will be referred as the vertical aspects of the analysis where focus is the interplay between the

---

[158]European Parliament and Council Regulation (EU) 2017/1369 of 4 July 2017 setting a framework for energy labelling and repealing Directive 2010/30/EU [2017] OJ L 198/1, recital 35.
[159]See Chap. 4.

different levels of the law,—i.e. mainly the EU level and national level. Strictly speaking, this line of analysis includes both vertical and horizontal aspects. The relationship between the different national jurisdictions in isolation though is the horizontal aspect.[160] However, due to presumed high level of harmonisation of European trademark law and as a matter of conceptual clarity, "vertical" will be taken to refer to the internal analysis of European trademark law. The vertical analysis accounts for the European legal method applied in this book. It includes analysing substantial European trademark law, which is taken to be EU trademark law and the trademark law of England and Wales, Sweden, Denmark and Norway.[161]

The inputs coming from outside of European trademark law will be referred as the horizontal aspects. The horizontal aspects include both an analysis of the average consumer vis-à-vis the "cousin" fictions in related areas of law, i.e. EU design law, European patent law and tort law. Also included is an analysis of how the average consumer as such is applied in the UCPD and the following the case law of the Court of Justice.

Perhaps it is fictitious to divide the analysis according to the vertical and horizontal dichotomy referring to the UCPD since the two areas of law in some areas overlap. For those two areas of law it makes sense to maintain the vertical/horizontal divide as analytical and conceptual tools. After all, European trademark law and consumer protection law, represented by the UCPD, are two separate areas of law with two mainly different policy underpinnings. The former mainly focuses on B2B relationships, protecting the senior trademark owner, whereas the latter focuses explicitly on B2C relationships protecting the presumptively weaker consumers.[162]

The point of departure for the analysis is *"how is the average consumer applied in European trademark law."* The analysis of this is approached from five angles to analyse:

First, *"what are the differences and similarities between the function of other related legal fictions in European law."* This query involves an overall analysis of the "informed user" in EU design law, the "person skilled in the art" in European patent law and the "reasonable person" in European tort law. Since the average

---

[160]Hence, McEvoy in setting out different categories of comparative law has described for instance a comparison of EU law and English law as a vertical comparison, whereas a comparison of English law and French law is a horizontal comparison. McEvoy, Sebastian., 'Descriptive and Purposive Categories of Comparative Law', in Monateri, P. G. ed., Methods of Comparative Law (1st edn, Edward Elgar, 2012), 144, p. 146.

[161]What is understood by European trademark law is further expanded on in Chaps. 2–4.

[162]The UCPD has thus been described as "a general clause to cover all economic harm caused to consumers by unfair practices" in B2C relations. Howells, Geraint G., Micklitz, Hans-W, and Wilhelmsson, Thomas, 'European Fair Trading Law the Unfair Commercial Practices Directive', (1st edn, Ashgate, 2006), preface.

consumer has been compared with the "rational actor" model from economics[163] and
to frame the analysis of the average consumer more broadly in social science, this
fiction is addressed at the end of the analysis.

Second, *"if the average consumer in European trademark law and European
consumer protection law harmonised horizontally."* This will be addressed referring
to the policy underpinning of European trademark law in consumer protection,
represented by the UCPD. This involves giving an account of *"what are the
differences and similarities between the average consumer in European trademark
law and the UCPD."*

Third, *"if the average consumer in European trademark law is harmonised
vertically."* Focus will be on an internal vertical analysis of European trademark
law. Part of this analysis linking to the law/fact divide described above is deciding if
"the average consumer in European trademark law is mainly normative or factual."
Also, to what extent *"the average consumer is applied consistently by the CJEU and
the national judiciaries in EU, represented by England and Wales, Sweden, Denmark and Norway."*

Fourth, *"if the average consumer in European trademark law is coherent with
European trademark law policy."* As set out above, policy is understood as the legal
and economic functions of *trademarks* and the functions of the *trademark system*.

Fifth, *"how the average consumer should applied in European trademark law."*

The first **four** angles encompass a descriptive and normative analysis of the
average consumer referring to mainly trademark law but also elements from other
areas of law. Based on the analysis, the **fifth** purely normative angle looks for
improvements of the average consumer in European trademark law through some
de lege ferenda and *de sententia ferenda* observations. It is not as such the aim of this
book to develop a new grand theory and practical average consumer model in
European trademark law. That said, an analysis of coherence and consistency will
solidify suggestions for improving the current average consumer. Included in this, is
the look for statements from European and non-European scholars operating in legal
systems that face the same key issue of framing a consumer image as part of deciding
likelihood of confusion in trademark law.[164]

---

[163] Among others, Davis, Jennifer, 'Revisiting the Average Consumer: An Uncertain Presence in
European Trade Mark', Intellectual Property Quarterly, no. 1, (2015), pp. 15, p. 16.

[164] See among others, on Canadian perspective, Corbin, Ruth M., 'The Moron in a Hurry – a
Creature of Law Or Science?', in Archibald, Todd L. and Echlin, Randall Scott eds., Annual
Review of Civil Litigation 2015 (1st edn, Carswell, 2015), 43 and on an Australian/European
perspective, Weatherall, Kimberlee, 'The Consumer as the Empirical Measure of Trade Mark Law',
Modern Law Review, vol. 80/no. 1, (2017), pp. 57.

1.7 Structure

This book is divided into five parts. Besides this introduction, *Part I* includes the methodology, legal sources and an account of the dynamics of European trademark law. *Part II* includes the horizontal analysis that may be divided in two sub-parts. In the first sub-part (Chaps. 5 and 6), the average consumer is seen in broader perspective through fiction theory followed by perspectives of other legal fictions and economics' rational actor model. The second sub-part (Chap. 7) analyses the average consumer as set out under the UCPD, and the other consumer models found in this directive. Of those other models, particular attention is paid to vulnerable consumers, represented by children, since this is an area where European trademark law and the UCPD clearly differ. *Part III* is the main part of the book designated to the vertical analysis. This part involves a historical account of the judicial development of the average consumer from *Cassis de Dijon* to *Sabel*. This is followed by an analysis of how the likelihood of confusion legislative standard sets the stage for the subsequent judicial development of the average consumer from *Sabel* onwards. The part closes with an account of how the General Court and national courts contextualise the average consumer as developed by the Court of Justice. Finalising the book is *Part IV* where the vertical and horizontal findings are discussed, and it is addressed if there is need for concern. This includes an addressing of if average consumer in European trademark law is coherent with trademark policy. After this, possible solutions are discussed bringing in solutions suggested by other scholars on how to approve the average consumer. Specific emphasis is here attached to aspects of law and economics.

Chapter 2
Methodology

2.1 Methodological Challenges

This chapter sets out the methodology best suited for the analysis and to select the relevant legal sources following from this methodology. The term "methodology" means a joint methodology created from aspects derived from other methods.[1] "Methods" and "aspects of methods" will be used as references to the different building blocks of the "methodology."

The legal method of this book is the legal dogmatic method necessitated by the vertical and horizontal analyses. The legal method has to distil the legal principles underlying the average consumer inferred from a European trademark in flux. Akin to Posner's understanding of legal method, this method has to create a "synthesis" of scattered legal materials of legislatures and judges.[2]

It is necessary in all European legal analysis to reach an understanding of, what is "valid European law?"[3] It raises the questions; what is European legal method, and what weight is to be attached to different legal sources? In EU, there will probably be at least the same number of answers as member states to the question, what is the

---

[1] For a distinction between "methodology" and "methods" see Watkins, Dawn, and Mandy Burton, 'Introduction', in Watkins, Dawn and Mandy Burton eds., Research Methods in Law (1st edn, Routledge, 2013), 1, p. 2-3 and Crotty, Michael, 'The Foundations of Social Research: Meaning and Perspective in the Research Process', (1st edn, Sage, 1998), pp. 2 and Gestel, Rob Van, Micklitz, Hans-W and Maduro, Miguel Poiares, 'Methodology in the New Legal World', EUI Working Papers, (2012/13), pp. 1, p. 2-3.

[2] EU law with its multitude of different sources could tentatively be compared to Common Law that in Posner's words "is more often inferred than positive," inferred from "scattered, sometimes inconsistent, and often ambiguous, incomplete, or poorly informed materials, mainly judicial opinions." Although Posner's analysis is aimed at US Common Law this point applies more generally to common law. The process of synthesising scattered legal materials has been described by Posner as the main task for legal scholars. Posner, Richard A., 'How Judges Think', (1st edn, Harvard University Press, 2008), p. 210.

[3] See below, Sect. 2.2.

© Springer Nature Switzerland AG 2020
R. D. Laustsen, *The Average Consumer in Confusion-based Disputes in European Trademark Law and Similar Fictions*, https://doi.org/10.1007/978-3-030-26350-8_2

appropriate European legal method? The term "legal dogmatic method" is a disputed term,[4] but it seems uncontroversial to regards it as part of the broader area of legal science.[5] In this book, "legal dogmatics" is understood as the analysis through systematisation of the legal sources of European trademark law. This systematisation will be done by way of employing Scandinavian Legal Realism, focusing on case law, but also by taking a broader perspective derived from Critical Legal Positivism, inferring legal principles not only from legal sources as they appear in case law. As part of the legal method, coherence and consistency will be used as tools to analyse the law.[6]

Moving outside of legal dogmatics, Hesselink argues that "the economic, political, comparative, historical and psychological and other analysis of law can contribute to solving a legal question in a satisfactory way" and that this "legal analysis becomes less formal."[7] The legal analysis of this book brings in aspects of comparative law to get a better understanding of the legal principles underlying the average consumer. Although not addressed as separate methods, historical aspects and aspects of economic theory are used where they contribute to the analysis.[8] For instance, when making some final *de lege ferenda* and *de sententia ferenda* observations in the final chapter, economic theory through the economic function of trademarks as lowering consumer search costs is used to tentatively suggest a more rigid contextualisation.

Giving an account on if the average consumer is harmonised vertically and horizontally requires aspects of comparative law. The vertical aspects are close to

---

[4]See among others, van Hoecke, Mark, 'Preface', in van Hoecke, Mark ed., Methodologies of Legal Research: What Kind of Method for what Kind of Discipline? (1st edn, Hart, 2011), p. vi. Siemns discusses the different roles of legal doctrinal analyses in Common Law and Civil Law landscapes arguing that doctrinal research is more prominent in the latter. Siems, Mathias M., 'A World Without Law Professors', in van Hoecke, Mark ed., Methodologies of Legal Research: What Kind of Method for what Kind of Discipline? (1st edn, Hart, 2011), 71, p. 80-81. According to Pattaro, doctrinal legal research may also be called for instance, "analytical study of law" or "doctrinal study of law." Furthermore, Pattaro has held that the term "legal dogmatics" is synonymous with "legal doctrine" that is a term most often used by continental legal theorists but less known among Anglo-American legal theorists. Pattaro, Enrico, A Treatise of Legal Philosophy and General Jurisprudence: Volume 4: Scientia Juris, Legal Doctrine as Knowledge of Law, (1st edn, Springer, 2005), p. 1-2.

[5]Legal science is also an ambiguous term. See Pattaro, Enrico, A Treatise of Legal Philosophy and General Jurisprudence: Volume 4: Scientia Juris, Legal Doctrine as Knowledge of Law, (1st edn, Springer, 2005), p. 1-2, Vaquero, Álvaro Núñez, 'Five Models of Legal Science', Revus, vol. 19 (2013), pp. 53 and Hesselink, Martijn W., 'A European Legal Method?: On European Private Law and Scientific Method', European Law Journal, vol. 15/no. 1, (2009), pp. 20, p. 21-22. Legal science is understood as referring more broadly to science dealing with law i.e. encompassing relevant to this book the methodological aspects of comparative law.

[6]See below Sect. 2.2.3.

[7]Hesselink, Martijn W., 'A European Legal Method?: On European Private Law and Scientific Method', European Law Journal, vol. 15/no. 1, (2009), pp. 20, p. 33. See also Gestel, Rob Van, and Micklitz, Hans-W, 'Revitalising Doctrinal Legal Research in Europe: What about Methodology?', in Neergaard, Ulla, Nielsen, Ruth and Roseberry, Lynn M. eds., European Legal Method – Paradoxes and Revitalisation (1st edn, Djøf Publishing, 2011), 25, p. 65-66.

[8]For the historical account of the average consumer, see Chap. 8. Economic theory is used in Chap. 1, Sect. 1.3.2 and Chap. 12, Sect. 12.6.

the core of traditional comparative law since different jurisdictions within the same area of law will be compared. The horizontal comparison between European trademark law and other areas of law is however not within the core of comparative law.[9]

The listed methods make it possible to address what is the law (*de lege lata*), the point of departure for this book analysis, but also how the average consumer should be applied by the legislatures (*de lege ferenda*) and the courts (*de sententia ferenda*).[10]

Initially, this chapter sets out the methodology seeking to make the methodological assumptions explicit.[11] Coherence and consistency are described as tools for analysing the law. The legal order and the division of European trademark law consisting of different levels, mainly EU law and national trademark law but also international law, provides the steer for the following chapter where the legal sources are set out.

2.2 European Legal Method: A Scandinavian Kaleidoscope

The legal dogmatic analysis of the law comprises a descriptive analysis of the "authoritative sources, such as existing rules, principles, precedents, and scholarly publications."[12] This analysis is conducted through a synthesis of Scandinavian

---

[9]See below Sect. 2.2.3.

[10]Ross, Alf, 'On Law and Justice', (1st edn, University of California Press, 1959), p. 46. There is no clear definition of these terms in particular due to discussions on the level of normativity vested in the different approaches. Peczenik has termed the distinction between *de lege lata* and *de lege ferenda* as a "cognitive inquiry" and held that "every legal scholar knows the distinction is difficult to consistently apply in the practice of legal research." That the terms used in legal argumentation are "ideal types" and not opposite to each other. Peczenik, Aleksander, 'Atheoryoflegaldoctrine', Ratio Juris, vol. 14/no. 14, (2001), pp. 75, p. 79. There seems to be no one attacking the conclusion that *de lege lata* is the most descriptive of the three terms. In this book though, it is at the same time acknowledged and made explicit that there is normativity vested in the *de lege lata* analysis in terms of choice of methods preceding the description and the clear normative elements vested in the analytical part of describing. In addition, Peczenik held that the result of an analytical description will be infused with normativity due to the choices made before and in reaching the result. *Ibid*. See also Pattaro, Enrico, A Treatise of Legal Philosophy and General Jurisprudence: Volume 4: Scientia Juris, Legal Doctrine as Knowledge of Law, (1st edn, Springer, 2005), p. 5 and Nielsen, Ruth, 'New European Legal Realism – New Problems, New Solutions?', in Neergaard, Ulla and Nielsen, Ruth eds., European Legal Method: Towards a New European Legal Realism? (1st edn, Djøf Publishing, 2013), 75, p. 99.

[11]Thus seeking to meet the invitation of doing so from Micklitz and Maduro who argue the importance of having a methodological debate in European legal scholarship. See e.g. Gestel, Rob Van, Micklitz, Hans-W and Maduro, Miguel Poiares, 'Methodology in the New Legal World', EUI Working Papers, (2012/13), pp. 1, p. 23.

[12]Gestel, Rob Van, and Micklitz, Hans-W, 'Revitalising Doctrinal Legal Research in Europe: What about Methodology?', in Neergaard, Ulla, Nielsen, Ruth and Roseberry, Lynn M. eds., European Legal Method – Paradoxes and Revitalisation (1st edn, Djøf Publishing, 2011), 25, p. 65.

Legal Realism[13] and Critical Legal Positivism. Legal dogmatics includes not only positive elements of describing the legal sources but also normative elements analysing these sources. The aim is through a systematisation to apply coherence and consistency as analytical tools to get a deeper understanding of the legal principles, not only the ones emerging from case law.[14]

In recent years, it has occupied scholars if a European legal method exists and if so, what it looks like[15] and rightly so considering the different legal traditions in the EU member states and the overarching EU law. Hesselink states that a European legal method has to be anchored solidly to the context of its specific legal culture capturing for instance the underlying values of European law.[16] Nielsen has claimed that, "EU law belongs to the category dynamic norm setting" and that "[i]t cannot be interpreted as a hierarchy of legal sources" since "it has a more complex structure with important and other non-hierarchical elements."[17] Adding to this, Tuori has stated that EU law is "intertwined with the domestic legal systems of the member

---

[13]For a comparison of Scandinavian Legal Realism and American Legal Realism, see Alexander, Gregory S, 'Comparing the Two Legal Realisms-American and Scandinavian', the American Journal of Comparative Law, vol. 50/no. 1, (2002), pp. 131, p. 132. For a further historic account of Scandinavian Legal Realism, see Tuori, Kaarlo, 'Ratio and Voluntas: the Tension between Reason and Will in Law', (1st edn, Ashgate, 2010), p. 124-125, Tvarnø, Christina D., and Nielsen, Ruth, 'Retskilder Og Retsteorier', (5th edn, Jurist- og Økonomforbundets Forlag, 2017), p. 371 and more broadly on the theory of the sources of law in a Nordic perspective, Evald, Jens, 'Juridisk Teori, Metode og Videnskab', (1st edn, Jurist- og Økonomforbundets Forlag, 2016), p. 27–33.

[14]Westerman emphasises the difference between "ordering" and "understanding" and emphasises the role of "understanding" to doctrinal legal research – i.e. moving beyond "arriving at a coherent order" is more than merely "ordering." "Ordering" is similar to the term "systematisation" used in this book. Westerman, Pauline C., 'Open or Autonomous? The Debate on Legal Methodology as a Reflection of the Debate on Law', in van Hoecke, Mark ed., Methodologies of Legal Research: What Kind of Method for what Kind of Discipline? (1st edn, Hart, 2011), 87, p. 91.

[15]Hesselink, Martijn W., 'A European Legal Method?: On European Private Law and Scientific Method', European Law Journal, vol. 15/no. 1, (2009), pp. 20, p. 20, the European Legal Method trilogy from 2009, 2011 and 2013 edited by Nielsen and Neergaard; Gestel, Rob Van, Micklitz, Hans-W and Maduro, Miguel Poiares, 'Methodology in the New Legal World', EUI Working Papers, (2012/13), pp. 1 and Pila, Justine, 'A Constitutionalized Doctrine of Precedent and the Marleasing Principle as Bases for a European Legal Methodology', in Ohly, Ansgar and Pila, Justine eds., The Europeanization of Intellectual Property Law: Towards a European Legal Methodology (1st edn, Oxford University Press, 2013), 227, p. 230-231.

[16]Hesselink, Martijn W., 'A European Legal Method?: On European Private Law and Scientific Method', European Law Journal, vol. 15/no. 1, (2009), pp. 20, p. 36-37, 42 and 44. See also Pila, Justine, 'A Constitutionalized Doctrine of Precedent and the Marleasing Principle as Bases for a European Legal Methodology', in Ohly, Ansgar and Pila, Justine eds., The Europeanization of Intellectual Property Law: Towards a European Legal Methodology (1st edn, Oxford University Press, 2013), 227, referring to Hesselink 2009.

[17]Nielsen, Ruth, 'New European Legal Realism – New Problems, New Solutions?', in Neergaard, Ulla and Nielsen, Ruth eds., European Legal Method: Towards a New European Legal Realism? (1st edn, Djøf Publishing, 2013), 75, p. 84.

states."[18] In similar veins, Maduro has argued, former Advocate General of the Court of Justice, that "EU law cuts across traditional boundaries of private and public law, state-made law and non-state law and so on." Moreover, that "[o]ne has to understand the co-actorship between national lawmakers and EU-institutions and be able to think beyond the boxes and categories of national law."[19]

The overall development of areas of law highly influenced by EU law takes place in a dynamic setting as an interplay between the member states and the overarching EU level.[20] As pointed out by Dinwoodie, this dynamics cuts through the EU infrastructure at large and to fully understand the dynamic setting it is necessary to consider "the legal and institutional context in which the [harmonisation] process occurs, and why harmonization is being attempted."[21] The formal reasons for harmonising European trademark law are reflected in the recitals of the legislative acts.[22] One formal reason was the differences in national law that caused an impediment to free movement of goods and services and distortion of competition in the common market.[23] To get a full understanding though of "the motivations for harmonization it is required to go beyond these formal statements."[24] The findings of Dinwoodie are important to remember when framing the legal method. If too much weight is attached to the legislative wording (in the preamble and main text), the analysis may fail to expose the underpinning principles of European trademark law.

The legal method has to account for the overall distinction between the legal traditions of the Common Law and Nordic legal families[25] and the overarching EU trademark law. The perception of the average consumer as a legal fiction has

---

[18]Tuori, Kaarlo, 'Law and Beyond the Nation-State', in Modéer, Kjell Å and Diestelkamp, Bernhard eds., Liber Amicorum Kjell Å Modéer (1st edn, Juristförlaget, 2007), 691, p. 697 similar to Dinwoodie below who refers specifically to trademark law. See footnote 21.

[19]Gestel, Rob Van, Micklitz, Hans-W and Maduro, Miguel Poiares, 'Methodology in the New Legal World', EUI Working Papers, (2012/13), pp. 1, p. 15.

[20]See Chap. 4.

[21]Dinwoodie, Graeme B, 'The Europeanization of Trade Mark Law', in Ohly, Ansgar and Pila, Justine eds., The Europeanization of Intellectual Property Law: Towards a European Legal Methodology (1st edn, Oxford University Press, 2013), 72, p. 75-76. The dynamic legal development, in which the average consumer is set in European trademark law, is addressed in Chap. 4.

[22]Ibid, p. 76, including footnote 1 of the text.

[23]Recital 3 of the TM Regulation and recital 2 of the TM Directive 2008. A further analysis of the purpose of EU trademark law was given in Chap. 1, Sect. 1.3.

[24]Dinwoodie, Graeme B, 'The Europeanization of Trade Mark Law', in Ohly, Ansgar and Pila, Justine eds., The Europeanization of Intellectual Property Law: Towards a European Legal Methodology (1st edn, Oxford University Press, 2013), 72, p. 76, including footnote 1 of the text. In a US context, Grynberg has advocated in favour of a broader debate of the effectiveness of trademark law reaching "some consensus about what the courts or legislators are trying to maximize." Grynberg, Michael, 'The Judicial Role in Trademark Law', Boston College Law Review, vol. 52, (2011), pp. 1283, p. 1299.

[25]See below Sect. 2.3 and Siems, Mathias, 'Comparative Law', (1st edn, Cambridge University Press, 2014), p. 79.

implications for the legal method.[26] It has been argued by del Mar that legal fictions may be seen "as helpful modes of legal change, but then quickly denigrated as signs of an immature legal system – one that has not yet achieved the explicitness and coherence of principle that characterises a fully-grown legal order."[27] Del Mar continues to argue, that legal fictions "when used wisely, are inherently dynamic resources that allow courts, over time, to balance flexibility and responsiveness with stability and predictability."[28] To capture these complex and subtle elements of the average consumer, a broader view of the legal sources is needed.

2.2.1 Scandinavian Legal Realism

One of the predominant legal methods in Scandinavia is Scandinavian Legal Realism as represented by the Dane Alf Ross and inspired by this the subsequent Analytical Legal Positivism.[29] According to Ross, legal science should get nearer to empirical sciences in order to "interpret legal thinking formally in terms of the same logic as that on which other empirical sciences are (*is*-propositions)."[30] Ross asserted, "that the doctrinal study of law must be recognised as an empirical social science."[31] According to Ross the doctrine on the legal sources has to focus on that "legal science should be analytical descriptive (as opposed to normative) science about norms, not a science that expressed itself in norms."[32] Under the doctrine of the sources of law, legal method has to focus on predicting the result of a hypothetical court case. This prediction is essentially a prognosis of why "the judge decides to base his decision on one rule rather than another."[33] The assumption is that scholars

---

[26]This leaves aside the discussion on legal fictions as a combination of normativity and facts addressed in Chap. 5.

[27]Del Mar, Maksymilian, 'Legal Fictions and Legal Change in the Common Law Tradition', in Del Mar, Maksymilian and Twining, William eds., Legal Fictions in Theory and Practice (1st edn, Springer, 2015), 225, p. 226.

[28]*Ibid*, p. 227.

[29]Jääskinen, Niilo, 'Back to the Begriffshimmel? A Plea for an Analytical Perspective in European Law', in Prechal, Sacha and van Roermund, G. eds., The Coherence of EU Law: The Search for Unity in Divergent Concepts (1st edn, Oxford University Press, 2008), 451, p. 453.

[30]Ross, Alf, 'On Law and Justice', (1st edn, University of California Press, 1959), preface p. x.

[31]*Ibid*, p. 40.

[32]Nielsen, Ruth, 'New European Legal Realism – New Problems, New Solutions?', in Neergaard, Ulla and Nielsen, Ruth eds., European Legal Method: Towards a New European Legal Realism? (1st edn, Djøf Publishing, 2013), 75, p. 94. See also Tvarnø, Christina D., and Nielsen, Ruth, 'Retskilder Og Retsteorier', (5th edn, Jurist- og Økonomforbundets Forlag, 2017), p. 377-379.

[33]Ross, Alf, 'On Law and Justice', (1st edn, University of California Press, 1959), p. 75. For a discussion on other scholars with a significant influence on developing of Scandinavian Legal Realism see Alexander, Gregory S, 'Comparing the Two Legal Realisms-American and Scandinavian', the American Journal of Comparative Law, vol. 50/no. 1, (2002), pp. 131, p. 148-149.

can predict the result of hypothetical court cases, including which legal sources will be applied by the judges, and how they will be interpreted.[34]

One purpose of Ross' theory was to set out a jurisprudence that could be verified akin to findings in empirical sciences.[35] Hence, according to his view on jurisprudence, the decisions on what "valid law" is have to be made by judges.[36] This matter has led to criticism by e.g. Dalberg who has claimed that too much weight in Ross' theory is put on judicial decisions being correct.[37] From Ross' viewpoint, focus should be on the analysis of *de lege lata* to discover what valid law is. On the other hand, *de lege ferenda* and *de sententia ferenda* are normative considerations on the law moving away from the analysis of what is valid law.[38] Ross' opposition to *de lege ferenda* and *de sententia ferenda* analysis of law does not mean that "pragmatic factors" cannot be considered in interpreting the law.[39] It would be a pragmatic factor if "teleological interpretation" meant considering not only the purpose of the statute but all relevant considerations.[40]

According to Nielsen, applying the Scandinavian Legal Realist theory to a broader EU legal context presents a challenge since enforcement of the law takes place in the member state courts. This is certainly also true for European trademark law.[41] Hence, the decisions of the Court of Justice are "primarily a statement of the legal ideology of the CJEU and lacks the factual dimension of law unless a national legal/state system chooses to add a factual dimension to the ideological statement of the CJEU."[42]

---

[34]Nielsen, Ruth, 'Legal Realism and EU Law', in Koch, Henning *et al* eds., Europe: The New Legal Realism: Essays in Honour of Hjalte Rasmussen (1st edn, Djøf Publishing, 2010), 545, p. 545-546.

[35]Ross, Alf, 'On Law and Justice', (1st edn, University of California Press, 1959), p. 34-38.

[36]*Ibid*, p. 40.

[37]Dalberg-Larsen, Jørgen, 'Perspektiver på ret & retsvidenskab – Retssociologiske og retsteoretiske artikler', (1st edn, Jurist- og Økonomforbundets Forlag, 2009), p. 121. Similarly, Evald has held that the issue with Ross' theory is, that it is left for the courts to decide what weight to attach to different legal sources. Evald, Jens, 'Juridisk Teori, Metode og Videnskab', (1st edn, Jurist- og Økonomforbundets Forlag, 2016), p. 29-30.

[38]Ross, Alf, 'On Law and Justice', (1st edn, University of California Press, 1959), p. 49.

[39]*Ibid*, p. 146.

[40]*Ibid*, p. 147-148. Expanding on what is pragmatic interpretation, Ross stated that "[p]ragmatic interpretation might consider not only foreseeable social effects, but also the technical acuity of the interpretation and its harmony with the legal system and the cultural ideas on which the system is built." *Ibid*, p. 146.

[41]See Calboli, Irene, 'The Role of Comparative Legal Analysis in Intellectual Property: From Good to Great?', in Dinwoodie, Graeme B. ed., Methods and Perspectives in Intellectual Property (1st edn, Edward Elgar, 2013), 3, p. 20.

[42]This is at least true for the decisions of the Court of Justice relevant to the substantial analysis of the book, i.e. preliminary rulings under art. 265 of the TFEU, and when the court acts as appeal court to the General Court in disputes on registration of EU trademarks. Nielsen, Ruth, 'New European Legal Realism – New Problems, New Solutions?', in Neergaard, Ulla and Nielsen, Ruth eds., European Legal Method: Towards a New European Legal Realism? (1st edn, Djøf Publishing, 2013), 75, p. 112. It seems that Nielsen is referring to the Court of Justice, and not to the CJEU as a whole. For a discussion of the CJEU term, see Chap. 1, footnote 11. See also Nielsen, Ruth, 'Legal

Former Advocate General of the Court of Justice, Jääskinen,[43] has analysed the potential beneficial influence of applying Analytical Legal Positivism to EU law. This line of positivism is a theoretical continuation of Scandinavian Legal Realism. That legal concepts are developed in European legal systems encompassing different legal traditions is not as such a "terminological and conceptual" problem under Analytical Legal Positivism. Still, what is problematical is that "behind conceptual or terminological problems important teleological conflicts between actors and normative systems are often hidden."[44] Following Analytical Legal Positivism, it is impossible to reach "'pure' i.e. value-free legal science" Due to this "inherently necessary teleology in law, it had to be made open and transparent" what are "the valuations and ideological elements that are inherent in legal concepts and legal reasoning." Part of this transparency process meant, according to Jääskinen, that deciding between different interpretations the choice "had to be justified openly, preferably with reference to the factual societal effects of the alternatives and their practical importance."[45]

Jääskinen concluded that studies of EU law "could learn something from the Finnish analytical legal positivists or any similar school inspired by logical-analytic philosophy,"[46] including the theory of Ross. This conclusion is based on the claim that to create legal concepts "that are universally applicable" legal concepts "should be derived from legal sources and methodologically controlled argumentation." This approach would prevent too much influence from diverging legal cultures that are an inherent part of European law "when national meanings are attributed to European legal terms."[47] Transparency in Analytical Legal Positivism as set out by Jääskinen is in line with Ross' theory of "valid law."[48]

Realism and EU Law', in Koch, Henning *et al* eds., Europe: The New Legal Realism: Essays in Honour of Hjalte Rasmussen (1st edn, Djøf Publishing, 2010), 545, p. 545.

[43]These findings are made by Jääskinen before he was appointed Advocate General of the Court of Justice in October 2009. A position he held until October 2015.

[44]Jääskinen, Niilo, 'Back to the Begriffshimmel? A Plea for an Analytical Perspective in European Law', in Prechal, Sacha and van Roermund, G. eds., The Coherence of EU Law: The Search for Unity in Divergent Concepts (1st edn, Oxford University Press, 2008), 451, p. 452.

[45]*Ibid*, p. 458-459.

[46]Jääskinen, Niilo, 'Back to the Begriffshimmel? A Plea for an Analytical Perspective in European Law', in Prechal, Sacha and van Roermund, G. eds., The Coherence of EU Law: The Search for Unity in Divergent Concepts (1st edn, Oxford University Press, 2008), 451, p. 459.

[47]*Ibid*, p. 460, in Coherence of EU Law. A successful example of a legal concept not suffering this fate is according to Jääskinen "undertaking" under European competition law. *Ibid*, footnote 12 of the text.

[48]As per above for Ross' understanding of teleological interpretation. Ross, Alf, 'On Law and Justice', (1st edn, University of California Press, 1959), p. 147. It will be recalled that "valid law" according to Ross has to be made visible in national court decisions, e.g. through teleological interpretation by the court. With the focus on the role of national case law, what is then the role of judges? Comparing judges and academics Schlag has stated that "[c]ourts have dockets. Legal academics have time. Given this asymmetry, the academics could always outdo the courts in the intricacy of their analysis." Schlag, Pierre, 'Essay and Responses – Spam Jurisprudence, Air Law, and the Rank Anxiety of Nothing Happening (A Report on the State of the Art)', Geo. L.J., vol. 97/no. 3, (2009), pp. 803, p. 822. Although the statement brings the qualifications of academics and

2.2.2   *Critical Legal Positivism*

Standing on the shoulders of *inter alia* Scandinavian Legal Realism, a Finnish theory was developed adopting "some kind of a communitarian understanding of legal language and legal concepts, emphasizing their common cultural and societal meanings and functions." The Finnish Kaarlo Tuori has supported this theory with his Critical Legal Positivism focused on the different layers of law.[49] Tuori sees the law as "multi-layered" divided into three layers, i.e. the "explicit surface-level material," "legal-cultural layers" and the "deep structure."

The explicit surface-level consists *inter alia*, of specific legislation, case law, and normative scholarly works. The legal-cultural layers comprise "normative, conceptual and methodological ingredients: general legal principles, concepts and theories; doctrines of legal sources; and distinct patterns of legal argumentation." Finally, the "deep structure" comprises a common legal core shared by different legal cultures. That is, Tuori regards the positive law as not only the changeable law on the explicit surface-level but also the law rooted in deeper values of the legal system.[50]

The analysis of legal validity cannot be decimated to a descriptive analysis of case law, which is roughly the approach of Scandinavian Legal Realism. Valid law under Critical Legal Positivism encompasses a "substantive dimension" that has to be analysed against "its harmony with the principles of the law's sub-surface layers,"[51] and it has to be "justified in light of the substantive normative yardsticks" deriving from the deeper layers of the law.[52] Thus, it is considering that "legal science not

---

judges to a head it is true to say that judges and private practitioners focus on specific decisions based on specific facts and only if it is necessary for the case at hand do they regard the law with the same intricacy and coherency as academics. This argument could be true of the trial court judges whereas appeal court judges assess points of law only. For practitioners, the key purpose of a dogmatic analysis is to preserve the interests of the client and hence an assessment of the facts in a subjective light. See Pattaro, Enrico, A Treatise of Legal Philosophy and General Jurisprudence: Volume 4: Scientia Juris, Legal Doctrine as Knowledge of Law, (1st edn, Springer, 2005), p. 4.

[49] See Jääskinen, Niilo, 'Back to the Begriffshimmel? A Plea for an Analytical Perspective in European Law', in Prechal, Sacha and van Roermund, G. eds., The Coherence of EU Law: The Search for Unity in Divergent Concepts (1st edn, Oxford University Press, 2008), 451, p. 456.

[50] Tuori, Kaarlo, 'Ratio and Voluntas: the Tension between Reason and Will in Law', (1st edn, Ashgate, 2010), p. 7. On the connection between the different layers of law Tuori states that "[n]ew regulations, new decisions by the courts and new ideas from legal scholars contain seeds which can grow into new components of the deep structure. There is a constant tension between established and emerging elements within the deep structure, and it is this tension that clears space for a reconstructive legal philosophy which maintains the attitude of normative criticism." Tuori, Kaarlo, 'Critical Legal Positivism', (1st edn, Ashgate, 2002), p. 321. See also Olsen, Henrik Palmer, 'Nyere Nordisk Retsfilosofi', in Hammerslev, Ole and Olsen, Henrik Palmer eds., Retsfilosofi: Centrale Tekster og Temaer (1st edn, Hans Reitzels Forlag, 2011), 571, p. 587.

[51] Tuori, Kaarlo, 'Critical Legal Positivism', (1st edn, Ashgate, 2002), p. 288.

[52] *Ibid*, p. 289.

only studies norms but also produces statements requiring normative justification."[53]

It is stated by Tuori that there is a clear link between law and the state and that "[m]odern, positive law would not have been possible without the legislative, adjudicative and administrative bodies of the state" and vice versa.[54] It applies despite the Court of Justice denoting EU law "as an independent legal order, distinct both from the municipal legal order of the Member States and from international law."[55] Hence, an analysis of national law and EU law should reflect that national law has not been discarded but that the law consists of different levels, including the transnational EU law.[56] How much room for manoeuvring EU law leaves to national law is a central query addressed throughout this book, since this directly affects the development of the average consumer.

Specifically, when analysing the law of the member states not only the directives as implemented into national law should be considered but also "for instance, EU regulations [and] preliminary rulings of the European Court of Justice".[57] When national courts apply EU norms more broadly, "they act simultaneously as institutions of both the municipal and the EU legal system."[58] In an analysis of law in the interface between EU and national levels it is not "possible, nor perhaps even necessary, to achieve precision in the separation of law from non-law and state law from non-state law" and the fragile boundaries "between both normative orders and institutional structures."[59]

2.2.3 Coherence and Consistency

Coherence and consistency are appropriate measures for analysing the multi-level legal order surrounding and underpinning the average consumer. As already stated coherence and consistency are used both theoretically and in practice as tools for dogmatically deciding if there is order in the system of law. The measures of

---

[53]*Ibid*, p. 293. Tuori has also stated more generally that "[l]egal science without any normative commitments and implications, and approaching the law from an external observer's position, is and remains an illusion". *Ibid*, p. 295.

[54]Tuori, Kaarlo, 'Ratio and Voluntas: the Tension between Reason and Will in Law', (1st edn, Ashgate, 2010), p. 287.

[55]*Ibid*, p. 300.

[56]*Ibid*, p. 305.

[57]*Ibid*, p. 301.

[58]Tuori, Kaarlo, 'Can we Still Speak of the Coherence of Law?', in Modéer, Kjell Å ed., Aleksander Peczenik Memorial Seminar: Pufendorf Seminar, Lund, March 10, 2006 (1st edn, Corpus Iuris, 2007), pp. 56, p. 67.

[59]Tuori, Kaarlo, 'Ratio and Voluntas: the Tension between Reason and Will in Law', (1st edn, Ashgate, 2010), p. 306.

coherence and consistency will be applied in the legal analysis of European trade-mark law.[60]

It has been argued by Prechal (currently a judge of the Court of Judge) that EU law, as part of a broader European legal order, requires coherence as any other legal order.[61] According to Maduro, the teleological interpretation by the Court of Justice forces it to make explicit its normative perception of EU legal order to create "a yardstick to better assess the coherence and consistency of its case law."[62] Westerman states that coherence and consistency are among legal principles that pursue two aims, i.e. "they guide legal reasoning by legal officials, but they also serve as point of orientation in doctrinal research"[63] and as part of this aim, coherence is "indispensable for legal doctrine."[64] The latter aim of coherence and consistency is the more prominent in this book. There is no clear definition in theory or practice though of coherence and consistency.[65]

---

[60]Besides coherence and consistency, other measures could have been brought in for the legal dogmatic analysis. For instance, in terms of the functions of legal fictions it is argued that they serve as "dynamic resources that allow courts, over time, to balance *flexibility and responsiveness with stability and predictability.*" Del Mar, Maksymilian, 'Legal Fictions and Legal Change in the Common Law Tradition', in Del Mar, Maksymilian and Twining, William eds., Legal Fictions in Theory and Practice (1st edn, Springer, 2015), 225, p. 227 (italics added) and see Chap. 5. Arguably stability and predictability are criteria overlapping with coherence and consistency.

[61]Prechal, Sacha, 'Binding Unity in EU Legal Order: An Introduction', in Prechal, Sacha and Roermund, G. van eds., The Coherence of EU Law: The Search for Unity in Divergent Concepts (1st edn, Oxford University Press, 2008), 1, p. 1. In fact, Prechal argues that European legal order requires "a special kind of coherence, namely convergence."

[62]Maduro, Miguel Poiares, 'Interpreting European Law – on Why and how Law and Policy Meet at the European Court of Justice', in Koch, Henning *et al* eds., Europe: The New Legal Realism: Essays in Honour of Hjalte Rasmussen (1st edn, Djøf Publishing, 2010), 457, p. 472. Pila argues that instead of focusing on the limits of legal systems when deciding the methodology "it would be better to focus on the potential role which legal methodology might play in bringing order and coherence to the complex reality of the European legal order that exists." Pila, Justine, 'A Constitutionalized Doctrine of Precedent and the Marleasing Principle as Bases for a European Legal Methodology', in Ohly, Ansgar and Pila, Justine eds., The Europeanization of Intellectual Property Law: Towards a European Legal Methodology (1st edn, Oxford University Press, 2013), 227, p. 232.

[63]Westerman, Pauline C., 'Open or Autonomous? The Debate on Legal Methodology as a Reflection of the Debate on Law', in van Hoecke, Mark ed., Methodologies of Legal Research: What Kind of Method for what Kind of Discipline? (1st edn, Hart, 2011), 87, p. 93.

[64]*Ibid*, p. 104. Vranken, on the other hand, has a broader approach to what may be categorised as legal doctrinal research and has advocated for more interdisciplinary aspects to be encompassed by legal doctrinal research. Vranken, Jan, 'Methodology of Legal Doctrinal Research: A Comment on Westerman', in van Hoecke, Mark ed., Methodologies of Legal Research: What Kind of Method for what Kind of Discipline? (1st edn, Hart, 2011), 111, p. 118 and p. 120.

[65]For an in depth discussion on the differences between the terms see Hillion, Christophe, 'Tous Pour Un, Un Pour Tous! Coherence in the External Relations of the European Union', in Cremona, Marise ed., Developments in EU External Relations Law (1st edn, Oxford University Press, 2008), 10, p. 13, including the sources in footnote 18 of the text. The lexical meaning adds to this unclarity, i.e. a "coherent" "argument, theory, or policy" is thus stated to be "logical and consistent" and

When defining coherence Missoli contends that the term "implies positive connections" and compared to consistency "is more about synergy and adding value."[66]
Along those lines, McCormick has stated that "rules can be consistent without the
system being coherent as a means of social ordering, if 'order' involves organization
in relation to intelligible and mutually compatible values."[67] If coherence is linked to
the distinction between *de lege lata* and *de lege ferenda* Peczenik has claimed that
both "aim at producing coherent theories."[68] Although Peczenik did not address *de
sententia ferenda,* its aim—akin to *de lege lata* and *de lege ferenda*—is also the
production of coherent theories.

As for consistency, Missoli has argued that "in principle" it means the "absence of
contradiction" and compared to coherence it "is more about compatibility and
making good sense."[69] Describing consistency McCormick has stated more strictly
that as a starting point a ruling is accepted "if it is not contradictory of some valid and
binding rule of the system." This however, does not apply to presumably "contradictory precedent [which] may be "explained" and "distinguished" to avoid such a
contradiction, or an ostensibly conflicting statute interpreted in a way which avoids
such contradiction."[70] Generally, there is a more clear-cut answer to whether
something is consistent or not whereas coherence is elastic in that, something may
be "more or less coherent."[71]

Coherence and consistency are not unfamiliar tools in European trademark law.[72]
Thus, a report made by the Max Planck Institute from 2011 on the functioning of the

---

"consistency" is referred to as being synonymous with "coherence." Oxford Dictionary of English
online version.

[66]Missiroli, Antonio, 'European Security Policy: The Challenge of Coherence', European Foreign
Affairs Review, vol. 6/(2001), pp. 177, p. 182.

[67]MacCormick, Neil, 'Legal Reasoning and Legal Theory', (1st edn, Oxford University Press,
1978), p. 107. See also Adams, Maurice, 'Doing what Doesn't Come Naturally on the Distinctiveness of Comparative Law', in van Hoecke, Mark ed., Methodologies of Legal Research: What Kind
of Method for what Kind of Discipline? (1st edn, Hart, 2011), 229, p. 229, Tuori, Kaarlo, 'Ratio and
Voluntas: the Tension between Reason and Will in Law', (1st edn, Ashgate, 2010), p. 314 and in
similar to Adams Tuori, Kaarlo, 'Can we Still Speak of the Coherence of Law?', in Modéer, Kjell Å
ed., Aleksander Peczenik Memorial Seminar: Pufendorf Seminar, Lund, March 10, 2006 (1st edn,
Corpus Iuris, 2007), pp. 56, p. 72.

[68]Peczenik, Aleksander, 'Atheoryoflegaldoctrine', Ratio Juris, vol. 14/no. 14, (2001), pp. 75, p. 79.

[69]Missiroli, Antonio, 'European Security Policy: The Challenge of Coherence', European Foreign
Affairs Review, vol. 6/(2001), pp. 177, p. 182.

[70]MacCormick, Neil, 'Legal Reasoning and Legal Theory', (1st edn, Oxford University Press,
1978), p. 106.

[71]Missiroli, Antonio, 'European Security Policy: The Challenge of Coherence', European Foreign
Affairs Review, vol. 6/(2001), pp. 177, p. 182. See also Hillion who calls the deciding of coherence
"a matter of degree" and consistency a "static notion." Hillion, Christophe, 'Tous Pour Un, Un Pour
Tous! Coherence in the External Relations of the European Union', in Cremona, Marise ed.,
Developments in EU External Relations Law (1st edn, Oxford University Press, 2008), 10, p. 14.

[72]Thus, a memorandum preceding the TM Regulation 1994 stated that it was "*consistent* with one
of the main objectives of the European Economic Community that steps should be taken to remove
wherever possible national barriers created by the existence of different industrial property laws."

European trademark system as part of the undergoing trademark reform ("the Max Planck TM Report")[73] operates with a criterion of coherence. Under the main heading "coherence" and the subheading, "coherence between TMD and CTMR"[74] it is held that "European trade mark legislation has come a long way in its goal to remove barriers to free movement of trade and competition by harmonization (. . .)."[75] Under the subheading "coherence with adjacent areas" of law, it is stated in the Max Planck TM Report that "[t]rade mark law stands in close interaction with other legal fields, in particular with regulations of marketing practices. Coherence must therefore also be ensured regarding European legislation concerning those adjacent fields," including the UCPD. When the differences between trademark law and the UCPD are pinpointed in the Max Planck TM Report, it is stated that the UCPD "does not cover or affect national regulations on commercial practices which harm only competitors' economic interests or which relate to a transaction between traders." That said, the UCPD "forms part of the overall legal framework to be observed, so as to provide for coherence and legal consistency. This becomes particularly relevant where the UCPD and trade mark law overlap, such as in case of use of signs creating a likelihood of confusion or deception."[76]

As for consistency, the Max Planck TM Report states that the results of the decisions of European trademark offices "should not depend on the administrative authority dealing with the mark or the individual examiner called upon to make the decision" and that "[u]nder the same factual circumstances the outcome should be the same."[77] It was furthermore stated that "[w]hile consistency is not the sole yardstick for the quality of decisions in trade mark matters, it is nevertheless a crucial element." Ensuring "consistency and quality of decisions and administrative

---

The TM Memorandum 1976, para 26 p. 20. In addition, it was stated in the memorandum that it was "*consistent* with the majority of the views expressed by commercial interests." *Ibid*, para 61 p. 18 (italics added). As for the TM Directive, the Commission stated in its proposal for the TM Directive 1989 that "[t]he current case-law in several of the Member States affords to trade marks a degree of protection which is to some extent *inconsistent* with the specific purpose of trade marks law." Commission Proposal for a first Council Directive to approximate the laws of the Member States relating to trade marks of 31 December 1980, [1980] OJ C 351/1 (the "TM Directive Proposal 1980"), p. 2. For other usages of consistency terminology in similar ways, see the TM Memorandum 1976, para 114 and 116, p. 29 and EESC opinion on the proposal for a first Council Directive to approximate the laws of the Member States relating to trade marks and the proposal for a Council Regulation on Community trade marks of 30 November 1981, [1981] OJ C 310/22, p. 22.

In the above references from preparatory texts of EU trademark law consistency is used in the theoretical meaning of "coherence" laid out above in that reference is made to consistency, given the purpose of the legislative acts. According to this book and the above theory, this line of analysis is a matter of coherence (a matter of degree) if a legislative act or decision is in accordance with its underlying policy.

[73]Study on the Overall Functioning of the European Trade Mark System presented by Max Planck Institute for Intellectual Property and Competition Law Munich 15 February 2011.

[74]I.e. the TM Directive 2008 and 2009 TM Regulation respectively.

[75]The Max Planck TM Report para 1.19, p. 49.

[76]*Ibid*, para 1.21, p. 50.

[77]*Ibid*, para 2.1, p. 244.

practices" (...) "would benefit the interests of users and the public at large, and it would also contribute to strengthening the coexistence between the EUTM and national trade mark regimes."[78] This way of using consistency is in line with the approach taken in this book in that a consistency analysis is an "either or question." That is to say, consistency exists if the decisions based on comparable "operative facts" have the same results.[79] In realty though, it is not straightforward to distil the operative facts. In McCormick's words selecting the relevant facts, is a process of selecting from a "bewildering and infinitely complex continuum of facts."[80]

2.2.4 Summarising Discussion

The analyses address the inherent tension vested in the average consumer manifested in the principles set out by the Court of Justice and applied by the General Court and national courts when they flesh out the average consumer. In this context, it is important to consider the lesson learnt from Scandinavian Legal Realism and the subsequent Analytical Legal Positivism. First, in terms of descriptively analysing how the current state of the law is; is it at all transparent at an EU level how the average consumer is framed? Second, from a normative perspective, could the average consumer at EU level be more transparent? The importance of this line of analysis is stressed by the fact that the average consumer in European trademark law has been developed incrementally and inconsistently. The Court of Justice introduced the average consumer into European trademark law it had immaturely been developed by the court in consumer protection law and unfair competition law. This line of development of the average consumer leaves a murky state of the law.[81]

Scandinavian Legal Realism also presents an argument for focusing the analysis primarily on predicting how national courts will apply the average consumer based on the guiding principles laid out by mainly the Court of Justice. It would be problematical if solely the method of Scandinavian Legal Realism was applied to the analysis of case law of the Court of Justice since the average consumer is fleshed out by the General Court and national courts. As a starting point though, it is relevant to lay out the legal sources made transparent by the Court of Justice when it sets out the legal principles of the average consumer. That said, the decisions of the Court of Justice and the Nordic courts are in general briefly reasoned and seemingly, it is not

---

[78] *Ibid*, para. 2.2, p. 244.

[79] McCormick described the "operative facts" as the "requite" facts and circumstances for the "legal consequences (...) to follow." MacCormick, Neil, 'Legal Reasoning and Legal Theory', (1st edn, Oxford University Press, 1978), p. 45.

[80] *Ibid*, p. 47.

[81] On this development, see Chap. 8.

fully transparent upon which legal sources and which grounds the decisions are based (*ratio decidendi*).[82] Therefore, applying Scandinavian Legal Realism narrowly to the analysis of case law of not only the Court of Justice but also of the national courts would leave out the opportunity of reaching a deeper understanding of the legal principles underlying the average consumer. More severely, this would make it less likely to understand reach an understanding of those legal principles.

In line with Scandinavian Legal Realism, analysis of case law of the Court of Justice and the national courts will be the focal point of the analysis. To get a broader picture of the legal principles underlying the average consumer in European trademark law though it is not sufficient merely to focus narrowly on predicting the results of court decisions as within Scandinavian Legal Realism.

Although Tuori's division of law into three layers will not be used as a rigid model in this book, it serves as a valuable conceptual yardstick for the legal analysis. The analysis has to consider the "explicit surface-level material" and the "legal-cultural layers" and "deep structure" to determine the underlying legal principles of the average consumer. In addition, Tuori's division of the law captures the "differences and internal relationships between EU and national judiciaries" inherent in the European trademark system.[83] The theory of how EU law is multi-level and consists of some underlying principles[84] is adaptable to the creation and analysis of the average consumer in European trademark law. This is in particular true since the average consumer as addressed above has been created incrementally and inconsistently in case law. Some of the cases are—briefly reasoned and do not make their normative foundation fully transparent. The dynamics of the development of the law between its different levels is addressed in Chap. 4.

In this book, coherence will be used as a broader tool for deciding if European trademark law is in line with its underlying policy. As laid out by theory this will be a matter of degree and discretion. As well, coherence is used to determine if European

---

[82]Bridge has stated that the tradition of the EU legal system very much stands on the shoulders of the Civil Law legal tradition. Bridge, John, 'National Legal Tradition and Community Law: Legislative Drafting and Judicial Interpretation in England and the European Community', Journal of Common Market Studies, vol. XIX/no. 4, (1981), pp. 351, p. 352-353 and p. 361-362. See also Levitsky, Jonathan E., 'The Europeanization of the British Legal Style', Am. J. Comp. L., vol. 42/no. 2, (1994), pp. 347, p. 351, Conway, Gerard, 'The Limits of Legal Reasoning and the European Court of Justice', (1st edn, Cambridge University Press, 2012), p. 162, Arnull, Anthony, 'The European Union and its Court of Justice', (2nd edn, Oxford University Press, 2006), p. 11. See also the discussion in Chap. 4, Sect. 4.3 on the role of the CJEU. The understanding of *ratio decidendi* is addressed below in Chap. 4, Sect. 4.3.3.

[83]Pila, Justine, 'A Constitutionalized Doctrine of Precedent and the Marleasing Principle as Bases for a European Legal Methodology', in Ohly, Ansgar and Pila, Justine eds., The Europeanization of Intellectual Property Law: Towards a European Legal Methodology (1st edn, Oxford University Press, 2013), 227, p. 232. Pila's quote refers more generally to European intellectual property law. However, her statement applies equally to European trademark law.

[84]This theory is partly developed by Tuori, who stresses the importance of different layers of law. Aspects of how European law develops between different levels (EU, national and international) is addressed in Chap. 4.

trademark law is harmonised vertically. Coherence is equally relevant, as shown by the Max Planck TM Report, to decide if European trademark law correlates with overlapping areas of law, in this book mainly the UCPD. In this instance, coherence is a relevant tool for deciding if trademark law is harmonised horizontally.

Consistency will be applied throughout the book to determine if comparable operative facts in case law lead to the same results. This approach poses a problem since the Court of Justice should not assess facts but only decide on the interpretation of legal matters. That this is not always the case is another matter.[85] Hence, this book seeks to detect if there is consistency on three levels. First, is there consistency in the cases of the Court of Justice when it sets out the general principles that frame the average consumer? This is *inter alia* to detect if the Court of Justice, in Geiger's words, is a "vector of incoherence."[86] Second, is there consistency between these principles when they cascade into the national courts and to the General Court?[87] Third, is there consistency in the case law across the different member states? It is the stance of this book that since European trademark law is infused with a high degree of "indefinite" legal and factual data, and since it belongs to an area of law in significant flux, it is impossible to obtain a fully logically coherent and consistent law.[88]

---

[85]The Court of Justice in Tritton *et al*'s words, may provide ""helpful guidance" applying its interpretation to a particular set of facts!" Davis, Richard, St Quintin, Thomas and Tritton, Guy, 'Tritton on Intellectual Property in Europe', (5th edn, Sweet & Maxwell, 2018), p. 23, footnote 95. See also Chap. 4, Sect. 4.3.

[86]Geiger, Christophe, 'The Construction of Intellectual Property in the European Union: Searching for Coherence', in Geiger, Christophe ed., Constructing European Intellectual Property: Achievements and New Perspectives (1st edn, Edward Elgar, 2013), 5, p. 13.

[87]As explained in Chap. 1, it is not the main purpose to analyse case law related to registration disputes, however, for completion, these cases will be included in the analysis.

[88]An example of lack of consistency is the vertical development – the interplay between the Court of Justice and the national infringement courts – and the horizontal development – the influence from the UCPD. Another variable is the level of normativity vested in the average consumer as a legal fiction. See Chap. 5. In general, the inherent conceptual divergence as explained by Prechal is also a significant variable. It is thus stated by Prechal that EU "prima facie (. . .) in particular seems to be jeopardized by conceptual divergence: [i] Multi-lingualism in EC legislation leads to incorrect, at times impossible, translations. These may incite lawyers to 'walk on the wild side' in advising or representing clients. [ii] EU law has its own terminology, different from Member States', jurisdictions. To a certain extent, it has developed outside of the system of checks and balance built into national legal traditions. [iii] While the law is enacted at the supra-national level, powers of application and enforcement are delegated to national authorities. [iv] Common education and common culture with respect to EU law are in statu nascendi, if not embryonic. They are certainly not part of the acquis communautaire. [v] Socio-political constellations, aspirations, and ideologies differ greatly from one Member State to another." Prechal, Sacha, 'Binding Unity in EU Legal Order: An Introduction', in Prechal, Sacha and Roermund, G. van eds., The Coherence of EU Law: The Search for Unity in Divergent Concepts (1st edn, Oxford University Press, 2008), 1, p. 1. As a general observation, Hoecke has stated, that too much "(. . .) legal data are too indefinite to enable us to conceive legal doctrine as a purely logical discipline. (. . .) Anyway, logical coherence is a characteristic of scientific research in any discipline and not just typical for the legal sciences." Van Hoecke, Mark, 'Legal Doctrine: Which Method(s) for what Kind of Discipline?', in van Hoecke,

2.3   Aspects of Comparative Law

Aspect of comparative law will permeate this book. Prechal states that "[i]n the context of collaboration of lawyers originating from different legal systems within the (legal services of the) EU institutions, issues of possible conceptual divergence can emerge rather easily." Prechal continues to explain that the CJEU "composed of members with roots in different legal systems, are often described as a 'comparative law laboratory'"—she refers to European trademark law as an example of this.[89] The quotes by Prechal capture the importance of comparative law not in the sense of a theoretical discipline, but as a key element in developing European law by the CJEU. According to Calboli, applying comparative law also makes it possible "to better define the contours of specific subject matters at issue at the national level" and "the reasons for the possible differences among national and foreign laws."[90]

The reason for applying comparative law is that the average consumer is developed in a multi-level legal order as an interplay between the Court of Justice and the national courts.[91] At the end, the comparative aspects will provide a better understanding of the national differences and the European legal "contours" of the average consumer. With the vertical analysis the comparative aspects should give an insight into how the average consumer is fleshed out by national courts that apply the broader principles laid out by the Court of Justice together with substantial law of the respective jurisdictions. Through the comparative aspects of the horizontal analysis, the purpose is to get an insight into how the average consumer differs from similar fictions in other areas of law, and how the legal principles differ between European trademark law and the UCPD.

It is debatable if comparative law is a separate method for analysing law or if it should be regarded as a separate area of law with its own methods. Despite this

---

Mark ed., Methodologies of Legal Research: What Kind of Method for what Kind of Discipline? (1st edn, Hart, 2011), 1, p. 9.

[89]Prechal, Sacha, 'Binding Unity in EU Legal Order: An Introduction', in Prechal, Sacha and Roermund, G. van eds., The Coherence of EU Law: The Search for Unity in Divergent Concepts (1st edn, Oxford University Press, 2008), 1, p. 31. When the General Court (previously the Court of First Instance ("CFI")) was given jurisdiction to decide certain matters under the TM Regulation 1994, Prechal explains that "the judges of one of the chambers of the CFI decided to write a brief note about 'their' national system of intellectual property rights protection, inter alia, in order to make their legal background in these matters more explicit." This shows a very simple and none-theoretical importance of comparative law and specifically referring to European trademark law. See also Jacob, Marc A., 'Precedents and Case-Based Reasoning in the European Court of Justice: Unfinished Business', (1st edn, Cambridge University Press, 2014), p. 16, including the sources in footnote 28 of the text.

[90]Calboli, Irene, 'The Role of Comparative Legal Analysis in Intellectual Property: From Good to Great?', in Dinwoodie, Graeme B. ed., Methods and Perspectives in Intellectual Property (1st edn, Edward Elgar, 2013), 3, p. 26.

[91]Also, as stressed by Calboli: "The role of comparative legal analysis in this area [in intellectual property law] continues to be crucial and is even more necessary today for scholars and legal actors than ever before." *Ibid*, p. 11.

disagreement there seems to be an agreement on the main purposes of comparative law one of which is to reach a better understanding of the law.[92] Specifically, Siemns has identified the purpose of comparative law as broadening "the understanding of how legal rules work in context" and as developing "an understanding of law as a general phenomenon, with individual legal systems existing as mere variations on the same theme."[93] Also, Siemns has argued that comparative legal analysis may provide practical use at the national level, e.g. for national legislatures, and at international level, e.g. at EU level, as guidelines on how workable a given area of law is.[94]

The aim of the analyses in this book determines the relevant aspects of comparative legal method. Hence, the methodological considerations required by the vertical analysis that compares the same area of law, differ from the considerations required by the horizontal analysis that compares different areas of law. For instance, it has been argued that comparing two areas of law is outside of comparative law as such.[95]

2.3.1 The Vertical Analysis

The vertical analysis of European trademark law takes its starting point in the overarching EU law. It involves an initial analysis of the EU legislation related to the likelihood of confusion standard and subsequently an analysis on the ruling of the Court of Justice.[96]

On the legislative level, the comparative analysis entails looking into the TM Directive and the national legislations that implement the directive.[97] In contrast to the TM Regulation, which has to be applied by courts in cases related to infringement of EU trademarks, the implementation process of the TM Directive opens for potential divergence between the member state jurisdictions.[98] In this process, "[l] inguistic differences may (. . .) cause apparent non-uniformity in the application of

---

[92]*Ibid*, p. 8. See also Siems, Mathias, 'Comparative Law', (1st edn, Cambridge University Press, 2014), p. 5-6 and Zweigert, Konrad, and Kötz, Hein, 'Introduction to Comparative Law', (3rd edn, Oxford University Press, 1998), p. 15-16. Kiikeri argues that the purpose is "the systematization of different legal orders and legal systems." Kiikeri, Markku, 'Comparative Legal Reasoning and European Law', (1st edn, Springer, 2001), p. 2.

[93]Siems, Mathias, 'Comparative Law', (1st edn, Cambridge University Press, 2014), p. 3.

[94]*Ibid*, p. 3-4.

[95]I.e. in this book, the horizontal comparison. *Ibid*, p. 13-14.

[96]The role of the Court of Justice as a lawmaker is addressed in Chap. 4, Sect. 4.3.

[97]Also, this involves looking into the mirror of this provision in registration matters, art. 5(1)(b) of the TM Directive.

[98]As per the general role of regulation in the EC Treaty Art. 249. For a recent account of the EU trademark system, see among others, Firth, Alison, Lea, Gary R. and Cornford, Peter, 'Trade Marks: Law and Practice', (4th edn, Jordans, 2016), chapter 14, in particular p. 322-330.

the harmonised national laws to specific marks in different member states."[99] It will
be detected if there among the selected jurisdictions are differences between the
ways the likelihood of confusion standard have been phrased by the national
legislatures. The analyses of the national adjudications mainly involve an analysis
on how the national courts decide infringement and registration under national
legislation and sporadically infringement under the TM Regulation.

Although the national court decisions are not formal legal sources in other
member state jurisdictions, there is still an overlap and an interplay between the
cases of the different member states: First, European legal method claims that
European trademark law develops as a joint enterprise between the overarching
EU law and national law.[100] Second, the national case law of one member state may
be referred to by counsels in similar cases in other member states on a more
anecdotal level (i.e. not as a formal legal source).[101] Although these foreign decisions are not seen as formal legal sources by a judge they may either way have some
impact on the result of the case.[102] Third, although varying in significance according
to different legal traditions, scholarly works that consider e.g. comparative perspectives when trademark law of one member state is analysed may affect the results of
the national decisions.[103] For instance, the NO Supreme Court time after time
explicitly refers to legal literature that draws on EU and national legal sources.[104]

The above differences between the TM Regulation and the TM Directive, including the implementation process, provide an argument for separately analysing not
only the legislation but also more important the case law of the CJEU and the
member states. However, as addressed in Chap. 10, there is a significant overlap
between the case law on the TM Regulation and the TM Directive.[105] Consequently,
it is necessary to find a middle-way between the presumed significant judicial

---

[99] *Ibid*, p. 295.

[100] In this perspective, e.g. a Danish preliminary reference to the Court of Justice may affect how the
average consumer is developed not only in Denmark but also in other EU jurisdictions.

[101] In the trademark dispute *Interflora High Court*, the English Arnold J stated that "the average
consumer provides what the EU legislature has described in recital (18) of the Unfair Commercial
Practices Directive as a "benchmark"." Interflora v. Marks & Spencer, [2013] EWHC 1291 (Ch),
para 209.

[102] See among others, Siemns referring to scholars measuring the "foreign influence related to
academic research." Siems, Mathias, 'Comparative Law', (1st edn, Cambridge University Press,
2014), p. 154-155.

[103] See *ibid*, p. 46-47.

[104] A recent example is Pangea Property Partners v. Klagenemnda, HR-2016-01993-A, [2016],
NOSC, paras 52-53. Here the court referred to the go-to textbook on Norwegian trademark law by
Lassen and Stenvik and a recent book on EU trademark law edited by Hasselblatt. Respectively,
Lassen, Birger Stuevold and Stenvik, Are, 'Kjennetegnsrett', (3rd edn, Universitetsforlaget, 2011)
and Hasselblatt, Gordian N., 'Community Trade Mark Regulation (EC) no 207/2009: A Commen-
tary', (1st edn, Beck/Hart, 2015).

[105] See Chap. 10, Sect. 10.2.2. Also, the clear resemblance (almost identity) between the wording of
the relevant provisions in the TM Regulation and the TM Directive, and the way the average
consumer has been developed under these secondary legislative acts.

resemblances due to the relatively high degree of harmonisation of European trademark law vis-à-vis the "latitude" left for the member states. Although no strict "country-by-country" comparison will be made, the countries will for the main part be dealt with separately. Due to the differences between the UK legal family and the Nordic legal families, and the resemblances between the Nordic jurisdictions, a certain division between the two families will be made.[106] Despite the resemblance between the Nordic jurisdictions, they are internally different as well therefore; a certain division between the Nordic jurisdictions will be upheld. As mentioned in the delimitation, the analysis does not include national procedural rules.[107]

2.3.1.1 The Chosen Jurisdictions

Although the different legal families are not named consistently, England and Wales are taken to represent the UK Common Law legal family and Sweden, Denmark and Norway the Nordic legal family.[108] The legal sources of the chosen countries are addressed in the following chapter. At this general stage, some overall key features of the different legal families will be highlighted.

Traditionally, Common Law has been developed through uncodified law under the *stare decisis* doctrine.[109] According to this doctrine, lower courts are bound by decisions of higher courts, and if principles laid down in previous decisions of higher courts are to be changed it is for the higher courts to do so.[110] With the starting point

---

[106]This comparative method is also called the "länderbericht" method. See Lando, Ole, 'Kort Indføring i Komparativ Ret', (3rd edn, Jurist- og Økonomforbundets Forlag, 2009), p. 206-207.

[107]See Chap. 1, Sect. 1.5.4.

[108]Siemns has created an overview of the different terms used to describe the different legal families by various authors. Siems, Mathias, 'Comparative Law', (1st edn, Cambridge University Press, 2014), p. 76. The terms used in this book are taken from Zweigert, Konrad, and Kötz, Hein, 'Introduction to Comparative Law', (3rd edn, Oxford University Press, 1998), pp. 132, 180 and 276. Zweigert and Kötz base their divisions of the countries into legal families on these features of a country: "(1) its historical background and development, (2) its predominant and characteristic mode of thought in legal matters, (3) especially distinctive institutions, (4) the kind of legal sources it acknowledges and the way it handles them, and (5) its ideology." *Ibid*, p. 68. Ideally, more EU member state jurisdictions should be included, however this would require a broader and more expansive scholarly collaboration among EU universities – this is clearly beyond the scope of this book.

[109]Merryman, John Henry, 'The Civil Law Tradition: An Introduction to the Legal Systems of Western Europe and Latin America', (1st edn, Stanford University Press, 1985), p. 321-322.

[110]Cornish, William R., Llewelyn, David, and Alpin, Tanya, 'Intellectual Property: Patents, Copyright, Trademarks and Allied Rights', (8th edn, Sweet & Maxwell, 2013), p. 25-26. See also Merryman, John Henry, 'The Civil Law Tradition: An Introduction to the Legal Systems of Western Europe and Latin America', (1st edn, Stanford University Press, 1985), p. 22, David, René, and Brierley, John EC, 'Major Legal Systems in the World Today', (3rd edn, Free Press, 1985), p. 376-382 and Lundmark, Thomas, 'Charting the Divide between Common and Civil Law', (1st edn, Oxford University Press, 2012), p. 371-374.

of statutory interpretation taken in the "literal rule of interpretation,"[111] preparatory works play a limited role in the statutory interpretation.[112] Hoecke and Ost have pointed out that as part of an "acceleration of the law" "[i]n England, an important increase in statutory legislation is rapidly reducing the scope and impact of general principles and rules as they have been developed by the common law courts."[113] As for the preliminary references to the Court of Justice, Craig states that national courts in the UK "have come to think of themselves more in terms of being part of a Community [the EU] judicial hierarchy, in which certain matters are naturally dealt with by the ECJ [the Court of Justice]."[114] In similar veins, Bridge has stated that "[t] here is broad recognition that the interpretation of Community law requires a special approach, and that English courts must seek and accept the guidance of the European Court."[115]

For the Nordic jurisdictions, Zweigert and Kötz point out that there is a significant degree of legal harmony between those.[116] Furthermore, that this harmony is rooted in a similar historical development, close "cultural links," similar languages, "no serious political differences," comparable "population and economic power," and the geographical proximity and placement of the countries.[117] The Nordic legal family is said to be closer to Continental Law than to Common Law.[118] The Nordic jurisdictions are "representatives of the culture of legal positivism" that subscribe "to a particular doctrine of legal sources that is the supremacy of legislated acts passed by a formally competent legislative organ (national parliament) as the source of

---

[111]Bridge, John, 'National Legal Tradition and Community Law: Legislative Drafting and Judicial Interpretation in England and the European Community', Journal of Common Market Studies, vol. XIX/no. 4, (1981), pp. 351, p. 363.

[112]Merryman, John Henry, 'The Civil Law Tradition: An Introduction to the Legal Systems of Western Europe and Latin America', (1st edn, Stanford University Press, 1985), p. 333-334, with reference to the principle laid down in Pepper Hart.

[113]Van Hoecke, Mark, and Ost, Francois, 'Legal Doctrine in Crisis: Towards a European Legal Science, Legal Studies, vol. 18 (1998), pp. 197, p. 201.

[114]Craig, Paul, 'Report on the United Kingdom', in Slaughter, Anne-Marie, Stone, Alec and Weiler, Joseph H. eds., The European Court and National Courts: Doctrine & Jurisprudence: Legal Change in its Social Context (1st edn, Hart, 1998), 195, p. 221.

[115]Bridge, John, 'National Legal Tradition and Community Law: Legislative Drafting and Judicial Interpretation in England and the European Community', Journal of Common Market Studies, vol. XIX/no. 4, (1981), pp. 351, p. 372.

[116]Reference is made to Scandinavia, which however is a term used interchangeably with "Nordic" by Zweigert and Kötz. "Nordic" as referring to "Northern Europe" covers Denmark, Finland, Iceland, Norway and Sweden, whereas Scandinavia in the geographical sense does not cover Iceland and Denmark. Zweigert, Konrad, and Kötz, Hein, 'Introduction to Comparative Law', (3rd edn, Oxford University Press, 1998), p. 277 and p. 284.

[117]Ibid, p. 284.

[118]Husa, Jaakko, Nuotio, Kimmo and Pihlajamäki, Heikki, 'Nordic Law – between Tradition and Dynamism', in Jaakko, Husa, Nuotio, Kimmo and Pihlajamäki, Heikki eds., Nordic Law – between Tradition and Dynamism (1st edn, Intersentia, 2007), pp. 1, p. 8.

law."[119] The jurisdictions have even been denoted "a community of values"[120] where there is a focus on protecting the individual.[121] Although the differences should not be exaggerated, Nordic jurisdictions are said to "be more practical and policy oriented" compared to Civil Law families, such as the Germanic.[122] The most common perception is that the Nordic legal family "is distinct from both Civil Law and Common Law."[123] One important aspect of the legal sources of the Nordic jurisdictions is the prominent role given to preparatory works in contrast with ditto in other legal families, including as mentioned the Common Law family.[124] The prominent role of preparatory works "is probably one aspect of securing the necessary formalism, [and] the predictability of legal decision-making."[125]

Two overall differences emerge between the Common Law and the Nordic legal families: First, Common Law operates *stare decisis* in contrast with Nordic Law said to "be more practically and policy-oriented."[126] Second, preparatory works play in practice a very limited role in interpreting statutes in Common Law, but they play a significant role in Nordic law. Through the analysis it will be determined if these differences solidify in the average consumer.

2.3.1.2   Method

It is argued by Zweigert and Kötz that "[t]he basic methodological principle of all comparative law is that of functionality." Moreover, that "from this basic principle stem all the other rules determining the choice of laws to compare, the scope of the undertaking, the creation of a system of comparative law and so on." According to the functional method, the overall question of any comparative study has to be formulated "in purely functional terms."[127] When this method is applied no specific references to any specific national legal terminology can be included in the question.

---

[119] *Ibid*, p. 9.

[120] *Ibid*, p. 21.

[121] *Ibid*, p. 27-28.

[122] Smiths, Jan M., 'Nordic Law in a European Context: Some Comparative Observations', in Husa, Jaakko, Nuotio, Kimmo and Pihlajamäki, Heikki eds., Nordic Law – between Tradition and Dynamism (1st edn, Intersentia, 2007), 55, p. 61.

[123] Tamm, Ditlev, 'The Danes and their Legal Heritage', in Dahl, Børge *et al* eds., Danish Law in a European Perspective (1st edn, Thomson – GadJura, 1996), 33, p. 35.

[124] Husa only refers specifically to the "Roman-German" legal family, however, the role of the preparatory works is even less prominent in the Common Law legal family. Husa, Jaakko, Nuotio, Kimmo and Pihlajamäki, Heikki, 'Nordic Law – between Tradition and Dynamism', in Jaakko, Husa, Nuotio, Kimmo and Pihlajamäki, Heikki eds., Nordic Law – between Tradition and Dynamism (1st edn, Intersentia, 2007), pp. 1, p. 34.

[125] *Ibid*, p. 34.

[126] *Ibid*, p. 61.

[127] Zweigert, Konrad, and Kötz, Hein, 'Introduction to Comparative Law', (3rd edn, Oxford University Press, 1998), p. 34.

Zweigert and Kötz base their functional approach on the "presumption that the practical results are similar" across different jurisdictions.[128] Zooming in on EU law, Markesinis has argued that in several areas the law is approaching an "ius commune."[129] The claim is built on the assumption that "Community law is now affecting almost every branch of municipal law, but also because in various ways it is forcing national systems to converge in their solutions to particular problems."[130]

The above arguments support the application of the functional method of comparative law to the analysis. The functional method, however, is by no means accepted without criticism. One key point of critique is according to Legrand that "rules and concepts alone actually tell one very little about a given legal system and reveal even less about whether two legal systems are converging or not. They may provide one with much information about what is apparently happening, but they indicate nothing about the deep structures of legal systems."[131] As Samuel points out, Zweigert and Kötz's focus on the functional method as the basic methodological approach in comparative law is probably taking it too far.[132]

European trademark law has been developed standing on the shoulders of national trademark law traditions. To achieve a complete understanding of the development of the average consumer it is necessary to analyse its judicial development in all EU member states before its development in EU law. This analysis is outside of this book and historical aspects are only scarcely addressed. It is safe to say that EU law has lessened the differences between the legal families and the national legal systems of Europe. In particular, it is so in European trademark law. The two-tier model of a regulation and a directive has harmonised this area of law and created a distinct purpose underlying the law.[133] It is argued that substantive European trademark law is harmonised so much that it makes sense to apply the

---

[128]*Ibid*, p. 40. Maduro and Micklitz refer to the challenge of not being biased towards a specific nationality as "how to formulate a comparative research question avoiding ethnocentricity." Gestel, Rob Van, Micklitz, Hans-W and Maduro, Miguel Poiares, 'Methodology in the New Legal World', EUI Working Papers, (2012/13), pp. 1, p. 17.

[129]Markesinis, Basil S., 'Foreign Law and Comparative Methodology: A Subject and a Thesis', (1st edn, Hart, 1997), p. 365 and 382.

[130]*Ibid*, p. 209. For instance, as argued by Levitsky, the UK's membership of the EU and the subsequent obligations to follow and implement EU law, including the decisions of the Court of Justice, has caused "a subtle shift in judicial approach, toward substantive reasoning rather than formal rules." Levitsky, Jonathan E., 'The Europeanization of the British Legal Style', Am. J. Comp. L., vol. 42/no. 2, (1994), pp. 347, p. 369. Levitsky further analyses some key statements of Lord Denning on the shift towards a more substantive reasoning rather than a more formal approach.

[131]Legrand, Pierre, 'European Legal Systems are Not Converging', ICLQ, vol. 45 no. 1, (1996), pp. 52. See also Siems, Mathias, 'Comparative Law', (1st edn, Cambridge University Press, 2014), p. 37-38 and Samuel, Geoffrey, 'An Introduction to Comparative Law – Theory and Method', (1st edn, Hart, 2014), p. 79-80 with references.

[132]Samuel, Geoffrey, 'An Introduction to Comparative Law – Theory and Method', (1st edn, Hart, 2014), p. 81.

[133]See Chap. 3, Sect. 3.2.2.1.

functional method in the comparison of the different national jurisdictions. Some key functions are the likelihood of confusion standard assessed by national versions of the global appreciation test as laid out by the Court of Justice in *Sabel*.[134] In line with the functional method, the framing of the issues with the vertical aspects is based on functional features. The vertical aspects are not rooted in particular national jurisdictions, but in the common EU confusion standard in which the average consumer has its origin as a legal fiction. Also, the average consumer is not understood as a specific national term but as a term used by the Court of Justice. The term *average consumer* is therefore not assumed to skew any aspects of the vertical analysis in a specific national direction.

The outcome of comparative legal analysis depends on the eye of the beholder. It is the approach of the comparative analysis of this book though not to use the law of the "beholder" as a baseline but to seek a neutral perspective. This is in accordance with the functional method where the comparatists "must cut themselves loose from their own doctrinal and judicial preconceptions."[135] In the vertical analysis, attention will be drawn to the different characteristics of the national jurisdictions.

2.3.2 The Horizontal Analysis

The horizontal aspects include as specified in the previous chapter similar fictions of EU design law, European Patent law and European tort law as well the average consumer found in the UCPD. Although the areas of law have similarities, they are different areas of law after all.

According to Siemns, based on a reference to among others McEvoy, it is it not comparative law to compare "how different areas of law deal with a particular issue with the same country."[136] According to this finding, the horizontal analysis is not a comparative legal analysis since it does not involve different countries. That said, McEvoy has more broadly defined comparative law as "firstly and usually the comparison between two or several 'systems' or the laws of those systems on the same particular issues."[137] Such a system can be an internal system, including "horizontal branches of *a single legal system*."[138] Although McEvoy does not specifically call the EU a "system," it is arguably so since the intended purpose of the horizontal comparison is isolated to the overarching EU level.

---

[134]Sabel v. Puma, Case C-251/95, [1997] ECR I-6191, para 22.

[135]Zweigert, Konrad, and Kötz, Hein, 'Introduction to Comparative Law', (3rd edn, Oxford University Press, 1998), p. 17 and p. 26-27.

[136]Siems, Mathias, 'Comparative Law', (1st edn, Cambridge University Press, 2014), p. 13-14.

[137]McEvoy, Sebastian, 'Descriptive and Purposive Categories of Comparative Law', in Monateri, P. G. ed., Methods of Comparative Law (1st edn, Edward Elgar, 2012), 144, p. 145.

[138]*Ibid*, p. 149 (italics added).

The functional method applied to the vertical comparison does not fit well in the horizontal comparison. On the one hand, it is possible to presume some degree of the similarity between the average consumer in European trademark law and the respective fictions in adjacent areas of law. The cousin fictions applied in those different adjacent areas of law have functions unique to their specific area of law, but as it will be seen, there is a commonality in their functions as fictions.[139] The average consumer in European trademark law and the UCPD are similar to a degree higher than the cousin fictions. Primarily, this is so since the UCPD refers to the average consumer and since the average consumer was imported into European trademark law via the unfair competition law decision, *Gut Springenheide*.[140] On the other hand, it is significant that the two legal regimes pursue different aims and that the UCPD refers to consumer models other than the average consumer.[141]

The presumption of similarity under the functional method cannot be presumed under the horizontal analysis when comparing European trademark law with aspects of other areas of law. As seen though, some significant commonalities allow for a functional analysis. The similar fictions are functionally similar. Both the informed user of EU design law, the person skilled in the art of European Patent law and the reasonable person of European tort law serve the function of instructing the judges in "hard cases" involving a significant degree of discretion. The functional similarity between the average consumer under European trademark law and the UCPD is more profound, since both areas of law at least formally apply the same *average consumer* and serve overlapping purposes.[142]

2.4 Conclusion

The methodology of this book consists of methods derived from legal science with the legal dogmatic method as the core method. Adding to this are aspects of comparative legal methods, mainly the functional method.

The legal method is created as a synthesis between Scandinavian Legal Realism and Critical Legal Positivism to draw clear attention to legal sources as found in case law of the Court of Justice, General Court and selected national courts. Additionally, other legal sources are equally used to better understand the legal principles that underlie the average consumer in European trademark law. Coherence is used as a measure for deciding if European trademark law is in line with its policy

---

[139]See Chap. 6.

[140]Gut Springenheide and Tusky, Case C-210/96, [1998] ECR I-4657.

[141]On the UCPD, see Chap. 7.

[142]As already mentioned the UCPD refers to the average consumer – not only in the recitals but also in the main text, which is in contrast with EU trademark legislation. Siemns has referred to the comparison of the content of legal rules as the "formal dimension." Siems, Mathias, 'Comparative Law', (1st edn, Cambridge University Press, 2014), p. 20.

underpinning, whereas consistency is used to decide if decisions with the same operative facts háve the same results.

Aspects of the functional method of comparative law are used to decide if the average consumer is harmonised vertically by focusing initially at the overarching EU level and subsequently on the case law of the General Court and the selected courts of England and Wales, Sweden, Denmark and Norway. In contrast, the functional method will not be strictly applied in the horizontal comparison between European trademark law and the similar fictions of EU design law, European Patent law and European tort law and the average consumer in the UCPD.

Chapter 3
Legal Sources

3.1 Multi-Level Legal Sources

The purpose of this chapter is to lay out the relevant legal sources denoted the "explicit surface-level" by Tuori. This means, first a specification of the legislation and the courts whose decisions will be included in the analysis. In this process, it is necessary to account for the different legal levels of this book, i.e. mainly the EU and the national levels, but also the international level. This chapter hence lays out the primary and secondary EU law followed by national trademark law and listing the national courts. Finally, the international aspects of European trademark law are set out. Due to the prominence of the Court of Justice as a lawmaker, the following chapter separately addresses the dynamic development of European trademark law. The legal method of this book necessitates an account of not only the positive legal sources as they emerge in case law, but also sources relevant to interpreting European trademark law, such as preparatory works.

As for areas of law adjacent to European trademark law, this chapter only deals with the UCPD since this directive will undergo more scrutiny than the EU design law, European patent law and European tort law. The legal sources of the last three areas of law are addressed in Chap. 6.

3.2 EU Law

Relevant to the analysis of EU trademark legislation is the general EU distinction between primary law and secondary legislation.[1] Primary EU law consists of the treaties and some general principles developed by the Court of Justice, whereas secondary legislation consists of "ordinary legislation," i.e. regulations, directives

---

[1]Dashwood, Alan, 'Wyatt and Dashwood's European Union Law', (6th edn, Hart, 2011), p. 23-24.

© Springer Nature Switzerland AG 2020
R. D. Laustsen, *The Average Consumer in Confusion-based Disputes in European Trademark Law and Similar Fictions*, https://doi.org/10.1007/978-3-030-26350-8_3

and decisions, cf. art. 288 of the TFEU.[2] In the legislative analysis, the attention will be focused on the secondary EU trademark legislation. Before the secondary legislation is set out, it is necessary to elaborate on primary legislation.[3]

3.2.1 Primary EU Law

The overall purpose and role of secondary legislation, and the institutional framework and purpose of the CJEU emerge in primary EU law.[4] Adding to the analysis of the purpose of trademark law, some general policy statements are found in the primary EU legislation that feed into the policy of EU trademark law.[5] As for primary EU law, the focus of this book is the treaties, not the "general principles" of primary EU law. Besides these general principles in a "strict technical sense" are principles "of such constitutional importance for the nature and functioning of the European Union that jurisprudence surely deserves to be classified as another unwritten source of the Union's primary law."[6] Two of these are the principles of direct effect and supremacy (or primacy).[7] Both relate to the capacity of "Union

---

[2]See Conway, Gerard, 'The Limits of Legal Reasoning and the European Court of Justice', (1st edn, Cambridge University Press, 2012), p. 178.

[3]This is necessary since: First, due to the hierarchy of the legal order and due to the overall purpose and role of secondary legislation. As further dealt with below the purpose of directives is stipulated in art. 114, referring to art. 26 of the TFEU and the purpose of regulations in art. 118 of the TFEU, whereas the functions of directives and regulations are set out in art. 288 of the TFEU. Second, some significant provisions on the functions of the EU institutions are found in EU primary legislation. Of paramount relevance is the function of the CJEU, including the preliminary ruling procedure of the Court of Justice which has been/is crucial to developing the average consumer (see Chap. 4, Sect. 4.3). Third, for the subsequent analysis of the purpose of trademark law, some general policy statements are found in primary EU legislation.

[4]The institutional framework of the CJEU is set out in arts. 13 and 19 of the TEU (arts. 220-224 of the TEU Pre-Lisbon). A key function of the Court of Justice in creating the average consumer is the dialogue with the national courts through its preliminary rulings procedure in art. 267 of the TFEU (art. 234 of the TFEU Pre-Lisbon) as per art. 19(3)(b) of the TEU. Finally, as provided for in art. 281 of the TEU Protocol (No 3) on the Statute of the Court of Justice of the European Union (the "Statute of the CJEU").

[5]See Chap. 1, Sect. 1.3.3.

[6]The key principles of EU primary law are principles such as the principle of proportionality and the principle of legal certainty and legitimate expectation. According to Dashwood *et al*, principles such as the principle of direct effect and supremacy are outside the core of primary law principles but can still be considered primary law due to their importance for the EU constitutional infrastructure. Dashwood, Alan, 'Wyatt and Dashwood's European Union Law', (6th edn, Hart, 2011), p. 23-24, p. 37 (the quote in the main text) and p. 321-322. For a thorough analysis of the core EU primary law principles, see Tridimas, Takis, 'The General Principles of EU Law', (2nd, Oxford University Press, 2006). For a further analysis of what is understood by "principles," see chapter 1 of this source.

[7]"Supremacy" and "primacy" are interchangeable terms. See Dashwood, Alan, 'Wyatt and Dashwood's European Union Law', (6th edn, Hart, 2011), p. 235, footnote 1 and Witte, and

norms to produce independent legal effects within the *national* legal systems and to be enforced as such before *domestic* courts."[8] The principle of direct effect relates to the ability of "Union law to produce independent legal effects within the national systems"[9] whereas the principle of supremacy (or primacy) signifies the ability of a Union law norm "to overrule inconsistent norms of national law in domestic court proceedings."[10]

As argued by Tuori, the EU does not have a constitution in a formal sense but arguably in a substantive sense. Although the formal constitution, the EU Constitutional Treaty, was put to rest by its dismal in 2005,[11] substantive constitutional functions are manifested in the Lisbon Treaty entering into force on 1 December 2009.[12] Reference to the Lisbon Treaty means reference to the treaty as a whole, including most importantly a reference to the TEU[13] and the TFEU,[14] i.e. both as

---

Bruno de, 'Direct Effect, Primacy and the Nature of the Legal Order', in Craig, Paul and Búrca, Gráinne de eds., The Evolution of EU Law (1st edn, Oxford University Press, 2011), 323, p. 323, including footnote 1 of the text. The Court of Justice laid down the principle of direct effect in *Van Gend en Loos*. Van Gend & Loos, Case 26/62, [1963] ECR 3. The Court of Justice stated in this decision that "the Community constitutes a new legal order of international law for the benefit of which the states have limited their sovereign rights." *Ibid*, p. 12. The principle of supremacy was laid down by the Court of Justice in Costa v. ENEL, Case 6/64, [1964] ECR 1194, p. 593.

[8]Dashwood, Alan, 'Wyatt and Dashwood's European Union Law', (6th edn, Hart, 2011), p. 235 (italics added). It is furthermore stated by de Witte that "[t]he two principles are (. . .) closely linked, and are habitually considered in conjunction." Witte, and Bruno de, 'Direct Effect, Primacy and the Nature of the Legal Order', in Craig, Paul and Búrca, Gráinne de eds., The Evolution of EU Law (1st edn, Oxford University Press, 2011), 323, p. 323.

[9]Dashwood, Alan, 'Wyatt and Dashwood's European Union Law', (6th edn, Hart, 2011), p. 244. For an analysis of the principle of direct effect see *ibid*, chapter 8, in particular p. 244-270, Witte, and Bruno de, 'Direct Effect, Primacy and the Nature of the Legal Order', in Craig, Paul and Búrca, Gráinne de eds., The Evolution of EU Law (1st edn, Oxford University Press, 2011), 323, full text, but in particular p. 324-340 and Leczykiewicz, Chapter 9, in the Oxford Handbook of European Union Law, 2015.

[10]Witte, and Bruno de, 'Direct Effect, Primacy and the Nature of the Legal Order', in Craig, Paul and Búrca, Gráinne de eds., The Evolution of EU Law (1st edn, Oxford University Press, 2011), 323, p. 323. For an analysis of the principle of supremacy see *ibid* full text, but in particular p. 340-346, Dashwood, Alan, 'Wyatt and Dashwood's European Union Law', (6th edn, Hart, 2011), chapter 8, in particular p. 270-278, and Claes, Chapter 8, in the Oxford Handbook of European Union Law, 2015.

[11]The constitution that was "put to rest" in 2005 was the Treaty Establishing a Constitution for Europe [2004] (the "EU Constitutional Treaty"). The treaty was ratified by fifteen member states, but was rejected followed by referenda in France and the Netherlands in 2005. On the process from the EU Constitutional Treaty in 2005 to the Lisbon Treaty in 2009, see Craig, Paul P., 'The Lisbon Treaty: Law, Politics, and Treaty Reform', (1st edn, Oxford University Press, 2010), p. 20-25.

[12]Tuori, Kaarlo, 'Ratio and Voluntas: the Tension between Reason and Will in Law', (1st edn, Ashgate, 2010), p. 309. See also Griller, Stefan, 'Is this a Constitution? Remarks on a Contested Concept', in Griller, Stefan and Ziller, Jacques eds., the Lisbon Treaty: EU Constitutionalism without a Constitutional Treaty? (1st edn, Springer, 2008), 21, p. 32-33.

[13]For an overview of the infrastructure of the TEU, see among others, Dashwood, Alan, 'Wyatt and Dashwood's European Union Law', (6th edn, Hart, 2011), p. 24-30.

[14]For an overview of the infrastructure of the TEU, see among others, *ibid*, p. 30-32.

amended by the Lisbon Treaty as such and more recently in 2012.[15] The most recent TEU and TFEU before the Lisbon Treaty will be called respectively "TEU Pre-Lisbon"[16] and "TFEU Pre-Lisbon."[17] Unless necessitated by the context, reference in the main text throughout is made to the TEU and TFEU and, if applicable, to similar provisions in the TEU Pre-Lisbon. Reference to the other treaties will only be included where necessary for the provision of relevant subtext to the analysis.[18]

First, as for the purpose of EU trademark law, the TM Directive states that it is "to serve the objective of fostering and creating a well-functioning internal market."[19] This wording creates a clear link to free movement law and the sheer purpose of the EU being to "establish an internal market,"[20] including the free movement of goods,[21] and services.[22] The free movement of goods provisions have had a significant impact on developing the average consumer before *Sabel*.[23]

Second, art. 118 of the TFEU now explicitly refers to "intellectual property" and thus the legal basis to set forth the TM Regulation is ensured for the EU Commission. As for the TM Regulation 2009 the legal basis was found in the general provision of 308 of the TFEU Pre-Lisbon (as amended by art. 352 of the TFEU).

---

[15]For an overview of the infrastructure of the Lisbon Treaty among others, Craig, Paul P., 'The Lisbon Treaty: Law, Politics, and Treaty Reform', (1st edn, Oxford University Press, 2010), p. 25-28.

[16]Treaty on the European Union (consolidated version), [2006] OJ C 321 E/5 (the "TEU Pre-Lisbon").

[17]Treaty Establishing the European Community (consolidated version), [2006] OJ C 321 E/37 (the "TFEU Pre-Lisbon").

[18]The most important preceding treaties of the TEU and TFEU are the Treaty of Maastricht signed on 7 February 1992, [1992], OJ C191/01, the Treaty of Amsterdam, [1997], OJ C340/01 (the "Amsterdam Treaty") and the Treaty of Nice, [2002] OJ C 325/01 (the "Nice Treaty"). Besides the treaties just mentioned, the preceding treaties of the TFEU are the Treaty of Rome of 25 March 1957 establishing the European Economic Community (the "EEC Treaty") and the Single European Act.

[19]Recital 8 of the TM Directive. Although this purpose is not mentioned in the TM Regulation, the statement seems to apply to EU trademark law at large. The reason for this is that the recital states that to achieve this end, it is necessary to change both the TM Regulation and the TM Directive.

[20]Cf. art. 3(3) of the TEU (art. 2 of the TEU Pre-Lisbon). For an overview of the free movement rules in the TFEU, see Craig, Paul P., 'The Lisbon Treaty: Law, Politics, and Treaty Reform', (1st edn, Oxford University Press, 2010), p. 316-318.

[21]Cf. mainly arts. 34-36 of the TFEU. These Provisions "have been interpreted as preventing holders of intellectual property rights from using them to prevent import of goods into one Member State from the territory of another where the holder of the rights in question has consented to their being place on the market." Essentially, this is known as the principle of "exhaustion." Dashwood, Alan, 'Wyatt and Dashwood's European Union Law', (6th edn, Hart, 2011), p. 408. Arts. 28-30 of the TFEU Pre-Lisbon. For an account of the free movement of goods in general, see *ibid*, Chapter 14, p. 407-460 and with specific reference to intellectual property law, Davis, Richard, St Quintin, Thomas and Tritton, Guy, 'Tritton on Intellectual Property in Europe', (5th edn, Sweet & Maxwell, 2018), chapter 7, in particular p. 783-854.

[22]Cf. mainly art. 56 of the TFEU (art. 49 of the TFEU Pre-Lisbon).

[23]See Chap. 8.

The legal basis for the TM Directive is found in art. 114 of the TFEU.[24] These provisions are addressed further in the following chapter in which the different means for harmonising European trademark law through the TM Regulation and TM Directive will be analysed.

Third, the important preliminary rulings procedure of the Court of Justice emerges under art. 267 of the TFEU. The relevance of this procedure to the formation of the average consumer can hardly be underestimated and hence this procedure is independently discussed in the following chapter.

3.2.2   Secondary EU Legislation

3.2.2.1   Trademark Legislation

The average consumer has been developed as part of the legislative standard of likelihood of confusion that transpires from the two prongs of EU trademark legislation, i.e. the TM Regulation that creates a unitary EU wide trademark, and the TM Directive that harmonises national trademark law.[25] The TM Regulation and the TM Directive are taken to be the "EU trademark legislation." The pivotal starting point for the substantial legal analysis is the EU trademark legislation.[26]

Due to the differences between the trademark laws of EU member states significant questions arose before the introduction of EU trademark legislation, including how to solve disputes between "trademarks legitimately used in different parts of the Community."[27] As far back as 31 July 1959, the member states and the EU

---

[24]Cf. art. 95 of the TFEU Pre-Lisbon.

[25]See Chap. 9.

[26]For further introduction to the EU trademark system, see in particular: Mellor, James, David Llewelyn, Moody-Stuart, Thomas, *et al*, 'Kerly's Law of Trade Marks and Trade Names', (16th edn, Sweet & Maxwell, 2018), Chapter 8, p. 158-253, Mühlendahl, Alexander von, Dimitris Botis, Spyros M. Maniatis, *et al*, 'Trade Mark Law in Europe: A Practical Jurisprudence', (3rd edn, Oxford University Press, 2016), chapter 2, Bently, Lionel, Sherman, Brad, Gangjee, Dev and Johnson, Phillip 'Intellectual Property Law', (5th edn, Oxford University Press, 2018), p. 861-862, Firth, Alison, Lea, Gary R. and Cornford, Peter, 'Trade Marks: Law and Practice', (4th edn, Jordans, 2016), Chapter 14 on the TM Directive, mainly p. 259-268, Chapter 14 on the TM Regulation, Cornish, William R., Llewelyn, David, and Alpin, Tanya, 'Intellectual Property: Patents, Copyright, Trademarks and Allied Rights', (8th edn, Sweet & Maxwell, 2013), p. 24-25 and p. 637-639, Bøggild, Frank, and Staunstrup, Kolja, 'EU-Varemærkeret', (1st edn, Karnov Group, 2015), Chapter 1, and Hasselblatt, Gordian N., 'Article 1: Community Trade Marks', in Hasselblatt, Gordian N. ed., Community Trade Mark Regulation (EC) no 207/2009: A Commentary (1st edn, Beck/Hart, 2015), 4, p. 4-35, including the detailed listed scholarly sources referred to on p. 4. Overall, the book edited by Hasselblatt provides a commentary on the TM Regulation 2009 and introduces the trademark systems of the EU member states.

[27]Other questions were: "What priority should be given to those who would use Community-wide media to promote their products throughout the whole territory or major parts of it? What registration system was best designed to hold the balance between effectiveness and due respect

Commission started sabre rattling over the creation of a harmonised and unified industrial property law. In consequence, a trademark working group was formed and it started its operations in late 1961. The work group led to the drafting of the Preliminary Draft of a Convention for a European Trade Mark.[28] The first piece of EU trademark legislation however, was not a regulation that created an EU wide trademark but the TM Directive 1989.[29]

The key feature of the TM Regulation 1994 was the introduction of a Community trade mark with "a unitary Character" and "equal effect throughout the Community"[30] to be registered with the Office for Harmonization in the Internal Market ("OHIM").[31] Adding to the policy background of EU trademark legislation, not surprisingly, according to Schovsbo, that trademark law was the first area of intellectual property law to be fully Europeanised through a regulation and a directive, due to the significant financial value of trademarks.[32] In similar veins, Hasselblatt has claimed that "[t]o try to explain the importance of effective trade mark protection to modern world entrepreneurs is a bit like carrying coals to Newcastle. Successful business people know by heart that a powerful trade mark encapsulates the essential values of a brand."[33]

The TM Directive 1989 was followed by the second trademark directive, i.e. the TM Directive 2008.[34] The TM Regulation 1994 was amended and repealed by the second codified trademark regulation, i.e. the TM Regulation 2009.[35] The TM Regulation is a codification of the amendments made to the TM Regulation 2009, including amendments made in December 2015 in regulation (EU) 2015/2424 (the "TM Amendment Regulation"),[36] whereas the TM Directive is recast of the

---

for competing interests, large and small? What place would remain for legal protection of marks and names on the basis of use rather than registration, where national law so allowed?" Cornish, William R., Llewelyn, David, and Alpin, Tanya, 'Intellectual Property: Patents, Copyright, Trademarks and Allied Rights', (8th edn, Sweet & Maxwell, 2013), p. 638-639.

[28]The description of the early days of European trademark development is found in the TM Memorandum 1976, p. 6.

[29]Cf. art. 16(1) of the TM Directive 1989.

[30]Cf. art. 1(2) of the TM Regulation 1994.

[31]Cf. art. 2 of the TM Regulation 1994 that defined the OHIM (now EUIPO) and art. 25 of the TM Regulation 1994 that stated that an application for registration of a Community trademark ultimately had to be filed with the OHIM.

[32]Schovsbo, Jens, Rosenmeier, Morten and Petersen, Clement Salung, 'Immaterialret: Ophavsret, Patentret, Brugsmodelret, Designret, Varemærkeret', (5th edn, Jurist- og Økonomforbundets Forlag, 2018), p. 445.

[33]Hasselblatt, Gordian N., 'Article 1: Community Trade Marks', in Hasselblatt, Gordian N. ed., Community Trade Mark Regulation (EC) no 207/2009: A Commentary (1st edn, Beck/Hart, 2015), 4, p. 5.

[34]Recital 4 of the TM Directive 2008.

[35]Art. 166 of the TM Regulation 2009.

[36]EP and Council Regulation (EU) 2015/2424 of 16 December 2015 amending Council Regulation (EC) No 207/2009 on the Community trade mark and Commission Regulation (EC) No 2868/95 implementing Council Regulation (EC) No 40/94 on the Community trade mark, and repealing

amendments made to the TM Directive 2008.[37] In near future, probably, the legislative process at EU level comes to a halt with completing the trademark reform process that resulted in the TM Regulation and TM Directive. The TM Amendment Regulation renamed the Community trade mark the "European Union trade mark" ("EU trade mark"), and the OHIM is now the EUIPO.[38] The changes made to EU trademark legislation through the recent trademark reform do not affect the substantial likelihood of confusion standard in neither infringement nor registration.[39]

The commonly worded provisions of the TM Regulation and the TM Directive on likelihood of confusion cause an overlap in the jurisprudence on the average consumer as set out by the Court of Justice in the preliminary rulings procedure and as appeal court to the General Court.[40] Despite the overlap, the subsequent

---

Commission Regulation (EC) No 2869/95 on the fees payable to the Office for Harmonization in the Internal Market (Trade Marks and Designs), [2015] OJ L 341/21 (the "TM Amendment Regulation").

[37]Codification and recasting essentially are the same, but recasting indicates that the amendments reflected in the TM Directive are more substantial than the changes reflected in the TM Regulation.
See: http://ec.europa.eu/dgs/legal_service/recasting_en.htm (last visited 26 May 2019).

[38]Recital 2 of the TM Amendment Regulation, and now recital 27 and art. 1(1) of the TM Regulation. For obvious reasons commentators have welcomed the name change of the OHIM. For two things, OHIM (when not abbreviated) was a long name and it did not indicate that the office dealt with intellectual property law. Welcoming the renaming are among others, Dinwoodie, Graeme, and Gangjee, Dev, 'The Image of the Consumer in EU Trade Mark Law', in Leczykiewicz, Dorota, and Weatherill, Stephen eds., The Images of the Consumer in EU Law: Legislation, Free Movement and Competition Law (1st edn, Hart, 2016), 339, p. 342, footnote 12 of the text. Grappling with the name of the office does not seem to end with the recent renaming. In a LinkedIn post of MARQUES (a European association representing the interests of trademark owners) Phillips has (teasingly) stated: "Previously English-speakers would refer to the office as "o-him", though some preferred the more exotic acronym of its Spanish name, OAMI. How will EUIPO be pronounced? Any suggestions?" An "update e-mail" containing the post of the MARQUES blog was received by the author of this book 14 April 2016.

[39]One minor exception is the removal of the requirement that "any sign" to be registrable has to be "capable of being represented graphically." For an analysis of the consequences of this change on the likelihood of confusion, see Chap. 9, Sect. 9.3.1.1. For an account of the other changes introduced by the new EU trademark legislation, see Hasselblatt, Gordian N., 'Article 1: Community Trade Marks', in Hasselblatt, Gordian N. ed., Community Trade Mark Regulation (EC) no 207/2009: A Commentary (1st edn, Beck/Hart, 2015), 4, p. 18-23, Bøggild, Frank, and Staunstrup, Kolja, 'EU-Varemærkeret', (1st edn, Karnov Group, 2015), p. 29-32, Wallberg, Knud, 'The European Trademark Reform. An Overview from a Danish Perspective', NIR, vol. 1 (2015), pp. 107, Wallberg, Knud and Ravn, Michael Francke, 'Varemærkeret: Varemærkeloven og Fællesmærkeloven Med Kommentarer', (5th edn, Jurist- og Økonomforbundets Forlag, 2017), p. 52-54 and Moscona, Ron, 'Reforms to European Union Trade Mark Law', Intellectual Property & Technology Law Journal, vol. 28/no. 5, (2016), pp. 20.

[40]On the convergence of case law of the Court of Justice related to confusion-based disputes decided under the TM Regulation and the TM Directive, see e.g. LTJ Diffusion v. Sadas, Case C-291/00, [2003] ECR I-2799, para 41, Interflora v. Marks & Spencer, Case C-323/09, [2011] ECR I-8625, para 38, including case law cited here, and Fédération Cynologique v. Federación Canina, Case C-561/11, [2012], (opinion of AG Mengozzi), paras 56-57. See also Bently, Lionel, Sherman, Brad, Gangjee, Dev and Johnson, Phillip 'Intellectual Property Law', (5th edn, Oxford University

analysis will where relevant account for the differences between: First, the TM Regulation that creates a unified trademark, and the TM Directive that merely harmonises national trademark law. Second, the differences caused by the divide between registration and infringement.

The analysis of the purpose of EU trademark legislation took place as mentioned on the backdrop of the mere purpose and function of regulations and directives. As is well-known wisdom of the TFEU, "[a] regulation shall have general application. It shall be binding in its entirety and directly applicable in all Member States" whereas directives "shall be binding, as to the result to be achieved, upon each Member State to which it is addressed, but shall leave to the national authorities the choice of form and methods."[41] Presumptively, there is a higher degree of similarity between the member states' application of regulations and presumptively a leeway for differences in the case of directives, since they have to go through the process of national implementation. How much importance to attach to this depends on how the relevant provisions of the TM Regulation and the TM Directive have been formulated, and the route chosen for harmonisation.[42]

3.2.2.2 The UCPD

As it appears from the introduction, the UCPD explicitly refers to the average consumer in the preamble[43] and in the main text.[44] Besides this, the UCPD employs a more nuanced consumer image as it also refers to other consumer models.[45] Howells *et al* have described the UCPD as "a general clause to cover all economic harm caused to consumers by unfair practices" in B2C relations.[46]

3.3 National Trademark Law and Its Institutions

As the representative of the Common Law, the law of England and Wales is dealt with first. The laws of the Nordic countries are dealt with jointly due to their similarities. Focus will be on the presentation of the legislative sources relevant to interpreting the likelihood of confusion standard in registration and infringement.

Press, 2018), p. 1103-1104 and Firth, Alison, Lea, Gary R. and Cornford, Peter, 'Trade Marks: Law and Practice', (4th edn, Jordans, 2016), p. 130-131 and p. 297.

[41]Cf. art. 288 of the TFEU.

[42]See Chap. 9, Sect. 9.3.2.

[43]Recital 18 of the UCPD.

[44]Cf. arts. 5(2)(b), 6(1)(2), 7(1)(2) and 8 of the UCPD.

[45]See Chap. 7.

[46]Howells, Geraint G., Micklitz, Hans-W, and Wilhelmsson, Thomas, 'European Fair Trading Law the Unfair Commercial Practices Directive', (1st edn, Ashgate, 2006), preface.

Besides legislation, also some key preparatory works of legislation will be laid out—in particular when dealing with the Nordic countries.

3.3.1 England and Wales

Based on the Trademarks Act of 1938 (the "UK TM Act 1938")[47] the UK implemented the TM Directive 1989 into its Trade Marks Act of 21 July 1994 (the "UK TM Act 1994")[48] entering into force 31 October 1994,[49] which also made new provisions due to the TM Regulation 1994. The UK TM Act 1994 was recently amended e.g. to implement the TM Directive, and the act entered into force 14 January 2019.[50] The TM Regulation 1994 extends to the whole of the UK,[51] although the UK case law relevant to this book is issued by certain courts of England and Wales, save for *UK* Supreme Court case law. For simplicity reference throughout is made to UK trademark law. Since the UK and Denmark were EU members when the TM Directive 1989 was introduced,[52] their legislatures had to finalise the implementation of the directive no later than 28 December 1991.[53] The relevant provisions of the UK TM Act 1994 are on registration under "Relative grounds for refusal of registration," s. 5(2)(a)-(b) and on infringement under "Infringement of registered trade mark," s. 10(2)(a)-(b). Preceding the UK TM Act 1994, the UK legislature drafted the White Paper Reform of Trade Marks Law (the "UK TM White Paper").[54] This piece of preparatory work has only a limited role to play in the UK courts, which is in line with the limited role of preparatory works in Common Law as addressed in the previous chapter.[55] This is even more so the case with the entering into force of the TM Directive 1989.[56]

In the following seminal statement by Jacob J[57] in *British Sugar v. James Robertson*, he addressed the relevance of transcripts of parliamentary debates and the UK TM White Paper: "The intention of Parliament is to implement whatever the

---

[47]The Trade Marks Act 1938 (C. 22).

[48]The Trade Marks Act 1994 (consolidated version) (C.26).

[49]Cf. s. 2 of the Trade Marks Act 1994 Commencement Order, [1994] (No. 2550 C. 52), cf. s. 109 of the UK TM Act 1994.

[50]See the Trade Marks Regulations 2018, no. 825.

[51]Cf. art. 108(1) of the UK TM Act 1994.

[52]The UK and Denmark joined the EU 1 January 1973.

[53]Cf. art. 16(1) of the TM Directive 1989. Source: https://europa.eu/european-union/about-eu/countries_en (last visited 26 May 2019).

[54]Reform of Trade Marks Law, [1990] (Cm 1203).

[55]See Chap. 2, Sect. 2.3.

[56]See Mellor, James, David Llewelyn, Moody-Stuart, Thomas, *et al*, 'Kerly's Law of Trade Marks and Trade Names', (16th edn, Sweet & Maxwell, 2018), p. 4-5 and p. 562-564.

[57]As he was then before becoming Lord Justice of the UK Court of Appeal.

Directive means. Views expressed in parliament about the meaning, even by Minister, cannot assist in resolving any ambiguity, which stems from the Directive itself. Neither the courts of any other country whose 20 trade marks laws are supposed to implement the [1989 TM] Directive, or the European Court of Justice in interpreting it, would refer to what a British Minister said in Parliament in the course of implementation here. It would be irrelevant. What matters is the language of the Directive. That is why it is so important that those responsible for this kind of legislation make serious efforts to be clear. If they are 25 [now 28] not then the process of litigation imposed on industry will ensure an ultimate cost to the public of the Union."[58] This finding is important since it lists the obligations of the UK judiciaries vis-à-vis the Court of Justice. However, bearing in mind the duty of EU consistent interpretation addressed by the Court of Justice in *von Colsen* and *Marleasing*, the finding is uncontroversial.[59]

As pointed out by Mellor *et al* referring to *South Central Trains Ltd v Christopher Rodway*, Jacob's statement applies with a significant rider.[60] If interpreting member state legislation rooted in a directive cannot be made referring to the directive itself, including its preamble, Hansards (transcripts of British Parliamentary debates) may be used as part of the interpretation. Potentially, this has implications to the analysis of national law. The part of the average consumer not decided on by the Court of Justice under the likelihood of confusion standard may allow for somewhat different interpretations by the member state judiciaries, e.g. by reference to preparatory works. Dinwoodie has seen the approach of the UK courts as "deriding" "in the trade mark context the Member State flexibility inherent in the concept of a directive – which would allow different Member States to realise common goals through different jurisprudential devices."[61]

---

[58]British Sugar v. Robertson, [1996] RPC 281, (EWHC), p. 292.

[59]On the decisions, see footnotes 83 and 84 below.

[60]Mellor, James, David Llewelyn, Moody-Stuart, Thomas, *et al*, 'Kerly's Law of Trade Marks and Trade Names', (16th edn, Sweet & Maxwell, 2018), p. 4-5, footnote 14 of the text. In *South Central Trains v. Christopher Rodway* the UK Court of Appeal by Keene LJ stated that in analysing the directive at stake "[i]t is also clear that the Directive and the framework leave it to each member state to deal with the details, so that the situation in each such state may be taken into account." South Central Trains v. Christopher Rodway, [2005] WL 871041, (EWCA), para 32. After concluding that the relevant national provisions are not ambiguous (*ibid* para 35), Keene LJ stated that "[i]f, however, there were any ambiguity, then I would accept that the criteria set out in Pepper v Hart were met and I would in that situation have regard to the two ministerial statements. They seem to me to put the matter beyond any doubt." *Ibid*, para 36.

[61]Dinwoodie has based his assertion on *inter alia* the statements of Jacob J (as he was then) in British Sugar v. Robertson, [1996] RPC 281, (EWHC). Dinwoodie, Graeme B, 'The Europeanization of Trade Mark Law', in Ohly, Ansgar and Pila, Justine eds., The Europeanization of Intellectual Property Law: Towards a European Legal Methodology (1st edn, Oxford University Press, 2013), 72, p. 80, including footnote 14 of the text.

3.3.2   Nordic Trademark Law: Similarities and Differences

Although some differences emerge between the selected Nordic countries, it has to be borne in mind that among the countries a high degree of similarity exists in their legal traditions, but also in their substantial trademark law.[62] Thus, the origin of a common understanding of the likelihood of confusion standard can be traced back to an early piece of preparatory works from 1882, the joint Nordic proposal for new trademark acts of Sweden, Denmark and Norway (the "Nordic TM Proposal 1882").[63] Also in 1949, the Nordic countries started working together on an update of their trademark acts. The collaboration resulted in new trademark acts of Sweden in 1960 (the "SE TM Act 1960"),[64] Denmark in 1959 (the "DK TM Act 1959")[65] and Norway in 1961 (the "NO TM Act 1961").[66] A natural consequence of the Europeanisation of trademark law is that the main motor for harmonisation of the Nordic trademark law is no longer the Nordic collaboration but the EU.[67]

As an EU member, Denmark implemented the TM Directive 1989 into Varemærkeloven of 6 June 1991 (the "DK TM Act 1991")[68] entering into force 1 January 1992.[69] The picture is more opaque with Sweden and Norway.

Norway is not an EU member but is part of both the European Free Trade Association ("EFTA") and the European Economic Area ("EEA"). The EEA Agreement was signed 2 May 1992 and entered into force 1 January 1994. The agreement extended the EU Single Market to the five EFTA countries at the time, including Norway and Sweden, which before becoming an EU member was part of EFTA.[70] Under the EEA Agreement Norway and Sweden at the time had to follow certain

---

[62]See Chap. 2, Sect. 2.3.1.

[63]Motiver til det af de Svensk-Norsk-Dansk kommitterede Forslag til Lov om beskyttelse af Varemærker of 12 August 1882.

[64]Varumärkeslagen, No 644 of 2 December 1960. The act entered into force 1 January 1961. The 1961 SE TM Act has been changed many times since, last 1 August 2009 through 2009:0116. For an overview of the changes to the 1961 SE TM Act, see Karnov Commentary for the SE TM Act 2010 as updated 25 May 2018, the introductory note p. 29.

[65]Varemærkelov, Act. No 211 of 11 June 1959. The act entered into force 1 October 1959. The DK TM Act 1959 has been changed many times, the latest changes were made 17 April 1989 through LBK 249/14.4.1989.

[66]Varemerkeloven, Act No 4 of 3 March 1961. The 1961 DK TM Act entered into force 1 October 1961 as most recently amended 1 January by L17.06.2005 nr. 90.

[67]Grundén, Örjan, 'En Ny Nordisk Känneteckensrätt Inför 2000-Talet?', NIR, vol. 4 (1994), pp. 542, p. 544.

[68]Varemærkelov, Act No 341 of 6 June 1991.

[69]Cf. § 61 of the DK TM Act 1991.

[70]EFTA, 'This is EFTA 2015', (booklet on EFTA), available at: http://www.efta.int/publications/this-is-efta-2015 (last visited 26 May 2019), p. 8.

"specific provisions and arrangements concerning intellectual, industrial and commercial property," including the TM Directive 1989.[71]

Sweden became an EU member 1 January 1995 and hence, was not an EU
member when the TM Directive 1989 was introduced. Sweden initially implemented
the TM Directive 1989 into the TM Act 1960 due to its EEA Agreement obligations.
The TM Directive 2008 was implemented into the Swedish trademark act from 2010
(the "SE TM Act 2010") that also accounted for the 2009 TM Regulation.[72] The
adaption of Swedish trademark law before the SE TM Act 2010 meant that the
provisions that laid down the likelihood of confusion standard had already been
adapted to EU law.[73] Norway implemented the TM Directive 1989 into the NO TM
Act 1961 to meet its obligations under the EEA Agreement. Despite the influence of
the Europeanisation of trademark law, it was pointed out in 1994 by Koktvedgaard,
one of the founding persons of Nordic intellectual property law,[74] that the Nordic
countries offer a common business culture providing a solid starting point for
affecting the European state of the trademark law.[75] In continuation of this line of
argument, Grundén pointed out at the same time that some smaller companies had
the Nordic countries as their home markets.[76] Undoubtedly, this commercial reality
has changed since 1994, but the Nordic collaboration on trademark law has continued, not least informally, and still there exists a strong knowledge sharing across the
Nordic countries.[77] Also outside of its country of origin, Nordic case law may be

---

[71]Cf. art. 65(2), of the EEA Agreement of 1994, cf. Annex XVII s 4. Certain exemptions to this
obligation are not relevant to the substantial analysis of this book. Hence, "[t]he provisions of the
[1989 TM] Directive shall, for the purposes of the [EEA]Agreement, be read with the following
adaptations: (a) in Article 3(2), the term 'trade mark law' shall be understood to be the trade mark
law applicable in a Contracting Party; (b) in Articles 4(2)(a)(i), (2)(b) and (3), 9 and 14, the
provisions concerning the Community trade mark shall not apply to EFTA States unless the
Community trade mark extends to them; (c) Article 7(1) shall be replaced by the following:
    'The trade mark shall not entitle the proprietor to prohibit its use in relation to goods which have
been put on the market in a Contracting Party under that trade mark by the proprietor or with his
consent.'" *Ibid.*

[72]Varumärkeslagen, SFS 2010:1877 of 9 December 2010, as most recently amended by amending
act SFS 2018:287 entering into force 25 May 2018.

[73]I.e. § 6 of the SE TM Act 1960. Bet. 2009 10/225, p. 61.

[74]Schovsbo has described Koktvedgaard as the person with the most individual impact on Nordic
intellectual property law research. See Schovsbo, Jens, 'Forord', in Schovsbo, Jens ed.,
Netværksmødet 2003: Immaterialrettens Afbalancering (1st edn, Jurist- og Økonomforbundets
Forlag, 2003), 7, p. 8.

[75]The considerations by various scholars and practitioners on a reform of Nordic trademark law,
aired during a roundtable debate, were summarised by Hyllinge in Nordisk Immateriellt Rättsskydd
("NIR") 1994. Koktvedgaard's opinion was summarised on p. 552-554 in Hyllinge, Claus.
'Sammanfattning Av Diskussionen Rörande En Ny Nordisk Känneteckenrätt Inför 2000-Talet',
NIR, vol. 4/(1994), pp. 545.

[76]Grundén, Örjan, 'En Ny Nordisk Känneteckensrätt Inför 2000-Talet?', NIR, vol. 4 (1994),
pp. 542, p. 544.

[77]For instance, the Nordic journal on intellectual property (NIR) publishes academic articles and
case comments. Also, every year IPR network meetings are held among senior researchers and PhD

referred to mutually by counsels in other Nordic courts and provide relevant legal subtext—although not as a binding legal source.

Sweden and Denmark have implemented the TM Directive into new consolidated national trademark acts that entered into force 1 January 2019, both reflected in governmental proposals from June 2018, respectively the "SE TM Prop. 2018/ 18:267"[78] and "DK TM Prop. 261/2017-18."[79] Notwithstanding the similarities of the Nordic jurisdictions, as pointed out by Lassen and Stenvik, their trademark laws cannot be viewed in isolation from their legal environments. In this context, some key differences do exist among the jurisdictions.[80] Also, at member state level when the national courts flesh out the average consumer, they are left with a certain room for manoeuvring; potentially within this room, the Nordic courts move in different directions.

3.3.2.1 Sweden

The SE TM Act 2010 now appears in a consolidated version that entered into force 1 January 2019.[81] Regarding registration and infringement the relevant provisions of the SE TM Act 2010 are found respectively under "Other rights as grounds for refusal of registration" § 8(2), ch. 2 and under "Implications of exclusive rights" § 10 (2), ch. 1. A significant contribution to interpreting the provisions is found

---

candidates from originally the Nordic countries but now also from three German universities. Although these meetings are on general intellectual property, they inevitably also affect the academic collaboration on trademark law among the Nordic countries. On these meetings, see Schovsbo, Jens, 'Forord', in Schovsbo, Jens ed., Netværksmødet 2003: Immaterialrettens Afbalancering (1st edn, Jurist- og Økonomforbundets Forlag, 2003), 7, p. 7-8.

[78]Regeringens proposition 2017/18:267 Modernare regler om varumärken och en ny lag om företagsnamn, of 7 June 2018. The amendments are implemented into the consolidated Lag om ändring i varumärkeslagen (2010:1877), SFS 2018:1652 of 15 November 2018.

[79]Erhvervs-, Vækst- og Eksportudvalget 2017-18, ERU Alm.del Bilag 261, Udkast til Forslag til Lov om ændring af varemærkeloven, fællesmærkeloven, designloven og gassikkerhedsloven, of 25 June 2018. The amendments were approved by the legislature through Lov om ændring af varemærkeloven og forskellige andre love og om ophævelse af fællesmærkeloven, Act No 1533 of 18 December 2018.

[80]A key difference is, according to Lassen and Stenvik, that Danish and Norwegian trademark law has been regarded as part of the general law of marketing practices and general principles that prevent unfair competition. Sweden, on the other hand, has required a stricter legal basis for intervention and the trademark legislation has been more fenced off from general unfair competition law. The consequence of this is that "not even identical legal provisions would have led to full legal harmonization" between the countries. In Norwegian: "at selv ikke likelydende lovbestemmelser ville ha gitt full rettsenhet." Lassen, Birger Stuevold and Stenvik, Are, 'Kjennetegnsrett', (3rd edn, Universitetsforlaget, 2011), p. 28.

[81]The recent amendments were approved by the legislature through Lag om ändring i varumärkeslagen (2010:1877) SFS 2018:1652 of 15 November 2018 and appear in the consolidated SE TM Act 2010.

particularly in the 705 pages long governmental bill 2009/10:225 of 3 June 2010 on
inter alia, changing the SE TM Act 2010 ("SE TM Prop. 2009/10:225").[82]

When Sweden joined the EU, the Swedish judiciaries accepted the duty to carry
out EU consistent interpretation. This duty was laid down by the Court of Justice
inter alia in *von Colsen* that dealt with the intention of national legislation to
implement a directive[83] and subsequently in *Marleasing* that dealt with a directive
that had not yet been implemented by the national legislature.[84] The duty to carry out
EU consistent interpretation has been confirmed and elaborated on by Högsta
Domstolen (the "SE Supreme Court/SESC") in *Mast-Jägermeister v. Vin & Sprit*
on likelihood of confusion in light of the SE TM Act 1960[85] and more recently in in
IFX v. PN.[86]

3.3.2.2   Denmark

The DK TM Act 1991 has been amended several times and now appears in a
consolidated version that entered into force 1 January 2019.[87] Regarding registration
and infringement the relevant provisions of the DK TM Act 1991[88] on registration

---

[82]Regeringens proposition 2009/10:225 Ny varumärkeslag och ändringar i firmalagen, of
3 June 2010.

[83]In *von Colsen* the starting point for the ruling was that the directive at stake was not sufficient clear
for it to have direct effect. However, the Court of Justice stated: "It is for the national court to
interpret and apply the legislation adopted for the implementation of the directive in conformity
with the requirements of Community law, in so far as it is given discretion to do so under national
law." *Ibid*, para 28.

[84]The Court of Justice elaborated on the principle laid down in *von Colsen* and held that "in
applying national law, whether the provisions in question were adopted before or after the directive,
the national court called upon to interpret it is required to do so, as far as possible, in the light of the
wording and the purpose of the directive in order to achieve the result pursued by the latter and
thereby comply with the third paragraph of Article 189 of the Treaty [art. 288 of the TFEU]."
Marleasing, Case C-106/89, [1990] ECR I-4135, para 8. As for the question of direct applicability,
the Court of Justice initially stated that "a directive may not of itself impose obligations on an
individual and, consequently, a provision of a directive may not be relied upon as such against such
a person." *Ibid*, para 6.

[85]Mast-Jägermeister v. Vin & Sprit, T 2982-01, [2003], SESC. For further on this decision, see
Chap. 10, Sect. 10.3.2.1.

[86]IFX v. PN, T 2228-00, [2003], SESC, p. 565. For further on this decision, see Chap. 10, Sect.
10.3.2.1. On the relationship between Swedish intellectual property law and EU law in the
described transition period until Sweden became an EU member, see Bernitz, Ulf, Karnell, Gunnar,
Lars Pherson, *et al*, 'Immaterialrätt Och Otillbörlig Konkurrens', (14th edn, Jure Bokhandel, 2017),
p. 27-29.

[87]The recent amendments were approved by the legislature through Lov om ændring af
varemærkeloven og forskellige andre love og om ophævelse af fællesmærkeloven, Act No 1533
of 18 December 2018 and appear in Varemærkeloven, consolidated act of 29 January 2019. no 88.

[88]For an overview of the development of the DK TM Act 1991 and preceding trademark acts, see
Wallberg, Knud and Ravn, Michael Francke, 'Varemærkeret: Varemærkeloven og
Fællesmærkeloven Med Kommentarer', (5th edn, Jurist- og Økonomforbundets Forlag, 2017),

are found under "Grounds for refusal," § 15, sub-s,1 (2) and on infringement under "Contents of the trade mark right," § 4, sub-s 1 (2). Koktvedgaard has stated that the DK TM Act 1959 was "a good and visionary act," and that "it was at the same level as the development of the law in the main industrial countries." Hence, the white paper that preceded the DK TM Act 1959 is still considered one of the most important texts for the overall understanding of Danish trademark law and interpreting specific provisions.[89] This, of course, is not to say that the duty to carry out EU consistent interpretation is not acknowledged by the Danish courts.[90] The white paper is Betænkning nr. 199 of 18 April 1958 (the "DK TM Bet. 199/1958"). Recently, Højesteret (the "DK Supreme Court") in *Ajos*, an employment conflict between two private parties (employee and employer), reiterated firmly that there is no obligation based on the principle of EU consistent interpretation to interpret Danish law *contra legem*.[91] This principle stands even against EU principles leading to opposite result.[92] The court concluded: "The Supreme Court would be acting outside the scope of its powers as a judicial authority if it were to disapply the provision in this situation."[93] Essentially, the DK Supreme court chose not to follow the preliminary ruling in the case by the Court of Justice that stated referring

---

p. 49-51, Schovsbo, Jens, Rosenmeier, Morten and Petersen, Clement Salung, 'Immaterialret: Ophavsret, Patentret, Brugsmodelret, Designret, Varemærkeret', (5th edn, Jurist- og Økonomforbundets Forlag, 2018), p. 447-448 and the Karnov Commentary for the DK TM Act 1991 as updated 1 July 2017, p. 10-11.

[89]The quotes in Danish: "en god og visionær lov" and "[d]en var fuldt på højde med retsudviklingen i industriens hovedlande." Koktvedgaard, Mogens, and Wallberg, Knud, 'Varemærkeloven af 6. Juni 1991 og Fællesmærkeloven af 6. Juni 1991 med Indledning og Kommentarer', (1st edn, Jurist- og Økonomforbundets Forlag, 1994), p. 13.

[90]See for instance, *Grundfos v. CO-industri* where the DK Supreme Court assessed the duty to interpret Danish law in consistency with EU law, with the important limitation though following from Court of Justice case law, not to interpret national law contra legem. Grundfos v. CO-industri, U.2014.914H, [2013], (DKSC), p. 923-924. See also Sørensen, Karsten Engsig, Nielsen, Poul Runge and Danielsen, Jens Hartig, 'EU-Retten', (6th edn, Jurist- og Økonomforbundets Forlag, 2014), p. 170-174.

[91]Ajos, Case 15/2014, [2016], (DKSC), p. 44. The unofficial translation of the decision into English referred to here is available on the website of the DK Supreme Court: http://www.supremecourt.dk/supremecourt/nyheder/pressemeddelelser/Documents/Judgment%2015-2014.pdf (last visited 26 May 2019). The official Danish version of the decision, Ajos, Sag 15/2014, [2016], (DKSC), is also available of the website of the DK Supreme Court: http://www.hoejesteret.dk/hoejesteret/nyheder/Afgorelser/Documents/15-2014.pdf (last visited 26 May 2019). See also Evald, Jens, 'Juridisk Teori, Metode og Videnskab', (1st edn, Jurist- og Økonomforbundets Forlag, 2016), p. 62-65.

[92]The EU law principle at stake was the prohibition of discrimination due to age.

[93]Ajos, Case 15/2014, [2016], (DKSC), p. 48. The decision was reached with one out of nine judges dissenting. The dissenting judge found that there was ground under Danish law to disapply the disputed Danish provision. *Ibid*, p. 51.

to an EU legal principle that the DK Supreme Court had to not apply the relevant Danish provision.[94]

3.3.2.3   Norway: The EEA Connection

For Norway, the relevant act is "Lov om beskyttelse av varemerker" of 26 March 2010 entering into force 1 July 2010 (the "NO TM Act 2010").[95] Regarding registration and infringement the relevant provisions of the NO TM Act 2010 are found respectively under "Trademarks that conflict with the rights of others," § 16(1) (a), cf. § 4(1)(b) of the NO TM Act 2010 and under "Content of a trademark right," § 4(1)(b) of the NO TM Act 2010. A significant contribution to interpreting the provisions is found in particular in the 114 pages long governmental bill Ot.prp. nr. 98 (2008–2009) of 15 May 2009 on the NO TM Act 2010 ("NO TM Prop. 98/2008-09").[96]

The EEA Agreement was entered into as a treaty under international law. The overall purpose of the EEA as specified in the agreement is to promote a continuous and balanced strengthening of trade and economic relations between the Contracting Parties with equal conditions of competition, and the respect of the same rules, to create a homogeneous European Economic Area.[97] As further specified in the agreement, its specific objectives correspond to the key objectives of the EU, including the four freedoms.[98] That said, in practice, the objectives of the EU treaties and the EEA Agreement may be interpreted differently. Thus, For one thing, the Court of Justice has stated that despite the similarity between the EEC (now the "TEU") and the EEA Agreement, the EEA Agreement does not create a "new legal order," and the principles of direct effect and supremacy known from EU law do not apply to the EEA Agreement.[99] However, the objectives of the EEC extend beyond the main objectives of the EEA Agreement, i.e. "free trade and competition in economic and commercial realities between the Contracting Parties [of the EEA

---

[94]I.e. Ajos, Case C-441/14, [2016] (Grand Chamber), paras 33-37 and 43 as confirmed by the Court of Justice in Egenberger v. Evangelisches Werk für Diakonie und Entwicklung, Case C-414/16, [2018] (Grand Chamber), paras 72-73. See Ajos, Case 15/2014, [2016], (DKSC), p. 44.

[95]Varemerkeloven, Act No 8 of 26 March 2010, as most recently changed by Act No 65 of 19 June 2015.

[96]Om lov om beskyttelse av varemerker (varemerkeloven), Ot.prp. nr. 98 (2008–2009) of 15 May 2009.

[97]Cf. art. 1(1) of the EEA Agreement.

[98]Cf. art. 1(2) of the EEA Agreement where it is stated: "In order to attain the objectives set out in paragraph 1, the association shall entail, in accordance with the provisions of this Agreement: (a) the free movement of goods; (b) the free movement of persons; (c) the free movement of services; (d) the free movement of capital; (e) the setting up of a system ensuring that competition is not distorted and that the rules thereon are equally respected; as well as (f) closer cooperation in other fields, such as research and development, the environment, education and social policy."

[99]Opinion 1991/1, 1, para 21.

Agreement]."[100] It is beyond this book to go further into a comparison of interpreting the EU treaties and the objectives of the EEA Agreement.[101]

Since Norway is a signatory to the EEA Agreement and still not an EU member, the duty of EU consistent interpretation of the NO TM Act 2010 does not follow directly from the general EU law as touched upon above.[102] However, through Norway's obligation to implement the TM Directive 1989 and subsequently the TM Directive 2008[103] it has obligations under the directive comparable to the remainder of the national jurisdictions relevant to this book. Because of the EEA Agreement, the TM Directive 1989 was attached in a Norwegian version to the ratification agreement.[104] This translation is due to the EEA Agreement as authentic as the official EU translations.[105]

In *Godmorgon*, Høyesterett (the "NO Supreme Court/NOSC") stressed some of the significant obligations Norway has towards the EU under trademark law. In the decision, the NO Supreme Court had to decide if a company could register the wordmark GODMORGON[106] for among other goods, fruit drinks and juices. An important question was the role of EU trademark law in interpreting the NO TM Act 1961.

After remarking that the TM Directive 1989 was implemented into Norwegian trademark law, the NO Supreme Court compared the English and Danish versions of the directive with the Norwegian version.[107] The court concluded that the Norwegian version of the relevant provision was imprecise and could not be the basis of the

---

[100]*Ibid*, paras 15-16. Another difference is, according to the Court of Justice, that although both the EEC and the EEA Agreement have been established as international treaties, the EEC "constitutes the constitutional charter of the Community based on the rule of law." *Ibid*, para 21.

[101]On this, see Opinion of the Court of Justice 1/91 of 14 December 1991.

[102]For an overall discussion on the meaning of the EEA Agreement in light of the EU and intellectual property law, see Davis, Richard, St Quintin, Thomas and Tritton, Guy, 'Tritton on Intellectual Property in Europe', (5th edn, Sweet & Maxwell, 2018), p. 39-47.

[103]Cf. art. 65(2), of the EEA Agreement of 1994, cf. Annex XVII dated 8 July 2016, s 9(h), cf. footnote 42 of the text.

[104]In attachment no 2 to "om samtykke til ratifikasion av Avtale om Det europeiske økonomiske samarbeidsområde (EØS), undertegnet i Oporto 2. mai 1992, St.prp. nr. 100 (1991-1992)" of 15 May 1992 (the "NO Prop. 100 (1991-1992)").

[105]Cf. art. 129(1) of the EEA Agreement. As Stenvik has pointed out in a commentary to Klagenemnda v. Jo-Bolaget Fruktprodukter, HR-2001-1049, [2002], NOSC and referring to art. 129(1) of the EEA Agreement, the judge was not correct in claiming that the Norwegian translation of the 1988 Directive was unofficial. Lassen, Birger Stuevold and Stenvik, Are, 'Kjennetegnsrett', (3rd edn, Universitetsforlaget, 2011), p. 324.

[106]In English "good morning." For an in-depth analysis of the decision, see Stenvik in Rognstad, Ole-Andreas, Stenvik, Are and Lassen, Birger Stuevold, 'Fra norsk rettspraksis', NIR, vol. 3 (2002), p. 313-325.

[107]As mentioned by Stenvik, the issue here was that the Norwegian translation indicated a higher threshold for registration than did in particular the Danish version, but also the English version. Rognstad, Ole-Andreas, Stenvik, Are and Lassen, Birger Stuevold, 'Fra norsk rettspraksis', NIR, vol. 3 (2002), p. 310, p. 319 and 324.

decision.[108] Then the court turned towards EU case law to find decisions that interpreted the provision. The court stated that case law of the Court of Justice more recent than to 2 May 1992[109] was not formally binding but should be given much weight in the interpretation.[110]

Referring to e.g. *Godmorgon*, Lassen and Stenvik have held that there is no doubt that case law of the Court of Justice is essential when interpreting of the trademark directives, as they have been implemented into the Norwegian trademark acts.[111] This is in particular true for the provisions of the directives relevant to this book, since they are closely mirrored in Norwegian trademark legislation. It also appears from the preparatory works[112] and case law that the trademark directives have to be considered when interpreting Norwegian trademark legislation.[113]

The EU trademark regulations are not part of the EEA Agreement and as such not binding to Norway. However, the substantial overlap between the trademark directives and regulations means that Court of Justice decisions on the regulations are relevant to the interpretation of Norwegian trademark law. Thus, the NO Supreme Court acknowledged in *Godmorgon*[114] and in the preparatory works of the 2010 TM Act,[115] that Court of Justice case law on the trademark regulations has a significant role to play to Norwegian trademark law. The NO Supreme Court has recently confirmed this in *Pangea v. Klagenemnda*.[116]

Following from the EEA Agreement, the EFTA states parties to the EEA Agreement had to establish the EFTA Court.[117] Essentially, the EFTA Court has the same

---

[108]The relevant provision was § 13 of the NO TM Act 1961.

[109]The signatory date of the EEA Agreement.

[110]This is in accordance with art. 6 of the EEA Agreement. Klagenemnda v. Jo-Bolaget Fruktprodukter, HR-2001-1049, [2002], NOSC, p. 395-396. See also Gundersen, Aase, 'Norsk Varemerkerett i Lys Av EU-Utviklingen', NIR, vol. 1 (2005), pp. 106, p. 106 and Thorning, Louise Christina, and Finnanger, Solvår Winnie, 'Trademark Protection in the European Union with a Scandinavian View', (1st edn, Thomson Reuters, 2010), p. 36.

[111]Lassen, Birger Stuevold and Stenvik, Are, 'Kjennetegnsrett', (3rd edn, Universitetsforlaget, 2011), p. 31. The NO TM Act 1961 implemented the TM Directive 1989 which did not cause substantial changes to the NO TM Act 1961 relevant to this book. Ot. prp. 72 (1991-92), p. 54. The NO TM Act 2010 implemented the TM Directive 2008.

[112]Ot. prp. 72 (1991-92), p. 55.

[113]Klagenemnda v. Jo-Bolaget Fruktprodukter, HR-2001-1049, [2002], NOSC.

[114]*Ibid*, p. 396.

[115]NO TM Prop. 98/2008-09, p. 8. See also from literature, Lassen, Birger Stuevold and Stenvik, Are, 'Kjennetegnsrett', (3rd edn, Universitetsforlaget, 2011), p. 31-32 and Thorning, Louise Christina, and Finnanger, Solvår Winnie, 'Trademark Protection in the European Union with a Scandinavian View', (1st edn, Thomson Reuters, 2010), p. 36.

[116]Pangea Property Partners v. Klagenemnda, HR-2016-01993-A, [2016], NOSC, paras 42-43.

[117]Cf. art. 108(2) of the EEA Agreement: "The EFTA Court shall, in accordance with a separate agreement between the EFTA States, with regard to the application of this Agreement be competent, in particular, for: (a) actions concerning the surveillance procedure regarding the EFTA States; (b) appeals concerning decisions in the field of competition taken by the EFTA Surveillance Authority; (c) the settlement of disputes between two or more EFTA States."

function towards the EFTA countries as the Court of Justice has towards the EU members. The sole competence of both courts is to interpret the EEA Agreement in their respective territories.[118] The above findings on the obligations of Norwegian courts to apply EU trademark legislation and the practice of the CJEU have also recently been emphasised by the EFTA Court in *Vigeland*.[119] So far, the EFTA Court has only made five decisions on trademark law. Four relate to the exhaustion of trademark rights[120] The most recent decision, *Vigeland*, relates to distinctiveness, descriptiveness and the overlap between trademark law and copyright law. Here, the court applied the known terminology on the average consumer in the realm of distinctiveness and descriptiveness.[121] Since these five decisions of the EFTA Court are not on likelihood of confusion, they will not be dealt with further in this book.[122]

3.4 National Trademark Courts

The national decisions considered are made by courts that usually deal with trademark disputes on the likelihood of confusion standard. The natural starting point for EU members is found in the so-called EU Trademark Courts (previously the "Community Trademark Courts") allocated to deal with e.g. infringement of EU trademarks. These courts have been designated by EU member states to deal with this specialised area of law. Besides the EU Trademark Courts, other courts are included by all jurisdictions though. For Norway, the relevant courts are the ones adjudicating on disputes related to national trademarks. In line with the delimitation of the book, this section does not involve an analysis of the national procedural rules.[123]

Under the TM Regulation, each of the EU member states must designate EU Trademark Courts of first and second instance to adjudicate on matters assigned to

---

[118]The NO Prop. 100 (1991-1992), p. 329.

[119]Vigeland, Case E-5/16, [2017], paras 44-45.

[120]A search for decisions on "trademarks" has been conducted in the EFTA case law database 31 July 2018. The decisions on trademark law are: Mag Instrument, Case E-2/97, [1997], Paranova, Case E-3/02, [2003], L'Oréal, Joined Cases E-9/07 and Case E-10/07, [2008] and Vigeland, Case E-5/16, [2017].

[121]Vigeland, Case E-5/16, [2017], paras 139 and 141. For further on this decision, see Senftleben, Martin, 'Vigeland and the Status of Cultural Concerns in Trade Mark Law – The EFTA Court Develops More Effective Tools for the Preservation of the Public Domain', IIC, vol. 48/no. 6, (2017) pp. 683.

[122]For a recent perspective on the decisions of the EFTA Court on trademark law, see Rognstad, Ole-Andreas, 'Intellectual Property Law', in Baudenbacher, Carl ed., The Handbook of EEA Law (1st edn, Springer, 2016), 703, p. 703-720.

[123]See Chap. 1, Sect. 1.5.4.

them under the TM Regulation.[124] The starting point is that appeal of first instance decisions can be made to second instance EU Trademark Courts.[125] Should it be possible to appeal the decision of the second instance Community Trademark Courts, the member states do not have to designate that court as an EU Trademark Court.[126] UK and Sweden have not designated their highest courts as Community Trademark Courts, respectively the UK Supreme Court ("UKSC") and the SE Supreme Court.[127] The decisions of these courts though are naturally included in the analysis.

Denmark on the other hand, has specified Højesteret (the "DK Supreme Court/DKSC") as Community Trademark Court as the appeal court to Sø- og Handelsretten, i.e. the Danish Maritime and Commercial High Court/(the "DK MCH Court/DKMCHC").[128] It is a matter for national law to determine the conditions of appeal for first instance Community Trade Mark decisions.[129] According to Danish procedural rules, decisions of the DK MCH Court may not always be appealed to the DK Supreme Court but has to be appealed to Vestre or Østre Landsret, i.e. to the branch in either the eastern or the western part of Denmark (depending on jurisdiction), (jointly the "DK Court of Appeal/DKCA").[130] Hence, the DK Court of Appeal is also part of the national trademark courts of Denmark.[131]

---

[124]Cf. art. 123(1) of the TM Regulation.

[125]Cf. art. 133(1), cf. art. 124 of the TM Regulation.

[126]Cf. art. 133(3) of the TM Regulation.

[127]Essentially, appeal to the SE Supreme Court may only happen in rare occasions, including if the matter "is of importance for the guidance of the application of law that the Supreme Court considers the appeal," cf. § 10, sub-s 1(1) of the Swedish Code on Civil Procedure (Rättegångsbalk, 1942:740 of 18 July 1942 (as changed 15 November 2016)).

[128]On the Danish Community Trade Mark Courts, see Christiansen, Claus Barrett, 'Denmark', in Hasselblatt, Gordian N. ed., Community Trade Mark Regulation (EC) no 207/2009: A Commentary (1st edn, Beck/Hart, 2015), 1292, p. 1292-1293, Bøggild, Frank, and Staunstrup, Kolja, 'EU-Varemærkeret', (1st edn, Karnov Group, 2015), p. 455-462 and Schovsbo, Jens, Rosenmeier, Morten and Petersen, Clement Salung, 'Immaterialret: Ophavsret, Patentret, Brugsmodelret, Designret, Varemærkeret', (5th edn, Jurist- og Økonomforbundets Forlag, 2018), p. 671-673.

[129]Cf. art. 133(2) of the TM Regulation.

[130]Under the Danish Administration of Justice Act, it is only possible to appeal decisions of the DK MCC to the DK Supreme Court if they relate to a matter of principle or have general significance for the development or application of the law, Cf. § 368(3), of the Danish Administration of Justice Act (i.e. bekendtgørelse af retsplejeloven, Consolidated Act No 1257 of 13 October 2016). In 2014 there was a reform of the Danish Administration of Justice Act. In *VMR Products v V2H* it was found by the DK Court of Appeal that due to this reform interim appeals of matters in DK MCH Court decisions have to be made to the DK Court of Appeal. VMR Products v V2H, U.2016.679Ø [2015], (DKCA), p. 680.

[131]After a case has been heard by two instances, the case may only be heard by the DK Supreme Court after permission from the Appeals Permission Board, cf. § 371, stk. 1 of the Danish Administration of Justice Act.

For Norway, Oslo Tingsrett (the "NO District Court/NODC") is mandatory venue of decisions of the appeal board of the NO IP Office.[132] Borgarting Lagmannsrett (the "NO Court of Appeal/NOCA") hears appeals from the NO District Court and if permission is given, the NO Supreme Court may hear these decisions.[133]

Based on the above and a publication of the EU Trademark Courts relevant to the EU members,[134] the national trademark courts are:

England and Wales: the UK Supreme Court, the Court of Appeal of England and Wales (the "UK Court of Appeal/EWCA") and the High Court of England and Wales (the "UK High Court/EWHC").[135]

Sweden: the SE Supreme Court, Svea Hovrätt (the "SE Court of Appeal/SECA") and Stockholms Tingsrätt (the "SE District Court/SEDC").[136] From 1 September 2016 references to the SE District Court and the SE High Court means reference to respectively the first and second instance of Patent- och Marknadsdomstol, the new Swedish court specialised in intellectual property disputes, including trademark disputes.[137]

Denmark: the DK Supreme Court, the DK Court of Appeal and the DK MCH Court.

Norway: the NO Supreme Court, the NO Court of Appeal and the NO District Court.

---

[132]Cf. § 62 of the NO TM Act 2010 for: "a) actions concerning a review of a decision made by the Norwegian Board of Appeal for Industrial Property Rights as mentioned in Section 52" and "c) civil actions concerning infringements of a registered trademark."

[133]Only to a limited extent may decisions of the NO Appeal Court be appealed to the NO Supreme Court, including if the case relates to a principle matter. Also, on rare occasions permission may be given to an appeal directly from a district court to the Supreme Court. See chapter 30 of the Norwegian Civil Procedural Act (Lov om mekling og rettergang i sivile tvister (tvisteloven), No 90 of 17 June 2005 (as changed 22 April 2016)).

[134]Publication of the lists of Community trade mark courts and Community design courts in accordance with Article 95(4) of Council Regulation (EC) No 207/2009 on the Community trade mark and Article 80(4) of Regulation (EC) No 6/2002 of 24 September 2014 on Community designs [2014] C 332/06.

[135]For further on the UK Trade Mark Courts, see Scourfield, Tom, 'United Kingdom', in Hasselblatt, Gordian N. ed., Community Trade Mark Regulation (EC) no 207/2009: A Commentary (1st edn, Beck/Hart, 2015), 1443, p. 1443-1445 and Firth, Alison, Lea, Gary R. and Cornford, Peter, 'Trade Marks: Law and Practice', (4th edn, Jordans, 2016), p. 346-350.

[136]Cf. § 6(2) of the SE 2010 TM Act. Under (1) of this provision, the SE District Court is the residual court, in case "the Code of Judicial Procedure does not assign a Court competent to entertain a case concerning revocation of a trade mark registration, trade mark infringement or a declaration whether certain legal relations exist or not." The trademark disputes of the SE District Court are dealt with in the fifth chamber of the court specialised in intellectual property disputes.

[137]Prop. 2015/16:57, p. 1. This proposition sets out in detail the functions of the new court vis-à-vis the exiting courts. See also generally on the Swedish Community Trade Mark Court Dahlman, Magnus, 'Sweden', in Hasselblatt, Gordian N. ed., Community Trade Mark Regulation (EC) no 207/2009: A Commentary (1st edn, Beck/Hart, 2015), 1438, p. 1438-1439.

3.5   International Treaties

3.5.1   The Paris Convention and the TRIPS Agreement

Besides the harmonisation of intellectual property law at the regional EU level, there have been longstanding attempts to regulate at the last level of law not addressed so far, international law. Besides the EU harmonisation and the Nordic collaborations, the international conventions are significant to the similarity of trademark laws across a multitude of countries and the "compatibility" across different trademark systems rooted in different jurisdictional systems.[138] Two of the main treaties relevant in this context are the Paris Convention for the Protection of Industrial Property of 20 March 1883, as most recently amended on 28 September 1979 (the "Paris Convention") and the Agreement on Trade-Related Aspects of Intellectual Property Rights of 15 April 1994 entering into force 1 January 1995 (the "TRIPS Agreement").

The Paris Convention is administered by the World Intellectual Property Organisation ("WIPO")[139] that resides under the United Nations. The TRIPS Agreement is part of the Agreement establishing the World Trade Organisation ("WTO Agreement") as such.[140] In 1884–1885 all countries relevant to this book signed the Paris Convention[141] and as of 1 January 1995 all the countries and the EU as such[142] became members of the WTO.[143] The key provisions on trademarks of the Paris Convention[144] were incorporated into the TRIPS Agreement allowing for interpreting these provisions by the WTO panels and the WTO Appellate Bodies.[145]

---

[138]Phillips, Jeremy, 'Trade Mark Law a Practical Anatomy', (1st edn, Oxford University Press, 2003), p. 38.

[139]Before the Convention Establishing the World Intellectual Property Organization of 14 July 1967, it was the United International Bureau for the Protection of Intellectual Property (known as "BIRPI") that administered the Paris Convention.

[140]Annex 1C of the WTO Agreement.

[141]The *UK*: accession 17 March 1884, in force 7 July 1884. *Sweden and Norway*: accession 29 May 1885, in force 1 July 1885. *Denmark*: accession and in force on 1 October 1884.

[142]For the accession of the EU to TRIPS Agreement, see Davis, Richard, St Quintin, Thomas and Tritton, Guy, 'Tritton on Intellectual Property in Europe', (5th edn, Sweet & Maxwell, 2018), p. 47-55.

[143]For an overview of the WTO members per 29 July 2016 and their signatory dates, see: https://www.wto.org/english/thewto_e/whatis_e/tif_e/org6_e.htm
(last visited 26 May 2019).

[144]Cf. art. 2(1) of the TRIPS Agreement, art. 1 to 12 and 19 were incorporated into the TRIPS Agreement. Art. 6 to 10ter are the provisions on trademark protection and protection against unfair competition.

[145]See Ricketson, Sam, 'The Paris Convention for the Protection of Industrial Property: A Commentary', (1st edn, Oxford University Press, 2015), p. 155.

The approach of the Paris Convention was a "principle of minimum standards (. . .) ensuring a minimal intrusion on Member States sovereignty."[146] Equally, the TRIPS Agreement stipulates minimum standards that may be tightened by the legislation of the WTO member states but may not contravene the standards of the agreement.[147] It emerges directly from the TM Directive that the member states as signatories to the Paris Convention and the TRIPS Agreement must ensure that the directive is "entirely consistent with that Convention and that Agreement." Furthermore, that the "[t]he obligations of the Member States resulting from that Convention and that Agreement should not be affected by this Directive."[148]

The reasons for cornering the role of the Paris Convention and the TRIPS Agreement in this book is that although they provide a significant framework, "they pale in comparison with European initiatives, IP having been a central focus of EU Single Market policies over the past 60 years" as pointed out by Pila.[149] As is clear now, Pila's point is most certainly also valid for European trademark law.

3.5.2 The Nice Agreement

As for the classification of goods and services, most the EU member states,[150] and Norway, are parties to the Nice Agreement Concerning the International Classification of Goods and Services for the Purposes of the Registration of Marks (the "Nice Agreement" and the classification system as such the "Nice Classification") is administered by WIPO.[151] The Nice Classification is divided into 45 classes, classes

---

[146]Pila, Justine, 'Intellectual Property as a Case Study in Europeanization: Methodological Themes and Context', in Ohly, Ansgar and Pila, Justine eds., The Europeanization of Intellectual Property Law: Towards a European Legal Methodology (1st edn, Oxford University Press, 2013), 3, p. 7.

[147]Cf. art. 1(1) of the TRIPS Agreement: "Members may, but shall not be obliged to, implement in their law more extensive protection than is required by this Agreement, provided that such protection does not contravene the provisions of this Agreement." See also Wager, Hannu, and Jayashree, Watal, 'Introduction to the TRIPS Agreement', in Taubman, Antony, Hannu, Wager and Jayashree, Watal eds., A Handbook on the WTO TRIPS Agreement (1st edn, Cambridge University Press, 2012), 1, p. 13-14.

[148]Recital 43 of the TM Directive. Previously, the TRIPS Agreement was not referred to in the recitals of the directive. See recital 13 of the TM Directive 2008 and the EU Commission's proposal for the TM Directive COM(2013) 162 final, p. 9. As for the relationship between the Paris Convention and the TRIPS Agreement, and EU law, including the duty of interpreting EU law consistently with international law, see Davis, Richard, St Quintin, Thomas and Tritton, Guy, 'Tritton on Intellectual Property in Europe', (5th edn, Sweet & Maxwell, 2018), p. 47-55.

[149]Pila, Justine, 'Intellectual Property as a Case Study in Europeanization: Methodological Themes and Context', in Ohly, Ansgar and Pila, Justine eds., The Europeanization of Intellectual Property Law: Towards a European Legal Methodology (1st edn, Oxford University Press, 2013), 3, p. 8.

[150]Except Cyprus and Malta. The countries relevant to this book signed the Nice Agreement 15 June 1957.

[151]Nice Agreement Concerning the International Classification of Goods and Services for the Purposes of the Registration of Marks of 1 January 2017.

1–34 allocated to goods and classes 35–45 to services. The most recent version of the
Nice Agreement (the 11th ed.) 2019 version came into force 1 January 2019.

According to a longstanding practice of OHIM (now EUIPO), registrants of
CTMs (EU trademarks) had to use the Nice Classification.[152] However, now it
appears in both the TM Regulation and the TM Directive that the Nice Classification
is mandatory.[153] The Nice Classification is significant since it anchors the registered
trademarks to specific products.[154] In *IP Translator*, the Court of Justice (Grand
Chamber) confirmed that the purpose of the registration system, part of which is the
Nice Classification, is that "economic operators must be able to acquaint themselves,
with clarity and precision, with registrations or applications for registration made by
their actual or potential competitors, and thus to obtain relevant information about
the rights of third parties."[155]

It has now been specified by the EU legislature what is meant by similar and
dissimilar products: "Goods and services shall not be regarded as being *similar* to
each other on the ground that they appear in the same class under the Nice
Classification. Goods and services shall not be regarded as being *dissimilar* from
each other on the ground that they appear in different classes under the Nice
Classification."[156] As seen in the substantial analysis, the perception of the average
consumer is significant when deciding the similarity of the products.[157]

---

[152]Although the obligation to apply for the classification of the Nice Agreement for the registration
of EU Trademarks does not appear in the TM Regulation 1994 and TM Regulation 2009, it has been
the practice of the OHIM to require the use of the Nice Classification. See the Guidelines
Concerning Proceedings Before the Office for Harmonization in the Internal Market (Trade
Marks and Designs), Part B Examination, Final version April 2008, available at: https://euipo.
europa.eu/tunnel-web/secure/webdav/guest/document_library/contentPdfs/law_and_practice/guide
lines/ctm/examination_en.pdf (last visited 26 May 2019), p. 10-13.

[153]Cf. art. 33 of the TM Regulation and art. 39 of the TM Directive. See also the EU Commission's
proposal for the TM Directive COM(2013) 162 final, p. 9.

[154]For a recent discussion of the Nice classification in light of practice, see Heath, Guy *et al*,
'Annual Review of EU Trademark Law: 2015 in Review', Trademark Reporter, vol.
106/no. 2, (2016), p. 422-428.

[155]Chartered Institute of Patent Attorneys v. Registrar of Trade Marks, Case C-307/10, [2012], para
48. See overall paras 46-49 of the decision, including the case law referred to here, for a discussion
on the purpose of the trademark registration system. On the classification system, see Bently,
Lionel, Sherman, Brad, Gangjee, Dev and Johnson, Phillip 'Intellectual Property Law', (5th edn,
Oxford University Press, 2018), 932-934 and Firth, Alison, Lea, Gary R. and Cornford, Peter,
'Trade Marks: Law and Practice', (4th edn, Jordans, 2016), p. 114-115.

[156]Cf. art. 33(7) of the TM Regulation and art. 39(7) of the TM Directive (italics added).

[157]See Chap. 11, Sect. 11.3. Jaeger-Lenz, Andrea, 'Article 8: Relative Grounds for Refusal', in
Hasselblatt, Gordian N. ed., Community Trade Mark Regulation (EC) no 207/2009: A Commentary
(1st edn, Beck/Hart, 2015), 198, p. 215-221.

3.6 Soft Law: The Important Role of Registration Offices

Outside trademark litigation the average consumer, as part of the likelihood of confusion standard, is applied in matters of registration of EU trademarks by the EUIPO and national trademarks offices. The EUIPO,[158] UK IPO,[159] the Danish Patent and Trade Mark Office (the "DK IPO")[160] and the Norwegian Industrial Property Office[161] in contrast with the Swedish Patent and Registration Office[162] do not *ex officio* assess likelihood of confusion as part of the relative grounds for refusal of registration.[163] The disputes on the likelihood of confusion decided by boards of appeal in opposition and invalidation procedures provide a high number of decisions that apply case law of more legal weight, but also fill in the gaps left by this case law.

It has been claimed by Arnold J that the activities of the EUIPO as the European trademark administration institution are part of "soft harmonization."[164] As part of these activities, the EUIPO guidelines on current trademark practice in particular (the "EUIPO TM Guidelines")[165] are significant in the norm setting on European

---

[158]Cf. art. 43 of the TM Regulation. See also on the changes, Mühlendahl, Alexander von, Dimitris Botis, Spyros M. Maniatis, *et al*, 'Trade Mark Law in Europe: A Practical Jurisprudence', (3rd edn, Oxford University Press, 2016), p. 8.

[159]On a description of the practice of the DK IPO on the assessment of the relative grounds for refusal, see Schovsbo, Jens, Rosenmeier, Morten and Petersen, Clement Salung, 'Immaterialret: Ophavsret, Patentret, Brugsmodelret, Designret, Varemærkeret', (5th edn, Jurist- og Økonomforbundets Forlag, 2018), p. 455.458.

[160]On a description of the practice of the UK IPO on the assessment of the relative grounds for refusal, see Firth, Alison, Lea, Gary R. and Cornford, Peter, 'Trade Marks: Law and Practice', (4th edn, Jordans, 2016), pp. 9.

[161]Cf. § 20, cf. § 16 of the NO TM Act 2010.

[162]Cf. § 17, chapter 2, cf. § 10, ch. 1 of the SE TM Act 2010. See also 2009/10:225, p. 422-423.

[163]As pointed out by Firth *et al*, the lacking *ex officio* assessment leave "a predisposition to allow the market to regulate itself and for applicants to 'have a go' at registering borderline or, possibly, invalid marks." Firth, Alison, Lea, Gary R. and Cornford, Peter, 'Trade Marks: Law and Practice', (4th edn, Jordans, 2016), p. 9. See Chap. 1, Sect. 1.5.1.

[164]Other activities are: "OHIM's Guidelines (1996, periodically revised) and Manual of Trade Mark Practice (constantly revised); the publication of decisions of Boards of Appeal via the OHIM website; the Alicante News (monthly from November 2004); the European Trade Mark Judges' Symposia (1st 1999 to 7th 2011); OHIM seminars for Community trade mark judges and other educational initiatives; the academic analyses in books, journals, and conferences; private sector initiatives including the European Trade Mark Reports, conferences, Darts, blogs, and so on; and personal contacts among both judges and lawyers." Arnold, Sir Richard, 'An Overview of European Harmonization Measures in Intellectual Property Law', in Ohly, Ansgar and Justine Pila eds., The Europeanization of Intellectual Property Law: Towards a European Legal Methodology (1st edn, Oxford University Press, 2013), 25, p. 31. For an overview of the activities of the EUIPO, see also Manea, Ruxandra, 'Article 2: Office', in Hasselblatt, Gordian N. ed., Community Trade Mark Regulation (EC) no 207/2009: A Commentary (1st edn, Beck/Hart, 2015), 35, p. 37.

[165]The EUIPO Guidelines for Examination of European Union Trade Marks, Final Version 1.0 of 1 October 2017, available at: https://euipo.europa.eu/ohimportal/en/trade-mark-guidelines (last visited 26 May 2019).

trademark law. The guidelines are targeted at "users of the European Union trade mark system and professional advisers who want to make sure they have the latest information on our examination practices." There seems to be no doubt that the practice of EUIPO as manifested also in its guidelines is not a binding legal source at neither the EU nor the national level.[166]

The NO Supreme Court in *Vesta Forsikring v. Trygg-Hansa* addressed the value of the OHIM practice as a legal source. Part of the issue was if Vesta in bad faith had sought to have a mark registered that was confusingly similar to a junior trademark of Trygg-Hansa and hence was invalid.[167] Assessing bad faith the NO Supreme Court referred to *Budejovicky Budvar v. Anheuser-Busch* where it had rejected, as the clear general rule through interpretation, to read a criterion of unfairness into the legislative bad faith requirement.[168] The NO Supreme Court in *Vesta Forsikring v. Trygg-Hansa* stated that after *Budejovicky Budvar v. Anheuser-Busch* there had been a significant development at the EU level on interpreting the TM Directive 1989,[169] however, the optional bad faith requirement under the directive was not implemented in the NO TM Act 1961. For interpretative support of the bad faith requirement under the directive,[170] the court turned to OHIM (and its boards of appeal) that on several occasions had given its interpretation on the bad faith requirement under the TM Regulation 1994.[171] Going against its interpretation in *Budejovicky Budvar v. Anheuser-Busch*, the court held referring to OHIM practice that bad faith had to be interpreted restrictively.[172] As pointed out by Gundersen, it would have been "interesting" had the NO Supreme Court given an account of the legal weight of OHIM practice as a legal source. Also, it would be interesting to see how the issue would be dealt with by Swedish and Danish courts.[173] According to Lassen and Stenvik, the argument against attaching much legal weight to EUIPO and also General Court decisions is that the Court of Justice may overrule the decisions. Favouring the use of EUIPO practice is the consistency of the law in the EU,

---

[166]See also Bøggild, Frank, and Staunstrup, Kolja, 'EU-Varemærkeret', (1st edn, Karnov Group, 2015), p. 28.

[167]Cf. § 14(7) of the NO TM Act 1961 (as amended in § 16(b) of the NO TM Act 2010) and § 25 of the NO TM Act 1961 (§ 35 of the NO TM Act 2010).

[168]Budejovicky Budvar v. Anheuser-Busch, HR-1998-55-A, [1998], NOSC, p. 1814.

[169]Vesta Forsikring v. Trygg-Hansa, Rt 2006 1473, [2006], NOSC, para 45.

[170]The optional art. 3(2)(d) of the TM Directive 1989 (art. 4(2) of the TM Directive). The NO Supreme Court noted however, that the § 14(7) of the NO TM Act 1961 resembled art. 4(4)(g) of the TM Directive 1989 [the TM Directive art. 5(4)(c)]. The court noted that the bad faith requirement had to be interpreted the same way in both provisions of the directive. This, the court found, justified the link from Norwegian trademark, through art. 4(4)(g), to art. 3(2)(d) of the TM Directive 1989 and then finally to art. 51(1)(b) of the TM Regulation 1994.

[171]*Ibid*, para 47. TM Regulation 1994 art. 51(1)(b) (the TM Regulation art. 59(1)(b)).

[172]Also the Court of Justice added that the registration had to be against "fair trade practice." *Ibid*, para 61. The NO Supreme Court added that the interpretation in *Vesta Forsikring v. Trygg-Hansa* not only went against its interpretation in *Budejovicky Budvar v. Anheuser-Busch* but also the Danish and Swedish trademark acts. *Ibid*, para 62.

[173]Gundersen, Aase, 'Fra Norsk Rettspraksis', NIR, vol. 6/(2007), pp. 578, p. 580.

according to the authors. That said, the somewhat significant legal weight attached to the EUIPO practice by the NO Supreme Court in *Vesta Forsikring v. Trygg-Hansa* is stretched according to the authors.[174] In line with the just stated, the Court of Justice in *Ohim v. Nike*[175] and *American Clothing Associates v OHIM*[176] has stated that the guidelines of the EUIPO are not binding as such.[177]

Since *Vesta Forsikring v. Trygg-Hansa* and the scholarly analysis of this decision, the NO Supreme Court recently in *Pangea v. Klagenemnda* confirmed the importance of EUIPO practice to interpreting Norwegian trademark law.[178] The court also stated that as a "matter of homogeneity" with the EEA Agreement the EUIPO TM Guidelines are important when interpreting Norwegian trademark law and that the guidelines reflect recent Court of Justice and EUIPO practice.[179] Although the EUIPO TM Guidelines are not formally binding to the national courts, the NO Supreme Court in *Pangea v. Klagenemnda* on several occasions referred explicitly to the guidelines as means of interpretation.[180] The DK Supreme Court also recently has attached weight to the guidelines, although implicitly[181] whereas the UK Court of Appeal on interpreting the likelihood of confusion standard has referred to the guidelines of the UK IPO.[182]

Although this book will not as such analyse the practice of the EUIPO or the national registration offices, the EUIPO TM Guidelines are included as a document that describes and interprets the state of European trademark and the application of the average consumer. Although outside of this book, it would be relevant to see how the EUIPO fills the gaps left by the decisions of more legal weight, i.e. by the Court of Justice and the General Court. The gaps may be left for the EUIPO because these courts have not yet decided on a particular issue. Another reason could be that the Court of Justice does not regard certain issues to be within its competence as an

---

[174]Lassen, Birger Stuevold and Stenvik, Are, 'Kjennetegnsrett', (3rd edn, Universitetsforlaget, 2011), p. 32.

[175]OHIM v. NIKE, Case C-53/11 P, [2012], para 57.

[176]American Clothing v. OHIM, Joined Cases C-202/08 P and C-208/08 P, [2009], para 57.

[177]See also Arnold, Sir Richard, 'An Overview of European Harmonization Measures in Intellectual Property Law', in Ohly, Ansgar and Justine Pila eds., The Europeanization of Intellectual Property Law: Towards a European Legal Methodology (1st edn, Oxford University Press, 2013), 25, p. 31 and Bøggild, Frank, and Staunstrup, Kolja, 'EU-Varemærkeret', (1st edn, Karnov Group, 2015), p. 28.

[178]Pangea Property Partners v. Klagenemnda, HR-2016-01993-A, [2016], NOSC, para 45.

[179]In Norwegian: "homogenitetshensyn." Reference was made to art. 3 of the EEA Agreement. Pangea Property Partners v. Klagenemnda, HR-2016-01993-A, [2016], NOSC, para 46.

[180]*Ibid*, paras 59, 62 and 68.

[181]See for instance, Jensens Bøfhus v. Sæby Fiskehal, U.2014.3658H, [2014], (DKSC) where the OHIM Guidelines (now the EUIPO TM Guidelines) are referred to in the note to the summary of the decision as published in the Danish journal Ugeskrift for Retsvæsen. On the value of these notes as a legal source, see Chap. 10, Sect. 10.3.2.2.

[182]See for instance Specsavers v. Asda, [2012] EWCA Civ 24, para 52.

interpreter of the law and hence leaves the registration of EU Trademarks ultimately to the General Court and before this to the EUIPO Boards of Appeal.

3.7   Conclusion

In this chapter, the relevant legal sources have been laid out with emphasis on EU law as represented by primary and secondary EU law. The natural focal point of the secondary EU legal sources is for the vertical analysis the TM Regulation and the TM Directive and for the horizontal analysis the UCPD. As for the national legislation, it is seen that all countries have now formally implemented the TM directive 2008, which in substance for this book is identical to the TM Directive. Although Norway as part of the EEA Agreement is bound to follow the provisions of the trademark directives relevant to this analysis, Norway is not formally bound by such EU principles as the principles of direct effect and supremacy. The Norwegian courts still in general follow the case law of the Court of Justice on substantial trademark law though. Not least, the NO Supreme Court explicitly has included references to the EUIPO TM Guidelines to interpret Norwegian trademark law coherently and consistently with EU law.

Whereas this chapter gives a more static picture of the legal sources, the following chapter will address the dynamics under which the legal sources interplay in European trademark law at different levels relevant to developing the average consumer. The main focus will be on the EU and national levels.

Chapter 4
The Dynamics of the European Trademark Law

4.1 The EU as a Lawmaker

The complexity of analysing the average consumer in European trademark law is caused by this area of law being in flux in different aspects. This complexity is also manifested in the methodology and legal sources set out in the previous chapter. European intellectual property law, including European trademark law, may be regarded as a special area of law and "as a hybrid of continental and Anglo-American traditions and *mentalities*." The view of European intellectual property law as a special area of law is "exacerbated by the complexity of European law at the constitutional, theoretical, and doctrinal levels, and the diversity of European instruments of direct and indirect relevance to IP, both of which can make for an opaque and seemingly impenetrable legal field."[1] Pila has stated that "EU lies at the heart" of development of most European legislative development of intellectual property law, including trademark law.[2] European trademark law resulting from EU legislative developments has led to "an extensive and deep Europeanization" of this area of law resulting from "a dynamic law-making process and not a static legislative instrument."[3] Due to Europeanisation of trademark law and the vaguely formulated EU trademark legislation, this means that the Court of Justice is a key player in the EU law making process.

To capture the dynamic development of European trademark law relevant to the analysis it is necessary to look into: First, harmonisation through mainly EU

---

[1]Pila, Justine, 'Intellectual Property as a Case Study in Europeanization: Methodological Themes and Context', in Ohly, Ansgar and Pila, Justine eds., The Europeanization of Intellectual Property Law: Towards a European Legal Methodology (1st edn, Oxford University Press, 2013), 3, p. 6.
[2]*Ibid*, p. 9.
[3]Dinwoodie, Graeme B, 'The Europeanization of Trade Mark Law', in Ohly, Ansgar and Pila, Justine eds., The Europeanization of Intellectual Property Law: Towards a European Legal Methodology (1st edn, Oxford University Press, 2013), 72, p. 76.

© Springer Nature Switzerland AG 2020
R. D. Laustsen, *The Average Consumer in Confusion-based Disputes in European Trademark Law and Similar Fictions*, https://doi.org/10.1007/978-3-030-26350-8_4

trademark legislation and subsequently, harmonisation through the UCPD adjacent to European trademark law. Second, the CJEU as a lawmaker, including the preliminary ruling procedure, the appellate function of the Court of Justice, the role of the legal precedent, the interpretation by the Court of Justice of legal sources and the role of Advocates General's opinions.[4]

4.2 Harmonisation Through Legislation

4.2.1 EU Trademark Legislation

EU trademark legislation as being in the midst of EU harmonisation feeds into the analyses of the vertical and horizontal *harmonisation*. The former refers to the harmonisation in trademark law and the latter to the harmonisation with other areas of law.[5] Leaving aside the substantial analysis of the actual harmonisation of the average consumer for subsequent chapters,[6] how does the trademark legislative harmonisation fit into general EU law perspectives on harmonisation?[7]

In line with the broader purpose of regulations, the TM Regulation has been made "to provide uniform protection of intellectual property rights throughout the Union and for the setting up of centralised Union-wide authorisation, coordination and supervision arrangements," cf. art. 118 of the TFEU.[8] This provision provides a surer legal basis for introducing EU trademark law co-existing with national trademark law than the previous art. 308 of the TFEU Pre-Lisbon (as amended by art. 352 of the TFEU) referred to as the legal basis in the TM Regulation 2009. Hence,

---

[4]A key scholarly addressing of the Court of Justice as an activist lawmaker was Rasmussen, Hjalte, 'On Law and Policy in the European Court of Justice: A Comparative Study in Judicial Policymaking', (1st edn, Martinus Nijhoff, 1986). See also Weatherill, Stephen, and Beaumont, Paul, 'EU Law: The Essential Guide to the Legal Workings of the European Union', (3rd edn, Penguin, 1999), p. 193-194.

[5]These terms are further discussed in Chap. 1, Sect. 1.6.

[6]In particular Chaps. 8 and 9.

[7]The TM Regulation and TM Directive are formal "legislative act(s)" under the TFEU in that they both have been adopted under the ordinary legislative procedure. Hence, art. 289(3) states that "[l] egal acts adopted by legislative procedure shall constitute legislative acts." The main legislative procedure is the "ordinary legislative procedure," cf. art. 289(1), cf. art. 294 of the TFEU. As it appears from note 1 of the TM Regulation and note 2 of the TM Directive, they have both been adopted under the ordinary legislative procedure. For a further analysis of the legislative acts under the TFEU, including their hierarchy, see among others, Craig, Paul P., 'The Lisbon Treaty: Law, Politics, and Treaty Reform', (1st edn, Oxford University Press, 2010), p. 252-260 and Curtin, Deirdre, and Manucharyan, Tatevik, 'Legal Acts and Hierarchy of Norms in EU Law', in Arnull, Anthony and Chalmers, Damian eds., The Oxford Handbook of European Union Law (1st edn, Oxford University Press, 2015), 103, p. 104-110.

[8]Reference in the introductory note of the TM Regulation is made explicitly to art. 118 of the TFEU. As mentioned above art. 118 of the TFEU and art. 17(2) of the EU Charter include the first explicit treaty reference to "intellectual property." See above Sect. 4.2.1.

art. 352 of the TFEU "has often been referred to as the 'flexibility clause'" and has had to sustain claims of "competence creep."[9] However, the Court of Justice has previously contended that art. 308 of the TFEU Pre-Lisbon could be the legal basis for introduction of rights co-exiting with national rights, such as what was known as the Community Trademark system.[10] Since regulations create a separate regime with separate rights, they are technically not harmonising national law.[11] Therefore, the TM Regulation is technically not harmonisation.[12] Due to the co-existence of the TM Regulation and TM Directive though, and their substantial resemblance as addressed, the TM Regulation is brought into this section on harmonisation through EU legislation.

---

[9]Dashwood, Alan, 'Wyatt and Dashwood's European Union Law', (6th edn, Hart, 2011), p. 109, Bradley, Kieran St Clair, 'Powers and Procedures in the EU Constitution: Legal Bases and the Court', in Craig, Paul and Búrca, Gráinne de eds., The Evolution of EU Law (1st edn, Oxford University Press, 2011), 85, p. 104 and Craig, Paul, and Búrca, Gráinne de, 'EU Law: Text, Cases, and Materials', (6th edn, Oxford University Press, 2015), p. 90-93.

[10]The Court of Justice has previously ruled that the predecessor of art. 114 of the TFEU (art. 95 of the TFEU Pre-Lisbon) does not provide the legal basis for creating co-existing regimes, such as the Community Trade Mark system. Hence, the Court of Justice stated in European *Parliament v. Commission* "that the Community may use Article 308 EC as the basis for creating new intellectual property rights in addition to national rights." Furthermore, that "art. 308 EC as a legal basis is, by contrast, excluded where the Community act in question does not provide for the introduction of a new protective right at Community level, but merely harmonises the rules laid down in the laws of the Member States for granting and protecting that right." European Parliament v. Commission, Case C-436/03, [2006] ECR I-3733, (Grand Chamber) para 37, including the case law referred to here. As for art. 95 of the TFEU Pre-Lisbon, the Court of Justice moved on to state that it "empowers the Community legislature to adopt measures to improve the conditions for the establishment and functioning of the internal market and they must genuinely have that object, contributing to the elimination of obstacles to the economic freedoms guaranteed by the Treaty." European *Ibid*, para 38, including the case law referred to here. For further analysis of the "competence creep" and the "legal basis disputes," see among others, Dashwood, Alan, 'Wyatt and Dashwood's European Union Law', (6th edn, Hart, 2011), p. 105-114 and Bradley, Kieran St Clair, 'Powers and Procedures in the EU Constitution: Legal Bases and the Court', in Craig, Paul and Búrca, Gráinne de eds., The Evolution of EU Law (1st edn, Oxford University Press, 2011), 85, p. 103-104.

[11]This understanding is in accordance with recital 2 of the TM Regulation stating that the TM Regulation 2009 "created a system of trade mark protection specific to the Union which provided for the protection of trade marks at the level of the Union." Italics added. In contrast, it was further stated that the parallel TM Directive 2008 offered "protection of trade marks available at the level of the Member States according to the national trade mark systems, *harmonized*" by the TM Directive 1989 and TM Directive 2008 (italics added). See similarly recital 8 of the TM Amendment Regulation. From legal literature, see among others Azoulai, Loïc, 'The Complex Weave of Harmonization', in Arnull, Anthony and Damian Chalmers eds., The Oxford Handbook of European Union Law (1st edn, Oxford University Press, 2015), 589, chapter 23 and Arnull, Anthony, 'The European Union and its Court of Justice', (2nd edn, Oxford University Press, 2006), p. 187-188.

[12]An example of harmonisation parlance on regulations is found in the Max Planck TM Report. In the report on a discussion of the changing of the 2009 TM Regulation reference is made to the possibility of "an extension of those rules to the CTM system, *if full harmonisation were the ultimate goal*" (italics added). The Max Planck TM Report, p. 232.

The purpose of the TM Directive is in line with the broader purpose of directives, in art. 114(1) of the TFEU to "adopt the measures for the approximation of the provisions laid down by law, regulation or administrative action in Member States which have as their object the establishment and functioning of the internal market."[13] The purpose of the TM Directive 1989 was, according to its title, "to approximate the laws of the Member States relating to trade marks."[14] It was not regarded as necessary "to undertake full-scale approximation of the trade mark laws of the Member States," but as "sufficient" to limit approximation "to those national provisions of law which most directly affect the functioning of the internal market."[15] This phrasing was restated in the TM Directive 2008.[16] However, a similar limitation of the depth of the approximation is not found in the TM Directive, stating that "it is necessary to go beyond the limited scope of approximation achieved by Directive 2008/95/EC [the TM Directive 2008] and extend approximation to other aspects of substantive trade mark law governing trade marks protected through registration pursuant to Regulation (EC) No 207/2009 [the TM Regulation 2009]."[17]

Referring to EU trademark law, Firth et al have pointed out the difference between "harmonisation in theory and practice." Harmonisation in theory encompasses EU law-making framework, including rules on the legislative procedures and the operation of the CJEU. Harmonisation in practice takes place through courts and trademark authorities.[18] Recently, Weatherill has described harmonisation as "an exercise in deregulation. On the simplest model, 28 different (national) regimes are reduced to one common (EU) regime. However, the market is not simply deregulated, it is simultaneously also regulated because the EU rule becomes the (common) basis for the regulation of the sector in question. In fact, it is more helpful to describe this not as regulation, but as reregulation in order to capture the notion that the EU is reacting to and replacing diverse patterns of national regulation."[19]

There are different means of EU legislative harmonisation through directives, two of which are: First, minimum harmonisation with minimum standards under which

---

[13]Reference in the introductory note of the TM Directive is made explicitly to art. 114(1) of the TFEU (art. 95(1) TFEU Pre-Lisbon). Art. 114 (1) refers to art. 26 of the TFEU stating in (1) that "[t]he Union shall adopt measures with the aim of establishing or ensuring the functioning of the internal market, in accordance with the relevant provisions of the Treaties" (art. 14 of the TFEU Pre-Lisbon). "Measures" under art. 114(1) of the TFEU encompass directives and also regulations passed by the ordinary legislative procedure. Craig, Paul, and Búrca, Gráinne de, 'EU Law: Text, Cases, and Materials', (6th edn, Oxford University Press, 2015), p. 616.

[14]Cf. the title of the TM Directive 1989.

[15]Recital 3 of the TM Directive 1989.

[16]Recital 4 of the TM Directive 2008.

[17]Recital 8 of the TM Directive. It was thus farsighted when the EU legislature stated in recital 3 of the TM Directive 1989 that "at present" (in 1989) it was unnecessary to approximate the law further.

[18]Firth, Alison, Lea, Gary R. and Cornford, Peter, 'Trade Marks: Law and Practice', (4th edn, Jordans, 2016), p. 302-304.

[19]Weatherill, Stephen, 'Empowerment is Not the Only Fruit', in Leczykiewicz, Dorota and Weatherill, Stephen eds., The Images of the Consumer in EU Law: Legislation, Free Movement and Competition Law (1st edn, Hart, 2016), 203, p. 210.

member states may adopt stricter standards if they comply with primary EU law. Second, maximum harmonisation, also referred to as complete harmonisation, whereby member states may not introduce higher standards.[20] Weatherill has referred to the former as creating "a pattern of regulation which mixes both EU rules, setting a minimum floor below which Member States may not slip, and national rules, in so far as stricter standards are preferred" which may cause "a fragmented pattern of laws."[21] The latter, Weatherill has referred to as a legislative method "whereby the EU sets both floor and ceiling of regulatory protection"[22] and where the EU "switches off the competence for the Member States to pursue any goals other than those chosen by the EU."[23] This is in line with the Court of Justice in *Pubblico Ministerio v. Ratti* holding that maximum harmonisation is a signal to the national legislatures and subsequently national courts not to provide a more strict definition of the relevant rule.[24] EU trademark law is tightly harmonised. Dinwoodie has stated that "[t]he tightness of harmonization is determined by at least two variables: the strictness of judicial review of compliance (...), and the extent to which the harmonization instruments constrained regulatory space at both ends of the policy spectrum."[25] Another variable, as referred to above, is the formulation of the relevant provisions.

---

[20]Weatherill, Stephen, 'Consumer Policy', in Craig, Paul and Búrca, Gráinne De eds., The Evolution of EU Law (2nd edn, Oxford University Press, 2011), 837, p. 850-851. For a further discussion of minimum and maximum harmonisation, see Craig, Paul, and Búrca, Gráinne de, 'EU Law: Text, Cases, and Materials', (6th edn, Oxford University Press, 2015), p. 626-627, including the sources in footnote 93 of this source.

[21]The citation is taken from an analysis by Weatherill of EU consumer law, but it applies outside this area of law. Weatherill, Stephen, 'EU Consumer Law and Policy', (2nd edn, Edward Elgar, 2013), p. 25 and subsequently Weatherill, Stephen, 'Empowerment is Not the Only Fruit', in Leczykiewicz, Dorota and Weatherill, Stephen eds., The Images of the Consumer in EU Law: Legislation, Free Movement and Competition Law (1st edn, Hart, 2016), 203, p. 210.

[22]Weatherill, Stephen, 'EU Consumer Law and Policy', (2nd edn, Edward Elgar, 2013), p. 25.

[23]Weatherill, Stephen, 'Law and Values in the European Union', (1st edn, Oxford University Press, 2016), p. 276.

[24]In the preliminary ruling, *Pubblico Ministero v. Ratti* the Court of Justice had to decide if Italy had complied with a directive laying down the requirements on what to be affixed to the containers of solvents. Italy had provided a more stringent law, defining these requirements more stringently. The second question for the Court of Justice was: "Is it lawful, notwithstanding the provisions set out in the said article, to prescribe in national legislation obligations and limitations which are more precise and detailed than, or at all events different from, those set out in the directive, and might the foregoing be considered an obstacle to the free movement of and trade in the goods and products covered by that directive (...)." The Court of Justice held "that Member States are not entitled to maintain, parallel with the rules laid down by the said directive for imports, different rules for the domestic market." Pubblico Ministero v. Ratti, Case 148/78, [1979] ECR 1629, para 26.

[25]Dinwoodie, Graeme B, 'The Europeanization of Trade Mark Law', in Ohly, Ansgar and Pila, Justine eds., The Europeanization of Intellectual Property Law: Towards a European Legal Methodology (1st edn, Oxford University Press, 2013), 72, p. 78, including footnote 6 of the text.

It appears from the wording that a trademark *"shall* not be registered if (…)"[26] and that "[t]he registered trade mark *shall* confer on the proprietor exclusive rights therein. The proprietor *shall* be entitled to prevent all third parties not having his consent from using in the course of trade."[27] These provisions are in contrast with the optional provisions of EU trademark legislation.[28] As is clear from the above citations, the provisions relevant to this book as such *in theory* create a "floor and ceiling" through maximum.[29] From the phrasing of the provisions, the Court of Justice is given a somewhat open playing field as a matter of law to decide what constitutes "likelihood of confusion." Arguably, the formulation of the relevant provision *in practice* leaves the Court of Justice to set the "floor and ceiling." In case of the confusion standard, the Court of Justice in effect sets the floor and ceiling. Had it not been for the Court of Justice's key role as a harmonising motor, the EU member states would have been left with an EU trademark legislation that would presumably lead to an even higher degree of incoherence and inconsistency on the important matter of what constitutes likelihood of confusion. Presumably, this incoherence and inconsistency would ultimately solidify in how the scope of protection of the senior trademark owner were to be calibrated vis-à-vis competitors and other stakeholders of trademark law.

The way the Court of Justice sets the floor and ceiling of the legislative confusion standard through the average consumer fiction feeds directly into the substantial analysis of this book. The theory supporting the argument of the average consumer as a legal fiction is addressed in the following chapter. How does the Court of Justice set the floor and ceiling—what are the normative elements creating the floor and ceiling? Through the insights of the above section on primary EU law and the insights provided by Weatherill, it is clear that primary EU law in principle sets the outer limits of the confusion standard, including the free movement rules of the

---

[26]Cf. art. 8(1)(b) of the TM Regulation, TM Regulation 2009 and TM Regulation 1994 and art. 4(1)(b) of the TM Directive, TM Directive 2008 and TM Directive 1989 (italics added).

[27]Cf. art. 9(2)(b) of the TM Regulation and art. 9(1)(b) of the TM Regulation 2009 and TM Regulation 1994 and art. 5(1)(b) of the TM Directive, TM Directive 2008 and TM Directive 1989 (italics added).

[28]See for instance, art. 4(4) and 5(2) of the TM Directive, TM Directive 2008 and TM Directive 1989. Hence, art. 4 states that "[a]ny Member State *may provide* that a trade mark is not to be registered or, if registered, is liable to be declared invalid where, and to the extent that (…)." Italics added. As for art. 4(4)(a) and art. 5(2), it is explained by the Max Planck TM Report that "[a]ll Member States except Cyprus have made use of those options." The Max Planck TM Report, p. 95.

[29]See also Dinwoodie and Gangjee 2016, holding that on the face of it the TM Directive 2008 and TM Directive 1989 "purported to be a limited harmonisation of registered trade mark laws of the Member States. (…) However, it is increasingly apparent that the harmonisation was in fact close to maximum harmonisation, imposing both floors and ceilings on the extent of protection that Member States could provide under national law." Dinwoodie, Graeme, and Gangjee, Dev, 'The Image of the Consumer in EU Trade Mark Law', in Leczykiewicz, Dorota, and Weatherill, Stephen eds., The Images of the Consumer in EU Law: Legislation, Free Movement and Competition Law (1st edn, Hart, 2016), 339, p. 341-342.

TFEU.[30] As for trademark law though, the Court of Justice stated in *Matratzen Concord v. Hukla*, that "[a]ccording to settled case-law, in a field which has been exhaustively harmonised at Community level, a national measure must be assessed in the light of the provisions of that harmonising measure and not of those of primary law."[31] Hence, defining the "floor and ceiling" is part of the substantial analysis of the average consumer with reference mainly to EU trademark legislation. In this chapter, it is addressed from an institutional viewpoint, how the Court of Justice does this chiefly through its preliminary ruling procedure under art. 267 of the TFEU, but also as appeal court to the General Court.

4.2.2   The UCPD

The overall purpose of the UCPD, as with the TM Directive, is stipulated in arts. 95 and 14 of the TFEU Pre-Lisbon on "the completion of the internal market."[32] In contrast with the TM Directive, the UCPD has explicitly referred to art. 153(1) stipulating the importance of ensuring "a high level of consumer protection" and art. 153 (3)(a) of the TFEU Pre-Lisbon[33] referring to art. 95 of the TFEU Pre-Lisbon.[34] The preamble to the UCPD has stated that the purpose of the directive is the creation of a high level of consumer protection through a "high level of convergence achieved by the approximation of national provisions through this Directive [UCPD]."[35] That is to say, not only is the average consumer used as a benchmark, it is also clear that one purpose of the UCPD is to protect consumers as such. The Court of Justice in *Nemzeti v. Magyarország* has stated that the UCPD "seeks to ensure a high level of consumer protection by carrying out *a complete harmonisation* of the rules relating to unfair business-to-consumer commercial [B2C] practices."[36] According to Weatherill, "[t]he Commission has promoted this model as essential to the

---

[30]Cf. mainly for goods arts. 34-36 of the TFEU, and services, cf. mainly art. 56 of the TFEU.

[31]Matratzen Concord v. Hukla, Case C-421/04, [2006] ECR I-2303, para 20. See also Mellor, James, David Llewelyn, Moody-Stuart, Thomas, *et al*, 'Kerly's Law of Trade Marks and Trade Names', (16th edn, Sweet & Maxwell, 2018), p. 673, including footnote 33.

[32]I.e. art. 114, referring to art. 26 of the TFEU. The citation is taken from art. 95 of the TFEU Pre-Lisbon. Since the UCPD was adopted before the Lisbon Treaty, reference in the UCPD is made to arts. 95 and 14 of the TFEU Pre-Lisbon. Reference to art. 95 of the TFEU Pre-Lisbon is found in the introduction and recital 1 of the UCPD whereas reference to art. 14 of the TFEU Pre-Lisbon is found in recital 2 of the UCPD.

[33]I.e. art. 169 of the TFEU.

[34]*Ibid.*

[35]Recital 11 of the UCPD.

[36]Nemzeti v. Magyarország, Case C-388/13, [2015], para 32 (italics added), including the mentioned case law here. In the decision the Court of Justice had to decide as a matter of law if "the erroneous information, such as that at issue in the main proceedings, is capable of being classified as a 'misleading commercial practice', within the meaning of that directive [the UCPD], even though that information concerned only one single consumer." *Ibid*, para 31.

regeneration of EU consumer policy in light of its contribution to the integration of markets in Europe under a common set of rules."[37] Willett and Morgan-Taylor have stated that the UCPD is a "very significant further Europeanisation of (regulatory) trade practices law." Due to the level of harmonisation, Willett and Morgan-Taylor have claimed that "it becomes especially important to assess to what extent the fairness concepts are supposed to be interpreted so that practices are fair so long as they are transparent." Moreover, that due to the maximum harmonisation member states "must allow a practice so long as these transparency requirements are satisfied."[38]

4.3   The CJEU as a Lawmaker

As it has been seen, the trademark law relevant to this book has undergone maximum harmonisation. Despite this, the General Court and national courts, ultimately the Court of Justice, have been left with the vaguely formulated likelihood of confusion standard. Therefore, a significant number of "hard cases" have emerged as a result of national courts grappling with the confusion standard which have resulted downstream in a high number of appeal cases on registration of EU trademarks and references by national courts to the Court of Justice for preliminary rulings under art. 267 of the TFEU. As held anecdotally by Arnull, "hard cases make bad law."[39] Similarly, Robin Jacob has held that "the more you clarify one aspect the woollier become others."[40] A key investigation of this book is the prominence of the

---

[37]Weatherill, Stephen, 'Consumer Policy', in Craig, Paul and Búrca, Gráinne De eds., The Evolution of EU Law (2nd edn, Oxford University Press, 2011), 837, p. 855. See also Weatherill, Stephen, 'EU Consumer Law and Policy', (2nd edn, Edward Elgar, 2013), p. 25-26 and Howells, Geraint G., 'Europe's (Lack of) Vision on Consumer Protection: A Case of Rhetoric Hiding Substance?', in Leczykiewicz, Dorota, and Weatherill, Stephen eds., The Images of the Consumer in EU Law: Legislation, Free Movement and Competition Law (1st edn, Hart, 2016), 431, p. 436-437. Elsewhere, Weatherill has stated that the UCPD is an example of "a shift from minimum to maximum harmonisation – whereby the EU sets both floor and ceiling of regulatory protection." Weatherill, Stephen, 'EU Consumer Law and Policy', (2nd edn, Edward Elgar, 2013), p. 24.

[38]Willett, Chris, and Morgan-Taylor, Martin, 'Recognising the Limits of Transparency in EU Consumer Law', in Devenney, James and Kenny, Mel eds., European Consumer Protection: Theory and Practice (1st edn, Cambridge University Press, 2012), 143, p. 145.

[39]Arnull, Anthony, 'Arsenal Football Club Plc v. Matthew Reed, High Court, Chancery Division, Judgment of 6 April 2001, [2001] 2 CMLR 23; Case C-206/01, Arsenal Football Club Plc v. Matthew Reed, Court of Justice of the European Communities (Full Court), Judgment of 12 November 2002, [2003] 1 CMLR 12; Arsenal Football Club Plc v. Matthew Reed, High Court, Chancery Division, Judgment of 12 December 2002, [2003] 1 CMLR 13', Common Market Law Review, vol. 40/no. 3, (2003), pp. 753, p. 768.

[40]Robin Jacob makes this statement after referring to many cases dealt with by the Court of Justice as preliminary rulings and as appeal cases from the General Court. Jacob, Robin, 'IP and Other Things: A Collection of Essays and Speeches', (1st edn, Hart, 2015), p. 94.

uncertainty caused by the "hard cases" by analysing the coherence and consistency of case law.

When the operation of the Court of Justice is addressed, it involves looking into its means of operation for the two types of actions addressed in this book, i.e. preliminary rulings and appeal decisions.[41] Involved in this is also a negative demarcation of operating the court formally expressed through procedural sovereignty of the national courts and the fundamental distinction between law and its application to the facts. The former, as long as it relates to matters of EU law, is reserved ultimately to the Court of Justice whereas the latter is left to the national courts. It has been claimed by Pila that "the interaction between national and European legal sources and institutions is becoming increasingly complex and contested."[42] This is equally true for the Europeanisation of trademark law, which is rooted in the nature of trademark law as "fact-intensive" in infringement *per se* allocating significant power for the "national courts in applying the formulations enunciated by the CJEU."[43] The distinction between law and fact is of upmost importance to the substantial analysis of the average consumer and because it feeds into determining which court decides the normative and factual elements of the average consumer fiction. Roughly, is it as a matter of law ultimately the Court of Justice, and is it more fact-based, the national courts. The fact intensiveness of trademark law may in effect "actually reserve more law-making potential to national courts than is ordinarily the case."[44] Hence, "treatment of an issue as a question of fact or law dictates the ability of the Court of Justice to ensure high levels of uniformity throughout Europe."[45] As for law, the Court of Justice has shown little willingness to clearly steer development of European trademark law by spelling out the normative elements vested in the average consumer.[46] The Court of Justice has stated that "the Court will defer to national court application of its global appreciation test of confusion absent reliance on an incorrect principle of law, and national courts have begun to flesh out the test in ways that are more practically helpful than

---

[41]Other actions under section 5 of the TFEU are actions i) against member states in breach of EU Law, cf. arts. 258 and 259, ii) against an EU Institution for failure to act, cf. art. 265 of the TFEU, and iii) of annulment, cf. mainly art. 263 of the TFEU. For an account of these, including appeals and preliminary rulings, in light of European trademark law, see Mühlendahl, Alexander von, Dimitris Botis, Spyros M. Maniatis, *et al*, 'Trade Mark Law in Europe: A Practical Jurisprudence', (3rd edn, Oxford University Press, 2016), chapter 3, in particular p. 17-22.

[42]Pila, Justine, 'Intellectual Property as a Case Study in Europeanization: Methodological Themes and Context', in Ohly, Ansgar and Pila, Justine eds., The Europeanization of Intellectual Property Law: Towards a European Legal Methodology (1st edn, Oxford University Press, 2013), 3, p. 4.

[43]Dinwoodie, Graeme B, 'The Europeanization of Trade Mark Law', in Ohly, Ansgar and Pila, Justine eds., The Europeanization of Intellectual Property Law: Towards a European Legal Methodology (1st edn, Oxford University Press, 2013), 72, p. 100.

[44]*Ibid*, p. 93.

[45]*Ibid*, p. 94.

[46]See Chap. 11. This differs from the area of assessing distinctiveness as part of the absolute grounds for refusal of registration where the Court of Justice has made clear assumptions on how the average consumer will react confronted with different unconventional signs.

the formulaic incantations emanating from the CJEU."[47] If the average consumer is more to the factual end, this potentially decentralises the framing of the average consumer to the national courts whereas a more normative average consumer potentially vests more power with the Court of Justice.[48] As part of the fact/law divide, the development of the average consumer is affected by the reality that trademarks are practical devices used by most companies in the market place. Trademarks are used by companies for a multitude of different products in a multitude of markets, for instance, the online market, and represent key business assets transacted upon by many companies.[49] These market aspects affecting the average consumer are addressed as part of the contextualisation analysis.[50]

Focus of the below is the role of the Court of Justice giving preliminary rulings on the EU trademark legislation and as appeal court to the General Court on matters of registration of EU trademarks under the TM Regulation. As part of this analysis, the role of the Advocates General and the General Court is addressed. Further, the analysis includes a scrutiny of the overall role of precedents of the Court of Justice and its interpretative style. For additional scrutiny of the Court of Justice, attention is drawn to general[51] and specialised IP literature.[52]

---

[47]Dinwoodie, Graeme B, 'The Europeanization of Trade Mark Law', in Ohly, Ansgar and Pila, Justine eds., The Europeanization of Intellectual Property Law: Towards a European Legal Methodology (1st edn, Oxford University Press, 2013), 72, p. 92. See also Chap. 1, Sect. 1.5.1.

[48]See Dinwoodie, Graeme B, 'The Europeanization of Trade Mark Law', in Ohly, Ansgar and Pila, Justine eds., The Europeanization of Intellectual Property Law: Towards a European Legal Methodology (1st edn, Oxford University Press, 2013), 72, p. 93.

[49]Conley, James G., Bican, Peter M., and Ernst, Holger, 'Value Articulation: A Framework for the Strategic Management of Intellectual Property', California Management Review, vol. 55/no. 4, (2013), pp. 102. See also Posner, Richard A., 'Intellectual Property: The Law and Economics Approach', the Journal of Economic Perspectives, vol. 19/no. 2, (2005), pp. 57, p. 67.

[50]See Chap. 11.

[51]See among others, Bobek, Michal, 'The Court of Justice of the European Union', p. 153, chapter 7, Arnull, Anthony, 'Judicial Review in the European Union', 376, chapter 15 and Tridimas, Takis, 'Dialogue with National Courts: Dialogue, Cooperation and Instability', 403, chapter 16, all three in Arnull, Anthony and Damian Chalmers eds., The Oxford Handbook of European Union Law (1st edn, Oxford University Press, 2015), Burrows, Noreen, and Greaves, Rosa, 'The Advocate General and EC Law', (1st edn, Oxford University Press, 2007), Conway, Gerard, 'The Limits of Legal Reasoning and the European Court of Justice', (1st edn, Cambridge University Press, 2012), Mare, Thomas de la, and Donnelly, Catherine, 'Preliminary Rulings and EU Legal Integration: Evolution and Stasis', in Craig, Paul and Búrca, Gráinne de eds., The Evolution of EU Law (1st edn, Oxford University Press, 2011), 363, chapter 13, Arnull, Anthony, 'The European Union and its Court of Justice', (2nd edn, Oxford University Press, 2006) and Jacob, Marc A., 'Precedents and Case-Based Reasoning in the European Court of Justice: Unfinished Business', (1st edn, Cambridge University Press, 2014).

[52]See among others, Mühlendahl, Alexander von, Dimitris Botis, Spyros M. Maniatis, et al, 'Trade Mark Law in Europe: A Practical Jurisprudence', (3rd edn, Oxford University Press, 2016), chapter 3 and Davis, Richard, St Quintin, Thomas and Tritton, Guy, 'Tritton on Intellectual Property in Europe', (5th edn, Sweet & Maxwell, 2018), p. 7-39. Also Dinwoodie, Graeme B, 'The Europeanization of Trade Mark Law', 75, chapter 5, Wadlow, Christopher, 'The Impact of General EU Law on Industrial Property Law', 103, chapter 6, and Jacob, Robin, 'The Relationship between

4.3.1   Preliminary Rulings: A Dynamic Dialogue with National Courts

The "dialogue" between the Court of Justice and the national courts may take place "indirectly" or "directly." According to Tridimas, the "[i]ndirect dialogue takes place, more generally, through the process of adjudication" where a national court may make statements on EU law "or apply or refuse to apply EU law without making a reference." Focal point of this section though, is the "direct dialogue" that "takes place through the preliminary reference procedure" under art. 267 of the TFEU.[53] Elsewhere, Tridimas has explained that the "[n]ational courts control access to the Court of Justice by being gatekeepers of the preliminary reference procedure" and giving "effect to the Court's preliminary rulings."[54] Referring to the "dialogue between courts" through the preliminary ruling procedure, Advocate General Colomer in *Arsenal v. Reed* held that "the Court [of Justice], as the legitimate interpreter of Community law, must analyse the problem from a broader point of view and with greater flexibility so as to give a reply which will be of assistance to the national court which raises the questions and to the other courts in the European Union, in the light of the applicable Community provisions."[55]

The preliminary ruling procedure establishes a process driven by questions of law that may be posed to the Court of Justice by "any court or tribunal of a Member

European and National Courts in Intellectual Property Law', 185, chapter 10, all three in Ohly, Ansgar and Pila, Justine eds., The Europeanization of Intellectual Property Law: Towards a European Legal Methodology (1st edn, Oxford University Press, 2013).

[53]Tridimas, Takis, 'Dialogue with National Courts: Dialogue, Cooperation and Instability', in Arnull, Anthony and Chalmers, Damian eds., The Oxford Handbook of European Union Law (1st edn, Oxford University Press, 2015), 403, p. 404-405, and overall chapter 16 in this book. For a general analyses of the preliminary ruling procedure see Arnull, Anthony, 'The European Union and its Court of Justice', (2nd edn, Oxford University Press, 2006), Chapter 4, Tridimas, Takis, 'Bifurcated Justice: The Dual Character of Judicial Protection in EU Law', in Rosas, Allan, Levits, Egils and Bot, Yves eds., The Court of Justice and the Construction of Europe: Analyses and Perspectives on Sixty Years of Case-Law – La Cour de Justice et la Construction de l'Europe: Analyses et Perspectives de Soixante Ans de Jurisprudence (1st edn, T.M.C. Asser Press, 2013), 367, p. 367-379, Dashwood, Alan, 'Wyatt and Dashwood's European Union Law', (6th edn, Hart, 2011), Chapter 7 and de la Mare and Mare, Thomas de la, and Donnelly, Catherine, 'Preliminary Rulings and EU Legal Integration: Evolution and Stasis', in Craig, Paul and Búrca, Gráinne de eds., The Evolution of EU Law (1st edn, Oxford University Press, 2011), 363, chapter 13.

[54]Tridimas, Takis, 'Bifurcated Justice: The Dual Character of Judicial Protection in EU Law', in Rosas, Allan, Levits, Egils and Bot, Yves eds., The Court of Justice and the Construction of Europe: Analyses and Perspectives on Sixty Years of Case-Law – La Cour de Justice et la Construction de l'Europe: Analyses et Perspectives de Soixante Ans de Jurisprudence (1st edn, T.M.C. Asser Press, 2013), 367 and Tridimas, Takis, 'Knocking on Heaven's Door. Fragmentation, Efficiency and Defiance in the Preliminary Reference Procedure, Common Market Law Review, vol. 40, (2003), pp. 9, p. 26.

[55]Arsenal v. Reed, Case C-206/01, [2002] ECR I-10273, (opinion of AG Colomer), footnote 81 of the opinion and his subsequent opinion in Vedial v. OHIM, Case C-106/03 P, [2004] ECR I-9573, (opinion of AG Colomer), para 34.

State" based on domestic disputes.[56] As for the national trademark decisions, this means references are made from national courts.[57] The preliminary ruling procedure ensures the functioning of the internal mark by way of ensuring that EU law has "the same effect in all the Member States."[58] Its importance "is hard to exaggerate,"[59] and, not least, the preliminary rulings are "enormously important in IP."[60] In line with the Tridimas citation and the heading of this section, the procedure is seen by some as "co-operative rather than hierarchical in nature"[61] and by others as an "intra-judicial dialogue"[62] combining "both cooperative elements and hierarchical elements."[63] Whether or not the procedure relevant to this book is one or the other is a matter of substantial analysis. If the average consumer is found to be harmonised vertically and/or horizontally, this arguably indicates some hierarchical elements. Here, the Court of Justice framing the average consumer as a matter of law is

---

[56]The TFEU allows for a preliminary ruling procedure between the national courts and the General Court, cf. art. 253(3) of the TFEU (art. 225(3) of the TFEU Pre-Lisbon) for specific areas to be further specified in the Statute of the Court of Justice of the European Union, i.e. Protocol No. 3 of the TFEU. So far, however, the General Court has not been given jurisdiction under the statute of the CJEU to hear preliminary references. See Dashwood, Alan, 'Wyatt and Dashwood's European Union Law', (6th edn, Hart, 2011), p. 65 and p. 210 and Tridimas, Takis, 'Knocking on Heaven's Door. Fragmentation, Efficiency and Defiance in the Preliminary Reference Procedure', Common Market Law Review, vol. 40, (2003), pp. 9, p. 20-21. See in general on preliminary rulings, Dashwood, Alan, 'Wyatt and Dashwood's European Union Law', (6th edn, Hart, 2011), chapter 7 and Tridimas, Takis, 'Dialogue with National Courts: Dialogue, Cooperation and Instability', in Arnull, Anthony and Chalmers, Damian eds., The Oxford Handbook of European Union Law (1st edn, Oxford University Press, 2015), 403, chapter 16.

[57]Determining what is a "court or tribunal," the Court of Justice stated in *Miles v. European Schools*: "According to settled case-law, in order to determine whether a body making a reference is a court or tribunal for the purposes of Article 267 TFEU, which is a question governed by EU law alone, the Court takes account of a number of factors, such as whether the body is established by law, whether it is permanent, whether its jurisdiction is compulsory, whether its procedure is inter partes, whether it applies rules of law and whether it is independent." Miles v. European Schools, Case C-196/09, [2011], ECR I-5105, (Grand Chamber), para 37, including the case law referred to here. See also Tridimas, Takis, 'Knocking on Heaven's Door. Fragmentation, Efficiency and Defiance in the Preliminary Reference Procedure', Common Market Law Review, vol. 40, (2003), pp. 9, p. 27.

[58]Arnull, Anthony, 'The European Union and its Court of Justice', (2nd edn, Oxford University Press, 2006), p. 95.

[59]*Ibid*, p. 97.

[60]Pila, Justine, 'Intellectual Property as a Case Study in Europeanization: Methodological Themes and Context', in Ohly, Ansgar and Pila, Justine eds., The Europeanization of Intellectual Property Law: Towards a European Legal Methodology (1st edn, Oxford University Press, 2013), 3, p. 20.

[61]Same quote in Arnull, Anthony, 'The European Union and its Court of Justice', (2nd edn, Oxford University Press, 2006), p. 96 and Dashwood, Alan, 'Wyatt and Dashwood's European Union Law', (6th edn, Hart, 2011), p. 216.

[62]Tridimas, Takis, 'Dialogue with National Courts: Dialogue, Cooperation and Instability', in Arnull, Anthony and Chalmers, Damian eds., The Oxford Handbook of European Union Law (1st edn, Oxford University Press, 2015), 403, p. 406.

[63]*Ibid*, p. 407.

assumed to provide some substantial steer for the national courts. These assumptions are based on the thought that if a larger orchestra plays in the same tempo, there must be a conductor indicating the tempo. Here, the conductor has already been shown not to be the EU legislature, leaving the Court of Justice as the only remaining option.

The aim is for the Court of Justice to guide the national courts and tribunals by answering legal questions related to interpreting the primary and secondary EU law, and to examine legal acts of EU institutions.[64] Trademark disputes may directly cover questions of law relating to the EU trademark legislation and issues of legal compatibility with national legislation, case law and administrative practice. An important legal aim is always to ensure that EU law is interpreted and applied consistently in every EU country. The effect of a given Court of Justice interpretation under art. 267 of the TFEU has an intended cumulative effect extending (ideally) well beyond the questioning court to other national courts and legal systems.

Although the preliminary ruling procedure has created many cases, it is still for the national referring bodies to apply the law to the facts, taking the outcome of the preliminary ruling into account. This is rooted in the formulation of art. 267 of the TFEU, which explicitly distinguishes between *interpretation of law* and *application of law*. As for the fact/law divide, Arnull has stated that "each court has the last word on the matters falling within its jurisdiction: the national court on questions of *fact and of national law*, the Court of Justice on questions of *Community law*."[65] Furthermore, Arnull has addressed the distinct dilemma the Court of Justice is confronted with when deciding preliminary rulings: "If it gives preliminary rulings which are too abstract, it risks being criticized for not offering national courts sufficient guidance" whereas "if (. . .) it gives a ruling which is too closely tailored to the circumstances of the main action, it may find itself trespassing on the preserve of the referring court."[66] Preliminary rulings are complicated by the national courts posing questions in light of their national legal setting whereas the Court of Justice in Bakardjieva's words "is concerned to ensure an effective process of market (and legal) integration," causing the courts to "often talk at cross-purposes."[67]

---

[64]"The Court of Justice shall have jurisdiction to give preliminary rulings concerning (a) the interpretation of the Treaties; (b) the validity and interpretation of acts of the institutions, bodies, offices or agencies of the Union." Cf. art. 267 of the TFEU. For further information on preliminary rulings and the EU court system as regards trademark law, see Heath, Guy *et al*, 'Annual Review of EU Trademark Law: 2013 in Review', Trademark Reporter, vol. 104/no. 2, (2014), pp. 450.

[65]Arnull, Anthony, 'The European Union and its Court of Justice', (2nd edn, Oxford University Press, 2006), p. 96 (italics added).

[66]*Ibid*, p. 107.

[67]Engelbrekt, Antonina Bakardjieva, 'Fair Trading Law in Flux? National Legacies, Institutional Choice and the Process of Europeanisation', (1st edn, Stockholm University, 2003), p. 531. The key area covered by the citation is where the national courts must apply the TM Directive implemented into national legislation in contrast with infringement matters related to EU trademarks where the national courts must apply the TM Regulation directly. The latter instance presumptively limits the scope for manoeuvring of the national court. See also Chap. 3, Sect. 3.2.2.1 and Sect. 4.2.1 of this chapter.

As a matter of interpretation, it has to be borne in mind that inferring legal principles from preliminary rulings may be challenging. One reason for this is that the questions posed by the referring courts are concrete questions that not necessarily separate the EU legal issues from the facts of the case. Also, as pointed out by Robin Jacob,[68] the referring Court on their side may formulate questions that are too long, although he argues at large that the effort put into framing these questions should be acknowledged.[69] Even if it is assumed that the questions posed by the referring court are clear, the answers given by the Court of Justice may still leave the referring court grappling with the answers.[70] Put baldly, Robin Jacob has held that the Court of Justice rarely answers the questions and that "it can mean that there is real dispute on the return of the case to the national court about what the oracle really meant."[71] Beyond the actual national case subject to the preliminary ruling, the upshot of the potential uncertainty vested in the decision may be more severe in the end when other stakeholders seek to derive principles from the Court of Justice case law, be they judges or scholars. This may have a negative ripple effect on the consistency of the legal principles of European trademark law. This aspect should be viewed in the context of the lacking *ratio decidendi* of Court of Justice case law as addressed below.

Besides being a seminal decision on substantial trademark law, *Arsenal v. Reed* is equally seminal to illustrate the interplay between the Court of Justice and national judiciaries within the preliminary ruling procedure. In *Arsenal v. Reed*, it was for the English judiciaries to decide if Reed's sale of merchandise bearing the senior trademark owned by Arsenal Football Club would constitute trademark use, or if it "would be perceived as a badge of support, loyalty or affiliation to the trade mark proprietor a sufficient connection."[72] If the former was the case, no infringement would be found. Focusing on general EU law connotations of the decision, it illustrates the difficulty of framing preliminary questions. Hence, Arnull has criticised the questions of Laddie J. of the High Court for being "curiously constructed in view of Laddie J.'s account of the arguments of the parties." In addition, that "[t]he drafting of the questions may be seen as the first example of a lack of communication between the referring court and the Court of Justice which

---

[68]Lord Justice at the UK Court of Appeal of the UK until May 2011.

[69]Jacob, Robin, 'The Relationship between European and National Courts in Intellectual Property Law', in Ohly, Ansgar and Pila, Justine eds., The Europeanization of Intellectual Property Law: Towards a European Legal Methodology (1st edn, Oxford University Press, 2013), 185, p. 198.

[70]Even the more so, if the questions posed are unclear.

[71]Robin Jacob has furthermore stated: "I turn finally to how the court [of Justice] answers the questions. It is not very satisfactory. It seldom actually answers the questions sent. Indeed, I cannot recall an occasion when it did. Too often, we get the formula, 'By its first question (or 'by its first and third questions') the referring court is essentially asking . . . .', and a different question is posed and then answered. It does not always matter – the question actually asked is covered." *Ibid.*

[72]Arsenal v. Reed, Case C-206/01, [2002] ECR I-10273, the second preliminary question posed by the UK High Court.

was to blight the remainder of the proceedings."[73] Based on the preliminary questions, the Court of Justice concluded that the specific use of the trademark was "a use which the trade mark proprietor may prevent in accordance with Article 5(1) of the Directive."[74]

When returned to the High Court, Laddie J. took the view that "[t]he ECJ [the Court of Justice] has disagreed with the conclusions of fact reached at the trial and indicated that the claimant should win because Mr Reed's use was such as would be perceived by some customers or users as a designation of origin. If this is so, the ECJ has exceeded its jurisdiction and I am not bound by its final conclusion. I must apply its guidance on the law to the facts as found at the trial."[75] Laddie J. was of the opinion that the ECJ had been used as appeal court, and hence stated that "[t]he correct route of appeal is to the Court of Appeal. Unlike the ECJ, it will have all the evidence before it and will give the parties the opportunity to argue what the proper findings of fact should be."[76] When brought before the Court of Appeal, the court did not agree with Laddie J. on the matter of jurisdiction of the ECJ.[77]

Besides the uncertainty vested in the questioning/answering procedure, the tricky distinction between law and fact begs for caution when analysing decisions of the Court of Justice. The Court of Justice itself will reject deciding on the facts, unless they have been distorted. Hence, in *Lloyd* it was stated, based on what is now art. 267 of the TFEU,[78] that "the role of the Court of Justice is limited to providing the national court with the guidance on interpretation necessary to resolve the case before it, while it is for the national court to apply the rules of Community law, as interpreted by the Court, to the facts of the case under consideration." Furthermore, that "it is for the national court to rule on the question if there exists between the two

---

[73] Arnull, Anthony, 'Arsenal Football Club Plc v. Matthew Reed, High Court, Chancery Division, Judgment of 6 April 2001, [2001] 2 CMLR 23; Case C-206/01, Arsenal Football Club Plc v. Matthew Reed, Court of Justice of the European Communities (Full Court), Judgment of 12 November 2002, [2003] 1 CMLR 12; Arsenal Football Club Plc v. Matthew Reed, High Court, Chancery Division, Judgment of 12 December 2002, [2003] 1 CMLR 13', Common Market Law Review, vol. 40/no. 3, (2003), pp. 753, p. 757.

[74] I.e. art. 10 of the TM Directive. Arsenal v. Reed, Case C-206/01, [2002] ECR I-10273, para 60. The Court of Justice conclude that "[o]nce it has been found that, in the present case, the use of the sign in question by the third party is liable to affect the guarantee of origin of the goods and that the trade mark proprietor must be able to prevent this, it is immaterial that in the context of that use the sign is perceived as a badge of support for or loyalty or affiliation to the proprietor of the mark." *Ibid*, para 61.

[75] Arsenal v. Reed, [2002] EWHC 2695 (Ch) # III, para 27.

[76] *Ibid*, para 29.

[77] Hence, Aldous LJ concluded that "[a]s the ECJ pointed out, the actions of Mr Reed meant that goods, not coming from Arsenal but bearing the trade marks, were in circulation. That affected the ability of the trade marks to guarantee the origin of the goods. I therefore conclude that the result reached by the ECJ was inevitable once their judgment had made it clear that the material consideration was whether the use complained of was liable to jeopardise the guarantee of origin, not whether the use was trade mark use. The judge should have followed the ruling and decided the case in Arsenal's favour." Arsenal v. Reed, [2003] EWCA Civ 696, para 48.

[78] Art. 177 of the TEU as revised by the Maastricht Treaty.

marks at issue in the main proceedings a likelihood of confusion within the meaning of the Directive."[79]

If the Court of Justice is not explicitly refusing to answer preliminary questions (or appeals) referring to the questions being on the facts of the case, it is not a straightforward task to infer the legal principles from the decision. The main reason for this is that the answers given by the Court of Justice may prove to be affected by a set of complex and detail-oriented questions. The bald observation, though, is that if the Court of Justice ventures into answering the questions, they will presumptively relate to the law. It is from these answers that the legal principles may be derived.

4.3.2   The Court of Justice and Its Appellate Function

The Court of Justice also acts as appeal court to the General Court on matters related to the TM Regulation. This function is based on disputes decided by the EUIPO Boards of Appeal.[80] Relevant to this book, are the many appeals on the likelihood of confusion standard as part of registration heard by the Court of Justice.

It has to be borne in mind that there is a distinction between the TM Regulation and the TM Directive, since they pursue different objectives, as addressed above. In other words, the former creates a *unified* trademark system and the latter a *harmonised* trademark system. In European trademark law the core business of the Court of Justice as a harmoniser is formally the preliminary ruling procedure.[81] In reality, however, the different purposes of the TM Regulation and TM Directive do not feed into the assessment by the Court of Justice of matters related to the different substantial parts of the EU trademark legislation. The commonality in the wording of the TM Regulation and TM Directive provisions on the likelihood of confusion standard facilitates a significant overlap of the resultant jurisprudence produced from preliminary and appeal decisions.[82] Consequently, there is no clear line between the Court of Justice's dealings with matters of likelihood of confusion in preliminary

---

[79]Lloyd Schuhfabrik Meyer v. Klijsen Handel BV, Case C-342/97, [1999] ECR I-3819, para 11.

[80]Cf. art. 72(1) of the TM Regulation. According to art. 72(2) of the TM Regulation, actions under art. 72(1) may be brought to the Court of Justice "on grounds of lack of competence, infringement of an essential procedural requirement, infringement of the TFEU, infringement of this Regulation or of any rule of law relating to their application or misuse of power." See also Jääskinen, Niilo, 'The Future of European Intellectual Property Law Courts: Intellectual Property and the European Judicial Architecture', in Ohly, Ansgar and Pila, Justine eds., The Europeanization of Intellectual Property Law: Towards a European Legal Methodology (1st edn, Oxford University Press, 2013), 217, p. 218.

[81]Dinwoodie, Graeme B, 'The Europeanization of Trade Mark Law', 72, p. 91 and Arnold, Sir Richard, 'An Overview of European Harmonization Measures in Intellectual Property Law', 25, p. 31 both in in Ohly, Ansgar and Pila, Justine eds., The Europeanization of Intellectual Property Law: Towards a European Legal Methodology (1st edn, Oxford University Press, 2013).

[82]On the convergence of case law of the Court of Justice related to the TM Regulation and the TM Directive, see Chap. 10, Sect. 10.2.2.

rulings based on the TM Regulation or the TM Directive or as appeal court dealing with the TM Regulation on matters of registration of EU trademarks.[83]

In accordance with the general role of the Court of Justice, the court also only deals with points of law as appeal court to the General Court, causing the findings of facts by the General Court to be final.[84] Under "consistent case-law," facts not relied upon previously by the EUIPO or the EUIPO Boards of Appeal cannot be taken into account by the General Court,[85] unless the facts are a "matter of common knowledge."[86] Illustrating the convergence of the Court of Justice acting as appeal court with its actions as the body giving preliminary rulings, the Court of Justice has recently stated in *Shoe Branding v. Adidas*, that "[i]t should be observed that, in arguing that the average consumer of sports footwear displays a high level of attention, is aware of the brand affixed to a specialised goods item and pays particular attention to the advertising space such as the side of a shoe, *the appellant is, in reality, disputing the General Court's findings of fact, which falls outside the Court of Justice's jurisdiction in hearing an appeal.*"[87]

In sum, there is a functional and substantial overlap between the preliminary ruling and appellate procedures of the Court of Justice. Although there might not be a difference in substantial law between the legal instruments (the TM Regulation and the TM Directive) on likelihood of confusion, there is a key difference between registration and infringement disputes. Inevitably, registration disputes involve prediction on how the junior trademark will be used and not actually is used. Hence, Mellor *et al* state that the "global appreciation in relation to the relative grounds (...) must be made on the basis of fair and notional use of the earlier and

---

[83]Dinwoodie, Graeme B, 'The Europeanization of Trade Mark Law', in Ohly, Ansgar and Pila, Justine eds., The Europeanization of Intellectual Property Law: Towards a European Legal Methodology (1st edn, Oxford University Press, 2013), 72, p. 87-88.

[84]Hence, art. 58(1) of the Statute of the Court of Justice states that "[a]n appeal to the Court of Justice shall be limited to points of law. It shall lie on the grounds of lack of competence of the General Court, a breach of procedure before it which adversely affects the interests of the appellant as well as the infringement of Union law by the General Court." Art. 256(1) of the TFEU (art. 225 (1) of the TFEU Pre-Lisbon) states the same principle. See also Arnull, Anthony, 'The European Union and its Court of Justice', (2nd edn, Oxford University Press, 2006), p. 26.

[85]Hammarplast v. OHIM, Case T-499/04, [2006], para 17.

[86]*Ibid*, para 18.

[87]Shoe Branding v. Adidas, Case C-396/15 P, [2016], para 16 (italics added). In *Longevity Health Products v. OHIM*, the Court of Justice stated that "[u]nder Article 256(1) TFEU and the first paragraph of Article 58 of the Statute of the Court of Justice of the European Union, an appeal lies on a point of law only. The General Court thus has exclusive jurisdiction to find and appraise the relevant facts and to assess the evidence. The appraisal of those facts and the assessment of that evidence thus do not, save where the facts or evidence are distorted, constitute points of law subject, as such, to review by the Court of Justice on appeal." Longevity Health Products v. OHIM, Case C-81/11 P, [2012], para 27, including case law referred to here. See also, recently Meica Ammerländische Fleischwarenfabrik Fritz Meinen v. EUIPO, Case C-182/16 P, [2017], para 33.

later marks, rather than by taking into account, the actual use in the marketplace as required in the equivalent assessment in relation to infringement."[88]

4.3.3 Legal Precedent: Looking Backwards and Ahead

As for the Court of Justice, it has to be determined how it deals with its previous cases in developing the law. The consistency at Court of Justice level is then mainly a matter of determining the consistency of the legal principles bearing in mind the potential deviations caused by the operative fact of the cases of the court asking preliminary questions or the case under appeal from the General Court. An example of a relevant deviation based on the facts is the Court of Justice holding that in the internet setting the relevant public is the "reasonably well-informed and reasonably observant *internet users.*"[89] This finding by the Court of Justice is rooted in the relevant national decisions being related to the internet vis-à-vis the physical market.[90]

Above inherent threats to the consistency of Court of Justice case law were highlighted through the fact/law divide and the inherent complexities of the preliminary ruling procedure. Besides being aware of these issues, it has to be borne in mind that an essential part of determining consistency is the evolution of Court of Justice case law through its use of precedent. Essentially, this is a matter of determining the law created by the precedent of the court. The starting point, according to Arnull, "is and has always been that the Court of Justice is not bound by its previous decisions but that in practice it does not often depart from them."[91] Consequently, there is no formal *ratio decidendi*, according to which the Court of Justice is bound by the "reason for decision" in previous cases.[92] *Ratio decidendi* in the scope of this book is understood in accordance with the definition provided by Cross and Harris: "A *ratio decidendi* of a case is any rule of law expressly or

---

[88]Mellor, James, David Llewelyn, Moody-Stuart, Thomas, *et al*, 'Kerly's Law of Trade Marks and Trade Names', (16th edn, Sweet & Maxwell, 2018), p. 400. See also Chap. 10, Sect. 10.2.2.

[89]L'Oréal v. eBay International, Case C-324/09, [2011] ECR I-6011, para 94 (italics added).

[90]The substantial analysis of this finding will be expanded upon in Chap. 11, Sect. 11.5.

[91]Arnull, Anthony, 'The European Union and its Court of Justice', (2nd edn, Oxford University Press, 2006), p. 627. See also, Cross, Rupert, and Harris, J. W., 'Precedent in English Law', (4th edn, Oxford University Press, 1991), p. 17. It should be mentioned that there are limited examples where the Court of Justice explicitly has deviated from its previous case law. For instance, in *CNL-SUCA v. HAG*, the Court of Justice stated, "it should be stated at the outset that the Court believes it necessary to reconsider the interpretation given in that judgment in the light of the case-law which has developed with regard to the relationship between industrial and commercial property and the general rules of the Treaty, particularly in the sphere of the free movement of goods." CNL-SUCA v. HAG, Case C-10/89, [1990] ECR I-3711, para 10.

[92]Koopmans, Thijmen, 'Stare Decisis in European Law', in O'Keeffe, David and Schermers, Henry G. eds., Essays in European Law and Integration: To Mark the Silver Jubilee of the Europa Institute, Leiden, 1957-1982 (1st edn, Kluwer Law International, 1982), 11, p. 22.

impliedly treated by the judge as a necessary step in reaching his conclusion, having regard to the line of reasoning adopted by him."[93] Marc Jacob has claimed that *ratio decidendi* "may be shorthand, but it can only be the result of interpretation and argumentation and not the replacement thereof."[94] As furthermore pointed out by Jacob, "[o]f course no two situations will never be exactly the same. If there was no possibility of abstracting beyond specific circumstances, there could never be precedent-based reasoning together with any efficiency and coherence gains this might entail." The substantial upshot of what Jacob has denoted "universability" is the transcendence of "individual decisionism and arbitrariness."[95] The focal point of the precedent in this book is that related to the average consumer. As dealt with in Chap. 5, there is an overlap between the average consumer as a fiction and the mere function of precedent—they both cause a certain degree of *universability* moving beyond the "specific circumstances." Specifically, universability of precedent has two aspects. First, a temporal aspect, indicating the value of a decision to previous and future cases. Second, that the reasoning of the Court of Justice may be "beyond the individual case but beneath a general norm."[96] A general norm may be found in primary or secondary legislation, and "case rationales tend to be of a lower degree of abstraction than most treaty provisions or legislation."[97]

Although the Court of Justice does not operate under a formal *ratio decidendi*, what are then the universal applicable principles to be derived from its case law?[98] The likelihood of confusion standard may appear in practice, among other elements through the average consumer fiction, to be rule-like.[99] If the standard based on the subsequent substantial analysis is found to be rule-like, it indicates reliance on precedent and some level of legal certainty.

The Court of Justice itself rarely analytically discusses its previous cases, which makes it difficult to decipher on which grounds (*ratio*) it bases its decisions (*decidendi*). In addition, the decisions tend to be short and abstract. Of relevance

---

[93]The definition continues "…or is a necessary part of his direction to the jury." This latter part of the definition is not relevant to the EU judicial system not operating a jury. Adding "or" also means that the first part of the definition is relevant in its own right and not dependent on the latter part. Precedent in English Law, Cross, Rupert, and Harris, J. W., 'Precedent in English Law', (4th edn, Oxford University Press, 1991), p. 72.

[94]Jacob, Marc A., 'Precedents and Case-Based Reasoning in the European Court of Justice: Unfinished Business', (1st edn, Cambridge University Press, 2014), p. 72.

[95]*Ibid*, p. 72-73.

[96]Jacob, Marc A., 'Precedents and Case-Based Reasoning in the European Court of Justice: Unfinished Business', (1st edn, Cambridge University Press, 2014), p. 73-74.

[97]*Ibid*, p. 77. It should be mentioned that *ratio decidendi* is known to EU trademark law. Hence, art. 71(2) of the TM Regulation stipulates that "[i]f the Board of Appeal remits the case for further prosecution to the department whose decision was appealed, that department shall be bound by the ratio decidendi of the Board of Appeal, in so far as the facts are the same." See *ibid*, p. 72, including footnote 14 of the text (italics added).

[98]The statements by Jacob on the role of precedent links to the finding in Chap. 5 of the likelihood of confusion as a standard from the outset.

[99]See Chap. 5, Sect. 5.2.

to this book is that this line of reasoning is in stark contrast with particularly the decisions made by the UK courts, which are much more elaborative.[100] In contrast with the decisions of the national courts selected for this book, the cases of the Court of Justice do not reveal concurring and dissenting judgements.[101] Although the Court of Justice tends to follow its previous cases, it also at times departs from them.[102] Due to the shortly reasoned decisions, it may not always be clear if the Court of Justice in effect distinguishes a decision from previous decisions. A good example of this is the reference by the Court of Justice to the "reasonably well-informed and reasonably observant *internet users*."[103] From the reasoning of the Court of Justice, it is unclear if this phrasing deviates materially from previous case law or merely a "repackaged" version of its "regular" average consumer. Furthermore, the Court of Justice often refers to "the case-law cited" in a previous decision and uses the following formulation in their references to previous case law: "(. . .) according to settled case-law (. . .)."[104] These references make it necessary to follow the "red line" backwards in time in the decisions to determine how certain legal principles have been developed. Even when the origin the principle is determined, the actual content and scope of the principle may be unclear due to the very short *ratio*. In this instance, it is necessary to make sufficient caveats extracting the legal principles, in particular from Court of Justice case law, since without sufficient *ratio* it may prove difficult to decide if there in effect is consistency in the case law. A principle may appear so broad that it does not make sense to denote it a consistent legal principle. An illustration of the difficulty of following a red line backwards in

---

[100]Among others, Arnold J, one of the most influential judges in the UK, has handed down some of the significant trademark decisions relevant to this book on behalf of the UK High Court. For an overview of these decisions, see Chap. 1, footnote 14. Arnold J has also given lengthy analyses of Court of Justice and domestic case law, including case law on the average consumer. Hence, in *Interflora EWHC* Arnold J allocated 14 pages (!) to analysing the legal backcloth of the average consumer. Interflora v. Marks & Spencer, [2013] EWHC 1291 (Ch), paras 194-224.

[101]Cross, Rupert, and Harris, J. W., 'Precedent in English Law', (4th edn, Oxford University Press, 1991), p. 17-18.

[102]A prominent example of this is *Keck Mithouard* where the Court of Justice narrowed its interpretation of art. 30 (art. 34 of the TFEU) laid down in Dassonville, Case 8/74, [1974] ECR 837. Keck Mithouard, Joined Cases C-267/91 and C-268/91, [1993] ECR I-6097, in particular paras 14-17. As explained by Weatherill and Beaumont "[t]he Court [of Justice] in Keck has adjusted the respective competences of the Community and of the member states in the sphere of economic regulation and, 'contrary to what has previously been decided' [*ibid*, para 16], the member states enjoy competence untouched by Article (. . .) 30 [art. 34 of the TFEU] in the absence of an impediment felt especially by importers." Weatherill, Stephen, and Beaumont, Paul, 'EU Law: The Essential Guide to the Legal Workings of the European Union', (3rd edn, Penguin, 1999), p. 612. See overall on *Dassonville, Keck Mithouard* and other relevant decisions in *ibid* 1999, p. 608-619 and Dashwood, Alan, 'Wyatt and Dashwood's European Union Law', (6th edn, Hart, 2011), p. 409-421.

[103]L'Oréal v. eBay International, Case C-324/09, [2011] ECR I-6011, para 94 (italics added).

[104]Shoe Branding v. Adidas, Case C-396/15 P, [2016], para 21.

time in decisions of the Court of Justice relevant to developing the average consumer is found in Chap. 10.[105]

The lacking elaborative reasons in the Court of Justice decisions is part of the reason for choosing a legal method that is broader than Scandinavian Legal Realism and including Critical Legal Positivism. Critical Legal Positivism opens up for bringing in legal sources not clearly given as part of the reasons for the decisions. Also, it opens up for considering the broader purpose of trademark law often referred to by the Court of Justice and by the Advocates General.

4.3.4   Interpretation and the Use of Legal Sources

To understand how the Court of Justice sets out the average consumer, it is necessary to understand the interpretative methods of the court. This understanding will provide an understanding of the legal backcloth necessary to analyse the average consumer. As Maduro points out, "[i]nterpretation can perhaps be suggestively described as the software of Courts." More narrowly, "interpretation can be understood simply by reference to the methodologies to be employed in the interpretation of rules: the types of legal arguments used by Courts, their techniques of exegesis of the text and the rules of logic that make of legal reasoning a form of practical reasoning."[106] Maduro also finds that there is an upshot of interpretation "linked to the proper role of courts in a democratic society." This broader role of the courts according to Maduro "is a function of the hermeneutics, institutional constraints and normative preferences that determine judicial outcomes in the light of an existent body of rules."[107] In line with Maduro's understanding of "interpretation," it is in this book understood "in the broad sense in which it means the process of understanding and applying a given text, most typically, a piece of legislation or a part of constitutional document."[108] The role of interpretation is important to bear in mind since on the one hand it is necessary to know the interpretive techniques of the Court of Justice when it analyses case law that sets out the average consumer, including what arguments can be made with the relevant legal sources as set out in Chap. 3.[109] On the other hand, in particular the normative preferences of the Court of Justice arguably play a significant role in developing the average consumer.

---

[105]See Chap. 10, Sect. 10.2.3.

[106]Maduro, Miguel Poiares, 'Interpreting European Law: Judicial Adjudication in a Context of Constitutional Pluralism', European Journal of Legal Studies, vol. 1/no. 2, (2007), pp. 1, p. 2.

[107]Ibid, p. 3.

[108]This understanding is derived from Conway's analysis of "the Limits of Legal Reasoning and the European Court of Justice." Conway, Gerard, 'The Limits of Legal Reasoning and the European Court of Justice', (1st edn, Cambridge University Press, 2012), p. 13.

[109]Komárek, Jan, 'Legal Reasoning in EU Law', in Arnull, Anthony and Chalmers, Damian eds., The Oxford Handbook of European Union Law (1st edn, Oxford University Press, 2015), 28, p. 45.

Komarék has seen the average consumer as an example of "foundational facts" that "are used to justify a legal doctrine" based on a set of "empirical assumptions" about consumer behaviour.[110] Explaining the meaning of foundational facts, Sherry has held that "[s]hifts in the tectonic plates under the Earth's bedrock cause earthquakes. Shifts in the tacit factual assumptions underlying legal doctrine can produce equally seismic results." Sherry continues, "[j]ust as earthquakes were once the only observable sign of movement in the tectonic plates, sudden and seemingly inexplicable changes in doctrine may alert us to changes in underlying assumptions."[111] In part, the average consumer is developed based on precedent and through the technical interpretive techniques. As indicated by Komarék, the average consumer builds on a set of assumptions, which inevitably open for the broader interpretive function of the Court of Justice, in particular the normative preferences of the court. In Sherry's words, the normative preferences will be based on "tacit factual assumptions underlying legal doctrine."

Through an analysis of case law, it is possible to determine the technical side of interpretation, however, it becomes more opaque when deciding the residue left for the normative preferences—and more so, what are the normative preferences of the Court of Justice? This question is difficult to answer, in part due to the character of the Court of Justice decisions as set out above, in particular the fact that they are short and not substantially elaborative in their reasoning. As Maduro points out, the institutional setting of a court affects its means of interpretation.[112] For the Court of Justice, the institutional frames have been set out above where it appears that the court is the gatekeeper of interpreting EU law considering the values of the special area of law, given the core Internal Market values. In this book, this means the purpose of trademark law, given the reason for being of the Internal Market.

The technical side of interpretation has importance to how the Court of Justice from case to case reaches its decisions, as it was shown to be the case with precedent. This relates clearly to the consistency of case law. The broader role of interpretation as a normative exercise and the role of the Court of Justice in ensuring that trademark law is seen in light of the broader purpose of the Internal Market relate to consistency but mostly to coherence. As it was found in Chap. 2 referring to Missoli, coherence "implies positive connections" and compared to consistency "is more about synergy and adding value."[113] Translated into trademark law, this means the synergy of trademark law with its purpose as such and its purpose in a broader Internal Market setting.

---

[110]*Ibid*, p. 48.

[111]Sherry, Suzanna. 'Foundational Facts and Doctrinal Change', University of Illinois Law Review, vol. 2011/no. 1, (2011), pp. 145, p. 145-146.

[112]Maduro, Miguel Poiares, 'Interpreting European Law: Judicial Adjudication in a Context of Constitutional Pluralism', European Journal of Legal Studies, vol. 1/no. 2, (2007), pp. 1, p. 3.

[113]Missiroli, Antonio, 'European Security Policy: The Challenge of Coherence', European Foreign Affairs Review, vol. 6/(2001), pp. 177, p. 182. See Chap. 2, Sect. 2.2.3.

In sum, there is a connection between coherence and the technical side of interpretation, but in particular, interpretation may be a proxy for the normative preferences of the Court of Justice, given its institutional setting. The next task is then to demarcate the interpretative methods of the Court of Justice.

Interpretation ties together the legal method of this book with the mapping out of the legal sources. Similarly, when analysing MacCormick's theories, Spaak has perceived *legal method* as a method, which includes interpretation manifested in "interpretive arguments (principles of statutory interpretation)."[114] This understanding of interpretation somewhat coincides with Marc Jacob's perception above of how to derive at the *ratio decidendi* of preceding cases through "the result of interpretation and argumentation and not the replacement thereof."[115] Besides the legal method, interpretation is also closely connected to the vertical comparison between EU and national case law. As stated in the previous chapter, the national judiciaries have different ways of dealing with different legal sources, in particular precedent and preparatory works. These differences are ultimately rooted in different means of interpretation applied by the national judiciaries.[116] The linking to national judiciaries is addressed further below where national trademark law and its institutions are discussed.

Understanding the interpretive methods of the Court of Justice is a prerequisite for deducing the legal principles from its case law and deciding its coherence and consistency. Earlier in this chapter referring to Arnull and Robin Jacob, the grappling of courts with "hard cases" may cause even "woollier" law.[117] This coincides with the finding of Hoecke that uncertainty of law makes it impossible to perceive law as a purely logical discipline, since it much depends "on interpretation of legal principles, rules and concepts."[118] According to Maduro: "Legal interpretation at the Court of Justice is governed by text,[119] context and telos or purpose."[120] The last

---

[114]Spaak, Torben, 'Guidance and Constraint: The Action-Guiding Capacity of Neil MacCormick's Theory of Legal Reasoning', Law and Philosophy, vol. 26 (2007), pp. 343, p. 346. Spaak sees interpretation as part of the legal method which "is a set of norms, arguments, and concepts" which besides interpretation also includes "modalities of decision such as analogy and *argumentum e contrario*, interpretive presumptions such as 'The legislature does not intend absurd results,' conflict-solving maxims such as *lex superior, lex posterior* and *lex specialis*, the principle of legality, and the rule of lenity." *Ibid.* See also Conway, Gerard, 'The Limits of Legal Reasoning and the European Court of Justice', (1st edn, Cambridge University Press, 2012), p. 19.

[115]See above Sect. 4.3.3.

[116]See Chap. 2, Sect. 2.3.1.1.

[117]See above Sect. 4.3.

[118]See van Hoecke, Mark, 'Legal Doctrine: Which Method(s) for what Kind of Discipline?', in van Hoecke, Mark ed., Methodologies of Legal Research: What Kind of Method for what Kind of Discipline? (1st edn, Hart, 2011), 1, p. 9. See also Chap. 2, footnote 88.

[119]This is also called "linguistic," "grammatical," "semiotic," or "literal arguments." Komárek, Jan, 'Legal Reasoning in EU Law', in Arnull, Anthony and Chalmers, Damian eds., The Oxford Handbook of European Union Law (1st edn, Oxford University Press, 2015), 28, p. 45.

[120]Maduro, Miguel Poiares, 'Interpreting European Law: Judicial Adjudication in a Context of Constitutional Pluralism', European Journal of Legal Studies, vol. 1/no. 2, (2007), pp. 1, p. 4.

means of interpretation will be referred to in this book as "purposive interpretation."[121] Adding to these ways of interpretation, MacCormick and Summers have identified "arguments from intention" as a way of interpretation.[122] These means of interpretation provide the starting point for interpretation as understood by this book. It should be mentioned that there is an overlap between the means of interpretation. For instance, preparatory works and preambles are relevant in interpretation based on both context, purpose and intention.

The *textual interpretation* focuses on the meaning of the legal text, referred to by Conway as the "literary or ordinary" meaning.[123] Arriving at the meaning of specific provisions based on its literary meaning is often complicated due to the vague and ambiguous formulations used by the EU legislature. According to Maduro, some key reasons for this elusiveness are, "the particular constraints of the EU legal order"[124] and that the "EU law is also a function of a deeper normative ambiguity."[125] As stated in *Cilfit*, it has to be borne in mind that the different language versions of EU legislation are authentic. Hence, interpreting a specific provision "involves a comparison of the different language versions,"[126] i.e. currently 24 versions,[127] including English, Swedish and Danish. In addition, as stated by the Court of Justice in *Cilfit* it should also be borne in mind that "even where the different language versions are entirely in accord with one another, that Community law uses terminology which is peculiar to it." Also, "that legal concepts do not necessarily have the same meaning in Community law and in the law of the various Member States."[128]

Contextual interpretation, also referred to by Komarék as "systemic arguments,"[129] according to Bengoetxea builds on the assumption that "a legal provision

---

[121] As pointed out by Conway, teleological interpretation is often used in an EU context focusing on a "systemic level," whereas "purposive" interpretation may be used more locally. Conway, Gerard, 'The Limits of Legal Reasoning and the European Court of Justice', (1st edn, Cambridge University Press, 2012), p. 20 with reference in footnote 83 of the text to e.g. Lasser, Michel de, 'Judicial Deliberations: A Comparative Analysis of Transparency and Legitimacy', (1st, Oxford University Press, 2004), p. 288. Since this book focuses not only EU law, but on European law, the broader term "purposive" has been chosen.

[122] MacCormick, Neil, and Summers, Robert D., 'Interpretation and Justification', in MacCormick, Neil and Summers, Robert D. eds., Interpreting Statutes (1st edn, Routledge, 1991), 511, p. 512-516.

[123] Conway, Gerard, 'The Limits of Legal Reasoning and the European Court of Justice', (1st edn, Cambridge University Press, 2012), p. 19.

[124] Maduro, Miguel Poiares, 'Interpreting European Law: Judicial Adjudication in a Context of Constitutional Pluralism', European Journal of Legal Studies, vol. 1/no. 2, (2007), pp. 1, p. 8.

[125] *Ibid*, p. 9.

[126] CILFIT v. Ministry of Health, Case 283/81, [1982] ECR 3415, para 19.

[127] For an overview of the different languages, see the Commission website at: http://ec.europa.eu/dgs/translation/translating/officiallanguages/index_en.htm (last visited 26 May 2019).

[128] *Ibid*, para 19. See also Arnull, Anthony, 'The European Union and its Court of Justice', (2nd edn, Oxford University Press, 2006), p. 608.

[129] Komarék, Jan, 'Legal Reasoning in EU Law', in Arnull, Anthony and Chalmers, Damian eds., The Oxford Handbook of European Union Law (1st edn, Oxford University Press, 2015), 28, p. 46.

(...) is properly understood when it is placed in a wider context."[130] The wider EU law context of a provision leaves "clues as to the construction of such provision."[131] Part of the context according to Beck may be "recitals in the preamble, provisions in the same text, relevant other secondary legislation, general terms and concepts and general principles of EU law."[132]

Purposive interpretation, according to Maduro, forces the Court of Justice to make explicit its normative perception of the EU legal order and "creates a yardstick to better assess the coherence and consistency of its case law."[133] Purposive interpretation in Komárek's words "refer to the purpose of the legal norm, its function in the overall legal scheme and the consequences of the selected interpretation."[134] Conway has referred to this means of interpretation as "a process of standing back from the ordinary meaning to identify the aim or purpose of a legal provision."[135]

The idea of interpreting through *argument for intention* is, according to MacCormick and Summers, that where "a relevant legislative intention about a

---

[130]Bengoetxea, Joxerramon, 'The Legal Reasoning of the European Court of Justice: Towards a European Jurisprudence', (1st edn, Clarendon Press, 1993), p. 240.

[131]*Ibid*, p. 241.

[132]See Beck, Gunnar, 'The Legal Reasoning of the Court of Justice of the EU', (1st edn, Hart, 2012), p. 191-207. Included in this means of interpretation are also arguments drawing on norms of interpretation, such as *"per anologiam, a fortiori, lex specialis, lex superior, a contrario* etc." Bengoetxea, Joxerramon, 'The Legal Reasoning of the European Court of Justice: Towards a European Jurisprudence', (1st edn, Clarendon Press, 1993), p. 241. Komárek, Jan, 'Legal Reasoning in EU Law', in Arnull, Anthony and Chalmers, Damian eds., The Oxford Handbook of European Union Law (1st edn, Oxford University Press, 2015), 28, p. 46.

[133]Maduro, Miguel Poiares, 'Interpreting European Law – on Why and how Law and Policy Meet at the European Court of Justice', in Koch, Henning *et al* eds., Europe: The New Legal Realism: Essays in Honour of Hjalte Rasmussen (1st edn, Djøf Publishing, 2010), 457. See also Chap. 2, footnote 65 and its sources.

[134]Komárek, Jan, 'Legal Reasoning in EU Law', in Arnull, Anthony and Chalmers, Damian eds., The Oxford Handbook of European Union Law (1st edn, Oxford University Press, 2015), 28, p. 46.

[135]Conway, Gerard, 'The Limits of Legal Reasoning and the European Court of Justice', (1st edn, Cambridge University Press, 2012), p. 20. One such interpretation is found in *Davidoff v. Gofkid* where the Court of Justice interpreted the provision on protecting well-known trademarks purposively. In art. 5(2) of the TM Directive 1989 it was stated that "[a]ny Member State may also provide that the proprietor shall be entitled to prevent all third parties not having his consent from using in the course of trade any sign which is identical with, or similar to, the trade mark in relation to goods or services which are not similar to those for which the trade mark is registered, where the latter has a reputation in the Member State and where use of that sign without due cause takes unfair advantage of, or is detrimental to, the distinctive character or the repute of the trade mark." Substantially. it is identical to art. 4(4)(a) of the TM Directive 1989 related to registration. A key question in *Davidoff v. Gofkid* was if the provision also included "identical or similar goods or services." The Court of Justice stated that the "article cannot be given an interpretation which would lead to marks with a reputation having less protection where a sign is used for identical or similar goods or services than where a sign is used for non-similar goods or services." Davidoff v. Gofkid, Case C-292/00, [2003] ECR I-00389, para 25. In the TM Directive and TM Regulation, the EU legislature has corrected for the previous gap. See also Davis, Richard, St Quintin, Thomas and Tritton, Guy, 'Tritton on Intellectual Property in Europe', (5th edn, Sweet & Maxwell, 2018), p. 381-382.

particular statutory provision can be identified, a statutory provision ought to be interpreted so as to secure conformity with that interpretation of the legislature." This interpretation, the authors continue, has to be "(a) in accordance with some appropriate sense of intention and (b) in respect of some element which serves as the object of intention" which may be derived from textual or purposive interpretation.[136] As explained in Chap. 3, preparatory works play different roles in the member states represented in this book. At EU level, preparatory works in practice do not play a role when interpreting primary EU legislation whereas they have some role in interpreting secondary EU legislation.[137]

The Court of Justice has referred explicitly to preparatory works in *Billerud Karlsborg v Naturvårdsverket* related to the statutory right to impose penalties on companies for failing in due time to surrender certain allowances based on their greenhouse gas emission. Due to ambiguities of the relevant provision, the Court of Justice referred to a piece of preparatory work (a Commission memorandum) to support the reading of the relevant directive. Here, the preparatory work was not referred to in the directive.[138] This approach of the Court of Justice seems to be opposed to its earlier stricter view in *Antonissen*. In this decision, the Court of Justice held that a "declaration recorded in the Council minutes at the time of the adoption of the" relevant regulation and directive "cannot be used for the purpose of interpreting a provision of secondary legislation where, as in this case, no reference is made to the content of the declaration in the wording of the provision in question. The declaration therefore has no legal significance."[139] Subsequently, the Court of Justice has revisited *Antonissen* in *Queen v. Licensing Authority* holding that preparatory works may be used to "*clarify a general concept* such as that of an 'essentially similar medicinal product' [the disputed concept]" and "may be taken into consideration when interpreting that provision"[140] despite not being referred to in the relevant legislation.[141]

Although with some reluctance, it emerges according to Court of Justice case law, that preparatory works may have a role to play in interpreting secondary legislation.

---

[136]This means of interpretation has also been referred to by MacCormick and Summers as "transcategorical" since it draws on other means of interpretation. MacCormick, Neil, and Summers, Robert D., 'Interpretation and Justification', in MacCormick, Neil and Summers, Robert D. eds., Interpreting Statutes (1st edn, Routledge, 1991), 511, p. 515.

[137]Danielsen, Jens Hartig, 'Parallelhandel og Varernes Frie Bevægelighed', (1st edn, Jurist- og Økonomforbundets Forlag, 2005), p. 22-24.

[138]Billerud Karlsborg v. Naturvårdsverket, Case C-203/12, [2013], paras 39-40. See also Billerud Karlsborg v. Naturvårdsverket, Case C-203/12, [2013], (opinion of AG Mengozzi), paras 28-29.

[139]Antonissen, Case C-292/89, [1991] ECR I-745, paras 17-18.

[140]Queen v. Licensing Authority, Case C-368/96, [1998] ECR I-7967, para 27.

[141]*Ibid*, para 26. See also Conway, Gerard, 'The Limits of Legal Reasoning and the European Court of Justice', (1st edn, Cambridge University Press, 2012), p. 255. For a broader discussion on the role of preparatory works, see ibid, p. 255-258. Referring to trademark law, Tritton *et al* have discussed the role of preparatory works, given international exhaustion of trademark rights. Davis, Richard, St Quintin, Thomas and Tritton, Guy, 'Tritton on Intellectual Property in Europe', (5th edn, Sweet & Maxwell, 2018), p. 461-462, including the case law referred to in footnote 981 of the text.

The value of a piece of preparatory works as a legal source is arguably higher if the EU legislature has referred to it in the notes of secondary EU legislation. An example of this is the reference in EESC TM Opinion 2013.[142] From Court of Justice case law it is obvious that the court perceives the preambles of secondary EU legislation as significant to interpreting the objectives of secondary EU legal sources and their main text.[143] For instance, the court on several occasions has referred to the recitals of the preambles of EU trademark legislation in its interpretation of the likelihood of confusion standard of the main text of the legislation. Thus, for instance, the court referred to the preambles in EU trademark legislation in *Canon*, holding "that the function of the protection conferred by the mark is primarily to guarantee the indication of origin,"[144] and in *Sabel* on the relevance of the "numerous elements" to interpreting the likelihood of confusion standard.[145]

Based on the above, the Court of Justice has a limited room for interpreting the legislative likelihood of confusion standard, including defining the relevant public through the average consumer, e.g. based on preparatory works. However, there is more room to include preparatory works referred to in the EU trademark legislation, such as the EESC TM Opinion 2013 as a source of interpretation. Most significant as aids of interpretation of the TM Regulation and TM Directive and their purpose are their preambles since they emerge directly in the legislative acts.

4.3.5 Opinions of Advocates Generals

Advocates General have been an important voice in developing the average consumer by the Court of Justice.[146] Therefore, reference is made to Advocate General opinions. As for the duties of the Advocates General "[i]t shall be the duty of the Advocate General, acting with complete impartiality and independence, to make, in open court, reasoned submissions on cases which, in accordance with the Statute of

---

[142]The EESC is touched upon in Chap. 1, Sects. 1.3.1–1.3.2 and Sect. 4.3.4 of this chapter.

[143]On the role of preambles as part of purposive interpretation, Arnull, Anthony, 'The European Union and its Court of Justice', (2nd edn, Oxford University Press, 2006), p. 607-608 and Sjåfjell, Beate, 'Towards a Sustainable European Company Law: A Normative Analysis of the Objectives of EU Law, with the Takeover Directive as a Test Case', (1st edn, Kluwer Law International, 2009), p. 128-130. The latter source exemplifies how preambles are used to interpret the objectives of EU company and securities law.

[144]Canon Kabushiki Kaisha v. Metro-Goldwyn-Mayer. Case C-39/97, [1998] ECR I-5507, para 27 and further on preambles as a legal source Sect. 4.3.4 of this chapter.

[145]Sabel v. Puma, Case C-251/95, [1997] ECR I-6191, para 22 and further on this Chap. 10, Sects. 10.1 and 10.2.2.

[146]The role of the Advocates General has undergone much scrutiny. See in particular, Burrows, Noreen, and Greaves, Rosa, 'The Advocate General and EC Law', (1st edn, Oxford University Press, 2007), mainly chapter 6 with the heading "Advocate General Jacobs and intellectual property law," Arnull, Anthony, 'The European Union and its Court of Justice', (2nd edn, Oxford University Press, 2006), p. 14-19.

the Court of Justice of the European Union, require his involvement."[147] In the Statute of the CJEU it is stated that "[w]here [the Court of Justice] considers that the case raises no new point of law, the Court may decide, after hearing the Advocate General, that the case shall be determined without a submission from the Advocate General."[148] The opinions of the Advocates General on how cases should be decided are not binding. In contrast with the decisions of the Court of Justice, Advocates General opinions are more deliberative and personal.[149]

As EU judges, the Advocates General lack specialisation in intellectual property law.[150] However, Burrows and Greaves have pointed out, that in the early years of European trademark law from 1997 to 2005, Jacobs was the lead Advocate General, *de facto* making him a specialist on European trademark law.[151] Burrows and Greaves have regarded this as an indication that it is not only a matter of workload to which Advocate General a case is allocated.[152] Rosati has pointed out that the number of Advocates General opinions is decreasing.[153] A reason for this, Rosati speculates with specific reference to copyright law but also generally to intellectual property law, could be the lacking intellectual property law specialisation.[154]

---

[147]Cf. art. 252 of the TFEU (art. 222 of the TFEU Pre-Lisbon).

[148]Cf. art. 20 of the Statute of the CJEU. Before the Nice Treaty it was mandatory for the Court of Justice to hear the Advocates General. Hence, the wording of art. 222 of the EC as consolidated after implementing of the Amsterdam Treaty (i.e. before the Nice Treaty): "It shall be the duty of the Advocate General, acting with complete impartiality and independence, to make, in open court, reasoned submissions on cases brought before the Court of Justice, in order to assist the Court in the performance of the task assigned to it in Article 220."

[149]Bobek, Michal, 'The Court of Justice of the European Union', in Arnull, Anthony and Chalmers, Damian eds., The Oxford Handbook of European Union Law (1st edn, Oxford University Press, 2015), 153, p. 168. As a side remark, Michal Bobek was himself appointed as Advocate General as of 7 October 2015.

[150]Rosati points out that the number of Advocates General opinions is decreasing. Rosati speculates, with specific reference to copyright law but also more generally to intellectual property law, if the reason for this is lacking intellectual property law specialists among the Advocates General. Rosati, Eleonora, 'Luxembourg, we have a Problem: Where have the Advocates General Gone?', Journal of Intellectual Property Law & Practice, vol. 9/no. 8, (2014), pp. 619, p. 619. See also Arnold, Sir Richard, 'An Overview of European Harmonization Measures in Intellectual Property Law', in Ohly, Ansgar and Justine Pila eds., The Europeanization of Intellectual Property Law: Towards a European Legal Methodology (1st edn, Oxford University Press, 2013), 25, p. 30.

[151]Burrows, Noreen, and Greaves, Rosa, 'The Advocate General and EC Law', (1st edn, Oxford University Press, 2007), p. 148.

[152]*Ibid*, p. 157.

[153]The most recent statistics of the Court of Justice shows that in 2017 approximately 67 % of all cases of the Court of Justice were decided without hearing the Advocates General. Court of Justice of the European Union: Annual Report 2017 Judicial Activity. Synopsis of the judicial activity of the Court of Justice, the General Court and the Civil Service Tribunal, available at: https://curia. europa.eu/jcms/upload/docs/application/pdf/2018-04/_ra_2017_en.pdf (last visited 26 May 2019), p. 98.

[154]Rosati, Eleonora, 'Luxembourg, we have a Problem: Where have the Advocates General Gone?', Journal of Intellectual Property Law & Practice, vol. 9/no. 8, (2014), pp. 619, p. 619. See also Laustsen, Rasmus D., 'An Economic Analysis of EU Trademark Law; the Role of the

Compared to the Court of Justice, the Advocates General more broadly and openly critically assess the cases and give a broader steer for future developments of the law.[155] In trademark law, this assessment includes for instance considering scholarly works,[156] national case law emerged pre-dating the TM Directive 1989[157] and more broadly the role of trademarks, given their underlying economic rationale. Hence, the Advocates General have clearly referred to the economic function of trademarks as lowering consumer search costs.[158] Advocates General have also been an important voice in developing the average consumer by the Court of Justice.[159]

Based on these findings, reference throughout this book is made to Advocate General opinions as an important source of law. Formally, of course, the value of an

---

Average Consumer in Trademark Infringement between Two Confusingly Similar Trademarks', in Lyngsie, Jacob, Mortensen, Bent O. G. and Østergaard, Kim eds., Rets- og Kontraktøkonomi: Law & Economics an Anthology (Djøf Publishing, 2016), 37, p. 54, including footnote 64 of the text. In similar veins, Arnold J has raised it as a point of critique that the Advocates General lack specialisation in intellectual property law, "or even, in most cases, in commercial law more generally." Arnold, Sir Richard, 'An Overview of European Harmonization Measures in Intellectual Property Law', in Ohly, Ansgar and Justine Pila eds., The Europeanization of Intellectual Property Law: Towards a European Legal Methodology (1st edn, Oxford University Press, 2013), 25, p. 30.

[155]Tridimas, Takis, 'the Role of the Advocate General in the Development of Community Law: Some Reflections', Common Market Law Review, vol. 34/no. 6, (1997), pp. 1349, p. 1361.

[156]Ohly, Ansgar, 'Introduction: The Quest for Common Principles of European Intellectual Property Law – Useful, Futile, Dangerous?', in Ohly, Ansgar ed., Common Principles of European Intellectual Property Law (1st edn, Mohr Siebeck, 2012), 3, p. 10.

[157]The limited number of references to historical national case law found in Advocates General opinions and even more so in Court of Justice case law, shows in Dinwoodie's words a "desire to decouple contemporary European law from a particular national lineage for understandable political reasons." Dinwoodie, Graeme B, 'The Europeanization of Trade Mark Law', in Ohly, Ansgar and Pila, Justine eds., The Europeanization of Intellectual Property Law: Towards a European Legal Methodology (1st edn, Oxford University Press, 2013), 72, p. 96-97.

[158]Among others, Advocate General Szpunar in *Hauck v. Stokke,* referred to the role of trademarks in lowering consumer search costs. Hauck v. Stokke, Case C-205/13, [2014], (opinion of AG Szpunar), para 30. Szpunar referred to Landes, William M., and Posner, Richard A., 'The Economic Structure of Intellectual Property Law', (1st edn, Harvard University Press, 2003), and Griffiths, Andrew, 'An Economic Perspective on Trade Mark Law', (1st edn, Edward Elgar, 2011). Advocate General Jääskinen in *Interflora Court of Justice,* assessed trademark infringement based on balancing the interests of the trademark owner and its competitor referring to what is the Pareto optimal solution. Interflora v. Marks & Spencer, Case C-323/09, [2011] ECR I-8625 (opinion of AG Jääskinen), para 94. Jääskinen referred to a text by Daniel Klerman, i.e. 'Trademark Dilution, Search Costs, and Naked Licensing', Fordham Law Review, vol. 74/no. 4, (2006), pp. 1759. See also Laustsen, Rasmus D., 'An Economic Analysis of EU Trademark Law; the Role of the Average Consumer in Trademark Infringement between Two Confusingly Similar Trademarks', in Lyngsie, Jacob, Mortensen, Bent O. G. and Østergaard, Kim eds., Rets- og Kontraktøkonomi: Law & Economics an Anthology (Djøf Publishing, 2016), 37, p. 54 and Chap. 1, Sect. 1.3.2.

[159]See among others, Advocate General Colomer in *Linde*, Linde *et al*, Joined cases C-53/01 to C-55/01, [2002] ECR I-3161 (opinion of AG Colomer), para 12. On the importance of Colomer's opinion in *Linde* and for a substantial analysis of the opinion and subsequent decisions, see Chap. 11, Sect. 11.6.

Advocate General's opinion as a legal source is assessed according to its subsequent acknowledgement by the Court of Justice. Burrows and Greaves in stressing the potential influence of Advocate General Jacobs on European trademark law have mentioned that the Court of Justice substantially followed his opinions and reasoning.[160] Included in this bulk of Jacobs' opinions are his opinions in two decisions crucial to developing the average consumer, *Sabel*[161] and *Lloyd*.[162]

Be opinions acknowledged by the Court of Justice or not, their value as a legal source is taken to be prominent, in particular on policy arguments. Although an Advocate General's opinion is confirmed by the Court of Justice, the court in its decisions rarely enters into a conversation with the Advocates General on the broader policy-oriented remarks found in opinions, for instance the economic role of trademarks as just referred to. Therefore, besides Advocates General's opinions as more formalised legal sources when confirmed by the Court of Justice, the opinions are also acknowledged in this book for their informal role in broadly analysing case law and the policy underpinnings of trademark law. This is more so relevant in the high degree of "hard cases" populating European trademark law, where scholars reading Court of Justice decisions often look for more subtext, some of which may be found in Advocate General opinions.

4.4 Conclusion

In this chapter it has been analysed how EU trademark legislation has been harmonised by the EU legislature and by the CJEU in its role of as lawmaker. From the wording of the legislation, setting out the likelihood of confusion standard it is clear that the standard in *theory* has undergone maximum harmonisation where the legislature has set the floor and ceiling of the standard. However, it has equally been portrayed how the level of harmonisation is in *practice* left to the operation of mainly the Court of Justice and its role as lawmaker due to the vague wording of the legislation.

As for the UCPD as consumer protection legislation, it emerges from the wording of the UCPD as well the finding by the Court of Justice in *Nemzeti v. Magyarország*

---

[160]Burrows, Noreen, and Greaves, Rosa, 'The Advocate General and EC Law', (1st edn, Oxford University Press, 2007), p. 148. The reason for only referring to Jacobs' influence as "potential" is that Burrows and Greaves also address the potential influence of Gulmann stating that "it would be unwise, without clearer evidence, to attempt to apportion credit to either individual." Burrows, Noreen, and Greaves, Rosa, 'The Advocate General and EC Law', (1st edn, Oxford University Press, 2007), p. 165. In Chap. 8 it is pointed out that Mancini and Gulmann (both previous Advocates General and afterwards judges at the Court of Justice) may have affected the early development of the average consumer. See Chap. 8, Sect. 8.7.

[161]Sabel v. Puma, Case C-251/95, [1997] ECR I-6191, (opinion of AG Jacobs).

[162]Lloyd Schuhfabrik Meyer v. Klijsen Handel BV, Case C-342/97, [1998] ECR I-3819, (opinion of AG Jacobs).

that the directive seeks "a complete harmonisation" related to B2C protection against unfair commercial practices.

It was seen that the dialogue between the Court of Justice and national courts through the preliminary rulings procedure dynamically develops the likelihood of confusion standard in EU trademark law. In the dialogue with national courts, it was seen that an inherent uncertainty vests in the preliminary rulings procedure since it is not always straightforward to interpret the rulings, since they are based on specific, and sometimes unclear, questions from the national courts. Also, the Court of Justice adds to the dynamic development of the law as appeal court to the General Court on the likelihood of confusion standard in registration disputes on EU trademarks.

Part of the uncertainty in the Court of Justice decisions is caused by their lacking clear *ratios decidendi*, the decisions being shortly reasoned and leaving out dissenting judgements. In its judgements, it was concluded that the Court of Justice opens up for normative preferences through its means of interpretation. The means of interpretation emphasised were means of interpretation referring to text, context, purpose and arguments from intention.

Preparatory works and the preambles of secondary EU legislation may have a role to play as means of interpretation relying on context, purpose and intention. It was concluded with specific reference to the likelihood of confusion standard, including the relevant public, that preparatory works, e.g. EESC TM Opinion 2013, and preambles of EU trademark legislation are relevant in this perspective.

Opinions of Advocates General were identified as contributing to developing European trademark, not least Jacobs' opinions in its early years. The opinions are referred to throughout as relevant when followed by the Court of Justice, but also as valuable contributions to the understanding of European trademark law and its underlying policies.

Part II
Horizontal Analysis: One Among Other Fictions and the UCPD Consumer Models

Chapter 5
The Average Consumer as a Legal Fiction and Beyond

5.1 Introduction

Based on theory, what is the average consumer in European trademark law? As the introduction mentions, it is stance of this book that the average consumer is a legal fiction. This chapter will elaborate on why that is from a theoretical viewpoint, and why the average consumer is not a legal standard or a legal concept. Part of this grappling is clearly normative. Legal theory is itself ambiguous and so is the terminology used for describing the average consumer and its application in practice. As it will be recalled from the introduction, Leczykiewicz and Weatherill have argued that consumer images as legal fictions are either policy hidden behind a "masquerade" of "actual needs and characteristics of EU consumers" or a way for the law to find a workable "regulatory framework."[1] Preceding this argument is the bulk of theoretical underpinning dissecting the understanding of what a legal fiction is. So far, no one has stepped back from the term "average consumer" and analytically described, based on legal theory, what is the most covering term for denoting the average consumer—in this book why "legal fiction" is the most appropriate term.[2] In addition, a review of legal texts on the average consumer indicates the need for a better theoretical steer on how to denote the average consumer. The subject of this book nests in a Europeanised trademark law developed dynamically. This creates substantial and methodological challenges when framing the analysis.[3] On top of that—or most likely because of that—the terminology used for denoting the

---

[1] See Leczykiewicz, Dorota and Weatherill, Stephen, 'The Images of the Consumer in EU Law', in Leczykiewicz, Dorota and Weatherill, Stephen eds., The Images of the Consumer in EU Law: Legislation, Free Movement and Competition Law (1st edn, Hart, 2016), 1, p. 14 and above in Chap. 1, Sect. 1.2.

[2] This is probably rightfully so since the format of journal articles does not allow the combining of an in-depth contemporary analysis of the average consumer with an analysis of legal theory.

[3] See Chap. 4.

© Springer Nature Switzerland AG 2020
R. D. Laustsen, *The Average Consumer in Confusion-based Disputes in European Trademark Law and Similar Fictions*, https://doi.org/10.1007/978-3-030-26350-8_5

average consumer is in flux, inconsistent and to the mind of the author incoherent with underpinning legal theory.

The average consumer in trademark law and adjacent areas of law, i.e. in this book the UCPD, has thus been denoted a "legal fiction,"[4] "legal construct,"[5]

---

[4]In relation to trademark infringement, Burrell and Handler have argued that "(...) the average consumer by reference to whom infringement is judged is *a legal fiction* and that this hypothetical person does compare the mark as registered with the defendant's use." Burrell, Robert, and Handler, Michael, 'Making Sense of Trade Mark Law', Intellectual Property Quarterly, no. 4, (2003), pp. 388, p. 406. Analysing the average consumer in the realm of the UCPD, Sibony referring to "homo oeconomicus" in economics has stated that "EU consumer law still largely relies on the fiction that consumers are 'reasonably well-informed and reasonably observant and circumspect'." In addition, Sibony has claimed that although the average consumer "is an expression *of fiction*, this "average consumer" exists in reality, within all of us." Sibony, Anne-Lise, 'Can EU Consumer Law Benefit from Behavioural Insights? An Analysis of the Unfair Practices Directive', in Mathis, Klaus ed., European Perspectives on Behavioural Law and Economics. Foundations and Applications (1st edn, Springer, 2015), 71, p. 72. Dinwoodie has stated that the US cousin of the European average consumer, "the ordinarily prudent purchaser," elsewhere also denoted the "reasonable consumer" and sometimes just the "reasonable person," is "in large part a *legal fiction* that implements a vision of the degree of consumer protection regulation that Congress and the courts think appropriate without rendering commerce inefficient." Dinwoodie, Graeme B., 'What Linguistics can do for Trademark Law', in Bently, Lionel, Davis, Jennifer and Ginsburg, Jane C. eds., Trade Marks and Brands: An Interdisciplinary Critique (1st edn, Cambridge University Press, 2008), 140, p. 148. Indicating a critique of the US equivalent of the average consumer, Gallagher and Goodstein have even held that it is not only a legal fiction but a "science fiction." Gallagher, William E., and Goodstein, Ronald C., 'Inference Versus Speculation in Trademark Infringement Litigation: Abandoning the Fiction of the Vulcan Mind Meld', Trademark Reporter, vol. 94/no. 6, (2004), pp. 1229. The authors build on an analogy to the Star Treck character the Vulcan who by way of touching a person's head with his fingertips can identify and undergo that person's thoughts as if they were his own. In that light the authors call the US equivalent of the average consumer a "science fiction" (all italics in this footnote are added).

[5]Interflora v. Marks & Spencer, [2012] EWCA Civ 1501, paras 44 and 73. This finding was upheld by the UK Court of Appeal in Interflora v. Marks & Spencer, [2014] EWCA Civ 1403, para 113, and also by the UK High Court in Hearst v. A.V.E.L.A., [2014] EWHC 439 (Ch), para 60 and Enterprise v. Europcar, [2015] EWHC 17 (Ch), para 131. Davis, Jennifer, 'Revisiting the Average Consumer: An Uncertain Presence in European Trade Mark', Intellectual Property Quarterly, no. 1, (2015), pp. 15, p. 19. Analysing the average consumer in the UCPD, Micklitz has in similar terms called the average consumer "ECJ's construction." Micklitz, Hans-W., 'Unfair Commercial Practices and Misleading Advertising', in Micklitz, Hans-W, Reich, Norbert and Rott, Peter eds., Understanding EU Consumer Law (1st edn, Intersentia, 2009), 61, p. 87 and Reich, Norbert, Micklitz, Hans-W., and Rott, Peter, 'European Consumer Law', (2nd edn, Intersentia, 2014), p. 94.

"judicial construct,"[6] "hypothetical average consumer,"[7] "hypothetical person,"[8] "hypothetical intelligent individual,"[9] "legal standard," "standard,"[10] "a notional construct," "construct,"[11] "notional typical person,"[12] "objective notion,"[13]

---

[6]Heymann, in dealing with the US counterpart of the average consumer, has used the term "judicial construct." Heymann, Laura A., 'The Reasonable Person in Trademark Law', Saint Louis University Law Journal, vol. 52/no. 3, (2008), pp. 781, p. 786, including footnote 26 of the text, where Heymann refers to a draft of Dinwoodie's article where Dinwoodie has called the average consumer a legal fiction. Dinwoodie, Graeme B., 'What Linguistics can do for Trademark Law', in Bently, Lionel, Davis, Jennifer and Ginsburg, Jane C. eds., Trade Marks and Brands: An Interdisciplinary Critique (1st edn, Cambridge University Press, 2008), 140, p. 148 (the finalised article which Heymann referred to in draft format).

[7]Davis, Jennifer, 'Locating the Average Consumer: His Judicial Origins, Intellectual Influences and Current Role in European Trade Mark Law', Intellectual Property Quarterly, no. 2, (2005), pp. 183, p. 188. This has been reiterated based on recent case law by Davis, Jennifer, 'Revisiting the Average Consumer: An Uncertain Presence in European Trade Mark', Intellectual Property Quarterly, no. 1, (2015), pp. 15, e.g. p. 21.

[8]Mellor, James, David Llewelyn, Moody-Stuart, Thomas, et al, 'Kerly's Law of Trade Marks and Trade Names', (16th edn, Sweet & Maxwell, 2018), p. 54.

[9]Pila, Justine, 'The Subject Matter of Intellectual Property', (1st edn, Oxford University Press, 2017), p. 18.

[10]Advocate General Fennelly in Estée Lauder, dealing with national measures for deciding consumer confusion in unfair competition law, described the average consumer as a "standard (...) defined in community law." Estée Lauder, Case C-220/98, [1999] ECR I-117, (opinion of AG Fennelly), para 29. Gut Springenheide, a preliminary ruling related to the regulation "on certain marketing standards for eggs" was one of the first decisions to set out the average consumer. See further on the decision in Chap. 10, Sect. 10.2. As is clear from the title of the regulation it encompasses legal standards. These standards include, cf. Art. 10(2)(e) of Regulation 1970/90, the prevention of "statements designed to promote sales, provided that such statements and the manner in which they are made are not likely to mislead the purchaser." In further qualifying the preliminary question of the German Bundesverwaltungsgericht related to art. 10(2)(e), the Court of Justice stated that it was essentially being asked "to define the concept of consumer to be used as a standard for determining whether a statement designed to promote sales of eggs is likely to mislead the purchaser." Gut Springenheide and Tusky, Case C-210/96, [1998] ECR I-4657, para 27. See also, Wallberg, Knud, 'Brug af Andres Varemærker i Digitale Medier: Et Bidrag til Afklaring af Varemærkerettens Indhold og Grænseflader', (1st edn, Jurist- og Økonomforbundets Forlag, 2015), p. 211.

[11]See Mellor, James, David Llewelyn, Moody-Stuart, Thomas, et al, 'Kerly's Law of Trade Marks and Trade Names', (16th edn, Sweet & Maxwell, 2018), p. 60, and "legal construct" p. 180 with reference to Interflora v. M&S has used the term "legal construct." Analysing the average consumer in the UCPD, Micklitz refers in similar terms to describe the average consumer as "ECJ's construction." Micklitz, Hans-W., 'Unfair Commercial Practices and Misleading Advertising', in Micklitz, Hans-W, Reich, Norbert and Rott, Peter eds., Understanding EU Consumer Law (1st edn, Intersentia, 2009), 61, p. 87 and also Reich, Norbert, Micklitz, Hans-W., and Rott, Peter, 'European Consumer Law', (2nd edn, Intersentia, 2014), p. 94.

[12]Or merely "notional person." See Mellor, James, David Llewelyn, Moody-Stuart, Thomas, et al, 'Kerly's Law of Trade Marks and Trade Names', (16th edn, Sweet & Maxwell, 2018), p. 52.

[13]See Gut Springenheide and Tusky, Case C-210/96, [1998] ECR I-4657, para 14.

"concept," "conceptual model,"[14] "model,"[15] "consumer image,"[16] "benchmark"[17]

---

[14]Analysing harmonisation of European trademark law and the interplay between the EU level and national markets, Ohly has stated that "specific features of national markets can partly be taken into account when national courts apply *legal concepts* which relate to the impact on the average consumer (...)." Ohly, Ansgar, 'Concluding Remarks: Postmodernism and Beyond', in Ohly, Ansgar and Pila, Justine eds., The Europeanization of Intellectual Property Law: Towards a European Legal Methodology (1st edn, Oxford University Press, 2013), 255, p. 259. Dinwoodie and Gangjee have stated that the average consumer "is a normative *concept*, albeit one not detached from empirical reality." Dinwoodie, Graeme, and Gangjee, Dev, 'The Image of the Consumer in European Trade Mark Law', Social Science Research Network (SSRN), (draft of 3 November 2014), pp. 1, p. 8. In the final version of the article, Dinwoodie and Gangjee have left out this formulation now holding that "the average consumer offers a normatively infused vantage point from which to assess (more objectively) subjective empirical evidence relating to actual consumer perceptions and behaviours." Dinwoodie, Graeme, and Gangjee, Dev, 'The Image of the Consumer in EU Trade Mark Law', in Leczykiewicz, Dorota, and Weatherill, Stephen eds., The Images of the Consumer in EU Law: Legislation, Free Movement and Competition Law (1st edn, Hart, 2016), 339, p. 353. Analysing the average consumer in light of registration and distinctiveness, Davis has generally claimed that "the average consumer is not a *real* but a *legal concept*." Davis, Jennifer, 'Promoting the Public Interest and the European Trade Mark Directive: A Contradictory Approach', ERA Forum, vol. 14/no. 1, (2013), pp. 117, p. 122. The statement by Davis is made analysing registration of trademarks, however, the formulation of the sentence does not indicate that her statement only applies to the registration scenario. See also Mellor, James, Llewelyn, David, Moody-Stuart, Thomas *et al*, 'Kerly's Law of Trade Marks and Trade Names. 1st Supplement', (1st edn, Sweet & Maxwell, 2014), p. 2. Under the UCPD the average consumer is also denoted a "concept." See among others, Reich, Norbert, Micklitz, Hans-W., and Rott, Peter, 'European Consumer Law', (2nd edn, Intersentia, 2014), p. 52 and Glöckner, Jochen, 'The Law Against Unfair Competition and the EC Treaty', in Hilty, Reto M. and Henning-Bodewig, Frauke eds., Law Against Unfair Competition: Towards a New Paradigm in Europe? (1st edn, Springer, 2007), 77, p. 86. Glinski and Joerges have stated that the UCPD "by and large, totally harmonised this area of law, thereby also codifying, in its Article 5, the concept of the 'average consumer' as developed by the ECJ." Glinski, Carola, and Joerges, Christian, 'European Unity in Diversity?! A Conflicts-Law: Re-Construction of Controversial Current Developments', in Purnhagen, Kai, Rott, Peter and Micklitz, Hans-W eds., Varieties of European Economic Law and Regulation: Liber Amicorum for Hans-W Micklitz (1st edn, Springer, 2014), 285, p. 300. The UCPD has stated that one aim of the directive is "clarifying certain legal concepts at Community level" although not referring specifically to the average consumer. Recital 5 of the UCPD. Bakardjieva has called the average consumer a "conceptual model" which – due to it is reference to "concept" – is taken to mean the same as a "legal concept." Engelbrekt, Antonina Bakardjieva, 'Fair Trading Law in Flux? National Legacies, Institutional Choice and the Process of Europeanisation', (1st edn, Stockholm University, 2003), p. 533. In *Gut Springenheide* the Bundesverwaltungsgericht, referring three questions to the Court of Justice, has denoted the average consumer as "an objective concept." Gut Springenheide and Tusky, Case C-210/96, [1998] ECR I-4657, para 15 (all italics in this footnote are added).

[15]Micklitz, Hans-W., 'Unfair Commercial Practices and Misleading Advertising', in Micklitz, Hans-W, Reich, Norbert and Rott, Peter eds., Understanding EU Consumer Law (1st edn, Intersentia, 2009), 61, p. 87.

[16]See with focus on the UCPD, Engelbrekt, Antonina Bakardjieva, 'Fair Trading Law in Flux? National Legacies, Institutional Choice and the Process of Europeanisation', (1st edn, Stockholm University, 2003), p. 532.

[17]On trademark law: Stuyck, Jules, 'Consumer Concepts in EU Secondary Law', Working Paper (2014), pp. 1, p. 8. On the UCPD: Mak, Vanessa, 'Standards of Protection: In Search of the 'Average Consumer' of EU Law in the Proposal for a Consumer Rights Directive', European

and "yardstick."[18] The different terms are by no means mutually exclusive. That said, some of the terms refer to distinct legal theories, such as the theories of "rules/ standards," "fictions," "constructs" and "concepts" addressed below. At least, the terms formally link to underpinning legal theory, but it is uncertain whether that linkage has always been intended by the users of the terms. The following quote from the seminal article of Ponciobò and Incardona on the vulnerable consumer under the UCPD illustrates the terminological grappling with describing the average consumer: "the vulnerable consumer *concept* is a superfluous, paternalistic *notion* which accentuates the difficulties already present in the *fiction* of the average consumer *standard*."[19]

It is the stance of this book that using a terminology coherent with legal theory will create a more consistent average consumer. The key assumption is that there is something to be learnt from legal theory and that theory will enlighten the application of the average consumer in practice. The theoretical anchoring creates a better frame for analysing the average consumer more precisely in that the different theories require different means for the analysis. In addition, a better theoretical anchoring of the average consumer may solidify in the practical framing of the average consumer.

Review of Private Law, vol. 19/no. 1, (2011), pp. 25, p. 28, Abbamonte, Guiseppe B., 'The Unfair Commercial Practices Directive and its General Prohibition', in Weatherill, Stephen and Ulf Bernitz eds., The Regulation of the Unfair Commercial Practices Under EC Directive 2005/29 (1st edn, Hart, 2007), 11, p. 24, Engelbrekt, Antonina Bakardjieva, 'Fair Trading Law in Flux? National Legacies, Institutional Choice and the Process of Europeanisation', (1st edn, Stockholm University, 2003), p. 332, Incardona, Rossella, and Ponciobò, Cristina, 'The Average Consumer, the Unfair Commercial Practices Directive, and the Cognitive Revolution', Journal of Consumer Policy, vol. 30/no. 1, (2007), pp. 21, p. 45 and Scholes, Annette Nordhausen, 'Behavioural Economics and the Autonomous Consumer', Cambridge Yearbook of European Legal Studies, vol. 14/no. 1, (2011), pp. 297, p. 318. Duivenvoorde 2015 calling his PhD thesis "The Consumer Benchmarks in the Unfair Commercial Practices Directive." Duivenvoorde, Bram B., 'The Consumer Benchmarks in the Unfair Commercial Practices Directive', (1st edn, Springer, 2015). The UCPD has stated that "this Directive takes as a benchmark the average consumer, who is reasonably well-informed and reasonably observant and circumspect, taking into account...." Recital 18 of the UCPD.

[18]For the "yardstick" terminology see: On trademark law: Advocate General Colomer Mag Instrument v. OHIM, Case C-136/02 P, [2004] ECR I-9165, (opinion of AG Colomer), para 48, Maniatis, Spyros M., 'Competition and the Economics of Trade Marks', in Sterling, Adrian ed, Intellectual Property and Market Freedom, (1st edn, Sweet & Maxwell, 1997), 63, p. 88, Heymann on a US perspective, Heymann, Laura A., 'The Reasonable Person in Trademark Law', Saint Louis University Law Journal, vol. 52/no. 3, (2008), pp. 781. On the UCPD: Micklitz, Hans-W., 'Unfair Commercial Practices and Misleading Advertising', in Micklitz, Hans-W, Reich, Norbert and Rott, Peter eds., Understanding EU Consumer Law (1st edn, Intersentia, 2009), 61, p. 88 and Howells, Geraint G., Micklitz, Hans-W, and Wilhelmsson, Thomas, 'European Fair Trading Law the Unfair Commercial Practices Directive', (1st edn, Ashgate, 2006), p. 111.

[19]Incardona, Rossella, and Ponciobò, Cristina, 'The Average Consumer, the Unfair Commercial Practices Directive, and the Cognitive Revolution', Journal of Consumer Policy, vol. 30/no. 1, (2007), pp. 21, p. 29 (italics added). At this stage, no further scrutiny is made into the differences between the average consumer in trademark law and reference to vulnerable consumers under the UCPD. For an analysis of this aspect, see Chap. 7.

5.2   Rules and Standards

Before giving an account on what the average consumer is, it is unavoidable to address the question of what is "likelihood of confusion" in light of legal theory since this is the legal source of the average consumer. Also in the previous chapter, the vague legislative formulation of the likelihood of confusion was designated as a key source of the dynamic development of European trademark law as it leaves its content to be further specified by the CJEU and national courts, especially the Court of Justice.[20] As it appears, the Court of Justice, when it had to give its understanding of how to decide confusion, used the average consumer as "part of the public" in its global appreciation test.[21] In analysing the Europeanisation of certain legal terms, Azoulai has claimed that "[t]he texts adopted by the EU legislator abound with undefined terms. Yet, it remains unclear whether and when the interpretation of these terms will lead to specific and uniform cores of meaning or to divergent national conceptions." It is furthermore claimed by Azoulai that processes of Europeanisation of certain legal terms are "the processes of and mechanisms by which a meaning, arguably specific to EU law, is given to terms inserted in legal texts."[22] In a general perspective, it is claimed by Rose, that "the European model [of intellectual property law] seems to use *ex ante* legislation to crack down on rights holders' overextension of IP."[23] This terminological Europeanisation is what likelihood of confusion has been exposed to partly through the average consumer. To assess that statement for likelihood of confusion, it also begs the question if it makes sense to categorise likelihood of confusion as "*ex ante* legislation." Essentially, this is a question of whether this piece of legislation may be regarded as a rule or a standard.

Both rules and standards may be created by the legislature or subsequently by the judiciaries. As Kaplow states, "[w]hen legislators leave the details of law to courts (. . .), individuals may be left with little guidance for years or decades."[24] There is no bright line distinction between rules and standards.[25] A key tool for distinguishing

---

[20]See Chap. 4, Sect. 4.3.

[21]See in particular Chap. 10, Sect. 10.2.

[22]Azoulai, Loïc, 'The Europeanisation of Legal Concepts', in Neergaard, Ulla and Ruth Nielsen eds., European Legal Method in a Multi-Level EU Legal Order (1st edn, Djøf Publishing, 2012), 165, p. 165-166.

[23]The statement is made comparing European and US matters. Rose has claimed that US intellectual property law often offers an assessment "ex post through the judiciary" of what is protected. Rose, Carol M., 'Introduction: A Real Property Lawyer Cautiously Inspects the Edges of Intellectual Property', in Dreyfuss, Rochelle Cooper and Ginsburg, Jane C. eds., Intellectual Property at the Edge: The Contested Contours of IP (1st edn, Cambridge University Press, 2014), 1, p. 7.

[24]The quote continues: ", while substantial legal costs are incurred both in providing advice to actors and in adjudicating disputes over unresolved questions." This may be inserted when assessing the consequences of having a broad confusion standard. Kaplow, Louis 'Rules Versus Standards: An Economic Analysis', Duke Law Journal, vol. 42 (1992), pp. 557, p. 622.

[25]That the distinction between rules and standards is unclear, is illustrated by the following example set up by Kaplow: "[A]dvance determination of the appropriate speed on expressways under normal

the two is, according to Sullivan, "the relative discretion they afford to the decision maker." Categorising forms of law as rules or standards, Sullivan continues, is "to signify where they fall on the continuum of discretion."[26] This continuum has also been referred to as a "specificity-generality continuum" with rules as potentially highly specific and standards as general.[27] This section will not go deep into the discussion of the grey area in the distinction between rules and standards but will focus mainly on the more clear-cut and less abstract examples of rules and standards at each end of the continuum.[28] The essence of the distinction between rules and standards is whether the law is given *ex ante* or *ex post*—"before or after individuals act."[29]

According to Kaplow "a rule may entail an advance determination of what conduct is permissible, leaving only factual issues for the adjudicator."[30] The structure of rules involves generalising in specifying "the scope of the rule [and] the factual conditions triggering the application of the rule."[31] This has been referred to in Chap. 2 discussing consistency as the "operative facts."[32] Defining the operative facts involves, according to Schlag, "classifying phenomena into

---

conditions, or even of the criteria that will be relevant in adjudicating reasonable speed (safety and the value of time, but not the brand of automobile or the particular driver's skill), are "rule-like" when compared to asking an adjudicator to attach whatever legal consequence seems appropriate, given whatever norms and facts seem relevant. Yet the same advance determination would be "standard-like" when compared to a precise advance determination of what constitutes normal conditions and what constitutes reasonable speed under various exceptional circumstances." *Ibid*, p. 562.

[26]Sullivan, Kathleen M., 'The Justices of Rules and Standards', Harvard Law Review, vol. 106/no. 1, (1992), pp. 22, p. 57. See also, Cross, Rupert, and Harris, J. W., 'Precedent in English Law', (4th edn, Oxford University Press, 1991), p. 18 and Ehrlich, Isaac, and Posner, Richard A., 'An Economic Analysis of Legal Rulemaking', the Journal of Legal Studies, vol. 3/no. 1, (1974), pp. 257.

[27]Ehrlich, Isaac, and Posner, Richard A., 'An Economic Analysis of Legal Rulemaking', the Journal of Legal Studies, vol. 3/no. 1, (1974), pp. 257.

[28]For instance, Schauer's seminal philosophical analysis of rule-based decision making has been criticised by Rakowski for being "too abstract and taxonomic to interest legislators and regulators." Rakowski, Eric, 'Book Review of Schauer, Frederick. Playing by the Rules: A Philosophical Examination of Rules-Based Decision Making in Law and in Life', Ethics, vol. 103/no. 1, (1993), pp. 828.

[29]Kaplow, Louis 'Rules Versus Standards: An Economic Analysis', Duke Law Journal, vol. 42 (1992), pp. 557, p. 559-560.

[30]*Ibid*, p. 560. See also Shavell elaborating on the cost and flexibility of rules in Shavell, Steven. 'Law Versus Morality as Regulators of Conduct', American Law and Economics Review, vol. 4/no. 2, (2002), pp. 227.

[31]Schauer, Frederick, 'Playing by the Rules – A Philosophical Examination of Rule-Based Decision-Making in Law and in Life', (1st edn, Clarendon, 1992), p. 23.

[32]Above, operative facts are mainly referred to in the realm of case law, however, the understanding of operative facts is similarly relevant to the analysis of rules. See above Chap. 2, Sect. 2.2.3. See also Schauer, Frederick, 'Playing by the Rules – A Philosophical Examination of Rule-Based Decision-Making in Law and in Life', (1st edn, Clarendon, 1992), p. 23 and Schlag, Pierre, 'Rules and Standards', UCLA Law Review, vol. 33 (1985-1986), pp. 379, p. 381-382.

predetermined classifications."[33] In general, rules will clarify which facts will cause the consequence of the rule to manifest.[34] Rules create more predictability but the flipside of this effect is that rules make it possible for subjects encompassed by the rule to "walk the line." That is to say in Kelman's words, it is possible to use the rules for one's "own advantage, counterpurposively."[35] Rules may be over inclusive and/or under inclusive. A rule is over inclusive according to Schauer if "[i]t encompasses states of affairs that might in particular instances not produce the consequence representing the rule's justification" and under inclusive in the opposite scenario.[36] The more detailed the written rules are, the more probable, in Posner's perspective, it is that a judge will enforce the written rule "as written rather than using it as merely the starting point for the development of legal standards."[37] In describing how to assess the success of rules, Diver has set out three criteria. First, legislative words are "well-defined and universally accepted meanings within the relevant community." Second, the rule is "applicable to concrete situations without excessive difficulty or effort." Third, the legislature regarded as a policymaker will want to make sure that "the substantive content of the message communicated in his words produces the desired behavior."[38]

In contrast with rules, a standard, following Kaplow's analysis, "may entail leaving both specification of what conduct is permissible and factual issues for the adjudicator."[39] Standards are according to Schlag "based upon evaluative parameters or variables" and "operate (. . .) by identifying relations, tendencies, and directions."[40] One potential consequence of standards is that they may be "subject to

---

[33]Schlag, Pierre, 'Rules and Standards', UCLA Law Review, vol. 33 (1985-1986), pp. 379, p. 428.

[34]Hence, Schlag has stated that "[t]he paradigm example of a rule has a hard empirical trigger and a hard determinate response." *Ibid*, p. 382.

[35]Kelman, Mark, 'A Guide to Critical Legal Studies', (1st edn, Harvard University Press, 1987), p. 41.

[36]Schauer, Frederick, 'Playing by the Rules – A Philosophical Examination of Rule-Based Decision-Making in Law and in Life', (1st edn, Clarendon, 1992), p. 32.

[37]Posner, Richard A., 'How Judges Think', (1st edn, Harvard University Press, 2008), p. 137.

[38]Diver, Colin S., The Optimal Precision of Administrative Rules, The Yale Law Journal, vol. 93/no. 1 (1983), pp. 65, p. 67. It has furthermore been stated by Diver that ensuring this "is usually bought at the price of incongruity or ex ante rulemaking costs." *Ibid*, p. 91.

[39]Kaplow, Louis 'Rules Versus Standards: An Economic Analysis', Duke Law Journal, vol. 42 (1992), pp. 557, p. 560. See also Parisi, Francesco and Fon, Vincy, 'The Economics of Lawmaking', (1 edn, Oxford University Press, 2009), p. 9-12, Shavell, Steven. 'Law Versus Morality as Regulators of Conduct', American Law and Economics Review, vol. 4/no. 2, (2002), pp. 227, in particular, p. 234-236 on "Specificity and Flexibility of Rules" and Sullivan, Kathleen M., 'The Justices of Rules and Standards', Harvard Law Review, vol. 106/no. 1, (1992), pp. 22, p. 24-123. Sullivan has argued that rules based on *ex ante* perspectives create more clarity for "private actors" encompassed by the rules than standards based on *ex post* perspectives. *Ibid*, p. 62-64, including footnote 259 of the text and the sources referred to there.

[40]Schlag, Pierre, 'Rules and Standards', UCLA Law Review, vol. 33 (1985-1986), pp. 379, p. 428.

arbitrary and/or prejudiced enforcement."[41] In Posner's words, "a standard permits consideration of all, or at least most facts that are relevant to the standard's rationale."[42] In exemplifying standards in a US context, Cross has referred to the "multifactor test" as a "common standard" "in which doctrine tells lower courts to consider a series of factors as relevant to the decision's outcome but provides no explicit instructions about how those factors are to be weighed."[43] Such a multifactor test is manifested in US trademark law as a judicial means for testing likelihood of confusion.[44] The multifactor test in US trademark law is similar to the global appreciation test in European trademark law that similarly has been referred to as a "multi-factor approach."[45]

The above serves as a theoretical basis for categorising the likelihood of confusion provision in European trademark law in coherence with the underlying theory of rules and standards. Purpose at this stage is solely to highlight the differences between rules and standards, not to claim that one or the other is superior as such. This part of the analysis may only be done in the practice in which the relevant law resides.[46]

The stance of this book is that from the legislative outset, the legislation preventing "likelihood of confusion" is a typical example of a standard. The EU

---

[41]Kelman, Mark, 'A Guide to Critical Legal Studies', (1st edn, Harvard University Press, 1987), p. 41.

[42]Mindgames v. Western Publishing, 218 F.3d 652 (7th Cir.), [2000], p. 657. See also Cross, Rupert, and Harris, J. W., 'Precedent in English Law', (4th edn, Oxford University Press, 1991), p. 15-16.

[43]Cross, Frank, Jacobi, Tanja and Tiller, Emerson, 'A Positive Political Theory of Rules and Standards', University of Illinois Law Review, no. 1, (2012), pp. 1, p. 18. For a recent and thorough account of the multifactor test for deciding likelihood of confusion under US trademark law, see Beebe, Barton, 'Trademark Law: An Open-Source Casebook', Trademark Infringement (V3 edn, 2016), p. 35-85.

[44]Beebe has detected that there are inconsistencies in the multifactor test in US trademark law among the Federal Circuit Courts. Hence, Beebe stated in 2006 that "[c]ourts, commentators, and practitioners have all the while speculated about which factors, if any, actually drive the outcome of the test, how the factors interact, and most important, whether the different tests, given the same facts, would yield different outcomes." Beebe, Barton, 'An Empirical Study of the Multifactor Tests for Trademark Infringement', California Law Review, vol. 94 (2006), pp. 1581, p. 1584. The inconsistency of the multifactor test has been revisited by Matuszewski in 2016 holding, similar to Beebe, that "due to the test's frequent evolution, the individual circuits have split off and developed their own versions of likelihood of confusion." Matuszewski, Kenneth A. 'Casting out Confusion: How Exclusive Appellate Jurisdiction in the Federal Circuit would Clarify Trademark Law', INTA Papers (2016), pp. 1, p. 3.

[45]Dinwoodie, Graeme, and Gangjee, Dev, 'The Image of the Consumer in EU Trade Mark Law', in Leczykiewicz, Dorota, and Weatherill, Stephen eds., The Images of the Consumer in EU Law: Legislation, Free Movement and Competition Law (1st edn, Hart, 2016), 339, p. 355.

[46]As stated by Richard Posner: "No sensible person supposes that rules are always superior to standards, or vice versa, though some judges are drawn to the definiteness of rules and others to the flexibility of standards." Mindgames v. Western Publishing, 218 F.3d 652 (7th Cir.), [2000], p. 657. See also Cross, Frank, Jacobi, Tanja and Tiller, Emerson, 'A Positive Political Theory of Rules and Standards', University of Illinois Law Review, no. 1, (2012), pp. 1, p. 15-16.

legislature has thus solely stated that "likelihood of confusion includes the likelihood of association," indicating what the scope of the exclusivity is, and that the assessment has to be made referring to "part of the public."[47] Hence, it is more or less left open what *in fact* constitutes likelihood of confusion, leaving it open for *ex post* judicial assessment. Potentially, in accordance with Schlag's findings, this leaves the standard open for arbitrary enforcement. In the subsequent judicial application of the likelihood of confusion legislative standard, it is possible for the European judiciaries to draw the standard closer to the rule end of the rule/standard continuum. Placement of the legislative standard on this continuum is an integral part of the analysis of this book. If a high degree of vertical and horizontal harmonisation of the average consumer occurs, this indicates a high degree of coherence and consistency, which might make the confusion standard more rule-like. If the reverse is true, this might cause the legislative standard to remain as such after the judicial assessment.[48] As it has been stated above, it is argued by some that the average consumer is a legal standard in its own right. This viewpoint is contested in this book.[49] The average consumer is part of the relevant public used for deciding likelihood of confusion. It is the likelihood of confusion that is prevented. The average consumer, though, is a key tool when deciding likelihood of confusion and it is argued below that the average consumer is a legal fiction nesting in the likelihood of confusion standard.[50]

5.3   Legal Fictions

No matter how empirical the average consumer is deemed to be, it will always have a theoretical and normative underpinning. Even an average consumer framed in practice by way of evidence will still be based on a set of theoretical and normative assumptions. As held by Samuel, "[h]uman acts and facts are too complex to model in a way that makes accurate and relatively detailed prediction possible."[51] This is also true for *acts* and *facts* forming consumer behaviour. Due to the inherent vagueness of the average consumer as a way of legal modelling, it cannot be compared to models in hard sciences that can or cannot be confirmed through real

---

[47]Sabel v. Puma, Case C-251/95, [1997] ECR I-6191, para 18. See also Chaps. 9 and 10.

[48]On this point, see Chap. 4, Sect. 4.3.1.

[49]Therefore, the legislative requirement of likelihood of confusion is not an example of *ex ante* intellectual property legislation in line with the above finding by Rose.

[50]Discussing the development of the unfairness standard under the UCPD, Howells *et al* have stated that the average consumer is part of a test under the unfairness standard, i.e. implicitly stating that the average consumer is not a standard in its own right. Howells, Geraint G., Micklitz, Hans-W, and Wilhelmsson, Thomas, 'European Fair Trading Law the Unfair Commercial Practices Directive', (1st edn, Ashgate, 2006), p. 20-21.

[51]Samuel, Geoffrey, 'Does One Need an Understanding of Methodology in Law before One can Understand Methodology in Comparative Law?', in van Hoecke, Mark ed., Methodologies of Legal Research: What Kind of Method for what Kind of Discipline? (1st edn, Hart, 2011), 177, p. 205.

life testing.[52] To reflect actual consumer perception by way of "describing" it through evidence, it is necessary to have a common theoretical understanding and normative qualification of what conceptually is the average consumer when gathering evidence, e.g. survey evidence. This is even more so if the average consumer is pulled towards a purely normative end, not considering actual consumer perception. Here, the average consumer is based on assumptions by the European judges and more open to being infused with legal theory.

No matter what the empirical inputs are in creating the average consumer, it is created *in law*. It is still for the judges to decide whether the average consumer in law is likely to be confused, no matter how much the parties rely on empirical evidence.[53] The variables vested in the average consumer are highlighted in Chap. 1.[54] For instance in seeking to describe real life consumer behaviour, there is no agreed method for marketing research (quantitative or qualitative),[55] and there are no agreed inputs from neoclassical and behavioural economics on consumer rationality.[56] Also, there is no clear understanding of the terms *average* and *consumer* separately and taken together as an *average consumer*.[57] Vested in the average consumer are the tensions between normativity and empirical data and between law and reality. Hence, it is not the view of this book that the average consumer is bipolar—either fiction or fact. This stance seems to be taken by among others, Hannerstig, posing the bipolar question, "The Average Consumer – legal fiction or reality?"[58] It is more promising as stated by Dinwoodie, though, that: "With respect both to absolute grounds for refusal such as distinctiveness, and infringement tests such as likely confusion or association, trade mark law remains dominated by a *legal fiction* (the reasonably well-informed and reasonably observant and circumspect consumer) *that*

---

[52]For further discussion on the comparison between legal modelling and modelling in mainly economics, see Chap. 6, Sect. 6.6.

[53]See among others, Bakardjieva discussing a similar problem in light of deciding the legal standard of deception under German law by way of actual consumer perception. Engelbrekt, Antonina Bakardjieva, 'Fair Trading Law in Flux? National Legacies, Institutional Choice and the Process of Europeanisation', (1st edn, Stockholm University, 2003), p. 327-328.

[54]See Chap. 1, Sect. 1.2.

[55]See *ibid*, Sect. 1.2, including footnote 23.

[56]Towfigh, Emanuel V. and Petersen, Niels, 'Economic Methods for Lawyers', (1st edn, Edward Elgar, 2015), p. 18 and p. 25.

[57]For a discussion on the incremental development of the term average consumer in Court of Justice jurisprudence pre *Sabel*, and the inconsistent use of the term (or similar terms) in different linguistic versions of the decisions, see Chap. 8, in particular Sect. 8.7.

[58]Despite posing this key question in his thesis, Hannerstig does not from a theoretical viewpoint address what is understood by a "legal fiction." Hannerstig, Niclas, 'The Average Consumer – Legal Fiction or Reality? A Comparative Study between European and American Trademark Law', LUP Student Papers (2011). It should be mentioned, that although the paper by Hannerstig is not peer reviewed, it is included as a source due to the credibility of his comparative analysis of European and US law.

is a mix of factual realities and legal policy."[59] Furthermore, Dinwoodie and Gangjee have referred to the "consumer's schizophrenic existence as both the legal fiction driving the system and the actual real world object of trade mark protection."[60] It is argued in this book that legal fiction theory can accommodate these tensions and provide the best means for analysing the average consumer.

5.3.1 Defining "Legal Fiction"

Legal fiction theory has a long history.[61] Lind argues that legal fictions should "be understood as true legal propositions" considering that they may contravene the "true propositions." Further, Lind has described legal fictions as "simply a form of creative lawmaking, a phenomenon of legal (primarily judicial) technique employed to resolve trouble in the legal environment."[62] According to Samuel, narrowly speaking legal fictions "apply only to situations where a statement asserts something to be true that is patently untrue."[63] Similarly, Schauer has stated that "[f]ictions are, by definition, false, and thus a legal fiction is a legal falsehood." The falsehood, Schauer has claimed, is rooted in the "actual or potential divergence between what the law *says* and what the law or some legal actor *should do*."[64] In this light, legal

---

[59]Dinwoodie, Graeme B. 'The Europeanization of Trade Mark Law', in Ohly, Ansgar and Pila, Justine eds., The Europeanization of Intellectual Property Law: Towards a European Legal Methodology (1st edn, Oxford University Press, 2013), 72, p. 93 (italics added).

[60]Although reference is not made specifically to the *average* consumer, the reference by the authors is made finalising an analysis of the average consumer and therefore seems chiefly to be referring to the consumer in this version. Dinwoodie, Graeme, and Gangjee, Dev, 'The Image of the Consumer in EU Trade Mark Law', in Leczykiewicz, Dorota, and Weatherill, Stephen eds., The Images of the Consumer in EU Law: Legislation, Free Movement and Competition Law (1st edn, Hart, 2016), 339, p. 377.

[61]See among others, Vaihinger, Hans, 'The Philosophy of 'as if': A System of the Theoretical, Practical and Religious Fictions of Mankind', (1st edn, Harcourt Brace, 1924) (a translation of Vaihinger's original text in German from 1911), and Kelsen's response to Vaihinger, Kelsen, Hans, 'On the Theory of Juridic Fictions with Special Consideration of Vaihinger's Philosophy of the as-if', in Del Mar, Maksymilian and Twining, William eds., Legal Fictions in Theory and Practice (1st edn, Springer, 2015), 3 (a translation of Kelsen's original text in German from 1919) and Fuller, Lon L., 'Legal Fictions', (1st edn, Stanford University Press, 1967). Legal fictions. Stanford University Press: Stanford (first published as three journal articles from 1930-1931 in Illinois Law Review.).

[62]Lind, Douglas, 'The Pragmatic Value of Legal Fictions', in Del Mar, Maksymilian and Twining, William eds., Legal Fictions in Theory and Practice (1st edn, Springer, 2015), 83, p. 84.

[63]Samuel, Geoffrey, 'Is Law a Fiction?', in Del Mar, Maksymilian and Twining, William eds., Legal Fictions in Theory and Practice (1st edn, Springer, 2015), 31, p. 32.

[64]Schauer, Frederick, 'Legal Fictions Revisited', in Del Mar, Maksymilian and Twining, William eds., Legal Fictions in Theory and Practice (1st edn, Springer, 2015), 113, p. 126.

fictions facilitate closing the gap between legal language and what is considered a sound result.[65]

As for the assumption of legal fictions as inherently false, Lind has claimed, that it builds on a set of inherently false statements claiming that legal fictions should be measured against an objective "extralegal reality." This objective "extralegal reality" builds further on the statement that outside of law it will always be possible to infer this reality. If measured against an alleged objective "extralegal reality," there will most likely be an inconsistency between this reality and the legal fiction, at the end reducing the value of the latter.[66] Similar to Lind, Ross has argued that truth in fictions is irrelevant and stated that models such as "homo economicus" or "bonus pater familias" are simplifications diverging from reality.[67] In his analysis of the common law, Herbert has denoted these models "mythical figure[s]."[68] Despite the analogy to myths, Herbert has claimed that at least the reasonable man in tort law "rests upon solid and even, it may be, upon permanent foundations."[69] The reasonable man and homo economicus, according to Ross, are "only posed not affirmed," meaning, "that they are presented under conditions that make truth value irrelevant."[70] As addressed in the following chapter, there are similarities between the average consumer and these models from tort law and economics.[71]

Besides highlighting inconsistency as an inevitable issue using an objective extralegal reality as a benchmark for framing legal fictions, would it be possible at all to determine the actual reality to be used as benchmark? What is the true reality depends very much, on how the extralegal world is perceived. The pragmatists' view

---

[65]*Ibid*, p. 127.

[66]Lind, Douglas, 'The Pragmatic Value of Legal Fictions', in Del Mar, Maksymilian and Twining, William eds., Legal Fictions in Theory and Practice (1st edn, Springer, 2015), 83, p. 88 and p. 93.

[67]Ross, Alf, 'Legal Fictions', in Hughes, Graham ed., Law, Reason, and Justice: Essays in Legal Philosophy, (1st edn, Springer, 1969), 217, p. 231.

[68]Herbert, describing the reasonable man in tort law, called this model a "mythical figure", stating that this model "in another science is held by the Economic Man, and in social and political discussions by the Average or Plain Man." Herbert, A. P., 'Uncommon Law – being Sixty-Six Cases Revised and Collected in One Volume, Including Ten Cases Not Published before', (6th edn, Methuen & Co. Ltd, 1948), p. 2-3. It has to be borne in mind that not all find the "myth" analogy appropriate, analysing legal fictions. Hence, Scott has stated that "'legal myth" refers to false propositions that are erroneously taken to be true and acted upon as if true," i.e. the propositions are not recognised as being false. Hamilton, K. Scott, 'Prolegomenon to Myth and Fiction in Legal Reasoning, Common Law Adjudication and Critical Legal Studies', the Wayne Law Review, vol. 35 (1988-1989), pp. 1449, p. 1471.

[69]As opposed to the reasonable man, Herbert has argued that "while the Economic Man has under the stress of modern conditions almost wholly disappeared from view, his Reasonable cousin has gained in power with every case in which he has figured." Herbert, A. P., 'Uncommon Law – being Sixty-Six Cases Revised and Collected in One Volume, Including Ten Cases Not Published before', (6th edn, Methuen & Co. Ltd, 1948), p. 4.

[70]Ross, Alf, 'Legal Fictions', in Hughes, Graham ed., Law, Reason, and Justice: Essays in Legal Philosophy, (1st edn, Springer, 1969), 217, p. 231. See also Ross, Alf, 'Directives and Norms', (1st edn, Clark, 1968), p. 31-32.

[71]See below Chap. 6, Sects. 6.5–6.6.

on what is true reality is that it is in flux and that our stock of knowledge changes over time.[72] What is the truth has to be seen as a connection between an idea and an object and between an idea and context. Upon deciding context, it has to be considered what is the relevant "field, situation, system [and] surrounding."[73] According to the pragmatic approach, legal fictions are defined "as a legal proposition that is inconsistent in denotative meaning or otherwise in semantic conflict with some proposition(s) asserted as true within some extralegal linguistic system."[74] Samuel has concluded that fictions in law result from abduction—i.e. the best explanation resulting from the available data. Hence, it cannot logically be concluded from the available data what is the correct result. Abduction is also understood as "inference to the best explanation."[75] In this light, legal fictions are viewed "'as if' they were 'true'" to comprehend objects not comprehended otherwise.[76]

5.3.2   Why Use Fictions?

Besides offering the best explanation, why then are fictions used in law at all and what are their function? Samuel argues that legal fictions create consistency when judges have to decide like decisions and a predictable outcome of current and future decisions.[77] Del Mar has argued that "when used wisely, [fictions] are inherently dynamic resources that allow courts, over time, to balance flexibility and responsiveness with stability and predictability."[78] A way of doing this is through fictions to suspend evidence of operative facts. Thus, the judge may disregard the evidence and proceed allowing "the normative consequence to follow" from the fiction.[79] Essentially, legal fictions allow for some predictability, and fictions may be moulded case-by-case based on the facts of the case. This predictability is known from the function of *rules*, whereas the flexibility is known from the function of *standards*. These functions of fictions link to part of the legal method of this book. Thus, ideally, in line with a key aim of Scandinavian Legal Realism, the average consumer

---

[72]Lind, Douglas, 'The Pragmatic Value of Legal Fictions', in Del Mar, Maksymilian and Twining, William eds., Legal Fictions in Theory and Practice (1st edn, Springer, 2015), 83, p. 91.

[73]*Ibid*, p. 92.

[74]*Ibid*, p. 94.

[75]Stanford Philosophy Encyclopedia section 1. Available at: https://plato.stanford.edu/entries/abduction/ (last visited 26 May 2019).

[76]Samuel, Geoffrey, 'Is Law a Fiction?', in Del Mar, Maksymilian and Twining, William eds., Legal Fictions in Theory and Practice (1st edn, Springer, 2015), 31, p. 34.

[77]*Ibid*, p. 44.

[78]Mar, Maksymilian del, 'Legal Fictions and Legal Change', International Journal of Law in Context, vol. 9/no. 4, (2013), pp. 442, p. 444.

[79]*Ibid*, p. 445.

fiction would make it possible for European judges to categorise certain facts through the fiction, making it easier to predict the outcome of court decisions.[80]

Legal fictions as offering the best explanation based on the relevant data is in effect what the average consumer in European trademark law does. To a certain extent, the average consumer acts as a proxy for consumer perception of the relevant trademarks. At the end, the average consumer facilitates answering the question if the relevant public is likely to be confused over the use by the junior owner of its trademark vis-à-vis that of the senior trademark owner. Wilhelmsson has asked the following questions in relation to the average consumer under the UCPD: "Is the idea of an average European consumer a *legal fiction*, at least to some extent or for some situations? Can it be criticized for *presupposing a reality* that does not exist or exists to a lesser degree than presumed?"[81] Adding to the fact/law divide, Dinwoodie has concluded that based on the presumption of the average consumer as a legal fiction, "much law-making can be achieved by trial courts making factual determinations viewed through policy lenses without substantial intervention by appellate courts (unless those appellate courts are willing to police fact-finding by trial courts aggressively)."[82] This finding is in line with the general theoretical assumptions of Lind above. The average consumer is a way for the fact finding trademark courts to suspend and categorise certain facts when they make their "factual determinations," potentially attaching more weight to policy. As dealt with below, the average consumer seeks to explain the relevant consumer perception by way of introducing some consumer rationality and by contextualising the average consumer.

Judges arguably regard the average consumer as a fiction as if it was the true perception of the relevant consumer group. The average consumer is a way of conceptualising the consumer perception within the frame of the dispute between the senior trademark owner and the junior trademark owner, with the former arguing that the average consumer is confused by the use of the latter's trademark.

5.3.3 Evaluation

In evaluating models more broadly, Achinstein has argued that the value of a model "can be judged from two different, though related, viewpoints: how well it serves the purposes for which it is employed, and the completeness and accuracy of the

---

[80]On the importance to Scandinavian Legal Realism of predicting the outcome of court decisions, see Chap. 2, Sect. 2.2.1.

[81]Wilhelmsson, Thomas, 'The Average European Consumer: A Legal Fiction?', in Wilhelmsson, Thomas, Paunio, Elina and Pohjolainen, Annika eds., Private Law and the Many Cultures of Europe (1st edn, Kluwer Law International, 2007), 243, p. 247.

[82]On the fact/law divide, see for instance, Chap. 11, Sect. 11.1. Dinwoodie, Graeme B, 'The Europeanization of Trade Mark Law', in Ohly, Ansgar and Pila, Justine eds., The Europeanization of Intellectual Property Law: Towards a European Legal Methodology (1st edn, Oxford University Press, 2013), 72, p. 93.

representation it proposes."[83] In assessing legal fiction *models*, it may be asked according to Samuel to what extent, "fictions intervene in the legal perception of social reality."[84] Further, if legal fictions are justified not referring to real life objects but to perception of justice. Samuel has moreover stated that legal fictions creating consistency and predictability are valid—their validity may not be attacked solely due to the fictional character of the model.[85] In evaluating legal fictions, focus should be on the practical context in which they are used and whether they can effectively "remove or regulate some trouble in law while inflicting no harm on settled truths, meanings, or understandings in any extralegal realms with which they conflict in extensional meaning."[86] In similar veins, Lind has argued that legal fictions should not be assessed referring to inconsistency with reality since, despite inconsistency, they may still have value in law "to the extent they function beneficially within law and work no havoc on any general stock of beliefs outside law (or within)."[87] In addition, Lind has pointed out that the extralegal reality also mentioned above is not to be derived from a set of objective facts "but of criss-crossing realities – *nature, the sciences, economics, psychology, history, etc. – each with its own ways of investigating, interpreting, classifying, speaking, and judging truth.*"[88] Creating a "universal" benchmark for measuring extralegal reality is impossible, thus no one may "claim the status of reality extraordinaire."[89] Even if such a *"reality extraordinaire"* were to be found, it would not as such be valuable as benchmark for measuring "conceptual truths" in law, including legal fictions.[90] Hence, "[h]uman beings exist in natural reality" whereas "the basic classification 'person' does not."[91] Essentially, legal fictions have to be assessed according to their ability to create *workable*

---

[83] Achinstein, Peter, 'Theoretical Models', the British Journal for the Philosophy of Science, vol. 16/no. 62, (1965), pp. 102, p. 104-105.

[84] Samuel, Geoffrey, 'Is Law a Fiction?', in Del Mar, Maksymilian and Twining, William eds., Legal Fictions in Theory and Practice (1st edn, Springer, 2015), 31, p. 41.

[85] *Ibid*, p. 44.

[86] Del Mar, Maksymilian, 'Legal Fictions and Legal Change', International Journal of Law in Context, Vol. 9/no. 4, (2013), pp. 442, p. 457 and Lind, Douglas, 'The Pragmatic Value of Legal Fictions', in Del Mar, Maksymilian and Twining, William eds., Legal Fictions in Theory and Practice (1st edn, Springer, 2015), 83, p. 99. Upon contextually assessing legal fictions, it has to be borne in mind, according to Lind, that they may on the one hand be useful and workable in some contexts but confusing, harmful on the other or even in some contexts "stoke the flames of injustice." *Ibid*, p. 100.

[87] *Ibid*, p. 94. Part of this "general stock of beliefs" is "established truths, meanings, or understandings in some extralegal realm or within law." Lind, Douglas, 'The Pragmatic Value of Legal Fictions', in Del Mar, Maksymilian and Twining, William eds., Legal Fictions in Theory and Practice (1st edn, Springer, 2015), 83, p. 84.

[88] See Sect. 5.3.1 above.

[89] Lind, Douglas, 'The Pragmatic Value of Legal Fictions', in Del Mar, Maksymilian and Twining, William eds., Legal Fictions in Theory and Practice (1st edn, Springer, 2015), 83, p. 97 (italics in the first quote are added).

[90] *Ibid*, p. 98 (italics added).

[91] *Ibid*, p. 98.

solutions causing more efficient and functional improvements in law. In this assessment, it has to be accounted for if legal fictions *in law* actually generate "confusion or incoherence" as well if they go against settled truths in reality.[92]

In the same way, as argued by Lind, there is no singular underlying reality of the average consumer. If an analysis of the average consumer is mainly occupied with the gap between this legal model and reality, it will most likely be concluded that the average consumer is inconsistent with real life consumer perception. The average consumer should be taken for what it is—a legal model—and it should be evaluated accordingly. The average consumer is one such conceptual understanding of a person not existing in reality but only in the epistemic world, in this case within law. There is no one objective truth on what is the perception of the average consumer. This is so for several reasons. The "consumer" term "exists not only between the Member States, but even within some Member States and within the EC consumer acquis."[93] Also, consumer perception and consumer behaviour, including consumer confusion, may be judged differently according to the scientific eyes through which it is analysed. Two of the non-legal strains scarcely touched upon in this book are the law and economics' assumption of a "rational actor model" and the contrasting counterpart from behavioural science, the "behavioural man."[94] Although there is merit in discussing these areas of research, it is the stance of this book that there is no "reality extraordinaire" and that it is impossible to reach a "universal" benchmark against which to employ consumer behaviour relevant to deciding consumer confusion in trademark law.[95]

It may be questioned, what is then the value of the average consumer as a legal fiction and how is the value to be assessed? According to the outlined pragmatic approach as represented by Lind, the value has to be assessed not with the sole reference to the existing gap between reality and law. Rather from an internal viewpoint, the average consumer has to be assessed against its value *in law*. This theoretical approach underpins the analyses because they focus on an intersystemic analysis of the average consumer *in law*. Therefore, in line with legal fiction theory, the analyses focus on analysing the average consumer horizontally and vertically *in law* and not so much the gap between law and reality. That said, mainly as part of the

---

[92]*Ibid*, p. 100.

[93]Stuyck, Jules, 'Setting the Scene', in Micklitz, Hans-W. *et al* eds., Cases, Materials and Text on Consumer Law (1st edn, Ius Commune, 2010), 1, p. 29 and Reich, Norbert, Micklitz, Hans-W., and Rott, Peter, 'European Consumer Law', (2nd edn, Intersentia, 2014), p. 51. The latter authors have argued though that there are common features of the term "consumer" under Community law.

[94]See Chap. 6, Sect. 6.6.3.

[95]Even if a "reality extraordinaire" existed, it may not serve as benchmark for measuring "conceptual truths" found in law. Without pre-empting the analysis and the normative aspects of this book on how the average consumer should be, it is safe to say that the average consumer by definition is conceptualised by law. Therefore, it is not necessarily fruitful to measure this legal fiction against reality – an average consumer is not found in persona in real life as per the pragmatic theory underlying legal fictions.

contextualisation analysis[96] and normative analysis on how the average consumer *should be*,[97] the gap between law and reality will be addressed. This analysis includes a mapping out of the assumptions derived from market reality creating the foundation of the average consumer *in law*. It will be touched upon if the assumptions create an unnecessary wide gap between the average consumer and an "extra-legal" reality.

Based on the above, it is the stance that detecting a gap between the average consumer in law and real life consumer behaviour should not be the main focus of the legal analysis. As for all models that are not testable in real life, they are not intended to be replicas of real life but to create workable generalisations. The challenge is finding a workable average consumer fiction *in law*.

5.4   Legal Constructs

The terms "legal fiction" and "legal construct" both indicate something that is more or less detached from reality and something constructed in law. The terms are examples of expressions rooted in overlapping legal theory. However, there are subtle differences in how legal fictions and legal construct are perceived in legal theory. Kelsen thus stated that a legal fiction "is accompanied – or ought to be accompanied – by the awareness that reality does not agree with it." Referring to Vaihinger, Kelsen further stated that fictions "are not only in contradiction with reality but self-contradictory in themselves... To be distinguished from them are *constructs*, which only contradict reality as given, or deviate from, but are not themselves self-contradictory... The latter might be called half-fictions or semi-fictions."[98] Although from the citation it is possible to see subtle theoretical differences between fictions and constructs, it is impossible to tell whether references to "legal constructs"—by some used to describe the average consumer—are meant to be different from "legal fictions" in the meaning just outlined. In light of this book, what is most significant is that scholars and practitioners referring to legal fictions and legal constructs seem occupied with the average consumer as something detached from reality and not with the theoretical discussion of whether one or the other is "self-contradictory." Therefore, the two terms used to describe the average consumer in this book are taken to mean the same.[99]

---

[96]See Chap. 11.

[97]See Chap. 12, Sects. 12.4–12.6.

[98]Kelsen, Hans, 'General Theory of Norms', (Clarendon Press, 1991), p. 256, including footnote 2 of the text (italics added).

[99]As an illustration of the overlapping terminological use of "legal fictions" and "legal constructs" Heymann is stating "that as we teach students trademark law, we should remind them that, as in tort law, the "reasonable person" is a judicial construct-one purportedly based on empirical evidence, but a construct nonetheless." Calling the US counterpart of the average consumer a "judicial construct" Heymann refers to Dinwoodie denoting it a "legal fiction." Heymann, Laura A., 'The

5.5 Legal Concepts

The term "concept" is probably the broadest term used to describe the average consumer. As with standards, the theory underlying "concepts" also addresses the tension between rules and standards respectively deciding individuals' behaviour *ex ante* and *ex post*. This theory demarcates concepts according to whether concepts are applied by the legislature or judiciaries. Concept theory also divides concepts according to their level of abstractness and normativity. Hence, Frändberg has stated that concepts may have a "law-stating" function. Concepts with a law-stating function Frändberg has defined as "concepts that are used for stating the material legal content."[100] These law-stating concepts may be found in legal texts such as legislation.[101] Frändberg has denoted law-stating concepts as "official," if they are derived from official legal texts such as legislation, preparatory works and court decisions.[102] In terms of the abstractness of concepts, von der Pfordten has divided legal concepts into four groups according to their abstractness: First, the "most abstract concepts" (e.g. obligation). Second, "more concrete concepts" (e.g. negligence). Third, concepts "close to empirical sensations" (e.g. heavy). Fourth, the "very concrete concepts" (e.g. terms denoting chemical substances).[103]

In terms of the normative basis concepts, Tuori has stated that "in dogmatic theories and concepts, the mutual weight of the factual and the normative aspect may vary. However, the normative side is never wholly obliterated; dogmatic concepts are never exclusively about facts. Their use in adjudication has normative conse-quences, and the very enterprise of legal dogmatics has a normative."[104]

As mentioned above, "likelihood of confusion" in this book is regarded as legal standard used for steering the behaviour of individuals *ex post*. Applying Frändberg's theory to this standard, it may also be regarded as a law-stating concept used in legislation and decisions, i.e. an official law-stating concept. The average consumer also falls within the realm of an official law-stating concept, but it is only stated in court decisions. In terms of the abstractness, the average consumer may be regarded as a conceptual tool manifesting the likelihood of confusion standard into

---

Reasonable Person in Trademark Law', Saint Louis University Law Journal, vol. 52/no. 3, (2008), pp. 781, including footnote 26 of the text.

[100]Frändberg, Åke, 'An Essay on Legal Concept Formation', in Jaap C., Hage and von der Pfordten, Dietmar eds., Concepts in Law (1st edn, Springer, 2009), 1, p. 2. Concepts with a law-stating function Frändberg has also denoted "law-concepts", and "concepts of law" and concepts with a juridical-operative function are also denoted "juridical concepts" and "concepts about law."

[101]If law-stating concepts are found in legal texts, they are denoted "genuine law-stating concepts" and "official law-stating concepts." *Ibid*, p. 3.

[102]*Ibid*, p. 4.

[103]Pfordten, Dietmar von der, 'About Concepts in Law', in Hage, Jaap C. and Dietmar von der Pfordten eds., Concepts in Law (1st edn, Springer, 2009), 1, p. 29-30.

[104]Tuori, Kaarlo, 'Self-Description and External Description of the Law', NoFo vol. 2 (2006), pp. 27, p. 35.

something measurable and more concrete.[105] A red line running through this book is the average consumer imbued with normativity. In line with the claim by Tuori, the average consumer, if regarded as a concept, should not be built entirely on factual findings. At the end, the final judicial assessment of the average consumer is normative, including who/what is to be encompassed by the average consumer.[106] From a theoretical perspective as laid out above it has some merit to approach the average consumer as a concept. Using fiction theory though best encapsulates the average consumer as covering factual and normative elements. As important though, fiction theory resonates with the general use of models in other legal and scientific areas anchoring legal fictions to the broader context of scientific models. This linking is followed up on in the next chapter. Initially, the focus is on two of the neighbouring areas of trademark law, European design law and European patent law, where the "informed user" and the "person skilled in the art" respectively are found. This is followed by an account of the "reasonable person" in tort law. Outside of law, the linking finishes with an account of the "rational actor model" in economics.

---

[105]When creating concepts, Gerring has argued that linguistically concepts may be created from new or existing words. As for new words, it may be more troublesome to establish a common ground of understanding of what they mean and costlier to apply by judges and advisors. These concepts may seem arbitrary and not intuitive. Gerring, John, 'What Makes a Concept Good? A Criterial Framework for Understanding Concept Formation in the Social Sciences', Polity, vol. 31/no. 3, (1999), pp. 357, p. 361 and Kähler, Lorenz, 'The Influence of Normative Reasons on the Formation of Legal Concepts', in Hage, Jaap C. and von der Pfordten, Dietmar eds., Concepts in Law (1st edn, Springer, 2009), 81, p. 91-92. What is then often seen is the creation of concepts from words already known and combination of words where the first word qualifies the other. Murphy, Gregory L., 'The Big Book of Concepts', (1st edn, Bradford Books, 2004), p. 465. According to Kähler, "terminology constraints" may limit the number of words available for the creation of legal concepts. Kähler ibid, p. 92. On the linguistic aspects of the term "average consumer," see for instance, Chap. 8, in particular Sect. 8.7. Here it emerges that the average consumer has been developed from at least one word known to trademark law and EU law in general – "consumer." Obviously, "average" is also a known word but not from the legal world. "Average" qualifies "consumer" and on the surface, it gives the intuitive impression that it may be inferred using math who is the average consumer. As it appears, it is the stance of this book that this is not the case.

[106]As for other theories of concepts, e.g. Kähler has presented a promising theory of concepts as "evaluative" in the sense understood as "concepts that can be used both to approve and repudiate a situation or an action." The average consumer may also to a certain extent be evaluative in that it is used to decide if there is confusion or not. According to Stavropoulos, it makes more sense that a concept is developed along certain practices in a consistent manner than "invoking special, ad hoc concepts" in that "concepts don't lie around, as it were, to be picked up in support of different interpretations." Stavropoulos, Nicos, 'Objectivity in Law', (1st edn, Clarendon Press, 1996), p. 197. This presents an argument for operating a consistent average consumer in European trademark law.

5.6 Conclusion

It has been detected that the average consumer in European trademark law[107] is denoted inconsistently and incoherent with legal theory. A theoretical analysis of the average consumer was conducted, given the legislative requirement of likelihood of confusion referring to the theory of rules and standards. Initially, it was found that the legislative prevention of likelihood of confusion, judicially solidified in the global appreciation test, is a typical example of a legal standard. To be exact, the average consumer is not the legal standard as such—the legal standard is the legislative requirement of likelihood of confusion.

Subsequently, the average consumer was analysed in light of mainly legal fiction theory but also the theory of constructs and concepts. It was concluded that the average consumer in European trademark law is a legal fiction, although in this context the merit of the theories of constructs and concepts was not ruled out. Because of this, analysing the average consumer should not be seen as bipolar—as either fictional or factual—but as a model containing both normative and factual elements. That the average consumer is not found in real life is not as such a decisive finding. The focus should be to create a *workable* fiction *in law*. The analysis of trademark law in the below chapters will therefore focus on the ability of the average consumer fiction to create coherence and consistency *in law* as the main indicators of "workability." Two functions of legal fictions are particularly relevant in this context: First, to analyse the presumptions of reality used as part of the average consumer and second, intertwined with this function, the average consumer as a way of suspending certain operative facts. These functions feed into the judicial development of the average consumer. Potentially, the more normative the average consumer is, the more power is allocated to the appellate courts and the Court of Justice as the ultimate interpreter of EU trademark law. If the average consumer is more descriptive, potentially more power is left for the courts adjudicating disputes on their operative facts, i.e. the General Court and national courts within their areas of competence.

---

[107]This includes certain references to adjacent areas of law – i.e. the UCPD.

Chapter 6
The Average Consumer and Its More or Less Distant Cousins

6.1 Introduction

The discussion on legal fictions is not only relevant to European trademark law but also in other areas of law and in economics. One just has to turn to the neighbouring legal areas, EU design law and European patent law operating respectively "the informed user" and "the person skilled in the art" used to calibrate the protectability and scope of the exclusive rights. Referring to these legal fictions, LJ Lewison in *Interflora EWCA I* held that the average consumer "enters the pantheon of characters who inhabit the world of intellectual property alongside his fellows."[1] The discussion on these "fellow" fictions takes its starting in *PepsiCo v. Grupo Promer* from 2011 on the invalidity of a community design where the Court of Justice made an important statement on the characteristics of the informed user vis-à-vis the average consumer and the "sectoral expert" (the "person skilled in the art").[2] Outside of intellectual property law, in tort law, "the reasonable person" is used to decide the standard of care. In tort law parallels between the US trademark law cousin to the average consumer, "the reasonably prudent consumer," and the "reasonable man"

---

[1] Specifically, LJ Lewison referred to "internet users" in trademark law, but for this reference, this seemed to encompass the "character" usually "inhibiting" trademark law, i.e. the average consumer. Interflora v. Marks & Spencer, [2012] EWCA Civ 1501, para 13.

[2] See PepsiCo v. Grupo Promer, Case C-281/10 P, [2011] ECR I-10153, in particular paras 53 and 59. "Sectoral expert" is another phrasing used to describe the "person skilled in the art" in patent law. Discussing the subject of the laws of patents, designs and trademarks, Pila has recently also linked the "fellow fictions" in these areas of law, holding that "it is clear that the ability of a certain hypothetical intelligent individual to single out each subject matter for which protection is sought as a distinct object of perception is central to its legal status as a subject matter of protectable type." Pila, Justine, 'The Subject Matter of Intellectual Property', (1st edn, Oxford University Press, 2017), p. 18.

© Springer Nature Switzerland AG 2020   149
R. D. Laustsen, *The Average Consumer in Confusion-based Disputes in European Trademark Law and Similar Fictions*, https://doi.org/10.1007/978-3-030-26350-8_6

are commonplace.[3] Koktvedgaard has made a similar comparison in a Nordic perspective.[4] The comparison makes sense since a certain reasonableness is infused into the average consumer as its characteristics are *"reasonably* well-informed and *reasonably* observant and circumspect."[5]

The intention of paralleling the average consumer with its counterparts in other areas of intellectual property law and tort law is not to analyse these areas of law thoroughly, but to provide sufficient background knowledge to set out the purpose and application of those other fictions. As for the design law, focus will be on the *EU* design law, i.e. the "Design Regulation"[6] and "Design Directive"[7] (jointly "EU design legislation"), as interpreted by the CJEU, mainly the Court of Justice. The focus of patent law will be *European* patent law as manifested in the European Patent Convention (the "EPC")[8] as interpreted mainly by the European Patent Office (the "EPO") as part of registering European patents.[9]

Private law, including tort law, is not as such harmonised in the EU or Europe. As held by van Dam though, "European private law generally, and European tort law in particular, is buzzing with activity."[10] Some of those activities are certain "harmonization initiatives." One is the Principles, Definitions and Model Rules of European Private Law manifested in a Draft Common Frame of Reference with book VI designated to "Non-contractual liability arising out of damage cause to another" (in the 2009 edition the "DCFR").[11] Another is the Principles of European Tort Law of 2005 ("PETL") drafted by the European Group on Tort Law.[12] The committees behind the DCFR and PETL consist of a multitude of academics from mainly European countries. The DCFR and PETL express some general European

---

[3]On those findings based on case law, see among others, Heymann, Laura A., 'The Reasonable Person in Trademark Law', Saint Louis University Law Journal, vol. 52/no. 3, (2008), pp. 781, p. 782 and Kirkpatrick, Richard L., 'Likelihood of Confusion in Trademark Law', (1st edn, Practising Law Institute, 1995), p. 24-25, including footnote 76 of the text.

[4]See below, Sect. 6.5.

[5]See for instance, Gut Springenheide and Tusky, Case C-210/96, [1998] ECR I-4657, para 37 (italics added).

[6]Council Regulation (EC) No 6/2002 of 12 December 2001 on Community designs, [2002] OJ L 3/1.

[7]EP and Council Directive 98/71/EC of 13 October 1998 on the legal protection of designs, [1998] OJ L 289/28.

[8]The European Patent Convention 16th edition of June 2016.

[9]The definition of "European patents" is below in footnote 72.

[10]Dam, Cees van, 'European Tort Law', (2nd edn, Oxford University Press, 2013), p. 130. Van Dam continues in an almost poetic way holding that "[a]cademic bees are tirelessly collecting the pollen of national flowers and bringing it to the European hive where the queen bee of European harmony is looking on with approval." *Ibid.*

[11]Von Bar, Christian *et al* eds., 'Principles, Definitions and Model Rules of European Private Law – Draft Common Frame of Reference (DCFR) Outline Edition', (1st edn, Sellier European Law Publishers, 2009).

[12]European Group on Tort Law, Principles of European Tort Law, of May 2005, available at: http://civil.udg.edu/php/biblioteca/items/283/PETL.pdf (last visited 26 May 2019).

principles of tort law. Those principles and legal literature will be the basis of the analysis of the reasonable person in European tort law.[13]

Moving outside of law, fictions, also understood as models, are part of everyday scientific research. One such model is the "rational actor model" in Economics. Recently, Davies has suggested, "that when the TM Directive was adopted the idea of a *rational, average consumer was a key assumption of the prevailing neo-classical economic orthodoxy*," hence clearly linking the average consumer to economics' rational actor model.[14] Focus in this context will be distilling some principles from theoretical economics, enough to understanding the assumption made by Davies and others of the average consumer as rational in a "neo-classical economic" sense. In this context, insights from recent scholarship on behavioural law and economics challenging the assumptions underlying the rational actor model are also considered.[15] The aim of drawing on economics and behavioural economics is to create a better ground for understanding the average consumer in a broader scientific context, given other social science models.

Based on the connection between the above-mentioned fictions in other areas of law and in economics, this chapter will finish by establishing a link to those other fictions. As it appears in *PepsiCo v. Grupo Promer* and *Interflora EWCA I* and authoritative legal literature, the comparison with other legal fictions and the rational actor model is relevant. Essentially, this comparison is used to establish on which broader grounds the average consumer stands, and what the average consumer and its characteristics *is* and *is not*. The comparison with an economic model anchors the average consumer in a scientific tradition of using models. At least in social science, these models share some common characteristics. The result of the comparison will impart a more profound understanding of the average consumer relevant to the

---

[13]See Dam, Cees van, 'European Tort Law', (2nd edn, Oxford University Press, 2013), chapters 2 – 6. In van Dam's words the broader principles, e.g. expressed in DCFR and PETL, should only be "the new starting points for discussion." According to van Dam, differences between various jurisdictions are a symptom of underlying differences "economically, culturally, and politically." These general differences are addressed for the relevant trademark law jurisdictions in Chap. 2, Sect. 2.3. These differences in tort law should be appreciated in "respect for the role each system can play in an ever growing and intense discourse on the way forward in a diverse European tort law." *Ibid*, p. 163-164. The analysis in this section is intentionally kept at the overall European level of principles (the start point level).

[14]Davis, Jennifer, 'Revisiting the Average Consumer: An Uncertain Presence in European Trade Mark', Intellectual Property Quarterly, no. 1, (2015), pp. 15, p. 16 (italics added). See also Trzaskowski, Jan, 'Behavioural Economics, Neuroscience, and the Unfair Commercial Practises Directive', Journal of Consumer Policy, vol. 34/no. 3, (2011), pp. 377, p. 386-387 and Incardona, Rossella, and Poncibò, Cristina, 'The Average Consumer, the Unfair Commercial Practices Directive, and the Cognitive Revolution', Journal of Consumer Policy, vol. 30/no. 1, (2007), pp. 21, p. 30 referring to Posner. Concluding their analysis, Incardona and Poncibò have claimed that "[t]he average consumer test reflects the economists' idealistic paradigm of a rational consumer in an efficient marketplace." *Ibid*, p. 35.

[15]For a definition of the "rational actor model" and the challenges of this model, see Parisi, Francesco, 'The Language of Law and Economics. A Dictionary', (1st edn, Cambridge University Press, 2013), p. 245-246.

further analyses. As seen so far, the other legal and economic fictions referred to in this chapter are also referred to as the more or less distant "cousins" of the average consumer.[16]

6.2 EU Design Law: The "Informed User"

6.2.1 Background

Before introducing the EU design legislation, there were significant differences between the national design laws. According to a green paper on "the legal protection of industrial design" from 1991 drafted by the EU Commission (the "Design Green Paper"),[17] "[t]he fragmentation of the Community into different national markets is incompatible with the creation of Internal market conditions." Therefore, "[a] Community protection system with a single registration" was needed.[18] One significant purpose of a common EU design protection was described by the Design Green Paper as the opportunity of companies to "rely on legal protection for their products in order to recoup the investment which design development entails."[19] It has recently been pointed out by Campinos, executive director of the EUIPO, that with the increased importance of "product differentiation and product appeal," design protection has become more recognised.[20] In 2017 though, the total number of filings for registration of EU trademarks outdid ditto for registration of Community designs with approximately 37,000.[21] The ratio found in registration between EU trademarks and Community designs does not echo in the number of cases heard by the Court of Justice.[22]

As with EU trademark law, EU design legislation consists of two prongs, a regulation and a directive. Under the EU design legislation, it is possible to obtain both an unregistered Community Design Right[23] and via the EUIPO a registered

---

[16]On this phrasing, see below Sect. 6.6.2.

[17]Commission Green Paper on the legal protection of industrial design No 111/51311/91 of June 1991.

[18]*Ibid*, p. 2.

[19]*Ibid*, p. 33.

[20]Campinos, António, 'Foreword', in Hasselblatt, Gordian N. ed., Community Trade Mark Regulation (EC) no 207/2009: A Commentary (1st edn, Beck/Hart, 2015), p. vii.

[21]The total number of trademark filings (direct and through international designations) was 146,409 and ditto design filings 109,728. See 2017 EUIPO Annual Report, available at: https://euipo.europa.eu/tunnel-web/secure/webdav/guest/document_library/contentPdfs/about_euipo/annual_report/annual_report_2017_en.pdf (last visited 26 May 2019), respectively p. 19 and 22.

[22]A search conducted in the CURIA database indicates that in 2017 the number of trademark cases heard by the Court of Justice, including appeals and preliminary rulings, was 49 for trademarks and 3 for designs.

[23]Cf. art. 1(2)(a) of the Design Regulation.

design right.[24] Through the Design Directive, as implemented into national design legislation, it is possible to obtain a national design right via the national industrial property offices[25]; however, the directive leaves room for national protection of unregistered design rights.[26] In line with the focus on trademark law, this section only addresses the registered rights. Under the EU design legislation, a "design" is defined as "the appearance of the whole or a part of a product resulting from the features of, in particular, the lines, contours, colours, shape, texture and/or materials of the product itself and/or its ornamentation."[27]

The "informed user" in EU design law is, akin to the average consumer, relevant as part of a gatekeeper function in registration/validation and in the calibration of the scope of protection in infringement disputes.[28] For EU design legislation, as with EU Trademark Legislation, there is a mirroring of a standard between the registration and infringement scenarios. In EU Trademark Legislation, this is the likelihood of confusion standard, whereas in EU design legislation the legislative standard in registration and infringement is "the overall impression."[29]

Deciding the protectability, a design may be protected under the EU design legislation "to the extent that it is *new* and has *individual character*."[30] In qualifying *individual character* it emerges in the legislation that "[a] design shall be considered to have *individual character if the overall impression it produces on the informed user differs from the overall impression produced on such a user by any design which has been made available to the public.*"[31] In the recitals of the legislation it

---

[24]Cf. art. 1(2)(b) of the Design Regulation. Unlike the EU Trademark, the EU unified design right still bears the prefix Community.

[25]Cf. art. 2 of the Design Directive, the directive applies to the registered design rights.

[26]Cf. art. 16 of the Design Directive on the "[r]elationship to other forms of protection"

"The provisions of this Directive shall be without prejudice to any provisions of Community law or of the law of the Member State concerned relating to unregistered design rights, trade marks or other distinctive signs, patents and utility models, typefaces, civil liability or unfair competition."

[27]Cf. art. 3(a) of the Design Regulation and art. 1(a) of the Design Directive.

[28]Some general commentaries on the informed user: on the Design Regulation: in Stone, David, 'European Union Design Law. A Practitioners' Guide', (2nd edn, Oxford University Press, 2016), p. 209-229 and Hasselblatt, Gordian N., 'Article 5: Novelty', in Hasselblatt, Gordian N. ed., Community Design Law: A Commentary (1st edn, Beck/Hart, 2015), 67, p. 71-72 and Brückner-Hofmann, Johanna, 'Article 6: Individual Character', in Hasselblatt, Gordian N. ed., Community Design Law: A Commentary (1st edn, Beck/Hart, 2015), 78, p. 81-82. A Danish perspective: Schovsbo, Jens, and Svendsen, Niels Holm, 'Designret: Designloven Med Kommentarer', (2nd edn, Jurist- og Økonomforbundets Forlag, 2013), p. 122-125.

[29]Registration: art. 6(1) of the Design Regulation and art. 5(1) of the Design Directive. Infringement: art. 10(1) of the Design Regulation and art. 9(1) of the Design Directive.

[30]Art. 4(1) of the Design Regulation and art. 3(2) of the Design Directive. As for the novelty requirement, it appears in art. 4 of the Design Directive that "[a] design shall be considered new if no identical design has been made available to the public before the date of filing of the application for registration or, if priority is claimed, the date of priority. Designs shall be deemed to be identical if their features differ only in immaterial details." Also, art. 5(1)(b) and (2) of the Design Regulation.

[31]Cf. art. 6(1) of the Design Regulation and art. 5(1) of the Design Directive.

appears that this assessment is to be conducted "taking into consideration the nature of the product to which the design is applied or in which it is incorporated, and in particular the industrial sector to which it belongs and the degree of freedom of the designer in developing the design."[32] Subsequently, a design registration may be invalidated.[33]

Under EU design legislation, "[t]he scope of the protection conferred by a Community [or national] design shall include any design which does *not produce on the informed user* a different overall impression."[34] One important difference between "individual character" and "scope of protection" is that as part of the latter, "there is no degree of individual character." Deciding on the scope of protection requires an examination of "the distance between the design and existing design corpus. A Community design may have a small or a large scope of protection, but it cannot have a smaller or greater individual character."[35] A claim for invalidation rarely turns on the novelty requirement but on individual character, including the "the overall impression" produced "on the informed user." This aspect is also the key parameter in infringement disputes.[36]

It emerges that the legislation mentions the informed user and that the phrasing used for this design law model differs from the Court of Justice's phrasing on the average consumer. The *user* compared to *consumer* is neutral and broader. Also, there is no qualifying prefix of *informed* as seen in the early stages of the average consumer in "the *averagely well-informed* consumer,"[37] and the informed user does not resonate with the nowadays characteristics of the average consumer as "reasonably well-informed and reasonably observant and circumspect." It thus appears that the EU legislature in explicitly using the informed user as part of deciding the "overall impression" standard, and not leaving as big a gap to be filled out, ultimately the Court of Justice has sought to clearly distance the design law model from that of trademark law. It should be mentioned though, that a significant gap is still left for the Court of Justice to actually decide who/what is the informed user and his/its

---

[32]Recital 14 of the Design Regulation and recital 13 of the Design Directive. Reference to the "freedom of the designer" is also found in the legislation as such for registration: art. 6(2) of the Design Regulation and art. 5(2) of the Design Directive. For infringement: art. 10(2) of the Design Regulation and art. 9(2) of the Design Directive. On the understanding of "freedom of the designer," see in particular PepsiCo v. Grupo Promer, Case C-281/10 P, [2011] ECR I-10153, paras 43-45.

[33]There are several grounds for invalidity. One of them is that the design lacks novelty and individual character, cf. art. 25(1)(b), cf. arts. 4, 5 and 6 of the Design Regulation and art. 11(1) (b), cf. arts. 3, 4 and 5 of the Design Directive.

[34]Cf. art. 10(1) of the Design Regulation and art. 9(1) of the Design Directive (italics added).

[35]Brückner-Hofmann, Johanna, 'Article 6: Individual Character', in Hasselblatt, Gordian N. ed., Community Design Law: A Commentary (1st edn, Beck/Hart, 2015), 78, p. 80-81.

[36]See Stone, David, 'European Union Design Law. A Practitioners' Guide', (2nd edn, Oxford University Press, 2016), p. 206 and Brückner-Hofmann, Johanna, 'Article 6: Individual Character', in Hasselblatt, Gordian N. ed., Community Design Law: A Commentary (1st edn, Beck/Hart, 2015), 78, p. 116.

[37]See Van Bennekom, Case 227/82, [1983] ECR 3883, para 18 (italics added). On the development of the average consumer by the Court of Justice, see Chap. 8.

characteristics. The incentive to this distancing may have been spurred by substantial reasons as addressed below, but also by the jurisprudential environment at the time of introducing the Design Directive in October 1998 where the development of the immature average consumer model had taken place by.[38]

6.2.2 Pepsi v. Grupo Promer: Changing the Script?[39]

In *Pepsi v. Grupo Promer*, the Court of Justice for the first time interpreted what was to be understood by "individual character," including the informed user. This was much needed due to the EU design legislation not defining the informed user. This lacking definition provided a potential opening for a beating around the bush by the European judiciaries and industrial property offices. According to Stone,[40] some national courts before *Pepsi v. Grupo Promer* had solely negatively defined the informed user as *not* being: "a mere end user, designer manufacturer, product design expert, person in the street, person skilled in the art [or] an average consumer as discussed in trade mark cases."[41] The historical finding of Stone in design law is presumably more prominent if transferred to European trademark law, where the national courts pre-*Sabel* had even less guidance on the "character" "inhibiting" trademark law, i.e. "the relevant public" phrasing found in the recitals.[42]

In *Pepsi v. Grupo Promer*, Pepsi had obtained a registration of a Community design for certain "promotional item[s] for games." Based on a prior national right, Grupo sought to have the design registration invalidated.[43] OHIM upheld the invalidation whereas the OHIM Board of Appeal annulled that decision. The General Court annulled that decision of the board of appeal, since Pepsi's design

---

[38]The directive was introduced after all the decisions mentioned in Chap. 8 on "the early days of the average consumer," and before *Sabel* from November 1997 and *Gut Springenheide* from 1998.

[39]The latter part of the heading is inspired by the Pepsi slogan from 1996 "Change the Script."

[40]One of the most significant voices in European design practice and literature.

[41]Stone, David, 'European Union Design Law. A Practitioners' Guide', (2nd edn, Oxford University Press, 2016), p. 214-215. Stone has based his findings on the case law of the courts of England and Wales and Austria. Since it is beyond this book to go into national case law on design law, no independent analysis of the national decisions is conducted. Stone has also detected some positive definitions in national case law of the informed user.

[42]See Chap. 10.

[43]The legal basis for the invalidation claim was art. 25(1)(b) and (d) of the Design Regulation. "Article 25 (1) A Community design may be declared invalid only in the following cases: (b) if it does not fulfil the requirements of Articles 4 to 9; (...) (d) if the Community design is in conflict with a prior design which has been made available to the public after the date of filing of the application or, if a priority is claimed, the date of priority of the Community design, and which is protected from a date prior to the said date by a registered Community design or an application for such a design, or by a registered design right of a Member State, or by an application for such a right;" It will be recalled that "individual character" decided referring to the informed user is decided under art. 6 of the Design Regulation.

lacked individual character.[44] To be exact, the status before reaching the Court of Justice was an invalidation of Pepsi's design. A significant part of the decision of the Court of Justice turned around interpreting "individual character" and the understanding of "informed user."

The second ground of appeal before the Court of Justice concerned the informed user and "his" level of attention.[45] Before the Court of Justice, Pepsi submitted that the designs at stake "conveyed a different overall impression on the 'informed user'" and that the "informed user was not the average consumer known from trademark law or merely the end user of the goods at issue."[46] Countering this, Grupo submitted, "that the General Court did not apply criteria concerning trade mark law such as the likelihood of confusion between the two conflicting designs at issue." In addition, Pepsi submitted that the informed user was to conduct the comparison of the designs "side by side and, in contrast to the position in trade mark law, does not have to rely on an 'imperfect recollection'."[47] Grupo argued that the question on the informed user's recollection was a matter of fact and hence not a question to be decided on by the Court of Justice.[48]

The Court of Justice initially held that the informed user "must be understood as lying somewhere between that of the *average consumer*, applicable in trade mark matters, who need not have any specific knowledge and who, as a rule, makes no direct comparison between the trade marks in conflict, and the *sectoral expert*, who is an expert with detailed technical expertise." Based on this, "the informed user may be understood as referring, not to a user of average attention, but to a particularly observant one, either because of his personal experience or his extensive knowledge

---

[44]For further on the background of the decision, see PepsiCo v. Grupo Promer, Case C-281/10 P, [2011] ECR I-10153, paras 9-35.

[45]*Ibid*, paras 47-61.

[46]*Ibid*, para 47.

[47]*Ibid*, para 48. As party to the case, OHIM supported Pepsi's argument. *Ibid*, para 51.

[48]*Ibid*, para 52. Although Grupo Promer did not explicitly state that the consequence of being a matter of fact was that, the Court of Justice had to not assess the issue. However, this is the consequence of factual of matters, unless the facts have been distorted. See also Chap. 1, Sect. 1.5.4.

of the sector in question."⁴⁹ The informed user will only, to the extent it is practically possible, make a direct comparison of the designs at stake.⁵⁰

It is already clear that there is no "one-size-fit-all" informed user but that the informed user has to be moulded according to the factual scenario to which it is applied. With that in mind, in *Pepsi v. Grupo Promer,* the Court of Justice therefore did not challenge the General Court referring to the OHIM Board of Appeal upholding "that the informed user could be a child in the approximate age range of 5 to 10 or a marketing manager in a company that makes goods which are promoted."⁵¹ Seemingly unfounded, the board of appeal stated as accepted by the General Court, that "[i]t makes little difference which of these categories of person is

---

⁴⁹*Ibid*, para 53 (italics added). Reference is also made by the Court of Justice to the opinion of Advocate General Mengozzi preceding the decision, i.e. PepsiCo v. Grupo Promer, Case C-281/10 P, [2011] ECR I-10153, (opinion of AG Mengozzi), paras 43-44. Recently, the Court of Justice has confirmed this finding in Easy Sanitary Solutions v. Group Nivelles, Joined Cases C-361/15 P and C-405/15 P, [2017], para 124. See also Herbert Neuman and Andoni Galdeano v. OHIM, Joined Cases C-101/11 P and C-102/11 P, [2012], para 53. Interestingly, to support his opinion in PepsiCo v. Grupo Promer, Mengozzi referred to the preparatory works of the Commission Proposal for a European Parliament and Council Regulation on the Community Design COM(93) 342 final-COD 463 of 3 December 1993, (the "Design Regulation Proposal"), p. 20. As referred to by Mengozzi: "The person on whom an overall impression of dissimilarity must be made is an "informed user"." This may be, but is not necessarily, the end consumer who may be unaware of the appearance of the product for example if it is an internal part of a machine or a mechanical device replaced in the course of a repair. In such cases, the "informed user" is the person replacing the part. A certain level of knowledge or design awareness is presupposed depending on the character of the design. But the term "informed user" should indicate also that the similarity is not to be assessed at the level of "design experts". The Design Regulation Proposal, p. 12 referred to by Mengozzi in his opinion para 44, including footnote 16 of the opinion. It also appears in the proposal, elaborating on the scope of protection, that "the overall impression created on an ordinary consumer, in the sense that the "informed user" may find striking differences, which would totally escape the attention of an ordinary consumer. Much depends on the character of the design." The Design Regulation Proposal, p. 15-16.

⁵⁰PepsiCo v. Grupo Promer, Case C-281/10 P, [2011] ECR I-10153, para 55. The Court of Justice referred to Mengozzi holding that in case where "designs relating to goods which – because of their large size or because they have to be placed far apart – can never, generally speaking, be set alongside one another: an informed user will not always be in a position to make a direct comparison of, for instance, two boats or two large items of industrial equipment." PepsiCo v. Grupo Promer, Case C-281/10 P, [2011] ECR I-10153, (opinion of AG Mengozzi), para 51. Consequently, it may have to be decided based on the facts of the case that no side-by-side comparison will be made by the informed user. *Ibid*, para 52. See also the Court of Justice in Karen Millen v. Dunnes Stores, Case C-345/13, [2014], paras 26-27.

⁵¹PepsiCo v. Grupo Promer, Case C-281/10 P, [2011] ECR I-10153, para 54, cf. Grupo Promer v. OHIM, Case T-9/07, [2010], ECR II-981, para 64. The quote is taken from the General Court's decision. The Board of Appeal stated that the informed user "could be a child in the approximate age range of 5 to 10 years, since the products are promotional items intended for young children. Alternatively, the informed user could be a marketing manager in a company that makes biscuits or potato snacks, since these are the typical products which are promoted by giving away small flat disks known in Spanish as *tazos* and in English as 'rappers' or 'pogs'." Pepsi v. Grupo Promer, Case R 1003/2005-3, [2006], para 16.

treated as the informed user. The point is that both will be familiar with the phenomenon of rappers."[52]

The Court of Justice maintained that the informed user did not possess the same characteristics of neither the *average consumer* nor the "*expert* or *specialist* capable of observing in detail the minimal differences that may exist between the designs in conflict." Consequently, "the qualifier 'informed' suggests that, without being a designer or a technical expert, the user knows the various designs which exist in the sector concerned, possesses a certain degree of knowledge with regard to the features which those designs normally include, and, as a result of his interest in the products concerned, shows a relatively high degree of attention when he uses them."[53] As for the fact/law divide, the Court of Justice found that the General Court had not been incorrect "in defining the informed user," including its level of attention.[54]

The expansive reference to the arguments of the parties and the finding of the CJEU clearly link to a central question in intellectual property law highlighted in Chap. 1 referring to Fromer and Lemley. When is the junior right holder's intellectual property asset "too similar in some respect to the plaintiff's?" The "audience" according to Fromer and Lemley is decisive on this matter—i.e. *in casu* the informed user.[55] Hence, referring to European design law, Stone has stressed that if the informed user possesses a high degree of "product knowledge and experience" then it is more likely that a junior design will create an overall impression different from the senior design. Hence, it is more likely that the junior design will be registered. This consequence of a knowledgeable and experienced informed user in infringement is that it is less likely for there to be an infringement.[56] These findings resonate well with the average consumer in trademark law.

Judge Brücker-Hofmann has stated that, although the informed user is "in most decisions personalised, it seems that the Invalidity Division as well as the General Court and the Courts throughout the EU are about to adopt the definition of the CJ

---

[52]This finding was more or less repeated verbatim by the General Court. Grupo Promer v. OHIM, Case T-9/07, [2010], ECR II-981, para 65. It was furthermore stated by the Board of Appeal that "[t] he appellant [Pepsi] proved by means of documents annexed to its reply that it has been marketing its tazos since 1995 and that Spanish newspapers were talking about *tazomanía* as early as 1998." Pepsi v. Grupo Promer, Case R 1003/2005-3, [2006], para 17. The General Court did not explicitly refer to this finding but more general to paras 16-17 of the Board of Appeal decision.

[53]PepsiCo v. Grupo Promer, Case C-281/10 P, [2011] ECR I-10153, para 59. This finding was confirmed by the Court of Justice in Easy Sanitary Solutions v. Group Nivelles, Joined Cases C-361/15 P and C-405/15 P, [2017], para 125.

[54]*Ibid*, para 60. As for the specific comparison of the designs by the General Court with a "view from above," Pepsi held that the facts had been distorted allowing the Court of Justice to replace the factual assessment. The Court of Justice rejected this argument. See *ibid*, paras 76-82.

[55]Fromer, Jeanne C., and Lemley, Mark A., 'The Audience in Intellectual Property Infringement', Michigan Law Review, vol. 112/no. 7, (2014), pp. 1251, p. 1252. See Chap. 1, Sect. 1.1.

[56]Stone, David, 'European Union Design Law. A Practitioners' Guide', (2nd edn, Oxford University Press, 2016), p. 210. See also Bently, Lionel, Sherman, Brad, Gangjee, Dev and Johnson, Phillip 'Intellectual Property Law', (5th edn, Oxford University Press, 2018), p. 775.

[Court of Justice] and follow the idea of an informed user as a *fictional person* with certain knowledge as defined by the CJ." The judge has seen this as leading to more consistency in the EU.[57] *Pepsi v. Grupo Promer* has gotten an icier reception by Stone though. Stone has sharply criticised the position of the Court of Justice in *Pepsi v. Grupo Promer* in its endorsement of the informed user as consisting of two different user groups: "The approach is wrong, and should be abandoned."[58] Supporting this statement, Stone has argued that the informed user test should continue as "an objective legal assessment: not divorced from reality, but not weighed down with the imaginings of exactly who the informed user is."[59] Furthermore, there is no legislative support for arguing that there are more than one informed user.[60] In sum, "[t]he informed user is a *legal fiction*, to be objectively assessed. Only one is required. A range of personalities is not necessary"[61] and there is "no place for surveys of 'informed users' in design cases in European Union."[62] Along the lines of the opinion of Stone, Tritton *et al* have described the informed user test as objective, stressing, "that it is not the judge's personal overall impression but the impression on the "informed user". Thus, hypothetically, courts should always come to the same conclusion on this." According to Tritton *et al* though, "since the "informed user" will often not be the everyday public," expert evidence may be relevant.[63] In laying out the test of the informed user, Musker has held that it

---

[57]Brückner-Hofmann, Johanna, 'Article 6: Individual Character', in Hasselblatt, Gordian N. ed., Community Design Law: A Commentary (1st edn, Beck/Hart, 2015), 78, p. 82-83 (italics added). Similarly, the informed user is called in a "fictitious person" in the EUIPO guidelines of EU designs. See Guidelines for Examination of Registered Community Designs EUIPO on the Examination of Design Invalidity Applications, Draft Version 1.0 of 1 October 2018 are available at: https://euipo. europa.eu/ohimportal/da/draft-design-guidelines-2018 (last visited 26 May 2019), p. 34.

[58]Stone, David, 'European Union Design Law – Highlights of Recent Case Law from the Court of Justice', IP Litigator, vol. January/February (2013), pp. 32, p. 33. See also Stone, David, 'European Union Design Law. A Practitioners' Guide', (2nd edn, Oxford University Press, 2016), p. 219.

[59]Stone, David, 'European Union Design Law – Highlights of Recent Case Law from the Court of Justice', IP Litigator, vol. January/February (2013), pp. 32, p. 220. Stone builds his arguments in this context on findings of national courts.

[60]*Ibid*, p. 222.

[61]Stone, David, 'European Union Design Law. A Practitioners' Guide', (2nd edn, Oxford University Press, 2016), p. 222 (italics added) and earlier Stone, David, 'European Union Design Law – Highlights of Recent Case Law from the Court of Justice', IP Litigator, vol. January/February (2013), p. 33. See also Brückner-Hofmann holding that "this person [the informed user] is fictional, a legal construct and it is not defined in the CDR [Design Regulation]." Brückner-Hofmann, Johanna, 'Article 6: Individual Character', in Hasselblatt, Gordian N. ed., Community Design Law: A Commentary (1st edn, Beck/Hart, 2015), 78, p. 81.

[62]Stone, David, 'European Union Design Law. A Practitioners' Guide', (2nd edn, Oxford University Press, 2016), p. 229.

[63]Davis, Richard, St Quintin, Thomas and Tritton, Guy, 'Tritton on Intellectual Property in Europe', (5th edn, Sweet & Maxwell, 2018), p. 696-697.

is objective "rather than a subjective test, based on the conduct of the designer."[64] Recently, in *DOCERAM v. CeramTec*, the Court of Justice had to decide how to assess if a design was dictated exclusively by its technical function. Here, the Court of Justice indirectly revisited its understanding of the informed user. The court was asked by the Higher Regional Court, Düsseldorf if this assessment had to be made by "an "objective observer" (. . .) and, if so, how is such an observer to be defined?"[65] Although the substance of the provision as such is irrelevant for the analysis, the court and Advocate General Saugmandsgaard Øe giving the opinion in the case made some generally relevant observations on the informed user.

Initially, Saugmandsgaard Øe questioned if "whether or not reasoning should be based on a hypothetical person whose presumed assessment would serve as an archetype."[66] Leaning on the known "person" from EU design law, the informed user, the Advocate General stated that "the informed user is not necessarily able to distinguish, beyond the experience gained by using the product concerned, the aspects of the appearance of the product which are dictated by the product's technical function from those which are arbitrary." Also, that "[t]he application of Article 8(1) of Regulation No 6/2002 [EU Design Regulation] actually necessitates a technical assessment, which requires specific skills that even an 'informed' user does not always have."[67] As an *obiter dictum*, Saugmandsgaard Øe correctly noted that "if the 'objective observer' criterion were to be accepted, this would raise a whole series of additional difficulties in defining this artificially created category and how it should be used, if only as regards the type and level of knowledge that such a person should possess."[68] It was rejected by the Court of Justice (agreeing with Saugmandsgaard Øe) that an objective observer should not be applied for the assessment of technical functionality.[69]

Based on *DOCERAM v. CeramTec*, it appears that the applicable legal fiction in EU design law still is the informed user as it was laid down by the Court of Justice in *Pepsi v. Grupo Promer*, and not an objective observer (or other possible legal fictions).

---

[64]Musker, David C., 'Community Design Regulation, Art. 6', in Gielen, Charles and von Bomhard, Verena eds., Concise European Trade Mark and Design Law (2nd edn, Kluwer Law International, 2017), 640, p. 640.

[65]DOCERAM v. CeramTec, Case C-395/16, [2018], para 16.

[66]DOCERAM v. CeramTec, Case C-395/16, [2018] (opinion of AG Saugmandsgaard Øe), para 55. Saugmandsgaard Øe noted that the defendant introduced the "objective observer" terminology into the case based on legal literature and one OHIM Board of Appeal decision. *Ibid*, para 56.

[67]*Ibid*, para 58. This observation, Saugmandsgaard Øe based on General Court case law. See, *ibid*, including footnote 68 of the opinion.

[68]*Ibid*, para 61.

[69]DOCERAM v. CeramTec, Case C-395/16, [2018], paras 37-38.

6.3 European Patent Law: The "Person Skilled in the Art"

6.3.1 Background

The direct link to European patent law is the use in patent law of a "person skilled in the art" or the synonymous "sectoral expert" as referred to by the Court of Justice in *Pepsi v. Grupo Promer*. It is clear from the court's finding dealt with above that on a scale of attentiveness the average consumer in trademark law is the least attentive, the sectoral expert the most attentive with the informed user in design law nesting somewhere in between. It will be recalled based on *Pepsi v. Grupo Promer* that a sectoral expert "is an expert with detailed technical expertise."[70] The person skilled in the art is not found in *EU* law, but in *European* patent law. Leaving aside the international aspects of patent law, such as the minimum standards found in the Paris Convention and the TRIPS Agreement,[71] the relevant legislative text is the EPC as interpreted by the EPO when registering European patents.[72] Essentially, the *European patent* is a bundle of patents granted in certain designated European countries hence the term is "something of misnomer."[73] The focus of this section is analysing how the person skilled in the art in registration and opposition proceedings has been interpreted and framed by the EPO and its boards of appeals.[74] Some references for illustration are made though to national decisions and the protection of patented inventions against certain equivalent inventions outside the literal scope of the patent claims.

The EPC encompasses 38 European states, including all the EU members and Norway. Although the EPC lays down rules on issuing patents, it only stipulates the

---

[70]PepsiCo v. Grupo Promer, Case C-281/10 P, [2011] ECR I-10153, para 53 referring to the opinion of Advocate General Mengozzi preceding the decision, i.e. Pepsi v. Grupo Promer, Case C-281/10 P, [2011] ECR I-10153, (opinion of AG Mengozzi), paras 43-44. See also footnote 49 above.

[71]It appears in art. 27(1) of the TRIPS Agreement that, subject to certain discretionary exemptions, "patents shall be available for any inventions, whether products or processes, in all fields of technology, provided that they are new, involve an inventive step and are capable of industrial application."

[72]"European patents" are defined in art. 2 of the EPC: "(1) Patents granted under this Convention shall be called European patents. (2) The European patent shall, in each of the Contracting States for which it is granted, have the effect of and be subject to the same conditions as a national patent granted by that State, unless this Convention provides otherwise."

[73]Waelde, Charlotte, Brown, Abbe, Kheria, Smita *et al*, 'Contemporary Intellectual Property: Law and Policy', (4th edn, Oxford University Press, 2016), p. 374.

[74]Decisions of the EPO (the examining and opposition divisions) may be appealed to the boards of appeal. There are 28 technical boards of appeal, a legal board of appeal, the Enlarged Board of Appeal and finally the Disciplinary Board of Appeal. For a fuller description of the boards of appeals, see: https://www.epo.org/about-us/boards-of-appeal.html (last visited 26 May 2019).

legal effects of patents to a limited extent.[75] That is to say, the "European patents must be separately enforced through the national court systems."[76] Besides the European patent, the EU countries and the European Parliament (the "EU Parliament") in 2012 settled on a unitary EU patent introduced through two regulations having regard to art. 118 of the TFEU[77] and an agreement on the creation of a unitary patent court (the "Unified Patent Court") (jointly the "EU Patent Package").[78] The aim of the EU Patent Package is to prevent the detrimental effect to the Internal Market of "the fragmented market for patents and the significant variations between national court systems."[79] A tool to reach this end is "to improve the enforcement of patents and the defences against unfounded claims and patents which should be revoked and to enhance legal certainty by setting up a Unified Patent Court for litigation relating to the infringement and validity of patents."[80] When the EU patent package has entered into force,[81] a European patent and the new "European patent

---

[75]I.e. respectively "formal patent law" and "substantial patent law." Schovsbo, Jens, Rosenmeier, Morten and Petersen, Clement Salung, 'Immaterialret: Ophavsret, Patentret, Brugsmodelret, Designret, Varemærkeret', (5th edn, Jurist- og Økonomforbundets Forlag, 2018), p. 232.

[76]Mainly the provisions in part II, chapter III of the EPC. See also Arnold, Sir Richard, 'An Overview of European Harmonization Measures in Intellectual Property Law', in Ohly, Ansgar and Justine Pila eds., The Europeanization of Intellectual Property Law: Towards a European Legal Methodology (1st edn, Oxford University Press, 2013), 25, p. 27.

[77]EP and Council Regulation (EU) No 1257/2012 of 17 December 2012 implementing enhanced cooperation in the creation of unitary patent protection, [2012] OJ L361/1 ("Unitary Patent Regulation") having regard to art. 118(1) of the TFEU on the creation and uniformly protecting European intellectual property rights. Furthermore, Council Regulation (EU) No 1260/2012 of 17 December 2012 implementing enhanced cooperation in the creation of unitary patent protection regarding the translation arrangements, [2012] OJ L361/89 (the "Patent Translations Regulation") having regard to art. 118(2) of the TFEU on establishment of "language arrangements for the European intellectual property rights." On art. 118 of the TFEU, see Chap. 4, Sect. 4.2.1.

[78]Council Agreement on a Unified Patent Court (2013/C 175/01) of 20 June 2013, [2013] OJ C 175/1 (the "Agreement on the Patent Court"). The agreement was signed by 25 EU member states. For an overview of the signatories see: https://www.unified-patent-court.org/about (last visited 26 May 2019). For a recent analysis of the EU Patent Court and its procedural rules, see Plesner, Peter-Ulrik et al, 'Den Europæiske Patentdomstol: Retsplejen ved den Fælles Patentdomstol', (1st edn, Jurist- og Økonomforbundets Forlag, 2018) and for an analysis of the EU Patent Package, see the edited book by Ballardini, Rosa Maria, Marcus, Norrgård and Bruun, Niklas eds., Transitions in European Patent Law: Influences of the Unitary Patent Package (1st edn, Wolters Kluwer, 2015).

[79]Recital 2 of the Agreement on the Patent Court.

[80]Recital 5 of the Agreement on the Patent Court.

[81]As per art. 18(2) of the Unitary Patent Regulation and art. 7(2) of the Patent Translations Regulation, the regulations will enter into force from the date of the Agreement on the Patent Court enters into force. The Agreement on the Patent Court will enter into force when minimum 13 states have ratified the agreement. See recital 14 of the Agreement on the Patent Court. As of July 2018, 16 states have ratified the agreement, but no firm start date of the Unified Patent Court has been confirmed. For a status of the ratification visit: http://www.consilium.europa.eu/en/docu ments-publications/agreements-conventions/agreement/?aid=2013001 (last visited 26 May 2019).

with unified effect"[82] may be enforced by the Unified Patent Court.[83] The documents of the EU Patent Package do not relate to substantive patent law, and the Unified Patent Court is thus obliged to apply the EPC as material law in its decisions.[84] The EU Patent Package as such does not materially influence the person skilled in the art. That said, it may not be ruled out that the Unified Patent Court may interpret the EPC differently than the EPO, and that this could influence the framing of the person skilled in the art.[85]

Disregarding the unified patent system, Arnold J has pointed out that despite there currently being "no supranational court to harmonize national interpretations of EPC-derived provisions" a "soft harmonization has been slowly established by a variety of means."[86] Four of those means are i) the Guidelines for Examination in the EPO (the "EPO Guidelines"),[87] ii) the publication of a comprehensive overview of Case Law of the Boards of Appeal of the EPO (the "EPO Case Law"),[88] iii) "the increasing tendency of national courts to follow the actual decisions of the Boards of Appeal in parallel cases" and iv) the national courts attempting to issue decisions consistent with those of other jurisdictions.[89] In line with Arnold J's findings, this overview analysis of the person skilled in the art will focus on the EPC, and EPO

---

[82] As it appears in art. 2(c) of the Unitary Patent Regulation, a European patent with unified effect is to be understood as "a European patent which benefits from unitary effect in the participating Member States by virtue of this Regulation [the Unitary Patent Regulation]."

[83] Hence, recital 7 of the Unitary Patent Regulation states, that "[t]o ensure the uniform substantive scope of protection conferred by unitary patent protection, only European patents that have been granted for all the participating Member States with the same set of claims should benefit from unitary effect." For a thorough account of the background of the EU Patent Package, see Pila, Justine, 'An Historical Perspective I: The Unitary Patent Package', 9, chapter 2 and Wadlow, Christopher, 'An Historical Perspective II: The Unified Patent Court', 33, chapter 3, both in in Pila, Justine and Wadlow, Christopher eds., The Unitary EU Patent System (1st edn, Hart, 2015).

[84] Art. 24(1)(C) of the Agreement on the Patent Court. Art. 24 more broadly sets out the sources to be applied by the Unified Patent Court.

[85] See generally on the application by the Unified Patent Court of the legal sources, Plesner, Peter-Ulrik et al, 'Den Europæiske Patentdomstol: Retsplejen ved den Fælles Patentdomstol', (1st edn, Jurist- og Økonomforbundets Forlag, 2018), p. 36-40.

[86] Arnold, Sir Richard, 'An Overview of European Harmonization Measures in Intellectual Property Law', in Ohly, Ansgar and Justine Pila eds., The Europeanization of Intellectual Property Law: Towards a European Legal Methodology (1st edn, Oxford University Press, 2013), 25, p. 27.

[87] Guidelines for Examination in the European Patent Office of November 2017, available at: https://www.epo.org/law-practice/legal-texts/guidelines/archive/guidelines-2017.html (last visited 26 May 2019).

[88] Case Law of the Boards of Appeal of the European Patent Office 8th Edition of July 2016, available at: https://www.epo.org/law-practice/case-law-appeals/case-law.html (last visited 26 May 2019). The EPO Case Law has recently been supplemented by Supplement to the EPO Case Law published in Supplementary publication 3, Official Journal EPO 2018 (the "EPO Case Law Supplement"), available at: http://www.epo.org/law-practice/legal-texts/official-journal/2018/etc/se3/2018-se3.pdf (last visited 26 May 2019).

[89] Arnold, Sir Richard, 'An Overview of European Harmonization Measures in Intellectual Property Law', in Ohly, Ansgar and Justine Pila eds., The Europeanization of Intellectual Property Law: Towards a European Legal Methodology (1st edn, Oxford University Press, 2013), 25, p. 27.

Case Law may consequently be relevant not only narrowly in relation to the EPC, but to national jurisdictions.

Under the EPC, "patentable inventions" include "any inventions, in all fields of technology, provided that they are *new, involve an inventive step* and are *susceptible of industrial application."*[90] The person skilled in the art has some relevance deciding if the invention is novel,[91] but the focus of this analysis is the inventive step requirement where the person skilled in the art is mentioned explicitly in the EPC. Under the EPC, "[a]n invention shall be considered as involving an *inventive step* if, having regard to the state of the art, it is not *obvious to a person skilled in the art."*[92] Musker has compared the function of inventive step in patent law with that of the individual character in design law.[93]

According to Kroher, the purpose of inventive step is to ensure that the invention "must (. . .) stand out from the state of the art by virtue of more than mere novelty."[94] From using "state of the art" as a yardstick against which inventive step has to be assessed, it emerges following Kroher, that the provision has to be interpreted objectively. Furthermore, "[i]n the ideal situation, there is always only one correct decision, free of all subjective aspects."[95] In the early days of the EPC, Pagenberg, in a two-volume article advocated for a more objective inventive step standard.[96]

---

[90]Cf. art. 52(1) of the EPC. As per art. 52(2) of the EPC "[t]he following in particular shall not be regarded as inventions within the meaning of paragraph 1: (a) discoveries, scientific theories and mathematical methods; (b) aesthetic creations; (c) schemes, rules and methods for performing mental acts, playing games or doing business, and programs for computers; (d) presentations of information."

[91]Novelty is defined in art. 54 of the EPC. For instance, "[a] document takes away the novelty of any claimed subject-matter derivable directly and unambiguously from that document including any features *implicit to a person skilled in the art* in what is expressly mentioned in the document." EPO Guidelines, Part G – Chapter VI-2 (italics added).

[92]Cf. art. 56 of the EPC (italics added). For an analysis of inventive step test as laid by the EPO Guidelines, Björkwall, Pia, 'The Unified Patent Court and the Inventive Step', in Ballardini, Rosa Maria, Norrgård, Marcus and Bruun, Niklas eds., Transitions in European Patent Law: Influences of the Unitary Patent Package (1st edn, Wolters Kluwer, 2015), 85, p. 85-89. See also the references to the person skilled in the art in, Schovsbo, Jens, Rosenmeier, Morten and Petersen, Clement Salung, 'Immaterialret: Ophavsret, Patentret, Brugsmodelret, Designret, Varemærkeret', (5th edn, Jurist- og Økonomforbundets Forlag, 2018), p. 242-243, Lindgreen, Nicolai, Schovsbo, Jens and Thorsen, Jesper, 'Patentloven med Kommentarer', (2nd edn, Jurist- og Økonomforbundets Forlag, 2018), p. 276-278 and Riis, Thomas and Trzaskowski, Jan, 'Det markedsretlige persongalleri', in Dahl, Børge, Riis, Thomas and Trzaskowski, Jan eds., Liber Amicorum: Peter Møgelvang-hansen (1st edn, Ex Tuto Publishing, 2016), pp. 439, p. 457-462.

[93]Musker, David C., 'Community Design Regulation, Art. 6', in Gielen, Charles and von Bomhard, Verena eds., Concise European Trade Mark and Design Law (2nd edn, Kluwer Law International, 2017), 640, p. 640.

[94]Kroher, Jürgen, 'Article 56: Inventive Step', in Singer, Margarete and Stauder, Dieter eds., European Patent Convention: A Commentary: Volume 1 (1st edn, Sweet & Maxwell, 2003), 141, p. 142.

[95]*Ibid*, p. 143.

[96]Pagenberg, Jochen, 'the Evaluation of the "Inventive Step" in the European Patent System – More Objective Standards Needed: Part One', International Review of Industrial Property and

Building on other authors, Pagenberg assessed the calibration of the person skilled in art as either an *"average person* as the yardstick or *the head of a research team."* In sum, Pagenberg saw that "a person skilled in the art is someone who is verifiable, at least in theory, one who has had an education typical for that field of the art, possessing *average knowledge."*[97] However, Pagenberg disagreed with the finding of some, "that the inventive step can be objectively measured merely by the "yardstick of *the average person skilled in the art.""*[98] Similarly, Kransell has called the person skilled in the art an "average expert."[99] As is clear from these quotes there is some overlap with the *average* consumer, but under patent law, this "person" is *skilled* and has to be found *in the art* not among *consumers.* Put more baldly, this "person" according to the German version of the EPC has to be a "Fachmann" (expert/specialist).[100] Hence, at least in terms of parlance, using the "average person" in patent law indicates some overlapping of common ground between trademark law and patent law.

Lacking inventive step may be a ground for opposition to the registration[101] leading to revocation[102] or revocation of a European patent "with effect for a Contracting State" under national proceedings.[103] Revocation in the latter sense and infringement of European patents are decided by national courts.[104] The patent claims of a European patent are influenced by the person skilled in the art, for

---

Competition Law, vol. 9/no. 1, (1978), pp. 1 and Pagenberg, Jochen, 'the Evaluation of the "Inventive Step" in the European Patent System – More Objective Standards Needed: Part Two', International Review of Industrial Property and Competition Law, vol. 9/no. 2, (1978), pp. 121.

[97]Pagenberg, Jochen, 'the Evaluation of the "Inventive Step" in the European Patent System – More Objective Standards Needed: Part One', International Review of Industrial Property and Competition Law, vol. 9/no. 1, (1978), pp. 1, p. 16 (italics added).

[98]*Ibid*, p. 17 (italics added). As for the use of expert opinions as part of framing the skilled person, Pagenberg claimed that "[i]nstead of answering questions of fact, they give their opinion as to the legal question of whether the invention was obvious to an average person or not." Pagenberg, Jochen, 'the Evaluation of the "Inventive Step" in the European Patent System – More Objective Standards Needed: Part Two', International Review of Industrial Property and Competition Law, vol. 9/no. 2, (1978), pp. 121, p. 143 (italics added).

[99]Kransell, Arne, 'The Average Expert', NIR, vol. 2 (1982), pp. 196.

[100]This wording is in accordance with the legislative and judicial versions of this "person:" Sweden ("fackman," cf. e.g. § 8(2) of the Swedish Patent Act), Denmark ("fagmand," cf. e.g. § 8(2), of the Danish Patent Act) and Norway ("fagmann," cf. e.g. § 8(2) of the Norwegian Patent Act).

[101]Cf. art. 100(a), cf. art. 52(1), cf. art. 56 of the EPC.

[102]Cf. art. 101(2) of the EPC.

[103]Cf. art. 138(1)(a), cf. art. 52(1), cf. art. 56 of the EPC. See more broadly on revocation, Schennen, Detlef, 'Chapter II: Revocation and Prior Rights', in Singer, Margarete and Stauder, Dieter eds., European Patent Convention: A Commentary: Volume 2 (1st edn, Sweet & Maxwell, 2003), 560, p. 560-561.

[104]For infringement, see art. 64(3) of the EPC.

instance as part of deciding inventive step, and the claims have implications for the outcome of subsequent national revocation and infringement proceedings.[105]

One of the main purposes of protecting certain inventions by law is "to encourage [creators] to produce socially valuable works, thereby maximizing social welfare." Importantly, it is necessary to calibrate the scope of protection not to hamper competition.[106] According to Fromer and Lemley, there is a red line from the purpose of patent law just roughly sketched through to "patent law's choice of the expert as the audience."[107] According to art. 69(1) of the EPC, "[t]he extent of the protection conferred by a European patent or a European patent application shall be determined by the claims."[108]

A significant aid to interpreting art. 69 of the EPC is found in a protocol to the EPC (the "EPC Protocol").[109] According to the EPC Protocol, the wording of the claims should not be interpreted literally. At the same time, claims should not only

---

[105]Davis, Richard, St Quintin, Thomas and Tritton, Guy, 'Tritton on Intellectual Property in Europe', (5th edn, Sweet & Maxwell, 2018), p. 145-146.

[106]Fromer, Jeanne C., and Lemley, Mark A., 'The Audience in Intellectual Property Infringement', Michigan Law Review, vol. 112/no. 7, (2014), pp. 1251, p. 1262-1263. According to Kitch, this has been viewed as the "reward theory." Kitch, Edmund W., 'The Nature and Function of the Patent System', the Journal of Law & Economics, vol. 20/no. 2, (1977), pp. 265, p. 266. It is beyond the scope of this book to analyse the rationales of patent law. For an overview of the rationales, see Fromer, Jeanne C., and Lemley, Mark A., 'The Audience in Intellectual Property Infringement', Michigan Law Review, vol. 112/no. 7, (2014), pp. 1251, p. 1262-1267, including the sources referred to in this text. For another recent account, see also Burk, Dan L. 'Law and Economics of Intellectual Property: In Search of First Principles', Annual Review of Law and Social Science, vol. 8/(2012), pp. 397.

[107]Fromer, Jeanne C., and Lemley, Mark A., 'The Audience in Intellectual Property Infringement', Michigan Law Review, vol. 112/no. 7, (2014), pp. 1251, p. 1263.

[108]For an account of the different approaches to demarcating the "edge" of the patentee's rights: See from a US perspective on a "metes and bounds" (also "fence posting"), see Burk, Dan L., and Mark A. Lemley, 'Fence Posts or Sign Posts? Rethinking Patent Claim Construction', University of Pennsylvania Law Review, vol. 157 (2009), pp. 1743, p. 1744 and p. 1766-1777. The different "core/gist" approach (also "sign posting") opens for expanding the patent outside of the "fence posts" of the claims. Art. 69 of the EPC on interpretation of patent claims is said to lie somewhere between these approaches. Lindgreen, Nicolai, Schovsbo, Jens and Thorsen, Jesper, 'Patentloven med Kommentarer', (2nd edn, Jurist- og Økonomforbundets Forlag, 2018), p. 407-409. On the historical development, see also Stenvik, Are, 'Protection for Equivalents Under Patent Law – Theories and Practice', IIC, vol. 32/no. 1, (2001), pp. 1, p. 4-6. The significance of patent claims differs from trademark infringement where trademarks roughly are compared with other trademarks. Schovsbo, Jens, Rosenmeier, Morten and Petersen, Clement Salung, 'Immaterialret: Ophavsret, Patentret, Brugsmodelret, Designret, Varemærkeret', (5th edn, Jurist- og Økonomforbundets Forlag, 2018), p. 338-339. Germany is one jurisdiction said to have practiced the "core/gist" approach before the introduction of the EPC. Bleken, Håkon, 'Ekvivalens i Norsk Patentrett', NIR, vol. 2 (2010), pp. 108. For a brief account of the differences between the approach of Germany and English common law, see Lindgreen, Nicolai, Schovsbo, Jens and Thorsen, Jesper, 'Patentloven med Kommentarer', (2nd edn, Jurist- og Økonomforbundets Forlag, 2018), p. 408-409, including the sources referred to here.

[109]I.e. Protocol on the Interpretation of Article 69 EPC of 5 October 1973 as revised by the Act revising the EPC of 29 November 2001.

provide a "guideline" in the sense "that the actual protection conferred may extend to what, from a consideration of the description and drawings by a person skilled in the art, the patent proprietor has contemplated."[110] As Bently *et al* point out, the protocol says "cryptically, that the courts should adopt a position in between these extremes."[111] Stauder has stated that one principle of art. 69 is that interpreting the claims "is to be based on the knowledge and capabilities of the person skilled in the art on the date of priority or filing."[112] It also follows from the EPC Protocol that to interpret the scope of patent protection under art. 69 of the EPC, "due account shall be taken of any element which is equivalent to an element specified in the claims."[113] Especially, this provision together with art. 69 of the EPC, link to protecting certain equivalent inventions not narrowly emerging from the patent claims.[114] It should be borne in mind though, as recently pointed out by Kemppinen *et al*, that protecting equivalents has been developed on the backdrop of a long interpretive tradition of the European jurisdictions, such as restrictive and expansive interpretation. Therefore, according to the authors "'[e]quivalence interpretation' does not really mean anything."[115] The protection of equivalents is addressed below since the person skilled in the art has a prominent role to play in deciding what constitutes equivalents.

It is clear from the above that the person skilled in the art, akin to the average consumer in trademark law and the informed user in design law, has a prominent role to play in the calibration patent rights. Not only is the person skilled in the art relevant when deciding the patentability of inventions, *inter alia*, through the inventive step requirement, but also to the scope of protection through interpretation of the patent claims. Below, examples from EPO boards of appeal practice will be given of the interpretation and application of the person skilled in the art as part of deciding the inventive step and aspects of infringement.

---

[110]Cf. art. 1 of the EPC Protocol.

[111]Bently, Lionel, Sherman, Brad, Gangjee, Dev and Johnson, Phillip 'Intellectual Property Law', (5th edn, Oxford University Press, 2018), p. 660.

[112]Stauder, Dieter, 'Article 64: Extent of Protection', in Singer, Margarete and Stauder, Dieter eds., European Patent Convention: A Commentary: Volume 1 (1st edn, Sweet & Maxwell, 2003), 236, p. 240.

[113]Cf. art. 2 of the EPC Protocol. Also, that the EPC Protocol is an integral part of the EPC, cf. art. 164(1) of the EPC.

[114]See Stauder, Dieter, 'Article 64: Extent of Protection', in Singer, Margarete and Stauder, Dieter eds., European Patent Convention: A Commentary: Volume 1 (1st edn, Sweet & Maxwell, 2003), 236, p. 245-246, Kemppinen *et al*, in Ballardini *et al* 2015, chapter 9, Bently, Lionel, Sherman, Brad, Gangjee, Dev and Johnson, Phillip 'Intellectual Property Law', (5th edn, Oxford University Press, 2018), p., p. 659-666, Visser, Derk, 'The Annotated European Patent Convention', (23rd edn, H.Tel., 2015), p. 80-83.

[115]Kemppinen, Hikki, Kemppinen, Jukka and Kemppinen, Seppa, 'The Doctrine of Equivalents and the Interpretation of the Extent of Protection Conferred by a Patent', in Ballardini, Rosa Maria, Marcus, Norrgård and Bruun, Niklas eds., Transitions in European Patent Law: Influences of the Unitary Patent Package (1st edn, Wolters Kluwer, 2015), 167, p. 175.

6.3.2   Is the Skilled Person in Practice a Nerdy Android?

In the EPO Guidelines on what/who constitutes the skilled person in the art for the purpose of deciding inventive step, it is stated as an introductory definition: "The "person skilled in the art" should be presumed to be a *skilled practitioner* in the relevant field of technology, who is possessed of *average knowledge and ability and is aware of what was common general knowledge* in the art at the relevant date.[116] He should also be *presumed* to have had access to everything in the "state of the art", in particular the documents cited in the search report, and to have had at his disposal the means and capacity for routine work and experimentation which are normal for the field of technology in question. If the problem prompts the person skilled in the art to seek its solution in another technical field, the specialist in that field is the person qualified to solve the problem."[117] Therefore, the inventive step of a solution must be "based on that specialist's knowledge and ability."[118]

   From the above, it is clear that the person skilled in the art is found in a different information layer than the average consumer and the informed user. This "person" is indeed a "sectoral expert" that possesses a high degree of technical knowledge in the relevant field of expertise. As opposed to the average consumer, the person skilled in the art is clearly contextualised to the specific sector of the patented invention. It could appear that the person skilled in the art has to reflect a real life "skilled practitioner." This has, however, been rejected by the EPO boards of appeal. First, the boards have stated that the skilled person may be a team.[119] Second, although not stressed in the EPO Guidelines, it appears in the cases of the EPO boards of appeal that in the assessment of inventive step a "business person" may be relevant deciding if an invention is indeed technical.[120] Hence, the EPO boards of appeal have held

---

[116]See for instance, Sequis v. Inex, T 4/98, [2001] OJ 496813, para 12.3 and Suimitomo Rubber v. Michelin, T 676/94, [1996], para 10.

[117]See for instance, Lucent Technologies, T 1364/05, [2007], para 2.35. The collective quote is taken from the EPO Guidelines, Part G – Chapter VII-3 (italics added). See also EPO Case Law, p. 188.

[118]Alza v. Elf, T 26/98, [2002], para 6.2 referring to Fives-Cail Babcock v. Fontanié, T 32/81, [1982].

[119]In Gerber Scientific Instrument v. Rudolf Hell, T 222/86, [1987] related to a patent in the field of laser engraving of transmitted pictures, the EPO Board of Appeal held: "In the opinion of the Board, laser engraving represents an advanced technology, where it is appropriate to identify the skilled person to be a production team of these experts: a physicist, who is competent for the laser, an expert in electronics, who is competent for the scanning and modulation, and a chemist, who is competent for the photosensitive layer of the recording carrier." *Ibid*, para 4.2.1. See also the EPO Guidelines Part G – Chapter VII-3.

[120]The applicant made a claim for an invention consisting of a method with technical and non-technical features. Part of the issue was whether differences to prior art were non-technical driven by business considerations, which (if so) would disqualify for inventive step. CardinalCommerce Corporation, T 1463/11, [2016], para 12. In this context, the EPO board of appeal found that it had to be determined what the "business person" could "give to the technically skilled person". *Ibid*, para 13. See also the EPO Case Law Supplement, p. 12.

that "[t]he notion of the *skilled person* is an artificial one; that is the price paid for an objective assessment. So it is too with the *business person*, who represents an abstraction or shorthand for a separation of business considerations from technical. A real business person, a real technically-skilled person, or a real inventor does not hold such "considerations separately from one another"."[121] That is to say that the person skilled in the art is a "notional skilled person," (i.e. a fictional skilled person).[122] The gist of these findings resonate with the finding of Birss J in *Hospira v Genentech* in the UK High Court holding that "[t]he person skilled in the art is not a real person. The skilled person never sees what is inventive and never misses what is obvious. They represent part of the application of a legal standard to patents."[123]

In a seminal decision of an EPO Board of Appeal, the board elaborated on the definition of a "skilled person" vis-à-vis an "inventor." That is in German, the sole linguistic version of the decision, "Fachmann" vis-à-vis "Erfinder." After looking into different definitions of "Fachmann," the board concluded that the person skilled in the art, in contrast with the inventor, does not possess inventive skills.[124] The essential point is, according to the board of appeal, that if one were to use an inventor as the yardstick against which the inventive step had to be assessed, then (too) many technical developments would not involve an inventive step.[125] This is in line with *Mills & Rockley v. Technograph* where Lord Reid of the UK Supreme Court held that "the hypothetical addressee is a skilled technician who is well acquainted with workshop technique and who has carefully read the relevant literature. He is supposed to have an unlimited capacity to assimilate the contents of, it may be, scores of specifications *but to be incapable of a scintilla of invention*." In addition,

---

[121]CardinalCommerce Corporation, T 1463/11, [2016], para 15 (italics added).

[122]For instance, in Bayer Pharma v. Leon Farma, T 637/09, [2013], para 4.5.3 where it was held by the EPO Board of Appeal: "Thus, the technical knowledge of a particular scientific team which had been acquired during the development of a particular substance, but which has not been published at the time of the effective date of filing of the patent in suit does not reflect the knowledge of the notional skilled person to be taken into account for the assessment of inventive step." See also, EPO Board Appeal Case Law 2016, p. 188-189.

[123]Hospira v. Genentech, [2014] EWHC 3857 (Pat), para 225. The appeal, dealt with recently by the Court of Appeal turning on obviousness, was rejected. Hospira v. Genentech, [2016] EWCA Civ 780. Essentially, what is "obvious" does not involve an inventive step. "Obviousness" is taken in the EPO guidelines to mean "that which does not go beyond the normal progress of technology but merely follows plainly or logically from the prior art, i.e. something which does not involve the exercise of any skill or ability beyond that to be expected of the person skilled in the art." EPO Guidelines, Part G – Chapter VII-4.

[124]"Keine deutet an, daß er [the person skilled in the art] über erfinderische Fähigkeiten verfügt. Ganz im Gegenteil ist es eben das Vorhandensein solcher Fähigkeiten, das den Erfinder vom sogenannten Fachmann unterscheidet." Allied Colloids v. SNF Floerger, T 39/93, [1996], para 7.8.4. See also EPO Case Law, p. 188-189.

[125]In German (original language of the text): "Wenn man also die Fähigkeiten eines solchen Erfinders als Maßstab benutzen würde, dann würden wohl die meisten, wenn nicht gar alle technischen Entwicklungen, nicht auf einer erfinderischen Tätigkeit im Sinne von Artikel 56 EPÜ [EPO] beruhen." Allied Colloids v. SNF Floerger, T 39/93, [1996], para 7.8.4.

that this "addressee" is *an unimaginative man with no inventive capacity.*"[126] Building on this, Jacob LJ[127] held in *Rockwater v. Technip* that "[i]t is settled that this man, if real, would be very boring — a nerd."[128] Also in line with the EPO Boards of Appeal, that "[t]he man can, in appropriate cases, be a team — an assembly of nerds of different basic skills, all unimaginative. But the skilled man is not a complete android, for it is also settled that he will share the common prejudices or conservatism which prevail in the art concerned."[129] As a curiosity, Pill LJ[130] later in *Rockwater v. Technip* tussled on words with Jacob LJ on his use of the words "nerd" and "android" to describe the person skilled in the art concluding that he preferred the wording by Lord Reid from *Mills & Rockley v. Technograph* cited above.[131]

In *Rockwater v. Technip* Jacob LJ made a valuable point on the calibration vested in the decision on the obviousness of inventions (inventive step). It was held by Jacob LJ, that "sometimes the requirement that the skilled man be uninventive is used by counsel for a patentee in an attempt to *downgrade or dismiss the evidence of an expert called to say that a patent is obvious* — "my witness is more nerdlike than his" is the general theme. I do not find this a helpful approach."[132] Staying clear of the linguistic tussle between Jacob LJ and Pill LJ on the lexical meaning of "nerd" and "android," Jacob had a valid point in using those words to describe the person skilled in the art. This is especially so, if the person skilled in the art is compared with the average consumer. The person skilled in the art seems to be more anchored in reality. It would be expected that judges would need more external inputs to put themselves in the shoes of the person skilled in the art in comparison with the average consumer being by far the least attentive and knowledgeable of the two. This

---

[126]Mills & Rockley v. Technograph, [1971] FSR. 188, (UKSC), p. 193 (italics added).

[127]As he was then, when he was sitting at the bench of the UK Court of Appeal.

[128]Rockwater v. Technip, [2004] EWCA Civ 381, para 7.

[129]*Ibid*, para 10.

[130]As he was then, when he was sitting at the bench of the UK Court of Appeal.

[131]Hence, Pill LJ held that Jacob LJ had suggested, "that he [the skilled person] is part of the way to being an android." Referring to a dictionary, Pill LJ held that a "nerd" is ""a person who lacks social skills or is boringly studious" and an 'android', in the same work, as "(in science fiction) a robot with a human appearance". I hope that those working in this field will not regard "men skilled in the art" as figures from science fiction who lack social skills. Jacob LJ, will think me less than supportive of the development of the language of the law but I do respectfully prefer, for its clarity, Lord Reid's terminology cited at paragraph 7 of the judgment." I.e., the wording used by Lord Reid in Mills & Rockley v. Technograph, [1971] FSR. 188, (UKSC), p. 193. See the main text at footnote 126 above. Rockwater v. Technip, [2004] EWCA Civ 381, para 135. In a post on the IPKat blog made by Phillips after participating in an event where Jacob LJ elaborated on *Rockwater v. Technip*, it was put in a humorous way that: "The IPKat overheard a suggestion that the true definition of "nerd" is "anyone who looks up the word 'nerd' in a dictionary." Unfortunately, the post does not say if the suggestion came from Jacob LJ. See Phillips, Jeremy (responsible for the post), 'A Nerd By Any Other Name', The IP Kat (28 October 2004): http://ipkitten.blogspot.dk/2004/10/nerd-by-any-other-name.html (last visited 26 May 2019).

[132]Rockwater v. Technip, [2004] EWCA Civ 381, para 11.

is without prejudice to the fact that the area of consumer behaviour is highly complex in its own right.[133] As it emerged from the reference to the decision by the EPO Board of Appeal and the holding of Jacob LJ in *Rockwater v. Technip*, it matters a great deal if the person skilled in the art is imbued with inventive skills.[134] This finding is comparable to trademark law and design law where it also matters to what extent the average consumer and the informed user are highly attentive/informed or less so. In patent registration and infringement, the senior patent owner has an interest in a person skilled with as high degree of inventiveness as possible, and the junior owner the opposite.[135] The thought behind this is that the more inventive the person skilled in the art is, the less likely it is that junior inventions will involve inventive step and hence be registered. In infringement disputes, the patent claims, as mentioned, have to be interpreted referring to the person skilled in the art. Therefore, unless it is clear from the wording of the claims, the more knowledgeable and inventive the person skilled in the art is deemed to be, the more will be within the scope of the patent right. This is in particular true within the protection of equivalents.

Based on an international case law analysis, Stenvik has detected two steps involved in infringement. The first step is to define the patented invention. This is decided based on the claims. If the meaning of the claims "is not plain, the court must interpret the words and phrases used in the claim, as those words and phrases would normally be understood by a person skilled in the art."[136] The second step is to determine if infringement has occurred. Infringement may occur if the alleged infringing invention is "literally covered by the claims."[137] Outside of this, it is possible to find infringement by equivalent inventions as mentioned above referring to art. 69 of the EPC and art. 2 of the EPC Protocol. The state of this area of law at a European level is uncertain.[138] Adding to the uncertainty, is the question of what

---

[133]The evidential side of the average consumer is addressed in Chap. 1, Sect. 1.5.4.

[134]In similar veins, Björkwall has argued that it is important to understand the characteristics of the person skilled in the art in the assessment of inventive step, since "the relative level within certain technological fields will depend on how this fictive person is visualized in the mind of the examiner or judge in a specific technological context." Björkwall, Pia, 'The Unified Patent Court and the Inventive Step', in Ballardini, Rosa Maria, Norrgård, Marcus and Bruun, Niklas eds., Transitions in European Patent Law: Influences of the Unitary Patent Package (1st edn, Wolters Kluwer, 2015), 85, p. 98.

[135]References to "senior owner" and "junior owner" is upheld for the consistency with similar references under trademark law. Often the "senior patent owner" is called the "patentee." Groves, Peter, 'A Dictionary of Intellectual Property Law', (1st edn, Edward Elgar, 2011), p. 236.

[136]Stenvik, Are, 'Protection for Equivalents Under Patent Law – Theories and Practice', IIC, vol. 32/no. 1, (2001), pp. 1, p. 6. In this process, different documentation according to Stenvik, may be considered, such as "the description, drawings, examination process history and other objective circumstances." *Ibid*, p. 6-7.

[137]Also called "literal infringement" or "textual infringement." *Ibid*, p. 7.

[138]This uncertainty was pointed out by Stenvik in 2001, but still remains. *Ibid*. Mainly, the uncertainty on a European level seems to relate to the requirements for protection against equivalent inventions, not if there is a protection against such equivalents at all. More certainty in European

constitutes equivalents which links to the profound question of Fromer and Lemley referred to in the introduction—when is enough similarity enough for constituting infringement? This question is inherently difficult in European trademark law, EU Design Law and is the case here, European patent law.

An analysis of any common European ground of a rule of equivalents is outside of this book.[139] It is safe to say though, that the person skilled in the art across different European jurisdictions has a prominent role to play in protecting equivalents, be it as part of a more explicit or implicit judicial rule of equivalents. Stenvik has detected three lines that demarcate the protection offered by protecting equivalents.[140] Such protection of equivalents has been applied directly by the NO Supreme Court in *Esai v. Krka* from 2009[141] and the UK Supreme Court in *Actavis v. Eli Lilly* in 2017[142] and more implicitly by the DK Supreme Court in *Hedegaard v. Hardi* from 2014.[143] In a commentary to *Esai v. Krka*, Bleken has stated that the

---

law was created with the significant UK Supreme Court decision *Actavis v. Eli Lilly*, where Lord Neuberger (giving the principle decision) and a unanimous court clarified that protection may be extended outside the claims. See Actavis v. Eli Lilly, [2017] UKSC 48, para 66, questions i)-iii), and subsequently Justice Arnold applied this in *Generics Trading, Synthon v. Yeda Research and Development and Teva Pharmaceuticals*, [2017] EWHC 2629 (Pat), para 160. Despite the certainty added by *Actavis v. Eli Lilly*, Jadeja *et al* have pointed out that "Lord Neuberger's attempt at harmonizing the scope of protection across Europe therefore appears to have encountered a shaky start." Jadeja, Nicole *et al*, 'Cast back into the sea of uncertainty – A doctrine of equivalents in UK law? The Supreme Court ruling in Actavis v Eli Lilly', Journal of Intellectual Property Law & Practice, vol. 13/no. 7, (2018), pp. 564, p. 568. Before *Actavis v. Eli Lilly*, the uncertainty was manifested in *Kirin-Amgen v. Hoechst* from 2004 (and previous decisions), when Lord Hoffmann e.g. stated that "article 69 [of the EPC] which, as it seems to me, firmly shuts the door on any doctrine which extends protection outside the claims." Kirin-Amgen v. Hoechst, [2004] UKHL 46, (UKSC), para 44.

[139]For an analysis of the various European jurisdictions, in particular the UK, Germany and Finland, see Kemppinen, Hikki, Kemppinen, Jukka and Kemppinen, Seppa, 'The Doctrine of Equivalents and the Interpretation of the Extent of Protection Conferred by a Patent', in Ballardini, Rosa Maria, Marcus, Norrgård and Bruun, Niklas eds., Transitions in European Patent Law: Influences of the Unitary Patent Package (1st edn, Wolters Kluwer, 2015), 167, chapter 9. It should be mentioned that the analysis was made before the UK Supreme Court decision in Actavis v. Eli Lilly, [2017] UKSC 48 (see the foregoing footnote). For a recent analysis of the German and UK doctrine of equivalents after this decision, see Widera, Philipp, 'Has Pemetrexed revived the Doctrine of Equivalence?', Journal of Intellectual Property Law & Practice, vol. 13/no. 3, (2018), pp. 238.

[140]Stenvik, Are, 'Protection for Equivalents Under Patent Law – Theories and Practice', IIC, vol. 32/no. 1, (2001), pp. 1, p. 7 and also more recently in his Norwegian book on patent law in 2013. See Stenvik, Are, 'Patentrett', (3rd edn, Cappelen Damm, 2013), p. 359-389.

[141]Eisai v. Krka, HR-2009-1735-A, [2009], NOSC, paras 29-30.

[142]Actavis v. Eli Lilly, [2017] UKSC 48, para 66, question i)-iii).

[143]In the decision, the DK Supreme Court found that in determining the scope of the patent protection: i) account should be taken of what was "technical similar – equivalent – to the elements of the patent claims" and ii) that in this assessment it should be considered if the alleged infringing invention before the senior patentee obtained his right was part of the prior art. If the patent claims were unclear, it should be considered had the patentee himself interpreted the claims narrowly to fulfil the novelty and inventive step requirements. Hedegaard v. Hardi, U.2014.488H, [2013],

decision merely led protection of equivalents in Norway "back on track" in line with comparable European jurisdictions.[144]

The first line is against the state of the art, meaning that akin to the inventive step assessment under art. 56 of the EPC, "the doctrine may not be applied so broadly as to encompass the state of the art," including the "known" and "obvious solutions" (the "prior-art limitation").[145] In the assessment of this, it has to be decided what has been made accessible to the person skilled in the art. The second is that the doctrine is assumed not to cover "obvious modifications" of the patented invention but "new and independent inventions" (the "obviousness test").[146] The third is not allowing for protection against inventions leading to "unequal technical solutions" (the "same problem requirement").[147]

Against the prior art limitation, it is a fundamental principle that protection of an invention through patent law does not extend to the prior art already available to the person skilled in the art. There is no deviation from this principle under the

---

DKSC, p. 528-529. With this decision, Schovsbo has held that the Danish state of the law was brought somewhat in compliance with the Norwegian, and hence the European law. Schovsbo has pointed out though, that it is regrettable that the Danish courts in contrast with the Norwegian are more "taciturn" and hence not as explicit in stating the law. Schovsbo, Jens, Rosenmeier, Morten and Petersen, Clement Salung, 'Immaterialret: Ophavsret, Patentret, Brugsmodelret, Designret, Varemærkeret', (5th edn, Jurist- og Økonomforbundets Forlag, 2018), p. 344-346. In *Actavis v. Eli Lilly*, Lord Neuberger (giving the principal judgement) recently analysed the applicability of a doctrine of equivalents in France, Germany, Italy, the Netherlands and Spain. See Actavis v. Eli Lilly, [2017] UKSC 48, paras 44-52.

[144]Bleken, Håkon, 'Ekvivalens i Norsk Patentrett', NIR, vol. 2 (2010), pp. 108, p. 120. The decision is also commented on by Ørstavik, Inger Berg, 'Ekvivalenslærens Innhold som Rettsnorm i Norsk Patentrett', NIR, vol. 2 (2010), pp. 134, p. 134-149.

[145]Stenvik, Are, 'Protection for Equivalents Under Patent Law – Theories and Practice', IIC, vol. 32/no. 1, (2001), pp. 1, p. 8-9. In Norwegian "den frie teknikk." Stenvik, Are, 'Patentrett', (3rd edn, Cappelen Damm, 2013), p. 381-382.

[146]Stenvik, Are, 'Protection for Equivalents Under Patent Law – Theories and Practice', IIC, vol. 32/no. 1, (2001), pp. 1. In Norwegian "varianten må ha vært nærliggende for en fagmann." Stenvik, Are, 'Patentrett', (3rd edn, Cappelen Damm, 2013), p. 359-389.

[147]Stenvik, Are, 'Protection for Equivalents Under Patent Law – Theories and Practice', IIC, vol. 32/no. 1, (2001), pp. 1, p. 12-13. In Norwegian: "inngrepsgjenstanden må løse samme problem som oppfinnelsen." Stenvik, Are, 'Patentrett', (3rd edn, Cappelen Damm, 2013), p. 368-372. Eisai v. Krka, HR-2009-1735-A, [2009], NOSC, para 32. Eisai v. Krka could be read as if the NO Supreme Court introduces a fourth criterion, namely that the alleged infringing invention is a modification to the senior patented invention. See Eisai v. Krka, HR-2009-1735-A, [2009], NOSC, para 32 and the analyses of the decision in Bleken, Håkon, 'Ekvivalens i Norsk Patentrett', NIR, vol. 2 (2010), pp. 108, p. 125 and 133 and Østravik NIR 2010, p. 149. Kemppinen *et al* have argued that there are four questions, i.e. "there is no infringement if the allegedly infringing object does not: (I) lead to the same end result; (2) *by* the same means as the patented invention, and if the infringing object also (3) is part of the state of art; and (4) the person skilled in the art is not able to deduct it *by* looking at the patent." However, as held by the authors, the questions seem to be covered by i.a. Stenvik's questions. Kemppinen, Hikki, Kemppinen, Jukka and Kemppinen, Seppa, 'The Doctrine of Equivalents and the Interpretation of the Extent of Protection Conferred by a Patent', in Ballardini, Rosa Maria, Marcus, Norrgård and Bruun, Niklas eds., Transitions in European Patent Law: Influences of the Unitary Patent Package (1st edn, Wolters Kluwer, 2015), 167, p. 180.

protection of equivalents. This principle also underlies the inventive step requirement that has to be judged against the prior art.[148] The obviousness test is also closely connected to the inventive step requirement. Likewise, this test is a matter of deciding, based on the patent claims, what is an obvious modification to the patent. Competing inventions deemed obvious are within the scope of protection of the patent. As with the assessment of inventive step as part of registration, the person skilled in the art is essential to deciding what is obvious. In registration, if the competing invention is obvious, it will not be registered, whereas in infringement, if the competing invention is obvious there will be infringement, if the other requirements for finding infringement are fulfilled.[149] Stenvik has stated that when dealing with marginal patents involving little inventive step, there may be a difference between the assessment of obviousness under registration and infringement. The former assessment may be less restrictive, whereas the latter the opposite. The rationale behind this, Stenvik has advocated, is that it potentially has more severe consequences for a patentee if the scope of the patentee's right is subsequently limited through infringement proceedings.[150] Assessing infringement and a potentially stricter obviousness assessment advocates a tighter calibration of the person skilled in the art as part of that process.

One of the main points of the analysis of European trademark law in this book is the interaction between mainly the Court of Justice and the national courts in creating the average consumer and in this process, the room for manoeuvring by the national courts. For the person skilled in the art with the future introduction of the EU Unified Patent, this could mean an even more complex interaction between not only the Unified Patent Court and national courts, but also somewhat the Court of Justice.[151] However, the EPO and its boards of appeals remain key players in this process and the EU Unified Patent Court will be the central specialist court.[152]

---

[148]Stenvik, Are, 'Protection for Equivalents Under Patent Law – Theories and Practice', IIC, vol. 32/no. 1, (2001), pp. 1 and Stenvik, Are, 'Patentrett', (3rd edn, Cappelen Damm, 2013), p. 381.

[149]Stenvik, Are, 'Protection for Equivalents Under Patent Law – Theories and Practice', IIC, vol. 32/no. 1, (2001), pp. 1, p. 9-12.

[150]Stenvik, Are, 'Patentrett', (3rd edn, Cappelen Damm, 2013), p. 376-378.

[151]An analysis of the role of the Court of Justice under the EU patent system is found in Dimopoulos, Angelos, 'An Institutional Perspective II: The Role of the CJEU in the Unitary (EU) Patent System', in Pila, Justine and Wadlow, Christopher eds., The Unitary EU Patent System (1st edn, Hart, 2015), 57, chapter 5. Dimopoulos concludes that the Unified Patent Court, on matters of EU law, is subordinated to the Court of Justice, but not that the Court of Justice should be seen as an appeal court to the Unified Patent Court. On matters of EU law, the Unified Patent Court will be under the obligation to preliminarily refer questions to the Court of Justice under art. 267 of the TFEU procedure. References also encompass "EU or national patent law, the interpretation of which may conflict with TRIPS or another international agreement concluded by the EU." Ibid, p. 64. According to Dimopoulos this follows from art. 207 of the TFEU, under which the "EU holds exclusive competence over commercial aspects of IP." Ibid, p. 68.

[152]An analysis of the role of the EPO under the EU patent system is found in Luginbuehl, Stefan, 'An Institutional Perspective I: The Role of the EPO in the Unitary (EU) Patent System', in Pila, Justine and Wadlow, Christopher eds., The Unitary EU Patent System (1st edn, Hart, 2015),

Probably, the Unified Patent Court will decrease fragmentation and increase the consistency through a more unified interpretation of the provisions relevant to the person skilled in the art sketched in this section. Most likely, the interplay between the Unified Patent Court and the Court of Justice will not negatively influence the increased consistency, since the Unified Patent Court after all is the specialist court compared to the Court of Justice.

6.4 Informed or Skilled: Why Does It Matter to Trademark Law?

After having addressed the "persons" populating European intellectual property law, it is possible to draw out some overall conclusions relevant to mutually demarcating them from each other. Taking *Pepsi v. Grupo Promer* as a starting point, a detour from European trademark law was taken into EU design law and European patent law to analyse the legal fictions populating those areas of law. It emerges that the average consumer, informed user and the person skilled in the art are clearly related. They facilitate answering the inherently difficult question posed by Fromer and Lemley: When is enough similarity enough for refusing registration or finding infringement? A commonality of the three legal fictions is that they are regarded not as a legal standard in their own right, but *as part of* legal standards in their respective legal areas. In trademark law, the average consumer is part of assessing "likelihood of confusion" in registration and infringement. In EU design law, the informed user is used in registration as part of assessing "individual character" through the "overall impression." In infringement, the informed user is part of a broader "overall impression" assessment not referring to "individual character." Finally, in European patent law, the person skilled in the art is essential in registration to assessing "inventive step" and in a similar query in infringement assessing if protection should be awarded to certain equivalent inventions not within the literal scope of the patent claims. It is the stance of this book that the legislative requirements just set out relevant to deciding registration and infringement in design law and patent law, akin to likelihood of confusion in trademark law, are legal standards since they essentially leave it open for an *ex post* judicial assessment to decide if they are met.[153] In this *ex post* assessment, the informed user and the person skilled in the art, respectively, play significant roles. Below, the differences and similarities between the three "persons" are discussed. This is done to provide a better (negative)

45, chapter 4. Because of potential inconsistencies of substantial patent law due to the EU patent, Luginbuehl finds that "[t]his is certain to reopen the question of if the EPO and its Boards of Appeal should not in the long term be integrated into the EU system, provoking difficult political and institutional decisions on the part of the EPO Contracting States that are not members of the EU." *Ibid*, p. 56.

[153]This is in accordance with the definition of "legal standards" in Chap. 5, Sect. 5.2.

definition of the average consumer in European trademark law. Also, this is done to sum up some core insight into the informed user and person skilled in the art valuable for the subsequent discussion in Chap. 12 on how to improve the average consumer.

Although not clearly based on *Pepsi v. Grupo Promer*, there seems to be some consensus on the fact that the three "persons" are legal fictions; a stance that is not disputed in this book. It is a key difference that the average consumer is not mentioned by the EU legislature in trademark legislation. Both the informed user and the person skilled in the art on the other hand are mentioned in the legislation. At least for the informed user emerging in EU design legislation around the time of the premature version of the average consumer, it is argued that the EU legislature could have wanted to clearly indicate that the informed user differed from the average consumer. This temporal aspect is not valid for the person skilled in the art since the EPC precedes EU trademark legislation.

Building on the wording of European trademark legislation, the "persons" of European trademark law are to be found as part of "the relevant public," which may cover one or more potential purchasers of marketed products, including average consumers. It seems commonly accepted that in terms of certain specialised products, such as pharmaceuticals, the relevant public may consist of a "general public" and "specialists," the former being very close to the average consumer. Here, it is the level of attention of the least attentive party (the general public) that has to be used as the test for deciding likelihood of confusion. This follows the logic that the general public is the first likely to be confused since members of that group are less attentive.[154] This trademark law practice could translate well into EU design law and be adapted to *Pepsi v. Grupo Promer*. For the relevant user group here, children of 5–10 years old are by no means the spitting images of a marketing manager, and presumably, children in that age group would have a different "overall impression" of the disputed designs/products than a marketing manager. The Court of Justice has, as mentioned above, not contested the board of appeal's finding that it does not matter if the informed user consists of children of 5–10 years old or a marketing manager. From case law in trademark law allowing for different relevant publics and their perception, this is surprising. Not least, this assumption of the two different users seems to be stretched. As Stone observes though, it is correct that if the relevant public is the average consumer, there are no different *average consumers*.[155] In this case, it is the average consumer as such, that can be more or less attentive.[156] Therefore, the finding by Stone of a singular informed user seems to be in line with the use by the Court of Justice of the average consumer mainly in singular form

---

[154]See below in Chap. 11.

[155]Stone, David, 'European Union Design Law. A Practitioners' Guide', (2nd edn, Oxford University Press, 2016), p. 221.

[156]See below Chap. 11.

in trademark law[157] and the legislature of ditto in the UCPD and other areas of EU legislation, but not when the relevant public is purchasers of specialised products.[158] Here, the relevant public may be the general and specialist public. In patent law, it emerged that the *person* skilled in the art, as mentioned by the legislature, is a single "person" like the informed user and the average consumer. However, it emerged from case law of the EPC boards of appeal and some national decisions that the person skilled in the art may consist of a team of experts.

The level of attention is one aspect that differentiates the three fictions. Where the average consumer is the least attentive, the person skilled in the art is by far the most attentive of the three, and the informed user falling in between. The Court of Justice in *Pepsi v. Grupo Promer* sketched this. Digging deeper though, there are significant similarities in the level of attentiveness of the three fictions. Comparing the level of attentiveness of the fictions is, without providing some important subtext, comparing "false friends." If zooming in on the different populations from where the fictions are found, they are somewhat similar in their level of attentiveness. With the average consumer, the relevant population is the consumer population, whereas the population for the informed user seems to be somewhat broader, since *users* may consist of for instance younger consumer groups or marketing experts. With the person skilled in the art, the population consists of experts ("Fachmänner"). None of the legal fictions are, compared to their respective peers in the relevant population, the most attentive. The average consumer is not the consumer making a detailed comparison between different marks, but is, at the same time, not completely ignorant of details. The informed user is not a user knowing all about the relevant design/product markets or the opposite. Last, the person skilled in the art is solely a "nerd" expert, not an expert with inventive skills and not an expert of the sloppy kind. Tentatively, the average consumer in trademark law has *average* cousins, in design law, the *average* informed user, and in patent law, the *average* person skilled in the art. At least for patent law, this is in line with Pagenberg's early finding that the person skilled in the art had to be the "*average* person as the yardstick or the head of a research team," "*the average* person skilled in the art" possessing "*average* knowledge."[159] In sum, compared across the different areas as such, the average consumer is the least attentive and the person skilled in the art the most attentive. Looking at the different areas one-by-one, the different fictions are in terms of the level of attention well off compared with their peers in their respective areas, but not flawless. Their level of attention is *average*.

Although *Pepsi v. Grupo Promer* to some extent changed the "script" of understanding the three fictions, put in baldly, the decision provided nothing that cannot be deduced from an intuitive and none-trained reading of the terms "average consumer," "informed user" and "sectoral expert"—the last one by far is the most

---

[157]Examples of the plural form of the average consumer is found by the court e.g. in Freixenet v. OHIM, Joined cases C-344/10 P and C-345/10 P, [2011] ECR I-10205, para 46.

[158]For other use by the EU legislature of the average consumer term, see above Chap. 1, Sect. 1.5.5.

[159]See above Sect. 6.3.1.

attentive. Still, no clear understanding seems to exist on the framing of the relevant legal fictions. It was shown that in design law the senior right owner in registration has an interest in an informed user with as lower level of knowledge and experience as possible. This will make it more difficult for the junior design to pass the gatekeeper to registration to some degree represented by the informed user. The reason for this is that the less knowledgeable and experienced the informed user is deemed to be, the less likely it is that there is a difference in the overall impression between the senior and junior designs. The same is true in matters of infringement. It was seen that this differs from patent law where the senior patent owner in both registration and infringement has an interest in a person skilled in the art with as high degree of inventiveness as possible.

To provide surer conclusions on the DNA of the informed user and the person skilled in the art, more analysis of those fictions is needed. It would provide surer conclusions if the projects flipside to this project were conducted on the informed user and the person skilled in the art, taking on board more insight from national jurisprudence on how those fictions are calibrated in registration and infringement disputes. Not least, with the EU Patent Package it remains to be seen how the new level of patent law will affect European patent law, including the person skilled in the art.

6.5   The Reasonable Person in Tort Law

6.5.1   Background

Beside the fictions in intellectual property law, it is relevant to compare the average consumer with "the reasonable person" in tort law used to decide the standard of care.[160] It is important to note though the significant differences between the purpose

---

[160]The reasonable person is also denoted "bonus pater familias" or the "reasonable man." On the differences between those terms, including "reasonable person," see Calabresi, Guido, 'Ideals, Beliefs, Attitudes, and the Law: Private Law Perspectives on a Public Law Problem', (1st edn, Syracuse University Press, 1985), Chapter 2, in particular p. 23-24. Use of the term reasonable *man* has caused debate on whether that is acceptable. Among others, McGinley in a US common law context have addressed the debate on the distinction between a reasonable *man* and reasonable *woman*. McGinley, Ann C., 'Reasonable Men?', Connecticut Law Review, vol. 45/no. 1, (2012), pp. 1, p. 24. See also, Horsey, Kirsty, and Erika Rackley, 'Tort Law', (4th edn, Oxford University Press, 2015), p. 212-213 and Cane, Peter, 'The Anatomy of Tort Law', (1st edn, Hart, 1997), p. 43-44. Herbert has described the reasonable man as "an ideal, a standard, the embodiment of all those qualities which we demand of the good citizen." Herbert, A. P., 'Uncommon Law – being Sixty-Six Cases Revised and Collected in One Volume, Including Ten Cases Not Published before', (6th edn, Methuen & Co. Ltd, 1948), p. 2. In addition, Herbert has stated that "I have called him a myth; and, in so far as there are a few, if any, of his mind and temperament to be found in the ranks of living men, the title is well chosen. But it is a. myth which rests upon solid and even, it may be, upon permanent foundations." *Ibid*, p. 4. Since the reasonable person term is a model mainly stemming from the "bonus pater" in civil law countries and "reasonable man" in common law, this

of trademark law and tort law, and the use of their respective models. Whereas one key legal purpose of trademark law is preserving the origin function and the economic function of lowering consumer search costs,[161] a key purpose of tort law is to ensure the balance between liberty and security of "neighbours."[162]

As hinted at in the introduction (despite the difference between trademark law and tort law) the comparison of their respective models is relevant since the US cousin of the average consumer, the neutral "reasonable purchaser" or the less so, the "reasonable consumer"[163] by Heymann and Austin has been compared to the reasonable person in tort law. Consequently, Heymann has stated that "[t]he reasonable person in tort law is someone who sets a standard of care, who models how the law tells us we should act as we go about our lives. But the reasonable person in trademark law is more rule-like than standard-like."[164] Austin has stated that the US cousin of the average consumer, like the reasonable person in tort law, "is an amalgam of legal and policy aspirations, commitments and beliefs, distilled over time as doctrines emerge and legislators innovate." The former according to Austin is "a proxy for real people – the actual consumers who might be confused by the defendant's use of a contested symbol" and the latter is "recognized as an analytical tool."[165] Heymann, slightly

---

term is used to refer to the standard of care in tort law since it is the most neutral. Bussani, Mauro, and Infantino, Marta, 'The Many Cultures of Tort Liability', in Bussani, Mauro and Sebok, Anthony J. eds., Comparative Tort Law: Global Perspectives (1st edn, Edward Elgar, 2015), 11, p. 29, including footnote 84 of the text. That said, as pointed out by Horsey and Rackley that the "reasonable person" is not entirely neutral, since it still may be questioned, "what is her or his race, religion, class, sexual orientation, age, education and so on?" Horsey, Kirsty, and Erika Rackley, 'Tort Law', (4th edn, Oxford University Press, 2015), p. 212.

[161] See below Chap. 1, Sect. 1.3.2.

[162] Moran has addressed other purposes of tort law, such as "deterrence" (p. 31-34), "compensation" (p. 34-39) and "equality" (p. 49-54). All page numbers refer to Moran, Mayo, 'Rethinking the Reasonable Person: An Egalitarian Reconstruction of the Objective Standard', (1st edn, Oxford University Press, 2003).

[163] Beebe, Barton, Thomas F. Cotter, Mark A. Lemley, et al, 'Trademarks, Unfair Competition, and Business Torts', (1st edn, Aspen, 2011), p. 176-177. Other terminology used to describe this "reasonable purchaser" is according to Heymann's analysis of case law, the "reasonably prudent consumer," "reasonable consumer" or "reasonable person." Heymann, Laura A., 'The Reasonable Person in Trademark Law', Saint Louis University Law Journal, vol. 52/no. 3, (2008), pp. 781, p. 781. See also Austin, Graeme W., 'Trademarks and the Burdened Imagination', Brooklyn Law Review, vol. 69/no. 3, (2004), pp. 827, p. 832.

[164] Heymann, Laura A., 'The Reasonable Person in Trademark Law', Saint Louis University Law Journal, vol. 52/no. 3, (2008), pp. 781, p. 782-783. The backing for this finding, Heymann has found in Austin's article from 2004 (right below) and Kaplow's analysis of the differences between rules and standards referred to above in Chap. 5, Sect. 5.2. Wallberg has made a similar comparison between the average consumer in European trademark law and the reasonable person. Wallberg, Knud, 'Brug af Andres Varemærker i Digitale Medier: Et Bidrag til Afklaring af Varemærkerettens Indhold og Grænseflader', (1st edn, Jurist- og Økonomforbundets Forlag, 2015), p. 211, including footnote 614 of the text.

[165] In addition, Austin has stated that the trademark law model "minimize the relevance of consumers' own independent thinking" since this model "is very often less than prudent, exhibiting instead unthinking and irrational responses to branding messages." Austin, Graeme W.,

disagreeing, has stated that Austin's finding "descriptively" makes sense, but that it is also fair to regard the US version of the average consumer "as a yardstick against which conduct is measured."[166] Although the scholarly arguments will not be comparatively tested in this section, it is addressed how well they resonates in European tort and trademark law. In addition, the reasonable person aspects are relevant due to the "reasonableness" of the average consumer.[167] In analysing the likelihood of confusion in trademark law, Koktvedgaard stated in 1965 that, with reference to the "relevant group of consumers" in this context, "a certain *"bonus pater"* discretion emerges in trademark law that dictates the detection and elimination of the *"standard errors"* of the ordinary purchaser."[168]

As a "basic norm," a person "legally attributable" to causing damage to another "is liable to compensate that damage,"[169] if the damage is caused by "conduct constituting fault."[170] To be held liable requires i) a "[l]oss, whether economic or non-economic, or injury,"[171] ii) "causation," i.e. "an activity or conduct (. . .) is a cause of the victim's damage if, in the absence of the activity, the damage would not have occurred,"[172] iii) foreseeability. In the determination of "whether and to what extent damage may be attributed to a person depends on factors such as (. . .) the foreseeability of the damage to a *reasonable person* at the time of the activity"[173] and iv) fault, i.e. "[a] person is liable on the basis of fault for intentional or negligent violation of the required standard of conduct."[174]

The reasonable person nests in the last requirement of fault, i.e. negligence where a "particular standard of care [is not] provided by a statutory provision whose purpose is the protection of the person suffering the damage from that damage."[175]

'Trademarks and the Burdened Imagination', Brooklyn Law Review, vol. 69/no. 3, (2004), pp. 827, p. 832.

[166]Heymann, Laura A., 'The Reasonable Person in Trademark Law', Saint Louis University Law Journal, vol. 52/no. 3, (2008), pp. 781, p. 783, including footnote 8 of the text.

[167]As explained in the introduction, reasonableness is infused into the average consumer since its characteristics are *"reasonably* well-informed and reasonably observant and circumspect." See Sect. 6.1 of this chapter.

[168]In Danish: "vedkommende forbrugerkreds" and "en slags *"bonus pater"* skøn i varemærkeretten, der bl.a. tilsiger at opfange og eliminere den almindelige købers *"normalfejl"*." Koktvedgaard, Mogens, 'Konkurrenceprægede Immaterialretspositioner: Bidrag til Læren om de Lovbestemte Enerettigheder og Deres Forhold til den Almene Konkurrenceret', (1st edn, Juristforbundet, 1965), p. 176-177. See also, *ibid*, p. 123.

[169]Cf. art. 1:101(1) of the PETL.

[170]Cf. art. 1:101(2)(a) of the PETL. See also art. VI.–1:101 of the DCFR.

[171]Cf. art. VI. – 2:101 of the DCFR. See in general chapter 2 of the DCFR and chapter 2 of the PETL.

[172]Cf. art. 3:101 of the PETL. See in general chapter 3 of the PETL and chapter 4 of the DCFR.

[173]Italics added. In the assessment of foreseeability, it has to be taken "into account in particular the closeness in time or space between the damaging activity and its consequence, or the magnitude of the damage in relation to the normal consequences of such an activity." Cf. art. 3:201 of the PETL.

[174]Cf. art. 4:101 of the PETL. See also chapter 3 on "accountability" of the DCFR.

[175]Cf. art. VI. – 3:102(a) of the DCFR.

The assessment of negligence is based on using the conduct of the "reasonable person" as a yardstick. In Ripstein's words, the reasonable person facilitates the process solving the conflict: "If one person injures another and is unwilling to pay damages, the question is not whether the injurer is really willing to pay after all, but under what conditions it is legitimate to require payment."[176] Essential to the negligence standard is the concept of "risk." The negligence standard allows for some degree of risk, in Cane's words referring "to the "chance", or "possibility", or "probability", or "likelihood" (less than 100 per cent) that some undesirable event will occur." Cane continues that "[n]egligence consists of imposing an "unreasonable" level of risk, of engaging in an activity which generates an unacceptable degree of risk without taking reasonable precautions to prevent the risk materializing in an adverse event."[177] Even if risk in this sense could be quantified, it is not to be understood in a mathematical sense, but "is inevitably a matter of judgement."[178]

Following the DCFR, it has to be decided if the action "does not otherwise amount to such care as could be expected from a reasonably careful person in the circumstances of the case."[179] Under the PETL, "[t]he required standard of conduct is that of the reasonable person in the circumstances." In contrast with the DCFR, the PETL exemplifies the elements of the assessment of this "standard of conduct" that "depends, in particular, on the nature and value of the protected interest involved, the dangerousness of the activity, the expertise to be expected of a person carrying it on, the foreseeability of the damage, the relationship of proximity or special reliance between those involved, as well as the availability and the costs of precautionary or alternative methods."[180] The standard of conduct "may be adjusted when due to age, mental or physical disability or due to extraordinary circumstances the person cannot be expected to conform to it."[181]

6.5.2 The Objectified Reasonable Person

It has been held by Widmer that fault, including negligence, for the most part in Europe is an ""objectivated" notion (...) which takes as a yardstick an objective standard of conduct to which everybody has to conform, independently of his individual capacities and which, therefore—it may be argued—has nothing to do

---

[176]Ripstein, Arthur, 'Reasonable Persons in Private Law', in Bongiovanni, Giorgio, Sartor, Giovanni and Valentini, Chiara eds., Reasonableness and Law (1st edn, Springer, 2009), 255, p. 257.

[177]Cane, Peter, 'The Anatomy of Tort Law', (1st edn, Hart, 1997), p. 37.

[178]Ibid, p. 40.

[179]Cf. art. VI. – 3:102(b) of the DCFR.

[180]Cf. art. 4:102(1) of the PETL.

[181]Cf. art. 4:102(2) of the PETL. For similar adjustment for children under 18, see art. VI. – 3:103 of the DCFR.

anymore with blameworthiness." That said, Widmer has pointed out that a certain degree of "blameworthiness" emerges in many cases.[182] In the commentary to the DCFR, it is held that negligence standard referring to the "reasonably careful person" "is an objective one." Moreover, that "[i]t does not turn on the individual abilities of the person acting, rather it is based on what can be reasonably expected of that person."[183] Bear in mind that despite the objectiveness, as pointed out by van Dam, "the courts can gear the reasonable person up and down at their discretion."[184] This moulding of the reasonable person as "a functional standard of reference enables the judges to differentiate according to the social role of the defendant and the circumstances of the case."[185] This function is, according to Cane, connected to the broader role of the tort law as not only solving "bilateral disputes about events" but also providing future "guidance to citizens about how to lead their lives." Therefore, following Cane, tort law conflicts should be resolved in "the social context of the lives of those subject to it" and "individuals" should not be treated as ""islands onto themselves" but as social creatures."[186]

---

[182]See Widmer, Pierre, 'Liability Based on Fault: Introduction', in European Group on Tort Law ed., European Group on Tort Law: Principles of European Tort Law: Text and Commentary (1st edn, Springer, 2005), 64, p. 65-66. See also Koziol, Helmut, 'Liability Based on Fault: Subjective or Objective Yardstick?', the Maastricht Journal of European and Comparative Law, vol. 5 (1998), pp. 111, p. 112 and 128.

[183]Bar, Christian von, and Clive, Eric, 'Principles, Definitions and Model Rules of European Private Law Draft Common Frame of Reference (DCFR)', (1st edn, Oxford University Press, 2010), p. 3278. Horsey and Rackley have stated that it must be decided "what level of care and skill did the activity the defendant was undertaking require?", Horsey, Kirsty, and Erika Rackley, 'Tort Law', (4th edn, Oxford University Press, 2015), p. 213. In a US context Farnsworth and Grady have similarly seen *"[n]egligence as conduct, not state of mind"* and held that "[a] bad state of mind is neither necessary nor sufficient to show negligence,' and conduct is everything." Furthermore, that "[t]he legal concept of negligence as unduly risky conduct distinct from state of mind reflects the law's strong ·commitment to an objective standard of behavior." Farnsworth, Ward and Grady, Mark F., 'Torts: Cases and Questions', (2nd edn, Aspen, 2009), p. 275. Von Eyben and Isager explain that under Danish law, the defendant's behaviour (the tortfeasor) as part of the negligence standard is not to be viewed as an "average behaviour" ("gennemsnitsadfærd"), but as a matter of whether the defendant's action or omission deviate from recognised behavioural patterns – e.g. recognised in legislation, case law or customs. Eyben, Bo von, and Isager, Helle, 'Lærebog i Erstatningsret', (8th edn, Jurist- og Økonomforbundets Forlag, 2015), p. 91.

[184]Dam, Cees van, 'European Tort Law', (2nd edn, Oxford University Press, 2013), p. 235. It has also been claimed by Cane that "[r]easonableness is an "objective" (as opposed to a "subjective") standard – the test is not whether the defendant thought any precautions taken were reasonable, but whether the court thinks so." Cane, Peter, 'The Anatomy of Tort Law', (1st edn, Hart, 1997), p. 40-41.

[185]Dam, Cees van, 'European Tort Law', (2nd edn, Oxford University Press, 2013), p. 266. In a section on "objective typical care" (In German: "Objectiv-typisierte Sorgfalt (Gruppenfahrlässigkeit)"), it has been explained by Deutsch that this objectified person may in various instances have different characteristics, e.g. in some instances characteristics of an amateur and in other those of a professional. See Deutsch, Erwin, 'Allgemeines Haftungsrecht', (2nd edn, Heymanns, 1996), p. 259-260.

[186]Cane, Peter, 'The Anatomy of Tort Law', (1st edn, Hart, 1997), p. 38.

As it has emerged, the reasonable person on the surface is objective and as such not moulded case-by-case. However, what does the objectivity cover? It has been held by Ripstein, commenting on objectivity in private law in general, that "[a]ny such (...) objectivity might well be suspected of being little more than a smokescreen for interests that are already well-entrenched." Ripstein continues holding that: "Precisely because the fault standard turns on substantive views about the importance of various activities, its contours will always be open to debate." Moreover, that the standard "is objective in a negative sense, inasmuch as it is not subjective, that is, the limits of liability are not fixed by the views, interests, or abilities of either of the parties to a tort action. Instead, it protects the interests in both liberty and security that everyone is assumed to have."[187] Calibrating the standard of care is a question of "whether I am being appropriately careful in light of my neighbour's interests in security and mine in liberty."[188] Moran has specifically held that "[t]he way that the reasonable person seamlessly intertwines the normative and descriptive may be one source of his appeal, but this very feature makes disentanglement difficult when the actual person no longer so closely resembles his 'legal' counterpart."[189] Samuel has held that the reasonable person is a "recourse" to a "fictional character" illustrating that there is a "gap between what a court thinks and social reality." In tort law, this gap is illustrated by judicial fall back on policy arguments by way of awarding damages caused by certain actions and not by others.[190]

It is the viewpoint of this book that the average consumer in trademark law is a legal fiction leaving room for descriptive and normative elements.[191] A strain addressed running through this chapter is the distinction between rules and standards. Above it is concluded that the fictions in intellectual property are part of

---

[187]Ripstein, Arthur, 'Reasonable Persons in Private Law', in Bongiovanni, Giorgio, Sartor, Giovanni and Valentini, Chiara eds., Reasonableness and Law (1st edn, Springer, 2009), 255, p. 276. Similarly, Moran has held that the reasonable person may illustrate the forming of "the boundary between the core concerns of negligence: liberty and security." As illustration of this, Moran has referred to the use of the reasonable person in relation to the mentally disabled. Moran, Mayo, 'Rethinking the Reasonable Person: An Egalitarian Reconstruction of the Objective Standard', (1st edn, Oxford University Press, 2003), p. 6.

[188]Ripstein, Arthur, 'Reasonable Persons in Private Law', in Bongiovanni, Giorgio, Sartor, Giovanni and Valentini, Chiara eds., Reasonableness and Law (1st edn, Springer, 2009), 255, p. 269. In similar veins, Widmer has held that the reasonable person may also be seen as a significant calibration device balancing the ""activity interest" which corresponds to the liberty of developing one's personality and displaying economic, sportive or artistic activities" with "the "integrity interest", corresponding to the liberty to enjoy one's own physical and psychic capacities and one's property without being disturbed." Widmer, Pierre, 'Liability Based on Fault: Introduction', in European Group on Tort Law ed., European Group on Tort Law: Principles of European Tort Law: Text and Commentary (1st edn, Springer, 2005), 64, p. 76.

[189]Moran, Mayo, 'Rethinking the Reasonable Person: An Egalitarian Reconstruction of the Objective Standard', (1st edn, Oxford University Press, 2003), p. 2.

[190]Samuel, Geoffrey, 'Is Law a Fiction?', in Del Mar, Maksymilian and Twining, William eds., Legal Fictions in Theory and Practice (1st edn, Springer, 2015), 31, p. 47.

[191]See Chap. 1, Sect. 1.2 and Chap. 5.

legislative standards and not standards in their own right. Similarly, it could be argued for tort law that the legislative standard is the negligence standard and part of that standard is the reasonable person fiction. However, it appears from the above analysis of the tort law principles that compared to the fictions in intellectual property law, the reasonable person is more proximate to the legal standard of negligence since the assessment hereof more or less is: "If the injurer's action in accordance with that of the reasonable person, the action is not negligent (the action meting or being above the threshold). If the action is not at least in accordance with the action of the reasonable person, the action is negligent (the action being below the threshold)."[192] It emerged above that a multitude of elements may be considered in assessing the actions of the injurer. This was exemplified by the non-exhaustive list of elements in the PETL.

The way the standard of care is assessed in European tort law by way of a multitude of elements, has certain functional resemblance with the multifactor test of likelihood of confusion in European trademark law (the global appreciation test).[193] Based on the findings in this section, it is viable to hold that the reasonable person in tort law is almost identical to the negligence standard and as such is not merely part of a standard as with the intellectual property law fictions. It is beyond this book though to analyse potential differences between the negligence standard and the reasonable person. Based on these findings, it seems justified that Heymann has claimed that the reasonable person "set a standard of care" and Austin's finding that it is an "analytical tool." The viability of Heymann's finding that the reasonable person is paternalistic manifesting "how the law tells us we should act as we go about our lives" depends somewhat on the normativity and objectivity of the reasonable person. Heymann has clearly attached much weight to the reasonable person as normative.

As per above, it is the starting point that the reasonable person standard is objective, hence leaving little room for descriptive elements understood as elements derived from the facts of each case. What is the normative side of the reasonable person, if any? As Ripstein metaphorically questions: what (normative) interests are hidden behind the "smokescreen?" From the viewpoint of this book, the normativity left for the judiciaries in framing the reasonable person can be set up in a sliding scale. Should it clearly emerge from e.g. legislation what is the standard of conduct in a given area, the judges may rely heavily on this legislation and hence less on a broader discretion of the *reasonableness* of the conduct. If not, the broader and more discretionary elements of the multifactor test of the reasonable person may play a more prominent role. These elements seem to have matured in different jurisdictions as reflected by the PETL, and basically, it is for the judicial assessment to decide how the elements are balanced against each other. In this balancing process, room is left

---

[192]This statement only addresses the starting point for assessing negligence and does not consider the defenses of the injurer. Such defenses could be "self-defense" and "self-help," cf. respectively art. 7:101(1)(a) and (b) of the PETL.

[193]This was introduced in the introduction, Sect. 6.1 of this chapter.

for some normativity. As the commentary to the DCFR points out, this normativity is reined in since "the requirements of necessary care may not be arbitrarily raised." Arbitrariness would "emphatically hinder human activity; people would scarcely be able to move freely, constantly in fear of possibly encountering liability."[194] With the caveats just stated, Heymann's findings of the reasonable person standard being normative are viable.

As for the "reasonable consumer" in US trademark law, as mentioned, Heymann has found this model to be "more rule-like than standard-like" disagreeing with Austin holding that this model is a "proxy for real people." For the reasons given above, this book does not contend that the average consumer in European trademark law is rule-like since it is a fiction forming part of the likelihood of confusion standard. That said, it is contended that the average consumer fiction is used, in Austin's words, as "a yardstick against which conduct is measured."

In Heymann's comparison referred to above, she has made a similar point that in trademark law "the conduct [under judicial assessment] is of *parties not directly before the court.*"[195] Although, Heymann has made the argument subtly in a footnote, the upshot of this is significant. The argument seems to relate to the fact that in applying the likelihood of confusion standard, the relevant party is the consumer group, in Europe somehow represented by the average consumer fiction. Therefore, when the relevant public is the average consumer, this fiction is used not only to calibrate the interests of the immediate parties of a dispute but also the interests of their consumers.[196]

The understanding of negligence and the *reasonable* person involves, in Cane's terms, a certain *risk* (also in the sense of *likelihood*) in a non-quantifiable way. This translates well into trademark law's *likelihood* of confusion standard, including the average consumer, essentially being non-quantifiable. Where the reasonable person is accepted to take some risks without acting negligently, the average consumer is also accepted to be somewhat confused without likelihood of confusion emerging in the legislative sense.

An important takeaway from this analysis is the move in tort law towards objectiveness and away from "blameworthiness," although this aspect still plays a role. It is relevant that a non-exhaustive list of European principles relevant to the assessment of the reasonable person feed objectiveness into the assessment of the *reasonableness* of this person. As it will be seen, the average consumer could use a

---

[194]Bar, Christian von, and Clive, Eric, 'Principles, Definitions and Model Rules of European Private Law Draft Common Frame of Reference (DCFR)', (1st edn, Oxford University Press, 2010), p. 3279. Another reason is that arbitrariness blurs the distinction between negligence and strict liability.

[195]Heymann, Laura A., 'The Reasonable Person in Trademark Law', Saint Louis University Law Journal, vol. 52/no. 3, (2008), pp. 781, p. 783, including footnote 8 of the text (italics added).

[196]This point is addressed below through a discussion of the importance of considering the value of the non-confused consumers in assessing likelihood of confusion. See Chap. 12, Sect. 12.5.

better steer. For instance, infusing the average consumer with some non-exhaustive objective principles could serve as inspiration for this steer.[197]

6.6 Rational Actor Model

6.6.1 *Background*

In science, models are used to explain and predict the behaviour of an object.[198] In "hard sciences," the purpose of models is to explain the phenomena, and the criterion of success is that the model corresponds with the examined object. In contrast, the purpose of models in "soft sciences" (behavioural and social science), including economics and law, is "different because the object of the conceptual scheme are humans whose free will behaviour makes causal analysis extremely difficult and controversial" and those models "can never bring together representation and reality" as "a causal, scheme of intelligibility." This causes models in social sciences to be "fictional."[199] From introducing the models by legislatures or judiciaries, this aspect also causes downstream discussions on how legal models are to be understood and applied. In Jacob's terminology, this may lead to "woolly areas" of law.[200] As illustrated by the models discussed so far in this chapter, they all are inherently "woolly." One reason for this is that the "phenomena in soft sciences" are "not tangible and rarely permit precise measurement;" an example of such a phenomenon according to Jacoby is the sense of "confusion."[201] Metaphorically, Phillips has

---

[197]The lacking steer in a purely normative fiction has been illustrated by Trzaskowski holding that "the average consumer is in fact merely a 'normative abstraction' setting a standard for; not how consumers do behave, but how they should behave. This resembles the notion of the *Bonus Pater Familias* in tort law, and which represent how (an average) citizen should behave in order not to be met with civil liability." Trzaskowski, Jan, 'The Unfair Commercial Practices Directive and Vulnerable Consumers', Conference Paper, (2013), pp. 1, p. 10. This finding is addressed in the following chapter.

[198]Samuel, Geoffrey, 'Is Law a Fiction?', in Del Mar, Maksymilian and Twining, William eds., Legal Fictions in Theory and Practice (1st edn, Springer, 2015), 31, p. 33.

[199]Samuel, Geoffrey, 'Is Law a Fiction?', in Del Mar, Maksymilian and Twining, William eds., Legal Fictions in Theory and Practice (1st edn, Springer, 2015), 31, p. 33-34. In describing the difference between "hard science" and "soft science," Jacoby has stated: "Because the phenomena (e.g., atoms, planets, genes, the heart) that are the focus of the natural (biological and especially physical) sciences are tangible and generally permit relatively precise measurement, they are usually are referred to as the "hard" sciences. In contrast, many of the phenomena studied in the behavioral and social sciences are more "fuzzy," defined by people rather than nature." Jacoby, Jacob, 'Trademark Surveys Volume I: Designing, Implementing, and Evaluating Surveys', (1st edn, American Bar Association, 2013), p. 191. On models of microeconomics, see Pindyck, Robert and Rubinfeld, Daniel, 'Microeconomics', (9th edn, Pearson, 2018), p. 27-28.

[200]See Chap. 1, Sect. 1.1.

[201]Jacoby, Jacob, 'Trademark Surveys Volume I: Designing, Implementing, and Evaluating Surveys', (1st edn, American Bar Association, 2013), p. 191. Although Jacoby writes on using surveys

described the average consumer in trademark infringement related to confusion as "a piece of human litmus paper, dipped into the market place and employed as an acid test of whether the trade mark owner can successfully sue the maker or seller of the allegedly similar product (...)."[202] Due to the profound differences between a model used in the hard sciences and law, the comparison between the average consumer and a model from the hard sciences (a pH test) is not appropriate.[203]

The average consumer as a legal model has been connected with a model from another area of social science, the rational actor model from economics, hence also falling in the category of fictional social science models.[204] The alleged rationality of the average consumer, according to some authors, can be traced back to the fundamental decisions on free movement of goods and consumer protection law dealt with

---

in trademark law, reference here to "confusion" is not merely to the legal sense of the word. Hence, the full list of examples is "motives, morale, creativity, frustration, *confusion*, deception, etc." *Ibid* (italics added).

[202]The quote continues: "or a canary in a cage, taken down the coal mine to see if the air is wholesome." If the canary survives, the air is wholesome. As further explained by Phillips, the miners represent the alleged infringer, i.e. the junior trademark owner, using a trademark potentially being confusingly similar to that of the senior trademark owner. Phillips finished by holding that "[n]either the consumer nor the canary derives any personal benefit from its experience." Of course, scholarly metaphors should not be overanalysed (including that of Phillips) one of the most influential intellectual property personalities in past years. However, given this chapter on models in law and more broadly in science, the metaphor overlooks a profound difference between models in law and the hard sciences. Phillips, Jeremy, 'Trade Mark Law a Practical Anatomy', (1st edn, Oxford University Press, 2003), p. 20. This has been reiterated by Phillips the IP Kat blog. See Phillips, Jeremy (responsible for the post), 'The Consumer Protection Function of Trade Marks: Just so?', The IP Kat (21 November 2014): http://ipkitten.blogspot.dk/2014/11/the-consumer-protection-function-of.html (last visited 26 May 2019).

[203]Arguably, a pH test is a *method* for testing the model of pH value and measurement.

[204]The term "rational actor" is used by among others Parisi, Francesco, 'The Language of Law and Economics. A Dictionary', (1st edn, Cambridge University Press, 2013), p. 245-246, Finkelstein, Claire, 'Legal Theory and the Rational Actor', in Mele, Alfred R. and Rawling, Piers eds., The Oxford Handbook of Rationality (1st edn, Oxford University Press, 2004), 399, chapter 21, Jacoby, Jacob, 'Is it Rational to Assume Consumer Rationality? Some Consumer Psychological Perspectives on Rational Choice Theory', Roger Williams University Law Review, vol. 6 (2000-2001), pp. 81, p. 127 and Elster, Jon, 'Reason and Rationality', (1st edn, Princeton University Press, 2009), p. 2 and 6. For use of the term "homo oeconomicus/economicus," see Sibony, Anne-Lise, 'Can EU Consumer Law Benefit from Behavioural Insights? An Analysis of the Unfair Practices Directive', in Mathis, Klaus ed., European Perspectives on Behavioural Law and Economics. Foundations and Applications (1st edn, Springer, 2015), 71, p. 72, Ross, Alf, 'Legal Fictions', in Hughes, Graham ed., Law, Reason, and Justice: Essays in Legal Philosophy, (1st edn, Springer, 1969), 217, p. 231, Golecki, Mariusz J., 'Homo Economicus Versus Homo Iuridicus Two Views on the Coase Theorem and the Integrity of Discourse Within the Law and Economics Scholarship', in Mathis, Klaus ed., Law and Economics in Europe: Foundations and Applications (1st edn, Springer, 2014), 69, chapter 4, and Engelbrekt, Antonina Bakardjieva, 'The Scandinavian Model of Unfair Competition Law', in Hilty, Reto M. and Henning-Bodewig, Frauke eds., Law Against Unfair Competition: Towards a New Paradigm in Europe? (1st edn, Springer, 2007), 161, p. 173. For use of the term "Rational man," see Posner, Richard A., 'Rational Choice, Behavioral Economics, and the Law', Stanford Law Review, vol. 50 (1997-1998), pp. 1551, p. 1559. In this book, the terms are regarded as interchangeable.

in Chap. 8 laying the foundation of this consumer image. Some of the decisions, Incardona and Poncibò, have seen as forming part of an "'information model," which incorporates the concept of a well-informed, critical, and attentive consumer."[205] Wilhelmsson has seen *Clinique* as indicating: "What 'rational' average consumers in one Member State can be expected to familiarize themselves with and take into account, may in another Member State fall far outside the scope of information which average consumers tend to look at."[206] Along those lines, Advocate General Fennelly in *Estée Lauder*, according to Davis, assumed the average consumer to be rational by finding that a "model of a hypothetical average consumer for cases of alleged confusion that is likely to be of the greatest *utility* both to national courts and to the Court [of Justice], in the latter case to obviate the need to decide such cases on an individual basis."[207] Referring to e.g. *Gut Springenheide*, Incardona and Poncibò have held that "[i]t seems that the ECJ relied upon the traditional law and economics analysis which suggests that consumers make decisions based on their anticipation of the expected outcomes of their decisions."[208]

---

[205]Incardona, Rossella, and Poncibò, Cristina, 'The Average Consumer, the Unfair Commercial Practices Directive, and the Cognitive Revolution', Journal of Consumer Policy, vol. 30/no. 1, (2007), pp. 21, p. 29. The authors refer to Rewe-Zentral AG v. Bundesmonopolverwaltung für Branntwein, Case 120/78, [1979] ECR 649, X (Nissan), Case C-373/90, [1992], ECR I-131, Schutzverband v. Yves Rocher, Case C-126/91, [1993] ECR I-2361, Verband Sozialer Wettbewerb v. Clinique Laboratoires, Case C-315/92 [1994] ECR I-317 and Verein gegen Unwesen in Handel und Gewerbe v. Mars, Case C-470/93, [1995] ECR I-1923.

[206]Wilhelmsson, Thomas, 'The Average European Consumer: A Legal Fiction?', in Wilhelmsson, Thomas, Paunio, Elina and Pohjolainen, Annika eds., Private Law and the Many Cultures of Europe (1st edn, Kluwer Law International, 2007), 243, p. 262. The decision is dealt with below in Chap. 8, Sect. 8.6 in the analysis of the judicial history of the average consumer pre *Sabel*. For a recent reference to these decisions, given the rationality, see Mak, Vanessa, 'The Consumer in European Regulatory Private Law', in Leczykiewicz, Dorota, and Weatherill, Stephen eds., The Images of the Consumer in EU Law: Legislation, Free Movement and Competition Law (1st edn, Hart, 2016), 381, p. 384 – 389. See also on consumers in unfair trading law, Engelbrekt, Antonina Bakardjieva, 'Fair Trading Law in Flux? National Legacies, Institutional Choice and the Process of Europeanisation', (1st edn, Stockholm University, 2003), p. 82 and p. 524-525.

[207]Estée Lauder, Case C-220/98, [1999] ECR I-117, (opinion of AG Fennelly), para 26 (italics added). Davis tacitly makes the point in her 2015 article where she refers to her findings in her 2005 article on the average consumer as supporting the argument of a rational consumer model. See Davis, Jennifer, 'Revisiting the Average Consumer: An Uncertain Presence in European Trade Mark', Intellectual Property Quarterly, no. 1, (2015), pp. 15, p. 21, where she in footnote 54 of that text refers to her 2005 article p. 197, where she in footnote 77 of that text has set out the quote by Fennelly from *Estée Lauder*.

[208]Incardona, Rossella, and Poncibò, Cristina, 'The Average Consumer, the Unfair Commercial Practices Directive, and the Cognitive Revolution', Journal of Consumer Policy, vol. 30/no. 1, (2007), pp. 21, p. 30. Referring to Posner, the authors have explained that "[i]n this model, consumers are viewed as rational actors able to estimate the probabilistic outcomes of uncertain decisions and to select the outcome which maximises their sense of well-being at the time the decision is made. As a consequence of their assumed rationality, consumers would largely be held responsible for their own actions, and the potential liability for the company would be greatly reduced." *Ibid*. See also Mak, Vanessa, 'The Consumer in European Regulatory Private Law', in

Recently, Mak has put forward the overall assumption that "[t]he prevailing image in EU law appears to be that of the consumer as a 'rational actor,'" including the average consumer.[209] In her more recent analysis of the average consumer in trademark law from 2015, Davis has worked from the starting point that "when the [1989] TM Directive was adopted the idea of a rational, average consumer was a key assumption of the prevailing neo-classical economic orthodoxy. There was also a belief that, in post-war society, inequalities of wealth and class, which might affect consumer behaviour and understanding, were no longer relevant."[210] Moreover, that the average consumer as a "rational, utility-maximising individual" "is the default position in European trade mark law" and that "[t]his assumption allows the judge to treat the consumer as a legal construct."[211] Based on the assumption of rationality of the average consumer, Abbamonte has held that it is assumed that consumers "should inform themselves about the quality and price of products and make efficient choices."[212]

Countering the above rationality assumptions of the average consumer, Alvisi has conclusively seen the average consumer as closer to the reasonable person than the rational actor holding that "[t]he average consumer is deemed a *reasonable* man as he makes conscious choices. However, although reasonable, he may not be rational."[213]

6.6.2   The Average Consumer and the Rational Actor: Distant Cousins?

Referring to *Gut Springenheide*, Mathis has claimed that "[t]he figure of the average consumer created by the Court [of Justice] is a not so distant cousin of *homo*

Leczykiewicz, Dorota, and Weatherill, Stephen eds., The Images of the Consumer in EU Law: Legislation, Free Movement and Competition Law (1st edn, Hart, 2016), 381, p. 385.

[209]Mak, Vanessa, 'The Consumer in European Regulatory Private Law', in Leczykiewicz, Dorota, and Weatherill, Stephen eds., The Images of the Consumer in EU Law: Legislation, Free Movement and Competition Law (1st edn, Hart, 2016), 381, p. 384.

[210]Davis, Jennifer, 'Revisiting the Average Consumer: An Uncertain Presence in European Trade Mark', Intellectual Property Quarterly, no. 1, (2015), pp. 15, p. 16.

[211]*Ibid*, p. 25.

[212]Abbamonte, Guiseppe B., 'The Unfair Commercial Practices Directive and its General Prohibition', in Weatherill, Stephen and Ulf Bernitz eds., The Regulation of the Unfair Commercial Practices Under EC Directive 2005/29 (1st edn, Hart, 2007), 11, p. 24.

[213]Alvisi, Chiara, 'The Reasonable Consumer Under European and Italian Regulations on Unfair Business-to-Consumer Commercial Practices', in Bongiovanni, Giorgio, Giovanni Sartor and Chiara Valentini eds., Reasonableness and Law (1st edn, Springer, 2009), 283, p. 292. Alvisi's findings are based on an analysis of the average consumer under the UCPD. However, the findings turn around some of the general characteristics of the average consumer also known to the trademark law version of the average consumer.

oeconomicus."[214] Although, the above references to the average consumer as rational are mainly made to the fiction populating consumer protection law, it is still conceptually relevant to European trademark law. The gist is that the common characteristics "reasonably well-informed and reasonably observant and circumspect" seem to lead certain authors to conclude that the average consumer in a neo classical economic sense is rational. There seems to be an implicit tendency to equate the average consumer as rational with the ability of judges to "treat the consumer as a legal construct."[215] In essence, does it make sense to translate the average consumer and its characteristics into the rational actor model and to describe the two metaphorically as "distant cousins"? It should be borne in mind that from the outset both the average consumer and the rational actor model are modelled around the same consumers. The following sections address the way the modelling has been done.

Initially, it is not correct that it is the rationality assumption that allows judges to assume a fictional consumer model in trademark law and other areas of law. The model has a more prominent and profound origin in the sheer purpose of using models in soft sciences and specifically in law. In trademark law, the average consumer is a crude model for measuring (describing) confusion that, as mentioned, does not allow for an exact measurement. This purpose represents the factual side of the average consumer imbued with an external reality. Just as important, the normative side of the average consumer fiction as analysed above allows for coherence and consistency over different cases. Part of framing the average consumer fiction has been imbuing it with certain assumed characteristics. This consumer fiction could in principle be a gullible "Homer Simpson" or a "moron in a hurry" with a different level of rationality.[216] Those fictions would presumably be

---

[214]Golecki, Mariusz J., 'Homo Economicus Versus Homo Iuridicus Two Views on the Coase Theorem and the Integrity of Discourse Within the Law and Economics Scholarship', in Mathis, Klaus ed., Law and Economics in Europe: Foundations and Applications (1st edn, Springer, 2014), 69, p. 72. Referring to misleading advertisement, Bagardgjieva has held that "[t]he average consumer is, however, not seen as a rational 'homo economicus' fully detached from reality. This consumer is considered not to have particular experience of the product in question and is presumed to read adverts casually. Therefore it is the aggregate overall impression by casual contact that is important." Engelbrekt, Antonina Bakardjieva, 'The Scandinavian Model of Unfair Competition Law', in Hilty, Reto M. and Henning-Bodewig, Frauke eds., Law Against Unfair Competition: Towards a New Paradigm in Europe? (1st edn, Springer, 2007), 161, p. 173.

[215]Davis, above in footnote 207 and Davis, Jennifer, 'Revisiting the Average Consumer: An Uncertain Presence in European Trade Mark', Intellectual Property Quarterly, no. 1, (2015), pp. 15, p. 25.

[216]The phrase "moron in a hurry" originates from *Morning Star v Express Newspapers*, a media case involving two newspaper publications. The telling quote from the Justice Foster goes: "[i]f one puts the two papers side by side, I for myself would find that the two papers are so different in every way that only a *moron in a hurry* would be misled." Morning Star v. Express Newspapers, [1979] FSR 113, (EWHC), p. 117 (italics added). As for the reference to "Homer Simpson," it originates in the Canadian decision *Atomic Energy v. Areva*, where Zinn J, after referring to the "moron in a hurry," held that "[i]n this industry [the nuclear power industry], the fact that Homer Simpson may be confused is insufficient to find confusion." Atomic Energy v. Areva, [2009] FC 980, para 28. Corbin has elaborated on these cases in an article on the Canadian version of the average consumer.

further away from reflecting actual consumer behaviour; however, they could still work as fictions in law allowing for consistency in different cases. As calibration devices reflecting the policy of trademark law, they would not function well. The point of bringing forward these other imagined fictions is that it is not the rationality assumptions that in Davis' words allow "the judge to treat the consumer as a legal construct" and in Fennelly's words, as referred to by Davis, to "obviate the need to decide such cases on an individual basis."[217] This function is owing to the mere function of fictions in law. Davis' reference to Fennelly is finding that the average consumer creates "*utility* both to national courts and to the Court [of Justice]" connotes with law and economics' use of "utility" whose level is measured through e.g. "Pareto" or "Kaldor-Hicks" efficiency.[218] Inevitably, the average consumer could be analysed in a strict law and economics sense through its impact on efficiency. However, in the way used by Fennelly, "utility" is arguably solely made in the sense of the word meaning "usefulness." Although it may be coincidental, this is supported by the Danish version of Fennelly's opinion simply translating "utility" into "help" ("hjælp"), but not in other linguistic versions.[219] On the face of it that is the gist of the average consumer as a legal fiction—it is *useful* "both to national courts and to the Court of Justice."

Before addressing how, if at all, the average consumer and its characteristics translate into economics and the rational actor model, it is necessary to establish an understanding and function of this model. Economic analysis of intellectual property law has so far been governed by "neoclassical approaches," including "rational actor models."[220] This model assumes that people try to act rationally, maximising their utility. This is rooted in the assumption, according to Stigler, that e.g. "[t]he householder who buys a consumer good on *average* knows better what and where

---

Corbin, Ruth M., 'The Moron in a Hurry – a Creature of Law Or Science?', in Archibald, Todd L. and Echlin, Randall Scott eds., Annual Review of Civil Litigation 2015 (1st edn, Carswell, 2015), 43, p. 43. See also Beebe, Barton, 'Trademark Law: An Open-Source Casebook', Trademark Infringement (V3 edn, 2016), p. 49.

[217]Estée Lauder, Case C-220/98, [1999] ECR I-117, (opinion of AG Fennelly), para 26 and see above footnote 207.

[218]As explained by Devlin, a Pareto improvement is understood as "given a pre-existing resource distribution, an exchange effect a Pareto improvement if it satisfies at least one person's preference without making any other individual worse off." Devlin, Allan, 'Fundamental Principles of Law and Economics', (1st edn, Routledge, 2014), p. 32. Kaldor-Hicks efficiency emerges "when an action increases the net welfare of society, but harms at least one person." *Ibid*, p. 33. See also Parisi, Francesco, 'The Language of Law and Economics. A Dictionary', (1st edn, Cambridge University Press, 2013), p. 162, Posner, Richard A., 'Economic Analysis of Law', (9th edn, Aspen, 2014), p. 14-15 and Griffiths, Andrew, 'An Economic Perspective on Trade Mark Law', (1st edn, Edward Elgar, 2011), p. 40.

[219]It cannot be ruled out that the Danish translation is purely an example of an imprecise translation. Other linguistic versions use words similar to "utility," hence Deutsh ("nuttigst"), French ("utile"), German ("Nutzen") and Swedish ("nytta").

[220]Burk, Dan L. 'Law and Economics of Intellectual Property: In Search of First Principles', Annual Review of Law and Social Science, vol. 8/(2012), pp. 397, p. 398.

to buy than the best home economist." Stigler has explained that "[t]he basis of the credo is simply the fact than an economic actor on *average* knows better the environment in which he is acting and the probable consequences of his actions than an outsider, no matter how clever the outsider may be."[221] In Posner's words rational actors are assumed to be "rational maximizers of their ends life, their satisfactions – equivalently, their "self-interest," which should however not be confused with selfishness. The happiness—or for that matter the misery—of other people may be part of one's satisfactions, although to avoid confusion economists generally prefer to speak of "utility" than self-interest."[222] According to Cooter and Ulen, "a rational actor can rank alternatives according to the extent they give her [or him] what she [or he] wants." For instance, "rational consumers can rank alternative bundles of consumer goods, and the consumer's budget constraints her [or his] choice among them."[223] Consumer utility maximisation means as put baldly by Jacoby, "seeking the most bang for the buck"[224] and also "buying when prices are lowered and refraining when prices rise."[225] According to Posner, the only people deviating from the starting point of being "rational maximizers of satisfactions" are "small children and the profoundly retarded" and people "under the influence of psychosis or similarly deranged through drug or alcohol abuse."[226] Price undoubtedly has an influence on the rational actor, however, according to Jacoby, "[r]egardless of how much the price is reduced, having previously purchased a product (or brand of a product) only to have it prove highly unsatisfactory, the consumer may

---

[221] Stigler, George J., 'Economists and Public Policy', AEI Journal on Government and Society, vol. May/June (1982), pp. 13, p. 16 (italics added). In similar veins Ramsay has held that "[e]ach individual in the market is assumed to be the best judge of his own interests and to act rationally, maximising his utility (or personal satisfaction) within the constraints of his economic resources." Ramsay, Iain, 'Consumer Law and Policy: Text and Materials on Regulating Consumer Markets', (3rd edn, Hart, 2012), p. 47. Reference at this point is made to a previous book of his from 1984, Ramsay, Iain, 'Rationales for Intervention in the Consumer Marketplace', (1st edn, Office of Fair Trading, 1984), p. 22-24. It is based on this finding that Mak has made her finding referred to above that consumers in EU law are assumed to be rational actors. Mak, Vanessa, 'The Consumer in European Regulatory Private Law', in Leczykiewicz, Dorota, and Weatherill, Stephen eds., The Images of the Consumer in EU Law: Legislation, Free Movement and Competition Law (1st edn, Hart, 2016), 381, p. 384.

[222] Posner, Richard A., 'Economic Analysis of Law', (9th edn, Aspen, 2014), p. 3. See also Parisi, Francesco, 'The Language of Law and Economics. A Dictionary', (1st edn, Cambridge University Press, 2013), p. 245 and Ariely, Dan, 'The Upside of Irrationality: The Unexpected Benefits of Defying Logic at Work and at Home', (1st edn, Harper Perennial, 2010), p. 5-6. It should be mentioned though that Ariely is not supportive of this kind of rationality assumption.

[223] Cooter, Robert, and Ulen, Thomas, 'Law and Economics', (6th edn, Pearson, 2014), p. 13.

[224] Jacoby, Jacob, 'Is it Rational to Assume Consumer Rationality? Some Consumer Psychological Perspectives on Rational Choice Theory', Roger Williams University Law Review, vol. 6 (2000-2001), pp. 81, p. 87.

[225] *Ibid*, p. 88.

[226] Posner, Richard A., 'The Problems of Jurisprudence', (1st edn, Harvard University Press, 1990), p. 353.

decide never to purchase that item again."[227] In particular, for products bought by the same consumer regularly, trademarks, in this context, according to Economides, "function directly through the previous experience of the consumer." Goods such as experience goods represent goods often purchased by consumers. For example, a bottle of diet COKE does not as such have a label that signal the taste however, from previous experiences with the product, the consumer is aided by the trademark "able to decide *rationally* as an informed consumer about his future choices between diet COKE and all other goods."[228] On the owner side, according to Burk, it is assumed that the "trademark owner (...) has a rational interest in seeing the intangible associations maintained, fostered, and developed." Those owners will be "in a position to coordinate the use and development of the mark"[229] in existing or new markets.[230]

In words familiar with the reason for being of legal models, Stigler has held that expanding the assumption of "rational behaviour to all areas of man's behaviour" is "a powerful and versatile theory which can produce suggestive hypotheses to tackle new problems, and it provides also the methods for studying these hypotheses."[231] Laurence Friedmann has claimed that "[r]ationally self-interested behavior still lies at the core of the science" and that "[n]o other social science, as far as I know, has been so successful, and so explicit, in finding core concepts and assumptions to work from."[232] In similar veins, Cooter and Ulen have argued that "[e]conomists often say that models assuming maximizing behavior work because most people are rational,

---

[227]Jacoby, Jacob, 'Is it Rational to Assume Consumer Rationality? Some Consumer Psychological Perspectives on Rational Choice Theory', Roger Williams University Law Review, vol. 6 (2000-2001), pp. 81, p. 94.

[228]Economides, Nicolas, 'The Economics of Trade Marks', Trademark Reporter, vol. 78 (1987), pp. 523, p. 528 (italics added).

[229]Burk, Dan L. 'Law and Economics of Intellectual Property: In Search of First Principles', Annual Review of Law and Social Science, vol. 8/(2012), pp. 397, p. 410.

[230]The economic function of trademarks as lowering consumer search costs is addressed in Chap. 1, Sect. 1.3.2. Within intellectual property management, it has been suggested that trademarks are key business assets. By way of the goodwill attached to trademark, it is possible for the trademark owner to create a strong brand and to leverage from existing markets (so-called "red ocean markets") into new markets (so-called "blue ocean markets"). Trademarks also facilitate the process for the owner of a patent protected invention in the duration of the protection to increase demand not only for the protected invention, but also for the brand under which it is sold. Thereby it is possible for the patent owner to leverage protection outside the duration of the patent protection, increasing market shares in existing markets. This mechanism of trademarks has been analysed further in the following article: Conley, James G., Bican, Peter M., and Ernst, Holger, 'Value Articulation: A Framework for the Strategic Management of Intellectual Property', California Management Review, vol. 55/no. 4, (2013), pp. 102. See also Posner, Richard A., 'Intellectual Property: The Law and Economics Approach', the Journal of Economic Perspectives, vol. 19/no. 2, (2005), pp. 57, p. 67.

[231]Stigler, George J., 'Economists and Public Policy', AEI Journal on Government and Society, vol. May/June (1982), pp. 13, p. 17.

[232]Friedman, Lawrence M. 'Law, Economics and Society', Hofstra Law Review, vol. 39 (2010-2011), pp. 487, p. 489.

and rationality requires maximization."[233] The "tough logic" underlying the rationality assumption, according to Stigler, replaces "ad hockery" providing "special explanations" and "exceptions."[234]

Based on the rational actor model, some assumed patterns of consumer behaviour might be detected. According to Mathis, "it is possible to assume that individuals' behaviour will follow a normal distribution curve, and that economic theory will explain the behaviour of the *average individual*," including consumers. This is based on the assumption, that "[i]n terms of distribution, the bulk of individuals cluster around the mean value, and if distribution is symmetrical, the highly variant behaviours at both extremities of the distribution cancel each other out, which is why they are of little consequence for the *average*."[235] On the face of it, this numerical way of using "average" in the sense of placing behaviour on a "normal distribution curve" resonates well with the behaviour of an *average* consumer in a descriptive sense. However, this does not fit well with the significant normative end of the average consumer in trademark law where "average" is not to be understood in the mathematical sense.[236]

As it emerges from the above, the "average consumer" is not a term well recognised in economic parlance. In European trademark law, this term emanates from the judicial vocabulary. However, some significant mentioning of the average consumer in economic theory has emerged.

6.6.3   The Critique from Behavioural Economics

The neoclassical assumptions underlying the rational actor model have been criticised by behavioural economics, or focused on the analysis of law, *behavioural law and economics*. In essences, the behavioural approach attacks the rationality assumptions infusing neoclassical economics. This new direction of economics seeks to test the rationality assumptions and "attempts to test them empirically and to modify and enhance them with insights from behavioral science."[237] Behavioural

---

[233]Cooter, Robert, and Ulen, Thomas, 'Law and Economics', (6th edn, Pearson, 2014), p. 12.

[234]Stigler, George J., 'Economists and Public Policy', AEI Journal on Government and Society, vol. May/June (1982), pp. 13, p. 17.

[235]Mathis, Klaus, 'Efficiency Instead of Justice – Searching for the Philosophical Foundations of the Economic Analysis of Law', (1st edn, Springer, 2009), p. 14 (italics added).

[236]Below, the meaning of the term "average" as part of the average consumer is discussed, given a numerical average, where it is concluded that the term is not to be understood as a numerical average. See Chap. 11, Sect. 11.2.2.

[237]Towfigh, Emanuel V. and Petersen, Niels, 'Economic Methods for Lawyers', (1st edn, Edward Elgar, 2015), p. 177. See also Mathis, Klaus ed., European Perspectives on Behavioural Law and Economics. Foundations and Applications (1st edn, Springer, 2015), foreword, p. ix-xi.

economics can be said to employ a "behavioral man"[238] or similarly a "behavioral model."[239] As such, behavioural law and economics is not analysed in this book. However, looking for improvements of the average consumer model through better ways of anchoring the model in science and enhancing its coherence and consistency more broadly, in the final chapter, reference will be made to solutions suggested by scholars drawing on behavioural law and economics, among others Weatherall.[240]

In an article by Thaler, together with Sunstein,[241] one of the most acclaimed behavioural economists today, he has criticised the rationality assumptions sketched in the previous section. Thaler has held that economists tend to employ the rational actor model normatively, i.e. with reference to describing what "rational consumers *should do.*" In addition, the model also often pretends to be descriptive, i.e. predicting, "what consumers in fact do."[242] According to Thaler, there are different consumer groups with different knowledge, including "experts" and "novices" (potentially children).[243] Thaler has criticised the "orthodox model of consumer behavior" for being "a model of robot-like experts. As such it does a poor job of predicting the behavior of the *average consumer.*" This, Thaler continues, "is not because the *average consumer* is dumb, but rather that he does not spend all of his time thinking about how to make decisions. A grocery shopper (. . .) spends a couple of hours a week shopping and devotes a rational amount of (scarce) mental energy."[244] Adding to this, Jacoby has held that "[f]rom the perspective of the behavioral sciences, while Economic Man Theory may apply across some to-be-defined aggregate, it falls apart when considering individual consumer behavior."[245]

---

[238]Posner, Richard A., 'Rational Choice, Behavioral Economics, and the Law', Stanford Law Review, vol. 50 (1997-1998), pp. 1551, p. 1559.

[239]Towfigh, Emanuel V. and Petersen, Niels, 'Economic Methods for Lawyers', (1st edn, Edward Elgar, 2015), p. 18.

[240]Weatherall, Kimberlee, 'The Consumer as the Empirical Measure of Trade Mark Law', Modern Law Review, vol. 80/no. 1, (2017), pp. 57. See also Sibony, Anne-Lise, 'Can EU Consumer Law Benefit from Behavioural Insights? An Analysis of the Unfair Practices Directive', in Mathis, Klaus ed., European Perspectives on Behavioural Law and Economics. Foundations and Applications (1st edn, Springer, 2015), 71.

[241]Thaler, Richard H. and Sunstein, Cass R., 'Nudge: Improving Decisions about Health, Wealth, and Happiness', (1st edn, Yale University Press, 2008).

[242]Thaler, Richard, 'Toward a Positive Theory and Consumer Choice', in Kahneman, Daniel and Tversky, Amos eds., Choices, Values, and Frames (1st edn, Cambridge University Press, 2000), 269, p. 269. For the divide between positive and normative analysis, see also Pindyck, Robert and Rubinfeld, Daniel, 'Microeconomics', (9th edn, Pearson, 2018), p. 28-29.

[243]Thaler has built his argument around an example by Milton Friedman and Savage referring to the predictability of a billiard player's next shots. With that in mind, Thaler has held that there are *expert* and *novice* players. However, his argument has broader implications going beyond the billiard example. Thaler, Richard, 'Toward a Positive Theory and Consumer Choice', in Kahneman, Daniel and Tversky, Amos eds., Choices, Values, and Frames (1st edn, Cambridge University Press, 2000), 269, p. 286-287 (italics added).

[244]*Ibid*, p. 269 (italics added).

[245]Jacoby, Jacob, 'Is it Rational to Assume Consumer Rationality? Some Consumer Psychological Perspectives on Rational Choice Theory', Roger Williams University Law Review, vol. 6 (2000-

Sunstein has argued that consumers are not rational in the traditional sense, but that they display a "bounded rationality, and that for many purposes, bounded rationality is just fine, producing outcomes that are equal to or perhaps even better than what would emerge from efforts to assess all costs and benefits."[246]

Posner has presented a key counter to the use of the "behavioral man," holding that "it is profoundly unclear what "behavioral man" would do in any given situation" and that there is no clear model of the "decisional structure" of this more empirically base model.[247]

6.6.4   Summarising Discussion

The above-analysis shows that the rational actor model differs somewhat from the average consumer, but that it may still be seen as a "distant cousin of the average consumer." In the characteristics of the average consumer as "reasonably well-informed and reasonably observant and circumspect," there is an inbuilt lower level of attention[248] compared to a highly attentive consumer, purchasing e.g. pharmaceuticals, or indeed compared with the informed user and the sectoral expert as stipulated by *Pepsi v. Grupo Promer*.[249] The rational actor model though

---

2001), pp. 81, p. 90. Burk has furthermore held that "[a]s it does in other areas of law, behavioral law and economics is challenging rational actor models in intellectual property to offer a more nuanced, realistic account of incentives and their effects." Burk, Dan L. 'Law and Economics of Intellectual Property: In Search of First Principles', Annual Review of Law and Social Science, vol. 8/(2012), pp. 397, p. 412. Along those lines, Laurence Friedman has held that "some human behavior is culturally determined, and all human behavior is culturally grounded. Human behavior always depends on time and place. None of it takes place in that clean, clear, abstract world which mathematical models describe. Not that these models do not work at all, but their zone is distinctly limited. The domain of free choice, of rational behavior, can expand or contract." Friedman, Lawrence M. 'Law, Economics and Society', Hofstra Law Review, vol. 39 (2010-2011), pp. 487, p. 491 and also p. 494.

[246]Sunstein, Cass R., 'Why Nudge? The Politics of Libertarian Paternalism', (1st edn, Yale University Press, 2014), p. 11.

[247]Posner, Richard A., 'Rational Choice, Behavioral Economics, and the Law', Stanford Law Review, vol. 50 (1997-1998), pp. 1551, p. 1559. This countering argument by Posner emerged as part of a response to one of the bedrock articles on behavioral economics, the article from 1998 by Jolls, Christine, Sunstein, Cass R. and Thaler, Richard, 'A Behavioral Approach to Law and Economics', Stanford Law Review, vol. 50/no. 5, (1998), pp. 1471.

[248]Hence, it has recently been claimed by Sibony and Helleringer that the average consumer "is deemed to have enough slack in his bandwidth to be 'reasonably well-informed and reasonably observant and circumspect'." Sibony, Anne-Lise, and Helleringer, Geneviève, 'EU Consumer Protection and Behavioural Sciences: Revolution Or Reform?', in Alemanno, Alberto and Sibony, Anne-Lise eds., Nudge and the Law: A European Perspective (1st edn, Hart, 2016), 209, p. 214.

[249]Mak (in a similar way analysing the rational consumer in EU law) has held that in areas of intellectual property law, besides trademark law, the "standard of informed reasonable behaviour from the consumer (...) is higher than that of the 'average consumer,' albeit to different degrees." Mak, Vanessa, 'The Consumer in European Regulatory Private Law', in Leczykiewicz, Dorota, and

allows for lower levels of attention than an expert consumer in its broad definition of "self-interest," including their satisfactions. Such satisfaction may be finishing grocery shopping fast and thus rushing through the supermarket not paying much attention to the marks of the products stacked in the trolley. As addressed in the introduction, the Court of Justice has held that "the average consumer's level of attention is likely to vary according to the category of goods or services in question."[250] The General Court has downstream used this to imbue the average consumer purchases of "everyday consumer goods" with an "average" attention[251] and at times lower than average attention.[252] The law in this matter accommodates the average consumer pursuing a "self-interest" in wrapping up quickly in the supermarket. An interest probably pursued by many everyday grocery shoppers as also noted by Thaler.

The danger though, as pointed out by Thaler, is that to the extent the rational actor model is deemed to be "a model of robot-like experts," it does not mirror the average consumer since this does not accommodate its inbuilt gaps of attentiveness of this model. From the broad definitions of self-interest of the rational actor, this model seems to move away from the "orthodox" rational actor model portrayed by Thaler. A highly relevant point though is Thaler claiming that the average consumer may in fact "not spend all of his time thinking about how to make decisions." This means that for instance in the grocery shopping scenario, the average consumer does potentially not even reach the decision making stage where relevant to trademark law, trademarks of two competing products are even considered before one product is tossed in the trolley. How does it then make sense in this scenario to talk about "likelihood of confusion"? Here, the average consumer can hardly be said to be other than purely a normative fiction, not describing what actually goes on.

Weatherill, Stephen eds., The Images of the Consumer in EU Law: Legislation, Free Movement and Competition Law (1st edn, Hart, 2016), 381, p. 386. Mak at this point refers to an "informed consumer" and then refers to Herbert Neuman and Andoni Galdeano v. OHIM, Joined Cases C-101/11 P and C-102/11 P, [2012] – a design case where the court of justice essentially has referred to the informed user as set out in *Pepsi v. Grupo Promer*. See for instance PepsiCo v. Grupo Promer, Case C-281/10 P, [2011] ECR I-10153, para 53.

[250]Lloyd Schuhfabrik Meyer v. Klijsen Handel BV, Case C-342/97, [1999] ECR I-3819, para 26. See also recently the General Court in BMB v. EUIPO, Case T-695/15, [2017], para 32 and Şölen Çikolata Gıda Sanayi ve Ticaret v. EUIPO, Case T-794/16, [2018], para 29.

[251]See for instance, Adidas v. OHIM (Shoe Branding), Case T-145/14, [2015], para 33. The decision relates to sports shoes and clothing in class 25 of the Nice Agreement.

[252]See for instance, Mederer v. OHIM (Gummy), Case T-210/14, [2016], para 28. The decision relates to certain confectioneries in class 30 of the Nice Agreement. The level of attention of the average consumer is dealt with further in Chap. 11.

6.7   Conclusion

The Court of Justice in *Pepsi v. Grupo* on the Design Regulation found that there is a similarity between the average consumer in trademark law, the informed user in design law and the sectoral expert (the person skilled in the art) in patent law. On a continuum of attentiveness, the Court of Justice placed the average consumer as the least attentive, the person skilled in the art as the most attentive and the informed user as falling between the two. When analysing those fictions, it emerged first that the average consumer as such is a singular "person" opposite the informed user and the person skilled in the art that may consists of different personal groups. As will be further analysed this is different in trademark law when the relevant public is not the *average consumer* but the somewhat similar *general public* and specialised purchasers. Second, focusing on the different fictions and their level of attention compared to their peers in their respective areas, as with the *average* consumer, roughly the informed user is the *average* user and the person skilled in the art is the *average* person skilled in the art. The fictions therefore are similar mechanisms in their respective legal environments. Third, it was shown that the fictions are significant calibration mechanisms for both the senior and junior owners in registration and infringement. The parties have an interest in moulding the relevant fiction to fit their claims.

Based on the European tort law principles laid down in the DCFR and PETL, the relationship between the average consumer and the reasonable person was analysed. It was concluded that the average consumer deemed to be "*reasonably* well-informed and *reasonably* observant and circumspect" is as the *reasonable* person infused with a certain reasonableness. Both are fictions and involve a non-quantifiable aspect. Thus, without breaching the "*likelihood* of confusion" standard in European trademark law, it is accepted for the average consumer to be somewhat confused and without breaching the negligence standard in European tort law it is accepted for the reasonable person to take some "*risks.*" In balancing what is "acceptable," both "likelihood" and "risk" indicate something non-quantifiable. It was found that the reasonable person was closely intertwined with the negligence standard, closer than the average consumer within the likelihood of confusion standard. As for the improvement of the average consumer addressed in the final chapter, potentially inspiration can be found in the objectiveness of the reasonable person.

Last, the average consumer was compared with another fiction, outside of law but within social science, the rational actor model from economics. The findings in literature that the average consumer is based on the self-maximizing rational actor model were not as such refuted. Hence, it makes sense to talk about the average consumer metaphorically as the "not so distant cousin of *homo oeconomicus.*" However, it must be noted that the average consumer is a legal term only to a limited extent found in economics. The characteristics of the average consumer given *in law* allow for some deviation in its attentiveness not fully resonating with the rational actor. Finally, the generalisations inherent in the average consumer are not allowed, as suggested by some, because of the resemblance between the average consumer and the rational actor model. The generalisations are allowed due to the broader role of social science models, including legal fictions.

The analysis of neighbouring legal fictions and the rational actor model has shown that the average consumer is not to be understood in a scientific vacuum but in a broader scientific picture. In particular since the models addressed in this chapter are all social science models with common features of finding *workable* solutions in their respective areas not striving at a one-to-one explanation of real world phenomena. This general pedigree of the average consumer is important to bear in mind throughout the subsequent analyses. The average consumer cannot only be analysed in a trademark law vacuum without bearing the broader role of social science models in mind.

Chapter 7
The UCPD and Trademark Average Consumers: Two of a Kind?

7.1 Introduction

This chapter analyses the UCPD version of the average consumer in contrast with the trademark law version. The UCPD is outside the domain of EU trademark law, and this piece of *lex generalis* EU legislation is within a much broader and less clearly defined realm of EU unfair competition law. It stands out how much scholarship exists on the UCPD average consumer compared to the European trademark law version[1] and, paradoxically, how little case law from the Court of Justice is available on the UCPD version. As Duivenvoorde notes, "[a]s a matter of fact, the notion of

---

[1]See among others, Friant-Perrot, Marine, 'The Vulnerable Consumer in the UCPD and Other Provisions of EU Law', in van Boom, Willem, Garde, Amandine and Akseli, Orkun eds., The European Unfair Commercial Practices Directive: Impact, Enforcement Strategies and National Legal Systems (1st edn, Farnham, Ashgate, 2014), 89; Trzaskowski, Jan, 'Behavioural Economics, Neuroscience, and the Unfair Commercial Practises Directive', Journal of Consumer Policy, vol. 34/no. 3, (2011), pp. 377, Trzaskowski, Jan, 'The Unfair Commercial Practices Directive and Vulnerable Consumers', Conference Paper, (2013), pp. 1; partly Mak, Vanessa, 'Standards of Protection: In Search of the 'Average Consumer' of EU Law in the Proposal for a Consumer Rights Directive', European Review of Private Law, vol. 19/no. 1, (2011), pp. 25; Incardona, Rossella, and Poncibò, Cristina, 'The Average Consumer, the Unfair Commercial Practices Directive, and the Cognitive Revolution', Journal of Consumer Policy, vol. 30/no. 1, (2007), pp. 21; Wilhelmsson, Thomas, 'The Average European Consumer: A Legal Fiction?', in Wilhelmsson, Thomas, Paunio, Elina and Pohjolainen, Annika eds., Private Law and the Many Cultures of Europe (1st edn, Kluwer Law International, 2007), 243, Duivenvoorde, Bram B., 'The Consumer Benchmarks in the Unfair Commercial Practices Directive', (1st edn, Springer, 2015). More broadly not only focus on the UCPD average consumer: Böhler, Christian, 'A Thin Line between the Rationalization of Consumer Choices and Overburdening Market Participants. Are the Courts Able to Keep the Balance?', European Food and Feed Law Review, vol. 10/no. 1, (2015), pp. 34 and Wiebe, Andreas, 'How Much Nature for the Consumer? Misleading Advertising, Trademark Law, the European Average Consumer Standard in the Food Sector', Corporate Governance eJournal, no. 32, 2015, (2015), pp. 1 and Howells, Geraint, Twigg-Flesner, Christian, Wilhelmsson, Thomas, 'Rethinking EU Consumer Law', (1st edn, Routledge, 2018), p. 27-31 and p. 66-73.

© Springer Nature Switzerland AG 2020

R. D. Laustsen, *The Average Consumer in Confusion-based Disputes in European Trademark Law and Similar Fictions*, https://doi.org/10.1007/978-3-030-26350-8_7

the 'average consumer' is referred to more often in trademark cases than in all other fields taken together."[2] One immediate reason for this is the different stakeholder interests vested in the two regimes addressed in this chapter.

As for the definition of "unfair competition," Henning-Bodewig have pointed out, that there are "no significant differences in terms of content between 'unfair competition' and other terms, such as the term frequently used by the ECJ, 'the fairness of commercial transactions' or the term 'unfair commercial practices' used in [the UCPD]."[3] It is the purpose of this chapter to determine to what extent the average consumer in European trademark law is harmonised with that of the UCPD. This involves looking into the policy underpinning of the UCPD. The Court of Justice has provided little guidance specifically on the UCPD and its average consumer. Therefore, the following mainly addresses how the EU legislature in the directive has laid out this average consumer. The key reason for the analysis of the UCPD is that the directive explicitly refers to the average consumer and the broad implications of the directive. Recital 18 of the UCPD thus crucially states that "this Directive takes as a benchmark the average consumer, who is reasonably well-informed and reasonably observant and circumspect, taking into account social, cultural and linguistic factors, as interpreted by the Court of Justice."[4] Several overall similarities and differences make the UCPD relevant to analyse from a European trademark law perspective.

Initially, there is a common judicial origin of the average consumer found in the early Court of Justice decisions on consumer protection law and unfair competition law, most importantly *Gut Springenheide* on unfair competition law.[5] Most noticeably, the above quote from recital 18 of the UCPD indicates that this "average consumer" and its characteristics is identical to the one in European trademark law. It also resonates well with European trademark law that the recital states that "[t]he average consumer test is not a statistical test."[6] Another familiar finding when bearing in mind the contextualisation in European trademark law, one is that under the UCPD the "[n]ational courts and authorities will have to exercise their own faculty of judgement, having regard to the case-law of the Court of Justice, to determine the typical reaction of the average consumer in a given case."[7] The similarities between the two versions of the average consumer were also stressed in the UK trademark dispute, *Interflora EWHC*, where Arnold J referred to recital 18 of the UCPD in laying out the average consumer.[8]

---

[2]Duivenvoorde, Bram B., 'The Consumer Benchmarks in the Unfair Commercial Practices Directive', (1st edn, Springer, 2015), p. 52.

[3]Henning-Bodewig, Frauke, 'Unfair Competition Law: European Union and Member States', (1st edn, Kluwer Law International, 2006), p. x.

[4]Recital 18 of the UCPD.

[5]For an account of the early decisions of the Court of Justice, see the following chapter.

[6]Recital 18 of the UCPD.

[7]*Ibid.*

[8]Interflora v. Marks & Spencer, [2013] EWHC 1291 (Ch), para 209. The defendant (M&S) referred to recital 18 of the UCPD as a ground for finding that the average consumer test is normative and involves the usual characteristics. Arnold J affirmed this.

The codification of the average consumer under the UCPD, but not in European trademark law, is a key difference. It has been held by the EU Commission that this codification took place "to give national authorities and courts common criteria to enhance legal certainty and reduce the possibility of divergent assessments."[9] The UCPD (and its preparatory works) does add more legal content and context than the well-known characteristics. This might provide an understanding of what the average consumer means in the UCPD and in the trademark law. A relevant difference is also the mentioned high quantity of scholarship on the UCPD, and more broadly unfair competition law.[10] Finally, the UCPD, at least formally, includes not only the average consumer model, but also other consumer models, such as the "vulnerable consumer." The vulnerable consumer as a consumer model, represented by children, is separately analysed since this consumer group in several ways represents a special case under both the UCPD and European trademark law.

7.2 Purpose of the UCPD

Under the UCPD, it is clear that the consumer is the focus of the EU legislature's protective attentions. When regulating B2C relations encompassed by the UCPD, consumers are the direct legal beneficiaries of protection, in contrast with trademark law in confusion-based disputes addressing the senior trademark owner versus a competitor. Besides being beneficiaries of protection, consumers also have legal standing in the UCPD if they have a legitimate interest in opposing to a commercial practice.[11]

The Preamble of the UCPD states that the purpose of the directive is the creation of a high level of consumer protection through a "high level of convergence achieved by the approximation of national provisions through this Directive [UCPD]".[12] This indicates that the average consumer is not only used as a benchmark, it is also a clear purpose of the UCPD to protect consumers as such. The UCPD explicitly seeks to "achieve a high level of consumer protection."[13] As

---

[9]Commission Staff Working Document Guidance on the Implementation/Application of Directive 2005/29/EC on Unfair Commercial Practices Accompanying the document "Communication From the Commission to the European Parliament, the Council, the European Economic and Social Committee and the Regions – A comprehensive approach to stimulating cross-border e-Commerce for Europe's citizens and businesses" (COM(2016) 320 final) of 25 May 2016 SWD(2016) 163 final, p. 37.

[10]See above footnote 1.

[11]Arts. 11-13 of the UCPD.

[12]Recital 11 of the UCPD.

[13]See art. 1 of the UCPD, and the Preamble in general. More precisely, in recital 6 it is stated that "[i]n line with the principle of proportionality, this Directive protects consumers from the consequences of such unfair commercial practices where they are material but recognises that in some cases the impact on consumers may be negligible. It neither covers nor affects the national laws on

Howells *et al* have described, the UCPD is "a general clause to cover all economic harm caused to consumers by unfair practices" in B2C relations.[14] In *Magyarország v. Nemzeti*, the Court of Justice interpreted B2C relations, referring to the broadly phrased UCPD, to include commercial practices where only one consumer is affected.[15] The court even stated that the UCPD is "designed with the consumer as the *target and victim* of unfair commercial practices in mind."[16] This indicates the B2C sphere of the UCPD, but also the central framing of the consumer.

While consumers are the main beneficiaries of protection in the UCPD, "it also indirectly protects legitimate businesses from their competitors who do not play by the rules in this Directive and thus guarantees fair competition in fields coordinated by it."[17] Besides aiming at a high level of consumer protection and, indirectly protecting fair business, the UCPD also has the explicit aim of preserving, "[t]he development of fair commercial practices within the area without internal frontiers is vital for the promotion of the development of cross-border activities".[18]

As EU harmonisation, the UCPD was necessitated to strengthen the internal market, since "unfair commercial practices show marked differences which can generate appreciable distortions of competition and obstacles to the smooth functioning of the internal market."[19] An EU Commission working paper from 2003 drafted as part of preparing the UCPD ("the UCPD Working Paper 2003") stated that "[i]n brief, specific legal barriers caused by the fragmented regulation of unfair commercial practices cause cost, complexity and uncertainty for firms and a lack of consumer confidence in cross-border transactions."[20] These policy points of departure are comparable to those of EU trademark legislation, i.e. the aim is to remove national barriers for EU interstate trade.[21] However, a very visible difference

---

unfair commercial practices which harm only competitors' economic interests or which relate to a transaction between traders." See also Nemzeti v. Magyarország, Case C-388/13, [2015], paras 32 and 51, including referred case law in para 32.

[14]Howells, Geraint G., Micklitz, Hans-W, and Wilhelmsson, Thomas, 'European Fair Trading Law the Unfair Commercial Practices Directive', (1st edn, Ashgate, 2006), preface.

[15]Nemzeti v. Magyarország, Case C-388/13, [2015], paras 31-37. The Court of Justice clearly disagreed with the conclusion of Advocate General Wahl that stated: "It is (. . .) my understanding that B2C conduct such as the communication of erroneous information to a single consumer cannot, to the extent that it constitutes an isolated event, be regarded as a 'commercial practice' within the meaning of the UCP Directive." Nemzeti v. Magyarország, Case C-388/13, [2015] (opinion of AG Wahl), para 35.

[16]Nemzeti v. Magyarország, Case C-388/13, [2015], para 52 (italics added). See also BKK Mobil Oil v. Zentrale, Case C-59/12, [2013], para 36.

[17]Recital 8 of the UCPD.

[18]Recital 2 of the UCPD.

[19]Recital 3 of the UCPD.

[20]Commission Staff Working Paper Extended Impact Assessment on the EP and Council Directive on unfair business-to-consumer commercial practices in the Internal Market and amending directives 84/450/EEC, 97/7/EC and 98/27/EC (the Unfair Commercial Practices Directive) of 18 June 2003, COM(2003)356 final. *Ibid*, p. 3.

[21]See Chap. 1, Sect. 1.3.3.

is the UCPD's cumulative purpose of making consumers sure of their rights, since "[s]uch barriers also make consumers uncertain of their rights and undermine their confidence in the internal market."[22]

In line with the focus of the EU Parliament on "maximum harmonisation" of consumer protection legislation,[23] the UCPD is a maximum legal harmonisation measure in that respect.[24] In *Mediaprint v. 'Österreich'-Zeitungsverlag*, Advocate General Trstenjak stated that the recitals of the UCPD with certain very limited exceptions seek a "full harmonisation" that "not only aims at *minimum harmonisation*, but also seeks to achieve *maximum approximation* of national provisions which prohibit the Member States, apart from certain exceptions, from retaining or introducing stricter rules, even in order to achieve a higher level of consumer protection."[25]

7.3 Transaction Timing and Likelihood of Harm

One prominent difference between European trademark law and the UCPD is the timing. This is apparent from the UCPD's extended *ex ante* view of the relevant transaction. The UCPD is concerned with a "transactional decision," which it defines as "any decision taken by a consumer concerning whether, how and on what terms to purchase, make payment in whole or in part for, retain or dispose of a product or to exercise a contractual right in relation to the product, *whether the consumer decides to act or to refrain from acting.*"[26] Unfair commercial practices are in particular

---

[22]Recital 4 of the UCPD.

[23]See UCPD Working Paper 2003, footnote 33 where reference is made to a green paper drafted by the EU Parliament on consumer protection law.

[24]Weatherill has stated that the UCPD is an example of "a shift from minimum to maximum harmonisation – whereby the EU sets both floor and ceiling of regulatory protection." Weatherill, Stephen, 'EU Consumer Law and Policy', (2nd edn, Edward Elgar, 2013), p. 25. See also Nemzeti v. Magyarország, Case C-388/13, [2015], para 32 and Howells, Geraint G., 'Europe's (Lack of) Vision on Consumer Protection: A Case of Rhetoric Hiding Substance?', in Leczykiewicz, Dorota, and Weatherill, Stephen eds., The Images of the Consumer in EU Law: Legislation, Free Movement and Competition Law (1st edn, Hart, 2016), 431, p. 436-439. For a recent analysis of the scope and gaps of the maximum harmonisation of the UCPD, see Howells, Geraint, Twigg-Flesner, Christian and Wilhelmsson, Thomas, 'Rethinking EU Consumer Law', (1st edn, Routledge, 2018), p. 47-48 and 73-84.

[25]Mediaprint v. 'Österreich'-Zeitungsverlag, Case C-540/08, [2010] ECR I-10909, (opinion of AG Trstenjak), para 61. Trstenjak has based this finding on recitals 11, 12, 14, 15 and arts. 1 and 4 of the UCPD. *Ibid*, paras 62-64. See also the Court of Justice in Europamur Alimentación v. Dirección General de Comercio y Protección del Consumidor, Case C-295/16, [2017], para 39 and the earlier opinion of Trstenjak in Zentrale zur Bekämpfung unlauteren Wettbewerbs v. Plus Warenhandelsgesellschaft, Case C-304/08, [2010] ECR I-217, (opinion of AG Trstenjak), paras 69-72.

[26]Cf. art. 2(k) of the UCPD (italics added).

misleading commercial practices,[27] including misleading actions[28] and misleading omissions,[29] and aggressive commercial practices,[30] including use of harassment, coercion and undue influence.[31] Added to this is a "blacklist" of commercial practices "which shall in all circumstances be regarded as unfair."[32]

Specifically relevant to the trademark law analysis is that misleading actions include practices in "any marketing of a product, including comparative advertising, *which creates confusion with any* products, *trade marks*, trade names or other distinguishing marks of a competitor."[33] In 2007, Bernitz stated that "[m]ost likely, the ECJ will use its present trade mark law jurisprudence on confusion and deception as an important point of departure."[34] So far, the Court of Justice has not ruled on the understanding of the UCPD confusion standard nor its interaction with the trademark law likelihood of confusion standard. Although the standard in EU trademark law is more mature than that of the UCPD, the future development of the latter may affect and negatively define the former. Art. $10^{bis}(3)(1)$ of the Paris Convention, which is said to be the confusion standard now manifested in the UCPD, is also relevant to interpreting the trademark confusion standard.[35]

A commercial practice is deemed unfair if it "*materially distorts or is likely to materially distort* the economic behaviour with regard to the product of the *average consumer* whom it reaches or to whom it is addressed, or of the *average member of the group* when a commercial practice is directed to a particular group of consumers."[36] The unfair commercial practices need not be an actual cause for an average consumer to make a transactional decision. Hence, it suffices that the unfair commercial practice is "*likely to cause him* [the average consumer] to take a transactional decision that [he] would have not have taken otherwise."[37]

The *likelihood* element is obviously also a key element in the trademark law confusion standard. It has appeared, though, that European trademark law is concerned with the likelihood of confusion in the *purchase situation*. The UCPD, on the other hand, focuses not only on the "transaction decision," but also on whether the unfair commercial practice in an *ex ante* perspective is "*likely to*

---

[27]Cf. art. 5(4)(a), cf. arts. 6 and 7 of the UCPD.

[28]Cf. art. 6 of the UCPD.

[29]Cf. art. 7 of the UCPD.

[30]Cf. art. 5(4)(b), cf. arts. 8 and 9 of the UCPD.

[31]Cf. art. 9 of the UCPD.

[32]Cf. art. 5(5) of the UCPD. Those practices are set out in Annex I of the UCPD.

[33]Cf. art. 6(2)(a) of the UCPD (italics added).

[34]Bernitz, Ulf, 'The Unfair Commercial Practices Directive: Its Scope, Ambitions and Relation to the Law of Unfair Competition', in Weatherill, Stephen and Bernitz, Ulf eds., The Regulation of the Unfair Commercial Practices Under EC Directive 2005/29 (1st edn, Oxford, Hart, 2007), 33, p. 42.

[35]See Chap. 9, Sect. 9.2.1.

[36]Cf. art. 5(2)(b) of the UCPD (italics added). Covered is also a commercial practice which "is contrary to the requirements of professional diligence." Art. 5(1)(a) of the UCPD.

[37]Cf. arts. 6(1), 7(1) and 8 of the UCPD (italics added).

cause" the average consumer to make a transaction decision in a broad sense.[38] Particularly, this to some extent resembles the "initial interest confusion" doctrine first raised in US trademark law practice.[39] The gist of this is that "[US] courts have allowed findings of trademark infringement solely on the basis that a consumer might initially be "interested," "attracted," or "distracted" by a competitor's, or even a non-competitor's, product or service," but not at the time of purchase.[40] The initial interest confusion doctrine was rejected at national level by the UK Court of Appeal in *Interflora EWCA III*. The court found the doctrine to be "an unnecessary and potentially misleading gloss" and not in accordance with Court of Justice case law.[41]

7.4 The Average Consumer

From the wording of the UCPD, it appears that the average consumer is the starting point consumer model under the directive.[42] Other conceivable consumer models in the UCPD are a "confident consumer,"[43] an "average member" of "a particular group of consumers"[44] and certain "vulnerable consumers."[45] In the UCPD, the legislature appears to have narrowed the average consumer, since reference is made explicitly to how the average consumer has been interpreted by the Court of Justice.[46] It is thus assumed that the EU legislature did not by way of the UCPD

---

[38]Hence, in a 2016 working paper on the UCPD, the EU Commission stated that "[n]ational enforcement authorities should therefore investigate the facts and circumstances of the individual case (i.e. in concreto), but assess also the 'likelihood' of the impact of that practice on the transactional decision of the average consumer (i.e. in abstracto)." The UCPD Working Paper 2016, p. 36.

[39]McKenna, Mark P., 'A Consumer Decision-Making Theory of Trade Mark Law', Virginia Law Review, vol. 98 (2012), pp. 67, Petty, Ross D., 'Initial Interest Confusion Versus Consumer Sovereignty: A Consumer Protection Perspective on Trademark Infringement', Trademark Reporter, vol. 98/no. 3, (2008), pp. 757, Glazer, Daniel C., and Dhamija, Dev R., 'Revisiting Initial Interest Confusion on the Internet', Trademark Reporter, vol. 95/no. 5, (2005), pp. 952 and Klein, David M., and Glazer, Daniel C., 'Reconsidering Initial Interest Confusion on the Internet', Trademark Reporter, vol. 93/no. 5, (2003), pp. 1035. Fhima, Ilanah S., 'Initial Interest Confusion', Journal of Intellectual Property Law & Practice, vol. 8/no. 4, (2013), pp. 311.

[40]Rothman, Jennifer E., 'Initial Interest Confusion: Standing at the Crossroads of Trademark Law', Cardozo Law Review, vol. 27/no. 1, (2005), pp. 105, p. 108.

[41]Interflora v. Marks & Spencer, [2014] EWCA Civ 1403, para 158, and overall paras 150-158. The decision overrules the finding by Arnold J in *Och-Ziff v. Och Capital* where it was concluded that initial interest confusion was actionable. Och-Ziff v. Och Capital, [2010] EWHC 2599 (Ch), para 101.

[42]See recital 18 and arts. 5(2)(b), 6(1)(2), 7(1)(2) and 8 of the UCPD.

[43]See recitals 4 and 13 of the UCPD.

[44]See recitals 18 and 19, and art. 5(2)(b) of the UCPD.

[45]See recital 18 and art. 5(3) of the UCPD.

[46]Recital 18 of the UCPD.

seek to significantly change the average consumer as developed by the Court of Justice at the time of introducing the directive and the average consumer as it was found in key decisions, such as *Sabel*, *Gut Springenheide* and *Lloyd*.[47] However, it is naturally important that the EU legislature in the UCPD, the maximum harmonising directive, referred not only to the average consumer, but also to its characteristics. The EU Commission in the UCPD Working Paper 2003 elaborated on the reasons for this. The EU Commission initially stated that the average consumer should be the "benchmark" for assessment of the fairness of commercial practices to ensure a balance between consumer interests and a "freedom of business to assume a certain level of understanding their commercial practices."[48] Subsequently, the EU Commission has sought to explain the well-known characteristics of the average consumer holding that the average consumer "is a reasonably critical person, conscious and circumspect in his or her market behaviour."[49]

Besides these well-known characteristics, the UCPD states that account should also be taken of "social, cultural and linguistic factors, as interpreted by the Court of Justice."[50] These factors have been traced back to the pre UCPD decision *Clinique* on misleading advertising, including its opinion by Advocate General Gulmann.[51] For instance, the Court of Justice deemed linguistic factors to be relevant under European trademark law in *DHL Express v. Chronopost*,[52] and all factors were referred to by the court in *Matratzen Concord v. Hukla* as relevant in the assessment of distinctive character of marks.[53] Recently, in *Ornua v. Tindale & Stanton*, the Court of Justice had to decide e.g. if "the geographical, demographic, economic or other circumstances of the States in which the coexistence has occurred be taken into consideration for the purpose of assessing the likelihood of confusion, so that the absence of a likelihood of confusion in those Member States can be extended to a third Member State, or to the European Union as a whole."[54] The court stated that "where the market conditions and the *sociocultural or other circumstances contributing to the overall impression produced by the EU trade mark and the sign at issue on the average consumer do not vary significantly*" such factors may considered when deciding if the senior trademark owner can prevent a junior trademark from

---

[47]Therefore, the average consumer in the UCPD, as it has been seen, is also "reasonably well-informed and reasonably observant and circumspect." Recital 18 of the UCPD.

[48]See the UCPD Working Paper 2003, p. 26.

[49]The UCPD Working Paper 2016, p. 38.

[50]Recital 18 of the UCPD. See on the UCPD Konsumentombudsmannen v. Ving Sverige, Case C-122/10, [2011] ECR I-3903, para 22 and Canal Digital Danmark, Case C-611/14, [2016], para 39.

[51]See Chap. 8, Sect. 8.6.

[52]DHL Express v. Chronopost, Case C-235/09, [2011] ECR I-2801, paras 47-48. Advocate General Jacobs also addressed this factor in *Lloyd*. Lloyd Schuhfabrik Meyer v. Klijsen Handel BV, Case C-342/97, [1998] ECR I-3819, (opinion of AG Jacobs), para 12.

[53]Matratzen Concord v Hukla, Case C-421/04, [2006] ECR I-2303, paras 25 and 32.

[54]Ornua v. Tindale & Stanton, Case C-93/16, [2017], para 2, second question.

being used in part of the whole of the EU.[55] In the UK (before *Ornua v. Tindale & Stanton*), Arnold J has even stated in a trademark context in *Enterprise v. Europcar* that "[i]t is *settled* that, in assessing matters from the perspective of the average consumer, the court must have regard to the *social, linguistic, cultural and economic conditions* in the Member State concerned, which may well vary as between Member States."[56]

The factors are critical since they illustrate that it is allowed for the national judiciaries to mould the average consumer to a diversified national and regional reality. Also, that despite full harmonisation there is no such thing as a "one-size-fits-all" average consumer. Wilhelmsson has found that these factors make the average consumer under the UCPD "partially culturebound."[57] Potentially, according to Wilhelmsson, many cultural "intra-European cultural variations" feed into this cultural binding of the average consumer.[58] Although national judiciaries may take in for instance "relevant cultural factors," as stated by the EU Commission, this "does imply that national courts should be assessing the effect of commercial practices on the ordinary consumer who is expected to be reasonably able to protect their own interests and not on consumers who are particularly vulnerable or gullible."[59]

The Court of Justice in *Magyarország v. Nemzeti* found that commercial practices under the UCPD include a practice whereby only one consumer is affected[60] and that this is in line with the "wide scope ratione materiae" of the UCPD.[61] Elaborating on this, the court furthermore stated that the average consumer was the benchmark (as usual) to be used also with only one consumer being affected.[62]

In *Purely Creative*, it was shown that psychological aspects are relevant. The claimant in the dispute was the UK Office of Fair Trading, at the time responsible for enforcing consumer protection laws, including the B2C practices under the UCPD ("OFT"). OFT claimed that distributing certain promotions by Purely Creative and others was an unfair commercial practice under the Consumer Protection from

---

[55]*Ibid*, para 42 (italics added). Here, the Court of Justice explicitly agreed with Advocate General Szpunar giving the opinion in the case. See Ornua v. Tindale & Stanton, Case C-93/16, [2017], (opinion of AG Szpunar), paras 41-42.

[56]Enterprise v. Europcar, [2015] EWHC 17 (Ch), para 139 (italics added).

[57]Wilhelmsson, Thomas, 'The Average European Consumer: A Legal Fiction?', in Wilhelmsson, Thomas, Paunio, Elina and Pohjolainen, Annika eds., Private Law and the Many Cultures of Europe (1st edn, Kluwer Law International, 2007), 243, p. 248.

[58]Wilhelmsson has mentioned "trust," "understanding communications," "rationality patterns," "role of commercial communications in decision-making" and "values and preferences." *Ibid*, p. 259-264.

[59]See the UCPD Working Paper 2003, p. 8.

[60]Nemzeti v. Magyarország, Case C-388/13, [2015], paras 39 and 41.

[61]*Ibid*, para 34, BKK Mobil Oil v. Zentrale, Case C-59/12, [2013], para 40 and Mediaprint Zeitungs- und Zeitschriftenverlag v. 'Österreich'-Zeitungsverlag, Case C-540/08, [2010] ECR I-10909, para 21.

[62]Nemzeti v. Magyarország, Case C-388/13, [2015], para 39.

Unfair Trading Regulations 2008 that implemented the UCPD into UK law.[63] In the distributed materials, the consumers were informed that they could claim a prize of minimum a few pounds and potentially much more. To claim the prize, consumers could e.g. call a premium rate phone number. The Court of Justice acknowledged that consumers do not always seem to act rationally. Hence, the court accepted there to be a "psychological effect caused by the announcement of the winning of a prize" causing the consumer to choose a more expensive way to reclaim the prize.[64] Furthermore, that the relevant consumer group is the average consumer or certain vulnerable consumers.[65] As Böhler points out referring to the German scholarly debate on the decision, this could be seen as giving room for "the consumer as some kind of impressionable idiot." In reality, Böhler continues, the decision is more an expression of the Court of Justice attaching too much weight to actual consumer behaviour and a "forced rationalization" of consumers and their application of a cost benefit analysis.[66]

In *Pereničová v. SOS financ spol*, SOS (a non-bank lender) in a loan agreement had stated an annual percentage rate of charge ("APR") lower than it was in fact. One question posed by the referring court to the Court of Justice was if that statement constituted "false information" under the UCPD.[67] If so, if the information "deceives or is likely to deceive the average consumer in relation to one or more of the elements listed in Article 6(1)" of the UCPD.[68] The Court of Justice initially found that it was false information, however, that it "is for the national court to ascertain, that false information must be regarded as a 'misleading' commercial practice under Article 6(1) of the directive."[69] The court thus clarified that this latter part of the assessment was part of the factual assessment residing with the referring court. On this point, the court disagreed with Advocate General Trstenjak who gave the opinion in the case. Trstenjak was not as reluctant to go into this assessment. It was thus held by Trstenjak that "[i]n a true-to-life situation, after all, it can be

---

[63]The Consumer Protection from Unfair Trading Regulations 2008, No. 1277 of 8 May 2008.

[64]Purely Creative v. Office of Fair Trading, Case C-428/11, [2012], paras 31 and 49. *Purely Creative* relates mainly to interpreting para 31 Annex I of the UCPD, including what is "false impression," and if a trader may impose a *de minimis* of costs on the consumer to claim a prize as seen in para 20 of Annex I. The commercial practices encompassed by Annex I are per se unfair, cf. art. 5(5) of the UCPD. The Court of Justice rejected that a *de minimis* of costs is allowed under para 31 of Annex I. *Ibid*, paras 36 and 42.

[65]*Ibid*, para 55. It may seem surprising that the Court of Justice has referred to the average consumer or vulnerable consumers, cf. art. 5(2)(b) of the UCPD, as benchmarks for the assessment of the information encompassed by the "black list" commercial practices in UCPD Annex I since these practices are per se unfair, cf. art. 5(5) of the UCPD stating: "Annex I contains the list of those commercial practices which shall in all circumstances be regarded as unfair."

[66]Böhler, Christian, 'A Thin Line between the Rationalization of Consumer Choices and Overburdening Market Participants. Are the Courts Able to Keep the Balance?', European Food and Feed Law Review, vol. 10/no. 1, (2015), pp. 34, p. 39.

[67]Cf. art. 6(1) of the UCPD.

[68]Pereničová v. SOS financ spol, Case C-453/10, [2012], para 40.

[69]*Ibid*, para 41.

assumed that an average consumer will normally obtain offers from a number of potential lenders and decide to take out a loan on the basis of a comparison of those offers, including the costs likely to be incurred." Therefore, "comparatively favourable credit conditions usually have a decisive influence on the opinion formed by the consumer."[70] The Court of Justice showed similar reluctance to assess the actual information in *Konsumentombudsmannen v. Ving Sverige*[71] and *Purely Creative v. OFT.*[72]

In *Canal Digital Danmark*, the Court of Justice assessed what constitutes under the UCPD a misleading omission "that causes or is likely to cause the average consumer to take a transactional decision that he would not have taken otherwise."[73] Canal Digital provided e.g. various television programme solutions to consumers and advertised these solutions via six advertisement campaigns as television and online banner advertisements. The programme solutions were offered at a monthly and 6-monthly charge. The issue was that the monthly charge was highlighted more clearly than the 6-monthly charge. In one of the three banner advertisements, the 6-monthly charge was not mentioned, however, by clicking on the banner, consumers were directed to the Canal Digital website where the full charge occurred.[74]

When the Court of Justice had to decide if the advertisements were misleading omissions under the UCPD, the court stated that a relevant factor was if the practice of a business results "in a significant asymmetry of information that is likely to confuse consumers."[75] When deciding if a misleading omission infringe the UCPD, the national court has to balance a multitude of elements considering the UCPD's aim to ensure "a high level of consumer protection." Therefore, "the limitations of time and space imposed by the communication medium used must be weighed against the nature and characteristics of the product in question, in order to determine whether the trader concerned in fact found it impossible to include the information at issue or to provide it in a clear, intelligible and unambiguous manner in the initial communication."[76] It was for the national court to balance these elements.

---

[70]Pereničová v. SOS financ spol, Case C-453/10, [2011], (opinion of AG Trstenjak), para 99.

[71]Konsumentombudsmannen v. Ving Sverige, Case C-122/10, [2011] ECR I-3903, para 59.

[72]It was thus stated by the Court of Justice in *Purely Creative v. OFT* on prize information that "[l]ike every other item of information provided by a trader to a consumer, information on the substance of the prize must be examined and assessed by the national courts in the light of recitals 18 and 19 in the preamble to the Unfair Commercial Practices Directive, and of Article 5(2)(b) of the directive. That concerns the availability of the information and how it is presented, the legibility and clarity of the wording and whether it can be understood by the public targeted by the practice." Purely Creative v. OFT, Case C-428/11, [2012], para 55.

[73]Canal Digital Danmark, Case C-611/14, [2016]. Besides assessing art. 7 on misleading omissions, the Court of Justice also assessed if art. 7 of the UCPD was correctly implemented into the Danish Marketing Practices Act. *Ibid*, paras 24-35. Further, the court assessed how the art. 7 was to be interpreted, given art. 6 of the UCPD on misleading actions. *Ibid*, para 42.

[74]On the facts of the case, see *ibid*, paras 13-23.

[75]*Ibid*, para 41.

[76]*Ibid*, para 62.

Interestingly, the Court of Justice in the decision explicitly refers to an information asymmetry between businesses and consumers which has implications to the economic underpinning of trademarks.[77] The UCPD should solve this asymmetry to ensure a high level of consumer protection and that "enough" information is given to the consumers on the specific product. It is clear that the Court of Justice envisages a narrow contextualization of the assessment where it matters what are the products and how they are advertised (television or online).

7.5   Other Consumer Models

How is the average consumer to be regarded in light of the other consumer models under the UCPD, the "confident consumer," the "vulnerable consumers" and an "average member" of "a particular group of consumers"?[78] At first glance, those models may seem to be legal novelties different from the average consumer in European trademark law. However, the trademark law analysis will show that the General Court in particular, but also by the national courts, mould the average consumer around the market realities (referred to as "contextualisation").[79] Is this merely what the legislature has emphasised in the UCPD with its broader range of consumer models: that the average consumer has to be contextualised? A bald answer is yes, and that those other models merely express what already applies as background law under European trademark law without the EU legislature's stipulation. However, in particular the vulnerable consumer model, as represented by children, is unique to the UCPD and a "misfit" in European trademark law.

7.5.1   The Models at a Glance

Several scholars have argued that the UCPD introduces a "confident consumer."[80] The confident consumer in consumer protection law, including the UCPD, according

---

[77]See Chap. 1, Sect. 1.3.2 and Chap. 12, Sect. 12.6.

[78]In the UCPD, the average consumer is referred to more broadly by the legislature, than is the case for the other consumer models under the UCPD only referred to in the general prohibition of unfair commercial practices. I.e. reference is made to the average consumer in relation to misleading actions (art. 6 of the UCPD), misleading omissions (art. 7 of the UCPD) and aggressive commercial practices (art. 8 of the UCPD), whereas the other consumer model are only referred to in the general prohibition of unfair commercial practices (art 5(2)(b) and (3) of the UCPD). See also Howells, Geraint, Twigg-Flesner, Christian and Wilhelmsson, Thomas, 'Rethinking EU Consumer Law', (1st edn, Routledge, 2018), p. 73.

[79]See Chap. 11.

[80]Wilhelmsson, Thomas, 'The Abuse of the "Confident Consumer" as a Justification for EC Consumer Law', Journal of Consumer Policy, vol. 27 (2004), pp. 317, Howells, Geraint G., 'Unfair

to Twigg-Flesner "is one who wishes to take advantage of the Single Market and is therefore, at least in principle a consumer interested in cross-border shopping."[81] It appears in the UCPD that consumers from the outset are rather confident.[82] "Supporting" consumer confidence though, provides a reason for harmonising this area of consumer protection law.[83] Critically, Wilhelmsson has stated that "against using the consumer confidence argument as a justification for harmonisation measures relates to doubts about consumers' knowledge of their rights even on a national level and about the impact of such (a lack of) knowledge on their behaviour." Furthermore, that it may be questioned, if consumers "know the content of their own legal system." Even a lack of such knowledge, will not discourage consumers "from shopping in their national surroundings."[84] If the wording of the UCPD is borne in mind, the confident consumer is merely regarded as a way of understanding the average consumer and the fundamental discounting of certain consumers vested in this model.[85]

The "average member" of "a particular group of consumers" is to some extent a specific consumer model of the UCPD. The EU Commission in the UCPD Working Paper 2003 stated that the starting point consumer model under the UCPD, the average consumer, "is however off-set by *modulating* the test when a trader targets a specific group of consumers. *Whether it is children or rocket scientists, the benchmark becomes an average member of that group*."[86] Keirsbilck has denoted this consumer group the "'modulated' average consumer benchmark."[87] Arguably, there is an overlap between this modulated average consumer and vulnerable consumers, for instance, in the case of children. As an example of this modulated group, Durovic has recently referred to "advertising male shaving equipment which is directed

---

Commercial Practices Directive – A Missed Opportunity?', in Weatherill, Stephen and Bernitz, Ulf eds., The Regulation of the Unfair Commercial Practices Under EC Directive 2005/29 (1st edn, Oxford, Hart, 2007), 103, p. 107-108 and Twigg-Flesner, Christian, 'The Importance of Law and Harmonisation', in Leczykiewicz, Dorota and Weatherill, Stephen eds., The Images of the Consumer in EU Law: Legislation, Free Movement and Competition Law (1st edn, Hart, 2016), 183 and chapter 7.

[81]Twigg-Flesner, Christian, 'The Importance of Law and Harmonisation', in Leczykiewicz, Dorota and Weatherill, Stephen eds., The Images of the Consumer in EU Law: Legislation, Free Movement and Competition Law (1st edn, Hart, 2016), 183, p. 185 and chapter 7.

[82]See ec. recital 4 of the UCPD.

[83]Recital 13 of the UCPD.

[84]Wilhelmsson, Thomas, 'The Abuse of the "Confident Consumer" as a Justification for EC Consumer Law', Journal of Consumer Policy, vol. 27 (2004), pp. 317, p. 325.

[85]On discounting, see Chap. 11, Sect. 11.2.

[86]The UCPD Working Paper 2003, p. 26 (italics added).

[87]Keirsbilck, Bert, 'The New European Law of Unfair Commercial Practices and Competition Law', (1st edn, Hart, 2011), p. 288. See also recently, Durovic, Mateja, 'European Law on Unfair Commercial Practices and Contract Law', (1st edn, Hart, 2016), p. 42.

exclusively at the male population above a certain age."[88] This is an example of a specific consumer group not being vulnerable at the same time.

Finally, the UCPD protects a "clearly identifiable group of consumers who are particularly vulnerable to the practice or the underlying product because of their mental or physical infirmity, age or credulity."[89] Advocate General Mengozzi has denoted protection of vulnerable consumers under the UCPD as "an ad hoc basis, for special protection for consumers."[90] An example of particularly vulnerable consumers is children.[91] The assessment of this group has to be made "from the perspective of the average member of that group."[92] In cases of vulnerable consumers, it is for the national judiciaries to extract the vulnerable consumer from the general consumer group. This is due to the legislature allowing "scope for suppression of practices that would not harm the average consumer in the general population but would have a particular impact within a clearly identifiable group of consumers."[93] The UCPD, however, does not offer protection against certain legitimate exaggerated advertisement.[94]

During the preparation of the UCPD, the EU Parliament suggested to further define certain "characteristics of a non-economic nature" making consumers particularly vulnerable. These characteristics, besides age, also include "disability, physical or mental conditions (including temporary ones) or level of literacy, which influence their assessment and/or reaction capacities" and factors that affect consumers' ability to understand sector specific "commercial communication."[95] That said, Twigg-Flesner has recently argued that today "[t]here is no recognition in the

---

[88]Durovic, Mateja, 'European Law on Unfair Commercial Practices and Contract Law', (1st edn, Hart, 2016), p. 42.

[89]Cf. art. 5(3) of the UCPD. The provision continues "in a way which the trader could reasonably be expected to foresee." On art. 5(3) of the UCPD, including its development, see Keirsbilck, Bert, 'The New European Law of Unfair Commercial Practices and Competition Law', (1st edn, Hart, 2011), p. 289-293. For an overview of how the vulnerable consumer appears in EU law, see Reich, Norbert, 'Vulnerable Consumers in EU Law', in Leczykiewicz, Dorota and Weatherill, Stephen eds., The Images of the Consumer in EU Law: Legislation, Free Movement and Competition Law (1st edn, Hart, 2016), 139 and more recently with specific reference to the vulnerable consumers under the UCPD, Howells, Geraint, Twigg-Flesner, Christian and Wilhelmsson, Thomas, 'Rethinking EU Consumer Law', (1st edn, Routledge, 2018), p. 70-73.

[90]Konsumentombudsmannen v. Ving Sverige, Case C-122/10, [2011] ECR I-3903, (opinion of AG Mengozzi), footnote 11 of the opinion.

[91]Recital 18 of the UCPD.

[92]Cf. art. 5(3) of the UCPD.

[93]Weatherill, Stephen, 'Empowerment is Not the Only Fruit', in Leczykiewicz, Dorota and Weatherill, Stephen eds., The Images of the Consumer in EU Law: Legislation, Free Movement and Competition Law (1st edn, Hart, 2016), 203, p. 215.

[94]Hence, art. 5(3) in fine of the UCPD states: "This is without prejudice to the common and legitimate advertising practice of making exaggerated statements or statements which are not meant to be taken literally."

[95]European Parliament legislative resolution on the proposal for a European Parliament and Council directive on unfair business-to-consumer commercial practices in the Internal Market and amending Directives 84/450/EEC, 97/7/EC and 98/27/EC (the Unfair Commercial Practices Directive) (COM

UCPD that most consumers can be vulnerable not because of a long-term personal attribute but rather because of a particular situation in which they find themselves."[96]

As for children, Abbamonte has argued that "[i]n the case of an advertisement of a toy during a TV programme for children, for example, one will have to take into account the expectations and the likely reaction of the average child of the group targeted and disregard those of an exceptionally immature or mature child belonging to the same group."[97] It has been found by Weatherill that the UCPD in targeting vulnerable consumers indicates, "that the Directive – as EU consumer law generally, in both legislative and judicial practice – is not blind to the needs of particular disadvantaged or vulnerable groups."[98] It is important to notice though, as pointed out by Schumacher, that the legislative steer for the vulnerable consumers is limited since the legislature has left the protection against conflicts over the legitimate exaggerated advertisements to judicial assessment.[99]

7.5.2 *Vulnerable Consumers Represented by Children*

The most important substantial difference between European trademark law and the UCPD is the inclusion in the UCPD of vulnerable consumers, for instance children. Interestingly, young children as opposed to elderly people probably rarely make any transactional decisions. Imagine a 6 year old child watching a TV program. This program in line with Abbamonte's example may contain an advertisement for a toy that may be considered an unfair commercial practice under the UCPD. Here, the advertisement, at least if targeted at young children, will be considered targeted at a specific consumer group *and* the target group consumer will also be considered vulnerable consumers. In reality, it is rare that any child who has watched the

---

(2003) 356 – C5-0288/2003 – 2003/0134(COD)) (Codecision procedure: first reading), P5_TA (2004)0298, art. 2(c).

[96]Howells, Geraint, Twigg-Flesner, Christian and Wilhelmsson, Thomas, 'Rethinking EU Consumer Law', (1st edn, Routledge, 2018), p. 71. Similarly, Wilhelmsson has stated when analysing the informed and the vulnerable consumer that "[o]ften a person needs protection not because he belongs to a certain group of people, but rather because he is in a certain situation.", Wilhelmsson, Thomas, 'the Informed Consumer v the Vulnerable Consumer in European Unfair Commercial Practices Law – A Comment', in Howells, Geraint *et al*, The Yearbook on Consumer Law 2007 (1st edn, Ashgate, 2007), 211, p. 212. For further on this "situational" analysis of the vulnerable consumer, see *ibid*, p. 211-215.

[97]Abbamonte in Weatherill 2007, p. 25. This example was also referred to by Advocate General Trstenjak in Mediaprint v. 'Österreich'-Zeitungsverlag, Case C-540/08, [2010] ECR I-10909, (opinion of AG Trstenjak), para 131, including footnote 102 of the opinion.

[98]*Ibid*, p. 216.

[99]Schuhmacher, Wolfgang, 'The Unfair Commercial Practices Directive', in Hilty, Reto M. and Henning-Bodewig, Frauke eds., Law Against Unfair Competition: Towards a New Paradigm in Europe? (1st edn, Springer, 2007), 127, p. 134. Art. 5(3) *in fine* of the UCPD. See above footnote 94.

advertisement will make any transactional decision on the advertised toy. Most likely, an adult will do that on their behalf. It has even been held in marketing literature by Underhill that "[t]hough technically adults are the ones who select and buy toys, the kids are the real decision-makers."[100] That the influence of children on their parents is probably significant in the selection of e.g. toys is another matter. The UCPD thus seems to accept a very vague standard of a transactional decision that does not necessarily have to equate to a real life transaction. Also, the UCPD with its reference to vulnerable consumers more narrowly contextualises the average consumer than European trademark law does.

Trademark law, in contrast with the UCPD, in a transaction scenario focuses on the time of purchase. Hence, as a clear starting point, if the average consumer is the relevant public, it has to be decided if the average consumer was likely to be confused at the time of purchase. The *ex ante* considerations before the time of purchase are thus not decisive. Earlier, Koktvedgaard has raised it as a "debatable" question if trademark law has to be contextualised to children.[101] Bøggild[102] and Staunstrup have addressed the issue of implementing the legislative approach to vulnerable consumers under the UCPD in European trademark law. It is advocated by Bøggild and Staunstrup that for instance a trademark dispute related to children's toys should be assessed referring to the "averagely attentive child."[103] At the same time they acknowledge, as shown by the above example, that where children are not the "actual buyers," the framing of the average consumer has to account for the perception of children.[104] They do not fully expand the argument, though. In this scenario, one would immediately expect the attention of a child to be lower than the attention of an adult, if the UCPD approach to children is followed. Following this logic, children would be the less attentive of the two. However, it is doubtful that this is so. As an example, children at an early age can presumably produce meticulous wish lists containing the names of toys based on scrutiny of catalogues from toy stores. In this case, it is probably the adult actually buying the toys mentioned in the those wish lists who is the weaker party in terms of the level of attention. Also, how would this argument play out if it was mainly the parents of the children buying their toys? Presumably, parents would know more about their children's favourite toys than a third party.

Phillips seems to be somewhat sceptical towards considering children in the assessment of likelihood of confusion in trademark law, at least if they are not themselves making the actual purchase. Hence, based on a European administrative

---

[100]Underhill, Paco, 'Why we Buy: The Science of Shopping: Updated and Revised for the Internet, the Global Consumer and Beyond', (1st edn, Simon & Schuster, 2009), p. 158.

[101]Koktvedgaard, Mogens, 'Lærebog i Immaterialret: Ophavsret, Patentret, Brugsmodelret, Mønsterret, Varemærkeret', (5th edn, Jurist- og Økonomforbundets Forlag), 1999, p. 338.

[102]One of the most prominent litigating counsels in Denmark in disputes on unfair commercial practices and trademark law.

[103]In Danish: "gennemsnitsoplyst barn." Bøggild, Frank, and Staunstrup, Kolja, 'EU-Varemærkeret', (1st edn, Karnov Group, 2015), p. 106. See also *ibid*, p. 105.

[104]*Ibid*, p. 106.

decision, Phillips has stated that with pet food, "the relevant consumer of that product is the purchaser of the pet food, not the pet itself." Based on a German decision, Phillips continues, "a German court has ruled that little girls of 4 years old and above are the 'relevant audience' for Betty dolls *even though many little girls may not be in a position to make their own purchase.*"[105] Phillips does not seem to accept the above argument that although children do not make the actual purchase, they may have a significant impact on the one (adult) who does. The above line of argument is of course different in trademark law for other potentially vulnerable consumers, such as mentally disabled or certain elderly people.

The relevance of young people and children in European trademark law does not seem to have been addressed by the Court of Justice. However, the General Court and national courts have made scattered references to them. Overall, the divide between adults and older children (assumed to be below 18 years old) may have an impact, for instance in relation to alcohol and tobacco. Thus, the General Court in *Companhia Muller de Bebidas v. OHIM* had to decide the relevant public for buying alcohol. The court found that "the sale of alcoholic beverages to children is generally prohibited and that therefore, solely by operation of law, the public concerned by those goods is limited to *adult consumers.*"[106] Similar findings for snuff was made by the SE District Court and recently affirmed by the SE Court of Appeal in *Swedish Match v. V2 Distribution*, where the court found the relevant public to be "those who use tobacco in the form of snuff and have turned 18 years old and so legally are allowed to buy goods of this kind."[107] Here, the courts rather mechanically let age dictated by laws on the legal age for purchase of alcohol and tobacco play a role in the framing of the relevant public. Those decisions provide no guidance on how a lower age may play a part. Essentially, the very tricky and interesting part is how in particular young children may be relevant to the relevant public.

On a few occasions, the General Court has also accepted a relevant public to be found among "young people." Hence, in *Bunker & BKR v. OHIM* the court found that for certain clothing items the relevant public was Austrian and "in particular, *young people* (...) familiar with English [and] (...) very aware of signs identifying clothing or footwear."[108] Similarly, in *Gauselmann v. OHIM* the General Court found that the relevant public was "the *younger generation* who are interested in computer and video games" with a higher attention than average.[109] In *J & Joy v. EUIPO*, the applicant unsuccessfully argued that e.g. clothing and headgear were

---

[105]Phillips, Jeremy, 'Trade Mark Law a Practical Anatomy', (1st edn, Oxford University Press, 2003), p. 353 (italics added).

[106]Companhia Muller de Bebidas v. OHIM, T-472/08, [2010] ECR II-3907, para 41 (italics added).

[107]In Swedish: "dem som använder tobak i form av snus och som har fyllt 18 år och därmed lagligen får köpa varor av detta slag." Swedish Match v. V2 Distribution, T 13352-1 and T 5357-12, [2013], p. 36 as affirmed by the SE Court of Appeal in Swedish Match v. V2 Distribution, T 768-14, [2015], SECA, p. 12.

[108]Bunker & BKR v. OHIM, Case T-423/04, [2005] ECR II-4035, para 25 (italics added).

[109]Gauselmann v. OHIM, Case T-106/09, [2010], para 20 (italics added). The decision also related to goods directed at a professional public. For further on the decision, see Chap. 11, Sect. 11.4.1.2.

"aimed at 'young and trendy' consumers" with a better understanding of the words
being part of conflicting figurative marks.[110] These decisions seem to presume that
for things that occupy young people they have a higher level of attention than
average. Crudely, it is easy to grasp that young people conceivably are occupied
with clothes and computer games. The General Court in those decisions did not
address the interesting question of how the situation is if the relevant public is not
buying the goods itself. This was not raised as an issue in the decisions.

The one time where the General Court seems to have addressed the relevance of
children not buying the goods themselves as the relevant public is in *Sadas v. OHIM*.
Here the court had to decide who was the relevant public for clothing goods for
children. The court found that "[t]o the extent that clothing goods for young children
are purchased by adults, the goods covered by the trade mark sought are just as much
for adults as for children."[111] Potentially, this is so, but normally when the court
concludes that there is a "dual relevant public," as is the case for a relevant public
consisting of e.g. consumers and professionals, then it is the attention of the public
with the lower level of attention that is decisive.[112] In Norway, the NO Court of
Appeal considered the perception of children in *Fetter Klovn v. TOP-TOY*.[113] This
decision related to the likelihood of confusion with the senior owner's (TOP-TOY)
three registered figurative trademarks including the word Superlek for
e.g. playthings, games, entertainment, services and other services. After the registration, the junior owner (Fetter Klovn) opened a toy store using different versions of
Superlek combined with Brio (its main supplier), including the words BRIO
SUPERLEK. In assessing likelihood of confusion, the NO Court of Appeal found
that "[c]hildren will probably notice Brio more than Superlek. Conversely, adults
will pay more attention to Superlek because it is a peculiar word which exactly
because of its unclear meaning stays in their mind."[114] The NO Supreme Court
affirmed this finding.[115] In this decision, the NO Court of Appeal clearly allowed for
the perception of children to play a role in the assessment of likelihood of confusion.
The court merely found, though, without further qualification that the perception of
children and adults was different.

---

[110]J & Joy v. EUIPO, Case T-389/15, [2017], para 23.

[111]Sadas v. OHIM, Case T-346/04, [2005] ECR II-4891, para 29. Bøggild and Staunstrup have also
solely referred to this decision in their account on the relevance of vulnerable consumers under
trademark law. Bøggild, Frank, and Staunstrup, Kolja, 'EU-Varemærkeret', (1st edn, Karnov
Group, 2015), p. 106.

[112]This problem is addressed in Chap. 11, Sect. 11.4.1.2.

[113]Fetter Klovn Karl v. TOP-TOY, HR-1999-34-A, [1999], NOSC.

[114]In Norwegian: "Barn vil nok kunne feste seg ved Brio mer enn med Superlek. På den annen side
vil voksne lett merke seg Superlek fordi det er et eiendommelig ord som nettopp på grunn av sin
uklare betydning fester seg i bevisstheten." Fetter Klovn v. TOP-TOY, LB-1997-3336, [1998],
NOCA, p. 4.

[115]Fetter Klovn Karl v. TOP-TOY, HR-1999-34-A, [1999], NOSC, p. 646.

The perception of children also played a significant role in the Danish decision *VN Legetøj v. Hasbro Europe*.[116] The senior owner (Hasbro) *inter alia* had a registered EU and Danish trademark, TRANSFORMERS, for play things.[117] Hasbro claimed that when the junior owner (VN Legetøj) used TRANSFORMAX for the same goods there was likelihood of confusion under the TM Regulation 2009 and the DK TM Act 1991 and that it was an unfair commercial practice under the Danish Marketing Practices Act implementing the UCPD.[118] Hasbro argued that "the target group is children that are more susceptible to influence than adults."[119] Furthermore, that in terms of "marketing, particular care has to be taken of children since children lack the critical faculties needed to distinguish between similar marks."[120] Referring to impartial expert evidence, the junior owner argued that "[t]he target group for play things is children and children are not less observant consumers than adults."[121] Part of the conclusion reached by one of the experts was that "it has to be assumed that the average Danish child [5 – 9 years old] will not relate the word "transformers" to the Danish word "transformator" unless he/she has parents who frequently use that word specifically in relation to their job."[122] The DK MCH Court found there to be a trademark infringement since there was likelihood of confusion, and equally that the practice of the junior owner was unfair. The DK Supreme Court affirmed this result.[123] It was not raised as an issue in neither *Fetter Klovn v. TOP-TOY* nor *VN Legetøj v. Hasbro Europe*, what happens in the scenario where adults buy the toys for children, i.e. more narrowly the actual purchase scenario.

Although the influence on adults of children not being present in the purchasing situations does not seem to have been explicitly addressed, the DK MCH Court subtly addressed this in an "adult-adult" scenario in *Ankenævnet v. Chantelle*. The court found that it could be taken into account "that a lot of expensive lingerie goods are purchased as Christmas gifts by men who refer orally to the name of the goods."[124]

---

[116]VN Legetøj v. Hasbro Europe, U.2012.107H, [2011], (DKSC).

[117]The Danish wordmark was more precisely THE TRANSFORMERS.

[118]Bekendtgørelse af markedsføringsloven, Act No 1216 of 25 September 2013.

[119]In Danish: "og produktets målgruppe er børn, som er væsentlig mere påvirkelige end voksne." VN Legetøj v. Hasbro Europe, U.2012.107H, [2011], (DKSC), p. 111.

[120]In Danish: "Ved markedsføring skal der udvises særlig omhu over for børn, da børn mangler kritisk sans til at skelne mellem mærker, der minder om hinanden." *Ibid.*

[121]In Danish: "Målgruppen for legetøjet er børn, og børn er ikke mindre observante forbrugere end voksne." *Ibid*, p. 112.

[122]In Danish: "Det må således formodes, at et gennemsnitligt dansk barn ikke vil relatere ordet "transformers" til det danske ord "transformator", medmindre han/hun har forældre, som jævnlig bruger dette ord konkret i forhold til deres arbejde." *Ibid*, p. 110.

[123]*Ibid*, p. 113.

[124]Ankenævnet v. Chantelle, U.2003.2366H, [2003], (DKSC), p. 2370. For further on the decision, see Chap. 11, Sect. 11.4.2.2.

7.6   Conclusion

It has been seen that there are many similarities and differences between the average consumer under European trademark law and the UCPD. The core of both models is the same. Both have the well-known characteristics "reasonably well-informed and reasonably observant and circumspect." The gist of both models is that when dealing with the average consumer, they discount the least and most attentive consumers. That the EU legislature has referred to the average consumer under the UCPD should not be overly emphasised—for one reason because in EU trademark legislation it would be more complex for the legislature to stipulate an average consumer. This at least would require significant caveats because, as shown in the following chapter, the relevant public in European trademark law is not always the average consumer. For another reason, the average consumer under European trademark law does not coincide with the direct beneficiaries of protection under the law, i.e. the senior and junior trademark owners. As for the B2C scenario under the UCPD, the beneficiaries are the consumers, less than the businesses.

Importantly, though, the EU legislature has sent a significant message to the national legislatures and judiciaries to be very careful in their contextualisation of average consumer. Besides the mentioning of the average consumer and its well-known characteristics, this is emphasised first by a reference to the "social, cultural and linguistic factors, as interpreted by the Court of Justice." It clearly indicates that there is no "one-size-fits-all" average consumer. Second, it is a difference between the European trademark and the UCPD that the latter refers to other consumer models, i.e. the "confident consumer," the "vulnerable consumers" and an "average member" of "a particular group of consumers." However, this difference only to some extent is manifested in substantial differences.

The "confident consumer" seems merely to reflect the average consumer starting point, i.e. its overall characteristics as confident compared to the gullible Homer Simpsons.[125] That the average consumer may be part of an average member of a group does not come as a surprise from a trademark law angle. As it will be seen, the average consumer can be part of the "general public" or "public at large" in contrast with a narrower group, such as "do-it-yourself" enthusiasts.[126] Of course, under the UCPD it is a clear message for the national judiciaries to be careful not to assess commercial practices in a too broad market making it less likely for the transactional decisions of the average consumer to be affected.

As for the vulnerable consumers, represented by children, this is an area where the UCPD and European trademark law are not harmonised. The UCPD more narrowly protects consumers, including children, whereas European trademark law protects senior and junior trademark owners. Under the UCPD, the weaker party in B2C involving children will be the latter. This is also emphasised with broader notion under the directive of transactional decisions. Although scattered examples

---

[125]See Chap. 11, Sect. 11.2.1.
[126]See Chap. 11, Sects. 11.1 and 11.4.1.2.

are found, it remains to be seen in European trademark law particularly what role children, mainly young children, are to play in likelihood of confusion where they are not present in the purchasing situation. Beside the reasons already given, another more pragmatic reason seems plausible. Under the UCPD, it should be possible for an (adult) judge to address if e.g. a business as part of TV advertisement tries to fool children with "alternative facts." Probably, it is more difficult for a judge to assess how young children would react confronted with two marked goods. Opening up for a narrower contextualisation under European trademark law, for instance to children, might complicate the likelihood of confusion assessment. Allowing for a contextualisation to children, would that also mean a narrow contextualisation to other consumer groups, such as the elderly?

Part III
Vertical Analysis: The Judicial Background and European Trademark Law

Chapter 8
The Early Beginnings of the Average Consumer Pre *Sabel*

8.1 What Is the Origin?

Although the book for the main analysis has been temporally delimited to 11 November 1997 onwards, where the Court of Justice issued its *Sabel* decision, the court had before this date sought to determine its stance on who/what was the average consumer. It has often been said that the average consumer as it is known today has its origin in the *Gut Springenheide* of 1998 residing in unfair competition law.[1] Not least, significant weight is attached to *Gut Springenheide* in *Lloyd*, the first decision where the Court of Justice set out the average consumer and its characteristics in EU trademark law. In many ways, *Gut Springenheide* provided a significant

---

[1]Davis has referred to *Gut Springenheide* as the starting point of the Court of Justice of the "hypothetical average consumer" but argues in a footnote that its origin is found in Mars. Davis, Jennifer, 'Locating the Average Consumer: His Judicial Origins, Intellectual Influences and Current Role in European Trade Mark Law', Intellectual Property Quarterly, no. 2, (2005), pp. 183, p. 185-186, including footnote 12 of the text. Similarly, Mak has argued that the development of the average consumer "culminated" in *Gut Springenheide* standing on the shoulder of a "further set of cases." Mak, Vanessa, 'Standards of Protection: In Search of the 'Average Consumer' of EU Law in the Proposal for a Consumer Rights Directive', European Review of Private Law, vol. 19/no. 1, (2011), pp. 25, Mak, Vanessa, 'The Consumer in European Regulatory Private Law', in Leczykiewicz, Dorota, and Weatherill, Stephen eds., The Images of the Consumer in EU Law: Legislation, Free Movement and Competition Law (1st edn, Hart, 2016), 381, p. 384-386. See also Incardona, Rossella, and Poncibò, Cristina, 'The Average Consumer, the Unfair Commercial Practices Directive, and the Cognitive Revolution', Journal of Consumer Policy, vol. 30/no. 1, (2007), pp. 21, p. 22, Hannerstig, Niclas, 'The Average Consumer – Legal Fiction or Reality? A Comparative Study between European and American Trademark Law', LUP Student Papers (2011), p. 36, Dinwoodie, Graeme, and Gangjee, Dev, 'The Image of the Consumer in EU Trade Mark Law', in Leczykiewicz, Dorota, and Weatherill, Stephen eds., The Images of the Consumer in EU Law: Legislation, Free Movement and Competition Law (1st edn, Hart, 2016), 339, p. 366, Wilhelmsson, Thomas, 'The Average European Consumer: A Legal Fiction?', in Wilhelmsson, Thomas, Paunio, Elina and Pohjolainen, Annika eds., Private Law and the Many Cultures of Europe (1st edn, Kluwer Law International, 2007), 243, p. 244.

© Springer Nature Switzerland AG 2020
R. D. Laustsen, *The Average Consumer in Confusion-based Disputes in European Trademark Law and Similar Fictions*, https://doi.org/10.1007/978-3-030-26350-8_8

steer to the future development of the average consumer, including on the distinction between law and fact and the characteristics of the average consumer.[2] However, the court did by no means invent the average consumer in that decision. As Advocate General Fennelly pointed out in *Estée Lauder* after the above decisions, the fact that the Court of Justice makes presumptions about consumer behaviour in the market is nothing new. Such presumptions have been made since *Cassis de Djion* and have developed over time in other decisions on protecting free movement of goods under art. 34 of the TFEU[3] and the exemption provision art. 36 of the TFEU, or on the additional grounds of exemption set out by the Court of Justice. Fennelly stated that as part of the EU consumer protection *acquis*, it has been favoured to disseminate information, "whether by advertising, labelling or otherwise, as the best means of promoting free trade in openly competitive markets." Favouring the dissemination of information has been done under the presumption *"that consumers will inform themselves about the quality and price of products and will make intelligent choices."*[4]

This chapter will analyse the relevant subtext of the average consumer found in some of the core decisions related to the free movement of goods, starting from *Cassis de Dijon* through to other decisions on consumer protection and unfair competition preceding *Sabel* where the average consumer was introduced to European trademark law. Besides, of purely historical interest, this analysis allows an answer to *why* and *how* the average consumer matured as an independent model and found its way into European trademark law. The findings are relevant to the vertical analysis in the understanding of the foundation of the average consumer. In addition, it is relevant to the horizontal analysis because it gives a clearer picture of why exportation of the average consumer from consumer protection and unfair competition law into European trademark law is not without friction. This analysis also provides important subtext to applying the average consumer under the UCPD analysed in the foregoing chapter. Inevitably, the analysis of this chapter involves touching upon some of the key issues of the free movement of goods, but the focus will be on the decisions relevant to the formation of the average consumer. A more comprehensive analysis of the free movement of goods is left for the general literature.[5]

---

[2] Gut Springenheide and Tusky, Case C-210/96, [1998] ECR I-4657, para 37.

[3] Art. 30 of the EEC Treaty.

[4] Estée Lauder, Case C-220/98, [1999] ECR I-117, (opinion of AG Fennelly), para 25. (italics in the latter quote added).

[5] See among others, Craig, Paul, and Búrca, Gráinne de, 'EU Law: Text, Cases, and Materials', (6th edn, Oxford University Press, 2015), chapter 19, Weatherill, Stephen, and Beaumont, Paul, 'EU Law: The Essential Guide to the Legal Workings of the European Union', (3rd edn, Penguin, 1999), Arnull, Anthony, 'Judicial Review in the European Union', 376, chapter 15, Tridimas, Takis, 'Dialogue with National Courts: Dialogue, Cooperation and Instability', 403, chapter 16, Craig, Paul, 'Accountability', 431, chapter 17, Armstrong, Kenneth, 'Governing Goods: Content and Context', 508, chapter 20, all four in Arnull, Anthony and Damian Chalmers eds., The Oxford Handbook of European Union Law (1st edn, Oxford University Press, 2015) and Barnard,

8.2   The Free Movement of Goods Framework

It permeates European trademark law that the free movement of goods and services have to be ensured. Common for developing the average consumer is that it has taken place in the realm of protecting the free movement of goods under art. 34 of the TFEU prohibiting between member states, "[q]uantitative restrictions on imports and all measures having equivalent effect" (the latter measures are referred to as "MEQR").[6] In *Dassonville* in 1974, one of the pivotal decisions defining "quantitative restrictions," the Court of Justice held that: "All trading rules enacted by Member States *which are capable of hindering, directly or indirectly, actually or potentially, intra-Community trade* are to be considered as measures having an effect equivalent to quantitative restrictions."[7] However, in an area of law not providing "a Community system guaranteeing for consumers the authenticity of a product's designation of origin," member states could introduce in that context "reasonable" measures preventing unfair practices.[8] According to Craig and de Búrca, "*Dassonville* sowed the seeds which bore fruit in *Cassis de Dijon*" in 1979, in which the Court of Justice qualified *Dassonville* further to include non-discriminatory rules in art. 34 of the TFEU.[9] Hence, as held by Weatherill and Beaumont, the court approached "market-partitioning rules that make no formal distinction between domestic and imported goods."[10]

Referring to its earlier case law starting with *Cassis de Dijon*, the Court of Justice in *Keck and Mithouard* in 1993 held that "obstacles to free movement of goods" included requirements stipulated in national non-harmonised rules, "such as those relating to designation, form, size, weight, composition, presentation, labelling, packaging."[11] In addition, the court specified that "the application to products from other Member States of national provisions restricting or prohibiting certain selling arrangements is not such as to hinder directly or indirectly, actually or potentially, trade between Member States within the meaning of the Dassonville

---

Catherine, 'The Substantive Law of the EU: The Four Freedoms', (5th edn, Oxford University Press, 2016), chapters 2, 4, 5 and 6.

[6]Art. 34 of the TFEU. MEQRs is an abbreviation found in legal literature of "measures equivalent to a quantitative restriction." See among others, Horspool, Margot, Humphreys, Matthew, and Wells-Greco, Michael, 'European Union Law', (10th edn, Oxford University Press, 2018), p. 314-321.

[7]Dassonville, Case 8/74, [1974] ECR 837, para 5. See Weatherill, Stephen, and Beaumont, Paul, 'EU Law: The Essential Guide to the Legal Workings of the European Union', (3rd edn, Penguin, 1999), p. 566 and Dashwood, Alan, 'Wyatt and Dashwood's European Union Law', (6th edn, Hart, 2011), p. 410-411.

[8]Dassonville, Case 8/74, [1974] ECR 837, para 6.

[9]Craig, Paul, and Búrca, Gráinne de, 'EU Law: Text, Cases, and Materials', (6th edn, Oxford University Press, 2015), p. 668.

[10]Weatherill, Stephen, and Beaumont, Paul, 'EU Law: The Essential Guide to the Legal Workings of the European Union', (3rd edn, Penguin, 1999), p. 566.

[11]Keck Mithouard, Joined Cases C-267/91 and C-268/91, [1993] ECR I-6097, para 15 referred to in Verband Sozialer Wettbewerb v. Clinique Laboratoires, Case C-315/92, [1994] ECR I-317, para 13.

judgment (. . .), so long as those provisions apply to all relevant traders operating within the national territory and so long as they affect in the same manner, in law and in fact, the marketing of domestic products and of those from other Member States."[12] In *Keck and Mithouard* the court is said to have refocused what is now art. 34 of the TFEU on "rules that affect patterns of trade across borders as such" and not "rules that affect patterns of trade generally without any special reference to national borders." The intention of the decision was allowing member states "to regulate markets in a manner that does not impede the interpenetration of national markets."[13]

Under art. 36 of the TFEU certain exemptions to art. 34 of the TFEU are allowed. Thus, following art. 36, art. 34 "shall not preclude prohibitions or restrictions on imports, exports or goods in transit justified" *inter alia*, on the ground of "(. . .) the protection of health and life of humans (. . .) or the protection of industrial and commercial property. Such prohibitions or restrictions shall not, however, constitute a means of arbitrary discrimination or a disguised restriction on trade between Member States."[14]

Adding to these treaty-based exemptions, the Court of Justice has approved additional exemptions such as consumer protection, if the compromise of the free movement of goods is non-discriminatory. Hence, in *Cassis de Dijon*, the court held that "[o]bstacles to movement within the Community resulting from disparities between the national laws relating to the marketing of the products in question must be accepted in so far as those provisions may be recognized as being necessary in order *to satisfy mandatory requirements relating in particular to the effectiveness of fiscal supervision, the protection of public health, the fairness of commercial transactions and the defence of the consumer.*"[15] In contrast with art. 36 of the TFEU, *Cassis de Dijon* is said to provide a non-exhaustive list of exemptions.[16] The decisions relevant to developing the average consumer initially dealt with defining, if at all certain national measures could be subsumed under art. 34 of the TFEU, and in the affirmative, if the legislative exception in art. 36 of the TFEU or the non-legislative exceptions set out by the Court of Justice applied. Based on the

---

[12]Keck Mithouard, Joined Cases C-267/91 and C-268/91, [1993] ECR I-6097, para 16.

[13]Weatherill, Stephen, and Beaumont, Paul, 'EU Law: The Essential Guide to the Legal Workings of the European Union', (3rd edn, Penguin, 1999), p. 612. See further on the implications of *Keck Mithouard, ibid*, p. 612-619, Dashwood, Alan, 'Wyatt and Dashwood's European Union Law', (6th edn, Hart, 2011), p. 418-421 and Arnull, Anthony, 'The European Union and its Court of Justice', (2nd edn, Oxford University Press, 2006), 427-441.

[14]Cf. Art. 36, of the TFEU.

[15]Rewe-Zentral AG v. Bundesmonopolverwaltung für Branntwein (*Cassis de Dijon*), Case 120/78, [1979] ECR 649, para 8 (italics added). For a further analysis of art. 36 and the "mandatory requirements" see among others, Barnard, Catherine, 'The Substantive Law of the EU: The Four Freedoms', (5th edn, Oxford University Press, 2016), chapter 6 and Craig, Paul, and Búrca, Gráinne de, 'EU Law: Text, Cases, and Materials', (6th edn, Oxford University Press, 2015), p. 695-711.

[16]Weatherill, Stephen, and Beaumont, Paul, 'EU Law: The Essential Guide to the Legal Workings of the European Union', (3rd edn, Penguin, 1999), p. 581 and p. 588-589.

principles laid down in *Dassonville*, *Cassis de Dijon* and *Keck and Mithouard*, the decisions relevant to developing the average consumer may be divided according to different taxonomies.[17] The below is divided according to the way the average consumer or more premature models have been used in the argumentation for derogating from art. 34 of the TFEU. This approach allows for some preliminary findings on the purposes of the early uses of the average consumer and the like. Further, the decisions in each section are set out according to their issuing date to be able to trace any temporal linearity.

Although this chapter, in line with the overall focus of this book, focuses on the free movement of *goods*, provisions similar to the ones on goods are found on *services*[18] in art. 56 of the TFEU stipulating that "restrictions on freedom to provide services within the Union shall be prohibited in respect of nationals of Member States who are established in a Member State other than that of the person for whom the services are intended."[19]

8.3 Cassis de Dijon: The "Beacon"

Although *Cassis de Dijon* from 1979 has taken up much space in the analysis of primary EU law on free movement of goods and under consumer protection law, analysis of the link between the decision and the average consumer in European trademark law is limited. That said, part of analysing consumer images in European law in general, Leczykiewicz and Weatherill have recently called *Cassis de Dijon*

---

[17]For an overview of the different taxonomies of art. 34 of the TFEU on MEQRs, see p. 74 and 89 and on different selling arrangements, see p. 124, 130, 136 and 145 (this page highlights the taxonomy the UCPD vis-à-vis the TFEU) of Barnard, Catherine, 'The Substantive Law of the EU: The Four Freedoms', (5th edn, Oxford University Press, 2016). See also Armstrong, Kenneth, 'Governing Goods: Content and Context', in Arnull, Anthony and Damian Chalmers eds., The Oxford Handbook of European Union Law (1st edn, Oxford University Press, 2015), 508, chapter 20.

[18]I.e., art. 49 of the TFEU Pre-Lisbon. What constitute services is defined in art. 57 of the TFEU (art. 50 of the TFEU Pre-Lisbon). See also art. 2(1) under directive (EC) No 2006/123 of 12 December 2006 on services of the Internal Market (the "Service Directive"). See on the definition of "service", Barnard, Catherine, 'The Substantive Law of the EU: The Four Freedoms', (5th edn, Oxford University Press, 2016), p. 428.

[19]It has been ruled by the Court of Justice that the freedom to provide services is not secondary to the freedom of movement of goods under art. 34 of the TFEU. See e.g., Omega v. Oberbürgermeisterin, Case C-36/02, [2004] ECR I-9609, para 26, including the case law referred to here. Certain derogations to the free movement of services may be allowed under the Service Directive "for reasons of public policy, public security, public health or the protection of the environment" (cf. art. 16(3) of the Service Directive) and on a "case-by-case" derogation may by way of "measures relating to the safety of services" (cf. art. 18(1) of the Service Directive). For an account of the Service Directive in a trademark context, see Elsmore, Matthew J., 'Intangible Assets for Intangible Deliverables: Trade Marks at Your Service', Journal of Intellectual Property Law & Practice, vol. 3/no. 9, (2008), pp. 580, in particular p. 585-586.

"the shining beacon of EU law's image of the consumer even two generations later."[20]

In Germany, legislation existed stipulating that fruit liqueur could only be sold as such if they contained an alcohol percentage of minimum 32. Cassis de Dijon, the well-known French liqueur, had an alcohol percentage below 15–20 meaning that in effect the German regulation hindered the import and sale in Germany of Cassis de Dijon. In a preliminary ruling, the Court of Justice had to consider if the German law complied with art. 30 of the EEC Treaty (art. 34 of the TFEU).[21]

The Court of Justice (Grand Chamber) held that "[i]n the absence of common rules relating to the production and marketing of alcohol despite a proposal for a regulation (...) it is for the Member States to regulate all matters relating to the production and marketing of alcohol and alcoholic beverages on their own territory."[22] The issue was a balancing exercise between different consumer interests; the consumer interests in ensuring free movement of goods against the interest of ensuring that German consumers were not confused about the alcohol percentage in liqueurs by way of ensuring a unified standard for liqueurs preserving public health and fair commercial practices.

As for the product requirements imposed by the German legislature on a minimum alcohol percentage, they were according to the court encompassed by art. 30 of the EEC Treaty.[23] Countering this, the German Government claimed that the German measures could be justified referring to public health and the prevention against unfair commercial practices. The Court of Justice did not accept the reference to public health since consumers already obtained other alcoholic beverages in the market with a low alcohol percentage.[24] On unfair competition, the Court of Justice stated that the German requirements would not be a "guarantee of the fairness of commercial transactions, since it is a simple matter *to ensure that suitable information is conveyed to the purchaser by requiring the display of an indication of origin and of the alcohol content on the packaging of products.*"[25] The Court of Justice reached the decision that "the requirements relating to the minimum alcohol content of alcoholic beverages do not serve a purpose which is in the general interest and such as to take precedence over the requirements of the free movement of goods, which constitutes one of the fundamental rules of the Community."[26] Moreover, that

---

[20]Leczykiewicz, Dorota and Weatherill, Stephen, 'The Images of the Consumer in EU Law', in Leczykiewicz, Dorota and Weatherill, Stephen eds., The Images of the Consumer in EU Law: Legislation, Free Movement and Competition Law (1st edn, Hart, 2016), 1, p. 3.

[21]If the German law did not comply with art. 30 of the EEC Treaty (art. 34 of the TFEU), it was a question of if it was encompassed by the exceptions set out in art. 36 of the EEC Treaty and TFEU.

[22]*Cassis de Dijon*, Case 120/78, [1979] ECR 649, para 8.

[23]*Ibid*, para 14.

[24]*Ibid*, para 11.

[25]*Ibid*, para 13 (italics added).

[26]Therefore, the German law constituted "an obstacle to trade which is incompatible with the provisions of Article 30 of the Treaty [TFEU art. 34]." *Ibid*, para 14.

the German product requirements were not proportionate to the objective of obtaining consumer protection.[27]

By its conclusion, the Court of Justice made assumptions on the knowledge of the "purchaser" which in effect meant consumers, who were the beneficiaries of protection of the German regulation. The court assumed that consumers could compute "*suitable* information." Although deciding what is *suitable* is a matter of discretion, the finding indicated that consumers were not "morons"[28] in need of being overly informed or individuals navigating the marketplace only with very limited information.[29] "Indication of origin" as a piece of important consumer information resonates well in European trademark law where the origin function is one of the key functions of trademarks.

As pointed out by Weatherill, it is impossible on an objective basis to conclude that the deregulation of the marketplace reached by the Court of Justice, e.g. in *Cassis de Dijon*, causes consumers to be left open for "practices from which protection should be afforded." The decision illustrates, according to Weatherill, "negative harmonisation" whereby the Court of Justice "prohibiting a national rule contributes to free trade without the need for the EU to adopt legislation in the area."[30] This stance, according to Weatherill, argues positive harmonisation by the EU legislature.[31] This, at the end, depends on the perception on how well consumers can look after themselves in the marketplace.[32] This finding is important in that the Court of Justice in *Cassis de Dijon* and other early decisions, such as *Drei Glocken*, *GB-Inno* and *Yves Rocher*, had to assess national (non-harmonised) law vis-à-vis

---

[27]Proportionate measures are measures "*necessary in order to satisfy mandatory requirements relating in particular to the effectiveness of fiscal supervision, the protection of public health, the fairness of commercial transactions and the defence of the consumer.*" *Ibid*, para 8.

[28]For an explanation of the expression "moron" as a reference to the phrase "moron in a hurry," see e.g. Chap. 6, Sect. 6.6.2, footnote 216.

[29]Advocate General Capotorti giving the opinion in *Cassis de Dijon* similarly held that "the idea of this widespread, if not general, incapacity on the part of the consumer seems to me to doom to failure any effort to protect him, unless it be to impose upon him a single national product the composition of which is constant and is rigorously controlled." Rewe-Zentral AG v. Bundesmonopolverwaltung für Branntwein (*Cassis de Dijon*), Case 120/78, [1979] ECR 649, (opinion of AG Capotorti), p. 673.

[30]Weatherill, Stephen, 'EU Consumer Law and Policy', (2nd edn, Edward Elgar, 2013), p. 44. See also Howells, Geraint G., 'Europe's (Lack of) Vision on Consumer Protection: A Case of Rhetoric Hiding Substance?', in Leczykiewicz, Dorota, and Weatherill, Stephen eds., The Images of the Consumer in EU Law: Legislation, Free Movement and Competition Law (1st edn, Hart, 2016), 431, p. 435 and Weatherill, Stephen, and Beaumont, Paul, 'EU Law: The Essential Guide to the Legal Workings of the European Union', (3rd edn, Penguin, 1999), p. 554-555.

[31]Also, Weatherill has pointed out that the decision illustrates the distinction between positive harmonisation conducted by the EU legislature and negative harmonisation conducted by the Court of Justice. Weatherill, Stephen, 'EU Consumer Law and Policy', (2nd edn, Edward Elgar, 2013), p. 44-45.

[32]*Ibid*, p. 45.

free movement stipulated by the treaty.[33] In many areas since, including consumer protection law, unfair competition law and trademark law, the EU legislature has chosen the route of harmonisation. As mentioned in Chap. 4, harmonisation of the law relevant to this book has taken the form of maximum harmonisation.[34] Hence, in most of the subsequent decisions on consumer protection and unfair competition, such as *Buet v. Ministère Public* in 1989,[35] *Van Bennekom, Commission v. Germany* in 1992, *Clinique* in February 1994, *Meyhui v. Schott Zwiesel Glaswerke* in August 1994, *Mars* in 1995 and *Graffione* in 1996 before *Gut Springenheide*, the Court of Justice had to assess national EU harmonised law or law unified through secondary EU legislation.

It is important to note in the context of harmonisation that looking narrowly at the average consumer, it is—as a model—still harmonised through case law and not through positively harmonised legislation. As Howells points out, the UCPD and the Unfair Terms in Contracts Directive are two examples of positive harmonisation of the average consumer.[36] The analysis of the average consumer as positively harmonised was made under the analysis of the UCPD in the foregoing chapter.

8.4   Drei Glocken: The Hard Balance

In 1988, the Court of Justice decided *Drei Glocken*.[37] For several reasons, the decision will be dealt with in some detail. On a more general level, *Drei Glocken* highlights the fine-tuned and difficult balance in weighing the interests in free movement of goods against the national legislation on product standards.[38] The difficulties in this exercise are illustrated by Advocate General Mancini and the

---

[33]Respectively, Drei Glocken, Case 407/85, [1988] ECR 4233, GB-INNO, Case C-362/88, [1990] ECR I-667 and Schutzverband v. Yves Rocher, Case C-126/91, [1993] ECR I-2361.

[34]See the general discussion on harmonisation in Chap. 4, Sect. 4.2.

[35]*Buet v. Ministère Public* is not dealt with separately below. A French salesman of English language teaching material conducted doorstep selling in France. This practice was prohibited under French law. The Court of Justice interpreted the directive (EEC) No. 85/577 of 20 December 1985 on protecting consumers in respect of contracts negotiated away from business premises (the so-called "doorstep selling directive") as allowing member states to introduce requirements more favourable to consumers. Based on this, the court decided that the French legislation was "not incompatible with Article 30 of the Treaty." Buet v. Ministère public, Case 382/87, [1989] ECR 1235, para 17. The doorstep directive subsequently underwent maximum harmonisation through directive 2011/83 of 25 October 2011.

[36]Howells, Geraint G., 'Europe's (Lack of) Vision on Consumer Protection: A Case of Rhetoric Hiding Substance?', in Leczykiewicz, Dorota, and Weatherill, Stephen eds., The Images of the Consumer in EU Law: Legislation, Free Movement and Competition Law (1st edn, Hart, 2016), 431, p. 435.

[37]Drei Glocken, Case 407/85, [1988] ECR 4233.

[38]See Davies, Gareth, 'Internal Market Adjudication and the Quality of Life in Europe', Columbia Journal of European Union Law, vol. 21/no. 2, (2014-2015), pp. 289, p. 291.

Court of Justice reaching opposite results—the former allowing the national measures and the latter prohibiting them. Also, being a dispute on national product requirements vis-à-vis free movement of goods, the decision is narrowly related to *Cassis de Dijon*. Not least, according to Mancini, in the decision, the average consumer represents a significant role of consumer perception.

A German manufacturer of pasta, Drei Glocken, had sold its pasta to an Italian retailer that had resold it on the Italian market. The issue was that Drei Glocken pasta consisted of a mixture of common wheat and durum wheat which, as alleged by the Italian authorities, infringed Italian legislation on the marketing and manufacture of pasta. This legislation stated among other things that dried pasta had to be made from only durum wheat. Essentially, the questions were whether the national measures complied with art. 30 of the EEC Treaty (art. 34 of the TFEU), and, if not, if any of the exemptions in art. 36 of the EEC Treaty applied as such or as expanded by *Cassis de Dijon*. It was quickly observed by the Court of Justice that the Italian measures infringed art. 30 of the EEC Treaty as interpreted by *Dassonville*.[39] Hence, the questions were whether any of the mentioned exemptions applied.[40]

The Court of Justice did not agree with Mancini who saw the Italian legislation as not infringing art. 30 of the EEC Treaty. Based on a lengthy analysis of different European traditions of consuming pasta, Mancini argued that "the Community must intervene directly in its own right and must do so by a means placed at its disposal by the [EEC] Treaty."[41] Meanwhile, it should be allowed for a member state, such as Italy, to "impose the obligation to use exclusively durum wheat for the manufacture of pasta products intended to be marketed within that State."[42] In his argumentation in favour of this result, Mancini referred to the different tastes of the *average consumer*. For instance, Mancini posed the rhetoric question: "ask *the average Community consumer* what cheese is; you can bet that his answer will not be 'Edam'. Immediately afterwards ask him what pasta is: the chances that he will reply 'spaghetti' are extremely high (whereas I repeat, in Naples or Milan the man in the street would reel off at least a dozen names)." Exemplifying the differences between pastas, Mancini referred to a Community customs regulation with the heading "Pasta ... such as spaghetti, macaroni, noodles, lasagne, gnocchi, ravioli, canneloni', and let no one tell me that it is merely an accident that the first pasta products mentioned in that list are precisely spaghetti and macaroni!"[43]

Assessing the exemptions, the Court of Justice rejected reference to "public health" under art. 36 of the EEC Treaty due to lack of proportionality.[44] It was further claimed by the Italian Government that the national requirements, *inter alia*,

---

[39]Drei Glocken, Case 407/85, [1988] ECR 4233, paras 9 and 11.

[40]*Ibid*, paras 10-11.

[41]Drei Glocken, Case 407/85, [1988] ECR 4233, (opinion of AG Mancini), p. 4272.

[42]*Ibid*, p. 4274.

[43]*Ibid*, p. 4269 (italics in the first quote added).

[44]Drei Glocken, Case 407/85, [1988] ECR 4233, para 14.

were introduced to ensure consumer protection and fair trading.[45] In addition, it was disputed that "suitable labels" would make the Italian consumers aware that foreign pastas, including that of Drei Glocken, did not consist exclusively of durum wheat.[46] The court rejected the arguments in favour of the Italian prohibition holding that "the Italian Government has at its disposal a less restrictive means of ensuring fair trading" by allowing only pastas made exclusively from durum wheat to be described. This would "enable to Italian consumers to express their preference."[47] The Court of Justice did not enter the conversation on the fragmented average consumer in EU as laid out by Mancini. This may seem surprising, since the court in the decision comparable to *Drei Glocken*, i.e. *German Beer Purity* from 1987, entered this conversation.[48] In this decision, the German Government argued that German consumers perceived "Bier" as a beverage produced by certain ingredients. Countering this argument, the Court of Justice held that "consumers' conceptions which *vary from one Member State to the other are also likely to evolve in the course of time within a Member State*. The establishment of the common market is, it should be added, one of the factors that may play a major contributory role in that development."[49] In contrast with Mancini in *Drei Glocken*, it should be mentioned that the court in *German Beer Purity* used the fragmented consumer perception countering the German standards of beer manufacturing.

As is clear, *Cassis de Dijon*, *Drei Glocken* and *German Beer Purity*[50] related to issues of a ban of certain products based solely on their quality not being justified referring to public health. Looking at them in hindsight in 2003, this group of decisions is, according to Davies, "the simplest group" of decisions that "can be dealt with shortly." In addition, Davies has suggested that these decisions are "of historical interest only."[51] That this for the most part is true has been seen with the harmonisation of product standards over the years, and not least, this is reflected in the 2016 communication of initiatives issued by the Commission on "European standards for the 21st century."[52] However, in terms of developing the average consumer, Mancini in *Drei Glocken* and the Court of Justice in *German Beer Purity*

---

[45]*Ibid*, paras 15-16.

[46]*Ibid*, para 19.

[47]*Ibid*, paras 22 and 28.

[48]Commission v. Germany ("German Beer Purity"), Case 178/84, [1987] ECR 1227.

[49]*Ibid*, para 32 (italics added).

[50]*Ibid*. For other decisions on similar standards, see Davies, Gareth, 'Internal Market Adjudication and the Quality of Life in Europe', Columbia Journal of European Union Law, vol. 21/no. 2, (2014-2015), pp. 289, p. 294, including footnote 28 of that text.

[51]Davies, Gareth, 'Consumer Protection as an Obstacle to the Free Movement of Goods', ERA Forum, vol. 4/no. 3, (2003), pp. 55, p. 58.

[52]One of the policy statements of the Commission in the communication is: "From goods to services and information and communication technologies (ICT), standards have proven to be a flexible way of raising quality and safety, improving transparency and interoperability, reducing costs and opening up markets for businesses, especially SMEs. Standards benefit consumers, companies and society at large." Commission, EP, Council, EESC and the Committee of the Regions

show one important aspect of the average consumer that has puzzled the judiciaries and legislatures, and still does so. This is the inevitable aspect of the average consumer as potentially reflecting different cultures. Mancini's exemplification of the perception of an "average Community [EU] consumer" of cheese and pasta highlights a profound difficulty of framing the average consumer. Essentially, in a broader picture, human perception of the world is (not surprisingly) in the eye of the beholder.[53] It is possible to perceive of an almost endless number of variables that define the "world" of the average consumer. Arguably, there is a positive correlation between the number of these variables and the size of the geographical area covered by the average consumer. Most notably, this establishes that if it is necessary in a dispute, be it on trademark law or the UCPD, the average consumer covers not only one EU member state but is an *EU* average consumer covering several EU member states. Some of these variables are used as parameters for the contextualisation analysis in Chap. 11.

Davies has questioned the approach of the Court of Justice in these standardisation decisions highlighting that "[t]he destruction of standards concerning pasta and chocolate – products not without cultural and symbolic importance in some Member States – follows the same analytic path as a decision on prizes for crosswords in magazines." Adding to this, Davies has highlighted the difference among the member states anecdotally illustrated by how "continental Europeans typically regard the British attachment to feet and pints." Furthermore, that "[c]hanging the ingredients of pasta is another such divisive issue, a cause for horror among Italians and shrugs elsewhere. What is self-evidently of passionate importance to one community is obscure to another." Potentially, this opens up for an ignorance of "the genuine values of national community" as part of the "transnational legal process."[54] Although it is outside the purpose of this book to normatively assess this argument, it illustrates the important role of consumers in the adjudication process. Consumers are the alleged beneficiaries of the national measures on consumer protection and protection against unfair commercial practices used to calibrate the free movement of goods. Besides being the beneficiaries, consumers have also been given assumed characteristics in some cases manifested as the average consumer. What kind of basic characteristics are consumers assumed

---

Communication on a Standardisation package. European Standards for the 21st Century of 1 June 2016, COM(2016) 358 final, p. 2.

[53] Among others, Kenyon and Sen have defined what they denote as a "user-based" quality "from a perceptual perspective" as: "quality is in the eye of the beholder. As individuals, we are all unique because of our genetic predispositions, cultural and social backgrounds, and our experiences." Therefore, "each one of us can best be satisfied with a product or service that deliver value based upon one's own particular preferences." Kenyon, George N., and Sen, Kabir C., 'The Perception of Quality: Mapping Product and Service Quality to Consumer Perceptions', (1st edn, Springer, 2015), p. 3.

[54] Davies, Gareth, 'Internal Market Adjudication and the Quality of Life in Europe', Columbia Journal of European Union Law, vol. 21/no. 2, (2014-2015), pp. 289, p. 309.

to have and how are they rooted in the different cultures of the member states or the EU as a whole? This is addressed throughout this book.

8.5 Medical Products and the "Public Health"

As seen in *Cassis de Dijon*, the Court of Justice assumed that consumers can compute "*suitable information*." This assumption was developed further when the Court of Justice had to interpret EU secondary legislation where the EU legislature had positively harmonised European law. Specifically, the Court of Justice issued decisions on whether to allow for national measures introduced under directive (EEC) No. 65/65 of 26 January 1965 on the approximation of provisions laid down by law, regulation or administrative action relating to proprietary medicinal products (the "Medical Product Directive 1965")[55] to derogate from art. 34 of the TFEU referring to "the protection of health and life of humans" under art. 36 of the TFEU. Although, in principle, since an "essential objective" of the Medical Product Directive 1965 was the protection of "public health", references to art. 36 of the TFEU were gradually made redundant.[56]

In *Van Bennekom* in 1983, the Court of Justice interpreted the Medical Product Directive 1965 and its definition of "medical product."[57] One of the six preliminary questions was whether products, which are "not "indicated or recommended" expressly as being suitable for curing, treating or preventing an infection, may none the less be substances "presented for treating or preventing disease in human being or animals" within the meaning of the Community definition of "medicinal product"."[58] The Court of Justice found that the criterion of the directive "of the

---

[55]Council Directive of 26 January 1965 on the approximation of provisions laid down by law, regulation or administrative action relating to proprietary medicinal products (65/65/EEC), [1965] OJ 369/65. It should be mentioned that the Medical Product Directive 1965 was codified in EP and Council Directive 2001/83/EC of 6 November 2001 on the Community code relating to medicinal products for human use, [2001] OJ L311/67.

[56]See Van Bennekom, Case 227/82, [1983] ECR 3883, para 14. An example of the redundancy of art. 36 of the TFEU is illustrated by *Commission v. Germany 1992* referred to below where the Court of Justice stated: "At the present stage of development of Community law, it is difficult to avoid the continued existence, for the time being and, doubtless, so long as harmonization of the measures necessary to ensure the protection of health is not more complete, of differences in the classification of products as between Member States." Commission v. Germany 1992, Case C-290/90, [1992] ECR I-3317, para 16. See similarly Monteil, Case C-60/89, [1991] ECR I-1547, paras 27-28 and Delattre, Case C-369/88, [1991] ECR I-1487, paras 28-29, both referred to subsequently in this section.

[57]The disputed products were certain "vitamin and multi-vitamin preparations which were in pharmaceutical form (tablets, pills and capsules) but were unaccompanied by any indication or recommendation" as required by the relevant law of the Netherlands. Van Bennekom, Case 227/82, [1983] ECR 3883, p. 3886.

[58]*Ibid*, para 16.

product's "presentation", is designed to cover not only medicinal products having a genuine therapeutic or medical effect but also those which are not sufficiently effective or which do not have the effect *which consumers would be entitled to expect in view of their presentation.*" The directive sought "to preserve consumers not only from harmful or toxic medicinal products as such but also from a variety of products used instead of the proper remedies. For that reason, the concept of the 'presentation' of a product must be broadly construed."[59] Against this background, the Court of Justice introduced the average consumer, holding "that a product is "presented for treating or preventing disease" within the meaning of Directive 65/65 not only when it is expressly "indicated" or "recommended" as such, possibly by means of labels, leaflets or oral representation, but also *whenever any averagely will-informed*[60] *consumer gains the impression*, which, provided it is definite, may even result from implication, that the product in question should, regard being had to its presentation, have an effect such as is described by the first part of the Community definition."[61]

In *Commission v. Germany 1992*, the Commission sued under art. 169 of the EEC Treaty (art. 258 of the TFEU) for non-fulfilment of an obligation following from the treaty.[62] The issue was whether an eye lotion produced by a French company was considered a "proprietary medical product" under the Medical Product Directive 1965.[63] If that was the case, Germany reserved the right to require prior authorisation of the product for it to be marketed in Germany. According to the Court of Justice (Grand Chamber),[64] the directive only constituted a "first stage in the approximation of national legislation"[65] and, due to lack of (maximum) harmonisation, it was unavoidable to find differences between the member states on the definition of medical products.[66] It was held by Germany that, due to the presentation and use

---

[59]*Ibid*, para 17 (italics in the first quote are added).

[60]It is assumed that "will-informed" is a misspelling of "well-informed," which is nowadays an accepted characteristic of the average consumer.

[61]*Ibid*, para 18 (italics added).

[62]Cf. art. 169 of the EEC Treaty. I.e. since the Commission was of the opinion that Germany had not complied with its obligations under the treaty.

[63]The 1965 Directive on Medicinal Products. The eye lotion could for instance be used for the removal of injurious substances from the eye through a rinsing process.

[64]The Court of Justice may sit in a Grand Chamber consisting of 13 judges, "presided over by the President of the Court. The Presidents of the chambers of five Judges and other Judges appointed in accordance with the conditions laid down in the Rules of Procedure," cf. art. 16(2) of the Statute of the CJEU. That the Court of Justice sits in the Grand Chamber illustrates either that it has been requested by "a Member State or an institution of the Union," cf. art. 16(3) of the Statute of the CJEU. Also, if the case before the Court of Justice "is of exceptional importance, the Court may decide, after hearing the Advocate General, to refer the case to the full Court," cf. art. 16(5) of the Statute of the CJEU. See also Bobek, Michal, 'The Court of Justice of the European Union', in Arnull, Anthony and Chalmers, Damian eds., The Oxford Handbook of European Union Law (1st edn, Oxford University Press, 2015), 153, p. 156-157.

[65]Commission v. Germany 1992, Case C-290/90, [1992] ECR I-3317, para 15.

[66]*Ibid*, para 16.

of the relevant lotions, "*the average well-informed consumer should infer from that that they have prophylactic or therapeutic properties.*"[67] The Court of Justice did not as such refer to the "average consumer" but held referring to its finding approximately one year earlier in *Upjohn* that, based on consumer "familiarity," it was "for the national authorities to determine, subject to review by the courts," the definition of what was understood by medical product.[68] In *Upjohn*, Advocate General Lenz held that "the only effects to be considered are those which the product has when applied to the part of the body to which, in the judgment of the *average user*, it is to be administered" and that children could be the relevant "average user."[69]

In the hearing report preceding *Commission v. Germany 1992* of Judge-Rapporteur Iglesias, the Commission had referred to the relevant directive as protecting "the unwary consumer against the possible damaging consequences of powerful chemical or biological preparations."[70] Interestingly, the hearing report, in contrast with the subsequent decision, stated referring to the Court of Justice in *Van Bennekom* that not only, the objective presentation of the medical products was relevant (i.e. what is "expressly indicated or recommended") "but also whenever *any averagely well-informed consumer gains the impression*" which "*may even result from implication.*"[71]

The Court of Justice has later referred to the finding and phrasing in *Van Bennekom* on many occasions in disputes on the Medical Product Directive 1965 or subsequent directives,[72] for instance, in *Delattre* in 1991,[73] *Monteil* in 1991[74] and *Commission v. Germany 2007*.[75]

---

[67] *Ibid*, para 11 (italics added).

[68] *Ibid*, para 17. Reference here was made to Upjohn, Case C-112/89, [1991] ECR I-1703, para 23. In *Upjohn* the main question was whether a hair restorer was a proprietary medical product under the 1965 Medical Product Directive, and/or a "cosmetic product" under directive (EEC) No. 76/768 of 27 July 1976 on approximation of the laws of the Member States relating to cosmetic products. EP and Council Regulation (EC) No 1223/2009 of 30 November 2009 on cosmetic products, [2009] OJ L342/59, cf. recital 69 of the regulation.

[69] Upjohn, Case C-112/89, [1991] ECR I-1703, (opinion of AG Lenz), para 63.

[70] Commission v. Germany 1992, Case C-290/90, [1992] (rapport for the hearing), ECR I-3317, p. 3324.

[71] *Ibid*, p. 3325 (italics added). Besides Germany, the Commission also referred to the relevance of the average consumer holding that "it must not be supposed that the 'average consumer' sees the eye-lotions as medicinal products or that he is entitled to expect that they are." *Ibid*.

[72] Alternatively, directive (EC) No 2001/83 among other directives on medical products codifying the 1965 Medical Product Directive.

[73] Delattre, Case C-369/88, [1991] ECR I-1487, paras 38-40 and 58.

[74] Monteil, Case C-60/89, [1991] ECR I-1547, paras 23-24.

[75] Commission v. Germany 2007, Case C-319/05, [2007] ECR I-9811, para 46.

8.6   Consumer Protection and Unfair Competition

Reich and Micklitz have stated that starting with *Cassis de Dijon*, the Court of Justice "has developed the broader *principle of consumer protection as an independent reason of justification* against national restrictions to free movement provided they are proportionate and non-discriminatory under Community law."[76] Micklitz has seen the decision as having "paved the way for the Internal Market project – market integration was achieved through mutual recognition" which subsequently was superseded by harmonisation.[77] The resulting harmonisation through secondary EU legislation has been interpreted by the Court of Justice in the below decisions. Part of that interpretation has been about how the presumptions to be made on consumer behaviour through the average consumer elevated from national to EU law by the Court of Justice.

The average consumer as introduced in *Van Bennekom* and the *Commission v. Germany 1992*[78] was narrowly related to the interest of consumer protection manifested in the protection of consumers' health. Besides this angle of consumer protection and the angle reflected in the standardisation decisions, there has been many significant decisions related to broader consumer protection and the prevention of unfair commercial practices, which are the most commonly claimed "mandatory requirements."[79] In these decisions, the Court of Justice has moved close to the assessment of how consumers perceive information, and which information is needed. Essentially, the court has followed its approach in *Cassis de Dijon* where it set out what is "suitable information" moving close to the factual assessment of cases.[80]

Referring to broader consumer protection, it has been claimed by Weatherill and Beaumont that the providing "of information is capable of restricting the free circulation of products in respect of which information is routinely provided in the country of origin."[81] Since the Court of Justice has prioritised the "informed consumer" spurring "the efficient operation of the market" it will most likely not uphold these rules.[82] It has been held by Mak that the informed consumer manifests "a standard of *informed reasonable behaviour from the consumer that is higher than*

---

[76]Reich, Norbert, Micklitz, Hans-W., and Rott, Peter, 'European Consumer Law', (2nd edn, Intersentia, 2014), p. 12.

[77]Micklitz, Hans-W., 'The Consumer: Marketised, Fragmentised, Constitutionalised', in Leczykiewicz, Dorota, and Weatherill, Stephen eds., The Images of the Consumer in EU Law: Legislation, Free Movement and Competition Law (1st edn, Hart, 2016), 21, p. 28.

[78]In addition, the decisions referring to these two decisions.

[79]Weatherill and Beaumont 1999, p. 588. As mentioned earlier, reference to "mandatory requirements" were first made by the Court of Justice in *Cassis de Dijon*, Case 120/78, [1979] ECR 649, para 8.

[80]These findings relate to the fact/law divide. See for instance, Chap. 11, Sect. 11.1.

[81]Weatherill, Stephen, and Beaumont, Paul, 'EU Law: The Essential Guide to the Legal Workings of the European Union', (3rd edn, Penguin, 1999), p. 583.

[82]*Ibid*, p. 584.

that of the 'average consumer', albeit to different degrees."[83] In dealing with in particular consumer notions of EU consumer protection law, de Vries has held that "[t]he basic notion of consumer in EU law is that the consumer is considered and defend their own interests."[84]

In 1990, the Court of Justice decided *GB-Inno* referring to e.g. *Cassis de Dijon*. *GB-Inno* concerned the legality of national legislation allegedly ensuring consumer protection and fairness of commercial practices vis-à-vis treaty protection of the free movement of goods.[85] The issue of the decision was measures of the Luxembourg unfair competition legislation "according to which sales offers involving a temporary price reduction may not state the duration of the offer or refer to previous prices."[86] GB-Inno, operating supermarkets in an area of Belgium close to Luxembourg, distributed certain advertisement leaflets in Belgium referring to price reductions of limited temporal validity and reduced prices compared to previous prices. A board claiming to act for the interests of Luxembourg traders held that the leaflets infringed the Luxembourg unfair competition legislation.

According to the Court of Justice: "The question thus arises whether national legislation which prevents the consumer from having access to certain information may be justified in the interest of consumer protection."[87] CCL and the Luxembourg Government argued that "[t]he purpose of the prohibition concerning the duration of the special offer is to avoid the risk of confusion."[88] Against this argument, GB-Inno and the Commission pointed out "that any *normally aware consumer knows* that annual sales take place only twice a year" and hence was not confused by the information provided in the leaflets.[89] In its assessment of these arguments, the Court of Justice referred to a community policy formulated to create "a close link between protecting the consumer and providing the consumer with information."[90] Among other aspects, the purpose of the programme was to protect "the economic interests of consumers" and "to ensure the accuracy of information provided to the consumer, but without refusing him access to certain information."[91] Referring to the

---

[83]Mak, Vanessa, 'The Consumer in European Regulatory Private Law', in Leczykiewicz, Dorota, and Weatherill, Stephen eds., The Images of the Consumer in EU Law: Legislation, Free Movement and Competition Law (1st edn, Hart, 2016), 381, p. 386 (italics added). The finding by Mak also relates to the "man skilled in the art" ("person skilled in the art") from patent law.

[84]Vries, Sybe Alexander de, 'The Court of Justice's 'Paradigm Consumer' in EU Free Movement Law', in Leczykiewicz, Dorota, and Weatherill, Stephen eds., The Images of the Consumer in EU Law: Legislation, Free Movement and Competition Law (1st edn, Hart, 2016), 401, p. 408.

[85]GB-INNO, Case C-362/88, [1990] ECR I-667.

[86]*Ibid*, para 2.

[87]*Ibid*, para 13.

[88]More specifically confusion "between special sales and half-yearly clearance sales the timing and duration of which is restricted under Luxembourg legislation." "CCL" is an abbreviation of "Confédération du Commerce Luxembourgeois." *Ibid*, para 11.

[89]*Ibid*, para 12 (italics added).

[90]*Ibid*, para 14.

[91]*Ibid*, para 16.

importance of consumer information and free movement of goods, national legislation that prevented certain consumer information could not be justified, according to the Court of Justice, despite the claim for consumer protection.[92] Although the Court of Justice did not explicitly refer to the "normally aware consumer," it took the side of the Commission and GB-Inno. Reich *et al* have seen the *GB-Inno* as an indication that "true information must not be withheld from the consumer."[93] The Court of Justice maintained its stance in *GB-Inno* in 1993 in *Yves Rocher* on national legislation that prevented the use of price comparisons of new and old prices.[94] As Weatherill pointed out at the time of the judgments, there was no common EU agreement on legislation on comparative advertisement; hence, this gave "a deep background diversity in practice among the Member States" with e.g. stringent German standards and less stringent UK ditto.[95]

The *Nissan* decision of 1992 related to misleading advertisement.[96] An exclusive importer of Nissan cars in the French market brought a claim against a French garage that advertised "along the lines of '*buy your new vehicle cheaper.*'"[97] The cars registered for importation were advertised as new and as guaranteed by the manufacturer, and they were sold at a lower price by the garage compared to other French dealers with fewer accessories though. The importer claimed that the owner of the garage had infringed French law by the way it had implemented a directive on misleading advertising.[98] The purpose of the directive was *inter alia*, to ensure consumer protection, free movement of goods and undistorted competition.[99]

---

[92]*Ibid*, paras 18 and 21.

[93]Reich, Norbert, Micklitz, Hans-W., and Rott, Peter, 'European Consumer Law', (2nd edn, Intersentia, 2014), p. 101. Although Reich *et al* have not referred to *Yves Rocher*, this decision also indicates that true information cannot be withheld from the consumer. See also Engelbrekt, Antonina Bakardjieva, 'Fair Trading Law in Flux? National Legacies, Institutional Choice and the Process of Europeanisation', (1st edn, Stockholm University, 2003), p. 439, Howells, Geraint G., and Weatherill, Stephen, 'Consumer Protection Law', (2nd edn, Routledge, 2005), p. 111-113.

[94]The French parent company of the German subsidiary of Yves Rocher sold via mail order its products in Germany. In connection with the sale, Yves Rocher circulated a catalogue where its previous prices were compared with its new prices. This price comparison was prohibited under German unfair competition law since it was "eye catching." The Court of Justice based its decision partly on its assessment in *GB Inno*. Schutzverband v. Yves Rocher, Case C-126/91, [1993] ECR I-2361, paras 10 and 12. The Court of Justice concluded that the interest in free movement of goods prevented national (non-harmonised) law from barring price comparisons. *Ibid*, para 23.

[95]Weatherill, Stephen, 'EU Consumer Law and Policy', (2nd edn, Edward Elgar, 2013), p. 51. Elaborating on the harmonisation of comparative advertisement regulation, Weatherill mentioned that the decisions related to the Directive on misleading advertising, which did harmonise comparative advertisement.

[96]X (Nissan), Case C-373/90, [1992], ECR I-131.

[97]X (Nissan), Case C-373/90, [1991] ECR I-131, (opinion of AG Tesauro), para 1.

[98]Directive (ECC) No. 84/450 of 10 September 1984 relating to the approximation of the laws, regulations and administrative provisions of the Member States concerning misleading advertising. This directive was later amended by the UCPD.

[99]X (Nissan), Case C-373/90, [1992], ECR I-131, para 9.

Specifically, the question was whether the three advertisement claims by the garage owner (new, cheaper—despite fewer accessories than for comparable cars—and guaranteed by the manufacturer) constituted misleading advertisement.[100] As for the first two claims, the Court of Justice stated that it was decisive whether "a significant number of consumers" were misled.[101] As for the guarantee, it could not be misleading if it was true.[102] The Court of Justice concluded that the directive did not as such preclude the sale of the imported cars as advertised.[103] The findings entailed that based on the facts it was for the national court to decide if the advertisement was misleading.[104]

Whereas the Court of Justice in *Nissan* referred to "a significant number of consumers," Advocate General Tesauro, who gave the preceding opinion, took a different approach. Tesauro stated that "the car market is characterized by a certain price transparency and *that the average consumer, who I am convinced is not wholly undiscerning, is inclined, not least in view of the considerable expense he is contemplating, to make a careful comparison of the prices on offer and to enquire of the seller, sometimes very meticulously, about the accessories with which the vehicle is equipped*." Furthermore, that "*vigiliantibus non dormientibus iura succurrunt*" ("the law benefits those who pay attention, not those who get distracted.")[105] As it subsequently became clear in Court of Justice case law, the finding of Tesauro was very much a prediction of how the average consumer was to be used in EU law. Here, it was flagged that there was a balance to be stroked between the inattentive and attentive consumers and that the law in general does not protect the inattentive consumers. Finally, Tesauro also indicated that consumers can be presumed to pay more attention (than normally) when buying cars. An assumption that has echoed in trademark law years later.

In *Clinique* of 1994, the issue was that German authorities sought to prevent Estée Lauder from selling its products on the German market bearing the name "Clinique." The legal basis for this was German unfair competition legislation that corresponded to some provisions in the directive on misleading advertising[106] and German law on foodstuff and consumer items that implemented the directive related to cosmetic

---

[100] *Ibid*, para 11.

[101] *Ibid*, paras 13-16.

[102] *Ibid*, para 17. See also GB-INNO, Case C-362/88, [1990] ECR I-667, para 17.

[103] X (Nissan), Case C-373/90, [1992], ECR I-131, para 19.

[104] *Ibid*, paras 15-16. See also referring to this Gut Springenheide and Tusky, Case C-210/96, [1998] ECR I-4657, para 34.

[105] X (Nissan), Case C-373/90, [1991] ECR I-131, (opinion of AG Tesauro), para 9 (italics added). The saying has initially been translated from Latin into the Italian "le leggi giovano a chi vigila, non a chi dorme" and from Italian into English. The Latin/Italian translation is taken from Paride, Bertozzi, 'Dizionario dei brocardi e dei latinismi giuridici', (6th edn, IPSOA, 2009).

[106] I.e. Directive (ECC) No. 84/450 of 10 September 1984 relating to the approximation of the laws, regulations and administrative provisions of the Member States concerning misleading advertising. See footnote 98 above. See Verband Sozialer Wettbewerb v. Clinique Laboratoires, Case C-315/92, [1994] ECR I-317, para 9.

products.[107] According to the Court of Justice, there was no doubt that restrictions on the use of the name Clinique did "affect free trade."[108] Based on the facts as presented to the Court of Justice, the court decided the case more closely based on the facts than suggested by Advocate General Gulmann who gave the opinion of the case.[109] Gulmann argued that account should be taken of "the fact that there may exist in this field linguistic, cultural and social differences."[110] Although the Court of Justice has referred to these factors subsequently,[111] and relevant to this book, the legislature under the UCPD, the Court of Justice in *Clinique* did not expressly refer to them.[112] The Court based its decision *inter alia*, on the facts that the Clinique products were sold in "Germany exclusively in perfumeries and cosmetic departments of large stores" and that the "products are ordinarily marketed in other countries under the name 'Clinique' and the use of that name apparently does not mislead consumers."[113] The Court of Justice paralleled the obstacles in *Clinique* to

---

[107]Council Directive of 27 July 1976 on the approximation of the laws of the Member States relating to cosmetic products (76/768/EEC), [1976] OJ L262/169. See Verband Sozialer Wettbewerb v. Clinique Laboratoires, Case C-315/92, [1994] ECR I-317, para 14. Since the introduction of the directive, the regulation of the cosmetic area has been expanded. For an overview of the current EU regulation on this area see: http://ec.europa.eu/growth/sectors/cos metics/legislation_en (last visited 26 May 2019).

[108]*Ibid*, para 19. The Court of Justice held that: "The fact that by reason of that prohibition the undertaking in question is obliged in that Member State alone to market its products under a different name and to bear additional packaging and advertising costs demonstrates that this measure does affect free trade." *Ibid*.

[109]Hence, Gulmann held that: "In order to give the national court the most appropriate answer, the Court can link the interpretation of Article 30 of the EEC Treaty closely to the specific facts of the case before the national court." Verband Sozialer Wettbewerb v. Clinique Laboratoires, Case C-315/92 [1993] ECR I-317, (opinion of AG Gulmann), para 9. "It is, however, necessary to bear in mind that the question in this case is not whether national legislation is generally compatible with Article 30; rather, the question concerns the application of national rules to a particular legal situation requiring a specific assessment of whether consumers are misled in the particular circumstances. It would in my opinion be wrong for the Court, in a case such as this, to link its interpretation of Article 30 too closely to the particular facts of the case." *Ibid*.

[110]*Ibid*, para 18. In *Graffione* related to the trademark "Contonelle" registered *inter alia* in Italy, Advocate General Jacobs explained referring to Gulmann's finding in *Clinique*: "The present name provides an excellent illustration as regards the linguistic factor. The name 'Cotonelle' might, arguably, cause a speaker of English, French or Italian to believe that a product is made of cotton. However, it could hardly have that effect on someone who understands only German or Spanish, since the words for cotton in those languages are 'Baumwolle' and 'algodón' respectively." Graffione, Case C-313/94, [1996] ECR I-6039, (opinion of AG Jacobs), para 10. For at outline of the facts of *Graffione*, see footnote 138 below.

[111]See for instance *Graffione* on the misleading nature of a trademark revoked under the Italian Trademarks Act implementing the TM Directive 1989. Graffione, Case C-313/94, [1996] ECR I-6039, para 22.

[112]See recital 18 of the UCPD and the analysis of the average consumer under the UCPD in Chap. 7.

[113]Verband Sozialer Wettbewerb v Clinique Laboratoires, Case C-315/92, [1994] ECR I-317, para 22.

the ones in *Keck and Mithouard*.[114] The court reached the decision that "clinical or medical connotations" of Clinique did not prohibit use of the word.[115]

Reich *et al* saw it as "obvious" that the Court of Justice "proceeded from the fact that the German consumer could not be misled by the term "Clinique"."[116] Based on the decision Weatherill found that the Court of Justice imagined "a rather robust, self-reliant consumer in the market who is able to enjoy the fruits of integration." This view of the court was in contrast with national measures that imagined the consumer as "more gullible."[117] Wilhelmsson has seen the *Clinique* decision as an indication of, "What '*rational' average consumers* in one Member State can be *expected* to familiarize themselves with and take into account, may in another Member State fall far outside the scope of information which average consumers tend to look at."[118] According to Bakardjieva, *Nissan* and *Clinique* show the willingness of the Court of Justice "to assume the role of an arbiter in drawing the border between free market and private ordering (when consumption patterns have to be adjusted to a new reality of integrated markets)."[119]

In contrast with *Clinique*, the Court of Justice expressly referred to the average consumer 6 months later in *Meyhui v. Schott Zwiesel Glaswerke*.[120] The decision related to interpreting a directive stipulating certain marketing standards of crystal glass.[121] Based on the directive, Belgium required that glass marketed in its territory should bear descriptive labels in the Belgian languages. Initially, the Court held that these requirements might constitute obstacles to the free movement of goods.[122] The Court held that for some categories of glass, the description was so much alike in the different languages, that it would be "easily recognizable" to the relevant consumers who were generally non-native speakers.[123] However, other descriptions would not be "*easily discernible to the average consumer for whom the purchase of crystal*

---

[114]*Ibid*, para 13.

[115]*Ibid*, para 23.

[116]Reich, Norbert, Micklitz, Hans-W., and Rott, Peter, 'European Consumer Law', (2nd edn, Intersentia, 2014), p. 99.

[117]Weatherill, Stephen, 'EU Consumer Law and Policy', (2nd edn, Edward Elgar, 2013), p. 52. See also Weatherill, Stephen, 'Who is the 'Average Consumer'?', in Weatherill, Stephen and Bernitz, Ulf eds., The Regulation of the Unfair Commercial Practices Under EC Directive 2005/29 (1st edn, Oxford, Hart, 2007), 115, p. 116.

[118]Wilhelmsson, Thomas, 'The Average European Consumer: A Legal Fiction?', in Wilhelmsson, Thomas, Paunio, Elina and Pohjolainen, Annika eds., Private Law and the Many Cultures of Europe (1st edn, Kluwer Law International, 2007), 243, p. 262 (italics added).

[119]Engelbrekt, Antonina Bakardjieva, 'Fair Trading Law in Flux? National Legacies, Institutional Choice and the Process of Europeanisation', (1st edn, Stockholm University, 2003), p. 605.

[120]Meyhui v. Schott Zwiesel Glaswerke, Case C-51/93, [1994] ECR I-3879.

[121]Directive (EEC) No 69/493 on the approximation of the laws of the Member States relating to crystal glass.

[122]Meyhui v. Schott Zwiesel Glaswerke, Case C-51/93, [1994] ECR I-3879, para 10, referring to Verband Sozialer Wettbewerb v. Clinique Laboratoires, Case C-315/92, [1994] ECR I-317, para 13.

[123]*Ibid*, para 17.

glass products is not a frequent occurrence." It was vital for the average consumer "to be given the *clearest information possible* as to what he is buying so that he does not confuse a product" in the different categories.[124] The Court of Justice thus rejected "the hypothesis" stated by the national court "that another language may be easily comprehensible to the purchaser is of only marginal importance."[125] In the decision, the Court did not refer to its previous decisions that set out the average consumer.[126] Although the Court of Justice in *Meyhui v. Schott Zwiesel Glaswerke* referred to the average consumer, it still found that the consumer needed the *clearest information possible*. A somewhat different approach seemed to have been taken by the Court in *Mars* dealt with below where it was assumed by the Court that the consumers were not to be overly informed.

Similar to *Clinique*, the Court of Justice in *Mars* in 1995 had to decide on the legality of German unfair competition law that prevented the marketing by Mars of certain ice cream snacks made and packaged in France. A German association sought an injunction in Germany against Mars due to Mars' marking of the packaging with "+10%" and claimed that it infringed German rules on unfair competition. One claim was that the marking "gave the consumer the impression that the product had been increased by a quantity corresponding to the coloured part of the new wrapping."[127] The Court of Justice did not accept that claim since the "*[r]easonably circumspect consumers may be deemed to know* that there is not necessarily a link between the size of publicity markings relating to an increase in a product's quantity and the size of that increase."[128] In line with the finding of the Court, Advocate General Léger in *Mars* advocated for imbuing the consumer with a certain common sense citing the view of the Commission, i.e. "it must also be clear to a *careful consumer* that a certain amount of exaggeration is inherent in any promotion of a product."[129] In *Gut Springenheide* the finding of the court in *Mars* has been referred to by Advocate General Mischo as an example of an "abstract, legal concept of a consumer."[130] Advocate General Fennelly in *Estée Lauder* saw that "[t]his identification of the level of protection required by the average consumer crystallised" in *Mars*.[131]

---

[124]*Ibid*, para 18 (italics added).

[125]*Ibid*, para 19.

[126]Advocate-General Gulmann did not at all refer to the average consumer as such.

[127]Verein gegen Unwesen in Handel und Gewerbe v. Mars, Case C-470/93, [1995] ECR I-1923, paras 8 and 22. The other claim was that consumers expected that the price of the marked snacks would not increase since a price increase would remove the advantage for the consumer. *Ibid*, para 7.

[128]*Ibid*, para 24 (italics added).

[129]Verein gegen Unwesen in Handel und Gewerbe v. Mars, Case C-470/93, [1995] ECR I-1923, (opinion of AG Léger), para 53 (italics added).

[130]Gut Springenheide and Tusky, Case C-210/96, [1998] ECR I-4657, (opinion of AG Mischo), para 55.

[131]Estée Lauder, Case C-220/98, [1999] ECR I-117, (opinion of AG Fennelly), para 27.

Reich *et al* have seen *Mars*, as a manifestation that "the reasonable consumer is required to identify objectively false information."[132] The consumer image in *Mars* has recently been depicted by Weatherill as "an instrumental consumer – a consumer who is empowered enough not to need regulation of the market in such circumstances and who is empowered further by the wider choice that is made available by opening up the local market to cross-border competition."[133] Even more strongly, Weatherill has continued his earlier critique of these examples of "over-regulation"[134] stating that the national rules in this context "do not deserve to stand. They do not deserve to be treated as measures of consumer protection at all. These cases involve absurd attempts to present protectionist rules that favour producer interests as measures of consumer protection."[135] Although not countering the scholarly critique by Weatherill as such, Bakardjieva has previously provided important subtext that explains the reason for the high number of German cases on unfair competition law. Hence, this is also indirectly an explanation of why many decisions through preliminary references have found their way to the Court of Justice: "One can say that the broad general clause in combination with a flexible enforcement mechanism, granting generous opportunities for collective representation of joint industry interests, proved to be the key to the success of the statute, if one equates 'success' with intensity of application of a piece of legislation in practice."[136] Adding to this, Bakardjieva has claimed that "it has been competitors and Wettbewerbsverbände that have systematically brought new cases before the courts and acted as avengers of the allegedly disadvantaged consumer minority."[137]

In *Graffione* of 1996, a key question was whether Italian unfair competition rules compromised free movement treaty rules.[138] However, referring to *Clinique* and

---

[132]Reich, Norbert, Micklitz, Hans-W., and Rott, Peter, 'European Consumer Law', (2nd edn, Intersentia, 2014), p. 101.

[133]Weatherill, Stephen, 'Empowerment is Not the Only Fruit', in Leczykiewicz, Dorota and Weatherill, Stephen eds., The Images of the Consumer in EU Law: Legislation, Free Movement and Competition Law (1st edn, Hart, 2016), 203, p. 206.

[134]Commenting on *Mars*, Weaterhill stated in 2013 that "[o]ne may wonder whether the court had become rather fed up of the German-sourced stream of indefensible examples of over-regulation spuriously depicted as measures of consumer protection."
    Weatherill, Stephen, 'EU Consumer Law and Policy', (2nd edn, Edward Elgar, 2013), p. 53.

[135]Weatherill, Stephen, 'Empowerment is Not the Only Fruit', in Leczykiewicz, Dorota and Weatherill, Stephen eds., The Images of the Consumer in EU Law: Legislation, Free Movement and Competition Law (1st edn, Hart, 2016), 203, p. 206.

[136]Engelbrekt, Antonina Bakardjieva, 'Fair Trading Law in Flux? National Legacies, Institutional Choice and the Process of Europeanisation', (1st edn, Stockholm University, 2003), p. 132.

[137]*Ibid*, p. 533. "Wettbewerbsverbände" refer to organisations prosecuting a wide variety of trade practices considered harmful to its members. For further on these organizations and their legal standing, see Engelbrekt, Antonina Bakardjieva, 'Fair Trading Law in Flux? National Legacies, Institutional Choice and the Process of Europeanisation', (1st edn, Stockholm University, 2003), p. 132-133.

[138]In Italy, the Italian company Scott sold *inter alia*, toilet paper bearing the trademark COTONELLE. An Italian court revoked the trademark since it, according to the court, misled

Mars, the starting point was that "the risk of misleading consumers" could compromise free movement if "that risk is sufficiently serious."[139] The Court of Justice in *Graffione* did not conduct the final balancing of free movement and the Italian rules on unfair competition. It stated though, that the Italian court had to consider "all the relevant factors, including the circumstances in which the products are sold, the information set out on the packaging of the products and the clarity with which it is displayed, the presentation and content of advertising material, and the risk of error in relation to the group of consumers concerned."[140]

8.7 Leaving a Legacy

As is clear from this chapter there has been no consistent development of the average consumer in the cases of the Court of Justice before *Sabel* and there has been no consistent use of the term "average consumer" and the assumed consumer characteristics. Therefore, this chapter provides no clear answer to the introductory question on *why* and *how* the average consumer model has matured, but the decisions leave some significant points relevant for the analysis.

In sketching the history of the average consumer, Fennelly in *Estée Lauder* claimed that "[i]t appears to have been Germany that first laid emphasis on the significance of the inference which 'the average well-informed consumer'" in *Germany v. Commission 1992*.[141] The first reference to this consumer model is not found in this decision though, but in *Van Bennekom* from 1983. That said, there is a clear connection from *Van Bennekom* through *Upjohn* from 1991 to *Germany v. Commission 1992*. The decisions are materially related since they all turn on protecting public health and interpreting the Medical Product Directive 1965. Besides the "birth date" of the average consumer, Fennelly seems to miss an important but subtle difference from the used terms.

---

consumers into assuming that the paper contained cotton. At EU level, the relevant trademark provision was found art. 12(2)(b) of the TM Directive 1989 (art. 20(b) of the TM Directive). Despite similar actions in France and Spain, the mark remained valid in those countries. An Italian wholesaler, Graffione, was due to the Italian decision unable to supply its customers with Cotonelle toilet paper etc. Fransa, that owned a supermarket in Italy, however, could continue the sale of these Cotonelle marked goods since it imported them into Italy from France. In an Italian court, Graffione sought an injunction against Fransa on the ground of Fransa's breach of unfair competition law. Fransa claimed that a prevention of its continuing sale of the Cotonelle goods would compromise free movement of goods.

[139]Graffione, Case C-313/94, [1996] ECR I-6039, para 24.

[140]*Ibid*, para 26.

[141]Estée Lauder, Case C-220/98, [1999] ECR I-117, (opinion of AG Fennelly), para 26, including footnote 37 of the text.

In *Van Bennekom* and *Commission v. Germany 1992*, the term used was the "averag*ely* well-informed consumer."[142] In this phrasing, *average* was used as an adverb to qualify *well-informed* meaning "having or showing much knowledge about a wide range of subjects, or about one particular subject."[143] Besides the mathematical sense of "average," the word may also be taken to mean "ordinary, standard, usual, normal, typical, regular [and] unexceptional."[144] This finding is relevant, since much of the subsequent debate about the average consumer has turn on whether this is a real or fictitious person. When referring to the "ordinary consumer" it has connotations that resemble the "reasonable person" in tort law as addressed earlier, and it seems to be accepted as an objectified test not fully moulded case-by-case.[145] "Average" as understood in math leaves the "average consumer" in the guise of a quantifiable reality.[146]

The English phrasing in *Van Bennekom* resonated well with other official language versions of the decision, such as the German,[147] French[148] and Dutch.[149] The Danish version though deviated from these versions stating that the relevant products had to be perceived through "en *fornuftig* gennemsnitsforbrugers øjne" translated into "the eyes of *a reasonable* average consumer."[150] The English wording in *Commission v. Germany 1992*, "the average well-informed consumer" did not use "average" as an adverb hence apparently did not qualify "well-informed" but "consumer." This was picked up by the Dutch version that referred to a "gemiddelde consument" ("average consumer") whereas the German[151] and French[152] versions kept its wording from *Van Bennekom*. The Danish version was "den almindeligt oplyste forbruger" ("the normally/ordinarily[153] informed consumer"), hence leaving out the reference in the Danish version of *Van Bennekom* to the average consumer as "reasonable." In *Meyhui v. Schott Zwiesel Glaswerke* where reference in the English

---

[142]Van Bennekom, Case 227/82, [1983] ECR 3883 and Commission v. Germany 1992, Case C-290/90, [1992] ECR I-3317 (italics added). See also Upjohn, Case C-112/89, [1991] (the hearing report), ECR I-1703. As mentioned, Fennelly referred to "the *average* well-informed consumer." Italics and emphasis added.

[143]Oxford University Press online English/English dictionary.

[144]*Ibid.*

[145]See Chap. 6, Sect. 6.5.

[146]See also in Chap. 11, Sect. 11.2.2.

[147]In German: "[B]ei einem durchschnittlich informierten Verbraucher."

[148]In French: "[A]ux yeux d'un consommateur moyennement avisé."

[149]In Dutch: "Gemiddeld onderscheidingsvermogen begiftigde consument."

[150]Italics added.

[151]In German: "[D]er durchschnittlich unterrichtete Verbraucher."

[152]In French: "[L]e consommateur normalement avisé."

[153]In Gyldendals Danish/English dictionary available online, "almindeligt" is translated into "commonly, generally, normally, ordinarily, averagely." In the general dictionary from Gyldendal, "averagely" is left out. Italics in the quote are added.

version was made to the "average consumer" as such, there was consistency in the different language versions.[154]

As depicted, there was an inconsistency in the different language versions of the Court of Justice case law setting out the early version of the average consumer. Besides a narrow linguistic interest, the differences depict that it was far from clear how to describe this new consumer image. Also, since the Court of Justice is the ultimate interpreter of EU law, that phrasing may have affected its substantial framing as either mainly a fiction or a real life consumer. Mellor *et al* have recently picked up on this line of linguistic analysis of the English, French and German versions of the *Gut Springenheide*, and found a similar inconsistency.[155]

Besides the wording "average consumer," Lenz used the term "average user" as mentioned in *Upjohn*. This phrasing has never solidified in Court of Justice case law. In trademark law related to likelihood of confusion, it has only been used scarcely.[156] Looking ahead, the term is interesting since "user" is neutral compared to "consumer" that has a more confined meaning and is thus more "mouldable" and open to include different kinds of consumers such as children or non-consumers as suggested by Lenz.[157]

As for consumer characteristics, some important points were raised by Mancini in *Drei Glocken* and Gulmann in *Clinique* namely that EU consumers are rooted in different countries. Differences may therefore emerge in terms of linguistic, cultural and social backgrounds. These differences have proven to be important to the subsequent development of the average consumer, and not least a significant obstacle. Hence, Wilhelmsson asked in his seminal article on the "Average *European* Consumer" that focused on the UCPD, "to what extent full harmonization can work well in the light of possible differences between national consumer cultures."[158]

When assessing the consistency of the case law set out in this chapter, it is necessary to step carefully. One consistent aspect in the decisions of the Court of Justice is the test of the national measures introduced to allegedly protect consumers, be it more broadly, their health or the protection against unfair commercial practices. Another consistent aspect is the reluctance of the Court of Justice to accept the national legislative measures, be they introduced purely as national law or national

---

[154]In German: "den durchschnittlichen Verbraucher," in French: "le consommateur moyen," in Dutch: "gemiddelde consument" and in Danish: "gennemsnitlige forbruger."

[155]Mellor, James, David Llewelyn, Moody-Stuart, Thomas, *et al*, 'Kerly's Law of Trade Marks and Trade Names', (16th edn, Sweet & Maxwell, 2018), p. 59-61.

[156]Hence, in the internet decisions, the Court of Justice has used the term "average internet user", see Chap. 11, Sect. 11.5. Recently, the General Court in *Pensa Pharma v. EUIPO* has also referred to the "average user" of soaps, pharmaceuticals etc. Pensa Pharma v. EUIPO, Joined cases T-544/12 and T-546/12, [2015], (judgment), para 117.

[157]See above in Sect. 8.5 on Upjohn, Case C-112/89, [1991] ECR I-1703, (opinion of AG Lenz).

[158]Wilhelmsson, Thomas, 'The Average European Consumer: A Legal Fiction?', in Wilhelmsson, Thomas, Paunio, Elina and Pohjolainen, Annika eds., Private Law and the Many Cultures of Europe (1st edn, Kluwer Law International, 2007), 243, p. 246 (italics added). For a further addressing of this query in the realm of the UCPD, see Chap. 7, Sect. 7.4.

law implementing EU directives.[159] In the development of the average consumer as such though, the consistency is much less prominent. All decisions refer to consumers as not only the beneficiaries of protection but also to their assumed abilities to process information. Based on the decisions in this chapter, it is possible to draw out some legal principles of these assumed abilities. It should be borne in mind though, that the fragmentation of the case law in this chapter inevitably influences the validity and reliability of these principles.

According to the Court of Justice, information available to consumers has to be "suitable information,"[160] and consumers' perception of the information may vary geographically across the EU member states and temporarily over time.[161] There are limits to what information consumers can be assumed to process since they may not see through "definite" information provided by "implication."[162] "Normally aware consumer[s]" are not easily confused by information, e.g. in leaflets on what goes on in the marketplace and should not be refused "certain information" by law but only be ensured the "accuracy of information provided."[163] The "reasonably circumspect consumers" can see through "publicity markings" in the marketing of products.[164] As for the price of the product, there is a positive correlation between price and the level of consumer attention. In essence, the Court of Justice has assumed that a higher price means a higher level of consumer attention.[165] Likewise, the Court has assumed that there is a positive correlation between the frequency by which a product is purchased and the information needed for the consumer not to be confused.[166]

There seems to be no doubt that the Court of Justice and its Advocates General have been an important motor in the early development of the average consumer, not least as part of negative harmonisation as addressed in this chapter.[167] Besides the importance of these institutions, it is also possible to point out certain persons as particularly important to the development.

---

[159]One exception mentioned in this chapter is Buet v. Ministère public, Case 382/87, [1989] ECR 1235.

[160]*Cassis de Dijon*, Case 120/78, [1979] ECR 649, see above Sect. 8.3.

[161]*Beer Purity*, Case 178/84, [1987] ECR 1227, see above Sect. 8.4.

[162]Van Bennekom, Case 227/82, [1983] ECR 3883, see above Sect. 8.4.

[163]GB-INNO, Case C-362/88, [1990] ECR I-667, see above Sect. 8.6.

[164]Verein gegen Unwesen in Handel und Gewerbe v. Mars, Case C-470/93, [1995] ECR I-1923, see above Sect. 8.6.

[165]X (Nissan), Case C-373/90, [1992], ECR I-131, see above Sect. 8.6. *Vice versa*, as addressed in Chap. 11, the General Court has repeatedly assumed that the level of attention of the average consumer is low when purchasing cheap "everyday consumer goods". See Chap. 11, Sect. 11.4.1.1.

[166]Meyhui v. Schott Zwiesel Glaswerke, Case C-51/93, [1994] ECR I-3879, see above Sect. 8.6. *Vice versa*, the General Court has made an assumption on consumer habits, when purchasing "everyday consumer goods." The assumption is that consumers need less information purchasing these products compared to other products. See Chap. 11, Sect. 11.4.1.1.

[167]See also generally on the role of the Court of Justice as a motor for harmonisation, Chap. 4, Sect. 4.3.

As part of the confirmation hearing of Judge Roberts in 2005 to become chief justice of the US Supreme Court, he famously said, "I will remember that it's my job to call balls and strikes, and not to pitch or bat."[168] Richard Posner, a judge himself, has seen this as a legalistic view "in the extreme sense."[169] In a European context, Jacob has referred to Roberts' phrasing as a description of a binary model for law making where "[t]he actors are typecast: state parties and legislators create law, adjudicators do not."[170] Bengoetxea, previously clerking for the Court of Justice, has held that "[i]n clear cases one can say that judges apply such rules [legal rules] almost unreflectively whereas in *hard cases* there is a need for reflection and some scope for discretion, and this makes judicial discretion more significant."[171] As rightfully pointed out by Jacob, "whether or not adjudicators actually 'make law' remains a topic for the ages."[172] Although this topic as such is beyond this book, it is worth mentioning some individuals that may have affected the formation of the average consumer.[173]

The operation of singling out individuals is naturally complicated by the less clear *ratio decidendi* and the lacking dissents of the Court of Justice.[174] The Advocate General opinions though are not anonymous. In this context, it is worth noting the pivotal opinion given by Mancini in *Drei Glocken* and Gulmann's opinion in *Clinique*[175] in their own right and since they both became judges of the Court of Justice. Thus, Mancini sat as judge as part of the Grand Chamber in *Commission v. Germany 1992*[176] and Gulmann sat as judge in *Mars*.[177] Later, Mancini and Gulmann sat as judges in *Sabel* and *Lloyd*, and Gulmann in *Gut Springenheide* that timewise fell between *Sabel* and *Lloyd*. These three decisions are an important

---

[168] Confirmation Hearing on the Nomination of John G. Roberts, Jr. to be Chief Justice of the United States. Committee on the Judiciary United States Senate, 109th Congress 1st session September 12-15, 2005, Serial No. J–109–37, p. 56.

[169] Posner, Richard A., 'How Judges Think', (1st edn, Harvard University Press, 2008), p. 78.

[170] Jacob, Marc A., 'Precedents and Case-Based Reasoning in the European Court of Justice: Unfinished Business', (1st edn, Cambridge University Press, 2014), p. 21. Jacob refers to Robert on p. 31.

[171] Bengoetxea, Joxerramon, 'The Legal Reasoning of the European Court of Justice: Towards a European Jurisprudence', (1st edn, Clarendon Press, 1993), p. 87 (italics added).

[172] Jacob, Marc A., 'Precedents and Case-Based Reasoning in the European Court of Justice: Unfinished Business', (1st edn, Cambridge University Press, 2014), p. 21.

[173] See Segal, Jeffrey A., 'Judicial Behaviour', in Goodin, Robert E. eds., The Oxford Handbook of Political Science (1st, Oxford University Press, 2011), 275, chapter 14.

[174] Ross has pointed out that "[t]he constructive part played by the judge" "to correct the directive of the statute is only rarely manifest." Ross, Alf, 'On Law and Justice', (1st edn, University of California Press, 1959), p. 151-152. Although this finding was made in a pre-EU setting, it is even more so relevant to the CJEU. See also in general the reasons in Chap. 2, Sect. 2.2.1.

[175] Gulmann also gave the opinion in Meyhui v. Schott Zwiesel Glaswerke, Case C-51/93, [1994] ECR I-3879, (opinion of AG Gulmann).

[176] Mancini was Advocate General from 1982 to 1988 and judge from 1988 to 1999.

[177] Gulmann was Advocate General from 1991 to 1994 and judge from 1994 to 2006.

basis for developing the average consumer in European trademark law.[178] Burrows and Greaves have stressed the significance of Gulmann, in his capacity as judge of the Court of Justice, to developing European intellectual property law, including trademark law.[179] Based on their opinions as Advocates General and subsequent roles as judges of the Court of Justice, it may be tentatively concluded that Mancini and Gulmann have affected the early formation of the average consumer.[180]

The remainder of this book will where relevant draw on the findings of this chapter that has depicted an early incremental development of the average consumer over almost two decades starting with *Cassis de Dijon* in 1979 and culminating in European trademark law with *Sabel* in 1997, *Gut Springenheide* in 1998 and *Lloyd* in 1999.[181]

---

[178]Chapter 10, in particular Sect. 10.2.

[179]The authors have also stressed that Advocate General Jacobs was important to developing European intellectual property law, including trademark law.

Burrows, Noreen, and Greaves, Rosa, 'The Advocate General and EC Law', (1st edn, Oxford University Press, 2007), p. 128. In fact, Burrows and Greaves refer anecdotally to the farewell reception in honour of Jacobs and Gulmann held in January 2006 where "the President of the European Court of Justice specifically praised their contribution to the development of the Community's trade mark case law." *Ibid*, footnote 16 of the text.

[180]This finding applies with the significant caveats set out in this section.

[181]Respectively, Sabel v. Puma, Case C-251/95, [1997] ECR I-6191, Gut Springenheide and Tusky, Case C-210/96, [1998] ECR I-4657 and Lloyd Schuhfabrik Meyer v. Klijsen Handel BV, Case C-342/97, [1999] ECR I-3819.

Chapter 9
Likelihood of Confusion: Legislative Harmonisation?

9.1 Introduction

It is necessary to analyse the legislative requirements of the likelihood of confusion standard before analysing the average consumer and its characteristics as it is applied in practice.[1] The legislative frame involves an analysis of how the average consumer as "part of the public" is anchored to the confusion standard and the aim is to get an understanding of what is the valid legal starting point (*de lege lata*).[2] As dictated by Critical Legal Positivism, the analysis of the standard will not only be based on the sources as strictly applied by the judiciaries, but will also involve looking into other sources such as preambles and preparatory works.

The focus of this analysis as stipulated in Chaps. 2 and 3 is EU trademark legislation, including how comparable standards of the Paris Convention and the TRIPS Agreement feed into the EU standard and downstream, how the EU standard via the TM Directive is implemented in national law. This latter aspect is paramount since the aspects of the applied functional comparative methods operate under a presumption of similarity between the national jurisdictions.[3] It is necessary to pressure test the validity of this presumption, initially through a legislative analysis. The analysis allows for a closer delimitation of what gap is left for the judiciaries to fill, i.e. a definition of the "floor and ceiling" of maximum harmonisation.[4] In the subsequent judicial analysis, the legislative standard will be a benchmark to see if it has changed its status from a "standard" into a "rule."[5] Reference in this chapter is

---

[1]This analysis is conducted applying the legal dogmatic method as it was set out in Chap. 2. See Chap. 2, Sect. 2.2.

[2]The understanding of *de lege lata* and what is understood as "valid law" is discussed in Chap. 2, Sects. 2.1 and 2.2.1.

[3]See Chap. 2, Sect. 2.3.

[4]On the understanding of "floor and ceiling," see Chap. 4, Sect. 4.2.1.

[5]On the distinction between "rule" and "standard," see Chap. 5, Sect. 5.2.

© Springer Nature Switzerland AG 2020

R. D. Laustsen, *The Average Consumer in Confusion-based Disputes in European Trademark Law and Similar Fictions*, https://doi.org/10.1007/978-3-030-26350-8_9

also made to the UCPD since the unfair competition law confusion standard of the Paris Convention is relevant to the UCPD and to European trademark law.[6]

9.2   The Likelihood of Confusion: An International Standard?

The Paris Convention and the TRIPS Agreement set out some minimum standards relevant to the analysis of the likelihood of confusion standard under EU trademark law. In contrast with the Paris Convention, the TRIPS Agreement entered into force 1 January 1995 after the finalisation of the TM Directive 1989 and the TM Regulation 1994.[7] Thus, the TRIPS Agreement as such did not affect early EU trademark legislation. Nowadays, it is directly stated in the preamble to the TM Directive that member states are bound by those treaties and that "[i]t is necessary that this Directive be entirely consistent with that [the Paris] Convention and that [the TRIPS] Agreement. The obligations of the Member States resulting from that Convention and that Agreement should not be affected by this Directive."[8] The recent revision of the EU trademark legislation included the reference to the TRIPS Agreement in this recital of the TM Directive.[9] The legal frame created in these treaties is even vaguer than the harmonisation initiatives of European trademark law. It is still relevant (and necessary) though to address the treaties since EU trademark legislation has to be interpreted consistently with them.[10]

The Paris Convention and the TRIPS Agreement have contributed to interpreting the likelihood of confusion standard. Most notably, Advocate General Jacobs in *Sabel*[11] used these international treaties in interpreting "association" in contrast with "confusion" as part of the likelihood of confusion standard. Jacobs built on this in his opinion in *Marca Mode v. Adidas.*[12] As it may be recalled, Jacobs has been considered important to the early development of European trademark law, including the average consumer.[13] Although the Court of Justice in their decisions did not

---

[6]I.e., art. 10bis(3)(1) of the Paris Convention.

[7]It should be mentioned though that the likelihood of confusion standard in art. 16(1) of the TRIPS Agreement was included in the draft agreement of July 23 1990. See Gervais, Daniel, 'The TRIPS Agreement: Drafting History and Analysis', (4th edn, Sweet & Maxwell, 2012), p. 326 setting out this draft of the provision in its entirety.

[8]Recital 41 of the TM Directive.

[9]The similar recital 13 of the TM Directive 2008.

[10]Recital 43 of the TM Directive. See also on this Chap. 3, Sect. 3.2.

[11]Sabel v. Puma, Case C-251/95, [1997] ECR I-6191, (opinion of AG Jacobs), paras 53-54.

[12]Marca Mode v. Adidas, Case C-425/98, [2000] ECR I-4861, (opinion of AG Jacobs), para 36, including footnotes 26 and 28 of the opinion where Jacobs referred to paras 53-54 respectively of his opinion in Sabel v. Puma, Case C-251/95, [1997] ECR I-6191, (opinion of AG Jacobs).

[13]See Chap. 4, Sect. 4.3.5.

refer explicitly to the Paris Convention and the TRIPS Agreement, they followed Jacobs' interpretation.

9.2.1 The Paris Convention

The likelihood of confusion standard relevant to this book does not as such appear in the Paris Convention. However, protecting well-known marks is rooted in art. $6^{bis}(1)$ of the Paris Convention *inter alia*, allowing a senior trademark owner "to prohibit the use, of a trademark which constitutes a reproduction, an imitation, or a translation, *liable to create confusion*, of a mark considered by the competent authority of the country of registration or use to be well known."[14] Although well-known trademarks are outside the scope of this book, this provision creates a relevant backcloth to the overall understanding of the European trademark law likelihood of confusion standard.[15] It has been pointed out by Ricketson that ""reproduction" or "imitation" point simply to the need for the trade mark to be the same or substantially the same" and that "adaptation" allows for protection of certain word marks linguistically looking dissimilar but in terms of meaning being precisely the same.[16] Finding no further aid of interpretation in the convention or the conference records, Ricketson has concluded that "liable to create" and "confusion" "suggest at least the likelihood or probability of confusion." Furthermore, that this goes "beyond the situation where a person (a consumer) *is actively mislead* into believing incorrectly that X is Y as distinct from the situation where he or she is left uncertain as to whether X is Y and vice versa."[17]

Despite the overlap between the meaning of "likelihood of confusion" in EU trademark legislation and "liable to create confusion" in art. 6bis of the Paris Convention, it must be noted the Court of Justice has not used the provision and the interpretation hereof in its interpretation of the EU standard.[18] Besides adding to

---

[14]Italics added. Art. 6bis of the Paris Convention, as per the wording of art. $6^{bis}(2)$, only applied to goods. However, art. 16(2) of the TRIPS Agreement has extended art. 6bis of the Paris Convention to services.

[15]See overall Ricketson discussing the meaning of "liable to create confusion" in connection with the "likelihood of confusion." Ricketson, Sam, 'The Paris Convention for the Protection of Industrial Property: A Commentary', (1st edn, Oxford University Press, 2015), p. 553-558. Art. 16(1) of the TRIPS Agreement extended the protection under art. 6bis of the Paris Convention to service marks.

[16]Ricketson, Sam, 'The Paris Convention for the Protection of Industrial Property: A Commentary', (1st edn, Oxford University Press, 2015), p. 554.

[17]*Ibid*, p. 555 (italics added).

[18]The Court of Justice though has applied the provision to determine what is understood by "well known" mark under art. 8(2)(c) of the TM Regulation and art. 5(2)(d) of the TM Directive and how "well known" is understood vis-à-vis marks with a reputation. For instance, in *General Motors v. Yplon* the Court of Justice preliminarily ruled on the meaning of "has a reputation" vis-à-vis the understanding of "well known" under art. 6bis of the Paris Convention. General Motors v. Yplon,

the understanding of the EU standard, the reference to the Paris Convention also highlights that understanding the "likelihood of confusion" (or similarly phrased terms) has been around long before the EU standard—with art. 6bis of the Paris Convention since 1925 where the provision was inserted by the Revision Conference of The Hague.[19] As addressed below, this is also the case for national confusion standards developed over long time before EU trademark legislation.

In 1999, the Assembly of the Paris Union for the Protection of Industrial Property and the General Assembly of WIPO issued joint recommendations on the protection of well-known marks as stipulated in art. 6bis of the Paris Convention (the "WIPO Recommendations").[20] The recommendations on deciding if a mark is well-known contain different factors to be included in this evaluation, including "the degree of knowledge or recognition of the mark in the relevant sector of the public."[21] The recommendations state that "(. . .) [r]elevant sectors of the public shall include, but shall not necessarily be limited to: (i) actual and/or potential consumers of the type of goods and/or services to which the mark applies; (ii) persons involved in channels of distribution of the type of goods and/or services to which the mark applies; (iii) business circles dealing with the type of goods and/or services to which the mark

---

Case C-375/97, [1999] ECR I-5421, paras 19-28See also more explicitly Advocate General Jacobs' preceding opinion, General Motors v. Yplon, Case C-375/97, [1999] ECR I-5421, (opinion of AG Jacobs), paras 30-44. After analysing the relevant provision of the Paris Convention and the TRIPs Agreement, Jacobs concluded that "the protection of well-known marks under the Paris Convention and TRIPs is accordingly an exceptional type of protection afforded even to unregistered marks. It would not be surprising therefore, if the requirement of being well-known imposed a relatively high standard for a mark to benefit from such exceptional protection. There is no such consideration in the case of marks with a reputation. Indeed, as I shall suggest later, there is no need to impose such a high standard to satisfy the requirement of marks with a reputation in Article 5(2) of the Directive." *Ibid*, para 33. Jacobs reiterated this point in his opinion in *Davidoff v. Gofkid*. See Davidoff v. Gofkid, Case C-292/00, [2003] ECR I-00389, (opinion of AG Jacobs), para 4, including footnote 4 of the opinion. See further on the well-known trademarks, Mellor, James, David Llewelyn, Moody-Stuart, Thomas, *et al*, 'Kerly's Law of Trade Marks and Trade Names', (16th edn, Sweet & Maxwell, 2018), p. 619-622 and Mühlendahl, Alexander von, Dimitris Botis, Spyros M. Maniatis, *et al*, 'Trade Mark Law in Europe: A Practical Jurisprudence', (3rd edn, Oxford University Press, 2016), p. 550-560. For a pre *Sabel* aspect, see Kur, Annette, 'Well-Known Marks, Highly Renowned Marks and Marks Having a (High) Reputation – What's It All About', IIC, vol. 23/no. 2, (1992), pp. 28.

[19]See Bodenhausen, Georg, 'Guide to the Application of the Paris Convention for the Protection of Industrial Property as Revised at Stockholm in 1967', (1st edn, World Intellectual Property Organization, 1968), p. 89.

[20]WIPO Joint Recommendation Concerning Provisions on the Protection of Well-Known Marks adopted by the Assembly of the Paris Union for the Protection of Industrial Property and the General Assembly of WIPO at the Thirty-Fourth Series of Meetings of the Assemblies of the Member States of WIPO September 20 to 29 1999. All countries relevant to this book were represented as parties to the process of making the recommendations, cf. annex II of the 1999 WIPO Joint Recommendations.

[21]Cf. art. 2(1)(b)(1) of the 1999 WIPO Joint Recommendations.

applies."[22] The recommendations express central elements akin to how the relevant public under European trademark law is to be framed ranging from consumers to parts of a "public" found in the supply chain of the relevant products. Although the recommendations are non-legally binding guidelines, they indicate that the mentioned elements are not only common to European trademark law but also elsewhere. The recommendations on the relevant public have been used as aids to interpretation of European trademark legislation by Advocate General Mengozzi in *Nieto Nuño v. Monlleó Franquet.*[23]

One aim of the Paris Convention, besides protecting trademarks, is "the repression of unfair competition."[24] The overall definition of "unfair competition" is found in art. $10^{bis}(2)$ of the Paris Convention stipulating that "unfair competition" is constituted by "[a]ny act of competition contrary to honest practices in industrial or commercial matters."[25] Examples of acts constituting unfair competition are "*all acts of such a nature as to create confusion* by any means whatever with the establishment, the goods, or the industrial or commercial activities, of a competitor," cf. art. $10^{bis}(3)(1)$ of the Paris Convention.[26] This provision is also addressed in relation to the UCPD analysis.[27] Referring to a an Italian decision from Corte di Cassazione, Bodenhausen in 1967 held that "[a]ny act of competition will have to be

---

[22]Cf. art. 2(2)(a)(i)-(iii) of the 1999 WIPO Joint Recommendations. The provision continues: "(b) Where a mark is determined to be well known in at least one relevant sector of the public in a Member State, the mark shall be considered by the Member State to be a well-known mark. (c) Where a mark is determined to be known in at least one relevant sector of the public in a Member State, the mark may be considered by the Member State to be a well-known mark. (d) A Member State may determine that a mark is a well-known mark, even if the mark is not well known or, if the Member States applies subparagraph (c), known, in any relevant sector of the public of the Member State."

[23]Nieto Nuño v. Monlleó Franquet, Case C-328/06, [2007] ECR I-10093, (opinion of AG Mengozzi), paras 6-7. After in those paragraphs setting out the recommendations on *inter alia* the "relevant sector of the public," Mengozzi seemed subsequently to use the recommendations implicitly in the understanding of "part of the public." *Ibid*, para 46. The recommendations have also been referred to by Advocate General Jacobs in Adidas-Salomon and Adidas Benelux v. Fitnessworld, Case C-408/01, [2003] ECR I-12537, (opinion of AG Jacobs), para 39, including footnote 18 of the opinion and by Advocate General Jääskinen in Interflora v. Marks & Spencer, Case C-323/09, [2011] ECR I-8625 (opinion of AG Jääskinen), para 129. See also the use of the recommendations by the General Court in J-M.-E.V. e hijos v. EUIPO, Case T-2/17, [2018], paras 65-71.

[24]Cf. art. 1(2) of the Paris Convention. The provision has rather broadly defined "[t]he protection of industrial property" as encompassing "the repression of unfair competition." On the background of the provision, see Correa, Carlos M., 'Trade Related Aspects of Intellectual Property Rights: A Commentary on the TRIPS Agreement', (1st edn, Oxford University Press, 2007), p. 38-39. The protection against unfair competition was extended with art. 39 of the TRIPS Agreement, *inter alia* offering protection of undisclosed information.

[25]For a discussion on the definition of unfair competition under the Paris Convention, see Ricketson, Sam, 'The Paris Convention for the Protection of Industrial Property: A Commentary', (1st edn, Oxford University Press, 2015), p. 694-696.

[26]Italics added.

[27]See Chap. 7, Sect. 7.3.

considered unfair if it is contrary to honest practices in industrial or commercial matters" and that "[t]his criterion is not limited to honest practices existing in the country where protection against unfair competition is sought."[28] Defining "principle of fairness in competition" under EU law, Micklitz has referred to the principle of unfair competition law in the Paris Convention. Micklitz has seen this principle cascading initially into Directive (ECC) No. 84/450 of 10 September 1984 relating to the approximation of the laws, regulations and administrative provisions of the Member States on misleading advertising[29] and, approximately 20 years later in 2005, into the UCPD.[30]

9.2.2   The TRIPS Agreement

The TRIPS Agreement harmonised substantive areas of trademark law.[31] The Court of Justice (Grand Chamber) stated in *Anheuser-Busch v. Budvar* that it is clear from art. 65(1) of the TRIPS Agreement that "the members were not obliged to apply the provisions of that agreement before the expiry of a general period of one year, that is to say, before 1 January 1996."[32] In the decision, the court clearly confirmed the duty to interpret EU law consistently with the TRIPS Agreement[33] parallel to the duty of

---

[28]Bodenhausen, Georg, 'Guide to the Application of the Paris Convention for the Protection of Industrial Property as Revised at Stockholm in 1967', (1st edn, World Intellectual Property Organization, 1968), p. 144.

[29]The full reference is Council Directive of 10 September 1984 relating to the approximation of the laws, regulations and administrative provisions of the Member States concerning misleading advertising, [1984] OJ L250/17. The directive was later amended by the UCPD. See Reich, Norbert, Micklitz, Hans-W., and Rott, Peter, 'European Consumer Law', (2nd edn, Intersentia, 2014), p. 72 and similarly Micklitz, Hans-W., 'Unfair Commercial Practices and Misleading Advertising', in Micklitz, Hans-W, Reich, Norbert and Rott, Peter eds., Understanding EU Consumer Law (1st edn, Intersentia, 2009), 61, p. 64.

[30]Reich, Norbert, Micklitz, Hans-W., and Rott, Peter, 'European Consumer Law', (2nd edn, Intersentia, 2014), p. 75 and Micklitz, Hans-W., 'Unfair Commercial Practices and Misleading Advertising', in Micklitz, Hans-W, Reich, Norbert and Rott, Peter eds., Understanding EU Consumer Law (1st edn, Intersentia, 2009), 61, p. 69. See also Djurovic, European Law on Unfair Commercial Practices and Contract Law, 2016, p. 74.

[31]Seville, Catherine, 'EU Intellectual Property Law and Policy', (2nd edn, Edward Elgar, 2016), p. 267.

[32]Anheuser-Busch v. Budvar, (Grand Chamber) Case C-245/02, [2004] ECR I-10989, para 4.

[33]Hence, the Court of Justice stated that "it follows from the Court's case-law that, when called upon to apply national rules with a view to ordering measures for the protection of rights in a field to which the TRIPs Agreement applies and in which the Community has already legislated, as is the case with the field of trade marks, the national courts are required under Community law to do so, as far as possible, in the light of the wording and purpose of the relevant provisions of the TRIPs Agreement." *Ibid*, paras 55 and 57, including the case law referred to here.

national courts to interpret the purpose of national trademark law, given the purpose of the directive as such.[34]

Whereas the Paris Convention was silent on rights conferred on trademark owners, the TRIPS Agreement was not. Thus art. 16(1) of the agreement states that "[t]he owner of a registered trademark shall have the exclusive right to prevent all third parties not having the owner's consent from using in the course of trade identical or similar signs for goods or services which are identical or similar to those in respect of which the trademark is registered where such use would result *in a likelihood of confusion*."[35] As Skrzydło-Tefelska and Żuk have pointed out, "protection against likelihood of confusion" is recognised by most trademark systems, including the TRIPS Agreement.[36] Without further ado, Tritton *et al* have claimed that art. 16(1) of the TRIPS Agreement is "self-explanatory."[37] The reason for this may be that the wording of the provision nowadays is familiar to the legislative wording of EU trademark legislation. Based on arts. 6bis and art. 10bis 3(1) of the Paris Convention[38] and art. 16(1) of the TRIPS Agreement, Jacobs concluded on the meaning of "association" as part of the EU likelihood of confusion standard that there is "no inconsistency between the [TM] Directive on the view I take and those international instruments."[39]

Above it was concluded that "liable to create confusion" under art. $6^{bis}(1)$ of the Paris Convention does not require proof of actual confusion. This was clarified even further under art. 16(1) of the TRIPS Agreement referring to "*likelihood* of confusion."[40] Although known to EU trademark legislation, according to Dratler, the TRIPS Agreement in certain areas broke "new ground," one of which was the introduction of "likelihood of confusion as a mandatory standard for infringement in international trademark law."[41] Malbon *et al* have also mentioned that since the

---

[34]*Ibid*, paras 56-57, including the case law referred to here.

[35]Italics added. The TM Directive refers directly to the conformity with art. 16(1) of the TRIPS Agreement, but not to the part of the provision on likelihood of confusion, but on priority. See recital 17 of the TM Directive.

[36]Skrzydło-Tefelska, Ewa, and Żuk, Mateusz, 'Article 9: Rights Conferred by a Community Trade Mark', in Hasselblatt, Gordian N. ed., Community Trade Mark Regulation (EC) no 207/2009: A Commentary (1st edn, Beck/Hart, 2015), 295, p. 298.

[37]Davis, Richard, St Quintin, Thomas and Tritton, Guy, 'Tritton on Intellectual Property in Europe', (5th edn, Sweet & Maxwell, 2018), p. 268.

[38]Ricketson has referred to art. 10bis of the convention as an aid for interpreting the term "confusion" in art. 16(1) of the TRIPS Agreement. Ricketson, Sam, 'The Paris Convention for the Protection of Industrial Property: A Commentary', (1st edn, Oxford University Press, 2015), p. 651. See also Correa, Carlos M., 'Trade Related Aspects of Intellectual Property Rights: A Commentary on the TRIPS Agreement', (1st edn, Oxford University Press, 2007), p. 186-187.

[39]Sabel v. Puma, Case C-251/95, [1997] ECR I-6191, (opinion of AG Jacobs), para 54.

[40]Italics added.

[41]Dratler, Jay, and McJohn, Stephen M., 'Intellectual Property Law: Commercial, Creative and Industrial Property: Volume One', (, Law Journal Press, 2016), p. 1A-75. See also Correa, Carlos M., 'Trade Related Aspects of Intellectual Property Rights: A Commentary on the TRIPS Agreement', (1st edn, Oxford University Press, 2007), p. 186, footnote 56 with a reference to Dratler.

provision stipulates "would result" and not "has resulted" indicates that there is no requirement of finding actual confusion.[42] They continue holding that "confusion" differs from "deception" occurring "when consumers are caused to believe a particular state of affairs to be the true state of affairs when it is not."[43] According to Correa, this rules out the senior trademark owner having to prove actual injury caused by the use of the junior mark.[44] As for the lower end of what the minimum requirement for confusion is, Correa has pointed out that "likelihood of confusion" "implies that a mere possibility of confusion is not sufficient for legitimizing the exercise of the exclusive rights."[45] Not having to prove actual confusion opens up for a broader view on what judicially constitutes confusion. This is essentially, what allows the use of an average consumer imbued with normative factors.

Although the Paris Convention and the TRIPS Agreement as such sketch the contours of the likelihood of confusion standard, they leave the difficult question open; how then is this standard to manifest itself in litigation? The WIPO Recommendations provide some guidance. There is no guidance on any potential differences in the understanding of the likelihood of confusion standard in registration and infringement. Bearing those differences in mind, the EU standard obviously emerges in registration and infringement, but more important, that EU trademark legislation has stipulated that the test is to be conducted referring to "part of the public."[46] Although matters of fleshing out a test for the average consumer has been left to the signatories to the Paris Convention and the TRIPS Agreement, Gervais has mentioned in his commentary on the TRIPS Agreement that the question is if "the average relevant consumer or buyer of the good or service in question may well be misled."[47] Gervais seems to indicate that "buyer" differs from "consumer" which is not always the case.

9.3   The European Likelihood of Confusion Standard

From a scrutiny of the likelihood of confusion standard as it has appeared at the international level, it clearly emerges that the standard develops in practice. Although the EU trademark legislation compared to the Paris Convention and the TRIPS Agreement provides more guidance on the application of the EU version of

---

[42]Malbon, Justin, Lawson, Charles and Davison, Mark, 'The WTO Agreement on Trade-Related Aspects of Intellectual Property Rights: A Commentary', (1st edn, Edward Elgar, 2014), p. 298.

[43]*Ibid*, p. 299. See also Correa, Carlos M., 'Trade Related Aspects of Intellectual Property Rights: A Commentary on the TRIPS Agreement', (1st edn, Oxford University Press, 2007), p. 187.

[44]Correa, Carlos M., 'Trade Related Aspects of Intellectual Property Rights: A Commentary on the TRIPS Agreement', (1st edn, Oxford University Press, 2007), p. 187.

[45]*Ibid*, p. 186.

[46]See right below Sect. 9.3.1 dealing with the EU standard.

[47]Gervais, Daniel, 'The TRIPS Agreement: Drafting History and Analysis', (4th edn, Sweet & Maxwell, 2012), p. 330.

the likelihood of confusion standard, it does not change this picture. It is necessary to analyse the EU trademark legislation to get a picture of the legislative requirements for testing the standard. In terms of the TM Directive, it is necessary to detect any variations in the implementation into national law. Despite the relevant provisions being maximally harmonised, there is still room for linguistic deviations.[48] That said, the interpretation of the legislative standard by the Court of Justice since the introduction of the TM Directive 1989 has reached a level of maturity that presumptively rules out significant deviations among the national trademark acts. Supporting this presumption is the prominence of the likelihood of confusion standard in the European trademark infrastructure.

9.3.1 The EU Standard

9.3.1.1 Introducing the Legislative Requirements

The origin function of trademarks allows consumers to navigate between products using trademarks as product identifiers.[49] The likelihood of confusion standard connects to this essential function of trademarks that allows trademarks to serve other broader purposes of the trademark system in the EU, such as enhancing competition. The focus of this analysis is the legislative requirements of the standard. This means how the standard plays out as part of the "relative grounds for refusal or invalidity" in art. 8(1)(b) of the TM Regulation[50] and art. 5(1)(b) of the TM Directive[51] and in infringement as part of the "rights conferred by a trade mark" in arts. 9(1) and (2)(b) of the TM Regulation[52] and arts. 10(1) and (2)(b) of the TM Directive.[53] The 2015 trademark reform left the provisions on registration as they were but introduced some changes of the infringement provisions that do not affect the substance of the likelihood of confusion though.[54] The specific uses prevented by

---

[48]For the earlier mentioning of these potential linguistic differences as part of implementing EU directives, see Chap. 2, Sect. 2.3.1 and on harmonisation Chap. 4, Sect. 4.2.1.

[49]See Chap. 1, Sect. 1.3.1.

[50]Ditto in the TM Regulation 2009 and TM Regulation 1994.

[51]Cf. art. 4(1)(b) of the TM Directive 2008 and TM Directive 1989.

[52]Cf. art. 9(1)(b) of the TM Regulation 2009 and TM Regulation TM Regulation 1994.

[53]Cf. art. 5(1)(b) of the TM Directive 2008 and TM Directive 1989.

[54]Accounting for the fact that the TM Regulation relates to protecting "EU trademarks," the changes of both the TM Regulation and TM Directive are the same. The changes are stipulated in the proposal for a new trademark directive with → and ← indicating the new insertions: "Article 510 Rights conferred by a trade mark 1. The ~~registered~~ → registration of a ← trade mark shall confer on the proprietor exclusive rights ~~therein~~.

→ 2. Without prejudice to the rights of proprietors acquired before the filing date or the priority date of the registered trade mark, ← ~~The~~the proprietor → of a registered trade mark ← shall be entitled

the infringement provisions emerge from art. 9(3)(a)-(f) of the TM Regulation and the identical art. 10(3)(a)-(f) of the TM Directive.[55]

In matters of infringement, it emerges from the TM Directive art. 9 that "[t]he registration of a trade mark shall confer on the proprietor exclusive rights therein.[56] (...) [T]he proprietor of that registered trade mark shall be entitled to prevent all third parties not having his consent from using in the course of trade, in relation to goods or services, any sign where[57] (...) the sign is identical with, or similar to, the trade mark and is used in relation to goods or services which are identical with, or similar to, the goods or services for which the trade mark is registered, if there exists a likelihood of confusion on the part of the public; the likelihood of confusion includes the likelihood of association between the sign and the trade mark."[58] Accounting for the fact that the TM Regulation relates to protecting "EU trade-marks," this provision of the TM Directive is identical with art. 9(1) and (2)(b) of the TM Regulation. It appears from the wording of the provision that it involves the following uses by "third parties" not having a consent from the "proprietor" of the senior mark: *(i)* "any sign" *(ii)* "in the course of trade," *(iii)* "in relation to goods or services" *(iv)* a minimum requirement of "similarity" between the senior trademark owner's trademark and the junior owner's sign and *(v)* their products as specified as part of registration, *(vi)* generally, that "the part of the public" is likely to be confused. "Any sign" *(i)* is a way for the legislature to indicate that essentially all junior signs are covered. This requirement should be read in connection with the broad definition of what may constitute a sign under the "[s]igns of which an EU trade mark may consist."[59] Although the 2015 trademark reform did not affect the

---

to prevent all third parties not having his consent from using in the course of trade → any sign in relation to goods or services where ←:

(b) ~~any~~ → the ← sign ~~where, because of its identity~~ → is identical ← ~~with~~, or ~~similarity~~ to, the trade mark and ~~the identity or similarity of the~~ → is used for ← goods or services ~~covered by~~ → which are identical with or similar to the goods or services for which ← the trade mark → is registered ← ~~and the sign,~~ → if ← there exists a likelihood of confusion on the part of the public; the likelihood of confusion includes the likelihood of association between the sign and the trade mark." EP and Council Proposal for a Directive to approximate the laws of the Member States relating to trade marks of 27 March 2013, COM(2013) 162 final 2013/89 (COD), p. 18-19.

[55]It emerges in art. 9(3)(a)-(f): "3.The following, in particular, may be prohibited under paragraph 2: (a) affixing the sign to the goods or to the packaging thereof; (b) offering the goods or putting them on the market, or stocking them for those purposes, under the sign, or offering or supplying services thereunder; (c) importing or exporting the goods under the sign; (d) using the sign as a trade or company name or part of a trade or company name; (e) using the sign on business papers and in advertising; (f) using the sign in comparative advertising in a manner that is contrary to Directive 2006/114/EC."

[56]Cf. art. 9(1) of the TM Regulation and art. 10(1) of the TM Directive.

[57]Cf. art. 9(2) of the TM Regulation and art. 10(2) of the TM Directive.

[58]Cf. art. 9(2)(b) of the TM Regulation and art. 10(2)(b) of the TM Directive.

[59]Cf. art. 4 of the TM Regulation and art. 3 of the TM Directive. Hence, art. 4 of the TM Regulation states that "[a]n EU trade mark may consist of any signs, in particular words, including personal names, or designs, letters, numerals, colours, the shape of goods or of the packaging of goods, or sounds, provided that such signs are capable of: (a) distinguishing the goods or services of one

substantial likelihood of confusion standard,[60] removal of the requirement that signs to be registrable have to be "capable of being represented graphically" may have downstream effects on the average consumer.[61] The change allows for registration of sounds as mentioned in the legislation, and potentially also smells.[62] Eventually, the Court of Justice must determine if registration of these signs as trademarks affects the framing of the average consumer in law, deciding the likelihood of confusion in registration and subsequently in infringement.[63]

The formulation "in the course of trade" *(ii)* as opposed to private use has been the focal point of European trademark since its early beginnings and hence the phrasing occurs several times in the early preparatory works.[64] As a means of interpreting the requirement, recital 18 of the TM Directive states that "[i]t is appropriate to provide that an infringement of a trade mark can only be established if there is a finding that the infringing mark or sign *is used in the course of trade for the purposes of distinguishing goods or services.*"[65] Based on this recital, there is a clear linking

---

undertaking from those of other undertakings; and (b) being represented on the Register of European Union trade marks ('the Register'), in a manner which enables the competent authorities and the public to determine the clear and precise subject matter of the protection afforded to its proprietor." In substance, the wording of art. 3 of the TM Directive is identical, although the TM Directive does not refer to "EU trade mark" but "trade mark" and "register" instead of "the Register of European Union trade marks."

[60]See above Chap. 3, Sect. 3.2.2.1, in particular footnote 39.

[61]That is, the removal of this requirement from art. 4 of the TM Regulation 2009 and TM Regulation 1994 and art. 2 of the TM Directive 2008 and TM Directive 1989. On registration of those and other unconventional marks, see Schovsbo, Jens, Rosenmeier, Morten and Petersen, Clement Salung, 'Immaterialret: Ophavsret, Patentret, Brugsmodelret, Designret, Varemærkeret', (5th edn, Jurist- og Økonomforbundets Forlag, 2018), p. 470-474 and Lunell, Erika, 'Okonventionella Varumärken : Form, Färg, Doft, Ljud', (1st edn, Stockholm, 2007).

[62]Hence, Danny Friedmann has argued that "[t]he reform of the trade mark system, by removing the graphical representation requirement, will bring the registration of non-traditional trade marks back to life, beginning with sound marks. Assessing the available paths of registration, which are linked to the advances of scent-emitting technology, it becomes clear that scent marks inevitably will make their comeback in the EU." This is with the caveat though, that an agreement can be reached on how to classify smells. See Friedmann, Danny, 'EU opens door for sound marks: will scent marks follow?', Journal of Intellectual Property Law & Practice, vol. 10/no. 12, (2015), pp. 931, p. 934 and the article at large for an analysis of the effect that the legislative change has on the ability to register smell marks.

[63]Instead, the requirement of representation now appears in art. 4(b) of the TM Regulation and art. 3 (b) of the TM Directive. The provision is set out above in footnote 59.

[64]For instance, the TM Memorandum 1976 stated that "[t]he exclusive right of the trade mark owner should, as in the 1964 Draft, be defined in general terms by means of the formula 'use in the course of trade' and not by an enumeration of individual kinds of use or of circumstances constituting infringements." The TM Memorandum 1976, p. 27. See also *ibid*, p. 13 and art. 3(1) of the TM Directive Proposal 1980.

[65]Italics added. The recital continues: "Use of the sign for purposes other than for distinguishing goods or services should be subject to the provisions of national law."

between using a mark "in the course of trade" and the essential function of trademarks.

Use in relation to goods and services *(iii)* has been interpreted as meaning that there has to be trademark use by the junior owner of its sign. This means that the use encompassed by the provision is use of the sign by the junior owner affecting the origin function of the senior mark.[66]

As is clear from the context of the provision, "similarity" between the junior sign and the senior mark and their products ((*iv*) and (*v*)) is something less than "identical."[67] It also appears that the minimum requirement under the likelihood of confusion standard is the finding of similarity between the mark and sign, and the products and that either of the two can be identical, and the other merely similar. Dissimilar products leave protection for marks with a reputation, and dissimilar marks are outside the scope of protection in general.[68] As mentioned in the introduction, deciding "similarity" is one of the main sources of "woolliness" in European trademark law.[69] The Court of Justice has confirmed e.g. in *Fundação Calouste Gulbenkian v. OHIM* that the finding of (as a minimum) similarity between the mark/sign and the products are cumulative conditions.[70]

---

[66]For instance, in *Céline SARL v. Céline SA*, the Court of Justice (Grand Chamber) stated that "there is use 'in relation to goods' within the meaning of Article 5(1) of the directive [art. 10(2) of the TM Directive] where a third party affixes the sign constituting his company name, trade name or shop name to the goods which he markets (see, to that effect, [Arsenal Football Club v. Reed, Case C-206/01, [2002] ECR I-10273], paragraph 41, and [Adam Opel v. Autec, Case C-48/05, [2007] ECR I-1017], paragraph 20). (. . .) In addition, even where the sign is not affixed, there is use 'in relation to goods or services' within the meaning of that provision where the third party uses that sign in such a way that a link is established between the sign which constitutes the company, trade or shop name of the third party and the goods marketed or the services provided by the third party." Céline SARL v. Céline SA, Case C-17/06, [2007] ECR I-7041, paras 22-23. See also Blomqvist v. Rolex, Case C-98/13, [2014], para 27 and Daimler v. Együd Garage, Case C-179/15, [2016], para 26, including the case law cited in both decisions. In *Mitsubishi v. Duma Forklifts*, the Court of Justice has recently significantly expanded "use" to include the debranding of goods not previously marketed in the EEA before placing the goods in circulation in the EEA. Mitsubishi v. Duma Forklifts, Case C-129/17, [2018], paras 42-49. See also further Skrzydło-Tefelska, Ewa, and Żuk, Mateusz, 'Article 9: Rights Conferred by a Community Trade Mark', in Hasselblatt, Gordian N. ed., Community Trade Mark Regulation (EC) no 207/2009: A Commentary (1st edn, Beck/Hart, 2015), 295, p. 309-310 and p. 362-365 and Bøggild, Frank, and Staunstrup, Kolja, 'EU-Varemærket', (1st edn, Karnov Group, 2015), p. 360-373.

[67]The understanding of "identical" taken within the "double identity" issues is addressed in the introduction Chap. 1, Sect. 1.5.1, in particular footnote 110.

[68]As for infringement of senior marks with "a reputation," see art. 9(2)(c) of the TM Regulation (art. 9(1)(c) of the TM Regulation 2009 and TM Regulation 1994) and art. 10(2)(c) of the TM Directive (art. 5(2) of the TM Directive 2008 and TM Directive 1989). As for registration, see the art. 8(5) of the TM Regulation (ditto of the TM Regulation 2009 and TM Regulation 1994) and art. 5(3)(a) of the TM Directive (art. 4(3) of the TM Directive 2008 and TM Directive 1989). See also Chap. 1, Sect. 1.5.1, in particular footnote 111.

[69]See Chap. 1, Sect. 1.1.

[70]Fundação Calouste Gulbenkian v. OHIM, Case C-414/14 P, [2015], para 48. See also earlier OHIM v. riha WeserGold Getränke, Case C-558/12 P, [2014], para 41, Kaul v. OHIM, Case C-193/

In recital 16 of the TM Directive, it has been stipulated that registered trademarks are given protection in particular of their indications of origin, and that the protection in the case of double identity conflicts is "absolute." This indicates that the "price" paid by the junior trademark owner in "double identity" conflicts is that the senior trademark owner need not establish likelihood of confusion. Under the likelihood of confusion standard though, it appears from the recital that "it is indispensable to give an interpretation of the concept of similarity in relation to the likelihood of confusion" and that the standard depends upon "the degree of similarity between the trade mark and the sign and between the goods or services identified."[71]

From the wording of the provision, the recital just mentioned is uncontroversial. In line with the recital, it appears from the wording of the provision that before assessing likelihood of confusion it is necessary to assess the entry requirements *(i)*– *(v)*. Although a significant gap is left by the legislature to the judiciaries on how to interpret the meaning of "a likelihood of confusion on the part of the public," some significant legislative interpretive aids are found in EU trademark legislation. These build on what has been stated above referring to the Paris Agreement and the TRIPS Agreement where it was concluded that actual confusion is unnecessary.

The substantial requirements of the provisions on infringement in EU trademark legislation are mirrored in the provisions on likelihood of confusion in registration.[72] However, it should be borne in mind that under registration *(ad i)* the junior owner's sign taken to be as specified in the application for registration, *(ad ii)* there is no requirement of "use in the course of trade", and *(ad iii)* "in relation to goods and services."[73] This is one reason why Bently *et al* have held that in infringement disputes that "focus is on specific real-life situation, rather than the speculative analysis called for in relation to many cases of relative grounds [for refusal of registration]."[74]

---

09 P, [2010] ECR I-2, para 43, Albert René v. OHIM, Case C-16/06 P, [2008] ECR I-10053, para 44, Alecansan v. OHIM, Case C-196/06 P, [2007], para 35, Ponte Finanziaria v. OHIM, Case C-234/06 P, [2007] ECR I-7333, para 48, Vedial v. OHIM, Case C-106/03 P, [2004] ECR I-9573, para 51 and Canon Kabushiki Kaisha v. Metro-Goldwyn-Mayer. Case C-39/97, [1998] ECR I-5507, para 22. Although the decisions relate to registration of trademarks, finding likelihood of confusion in infringement disputes also presupposes, as a minimum, a similarity between the mark/ sign and the products. This emerges from the identically worded provisions on registration and infringement.

[71]Recital 11 of the TM Directive and recital 8 of the TM Regulation 2009.

[72]Art. 8(1)(a) of the TM Regulation (ditto in the TM Regulation 2009 and TM Regulation 1994) and art. 4(1)(a) of the TM Directive (ditto of the TM Directive 2008 and TM Directive 1989).

[73]Mellor, James, David Llewelyn, Moody-Stuart, Thomas, *et al*, 'Kerly's Law of Trade Marks and Trade Names', (16th edn, Sweet & Maxwell, 2018), p. 589 and Bently, Lionel, Sherman, Brad, Gangjee, Dev and Johnson, Phillip 'Intellectual Property Law', (5th edn, Oxford University Press, 2018), p. 1104.

[74]*Ibid*. See also Bøggild, Frank, and Staunstrup, Kolja, 'EU-Varemærkeret', (1st edn, Karnov Group, 2015), p. 358 and Mellor, James, David Llewelyn, Moody-Stuart, Thomas, *et al*, 'Kerly's Law of Trade Marks and Trade Names', (16th edn, Sweet & Maxwell, 2018), p. 426 and 589.

9.3.1.2 Part of the Public

As it is the point of departure for the average consumer, it is necessary to scrutinise the last legislative requirement *(vi)* linking likelihood of confusion to "the part of the public."

In the first proposal for a trademark directive from 1980 it was qualified that in registration and infringement the "likelihood of confusion" had to be "serious."[75] As pointed out by Levin, the thought behind this was essentially to prevent that too many marks were confusingly similar, causing a meltdown of the trademark system.[76] The EESC opposed the "serious" qualification, stating in their opinion on the proposal that "[t]he Directive should not create the impression that there are cases where the likelihood of confusion is immaterial. *Economic operators who have no specialist knowledge, and particularly consumers, are entitled to be protected against any likelihood of confusion.*"[77] The opinion was made before qualifying likelihood of confusion as a standard that includes "likelihood association" which was the phrasing to be used in EU trademark legislation. Where "serious" seemed to elevate the threshold for finding confusion, "association" seems to do the opposite since association is something less than confusion—a mere "link."[78] Even after the reform EU trademark legislation still protects not only against "likelihood of confusion" but also against "likelihood of association." There is more agreement on the overall meaning of "confusion" in contrast with "association." This is not least the case since confusion is a commonly known term in international treaties as addressed above and in national law as addressed below. As for "association," Cornish *et al* have rightfully pointed out that the "word is a passport to clever speculation about the possible psychological impact of marking or get-up on this and that social group."[79] In elaborating on confusion in the recitals, the legislature has clearly indicated that the relevant confusion is confusion about the origin of products.[80] The meaning of "association" has been heavily interpreted by the Court of Justice, but already in *Sabel* the court stated "that the mere association which the

---

[75]Registration art. 8(1)(b) and infringement art. 3(1) of the TM Directive Proposal 1980.

[76]Levin, Marianne, 'Lärobok i Immaterialrätt: Upphovsrätt, Patenträtt, Mönsterrätt, Känneteckensrätt i Sverige, EU och Internationellt', (11th, Norstedts Juridik, 2017), p. 462. Levin continued holding that "from a European harmonisation perspective it is significant that national case law is aligned and not least, that likelihood of confusion is dealt with in a similar way and with the same strictness." In Swedish: "Ur ett europeiskt harmoniseringsperspektiv är det viktigt att nationell praxis blir likartad och inte minst att förväxlingsprincipen hanteras likartat och med lagom stränghet." *Ibid.*

[77]EESC opinion on the proposal for a first Council Directive to approximate the laws of the Member States relating to trade marks and the proposal for a Council Regulation on Community trade marks of 30 November 1981, [1981] OJ C 310/22, p. 24 (italics added).

[78]Looking up "association" in the Oxford University Press online English/English dictionary, it appears that "connection" and "link" are examples of synonyms to the word.

[79]Cornish, William R., Llewelyn, David, and Alpin, Tanya, 'Intellectual Property: Patents, Copyright, Trademarks and Allied Rights', (8th edn, Sweet & Maxwell, 2013), p. 768.

[80]Recital 11 of the TM Regulation and recital 16 of the TM Directive.

public might make between two trade marks as a result of their analogous semantic content is not in itself a sufficient ground for concluding that there is a likelihood of confusion."[81] Furthermore, that "[i]t follows from that wording that the concept of likelihood of association is not an alternative to that of likelihood of confusion, but serves to define its scope."[82]

The word confusion itself indicates a certain human processing and as such creates an opening for a referencing public. This is also explicitly indicated by the legislature referring to "the part of the public."[83] Importantly this sentence allows for the singling out of a *part* of the public different from the public *as a whole*. This allows for the singling out of an *average* consumer apart from *all consumers* although the average consumer is not mentioned as the public manifesting the relevant *part of the public*. It appears though that one of the key elements in the assessment of the "numerous elements" depends "in particular, on the recognition of the trade mark *on the market*."[84] To understand the relevant recognition, it is necessary to understand the relevant market. There is no clear definition of the "market" in the EU trademark legislation. Most prominently, this is opposed to competition law where the EU Commission in a notice[85] has provided a market definition as "a tool to identify and define the boundaries of competition between firms."[86]

As for the understanding of "market," EU trademark legislation does state the obvious distinction between the Internal Market as a whole and the market of the member states as parts of that whole. As explicitly stated in the EU trademark legislation, this relates to "[t]he coexistence and balance of trade mark systems at national and Union level [that] in fact constitutes a cornerstone of the Union's approach to intellectual property protection."[87] As it appears in Chap. 3, the TM Regulation relates to the registration of EU trademarks in the EU as a whole and the

---

[81]Sabel v. Puma, Case C-251/95, [1997] ECR I-6191, para 26.

[82]*Ibid*, para 18. See also Marca Mode v. Adidas, Case C-425/98, [2000] ECR I-4861, para 34 and recently in the appeal decision Moscow Confectionery Factory v. EUIPO, Case C-248/18 P, [2018], paras 18-22. For some recent texts on interpreting "association," see Mühlendahl, Alexander von, Dimitris Botis, Spyros M. Maniatis, *et al*, 'Trade Mark Law in Europe: A Practical Jurisprudence', (3rd edn, Oxford University Press, 2016), p. 304-311 and Jaeger-Lenz, Andrea, 'Article 8: Relative Grounds for Refusal', in Hasselblatt, Gordian N. ed., Community Trade Mark Regulation (EC) no 207/2009: A Commentary (1st edn, Beck/Hart, 2015), 198, p. 212-213.

[83]Along those lines, Maeyaert and Muyldermans have stated that "[t]he likelihood of must obviously be established in the mind of, or on part of the relevant public." Maeyaert, Paul, and Muyldermans, Jeroen, 'Likelihood of Confusion in Trademark Law: A Practical Guide Based on the Case Law in Community Trade Mark Oppositions from 2002 to 2012', Trademark Reporter, vol. 103/no. 5, (2013), pp. 1032, p. 1041.

[84]Recital 11 of the TM Regulation and recital 16 of the TM Directive (italics added).

[85]Commission Notice on the definition of relevant market for the purposes of Community competition law of 9 December 1997, [1997] OJ C372/03.

[86]*Ibid*, para 2.

[87]Recital 3 of the TM Directive. See also recital 39 of the TM Regulation.

TM Directive relates to one or more member states.[88] Apart from the fact that the market is defined according to territoriality, it is also clear that the relevant market in European trademark law is defined according to the products, be they goods or services as specified in the Nice Agreement. As part of contextualising the relevant public, it is necessary to define whose perception is relevant; this definition directly affects the assessment of the confusion standard.[89] In the words of the EESC as set out above, in particular consumers as "economic operators" are stakeholders to be protected against confusion. The EESC TM Opinion 2013 also emphasised the importance of consumer protection to European trademark law.[90] The EESC findings also emerge in case law of the CJEU and national courts where the average *consumer* is the most favoured relevant public.

Elsewhere in EU trademark legislation, the legislature has allowed "third parties" to argue, before registration of a trademark, why it should not be registered.[91] Those third parties are broadly defined as "[a]ny natural or legal person and any group or body representing manufacturers, producers, suppliers of services, traders or consumers."[92] Since confusion relates to human perception, this forecloses legal persons from the confusion standard but the remainder of the "third parties" exemplify well the potential *part of the public* whose perception could be relevant. Naturally, the mentioned third parties possess different characteristics. The consequence of preventing likelihood of confusion—besides protecting the origin function—is "allowing consumers to make informed choices only when they [the trademarks] are actually used on the market." The likelihood of confusion assessed referring to e.g. "traders" respectively "consumers" will not be the same."[93] Stakeholders of trademark law possess different characteristics affecting their level of attention, and there will be a difference between when "traders" and "consumers" can make an informed choice and when they *most likely* will be confused. These different levels of attention of different publics is a prominent theme in the practice addressed as part of contextualisation.[94]

The relevant "market" is only one but many of the "numerous elements" used in the assessment of likelihood of confusion. Other elements that "should constitute the specific condition for such protection" are "the association which can be made with the used or registered sign, the degree of similarity between the trade mark and the

---

[88]See Chap. 3, Sect. 3.2.2.1.

[89]See Chap. 10.

[90]The EESC TM Opinion 2013, p. 44. The aspect of consumer protection is addressed in Chap. 1, Sect. 1.3.3.

[91]Under art. 40(1) of the TM Directive, third parties are generally given a right of observation "on which grounds the trade mark should not be registered *ex officio*." The right of observation under art. 45(1) of the TM Regulation is limited to the grounds specified in arts. 5 and 7 of the TM Regulation.

[92]Cf. art. 45(1) of the TM Regulation and TM Directive.

[93]Recital 31 of the TM Directive. This recital is not found in neither the TM Regulation nor the TM Regulation 2009.

[94]See Chap. 10.

sign and between the goods or services identified."[95] These other elements are addressed in the following chapter as part of analysing the global appreciation test as it is applied in practice.

9.3.2 National Differences?

Since the likelihood of confusion standard of the TM Directive just analysed and European trademark jurisprudence have somewhat matured, it is presumed that there is a high degree of similarity between trademark acts of the selected Member States. The question on confusion between a senior and a junior mark seems universal in trademark law, also pre *Sabel* in national law. The historical importance of confusion has also been stressed by the early mentioning of confusion in the Paris Convention. Therefore, some main historical lines in national law pre *Sabel* will be outlined below to illustrate the national origin and prominence of the confusion standards. Earlier the differences between the UK Common law and Nordic legal families were addressed, and the national legal sources implementing the TM Directive 1989, TM Directive 2008 and the TM Directive were set out.[96] This section substantially analyses the result of the implementation processes, i.e. the EU likelihood of confusion standard as it has emerged after the implementation in national trademark legislation.

9.3.2.1 England and Wales

In UK law, the likelihood of confusion standard in trademark law is somewhat intertwined with a similar standard in the law of passing off. Recently, Dent has analysed the introduction of "confusion" in mainly UK case law in the late nineteenth century. Overall, Dent finds the division between "confusion" and "deception" to be somewhat correlating with "a firmer (...) division between the law of trade marks and that of passing off."[97] According to Wadlow, passing off relates to "misrepresentations made by one trader which damage the goodwill of another trader" consisting of what has been denoted the "classical trinity," i.e. misrepresentation, damage and goodwill.[98] Initially, the current focus on confusion in trademark law has made Dent observe that "[t]he individual, and not the

---

[95]Recital 11 of the TM Regulation and recital 16 of the TM Directive (italics added).

[96]See Chap. 3, Sect. 3.3. It is only the UK, Sweden and Denmark that recently have implemented the TM Directive.

[97]Dent, Chris, 'Confusion in a Legal Regime Built on Deception: The Case of Trade Marks', Queen Mary Journal of Intellectual Property, vol. 5/no. 1, (2015), pp. 2.

[98]"A representation is false if it is calculated to deceive in fact, even if it is literally true in some sense. Likewise, a representation is false if *it will deceive a substantial number of those to whom it is addressed, even if others will not be deceived.* Not every type of misrepresentation amounts to

actions of the defendant, has moved to the centre of the analysis."[99] The passing off of marks also focuses on the misleading of consumers.[100] The development of case law has further caused Dent to conclude that "the judges in the later nineteenth century were seeing consumers as more than mindless purchasers of goods – they had a mentality that was, in the end, capable of being confused."[101] In addition, that "[i]t is only after the courts accepted that individuals had interests that they could act upon (utilitarianism), that the individuals had a 'mentality', and that they possessed potentially erroneous knowledge as part of their inner life, that 'confusion' could be adopted as an external assessment of someone's state of being."[102]

In *Enterprise v. Eurocar* from January 2015, based on trademark law and passing off, Arnold J elaborated on the "standard of perspicacity" of purchasers under passing off. Specifically, Arnold J in the part of the decision on trademark infringement referred to the passing off decision *Seixo v. Provezende* from 1866 where Lord Cranworth LC found that "[[a]ll that courts of justice can do is to say that no trader can adopt a trade mark so resembling that of a rival, as that] *ordinary purchasers, purchasing with ordinary caution, are likely to be misled*."[103] During a presentation

---

passing-off." Wadlow, Christopher, 'The Law of Passing-Off: Unfair Competition by Misrepresentation', (5th edn, Sweet & Maxwell, 2016), p. 8 (italics added).

[99]Dent, Chris, 'Confusion in a Legal Regime Built on Deception: The Case of Trade Marks', Queen Mary Journal of Intellectual Property, vol. 5/no. 1, (2015), pp. 2, p. 6.

[100]Wadlow, Christopher, 'The Law of Passing-Off Unfair Competition by Misrepresentation', (5th edn, Sweet & Maxwell, 2016), p. 566-578. It is beyond the scope of this book to address the difference between passing off of marks and trademark infringement. Wadlow has addressed the differences in chapter 8 of his text, in particular pp. 631. See also Mellor, James, David Llewelyn, Moody-Stuart, Thomas, *et al*, 'Kerly's Law of Trade Marks and Trade Names', (18th edn, Sweet & Maxwell, 2018), chapter 20, in particular p. 748 and p. 785-787. Dent has seen several reasons for introducing confusion into trademark law, some of which relate to the rising importance of the individual. The claims related to the rising importance of the individual are: "[i]the acceptance, in the law, of members of society as individuals with specific attributes; [ii] the acknowledgement of the 'internal' life of those individuals; and [iii] the understanding that individuals possess knowledge and that knowledge may be incorrect." Dent, Chris, 'Confusion in a Legal Regime Built on Deception: The Case of Trade Marks', Queen Mary Journal of Intellectual Property, vol. 5/no. 1, (2015), pp. 2, p. 17 and expanded on in p. 17-26. Dent has offered three other reasons: "[i]the shift away from the 'moral' dimension of deception; [ii] the introduction of the trade mark registration system; [iii] and a breakdown in the rigidities that were a feature of the early nineteenth century." *Ibid*, p. 8 and expanded on in p. 8-17.

[101]Dent, Chris, 'Confusion in a Legal Regime Built on Deception: The Case of Trade Marks', Queen Mary Journal of Intellectual Property, vol. 5/no. 1, (2015), pp. 2, p. 23. This finding, is connected with the "quality function" of trade marks where customers see trademarks as not only a badge of origin but also a sign of quality. For this function to manifest itself requires "customers" "have the capacity to know quality when they see it" and that they "may be misguided as to the quality of a product based on their knowledge of a mark." *Ibid*, p. 26. For a further elaboration on the quality function, see Chap. 1, Sect. 1.3.1.

[102]*Ibid*, p. 26.

[103]Seixo v. Provezende, (1865-66) LR 1, Ch App 192, p. 196 (italics added). The quote from *Seixo v. Provezende* was provided by Arnold J in *Enterprise v. Europcar*, [2015] EWHC 17 (Ch), para 158.

immediately following *Enterprise v. Europcar* on the average consumer in trademark law and passing off, Arnold J built on this finding, claiming that the average consumer of today's European trademark law has been known in UK jurisprudence for around 150 years and that it does not originate from the Court of Justice case law.[104]

The likelihood of confusion standard of the UK TM Act 1938 was a matter of whether the junior mark was "likely to *deceive* or cause confusion."[105] As White and Jacob have pointed out, this phrase replaced the legislative phrase "*calculated to deceive*" that had previously been found in UK trademark acts. Based on case law it had appeared that "deceive" was not seen as involving any intent and should be seen as merely "*likely* to deceive." Moreover, that "deceive" had been covering issues rightfully seen as "causing confusion."[106]

The aim of introducing the UK TM Act 1994 according to the UK TM White Paper was "to provide, as far as possible, a new and self-sufficient law of trade marks, while at the same time simplifying the text of the law."[107] Along those lines, Jacob J held in *British Sugar v. Robertson* that "[t]he Trade Marks Act 1994, implementing an EC Directive, has swept away the old law."[108] Elaborating on the likelihood of confusion standard as part in infringement "Effects of registered trade mark," i.e. s. 10(2)(a)-(b), the UK TM White Paper stated that "[t]he extent of the protection of a registered trade mark should be, as closely as possible, whatever is needed to protect the legitimate interests of its proprietor and to prevent confusion of the public."[109] It is clear from the UK TM Act 1994 that, overall, the relevant provisions are with some differences narrowly mirroring those of the TM Directive. However, some different wording emerges on infringement. Hence, in *British Sugar v. Robertson* Jacob J commented on implementing what is now art. 10 of the TM Directive,[110] holding that "[f]or reasons which baffle me our Parliamentary draftsman did not simply copy this. He set about re-writing it. So, section 9(1) [of the UK Act 1994] has no exact equivalent in Article 5 [of the TM Directive 1989, now art. 10(2) of the TM Directive]." Further, that "[s]ection 9(1) is really no more than a chatty introduction to the details set out in section 10 [of the UK Act 1994], itself adding no more than that the acts concerned must be done without consent." As Jacob J stated this meant that the wording "by the use of the trade mark" in art. 9

---

[104]The presentation, where the author of this book was present, can be found at: Arnold, Richard, presentation under the heading 'The average consumer in passing off' as part of a conference under the heading 'The Average Consumer in Trade Mark Law and Passing Off' held at UCL in London 25 February 2015, at 17:50: https://www.youtube.com/watch?v=zqTC_-beZxk (last visited 26 May 2019), see from 18:25 onwards.

[105]In registration: s. 11 and 12(1) and infringement: s. 4(1) (italics added).

[106]White, T. A. Blanco, and Robin, Jacob, 'Kerly's Law of Trade Marks and Trade Names', (10th edn, Sweet & Maxwell, 1972), p. 451 (italics added).

[107]Recital 12 of the UK TM White Paper.

[108]British Sugar v. Robertson, [1996] RPC 281, (EWHC), p. 285.

[109]Cf. para 3.13 of the UK TM White Paper.

[110]Art. 5 of the TM Directive 1989 as elaborated on by Jacob J.

(1) of the UK TM Act 1994 did not occur in its current equivalent in art. 10(2) of the TM Directive. It emerges that the legislature has clarified the different scenarios in which infringement may occur, i.e. if the marks are identical but the products merely similar,[111] and *vice versa*.[112] Nothing is in the UK TM White Paper or the UK TM Act 1994 on the understanding of "the part of the public." Despite these differences, according to Jacob J, interpreting the UK provision one should disregard this "departure from the Directive."[113]

Since trademark use under registration is not a requirement, only the editorial differences between the TM Directive and the UK TM Act 1994 as just highlighted in infringement emerge in the "Relative grounds for refusal of registration," cf. s 5(2) (a)-(b) of the UK TM Act 1994. The recent amendments to the UK TM Act 1994 to implement the TM Directive do not change the provisions on the likelihood of confusion standard in registration or infringement.[114]

9.3.2.2 Nordic Countries

As it has emerged earlier there is and continue to be a substantive similarity of trademark law in the Nordic countries.[115] This similarity is manifested in the Nordic trademark acts and now affected by the increased Europeanisation of trademark law starting with the TM Directive 1989. Earlier the Nordic TM Proposal 1882 was said to contain the first common Nordic understanding of a likelihood of confusion standard.[116] The proposal for a provision building on existing practice and legislation of the countries stated that a mark (or a name) is infringed when it "in its entirety is imitated in such a way that a buyer easily will have the impression that the product is provided with the mark/stamp of the rightful manufacturer."[117] Exemplifying the outcome of the proposal at national level, the subsequent Danish Trademark Act

---

[111]Hence, it is stipulated in s 10(2)(a) of the UK TM Act 1994: "(2) A person infringes a registered trade mark if he uses in the course of trade a sign where because – (a) the sign is identical with the trade mark and is used in relation to goods or services similar to those for which the trade mark is registered, or (. . .)."

[112]In s 10(2)(b) of the UK TM Act 1994 it is stipulated: "(b) the sign is similar to the trade mark and is used in relation to goods or services identical with or similar to those for which the trade mark is registered, there exists a likelihood of confusion on the part of the public, which includes the likelihood of association with the trade mark." The latter sentence stipulating the likelihood of confusion requirement applies equally to both s. 10(2)(a) and (b).

[113]British Sugar v. Robertson, [1996] RPC 281, (EWHC), p. 291.

[114]See the Trade Marks Regulations 2018, no. 825 and above in Chap. 3, Sect. 3.3.1.

[115]See Chap. 2, Sects. 2.3.1, 2.3.1.1, and 2.3.2.

[116]See Chap. 3, Sect. 3.3.2.

[117]In Danish: "i sin Helhed er saaledes eftergjort, at en Kjøber let faar det Indtryk, at Varen er forsynet med den rette Tilvirkers Stempel." "Stempel" may be translated into English as "mark" or "stamp." The Nordic TM Proposal 1882, p. 41.

from 1890 ("the DK TM Act 1890")[118] stipulated that trademark infringement occurred under the following requirements: "when another's (...) registered trademark, although not depicted unchanged, but the changes are of no other nature, than the names or marks are imitated in their entirety, disregarding the difference in details, easily could be confused."[119] Similar phrasing was found in registration.[120]

It is clear from this historical account that a Nordic likelihood of confusion standard existed before the mentioning of confusion in the Paris Convention in 1925 and obviously long before the TRIPS Agreement and EU trademark legislation. Moreover, that the early confusion standard resonates with the EU standard referring not only to confusion, but also to the aspect that this had to be measured in its "entirety" referring to whether essentially the "buyer's" ability to decide the origin of the senior goods would be affected. A common feature of modern day Nordic trademark acts is that none of the current acts refer to "part of the public" although the respective national versions of the directive loyally have translated the phrase into similar national terms (Swedish: "allmänheten," Danish: "offentlighedens bevidsthed"[121] and Norwegian: "allmennheten"[122]). Interestingly though, none of the Nordic translations of the directive indicate that the relevant public is merely *part* of the public. Especially, the legislatures of Sweden and Denmark and the UK have narrowly kept the wording of the directive. As explained below, this is even more so the case with the update of the DK TM Act 1991 further aligning the wording of the likelihood of confusion provision with that of the TM Directive. As for Norway, the Norwegian legislature has kept a different structure on matters of registration.

Although the UCPD as implemented into national law is not analysed in this book, the directive authoritatively translates the average consumer term and its characteristics into Nordic language terms that all are more or less identical

---

[118]Varemærkeloven, Act. No 52 of 17 April 1890.

[119]In Danish: "en Andens (...) registrerede Varemærke vel ikke gengives uforandret, men Forandringerne ikke er af anden Beskaffenhed, end at Navnene eller Mærkerne i deres Helhed, uagtet Forskellen i Enkeltheder, let kunne forvexles." § 13 of the DK TM Act 1890. This provision included both a reference to "mark" and "name."

[120]See § 4(5) of the DK TM Act 1890. On the preparatory comments on this provision, see the Nordic TM Proposal 1882, pp. 31 and p. 19-20.

[121]Cf. art. 8(1)(b) and art. 9(2)(b) of the TM Regulation and art. 5(1)(b) and 10(2)(b) of the TM Directive of the Swedish and Danish versions.

[122]Cf. art. 4(1)(b) and art. 5(1)(b) of the TM Directive 1989 in Norwegian.

to the English terms (Swedish: "genomsnittskonsumenten," Danish: "gennemsnitsforbruger" and Norwegian:[123] "gjennomsnittsforbrukeren").[124]

9.3.2.2.1 Sweden

In infringement the legislature states in § 10 (2), ch. 1 of the SE TM Act 2010 that the likelihood of confusion ("risk för förväxling" or as stated in the SE TM Prop. 2009/10:225 "förväxlingsrisk")[125] includes "the risk that the sign *causes the perception* that there is an association between the one using the sign and the proprietor of the trademark."[126] The phrasing "causes the perception" is not known from EU trademark legislation but this, besides the word confusion itself, clearly indicates causality between use of the junior mark and confusion. Also, it stresses the human aspect of confusion. The legislature stressed in its proposal for the SE TM Act 2010 that it found this phrasing to a further extent than the TM Directive 2008 is in line with Court of Justice case law, indicating the elements to be included in the assessment of likelihood of confusion.[127] The Swedish provision makes it clearer than the directive that there has to be causality between the junior mark (its identity/similarity with the senior trademark) and the likelihood of confusion. The Swedish insertion of causality is not found in neither the DK TM Act 1991 nor the NO TM Act 2010.

In the proposal to the provision though, nothing is mentioned on the relevant public, merely that in relation to marks with a reputation, the assessment has to be made referring to the relevant purchasers ("omsättningskretsen").[128] The legislature also set out an aim for a narrow resemblance between the SE TM Act 2010 and the TM Directive 2008.[129] Although the SE TM Act 2010 does not refer to any relevant public (less so the average consumer) in relation to assessment of likelihood of

---

[123]The UCPD is part of the EEA Agreement, cf. art. 72 on consumer protection, cf. Annex XIX, para 7(g) of the EEA Agreement. The UCPD has been implemented into Norwegian law in the Norwegian Marketing Practices (Markedsføringsloven, Act No 2 of 9 January 2009, as most recently amended 1 July 2016). Although Norwegian is not an official language of the EU, the Norwegian legislature has made a Norwegian translation of the UCPD. This version is available at: https://www.regjeringen.no/no/dokumenter/Europaparlaments%2D%2Dog-radsdirektiv-200529EF-direktiv-om-urimelig-handelspraksis%2D%2D-forelopig-norsk-oversettelse/id500926/ (last visited 26 May 2019).

[124]Recital 18 of the UCPD. The translation in the Nordic languages is: Swedish: "genomsnittskonsumenten som är normalt informerad samt skäligen uppmärksam och upplyst," Danish: "almindeligt oplyst, rimeligt opmærksom og velunderrettet gennemsnitsforbruger" and Norwegian: "gjennomsnittsforbrukeren, som er rimelig velinformert og rimelig observant og kritisk."

[125]E.g. SE TM Prop 2009/10:225, p. 121.

[126]In Swedish: "inbegripet risken för att användningen av tecknet leder till uppfattningen att det finns ett samband mellan den som använder tecknet och innehavaren av varukännetecknet."

[127]*Ibid*, p. 122.

[128]*Ibid*, p. 117.

[129]*Ibid*, p. 121.

confusion, it is clearly stressed in the proposal that a key function of trademarks is "to prevent consumers from confusing different goods and services."[130] The mirroring provisions on registration in § 8 (2), ch. 2 of the SE TM Act 2010 narrowly reflect the TM Directive.

The update of the SE TM Act 2010 as in SE TM Prop. 2018/18:267 does not substantially change to the current legislative likelihood of confusion standard.[131]

9.3.2.2.2 Denmark

As referred to in Chap. 3, the predecessor of the DK TM Act 1991, the DK TM Act 1959, was considered by Koktvedgaard as a visionary piece of legislation. In the same vein the proposal of a new trademark act as part of implementing the TM Directive 1989 into Danish law mentioned that although the DK TM Act 1959 "overall had worked satisfactorily, it is still found to be correct at the same time to modernise the [1959] trademark act, in particular with the purpose of simplifying case handling."[132] Koktvedgaard was also part of the implementation process as chairman of an expert committee on Industrial Property.[133]

The provision on infringement in § 4, sub-s 1 (2) of the DK TM Act 1991 before the recent update of the act was similar to the corresponding provision in the SE TM Act 2010 hence leaving out a reference to "part of the public" relevant to deciding likelihood of confusion ("risiko for forveksling" or as stated in the DK TM Bet. 199/1958 "forvekslingsfare").[134] In a proposal for a new Danish trademark act from 1991 (the "DK TM Prop. 1990/2")[135] it is stated that the "likelihood of association" introduced in the TM Directive 1989 and implemented into the DK TM Act 1991 is a "formal innovation" in Danish trademark law. In reality though, this criterion could already be given weight in case law preceding the DK TM Act 1991. It was thus stated in the DK TM Bet. 199/1958 preceding the DK TM Act 1959 on the similarity of the marks that besides confusion it could be considered whether the junior mark indicated between the parties "a special affiliation or another commercial

---

[130]In Swedish: "från konsumentsynpunkt fyller ett varukännetecken en funktion genom att konsumenterna kan undvika att förväxla olika varor och tjänster." *Ibid*, p. 119. "Varukännetecken" is an umbrella term used for trademarks ("varumärken") and other trade signs, hence the heading of chapter 1 of the SE TM Act 2010 "Varumärken och andra varukännetecken m.m." ("trademarks and other trade signs etc.").

[131]See the SE TM Prop. 2018/18:267 on §10(2), ch. 1, p. 11 and § 8(2), ch. 2, p. 17 and above Chap. 3, Sects. 3.3.2 and 3.3.2.1.

[132]In Danish: "i det store og hele har fungeret tilfredsstillende, er det fundet rigtigt samtidig at gennemføre en modernisering af varemærkeloven, især med det formål at forenkle sagsbehandlingen." *Ibid*, para 1. See Chap. 3, Sect. 3.3.2.2.

[133]*Ibid*, para 4.

[134]The DK TM Bet. 199/1958, p. 107.

[135]Forslag til varemærkelov, No 1990/2 LSF 83 of 10 June 1991.

connection."[136] Furthermore, the DK TM Prop. 1990/2 stated that as part of assessing confusion and association, "consumers" ("forbrugerne") are the relevant public.[137] Since as shown by Danish case law, consumers are far from always the relevant public, this may arguably be a slip of the pen by the drafter of the proposal indicating what at the time was (and now is) most often the relevant public—the consumers. The DK TM Bet. 199/1958 referred to the more neutral "purchaser" ("køber").[138]

The mirroring provisions on registration in § 15, sub-s 1 (2) of the DK TM Act 1991 narrowly reflect the TM Directive and what has been said on the infringement disputes also applies here.

As part of the update of the DK TM Act 1991, the Danish legislature in the DK TM Prop. 261/2017–18 has wisely stated that the wording of the proposal for the update of the Danish trademark act is kept close to the TM Directive "as far as possible to reduce the risk of interpretive uncertainty."[139] This means keeping the wording on the likelihood of confusion standard in registration and infringement as set out in the Danish version of the TM Directive. Besides some minor adjustments of the of the provisions in the DK TM Act 1991 relevant to this analysis, it has now been stated in the DK TM Act 1991 that likelihood of confusion must be assessed referring to "the relevant public" ("offentlighedens bevidsthed").[140] Other than ensuring a better alignment with the TM Directive, nothing in the DK TM Prop. 261/2017–18 indicates any intention of the legislature to materially change the likelihood of confusion standard in the DK TM Act 1991.[141]

9.3.2.2.3   Norway

As it appeared in Chap. 3, Norway is according to the EEA Agreement obliged, due to certain modifications through the EEA Agreement, to implement the TM Directive 1989. Although the NO TM Act 1961 was already aligned with the TM Directive 1989, the NO TM Act 2010 was introduced to further adjust to the

---

[136]*Ibid*, p. 107. In Danish: "en særlig tilknytning eller anden kommerciel forbindelse." See also Koktvedgaard, Mogens, and Wallberg, Knud, 'Varemærkeloven af 6. Juni 1991 og Fællesmærkeloven af 6. Juni 1991 med Indledning og Kommentarer', (1st edn, Jurist- og Økonomforbundets Forlag, 1994), p. 65.

[137]The DK TM Prop. 1990/2, ad § 4(1). In Danish: "formelt en nydannelse."

[138]The DK TM Bet. 199/1958, p. 107.

[139]In Danish: "i videst muligt omfang bevares med henblik på at reducere risikoen for fortolkningstvivl." DK TM Prop. 261/2017-18, p. 24.

[140]*Ibid*, see on § 4, sub-s 1(2), p. 2-3 and § 15, sub-s 1(2), p. 8-9.

[141]See the DK TM Prop. 261/2017-18 on § 4, sub-s 1(2), p. 28-31 and p. 55-56 and § 15, sub-s 1(2), p. 37-41 and p. 73. See also above in Chap. 3, Sects. 3.3.2 and 3.3.2.2.

directive.[142] At the time of preparing the act it was the TM Directive 1989 that was annexed to the EEA Agreement, but currently it is the TM Directive 2008.[143]

The likelihood of confusion standard is set out in the NO TM Act 2010 § 4(1) (b) on infringement and in § 16(1)(a), cf. § 4(1)(b) on registration. These provisions resemble the TM Directive and the phrasing of the SE TM Act 2010 and the DK TM Act 1991. Hence, there is no mentioning of the "part of the public" relevant to deciding likelihood of confusion ("risiko for forveksling" or as stated in NO TM Prop. 98/2008–09 "forvekslingsrisiko").[144] Based on case law it is stated in NO TM Prop. 98/2008–09 on the comments on § 4 that deciding likelihood of confusion has to be done with reference to the relevant purchasers ("omsetningskretsen") and that in relation to ordinary consumer goods the relevant public is the average consumer ("gjennomsnittsforbruker").[145] This seems to build on the previous wording of § 4 (1) of the NO TM Act 1961 that confusion had to be assessed in the "ordinary market" ("alminnelige omsetning").

Structurally, in the registration scenario it is clarified that a sign is unregistrable if, without the consent of the senior trademark owner, "use of the trademark would infringe the right of another in this country to a trademark or business name or another business sign," cf. § 16(a), one of which is § 4(1)(b) on likelihood of confusion.[146] § 16(a) follows the logic of EU trademark legislation, i.e. that a junior mark that would infringe a senior mark cannot be registered. However, compared to the other national jurisdictions, this provision does not address the legislative differences mentioned in EU trademark legislation between the registration and infringement scenario.[147] There seems to be no reason other than structural and historical reasons for the different wording of this provision.[148]

9.4 Conclusion

It is clear from the historical accounts that confusion standards before EU trademark legislation were found in the UK, the Nordic countries and in the Paris Convention. The Paris Convention, and today also the TRIPS Agreement, are aids to interpreting the EU likelihood of confusion standard. This international backcloth has to some

---

[142]See the NO TM Prop. 98/2008-09, p. 5.

[143]EAA Agreement, Annex VII, para 9(h) of 8 July 2016.

[144]NO TM Prop. 98/2008-09, p. 42.

[145]*Ibid*, p. 42. In Norwegian "ordinary consumer goods" are called "alminnelige forbruksvarer."

[146]It appears in NO TM Prop. 98/2008-09 that § 16(a) e.g. implements art. 4(1) of the TM Directive 1989 (now art. 5(1) of the TM Directive). *Ibid*, p. 52.

[147]The fact as mentioned above that under registration i) the junior user's sign is specified based on its application for registration, ii) there is no requirement of "use in the course of trade," iii) and "in relation to goods and services." See Chap. 10, Sect. 10.2.2.

[148]As explained in NO TM Prop. 98/2008-09, the proposal essentially continues the previous law. NO TM Prop. 98/2008-09, p. 39.

degree harmonised the standard. Inevitably, the national pre EU standards have played into the international treaties, but also have an impact today on the ongoing dialogue between the Court of Justice and national courts through the preliminary rulings procedure.[149]

The TM Directive added important additional layers to the standard, both in terms of clarity and woolliness. It adds clarity that the likelihood of confusion standard has to be assessed with reference to "part of the public" and as per the recitals that this assessment consists of "numerous elements" "in particular, on the recognition of the trade mark on the market." Especially, this assessment has opened the door for the global appreciation test created by the Court of Justice. This test clearly stands on the shoulders of national judicial traditions and will be addressed further in the following chapter. Woolliness is added by including in the likelihood of confusion standard "likelihood of association," association not being a term known from the international treaties.

Like Jacob J, one can be "baffled" by national legislatures not clearly following the wording of the TM Directive, on the face of it even adding or removing requirements stipulated in the directive. It was seen how the UK legislature in infringement has added a requirement "by the use of the trade mark." It was seen how until recently, the Nordic trademark acts do not refer to "part of the public." This has changed with the update of the DK TM Act 1991 where the Danish legislature wisely has followed the wording of the TM Directive on the likelihood of confusion more closely, including the insertion of a reference to "the relevant public." Also, it has been seen that there are structural differences between the national trademark acts, most prominently by the UK dividing the provisions into a part on "identity of the marks/similarity of the products" and *vice versa*, and Norway in registration shortly stating that infringing marks are not registrable.

In particular, if the literal meaning of the current Nordic trademark acts were to be followed strictly, this could cause a significant substantial difference between the UK and the Nordic jurisdictions. This finding is caused by the legislative abandoning of references to *part of the public* as a required element in assessing likelihood of confusion. This legislative abandoning could even be a question of incorrect implementation of the TM Directive. However, first, from the preparatory works it is clear that the intention of the legislatures has been to fully implement the directive. Second, these preparatory works leave no doubt that there has been no intention of deviating from the requirement of applying part of the public in using the likelihood of confusion standard. Third, the preparatory works indicate that applying a reference public deciding confusion is not a novelty in the Nordic jurisdictions. This intention of the Danish legislature underlying the DK TM Act 1991 is now reflected directly in the legislation with the mentioned insertion of the reference to the relevant public as part of the likelihood of confusion standard.

The conclusion is that there is a high degree of legislative harmonisation between the relevant member states and it confirms the presumption of legislative similarity.

---

[149]See Chap. 4, Sect. 4.3.1.

Admittedly, it does not add to the coherence and consistency that the jurisdictions after all present differences. If the opposite situation was imagined where national legislatures had stipulated an exhaustive list of elements forming the global appreciation test, the coherence and consistency would certainly be increased. Probably though, such a legislative list would constitute incorrect implementation of the TM Directive, since it would narrow the fairly wide floor and ceiling left by the EU legislature for national legislatures and European judiciaries.

Some essential gaps left by the EU legislature for the European judiciaries are deciding which "numerous elements" constitute the test for likelihood of confusion and what role "part of the public" has to play. Also, the national legislatures have left gaps in terms of the mentioned inconsistencies for the national courts. Since on the surface the substantial legislative likelihood of confusion standard has not been changed since its introduction in EU trademark legislation through the TM Directive 1989, the residue of EU law potentially affected by national deviating standards has decreased. Essentially, since the Court of Justice frequently has interpreted the likelihood of confusion standard *in law* from *Sabel* onwards, the court has inevitably minimised the uncertainty where there is room for deviating national interpretations.

Chapter 10
The Average Consumer in a "Global" Perspective

10.1 Introduction

It emerged in the previous chapter that the likelihood of confusion standard under the EU trademark legislation has to be tested referring to "part of the public" and "numerous elements," one of which is "in particular, on the recognition of the trade mark on the market." Although reference to "numerous elements" has not been made in the main text of the legislation, but in the recitals, the Court of Justice has, starting from *Sabel,* used the recitals in developing "the global appreciation test."[1] How the judiciaries lay out this "multifactor test" referring to the average consumer is analysed in this chapter. The analysis is conducted through three central decisions by the Court of Justice from the late 1990s—*Sabel, Gut Springenheide* and *Lloyd* referred to as the "trinity" decisions. The decisions were important to developing the average consumer in EU trademark law and still stand as key precedents. In addition, it is analysed what role those decisions play into developing the average consumer in national jurisprudence. This analysis also addresses that the global appreciation test has not been developed in an EU legal vacuum but stands on the shoulders of longstanding national practice. The parts of the global appreciation test as such are not analysed but merely how the test from a broader perspective is implemented into national trademark law by national judiciaries. For an analysis of the different parts, attention is directed to general scholarly literature.[2]

---

[1]Sabel v. Puma, Case C-251/95, [1997] ECR I-6191, para 22.

[2]For instance, from current literature: Focusing mainly on the broader European level, Kur, Annette and Senftleben, Martin, 'European Trade Mark Law: A Commentary', (1st edn, Oxford University Press, 2017), p. 220-231, Mühlendahl, Alexander von, Dimitris Botis, Spyros M. Maniatis, *et al,* 'Trade Mark Law in Europe: A Practical Jurisprudence', (3rd edn, Oxford University Press, 2016), p. 311-370, Jaeger-Lenz, Andrea, 'Article 8: Relative Grounds for Refusal', in Hasselblatt, Gordian N. ed., Community Trade Mark Regulation (EC) no 207/2009: A Commentary (1st edn, Beck/Hart, 2015), 198, p. 211-245 (registration), in particular p. 247-255 and p. 367-372 (infringement), Bøggild, Frank, and Staunstrup, Kolja, 'EU-Varemærkeret', (1st edn, Karnov Group, 2015),

© Springer Nature Switzerland AG 2020
R. D. Laustsen, *The Average Consumer in Confusion-based Disputes in European Trademark Law and Similar Fictions*, https://doi.org/10.1007/978-3-030-26350-8_10

10.2   The Trinity Decisions: Sabel, Gut Springenheide and Lloyd

10.2.1   Frame of the Decisions

Before analysing the global appreciation test as introduced by *Sabel*, it should be mentioned that from a functional view, this test is not a legal novelty owing to neither European trademark law, nor trademark law in general. Hence, in exemplifying the understanding of standards in a US context, it has been established that with reference to Cross that the "multifactor test" is a "common standard" "in which doctrine tells lower courts to consider a series of factors as relevant to the decision's outcome but provides no explicit instructions about how those factors are to be weighed." An example of a multifactor test in US American jurisprudence is found in trademark law testing likelihood of confusion.[3] In a European context, it was found that to decide the negligence standard in tort law, the reasonable person (somewhat comparable to the average consumer) was applied as part of a multifactor test.[4] Essentially, the global appreciation test is a multifactor test. That the global appreciation test falls into the category of a multifactor test merely says something about the function of the test, not the substance. The global appreciation test serves a profound purpose in EU law, since it relates to the functional difference between the Court of Justice and the General Court and national courts. It will be recalled that the Court of Justice interprets EU law but refrains from going into the factual

---

245 – 332 and Davis, Richard, St Quintin, Thomas and Tritton, Guy, 'Tritton on Intellectual Property in Europe', (5th edn, Sweet & Maxwell, 2018), p. 369-380; the UK: Firth, Alison, Lea, Gary R. and Cornford, Peter, 'Trade Marks: Law and Practice', (4th edn, Jordans, 2016), p. 130-135, Bently, Lionel, Sherman, Brad, Gangjee, Dev and Johnson, Phillip 'Intellectual Property Law', (5th edn, Oxford University Press, 2018), p. 1031-1051 (registration) and p. 1103-1104 (infringement), Cornish, William R., Llewelyn, David, and Alpin, Tanya, 'Intellectual Property: Patents, Copyright, Trademarks and Allied Rights', (8th edn, Sweet & Maxwell, 2013), p. 736-738 (registration) and p. 764-769 (infringement) and Mellor, James, David Llewelyn, Moody-Stuart, Thomas, *et al*, 'Kerly's Law of Trade Marks and Trade Names', (16th edn, Sweet & Maxwell, 2018), p. 402-427 (registration) and p. 588-603 (infringement), and Chapter 3 on the average consumer consolidating the earlier supplement found in Mellor, James, Llewelyn, David, Moody-Stuart, Thomas *et al*, 'Kerly's Law of Trade Marks and Trade Mames. 1st Supplement', (1st edn, Sweet & Maxwell, 2014), section 1A: Bernitz, Ulf, Karnell, Gunnar, Lars Pherson, *et al*, 'Immaterialrätt Och Otillbörlig Konkurrens', (14th edn, Jure Bokhandel, 2017), p. 285-292 and Wessman, Richard, 'Varumärkeslagen: En Kommentar', (1st edn, Wolters Kluwer, 2014), p. 35-42 (infringement) and p. 73-75 (registration); Denmark: Wallberg, Knud and Ravn, Michael Francke, 'Varemærkeret: Varemærkeloven og Fællesmærkeloven Med Kommentarer', (5th edn, Jurist- og Økonomforbundets Forlag, 2017), p. 161-167 (infringement) p. 310-341 (registration) and Schovsbo, Jens, Rosenmeier, Morten and Petersen, Clement Salung, 'Immaterialret: Ophavsret, Patentret, Brugsmodelret, Designret, Varemærkeret', (5th edn, Jurist- og Økonomforbundets Forlag, 2018), p. 528-540 And; Norway: Lassen, Birger Stuevold and Stenvik, Are, 'Kjennetegnsrett', (3rd edn, Universitetsforlaget, 2011), Chapters 11-13, in particular p. 391-416.
[3]See Chap. 5, Sect. 5.2.
[4]See Chap. 6, Sect. 6.5.2.

assessment, although, as will emerge below, the distinction between *law* and *fact* is far from clear.[5] The definition by Cross of a multifactor test provides a valuable steer for the analysis of the global appreciation test. The factors of the test are set out by the Court of Justice, but their weighing in Europe is left to the General Court and the national courts. It is not always the case though that the Court of Justice refrains from going into weighing the different factors.

As is clear now, the average consumer before *Sabel* was gradually developed by the Court of Justice in a series of decisions on unfair competition law and consumer protection law.[6] Besides *Sabel* from November 1997, two early decision were essential to the formation in European trademark law of the global appreciation test and the average consumer, namely *Gut Springenheide and Tusky* ("Gut Springenheide")[7] from July 1998 and *Lloyd Schuhfabrik Meyer v. Klijsen Handel BV* ("Lloyd")[8] from June 1999. Important to these decisions are the opinions of Advocate General Jacobs in *Sabel* and *Lloyd* from April 1997 and October 1998 respectively and the opinion of Advocate General Mischo in *Gut Springenheide* from March 1998. Calling the decisions a "trinity" makes figuratively sense in that the decisions created a transition from the historical decisions on the average consumer into substantial European trademark law. Also, the decisions put flesh and bone to the average consumer fiction as part of the global appreciation test. Finally, *Gut Springenheide* is important, since the decision shows that the average consumer known today was not developed purely in trademark law. Since the Court of Justice in line with its general way of reasoning did not clearly express its *ratio decidendi* in *Gut Springenheide* and no clear explanation was provided by Mischo when he gave his opinion in the decision, it is difficult to tell why the average consumer was referred to by the Court of Justice. It is the stance of this book that the development of the average consumer in the three decisions owes a great deal to the fact that five of the judges sitting on the bench of the Court of Justice were the same in all three decisions,[9] and an additional five of the judges sitting on the bench in *Lloyd* also sat on the bench in *Sabel*.[10] That is, only three judges did only participate in *Sabel*.[11]

---

[5]See e.g. Chap. 11, Sect. 11.6.

[6]See Chap. 8.

[7]Gut Springenheide and Tusky, Case C-210/96, [1998] ECR I-4657.

[8]Lloyd Schuhfabrik Meyer v. Klijsen Handel BV, Case C-342/97, [1999] ECR I-3819.

[9]I.e., Almeida, Edward, Gulmann, Puissochet and Wathelet.

[10]I.e., Inglesias (President), Jann, Kapteyn, Mancini and Sevón.

[11]I.e., Hirsch, Murray and Ragnemalm.

10.2.2   *Interpretation of the Decisions*

The factual scenario in *Sabel* was that the senior trademark owner (Puma) had an earlier registered pictorial trademark in Germany for e.g. "leather and imitation leather, goods made therefrom (bags) and articles of clothing." The junior trademark owner (Sabel) had sought to register a pictorial mark for certain goods similar to those of Puma.[12]

The questioning German court (the Bundesgerichtshof) claimed that likelihood of confusion had to be considered referring to "the overall impression made by the respective signs." It was concluded by Advocate General Jacobs that "the [1989 TM] Directive requires that there be a likelihood of the consumer being misled in some way as to the origin of the goods." This assessment was considered by Jacobs as a matter of fact, although the principle of the "overall impression was a matter of law."[13] Hence, Jacobs held that this principle was "perhaps self-evident" but "[g] iven that the essential criterion is the likelihood of confusion, the Bundesgerichtshof must be correct in considering that what is important is the overall impression conveyed by the mark." This meant that as a matter of law it could not be ruled out that including a textual element in "one of two pictorial marks" ruled out the finding of a likelihood of confusion.[14] Jacobs did not refer to the relevance of the average consumer as part of the legal assessment. Although the Court of Justice did not explicitly refer to the opinion of Jacobs, it followed his reference to the principle of the "overall impression." The court stated that the legislative reference to "the part of the public" in the relevant provision and "numerous elements" in the recitals meant that "[t]he likelihood of confusion must therefore be appreciated globally, taking into account all factors relevant to the circumstances of the case."[15] The court continued finding that the "global appreciation of the visual, aural or conceptual similarity of the marks in question, must be based on the overall impression given by the marks, bearing in mind, in particular, their distinctive and dominant components." Moreover, that "[t]he wording (. . .) '. . . there exists a likelihood of confusion on the part of the public . . .' — *shows that the perception of marks in the mind of the average consumer of the type of goods or services in question plays a decisive role in the global appreciation of the likelihood of confusion.* The average consumer normally perceives a mark as a whole and does not proceed to analyse its various details."[16]

---

[12]I.e., "18 'Leather and imitation leather, products made therefrom not included in other classes; bags and handbags' and 25 'Clothing, including tights, hosiery, belts, scarves, ties/cravats and braces; footwear; hats'" (the numbers refer to the Nice Agreement). Sabel v. Puma, Case C-251/95, [1997] ECR I-6191, para 3.

[13]Sabel v. Puma, Case C-251/95, [1997] ECR I-6191, (opinion of AG Jacobs), para 9.

[14]*Ibid*, para 59.

[15]Sabel v. Puma, Case C-251/95, [1997] ECR I-6191, para 22.

[16]*Ibid*, para 23 (italics added). "Aural" has also been denoted "phonetic." See for instance MEGA Brands v. OHIM, Case C-182/14 P, [2015], para 31.

It has often been said that the average consumer as it is known today has its origin in *Gut Springenheide* residing in unfair competition law.[17] Not least, significant weight is attached to the decision in *Lloyd*, the first decision where the Court of Justice set out the characteristics of the average consumer in EU trademark law.[18] Whereas *Sabel* referred to the average consumer as nesting within the global appreciation test, it did not mention its characteristics that have shown to be paramount to applying the fiction in practice. In many ways, *Gut Springenheide* provided a significant steer to the future development of the average consumer on the distinction between law and fact and the characteristics of the average consumer.[19] *Gut Springenheide* turned on unfair competition law, specifically on a regulation on the promotion of eggs (the "Egg Regulation").[20] The Egg Regulation laid down certain mandatory rules relating to the information to be included on packs of eggs.[21] The regulation further stipulated some optional information allowed "on either inner or outer surfaces" of the packs, including "statements designed to promote sales, provided that such statements and the manner in which they are made *are not likely to mislead the purchaser*."[22] On its egg packs, Gut Springenheide had included the description "6-Korn – 10 frische Eier" (meaning "six-grain – 10 fresh eggs"). The Court of Justice paraphrased the three questions posed by the German court into a question on how the Court of Justice would "define the concept of consumer to be used as a standard for determining whether a statement designed to promote sales of eggs is likely to mislead the purchaser."[23]

After referring to the prevention against misleading advertising,[24] the Court of Justice referred to its previous case law where it had considered "whether a description, trade mark or promotional text is misleading under the provisions of the Treaty or of secondary legislation." Some of the cases referred to by the court were *GB-Inno*, *Yves Rocher*, *Clinique* and *Mars*, all forming part of the early development

---

[17]See Chap. 8, footnote 1.

[18]As was clear from Chap. 8 there had been no consistency in the development by the Court of Justice of the average consumer in its cases before *Sabel*, specifically, in using the term "average consumer" and its assumed characteristics.

[19]Gut Springenheide and Tusky, Case C-210/96, [1998] ECR I-4657, para 37.

[20]Council Regulation (EEC) No 1907/90 of 26 June 1990 on certain marketing standards for eggs, [1990] OJ L173. This regulation was repealed by a regulation from 2006. I.e. the Council Regulation (EC) No 1028/2006 of 19 June 2006 on marketing standards for eggs, [2006] OJ L186/1 (see recital 2 of the regulation). Rules for implementing this regulation were laid down in Commission Regulation (EC) No 557/2007 of 23 May 2007 laying down detailed rules for implementing Council Regulation (EC) No 1028/2006 on marketing standards for eggs, [2007] OJ L132/5.

[21]Cf. art. 10(1) of the Egg Regulation.

[22]Cf. art. 10(2)(e) of the Egg Regulation (italics added).

[23]I.e., in breach of art. 10(2)(e) of the Egg Regulation. The questioning German court was the Federal Administrative Court (Bundesverwaltungsgericht).

[24]Gut Springenheide and Tusky, Case C-210/96, [1998] ECR I-4657, para 29.

of the average consumer pre *Sabel.*[25] Referring to those and other decisions, the court held that "in order to determine whether the description, trade mark or promotional description or statement in question was liable to mislead the purchaser, the Court took into account the *presumed expectations of an average consumer who is reasonably well-informed and reasonably observant and circumspect, without ordering an expert's report or commissioning a consumer research poll.*"[26]

Where earlier formulations of the average consumer and its characteristics had been hesitant, the formulation used by the Court of Justice in *Gut Springenheide* has since this decision been the mechanical phrasing used by the court in trademark law when "part of the public" has been deemed to be the average consumer. Most notably, the phrasing has found its way into the UCPD.[27] The Court of Justice in *Gut Springenheide* also allowed that "a national court might decide, in accordance with its own national law, to order an expert's opinion or commission a consumer research poll for the purpose of clarifying whether a promotional description or statement is misleading or not."[28] In its reference directly back to some of the historical decisions on developing the average consumer, the court in *Gut Springenheide* leapfrogged *Sabel.* One reason for this could be that the court in *Sabel* did not deal specifically with the characteristics of the average consumer, which have been addressed in many of the historical decisions.[29] The opinion of Mischo in *Gut Springenheide* and the court's decision are significant to the understanding of the characteristics of the average consumer and what has been termed "discounting."[30]

In *Lloyd*, the Court of Justice clearly tied the knot between *Sabel* and *Gut Springenheide* and added important clarification to those decisions. As with *Sabel*, *Lloyd* related to the use of trademarks on goods targeted at consumers, however, *Lloyd* related to interpreting the likelihood of confusion standard in infringement.[31] In *Lloyd*, the senior trademark owner had registered the trademark LLOYD for shoes in Germany and sought to prevent the junior owner from using its mark LOINT'S for shoes and footwear in Germany, claiming likelihood of confusion. Specifically, the senior owner claimed "that 'Loint's' is likely to be confused with 'Lloyd' because of the aural similarity of the two signs and because of the enhanced distinctive character

---

[25]I.e., reference to respectively, GB-INNO, Case C-362/88, [1990] ECR I-667, Schutzverband v. Yves Rocher, Case C-126/91, [1993] ECR I-2361, Verband Sozialer Wettbewerb v. Clinique Laboratoires, Case C-315/92, [1994] ECR I-317 and Verein gegen Unwesen in Handel und Gewerbe v. Mars, Case C-470/93, [1995] ECR I-1923. Gut Springenheide and Tusky, Case C-210/96, [1998] ECR I-4657, para 30. See Chap. 8.

[26]Gut Springenheide and Tusky, Case C-210/96, [1998] ECR I-4657, para 31 (italics added).

[27]Recital 18 of the UCPD. For other areas where this phrasing has also been applied, see Chap. 1, Sect. 1.5.5.

[28]Gut Springenheide and Tusky, Case C-210/96, [1998] ECR I-4657, paras 35 and 37. See also Chap. 11, Sect. 11.2.2.

[29]See Chap. 8.

[30]See Chap. 11, Sect. 11.2.

[31]Cf. art. 5(1)(b) of the TM Directive 1989 (art. 10(2)(b) of the TM Directive).

of the 'Lloyd' mark, which arises from the absence of descriptive elements and from the high degree of recognition of the mark."[32] One question posed by the national court related to interpreting "similarity" of the senior and junior marks as part of the likelihood of confusion standard, including the aural similarity.[33]

Initially, the Court of Justice demarcated its competences by holding that "it is for the national court to rule on the question whether there exists between the two marks at issue in the main proceedings a likelihood of confusion within the meaning of the [1989 TM] Directive."[34] The court held that included in the legal assessment within its competence are "the criteria to be applied in assessing the likelihood of confusion within the meaning of Article 5(1)(b) of the Directive [art. 10(2)(b) of the TM Directive]."[35] As part of the likelihood of confusion standard, the court referred to the global appreciation test as laid down in *Sabel*.[36] Based on the recitals of EU trademark legislation, the court reiterated its finding in *Canon* from September 1998 that as part of the global appreciation test there is "some *interdependence between the relevant factors*, and in particular a similarity between the trade marks and between the goods or services covered. Accordingly, a lesser degree of similarity between those goods or services may be offset by a greater degree of similarity between the marks, and vice versa."[37]

The Court of Justice repeated the elements of the global appreciation test as set out in *Sabel*, finding that the average consumer was the relevant public.[38] Immediately after this, the court paired its finding on the global appreciation test in *Sabel* with its finding in *Gut Springenheide,* holding that "[f]or the purposes of that global appreciation, the average consumer of the category of products concerned is deemed to be reasonably well-informed and reasonably observant and circumspect."[39] Then the court added to *Sabel* some important aspects to the global appreciation test and the framing of the average consumer. Thus, the court stated that "the average consumer only *rarely has the chance to make a direct comparison between the different marks* but must place his trust in the imperfect picture of them that he has kept in his mind." In addition, that "[i]t should also be borne in mind that the average

---

[32]Lloyd Schuhfabrik Meyer v. Klijsen Handel BV, Case C-342/97, [1998] ECR I-3819, (opinion of AG Jacobs), para 4.

[33]Lloyd Schuhfabrik Meyer v. Klijsen Handel BV, Case C-342/97, [1998] ECR I-3819, para 10 (first question).

[34]*Ibid*, para 11.

[35]*Ibid*, para 12.

[36]*Ibid*, para 19.

[37]*Ibid* (italics added) referring to Canon Kabushiki Kaisha v. Metro-Goldwyn-Mayer. Case C-39/97, [1998] ECR I-5507, para 17.

[38]Lloyd Schuhfabrik Meyer v. Klijsen Handel BV, Case C-342/97, [1998] ECR I-3819, para 25 referring to Sabel v. Puma, Case C-251/95, [1997] ECR I-6191, para 23.

[39]Lloyd Schuhfabrik Meyer v. Klijsen Handel BV, Case C-342/97, [1998] ECR I-3819, para 26 referring to Gut Springenheide and Tusky, Case C-210/96, [1998] ECR I-4657, para 31.

consumer's *level of attention is likely to vary according to the category of goods or services in question.*"[40]

Although the Court of Justice in *Lloyd* provided a valuable interpretation of the likelihood of confusion standard and the average consumer, it was not explicit on the relationship between registration and infringement disputes.[41] However, one year after *Lloyd* in *Marca Mode v. Adidas* on the likelihood of confusion standard, the court clarified the relationship. After stating that the "[s]ubstantially identical terms are used"[42] in the provisions on registration and infringement, and "[a]ccordingly, *that* interpretation [in *Sabel*] must also apply" to infringement.[43] As for the relationship between the TM Regulation and TM Directive, the Court of Justice addressed this in the appeal decision *Ruiz-Picasso v. OHIM*. Stating the law in the decision, the court found that the provisions of the directive on the likelihood of confusion in registration and infringement "are formulated in terms essentially identical to" those of the regulation[44] and then the court applied as precedents *Sabel* and *Lloyd*.[45] Essentially, in his opinion of *Marca Mode v. Adidas* from January 2000 Jacobs expressed the current state of the law on the relationship between the likelihood of confusion standard under the TM Regulation and the TM Directive. Thus, Jacobs held that "[i]t is clearly appropriate that the provisions of the Directive should be interpreted in the same way as the corresponding provisions of the Regulation."[46]

10.2.3   How They Are Relevant Today

The importance of *Sabel*, *Gut Springenheide* and *Lloyd* to the development of the likelihood of confusion standard, including the global appreciation test and the average consumer, can hardly be underestimated. One common denominator of the decisions is that the consumer was very much in focus. Being preliminary

---

[40]Lloyd Schuhfabrik Meyer v. Klijsen Handel BV, Case C-342/97, [1998] ECR I-3819, para 26 (italics added).

[41]I.e. the court did not did not explicitly confirm Jacobs' preceding opinion that *Sabel* "provides much of the guidance required by the referring court [in *Lloyd*]" on provisions substantially identical. Lloyd Schuhfabrik Meyer v. Klijsen Handel BV, Case C-342/97, [1998] ECR I-3819, (opinion of AG Jacobs), para 15. See also Lloyd Schuhfabrik Meyer v. Klijsen Handel BV, Case C-342/97, [1998] ECR I-3819, para 4. *Sabel* related to the likelihood of confusion in registration and *Lloyd* to infringement.

[42]Marca Mode v. Adidas, Case C-425/98, [2000] ECR I-4861, para 26.

[43]*Ibid*, paras 27-28 (italics added).

[44]Ruiz-Picasso v. OHIM, Case C-361/04 P, [2006] ECR I-643, para 4.

[45]See also Matratzen Concord v. OHIM I, Case C-3/03 P, [2004] ECR I-3657, para 27, and Medion v. Thomson Multimedia, Case C-120/04, [2005] ECR I-8551, para 27 and the opinion of Jacobs, Medion v. Thomson Multimedia Sales, Case C-120/04, [2005] ECR I-8551, (opinion of AG Jacobs), para 18 and footnote 5 of the opinion.

[46]Marca Mode v. Adidas, Case C-425/98, [2000] ECR I-4861, para 35.

rulings, the decisions were naturally framed by the questions posed by the referring courts wanting clarification on interpreting the "likelihood of confusion" of "the relevant *public*" (*Sabel* and *Lloyd*) and the interpretation of a provision in unfair competition law on what constitutes "likely to mislead the *purchaser*" (*Gut Springenheide*), with "*public*" and "*purchaser*" being represented by consumers. In *Sabel* and *Lloyd* the relevant goods were goods targeted for sale to consumers, respectively such goods as clothing and shoes. In *Gut Springenheide* the consumer was the "purchaser" being protected when buying eggs. All the mentioned goods are mundane in the sense that probably most people can perceive a scenario of purchasing them.

In essence, the average consumer was introduced into trademark law in *Sabel* and merged with the findings in *Gut Springenheide*, somewhat based on the historical decisions on the average consumer. The merger was concluded in *Lloyd* where the average consumer with its characteristics well-known to European trademark law today was set out. After *Lloyd*, *Gut Springenheide* has had little importance as independent ground for interpreting the likelihood of confusion standard. This is not least so since the global appreciation test in European trademark law as paired with the average consumer is unique to this area of law. Even so, for instance *Gut Springenheide* has been referred to independently by the Court of Justice on the role of the average consumer in interpreting "distinctiveness" in *Phillips v. Remington*.[47] and *Proctor Gamble*.[48] On a national level, independent references to *Gut Springenheide* as an aid for interpreting the likelihood of confusion standard are found in the UK in *Interflora EWCA III*[49] and recently in Norway in *NYX v. Laboratoire Nuxe*.[50]

Overall, *Sabel* and *Lloyd* today form the precedents on interpreting the likelihood of confusion standard, including the global appreciation test and the average consumer. Obviously, this is clear from subsequent decisions of the Court of Justice referring directly to *Sabel* and *Lloyd*. Due to the way the court applies its precedents, though, it is not always clear from more recent decisions that they are based on *Sabel* and *Lloyd*. However, when the paths of precedents are followed backwards in time, this appears to be the case. One recent example illustrating this is the appeal decision *Shoe Branding v. Adidas* from February 2016.[51] The junior owner (Shoe Branding) sought to register a mark consisting of two stripes as an EU trademark for "footwear." The senior trademark owner (Adidas) opposed its application, *inter alia*, on the grounds of likelihood of confusion with its three-stripe trademark and that its mark had a reputation. At the EUIPO Board of Appeal, the registration was upheld,

---

[47]Koninklijke Philips Electronics v. Remington Consumer Products, Case C-299/99, [2002] ECR I-5475, para 63.

[48]Proctor Gamble, in joined cases C-468/01 P to C-472/01 P, [2004] ECR I-5173, para 57.

[49]Interflora v. Marks & Spencer, [2014] EWCA Civ 1403, (referred to in the main text as "Interflora EWCA III"), para 117.

[50]NYX v. Laboratoire Nuxe, TOSLO-2014-79765, [2015], NODC, p. 5.

[51]Shoe Branding v. Adidas, Case C-396/15 P, [2016].

but the decision was annulled by the General Court, thus rendering the junior mark unregistrable. Central to the dispute was the interpretation of the likelihood of confusion standard, including the average consumer, and its application. As part of interpreting the standard, the Court of Justice referred to the global appreciation test and its factors as its "settled case-law." In doing so, the court referred to *nfon v. Fon Wireless* "and the case-law cited here."[52] This decision referred to *OHIM v. Shaker*[53] and *Aceites del Sur-Coosur v. Koipe Corporación*.[54] Both decisions referred to *Medion v. Thomson Multimedia*[55] and *Matratzen Concord v. Hukla*.[56] *OHIM v. Shaker* also referred to *Marca Mode v. Adidas*[57] and *Mülhens v. OHIM*.[58]

Except for *Marca Mode v. Adidas, Mülhens v. OHIM*,[59] *nfon v. Fon Wireless* and *Shoe Branding v. Adidas*, all the mentioned decisions referred to *Lloyd* para 18. All decisions, except for *nfon v. Fon Wireless* and *Shoe Branding v. Adidas*, also referred to *Sabel* para 22, laying out the global appreciation test referred to in *Lloyd* para 18. The earliest of the decisions, *Marca Mode v. Adidas* issued one year after *Lloyd*,[60] included no references to *Lloyd*. One simple explanation for the lacking reference could be that Jacobs in his opinion *Marca Mode v. Adidas* did not include a reference to *Lloyd* specifically on the point of the global appreciation test. Besides serving as a rather confusing web of decisions, the above paths of precedents

---

[52]Specifically, the court stated that it should "be borne in mind that, according to *settled case-law*, the existence of a likelihood of confusion on the part of the public must be appreciated globally, taking into account all factors relevant to the circumstances of the case. That global assessment, in relation to the visual, aural or conceptual similarity of the marks in question, as in the present case, must be based on the overall impression given by the marks, bearing in mind, in particular, their distinctive and dominant components." Shoe Branding v. Adidas, Case C-396/15 P, [2016], para 26 (italics added).

[53]OHIM v. Shaker, Case C-334/05 P, [2007] ECR I-4529 referred to by nfon v. Fon Wireless, Case C-193/13 P, [2014], para 36.

[54]Aceites del Sur-Coosur v. Koipe Corporación, Case C-498/07 P, [2009] ECR I-7371 referred to by nfon v. Fon Wireless, Case C-193/13 P, [2014], para 36. *Aceites del Sur-Coosur v. Koipe Corporación* also referred to *OHIM v. Shaker*, para 34. Aceites del Sur-Coosur v. Koipe Corporación, Case C-498/07 P, [2009] ECR I-7371, para 59.

[55]I.e., Medion v. Thomson Multimedia, Case C-120/04, [2005] ECR I-8551, para 27, referred to by Aceites del Sur-Coosur v. Koipe Corporación, Case C-498/07 P, [2009] ECR I-7371, para 59 and OHIM v. Shaker, Case C-334/05 P, [2007] ECR I-4529, para 34.

[56]Matratzen Concord v. OHIM I, Case C-3/03 P, [2004] ECR I-3657, para 28, referred to by Aceites del Sur-Coosur v. Koipe Corporación, Case C-498/07 P, [2009] ECR I-7371, para 59 and OHIM v. Shaker, Case C-334/05 P, [2007] ECR I-4529, para 34.

[57]Marca Mode v. Adidas, Case C-425/98, [2000] ECR I-4861, para 40 referred to by OHIM v. Shaker, Case C-334/05 P, [2007] ECR I-4529, para 34.

[58]Mülhens v. OHIM, Case C-206/04 P, [2006] ECR I-2717, para 18 referred to by OHIM v. Shaker, Case C-334/05 P, [2007] ECR I-4529, para 34. At the mentioned paragraph, Mülhens v. OHIM also referred to paragraph 40 of the earlier Marca Mode v. Adidas, Case C-425/98, [2000] ECR I-4861.

[59]It should be mentioned that although *Mülhens v. OHIM* did not refer to *Lloyd* on the global appreciation, it referred to both *Sabel* and *Lloyd* on the specific factors of the test. See Mülhens v. OHIM, Case C-206/04 P, [2006] ECR I-2717, para 19.

[60]*Lloyd* was issued 22 June 1999 and *Marca Mode v. Adidas* 22 June 2000.

illustrate how the Court of Justice has developed the global appreciation test and that the test as interpreted in 2016 in *Shoe Branding v. Adidas* has its origin in *Sabel* and *Lloyd*.

In other areas, it is possible to trace similar paths of precedents backwards starting from *Shoe Branding v. Adidas*. Hence, the specific factors of the global appreciation test also lead back to *Sabel* and *Lloyd*, i.e. "[t]hat global assessment, in relation to the visual, aural or conceptual similarity of the marks in question, as in the present case, must be based on the overall impression given by the marks, bearing in mind, in particular, their distinctive and dominant components."[61] Besides the decisions mentioned above on the global appreciation test and its components, many other decisions by the Court of Justice have referred to the test.[62]

In *Lloyd*, the Court of Justice found that the legal assessment of the facts based on the global assessment test factors was to be conducted by the national courts. Subsequently, the court has expanded on the distinction between law and fact in this matter. It was thus stated by the court in *Union Investment v. OHIM* that "[w]hereas *the evaluation of those factors is an issue of fact* that cannot be reviewed by the Court [of Justice], failure to take all of those factors into account, on the other hand, constitutes *an error of law*."[63] In *Barbara Becker v. Harman*, the court found that the General Court had "erred in law in basing its assessment of the conceptual similarity of the marks on general considerations taken from the case-law without analysing all the relevant factors specific to the case, in disregard of the requirement of an overall assessment of the likelihood of confusion, taking account of all factors relevant to the circumstances of the case, and based on the overall impression produced by the marks at issue."[64] These findings have more recently been con-firmed by the court in *Fetim v. OHIM*.[65] Although the findings of the Court of Justice on the distinction between law and fact after *Lloyd* are made in the court's capacity as appeal court to the General Court, they are more broadly applicable. This is so since the role of the Court of Justice is interpreting the law, be it as part of the

---

[61]Shoe Branding v. Adidas, Case C-396/15 P, [2016], para 26, nfon v. Fon Wireless, Case C-193/13 P, [2014], para 36, Aceites del Sur-Coosur v. Koipe Corporación, Case C-498/07 P, [2009] ECR I-7371, para 60, OHIM v. Shaker, Case C-334/05 P, [2007] ECR I-4529, para 35, Mülhens v. OHIM, Case C-206/04 P, [2006] ECR I-2717, para 19, Medion v. Thomson Multimedia, Case C-120/04, [2005] ECR I-8551, para 28, Matratzen Concord v. OHIM I, Case C-3/03 P, [2004] ECR I-3657, para 29, Lloyd Schuhfabrik Meyer v. Klijsen Handel BV, Case C-342/97, [1998] ECR I-3819, para 25 and Sabel v. Puma, Case C-251/95, [1997] ECR I-6191, para 23.

[62]For instance, Ruiz-Picasso v. OHIM, Case C-361/04 P, [2006] ECR I-643, paras 18-19, Castellblanch v. OHIM, Case C-131/06 P, [2007], para 55, Barbara Becker v. Harman, Case C-51/09 P, [2010] ECR I-5805, paras 32-33, Calvin Klein v. OHIM, Case C-254/09 P, [2010] ECR I-7989, paras 44-45, Bimbo SA v. OHIM, Case C-591/12 P, [2014], para 21 and BGW Beratungs-Gesellschaft v. Bodo Scholz, Case C-20/14, [2015], para 35.

[63]Union Investment v. OHIM, Case C-317/10 P, [2011] ECR I-5471, para 45 (italics added) referring to Barbara Becker v. Harman, Case C-51/09 P, [2010] ECR I-5805, para 40.

[64]*Ibid.*

[65]Fetim v. OHIM, Case C-190/15 P, [2015], para 37.

preliminary rulings procedure or as appeal court.[66] The distinction between law and fact is also a reoccurring issue more narrowly related to the characteristics of the average consumer as part of contextualisation.[67]

10.2.4   The General Court

It follows from the above findings that the likelihood of confusion standard, including the global appreciation test factors and the relevant public, are part of *the law*. As such, the General Court is bound to follow decisions where the Court of Justice, as the ultimate interpreter of EU law, has interpreted the global appreciation test. Although the General Court has applied the legal principles laid down by the Court of Justice in *Sabel* and *Lloyd* on the global appreciation test, it has built on the principles inconsistently. The General Court practice on the likelihood of confusion standard is massive. In its decisions, the General Court tends to make "90 degrees references" to its own decisions, using precedents at a horizontal level appearing as its own precedents, but when following the reference backwards in time, the precedents appear to be vertical precedents derived from *Sabel* and *Lloyd*, and other early decisions of the Court of Justice. For instance, in *Claudia Oberhauser v. OHIM*, an early decision of the General Court from October 2002 on the likelihood of confusion standard, the court referred to the findings of the Court of Justice on the global appreciation test and applying the average consumer of *Sabel* and *Lloyd*.[68]

In *Laboratorios RTB v. OHIM* from July 2003, the General Court built on its findings in *Claudia Oberhauser v. OHIM* and the Court of Justice's findings in *Sabel* and *Lloyd*.[69] The background of the dispute was the junior mark owner (Giorgio Beverly Hills) seeking to register GIORGIO BEVERLY HILLS for numerous classes of goods, including class 3 of the Nice Agreement. The opposition to the registration was brought by Laboratorios based on senior registrations in Spain of

---

[66]See Chap. 4, Sect. 4.3.

[67]This issue is addressed in Chap. 11.

[68]Hence, the General Court held that "the likelihood of confusion on the part of the public must be assessed globally, taking into account all factors relevant to the circumstances of the case" and referred to Sabel v. Puma, Case C-251/95, [1997] ECR I-6191, para 16, Lloyd Schuhfabrik Meyer v. Klijsen Handel BV, Case C-342/97, [1999] ECR I-3819, para 18 and Marca Mode v. Adidas, Case C-425/98, [2000] ECR I-4861, para 40. *Claudia Oberhauser v. OHIM*, Case T-104/01, [2002] ECR II-4359, para 26. In addition, it was held by the General Court in *Claudia Oberhauser v. OHIM* that "the perception of marks in the mind of the average consumer of the goods or services in question plays a decisive role in the global assessment of the likelihood of confusion. The average consumer normally perceives a mark as a whole and does not proceed to analyse its various details." On this the General Court referred to Sabel v. Puma, Case C-251/95, [1997] ECR I-6191, para 23 and Lloyd Schuhfabrik Meyer v. Klijsen Handel BV, Case C-342/97, [1999] ECR I-3819, para 25. Claudia Oberhauser v. OHIM, Case T-104/01, [2002] ECR II-4359, para 28.

[69]Laboratorios RTB v. OHIM, Case T-162/01, [2003] ECR II-2821.

four figurative trademarks all containing the word "giorgi" against part of the goods covered by class 3 of the Nice Agreement, i.e. certain toiletries.[70] The status of the case before reaching the General Court was that the opposition against the registration had been dismissed. The reason for the dismissal by most recently the OHIM Board of Appeal was that despite identity between goods there was no likelihood of confusion between the marks. An essential part of the dispute turned on consumer perception. The senior owner claimed that the word "giorgi" was the "predominant component" of its trademarks and caused a "strong likelihood of confusion."[71] Furthermore, that the word was the "component which the consumer perceives with the greatest force" and "that most forcefully distinguishes the applicant's [the senior owner's] goods."[72] It was also claimed that consumers only use the abbreviation "giorgio" and leave out "Beverly Hills."[73] Based on a further analysis of the "visual and phonetic similarities between the conflicting marks, together with the fact that they designate goods within the same class, namely Class 3," the senior owner concluded that the conflicting marks "are liable to create a likelihood of confusion in the mind of the consumer."[74] OHIM contested the assessment, e.g. holding that consumers do not merely ask orally for the goods, and hence the arguments on the use in the market of the marks "does not reflect the way in which the market operates."[75]

When the General Court in *Laboratorios RTB v. OHIM* built on the law as stated by the Court of Justice in *Sabel* and *Lloyd*[76] and by itself in *Claudia Oberhauser v. OHIM*, it did so over three paragraphs essentially summing up the status of the global appreciation test and the use of the average consumer.[77] The General Court found that due to the registration of the senior marks in Spain "and that the goods in question are everyday consumer items, the targeted public by reference to which the likelihood of confusion must be assessed is composed of average consumers in

---

[70]Specifically, "[t]oilet soaps; perfumery, essential oils, cosmetics, hair lotions; dentifrices, deodorants for personal use and preparations for the cleaning, care, beautification of the skin, scalp and hair." *Ibid*, para 5.

[71]*Ibid*, para 16.

[72]*Ibid*, para 17.

[73]*Ibid*, para 20.

[74]*Ibid*, para 22.

[75]*Ibid*, para 26.

[76]The General Court in *Laboratorios RTB v. OHIM* also built on the decisions of the Court of Justice. *Ibid*, paras 30-33. The General Court referred to Canon Kabushiki Kaisha v. Metro-Goldwyn-Mayer. Case C-39/97, [1998] ECR I-5507, paras 16-17, where the Court of Justice built on its finding in Sabel v. Puma, Case C-251/95, [1997] ECR I-6191, para 22 and Marca Mode v. Adidas, Case C-425/98, [2000] ECR I-4861, para 40 where the Court of Justice also built on its finding in *Sabel* para 22 and *Canon* paras 17 and 19.

[77]Laboratorios RTB v. OHIM, Case T-162/01, [2003] ECR II-2821, paras 30-33.

Spain."[78] After applying the global appreciation test, the General Court concluded that there was no likelihood of confusion between the two marks.[79]

Laboratorios RTB v. OHIM is included in some length since it has formed an important precedent in the General Court case law on the likelihood of confusion standard since it was handed down until today. It is unclear why this is so. On its central points of legal interpretation, the decision adds nothing that had not already been laid down by the Court of Justice in *Sabel* and *Lloyd*. Adding to those decisions, the General Court included two references to *Claudia Oberhauser v. OHIM* that were merely circular references since the General Court had already included references to *Sabel* and *Lloyd* identical to the references to the decisions in *Claudia Oberhauser v. OHIM*.[80]

In sum, neither *Claudia Oberhauser v. OHIM* nor *Laboratorios RTB v. OHIM* added anything to the legal interpretation of the likelihood of confusion standard and the understanding of the average consumer. One thing the latter decision did add though, was that when dealing with "everyday consumer goods" the relevant public is the average consumer. This, however, as dealt with in the following chapter, is not a point in law but in fact. It is unclear why the General Court applied *Laboratorios RTB v. OHIM* as a precedent of law in many of its subsequent decisions.[81] Since

---

[78] *Ibid*, para 34.

[79] *Ibid*, para 54.

[80] Hence, the General Court in *Laboratorios RTB v. OHIM*, para 30 referred to Claudia Oberhauser v. OHIM, Case T-104/01, [2002] ECR II-4359, para 25 of Claudia Oberhauser v. OHIM, Case T-104/01, [2002] ECR II-4359 and in para 31 referred to *Claudia Oberhauser v. OHIM* para 26. *Claudia Oberhauser v. OHIM* para 25 referred to Canon Kabushiki Kaisha v. Metro-Goldwyn-Mayer. Case C-39/97, [1998] ECR I-5507, para 29 and Lloyd Schuhfabrik Meyer v. Klijsen Handel BV, Case C-342/97, [1999] ECR I-3819, para 17. On *Claudia Oberhauser v. OHIM* para 26, see footnote 68 above.

[81] On decisions not appealed to the Court of Justice. See for instance on goods: Koffiebranderij en Theehandel v. OHIM, Case T-66/03, [2004] ECR II-1765, para 21, 2004 July 13: Samar v. OHIM, Case T-115/03, [2004] ECR II-2939, para 29, New Look v. OHIM, Joined cases T-117/03 to T-119/03 and T-171/03, [2004] ECR II-3471, para 24, Wassen International v. OHIM, Case T-312/03, [2005] ECR II-2897, para 27, Cabel Hall Citrus v. OHIM, Case T-488/07, [2010], para 27, Ergo Versicherungsgruppe v. OHIM, Case T-220/09, [2011] ECR II-237, para 15, Infocit v. OHIM, Case T-85/14, [2015], para 26, Verus Eood v. OHIM, Case T-576/13, [2015], para 17, Iglotex v. OHIM, Case T-282/13, [2015], para 23, LG Developpement v. EUIPO, Case T-160/15, [2016], para 15, Nanu-Nana Joachim Hoepp v. EUIPO, Case T-39/16, [2017], para 55, Enoitalia v. EUIPO, Case T-707/16, [2018], para 16 and Republic of Cyprus v. EUIPO II, Case T-847/16, [2018], para 21. On services and both goods and services: Zitro IP v. OHIM, Case T-665/13, [2015], para 17, 1&1 Internet v. OHIM, Case T-61/15, [2016], para 19, Auyantepui v. EUIPO, Case T-8/15, [2016], para 16, Messe Friedrichshafen v. EUIPO, Case T-224/16, [2017], para 31, Apax Partners UK v. EUIPO, Case T-209/16, [2017], para 19 and Deutsche Post v. EUIPO, Case T-537/15, [2018], para 26. The same picture emerges in decisions appealed to the Court of Justice. For some recent examples see: Gat Microencapsulation v. OHIM, Case T-720/13, [2015], para 24, Meica Ammerländische Fleischwarenfabrik v. OHIM, Case T-247/14, [2016], para 33, Novomatic v. EUIPO, Case T-326/14, [2016], para 43, Banca Monte dei Paschi di Siena and Wise Dialog Bank, Case T-84/16, [2017], para 55 and Moscow Confectionery Factory v. EUIPO, Case T-795/16, [2018], 17.

there seems to be no legal explanation for this, it has created a somewhat inconsistent development of the average consumer in the decisions of the General Court. The court's continued emphasis on *Laboratorios RTB v. OHIM* on the surface indicates a significance of the decision which fades, though, since its legal interpretation merely masks the contribution of *Sabel* and *Lloyd*. Adding to the lacking significance of the decision is that it was not tried by the Court of Justice.[82]

Other comparable examples of the General Court using its own precedents exist. Thus, on the elements of the global appreciation test the General Court has often referred to *Phillips-Van Heusen v. OHIM* from October 2003.[83] It should be mentioned that the General Court starting from *Giorgio Beverly Hills v. OHIM*[84] referred to *OHIM v. Shaker*[85] of the Court of Justice instead of *Phillips-Van Heusen v. OHIM* on the factors of the global appreciation test.[86] Also with particular relevance to the contextualisation of the average consumer, the General Court has

---

[82]This was also the case with Claudia Oberhauser v. OHIM, Case T-104/01, [2002] ECR II-4359.

[83]Hence, the General Court in *Phillips-Van Heusen v. OHIM* stated that "it is clear from the case-law of the Court of Justice that the global assessment of the likelihood of confusion, as far as concerns the visual, aural or conceptual similarity of the marks in question, must be based on the overall impression given by the marks, bearing in mind, *inter alia*, their distinctive and dominant components." The General Court based its findings on Sabel v. Puma, Case C-251/95, [1997] ECR I-6191, para 23 and Lloyd Schuhfabrik Meyer v. Klijsen Handel BV, Case C-342/97, [1999] ECR I-3819, para 25. Phillips-Van Heusen v. OHIM, Case T-292/01, [2003] ECR II-4335, para 47. This finding has been referred to by the General Court in many decisions. As for decisions from the General Court not appealed to the Court of Justice on goods, see for instance: Grupo El Prado Cervera v. OHIM, Case T-117/02, [2004] ECR II-2073, para 44, Samar v. OHIM, Case T-115/03, [2004] ECR II-2939, para 32, Lidl Stiftung & Co. v. OHIM (REWE-Zentral), Case T-296/02, [2005] ECR II-563, para 62, Vincenzo Fusco v. OHIM, Case T-185/03, [2005] ECR II-715, para 48, Wassen International v. OHIM, Case T-312/03, [2005] ECR II-2897, para 32, Mundipharma v. OHIM, Case T-256/04, [2007] ECR II-449, para 52, Cabel Hall Citrus v. OHIM, Case T-488/07, [2010], para 32 and Copernicus-Trademarks v. OHIM, Case T-684/13, [2015], para 60. On both goods and services: Grupo Sada v. OHIM, Case T-31/03, [2005] ECR II-1667, para 47, 2006 June 13, Inex v. OHIM, Case T-153/03, [2006] ECR II-1677, para 26, Volvo v. OHIM, Case T-434/07, [2009] ECR II-4415, para 30 On this point, *Volvo v. OHIM* referred to *Phillips-Van Heusen v. OHIM*, but also to *Inex v. OHIM*. I.e. Inex v. OHIM, Case T-153/03, [2006] ECR II-1677, para 26. A similar picture emerges in decisions appealed to the Court of Justice on goods: Ruiz-Picasso v. OHIM, Case T-185/02, [2004] ECR II-1739, para 53, Vitakraft-Werke Wührmann & Sohn v. OHIM, Case T-356/02, [2005] ECR II-3445, para 49, L'Oréal v. OHIM, Case T-112/03, [2005] ECR II-949, para 63 and Longevity Health Products v. OHIM, Case T-363/09, [2010], para 26. On services: TeleTech Holdings v. OHIM, Case T-288/03, [2005] ECR II-1767, para 83.

[84]Giorgio Beverly Hills v. OHIM (WHG), Case T-228/06, [2008], para 19.

[85]OHIM v. Shaker, Case C-334/05 P, [2007] ECR I-4529, para 35. One exception to this though is N & C Franchise v. EUIPO, Case T-792/16, [2017], para 29.

[86]See for instance, the General Court's decisions appealed to the Court of Justice on goods: New Yorker SHK Jeans v. OHIM, Case T-415/09, [2011], para 48, Clorox Company v. OHIM, Case T-135/11, [2012], para 22, WeserGold Getränkeindustrie, Case T-278/10, [2012], para 43, Lancôme v. OHIM, Case T-204/10, [2012], para 22, Bimbo v. OHIM, Case T-569/10, [2013], para 55, Tetra Pharm (1997) v. EUIPO, Case T-441/16, [2017], para 38 and Moscow Confectionery Factory v. EUIPO, Case T-795/16, [2018], para 29. On services and both goods and services: Argo Group v. OHIM, Case T-247/12, [2014], para 32, Meica Ammerländische

often referred to *Mundipharma v. OHIM*.[87] Although neither *Phillips-Van Heusen v. OHIM* nor *Mundipharma v. OHIM* seem to add new law on the average consumer, the latter decision adds a significant aspect of contextualising the average consumer, and in this capacity it is dealt with in some depth in the following chapter.[88]

10.3   The Global Appreciation Test in a National Context

What has been stated above on the average consumer as part of a global appreciation test starting with *Sabel* built on what was already at the time known in the EU member states. Hence, when Jacobs in his opinion in *Sabel* addressed the principle of the "overall impression" expressed by the marks he stated: "The application of the principle that regard must be had to the overall impression conveyed by trade marks appears *to be common amongst Member States*; indeed that principle is perhaps self-evident."[89] Although an analysis of national case law before *Sabel* is outside the scope of this book, it is worth noticing, that national tests akin to the global appreciation test have been analysed intensively by national scholars before *Sabel*. All tests have involved fictions similar to the average consumer when they have been used to assess likelihood of confusion.

From a UK perspective, it has been mentioned referring to *Seixo v. Provezende* from 1866 that the average consumer in European trademark law seems to owe part of its origin to the UK law of passing off.[90] Analysing the requirements for infringement of registered trademarks under the likelihood of confusion standard in UK trademark law, Cornish stated in 1980 that with certain modifications the test was similar to that of passing off. Thus, decisive was "[t]he impressions created by the marks in terms of both sight and sound" which was to be "judged as they would

---

Fleischwarenfabrik v. OHIM, Case T-247/14, [2016], para 45 and Wise Dialog Bank, Case T-84/16, [2017], para 70.

[87]Without referring to *Lloyd*, the General Court has time and again referred to paragraph 42 from *Mundipharma v. OHIM* including a passage on the contextualisation of the average consumer: "As a preliminary point, it must be borne in mind that, in the global assessment of the likelihood of confusion, account should be taken of the average consumer of the category of products concerned, who is reasonably well informed and reasonably observant and circumspect. It should also be borne in mind that the average consumer's level of attention is likely to vary according to the category of goods or services in question (see, by analogy, Case C-342/97 *Lloyd Schuhfabrik Meyer* [1999] ECR I-3819, paragraphs 25 and 26)." Mundipharma v. OHIM, Case T-256/04, [2007] ECR II-449, para 42.

[88]See Chap. 11, Sect. 11.4.1.2, including the decisions mentioned in footnote 218.

[89]Sabel v. Puma, Case C-251/95, [1997] ECR I-6191, (opinion of AG Jacobs), para 59 (italics added). Later in his opinion Jacobs also stated that "[m]oreover, trade-mark protection in respect of conceptual similarity does not appear to be uncommon amongst Member States." *Ibid*, para 62. As addressed in Chap. 9, Sect. 9.3.2, the legislatures at the time had introduced the likelihood of confusion standard.

[90]See Chap. 9, Sect. 9.3.2.1.

be thought likely to strike customers in actual trade."[91] Furthermore, that the question was "what impact would the defendant's mark be likely to have on probable customers, given the expectations they already have and the amount of attention that they will pay."[92]

From a Nordic perspective, Nordic TM Proposal 1882 stated that when deciding "whether marks are so similar to be confused the overall impression should be decisive not the potential existing dissimilarities."[93] Decisive in this assessment is the perception of the "purchaser" and "public."[94] The principle of the "overall impression" and the relevance of the perception of the average consumer (or similar fictions) as applied in practice pre *Sabel* has been analysed in depth by Nordic scholars and it emerges from the literature that the principle is well established.[95] For instance, in a Swedish context Heiding stated in 1966 that

---

[91]Cornish pointed out that in infringement the actual use by the senior owner of its trademark did not matter in terms of trademark law whereas it did under passing off. Cornish, William R., 'Intellectual Property: Patents, Copyright, Trade Marks, Allied Rights', (1st edn, Sweet & Maxwell, 1981), p. 560. See similarly on registration, *ibid*, p. 530-532 (and the successor Cornish, William R., Llewelyn, David, and Alpin, Tanya, 'Intellectual Property: Patents, Copyright, Trademarks and Allied Rights', (8th edn, Sweet & Maxwell, 2013), p. 735-738) and White, T. A. Blanco, and Robin, Jacob, 'Kerly's Law of Trade Marks and Trade Names', (10th edn, Sweet & Maxwell, 1972), p. 174-175 (and the successor Mellor, James, David Llewelyn, Moody-Stuart, Thomas, *et al*, 'Kerly's Law of Trade Marks and Trade Names', (16th edn, Sweet & Maxwell, 2018), p. 426 and 589). The current scholarly accounts of trademark law deal with passing off and trademark law separately, and the likelihood of confusion standard is dealt with as distinct from passing off. This is not least so due to the influence of *Sabel* and the subsequent decisions introducing the global appreciation test. For an account of the distinction between passing off and trademark law in the UK, see Mellor, James, David Llewelyn, Moody-Stuart, Thomas, *et al*, 'Kerly's Law of Trade Marks and Trade Names', (16th edn, Sweet & Maxwell, 2018), p. 748.

[92]Cornish, William R., 'Intellectual Property: Patents, Copyright, Trade Marks, Allied Rights', (1st edn, Sweet & Maxwell, 1981), p. 486-487 (and the successor Cornish, William R., Llewelyn, David, and Alpin, Tanya, 'Intellectual Property: Patents, Copyright, Trademarks and Allied Rights', (8th edn, Sweet & Maxwell, 2013), p. 755-769). See also White, T. A. Blanco, and Robin, Jacob, 'Kerly's Law of Trade Marks and Trade Names', (10th edn, Sweet & Maxwell, 1972), chap. 17 (and the successor Mellor, James, David Llewelyn, Moody-Stuart, Thomas, *et al*, 'Kerly's Law of Trade Marks and Trade Names', (16th edn, Sweet & Maxwell, 2018), Chapter 3 and p. 588-603).

[93]In Danish: "hvorvidt Mærker ere hinanden saa lige, at de let kunne forvexles med hinanden, bør den afgjørende Vægt lægges paa Totalindtrykket og ikke paa de Uligheder, som muligt kunne findes." Nordic TM Proposal 1882, p. 41.

[94]In Danish: "Kjøber" and "Publikum."

[95]See among others, on Swedish law: Heiding, Sture, 'Om Registrerade Varumärken Och Inarbetade Kännetecken', (1st edn, Almqvist & Wiksells, 1946), p. 86-98, Heiding, Sture, 'Svensk Varumärkes Rätt', (3rd edn, Affärsekonomi, 1966), p. 40-51, Pherson, Lars, 'Varumärken från Konsumentsynpunkt: En Rättsvetenskaplig Studie', (1st edn, Liber Förlag, 1981), chapter 4 and Thommessen, Ø., 'Lovene om Varemerker og Fellesmerker av 3. Mars 1961', (1st edn, Gyldendal Norsk Forlag, 1961), p. 25-27 and p. 31-32. Danish law: Andreasen, Hardy, 'Varemærkeretten i Konkurrenceretlig Belysning. En Retssammenlignende Analyse Af Varemærkerettens Grundbegreber Og En Fremstilling Af Ejendomstetten Til Varemærker', (1st edn, Ejnar Munksgaard, 1948), 274-332, Carlsen, Rigmor, 'Varemærker : Registreringspraksis', (1st edn,

"differences in certain parts [of the marks]do not prevent that the marks are considered to be confusingly similar since it is a leading principle that confusing similarity has to be considered according to the *overall impression*."[96] In a Danish context analysing confusion, Andreasen in 1948 referred to the significance of the "fundamental doctrine denoted the doctrine of the *overall impression*."[97] Also in a Danish context, Koktvedgaard in 1988 described this principle as "sound and well but difficult to comply with"[98] since in practice the principle dictates that insignificant "differences in detail" should not be included, however, not dictating which elements are insignificant and hence not to be.[99] In a Norwegian context, Knopf stated in 1936 that "when deciding likelihood of confusion, ultimately the overall impression of the mark is decisive."[100] Based on an analysis of trademark law, including UK law and in particular Nordic law, Koktvedgaard stated in 1965 that "[i]n Nordic

---

Direktoratet for Patent- og Varemærkevæsenet, 1980), p. 48-62 (mainly on registration), Hude, Harry, and Olsen, Julie, 'Haandbog i Varemærkeret: Kommenteret Udgave Af Lov Om Varemærker Af 7. April 1936', (1st edn, Reitzel, 1945), p. 170-216 (registration) and 310-345 (infringement), Kobbernagel, Jan, 'Konkurrencens Retlige Regulering II: Mærkeretten', (1st edn, Nyt Nordisk Forlag, 1967), chapter 6, Koktvedgaard, Mogens, 'Konkurrenceprægede Immaterialretspositioner: Bidrag til Læren om de Lovbestemte Enerettigheder og Deres Forhold til den Almene Konkurrenceret', (1st edn, Juristforbundet, 1965), in particular p. 168-181, Koktvedgaard, Mogens, 'Lærebog i Immaterialret: Ophavsret, Fotoret, Patentret, Mønsterret, Varemærkeret', (1st edn, Jurist- og Økonomforbundets Forlag, 1988), p. 231-241 (and the successor, now Schovsbo, Jens, Rosenmeier, Morten and Petersen, Clement Salung, 'Immaterialret: Ophavsret, Patentret, Brugsmodelret, Designret, Varemærkeret', (5th edn, Jurist- og Økonomforbundets Forlag, 2018), p. 524-540), Koktvedgaard, Mogens, and Wallberg, Knud, 'Varemærkeloven af 6. Juni 1991 og Fællesmærkeloven af 6. Juni 1991 med Indledning og Kommentarer', (1st edn, Jurist- og Økonomforbundets Forlag, 1994), p. 23-28 (overall), p. 60-65 (infringement) and p. 117-127 (registration) (and the successor, now Wallberg, Knud and Ravn, Michael Francke, 'Varemærket: Varemærkeloven og Fællesmærkeloven Med Kommentarer', (5th edn, Jurist- og Økonomforbundets Forlag, 2017), p. 62-66 (overall), p. 161-178 (infringement) and p. 310-342 (registration)). Norwegian law: Knoph, Ragnar, 'Åndsretten', (1st edn, Nationaltrykkeriet, 1936), p. 454-459, Lassen, Birger Stuevold, 'Oversikt Over Norsk Varemerkerett', (2nd edn, Universitetsforlaget, 1997), chapter 11 (generally on confusion), chapter 12 (on confusion between the products) and chapter 13 (on confusion between the marks) (and the successor Lassen, Birger Stuevold and Stenvik, Are, 'Kjennetegnsrett', (3rd edn, Universitetsforlaget, 2011), same chapter numbers).

[96]In Swedish: "Skiljaktighet i vissa delar hindrar ej att märkena äro att anse som förväxlingsbara, ty en ledande grundsats är att man skall bedöma den förväxlingsbara likheten efter totalintrycket." Heiding, Sture, 'Svensk Varumärkes Rätt', (3rd edn, Affärsekonomi, 1966), p. 42.

[97]In Danish: "den fundamentale Læresætning, der benævnes *Helhedsgrundsætningen*." Andreasen, Hardy, 'Varemærkeretten i Konkurrenceretlig Belysning. En Retssammenlignende Analyse Af Varemærkerettens Grundbegreber Og En Fremstilling Af Ejendomstetten Til Varemærker', (1st edn, Ejnar Munksgaard, 1948), p. 284.

[98]In Danish: "sundt og godt, men vanskeligt at efterleve." Koktvedgaard, Mogens, 'Lærebog i Immaterialret: Ophavsret, Fotoret, Patentret, Mønsterret, Varemærkeret', (1st edn, Jurist- og Økonomforbundets Forlag, 1988), p. 236.

[99]In Danish: "detailforskelle." *Ibid.*

[100]In Norwegian: "Det er helhedsindtrykket av merket som til syvende og sidst blir avgjørende for forvekslingsmuligheten." Knoph, Ragnar, 'Åndsretten', (1st edn, Nationaltrykkeriet, 1936), p. 456.

and foreign law [including UK law] it is the normal understanding that the confusion test of trademark law has to be made on the basis of *the presumed reaction of the relevant normal/ordinary/average consumer.*"[101]

The global appreciation test, including the prominence of the average consumer, as manifested in *Sabel* and the subsequent decisions has solidified as such in national trademark practice. As is clear from the historical scholarly accounts just given, the test has not been introduced as a piece of law different from what was already known to national law pre *Sabel*.[102]

10.3.1   England and Wales

As it has been pointed out, the UK trademark law closely follows that of the EU.[103] This includes the global appreciation test. For instance, in *O2 v. Hutchison* on certain telecommunications services there was disagreement between the parties on the similarity of the mark and the sign[104] but agreement on the identity between the services.[105] Stipulating the law on likelihood of confusion, Lewison J[106] agreed with the counsels (one of which was Arnold QC, now Justice)[107] on the elements to be considered in globally testing the likelihood of confusion. Also, that an essential part

---

[101]In Danish: "Det er den almindelige opfattelse i nordisk og fremmed ret, at varemærkerettens forvexlingsprøve skal foretages på basis af *den antagelige reaktion hos vedkommende normalforbruger.*" The Danish word "normal" translates into the English words "normal," "ordinary," and "average." Koktvedgaard, Mogens, 'Konkurrenceprægede Immaterialretspositioner: Bidrag til Læren om de Lovbestemte Enerettigheder og Deres Forhold til den Almene Konkurrenceret', (1st edn, Juristforbundet, 1965), p. 177.

[102]The more specific judicial development of the average consumer, including its contextualisation, is analysed in the following chapter.

[103]See Chap. 9, Sect. 9.3.2.1.

[104]O2 v. Hutchison, [2006] EWHC 534 (Ch), paras 107-120.

[105]*Ibid*, para 121.

[106]Now Lord Justice with the UK Court of Appeal.

[107]Now Justice with the UK High Court.

of the test was the perception of the average consumer.[108] Jacob LJ in the UK Court of Appeal did not as such challenge this finding. Interestingly though, Lewison J left out the central reference to the varying attention of the average consumer as set out in *Lloyd*. Approximately 6 years later in 2012, Kitchin LJ in *Specsavers v. Asda* on optician's services also gave a similar summarising account of the elements to be included in the global appreciation test. With slight modifications, the elements were

---

[108]"Both Mr Arnold and Mr Hobbs agreed on the approach that the court should take in assessing the likelihood of confusion. They each subscribed to the following propositions, which I accept as accurately summarising the law:

  i) "the likelihood of confusion must be appreciated globally, taking account of all relevant factors;" [Sabel v. Puma, Case C-251/95, [1997] ECR I-6191, para 22];

  ii) the matter must be judged through the eyes of the average consumer of the goods/services in question; Sabel v. Puma, Case C-251/95, [1997] ECR I-6191, para 23; who is deemed to be reasonably well informed and reasonably circumspect and observant - but who rarely has the chance to make direct comparisons between marks and must instead rely upon the imperfect picture of them he has kept in his mind; [Lloyd Schuhfabrik Meyer v. Klijsen Handel BV, Case C-342/97, [1999] ECR I-3819, para 27];

  iii) the average consumer normally perceives a mark as a whole and does not proceed to analyse its various details; [Sabel v. Puma, Case C-251/95, [1997] ECR I-6191, para 23];

  iv) the visual, aural and conceptual similarities of the marks must therefore be assessed by reference to the overall impressions created by the marks bearing in mind their distinctive and dominant components; [Sabel v. Puma, Case C-251/95, [1997] ECR I-6191, para 23];

  v) a lesser degree of similarity between the marks may be offset by a greater degree of similarity between the goods/services and vice versa; [Canon Kabushiki Kaisha v. Metro-Goldwyn-Mayer. Case C-39/97, [1998] ECR I-5507, para 17];

  vi) there is a greater likelihood of confusion where the earlier trade mark has a highly distinctive character either per se or because of the use that has been made of it; [Sabel v. Puma, Case C-251/95, [1997] ECR I-6191, para 24];

  vii) mere association, in the sense that the later mark brings the earlier mark to mind, is not sufficient; [Sabel v. Puma, Case C-251/95, [1997] ECR I-6191, para 26];

  viii) further, the reputation of a mark does not give grounds for presuming a likelihood of confusion simply because of a likelihood of association in the strict sense; [Marca Mode v. Adidas, Case C-425/98, [2000] ECR I-4861, para 41];

  ix) but if the association between the marks causes the public to wrongly believe that the respective goods/services come from the same or economically linked undertakings, there is a likelihood of confusion; [Canon Kabushiki Kaisha v. Metro-Goldwyn-Mayer. Case C-39/97, [1998] ECR I-5507, para 29]." O2 v. Hutchison, [2006] EWHC 534 (Ch), para 122 (italics and emphasis added) (the case names are inserted to match those used in this book).

identical to the ones given by Lewison J in *O2 v. Hutchison*. However, included was also the finding of the varying attention of the average consumer from *Lloyd*.[109] This point was also referred to by Floyd LJ in *J.W. Spear v. Zynga* in March 2015.[110]

In *Comic Enterprises v. Twentieth Century Fox HC* in 2014 on certain entertainment services, Wyand QC (sitting as a Deputy High Court Judge) referred to the summary of the elements of the global appreciation test as found in a "standard summary" of the UK IPO, but held that "[t]he most accurate version, and the one

---

[109]"On the basis of these and other cases the Trade Marks Registry has developed the following useful and accurate summary of key principles sufficient for the determination of many of the disputes coming before it:

(a) the likelihood of confusion must be appreciated globally, taking account of all relevant factors;
(b) the matter must be judged through the eyes of the average consumer of the goods or services in question, who is deemed to be reasonably well informed and reasonably circumspect and observant, but who rarely has the chance to make direct comparisons between marks and must instead rely upon the imperfect picture of them he has kept in his mind, and whose attention varies according to the category of goods or services in question;
(c) the average consumer normally perceives a mark as a whole and does not proceed to analyse its various details;
(d) the visual, aural and conceptual similarities of the marks must normally be assessed by reference to the overall impressions created by the marks bearing in mind their distinctive and dominant components, but it is only when all other components of a complex mark are negligible that it is permissible to make the comparison solely on the basis of the dominant elements;
(e) nevertheless, the overall impression conveyed to the public by a composite trade mark may, in certain circumstances, be dominated by one or more of its components;
(f) and beyond the usual case, where the overall impression created by a mark depends heavily on the dominant features of the mark, it is quite possible that in a particular (an element corresponding to an earlier trade mark may retain an independent distinctive role in a composite mark, without necessarily constituting a dominant element of that mark);
(g) a lesser degree of similarity between the goods or services may be offset by a greater degree of similarity between the marks, and vice versa;
(h) there is a greater likelihood of confusion where the earlier mark has a highly distinctive character, either per se or because of the use that has been made of it;
(i) mere association, in the strict sense that the later mark brings the earlier mark to mind, is not sufficient;
(j) the reputation of a mark does not give grounds for presuming a likelihood of confusion simply because of a likelihood of association in the strict sense; and
(k) if the association between the marks causes the public to wrongly believe that the respective goods [or services] come from the same or economically-linked undertakings, there is a likelihood of confusion."

Specsavers v. Asda, [2012] EWCA Civ 24, para 52. The elements of the global appreciation test were derived from the following Court of Justice decisions without any references to specific paragraphs of the decisions: Sabel v. Puma, Case C-251/95, [1997] ECR I-6191, Canon Kabushiki Kaisha v. Metro-Goldwyn-Mayer. Case C-39/97, [1998] ECR I-5507, Lloyd Schuhfabrik Meyer v. Klijsen Handel BV, Case C-342/97, [1999] ECR I-3819, Marca Mode v. Adidas, Case C-425/98, [2000] ECR I-4861, Matratzen Concord v. OHIM I, Case C-3/03 P, [2004] ECR I-3657, Medion v. Thomson Multimedia Sales, Case C-120/04, [2005] ECR I-8551 and OHIM v. Shak05 P, [2007] ECR I-45/05 P, [2007] ECR I-4529. See *ibid*, para 51.

[110]J.W. Spear v. Zynga, [2015] EWCA Civ 290, para 34.

which was cited with approval by Kitchin LJ" was in *Specsavers v. Asda*.[111] The summary was also referred to by Floyd LJ in *J.W. Spear v. Zynga*.[112] The summary was amended by Kitchin LJ a few days later in *Maier v. ASOS* from April 2015.[113]

So far, it has emerged that the UK judiciaries explicitly have followed the global appreciation test, including the average consumer, as set out by the Court of Justice. As addressed in the following chapter, certain modifications to this are found when it comes to contextualisation.

10.3.2   The Nordic Countries

Until now, it has been established that the Nordic legislatures in their respective trademark acts have chosen not to refer to "part of the public" as stipulated in EU trademark legislation and that the Nordic judicial tradition of courts issue short decisions with at times tacit *ratios decidendi*.[114] Those two aspects make it more difficult to clearly compare the development of the Nordic jurisdictions with that of the EU and the UK. The Nordic jurisdictions only to a limited extent refer to EU case law and, if so, it may not be clear what legal principles are derived from the EU decisions. Of the three jurisdictions, the Danish judiciaries are the least explicit when framing the global appreciation test and the average consumer. Fortunately, for the analysis though, in all Nordic countries the supreme courts and courts of appeal have laid down their view on their respective versions of the global appreciation test and the average consumer.

10.3.2.1   Sweden

In the infringement decision, *Mast-Jägermeister v. Vin & Sprit* from 2003, the SE Supreme Court had to decide if the junior mark JÄGARDBRÄNNVIN was confusingly similar to the senior marks JÄGER and JÄGERMEISTER registered for beer

---

[111]Comic Enterprises v. Twentieth Century Fox, [2014] EWHC 185 (Ch), para 108. Wyand QC referred to the same decisions of the Court of Justice as Kitchin LJ in *Specsavers v. Asda. Ibid*, para 107.

[112]J.W. Spear v. Zynga, [2015] EWCA Civ 290, para 33.

[113]Hence, it was held by Kitchin LJ that to the points set out by him in *Specsavers v. Asda* "should be added the further guidance provided by the Court of Justice in [Canon Kabushiki Kaisha v. Metro-Goldwyn-Mayer. Case C-39/97, [1998] ECR I-5507, para 29] that the risk that the public might believe that the goods or services in question come from the same undertaking or, as the case may be, from economically-linked undertakings, constitutes a likelihood of confusion for the purposes of the provision." Maier v. ASOS, [2015] EWCA Civ 220, para 76.

[114]See Chap. 2, Sect. 2.2.4.

and alcoholic drinks.[115] Referring to the preparatory works of the SE TM Act 1960, the court held that "assessing the potential confusing similarity of a mark an overall assessment has to be made, i.e. all circumstances that may have an effect on the assessment of confusing similarity have to be tried."[116] Followed by this was a reference to the TM Directive 1989 and, although implicitly, to the "numerous elements" of its preamble. The court held that the Swedish TM Act had to be interpreted in accordance with Court of Justice case law referring to *Lloyd* and *Canon*.[117] After assessing the conceptual, aural and visual similarity, the court found that the "*group of buyers* may find that the alcoholic liquors come from a company being at least economically linked."[118] The SE Supreme Court disagreed with the SE Court of Appeal and found, with a one out of four dissent, that there was no likelihood of confusion.[119] Whereas the SE Supreme Court more generally referred to the "group of buyers," the Court of Appeal explicitly set out the relevant public referring to the "average consumer" and its varying attention depending on the relevant products.[120]

When the SE Supreme Court in *IFX v. PN* later in 2003 issued its decision, it based it partly on the same background law—i.e. the same preparatory works, the recital of the TM Directive 1989, *Lloyd* and *Canon*.[121] The decision related to certain services on "advertising; business management; business administration; office functions."[122] Despite the marks being almost identical (CHECK POINT and CHECK•POINT), the court found there was not sufficient similarity between the services.[123] There was a limited "risk that the average consumer of the services

---

[115]Classes 32 and 33 of the Nice Agreement. Mast-Jägermeister v. Vin & Sprit, T 2982-01, [2003], SESC. The decision was furthermore analysed earlier, given the duty to EU consistent interpretation. See Chap. 3, Sect. 3.3.2.1.

[116]In Swedish: "Vid bedömning av ett känneteckens förväxlingsbarhet skall en helhetsbedömning göras, dvs. alla föreliggande omständigheter som inverkar på frågan om förväxlingsbarhet skall prövas." Reference was made to NJA II 1960 s. 227.

[117]Mast-Jägermeister v. Vin & Sprit, T 2982-01, [2003], SESC, p. 3.

[118]In Swedish: "att omsättningskretsen kan tro att spritdryckerna kommer från företag med i vart fall ekonomiska band." *Ibid*, p. 5 (italics added).

[119]Mast-Jägermeister v. Vin & Sprit, T 799-99, [2001], SECA.

[120]*Ibid*, p. 6.

[121]IFX v. PN, T 2228-00, [2003], SESC, p. 4-5.

[122]Class 35 of the Nice Agreement.

[123]The court held that "the services in class 35 and IFX's service [the junior mark owner] do not compete with or complement each other even if the aim of both services arguably is to support the running of a company." In Swedish: "Tjänsterna i klass 35 och IFX's tjänst varken konkurrerar med eller kompletterar varandra även om ändamålen med dem kan sägas vara att utgöra ett stöd i driften av företag." *Ibid*, p. 8. The SE Supreme Court also stated in its conclusion that there was a "low degree" of confusion between the services. *Ibid*, p. 9.

would believe that they come from the same undertaking or from an economically linked company."[124]

In *Folksam v. Folkia*, part of the issue was whether the senior mark FOLKSAM registered in Sweden and the EU had been infringed by a series of junior marks, including FOLKIA. The senior mark was registered for certain insurance services and services related "to financial and monetary affairs,"[125] whereas the junior owner (Folkia) offered credit services for private persons. Legally, the decision turned on likelihood of confusion and if Folksam was offered an additional protection due to the reputation of its mark. The SE District Court in its assessment of infringement of the EU and Swedish trademarks made a thorough account of the background law known from *Sabel, Lloyd, Canon* and *Marca Mode v. Adidas*, referring to the importance of the overall assessment and the average consumer.[126] The parties agreed that the relevant "group of buyers consists of the Swedish general public, i.e. men and women living in all of Sweden and aged 18 years or more."[127] On the likelihood of confusion, it was concluded by the SE Court of Appeal that there was no risk of confusion and hence no risk that the relevant public would find that the services were from "economically-linked undertakings." Although leaving out the same extensive referencing to EU case law as found in the SE District Court, the SE Court of Appeal based this finding on a reference to *Canon*.[128] Like the SE District Court, the SE Court of Appeal concluded that there was no likelihood of confusion between FOLKSAM and FOLKIA.[129] The SE Court of Appeal found that FOLKSAM had a reputation and that FOLKIA was "detrimental to the distinctive character or the repute of the trade mark."[130] This was opposite to the SE District Court, which did not find this to be the case.[131] The SE Supreme Court has extraordinarily accepted to hear an appeal from Folkia, but so far has not adjudicated the appeal.[132] In the recent *Länsförsäkringar v. Matek* case the SE Supreme Court,

---

[124]In Swedish: "Risken för att genomsnittskonsumenten av tjänsterna skall tro att tjänsterna härstammar från samma företag eller från företag med ett ekonomiskt samband." IFX v. PN, T 2228-00, [2003], SESC, p. 8. The SE Supreme Court reversed the unanimous decision of the SE Court of the Appeal. Nihlmark v. IFX Infoforex Scandinavia, T 900-96, [2000], SECA.

[125]Cf. class 36 of the Nice Agreement.

[126]Folksam v. Folkia, T12057-11, [2012], SEDC, p. 44-45.

[127]In Swedish: "omsättningskrets utgörs av den svenska allmänheten, dvs. män och kvinnor boende i hela Sverige i åldern 18 år och äldre." *Ibid*, p. 4-5 and p. 39, Folksam v. Folkia, T 289-13, [2014], SECA, p. 10 (italics added).

[128]Folksam v. Folkia, T 289-13, [2014], SECA, p. 11. Reference was made to Canon Kabushiki Kaisha v. Metro-Goldwyn-Mayer. Case C-39/97, [1998] ECR I-5507, para 30.

[129]Folksam v. Folkia, T12057-11, [2012], SEDC, p. 45 and Folksam v. Folkia, T 289-13, [2014], SECA, p. 12.

[130]Cf. art. 9(1)(c) of the TM Regulation 2009 (art. 9(2)(c) of the TM Regulation) and § 10(3), ch. 1 of the SE TM Act 2010. Folksam v. Folkia, T 289-13, [2014], SECA, p. 15-16.

[131]Folksam v. Folkia, T12057-11, [2012], SEDC, p. 47-48.

[132]Aspects of the grounds given by Folkia (the junior owner) for the appeal touches upon some key aspects of applying the relevant public in context, and as such they are addressed in the following chapter.

deciding likelihood of confusion as part of an infringement of an EU trademark in Sweden, found that as part of its obligation to apply EU law it had to apply the average consumer as part of the global appreciation test.[133]

In *Swedish Match v. V2 Distribution*, the SE Court of Appeal had to decide as part of a registration dispute if the senior three dimensional mark of a black and white snuff can registered in Sweden for snuff was confusingly similar to that of the junior owner.[134] After initially assessing the absolute grounds for registration, the court assessed the likelihood of confusion and concluded that the relevant average consumer was "consumers of snuff."[135] Similarly, in the infringement dispute, *Kraft Foods v. Mars*, the SE Court of Appeal referred to the overall assessment and average consumer in its assessment of the likelihood of confusion standard.[136]

10.3.2.2   Denmark

In Denmark, the DK Supreme Court has applied a global appreciation test in several decisions. In *Lube v. Dansk Droge*, the DK Supreme Court had to give a ruling on trademark infringement as part of enforcement proceedings. The senior trademark owner (Lube) claimed that its wordmark had been infringed by that of the junior trademark holder (Droge).[137] Initially, the DK MCH Court in its short reason for the decision stated that "according to an overall assessment of the two marks the court does not find that there is a risk of confusion." Then the court shortly assessed certain

---

[133]Länsförsäkringar v. Matek, T 3403-14, [2017], SESC, paras 10-11. The SE Supreme Court merely confirmed the finding by the SE Court of Appeal in Matek v. Länsförsäkringar, T 3270-13, [2014], SECA, p. 5-6. The likelihood of confusion had to be decided between a senior EU trademark (Länsförsäkring's junior figurative mark) and a figurative national Swedish mark. The senior owner had its mark registered for certain services and goods, but the dispute concerned the similarity between its real estate affairs services vis-a-vis the services of the junior mark owner, i.e. the selling and making of pre-fabricated wooden houses.

[134]Class 34 of the Nice Agreement.

[135]Swedish Match v. V2 Distribution, T 768-14, [2015], SECA, p. 20.

[136]In Kraft Foods v. Mars, the SE Court of Appeal had to decide if there was a likelihood of confusion between a senior figurative mark and two junior figurative marks and a word mark. The senior mark was a stylised version of the letter "m" (used by Kraft) registered in Sweden for certain chocolate products in class 30 of the Nice Agreement. The junior figurative marks were stylised versions of the letter "m" and of the letters "m & m" and a wordmark M&M. The SE Court of Appeal concluded that there was a likelihood of confusion between the figurative marks but not between the senior figurative mark and the junior word mark. See in particular, Kraft Foods v. Mars, T 14298-09, [2015], SEDC, p. 11 and p. 13-16.

[137]Lube v. Dansk Droge, U.2000.506H, [1999], (DKSC), p. 506-510. The junior word mark was MEGASOL and the senior registered word mark PIKASOL. Both used their marks in relation to sale of fish supplement capsules.

aural and visual elements of the marks before concluding that there was no infringe-ment.[138] The DK Supreme Court without further substantial reason affirmed the decision of the DK MCH Court.[139]

Similar usages by the DK Supreme Court of the "overall impression" test with no further elaboration of the test are found in other decisions. In *Ankenævnet v. Chantelle*, the senior owner (Chantelle) sought cancellation of the mark of the junior owner (Anne Shantel). The names of the owner as just stated were equal to their respective word marks both registered for lingerie. Since the DK IPO maintained registration of the junior mark, the office was party to the case in the court decisions. The DK MCH Court agreed with Chantelle on its emphasis on aural similarity and a practice of abbreviating ANNE SHANTEL to "Shantel," hence rendering the mark closer to "Chantelle." Although not explicitly stating it, the court seemed to use the "ordinary consumer" referred to by the parties as the relevant public. The court referred to *Lloyd*, but it did so only to illustrate the interdependence between the similarity of the products and marks.[140] The DK Supreme Court found for the DK IPO Board of Appeal, stating that there was lacking proof that the "group of buyers" would abbreviate ANNE SHANTEL to "Shantel" and that "[a]fter an overall assessment, the Supreme Court hereafter finds that such a similarity between the marks and a risk of confusion has not been established."[141]

In the registration dispute, *Saint-Gobain v. Richter-System* from 2006 it had to be decided if there was likelihood of confusion between the senior registered mark ECOPHON and the junior mark EUROPHON for sound insulation. The DK IPO as upheld by its board of appeal found for the senior owner. As part of the procedure the senior owner referred e.g. to the global appreciation test of *Sabel*, *Lloyd* and *Canon* and the importance of EU law to interpreting Danish law.[142] The DK MCH Court found for the junior owner among other aspects based on the visual, aural and conceptual similarity.[143] Three of the five judges in the DK Supreme Court affirmed the findings of the DK MCH Court. The two dissenting judges found that due to the identity of the goods, a less strict assessment of mark similarity was needed and agreed with the majority that there was no conceptual similarity between the marks. "In our opinion, however, the marks as a whole are clearly confusingly similar based on a visual assessment."[144]

---

[138]In Danish: "Ud fra en samlet bedømmelse af de to mærker finder retten ikke, at der er risiko for forveksling." *Ibid*, p. 514.

[139]*Ibid*, p. 515.

[140]See Ankenævnet v. Chantelle, U.2003.2366H, [2003], (DKSC), p. 2370.

[141]In Danish: "Efter en helhedsvurdering finder Højesteret herefter, at der ikke er godtgjort en sådan lighed mellem mærkerne eller risiko for forveksling." Ankenævnet v. Chantelle, U.2003.2366H, [2003], (DKSC), p. 2371.

[142]Saint-Gobain v. Richter-System, U.2006.1203H, [2006], (DKSC), p. 1207.

[143]*Ibid*, p. 1208.

[144]In Danish: "Efter vores opfattelse er mærkerne som helhed imidlertid efter en visuel bedømmelse klart forvekslelige." *Ibid*, p. 1208-1209.

Similar ways of using the overall impression reference with no or merely scarce reference to the relevant public are found in many other Danish decisions appealed from the DK MCH Court to the DK Supreme Court.[145]

One of the few times the DK Supreme Court has used the term "average consumer" (gennemsnitsforbrugeren) is in *Ankenævnet v. Nestlé (prev. Novartis)*. The simple reason for this seems to be that the senior mark owner argued that reference had to be made to the "average consumer."[146] In *PUMA v. Coop Danmark*, the junior mark owner (Coop) argued that there was no infringement based on certain market surveys since "there is no risk that the *average consumer* will confuse the Coop shoe with Puma's shoe."[147] Although the DK MCH Court found for Coop and based its reasoning on the "overall assessment," it did not refer to the average consumer but merely to "consumers."[148] The DK Supreme Court affirmed the decision and did not refer to consumers (nor average consumer).[149]

Overall, DK Supreme Court decisions on likelihood of confusion only rarely refer to case law of the Court of Justice in the main text of the decisions. However, in the notes to the summaries of the decisions as published in the Danish Ugeskrift for Retsvæsen ("UfR")[150] there are references to EU case law and almost always relevant literature addressing aspects of EU law.[151] The notes have typically been made single-handedly by the judge(s), summarising the decision in its version

---

[145]Infringement: The DK MCH Court referred to a certain "market segment" and the DK Supreme Court referred to ""customers" in B-Young v. Mind Companies, U.2007.1477H, [2007], (DKSC), p. 1481-1482, and no reference was made by the DK MCH Court to the relevant public, but in assessing the facts the DK Supreme Court referred to the "groups of customers" of the parties in TBL Trailer v. TLT, U.2010.1908H, [2006] (DKSC), p. 1911. Registration: The DK MCH Court and DK Supreme Court referred to the "average consumer" in Ankenævnet v. Nestlé (prev. Novartis), U.2009.754, [2008], (DKSC), p. 756-757 and Elite Licensing v. Elite NYC, U.2012.3383H, [2012], (DKSC), p. 3889-3895.

[146]Ankenævnet v. Nestlé (prev. Novartis), U.2009.754, [2008], (DKSC), p. 756-757.

[147]In Danish: "Der er ingen risiko for, at gennemsnitsforbrugeren skulle forveksle Coop-skoen med Pumas sko." PUMA v. Coop Danmark, U.2011.3433, [2013], (DKSC), p. 3436 (the argument was made before the DK MCH Court) (italics added).

[148]In Danish: "Forbrugerne." *Ibid*, p. 3436-3437.

[149]*Ibid*, p. 3438.

[150]UfR publishes all significant decisions of the DK Supreme Court decisions and the principle decisions of lower courts.

[151]See for instance, the note in its entirety, in B-Young v. Mind Companies, U.2007.1477H, [2007], (DKSC) "U 1989.216 H, U 1998.1189 S, U 2003.2366 H, Samling af afgørelser fra EF-domstolen 1997 I s. 6191 (dom af 11/11 1997 i sag C-251/95 Sabel BV mod Puma AG), Retten i Første instans' dom af 16/3 2005 i sag T-112/03 l'Oreal SA mod Revlon SA, Palle Bo Madsen: Markedsret, Del 2, 4. udg. (2002), s. 164-65, 168-69, 177-79, Knud Wallberg: Varemærkeret, 3. udg. (2004), s. 30, 69, 95,98-99 og 189, Mogens Koktvedgaard: Lærebog i immaterialret, 7. udg. ved Jens Schovsbo (2005), s. 360, 395, 399."

published in the UfR, and therefore the notes do not have a significant value as a legal source.[152]

10.3.2.3   Norway

In Norway, the NO Supreme Court has on many occasions addressed the framing of the average consumer as part of the global appreciation test.

In *Klagenemnda v. W Pelz* of the NO Supreme Court the junior owner sought to register COSMEA in Norway for certain hygienic articles for women.[153] The senior owner objected to the registration based on the senior mark COMICA registered for goods, including "mainly pharmaceuticals and other preparations for medical or veterinary purposes."[154] The first judge to consider the case (Schei) found that confusion in registration had to be "decided according to an overall assessment where the degree of similarity between the goods and trademarks will be key elements."[155] The case was assessed under the NO TM Act 1961. The legislative requirement of the act stated that confusion had to be assessed in the "ordinary market" which meant that according to Norwegian case law and scholarly literature "it is required that one has to assume that a non-insubstantial part of the group of buyers will be misled."[156] Without further reference to the relevant public, the NO Supreme Court affirmed the NO District Court, concluding that there was confusion between the marks.[157] Similar phrasing was used by the NO Supreme Court in the infringement dispute on likelihood of confusion in *Fetter Klovn Karl v. TOP-TOY*.[158]

Ten years after *Klagenemnda v. W Pelz*, the NO Supreme Court revisited its finding on the assessment of the average consumer in *Søtt + Salt v. Pascal*.[159] The decision was a registration dispute where the court had to decide whether there was a likelihood of confusion between the senior mark SØTT + SALT and the junior mark

---

[152]For further on the notes of court decisions as published in UfR, see former DK Supreme Court judge, Zahle, in Zahle, Henrik, 'At Forske Ret - Essays Om Juridisk Forskningspraksis', (1st edn, Gyldendal, 2007), p. 56-60.

[153]Class 5 of the Nice Agreement.

[154]Class 3 of the Nice Agreement.

[155]In Norwegian: "avgjøres etter en samlet vurdering hvor graden av vareslagslikhet og graden av kjennetegnslikhet vil være sentrale elementer."

[156]In Norwegian: "kreves at man må regne med at en ikke ubetydelig del av omsetningskretsen vil bli villedet." Mozell, HR-1995-167-B, [1995], NOSC, 1916 and Lassen, Birger Stuevold, 'Oversikt Over Norsk Varemerkerett', (2nd edn, Universitetsforlaget, 1997), p. 266. See further on the legislative requirement of the NO TM Act 1961 in Chap. 10, Sect. 10.3.2.3.

[157]Klagenemnda v. W Pelz, HR-1998-63-A, [1998], NOSC, p. 1991-1993.

[158]Fetter Klovn Karl v. TOP-TOY, HR-1999-34-A, [1999], NOSC, p. 646.

[159]Søtt + Salt v. Pascal, HR-2008-1686-A, [2008], NOSC.

PASCAL SØTT & SALT.[160] The relevant provisions were found in the NO TM Act 1961, as with *Klagenemnda v. W Pelz*. The first judge to consider the case (Tønder) overall found that "I cannot see that the questions of this case beg other solutions under EU law than under Norwegian law disregarding EU law."[161] The judge hence saw the practice of the CJEU as a practice exemplifying the relevant "standard of assessment."[162] As for the assessment of confusion, Tønder held referring to *Lloyd* that "[a]s a starting point, a discretionary overall assessment has to be made based on the concrete circumstances."[163] Tønder then importantly found that he could see no "substantial difference" between the assessment of confusion under Norwegian and EU law, as the former used as part of its assessment the "non-insubstantial part of the group of buyers" and the latter "the perception of "the average consumer" of the actual type of products."[164] Consequently, it is decisive, as also laid down by the NO District Court in the case, "if an averagely educated,[165] reasonably observant and well-informed consumer of gourmet food and restaurant services etc. may confuse the marks."[166] Based on an assessment of the elements known from the EU global appreciation test, including visual, phonetic and conceptual similarity, it was concluded by the NO Supreme Court, with one of the five judges dissenting, that there was a likelihood of confusion between the marks. The dissenting judge (Bårdsen) disagreed with the weighing of the different elements but not with the overall finding of Tønder related to the average consumer and the relationship between Norwegian and EU law.[167]

Reference to the significance of the linking between the Norwegian practice, referring to a "non-insubstantial part of the group of buyers" and to the EU "average consumer" has later been made by the NO Court of Appeal in decisions decided under the NO TM Act 2010, for instance on infringement used on goods in

---

[160]The senior mark was registered for the following products: goods of classes 8, 16 and 21, and services of classes 35, 41 and 43 of the Nice Agreement. The junior mark was registered for the following products: goods of classes 29, 30 and 32, and services of classes 41 and 43 of the Nice Agreement.

[161]In Norwegian: "Jeg kan ikke se at de spørsmål som denne saken reiser, gir andre løsninger etter EU-retten enn det vi etter norsk rett ville ha kommet til uten EU-retten." Søtt + Salt v. Pascal, HR-2008-1686-A, [2008], NOSC, para 38.

[162]In Norwegian: "vurderingsnorm."

[163]In Norwegian: "Som utgangspunkt skal det her skje en skjønnsmessig helhetsvurdering med grunnlag i de konkrete forhold." *Ibid*, para 40. Tønder referred to Lloyd Schuhfabrik Meyer v. Klijsen Handel BV, Case C-342/97, [1999] ECR I-3819, para 19.

[164]The quotes in Norwegian: "realitetsforskjell," "en ikke ubetydelig del av omsetningskretsen" and ""gjennomsnittsforbrukeren" av den aktuelle produkttype vil oppfatte varemerkene." Søtt + Salt v. Pascal, HR-2008-1686-A, [2008], NOSC, para 41.

[165]The Norwegian "opplyst" may translate e.g. into the English "educated" and "well-informed."

[166]In Norwegian: "om en alminnelig opplyst, rimelig oppmerksom og velinformert forbruker av gourmetmat og restauranttjenester m.v. vil kunne blande merkene sammen." See Søtt + Salt v. Pascal, TOSLO-2006-86520, [2006], NODC, p. 6 and Søtt + Salt v. Pascal, HR-2008-1686-A, [2008], NOSC, para 41.

[167]The dissent appears in *ibid*, paras 68-80.

Esthetique v. Parfyme Handlernes Innkjøpssamarbeid[168] and on services in *Ranstad Holding v. Top Temp Holding*[169] and *Pangea Property Partners v. Klagenemnda.*[170] Although this last decision was heard by the NO Supreme Court, the court did not assess the relevant public since it did not find the services to be sufficiently similar for the legislative minimum threshold of similarity between the products to be met.[171] In *Pangea Property Partners v. Klagenemnda*, the NO Court of Appeal found that although *Søtt + Salt v. Pascal* was decided when the TM Directive 1989 applied, the TM Directive 2008 as such did not change the state of the law on the relevant public.[172]

10.4   Conclusion

The analysis of the "trinity" decisions *Sabel*, *Gut Springenheide* and *Lloyd* showed the fundamentals of the average consumer, with *Sabel* and *Lloyd* manifesting the average consumer in European trademark law as part of the global appreciation test. Especially, *Sabel* and *Lloyd* have been shown to form the foundation of the average consumer. Essentially, if the paths of precedents are followed backwards from more recent decisions on the likelihood of confusion of the Court of Justice and of the General Court, the paths often end at *Sabel* and *Lloyd*. The characteristics of the average consumer and its varying level of attention laid down in *Lloyd* are key takeaways important to the contextualisation analysed in the following chapter.

Moving into the national jurisdictions, the analysis has resulted in an initial conclusion of functional similarity between them. As seen through the legislative analysis of the likelihood of confusion standard, all jurisdictions have had similar standards before the TM Directive 1989 and pre *Sabel*. It clearly emerges from historical scholarly literature and references in national decisions that the global appreciation test in EU law is not a legal novelty. National judges appear to have solved the issue of how much similarity between two marks used for certain products is enough for there to be likelihood of confusion in a registration or infringement dispute through their versions of a global appreciation test referring to a relevant public. Bearing in mind the dynamic development of EU trademark law, not surprisingly, the Court of Justice has not imposed a new test of likelihood of

---

[168]Esthetique Norge v. Parfyme Handlernes Innkjøpssamarbeid, LB-2010-94902, NOCA, p. 6. The NO Supreme Court did not allow an appeal to the court.

[169]Ranstad Holding v. Top Temp Holding, LB-2012-154945, [2014], NOCA, p. 7. Although this decision does not refer explicitly to Søtt + Salt v. Pascal, HR-2008-1686-A, [2008], NOSC, para 41, it uses the same wording.

[170]Pangea Property Partners v. Klagenemnda, LB-2014-52230, [2015], NOCA, p. 5-6.

[171]Pangea Property Partners v. Klagenemnda, HR-2016-01993-A, [2016], NOSC, para 74.

[172]Pangea Property Partners v. Klagenemnda, LB-2014-52230, [2015], NOCA, p. 6.

confusion but merely through a dialogue with the national courts has built on what was already known to the member state jurisdictions.[173]

The analysis of national case law post *Sabel* leaves the impression that there is harmonisation between the different national jurisdictions. For different reasons the contours of the level of the harmonisation are murky, though.

First, the differences between the UK common law and the Nordic legal families seem to manifest themselves in the judicial framing of the respective versions of the global appreciation test and the average consumer. The UK courts are formalistic and have meticulous *ratios decidendi*. This was seen for instance in *O2 v. Hutchison*[174] in the UK High Court and in *Specsavers v. Asda*[175] in the UK Court of Appeal. The Nordic courts, not being so explicit on the *ratios decidendi,* have not been as explicit in their stipulation of a version of a global appreciation test and the average consumer. Explicit references to the average consumer has been found in supreme court decisions, e.g. by the SE Supreme Court in *IFX v. PN,*[176] the DK Supreme Court in *Ankenævnet v. Nestlé (prev. Novartis)*[177] and the NO Supreme Court in *Søtt + Salt v. Pascal.*[178] That said, explicit references to the average consumer or more generally the relevant public is rarest in Danish case law.

Whereas the UK judiciaries have been consistent in their reference to the average consumer if deemed the relevant public, the Nordic judiciaries have been far less consistent. For instance, in Sweden the SE Court of Appeal in *Mast-Jägermeister v. Vin & Sprit* referred to the "average consumer"[179] as set out by the Court of Justice, the "group of buyers,"[180] "consumers"[181] and buyers.[182] In Denmark, the Supreme Court in *PUMA v. Coop Danmark* referred to "ordinary consumer"[183] and merely "consumers,"[184] in *Ankenævnet v. Chantelle* "group of buyers"[185] and in *Coop Danmark v. Puma* "the relevant group of customers."[186] In Norway in *Pelz*

---

[173]It has to borne in mind though that the conclusions on the historical aspects are merely tentative, since no historical analysis as such has been conducted. See Chap. 4, Sect. 4.3.

[174]O2 v. Hutchison, [2006] EWHC 534 (Ch), para 122.

[175]Specsavers v. Asda, [2012] EWCA Civ 24, para 52.

[176]IFX v. PN, T 2228-00, [2003], SESC, p. 8.

[177]Ankenævnet v. Nestlé (prev. Novartis), U.2009.754, [2008], (DKSC), p. 756-757.

[178]Søtt + Salt v. Pascal, HR-2008-1686-A, [2008], NOSC, para 41.

[179]In Swedish: "genomsnittskonsument."

[180]In Swedish: "omsättningskretsen." Mast-Jägermeister v. Vin & Sprit, T 799-99, [2001], SECA, p. 6.

[181]In Swedish: "konsumenterna." *Ibid*, p. 7-8.

[182]In Swedish: "köpare." *Ibid*, p. 8.

[183]In Danish: "normale forbruger."

[184]In Danish: "forbrugere." PUMA v. Coop Danmark, U.2011.3433, [2013], (DKSC), p. 3438.

[185]In Danish: "omsætningskreds."Ankenævnet v. Chantelle, U.2003.2366H, [2003], (DKSC), p. 2371.

[186]In Danish: "kundekreds" Coop Danmark v. Puma, U.2008.446H, [2007], (DKSC), p. 453.

v. Klagenemnda, the NO Court of Appeal referred to the "buying public."[187] In *Søtt + Salt v. Pascal* before the NO Supreme Court the claimant referred to "usual consumer,"[188] the defendant to the "average consumer"[189] and the court to the "average consumer" and the Norwegian phrasing "non-insubstantial part of the group of buyers."[190] Based on the theoretical grappling with the average consumer in light of fiction theory, it was concluded that language is important, not least judicial language, and that linguistic inconsistencies may solidify in practical inconsistencies.[191] Besides the different terminology set out above, it does create some conceptual uncertainty when the Norwegian judges refer to a "non-insubstantial part of the group of buyers," and Danish judges most rarely address the relevant public. The lacking references to the relevant public sometimes though reflect that the parties do not base their claims on weighty arguments on the relevant public or agree on it. To flesh out the relevant public is a matter for the fact finding courts. However, the EU legislature has left no doubt that the relevant public is part of assessing the likelihood of confusion standard. The Court of Justice case law starting with its "trinity" decisions equally leaves no doubt that the relevant public as part of the likelihood of confusion standard is manifested in the global appreciation test and that often the average consumer represents the relevant public. In other words, although the parties in a judicial dispute do not address the relevant public, the courts by including unclear references to the relevant public, or no references, leave the law in this area uncertain.

Second, the UK judiciaries have clearly implemented the likelihood of confusion standard narrowly as set out by the Court of Justice. Also, it must be borne in mind that the legislative analysis of the UK TM Act 1994 showed that the act narrowly mirrors the standard of the TM Directive 1989. In contrast, the Nordic legislatures did not include references to the relevant public. The Swedish decisions included many references to Court of Justice decisions. Danish decisions, though, only included scarce references to case law of the Court of Justice in the main text of the decisions but more often in notes to the decisions as published in UfR, thus having a limited value as a legal source. In Norway, the Supreme Court took a rare opportunity in a Nordic perspective to explicitly address the relationship between national and EU trademark law in *Søtt + Salt v. Pascal* with its analysis of *Lloyd* in light of previous national practice.[192]

Based on the analysis in this chapter the national jurisdictions overall seem to comply with the global appreciation test. This seems so due to Court of Justice case

---

[187]In Norwegian: "kjøpende publikum." Pelz v. Klagenemnda, LB-1997-2383, [1998], NOCA, p. 4-5.

[188]In Norwegian: "vanlige forbruker." Søtt + Salt v. Pascal Drift, HR-2008-1686-A, [2008], NOSC, para 13.

[189]In Norwegian: "gjennomsnittsforbrukeren." *Ibid*, para 24.

[190]*Ibid*, para 41.

[191]See Chap. 5, Sect. 5.6 and Chap. 6, Sect. 6.7.

[192]Søtt + Salt v. Pascal Drift, HR-2008-1686-A, [2008], NOSC, para 41.

law, but as important the pre *Sabel* national background law. When it comes to the relevant public often represented by the average consumer, the consistency is murkier. On a continuum, the UK judiciaries at one end have clearly implemented the EU relevant public whereas at the other end the Danish judiciaries rarely address the relevant public. Sweden and Norway would fall between the two, however, none of the Nordic judiciaries are always clear that, when relevant, they use the average consumer as set out by the Court of Justice.

Chapter 11
Contextualisation of the Average Consumer

11.1 Introduction

The "trinity" decisions of the Court of Justice are equally relevant to what was defined in the introduction as "contextualisation" of the average consumer, meaning how European judiciaries as a combination of law and fact have adapted the average consumer to the different market realities.[1] The entrance point is that choosing the average consumer as the *relevant* public in itself begs a certain contextualisation since *relevance* depends on the context.[2]

Essential to contextualisation, is the finding in *Lloyd* building on *Gut Springenheide* that the average consumer as a starting point is "reasonably well-informed and reasonably observant and circumspect" and in *Lloyd* that its "level of attention is likely to vary according to the category of goods or services in question."[3] Also that the average consumer is someone who accounts for distinctive and dominant components of a trademark. According to the Court of Justice, this normally means perceiving a trademark as a whole and not analysing its various details and the visual, aural or conceptual similarity of the trademarks in question.

---

[1] See Chap. 1, Sect. 1.4.

[2] Bøggild and Staunstrup have mapped out the average consumer mainly referring to case law of the General Court in relation to different products and purchasers. See Bøggild, Frank, and Staunstrup, Kolja, 'EU-Varemærkeret', (1st edn, Karnov Group, 2015), p. 100-108. See also the EUIPO TM Guidelines, Part C, Section 2, Opposition, 'Double Identity and Likelihood of Confusion, Chapter 3, Relevant Public and Degree of Attention', and Maeyaert, Paul, and Muyldermans, Jeroen, 'Likelihood of Confusion in Trademark Law: A Practical Guide Based on the Case Law in Community Trade Mark Oppositions from 2002 to 2012', Trademark Reporter, vol. 103/no. 5, (2013), pp. 1032, p. 1043-1051.

[3] Lloyd Schuhfabrik Meyer v. Klijsen Handel BV, Case C-342/97, [1999] ECR I-3819, para 26. The Court of Justice referred to Gut Springenheide and Tusky, Case C-210/96, [1998] ECR I-4657, para 31.

© Springer Nature Switzerland AG 2020
R. D. Laustsen, *The Average Consumer in Confusion-based Disputes in European Trademark Law and Similar Fictions*, https://doi.org/10.1007/978-3-030-26350-8_11

This is further characterised as "imperfect recollection."[4] Kitchin LJ in *Specsavers v. Asda* has put firmly that in assessing the likelihood of confusion in infringement "from the perspective of the average consumer of the goods or services in question" account should be taken of "all the circumstances of that use that are likely to operate in that average consumer's mind when considering the sign and the impression it is likely to make on him. *The sign is not to be considered stripped of its context.*"[5] Arnold J has denoted this "contextual assessment."[6]

It must be borne in mind that from the outset there is a difference between "contextualising" the average consumer in registration and infringement, although the substantial provisions on likelihood of confusion are the same. In registration, the contextualisation is notional since according to the Court of Justice in *O2 v. Hutchison 3G* it is the *assumed* use of the junior mark that has to be considered, whereas in infringement it is the *actual* use of the junior mark in the marketplace.[7] The distinction is not a theme in this chapter on contextualisation since the aim is to analyse some key contextual aspects equally relevant to registration and infringement. This includes how the relevant public is moulded around the market in which goods bearing the marks *will be* or *are* marketed. Comparing trademark law with other intellectual property law disciplines Koktvedgaard has stated that "[t]he practical work with trademark law naturally leads to a more realistic perception of the structure and method of this legal discipline."[8] In line with Koktvedgaard's finding is the gist of contextualisation that the average consumer has to be applied to the market realities in which the specific decisions nest.

The process of contextualising the average consumer in a dispute on likelihood of confusion based on the facts is, as a clear rule of thumb, not a matter for the Court of Justice, but for the General Court and national courts. In the appeal decision *Shoe Branding v. Adidas*, the junior owner (Shoe Branding) disputed how the General Court had assessed how the average consumer perceived trademarks used for sports clothing. Responding to this claim, the Court of Justice stated that "[a]ccording to settled case-law, findings relating to the characteristics of the relevant public and to consumers' degree of attention, perception or attitude represent appraisals of fact."[9]

---

[4]Lloyd Schuhfabrik Meyer v. Klijsen Handel BV, Case C-342/97, [1999] ECR I-3819, paras 26-27.

[5]Specsavers v. Asda, [2012] EWCA Civ 24, para 87. The finding by Kitchin LJ has been referred to by the UK Court of Appeal in Interflora v. Marks & Spencer, [2012] EWCA Civ 1501, para 37, J.W. Spear v. Zynga, [2015] EWCA Civ 290, para 34, Maier v. ASOS, [2015] EWCA Civ 220, para 79 and Comic Enterprises v. Twentieth Century Fox, [2016] EWCA Civ 41, para 33.

[6]See e.g. Arnold J in Och-Ziff v. Och Capital, [2010] EWHC 2599 (Ch), para 76 and Supreme Petfoods v. Henry Bell, [2015] EWHC 256 (Ch), para 77.

[7]O2 v. Hutchison 3G, Case C-533/06, [2008] ECR I-4231, paras 63-67.

[8]In Danish: "Det praktisk arbejde med varemærkeretten, fører naturligt frem mod en mere realistisk opfattelse af denne retsdisciplins struktur og metode." Koktvedgaard, Mogens, 'Konkurrenceprægede Immaterialretspositioner: Bidrag til Læren om de Lovbestemte Enerettigheder og Deres Forhold til den Almene Konkurrenceret', (1st edn, Juristforbundet, 1965), p. 160.

[9]Shoe Branding v. Adidas, Case C-396/15 P, [2016], para 15.

Among other decisions, the court referred to *Henkel* on distinctiveness of a non-traditional mark where the court held that it was for the "competent authority" to "undertake a specific assessment of the distinctive character of the trade mark at issue, referring to the perception of the average consumer."[10] Paradoxically, *Henkel* at the same time provides a rare example of the court actually making assumptions on the level of attentiveness of the average consumer and its characteristics in a factual context, namely that of perceiving non-traditional marks.[11] Another caveat is found by the Court of Justice in *Libertel* based on *Lloyd*, stating that where the "goods and services [are] intended for all consumers (. . .) the relevant public in this case must be deemed to be composed of the average consumer."[12] *Henkel, Libertel* and similar decisions are addressed below to illustrate how the Court of Justice speaks with two tongues on the distinction between fact and law, given the perception of the average consumer.[13]

Throughout this book, it has been addressed that many variables derived from the market reality feed into the framing and application of the average consumer. Thus, during the analysis of the average consumer under the UCPD, it was established that here and under European trademark law, the Court of Justice deems "social, cultural and linguistic" and "other circumstances" as relevant.[14] When adapting the average consumer to the market reality, it is essential to decide; what is the relevant population in which the relevant public is found? More broadly, in light of the analysis of the cousins of the average consumer in EU design law and European patent law, it was illustrated that populations from which to derive the relevant audience can be "experts," "users," or, as most often is the case in European trademark law, "consumers."[15] Since the General Court often has given its stance on who the relevant public is in likelihood of confusion disputes, many examples are found in its case law on this. The case law of the General Court manifests that there is an overall distinction to be made between a specialist public and a consumer public. Between the two, the consumer public may be more or less specialised. At the former end of the spectrum the General Court has found that the relevant public may be

---

[10]Henkel, Case C-218/01, [2004] ECR I-1725, para 51. The Court of Justice in *Shoe Branding v. Adidas*, also referred to Longevity Health Products v. OHIM, Case C-84/10 P, [2010], para 29 and Big Line v. Demon, Case C-170/14 P, [2014], para 42. Ultimately those decisions merely refer to *Henkel*, para 51.

[11]Henkel, Case C-218/01, [2004] ECR I-1725, para 52.

[12]Libertel, Case C-104/01, [2003] ECR I-3793, para 46 referring to Lloyd Schuhfabrik Meyer v. Klijsen Handel BV, Case C-342/97, [1999] ECR I-3819, para 26. See also Alcon v. OHIM, Case C-412/05 P, [2007] ECR I-3569, para 62 referring to SAT.1 v. OHIM, Case C-329/02 P, [2004] ECR I-8317, para 24 and Procter & Gamble v. OHIM, Joined cases C-473/01 P and C-474/01 P, [2004] ECR I-5173, para 62.

[13]See Sect. 11.6.

[14]See Chap. 7, Sect. 7.4.

[15]See Chap. 6, Sect. 6.3–6.4.

"professionals,"[16] a "professional public,"[17] "specialists,"[18] "professionals and man-ufacturers,"[19] "business professionals," such as "directors or managers of large or small undertakings,"[20] "business consumers"[21] or "specialist consumer."[22] At the

---

[16]Alcon v. OHIM, Case T-130/03, [2005] ECR II-3859, para 49, Devinlec Développement Innovation v. OHIM, Case T-147/03, [2006] ECR II-11, paras 62-63, AMS Advanced Medical Services v. OHIM, Case T-425/03, para 51, Vimeo v. OHIM, Case T-96/14, [2015], para 26, Air Products and Chemicals v. OHIM, Joined Cases T-305/06 to T-307/06, para 34, Deepak Rajani v. OHIM, Case T-100/06, [2008], para 58, Harman International Industries v. OHIM (Babara Becker), Case T-212/07, [2008] ECR II-3431, para 26, Wellcome Foundation *et al* v. OHIM, Joined cases T-493/07, T-26/08 and T-27/08, [2009], para 49, Gauselmann v. OHIM, Case T-106/09, [2010], para 20, Longevity Health Products v. OHIM, Case T-363/09, [2010], para 23, Three-N-Products Private v. OHIM, Case T-313/10, [2011], para 27, Fetim v. OHIM, Case T-395/12, [2015], para 19, Skype v. OHIM, Case T-184/13, [2015], para 22, Pensa Pharma v. EUIPO, Joined cases T-544/12 and T-546/12, [2015], 69 Gat Microencapsulation v. OHIM, Case T-720/13, [2015], para 31, Azanta v. EUIPO, Case T-49/16, [2017], para 28, Environmental Manufacturing v. EUIPO, Case T-681/15, [2017], para 33, Forest Pharma v. EUIPO, Case T-36/17, [2017], paras 49-50, Sports Division SR v. EUIPO, Case T-139/16, [2017], para 39, Yusuf Pempe v. EUIPO, Case T-271/16, [2017], para 30, Laboratorios Ern v. EUIPO II, Case T-700/16, [2017], para 25 and Dimitrios Mitrakos v. EUIPO, Case T-15/17, [2018], para 24.

[17]Gauselmann v. OHIM, Case T-106/09, [2010], para 20, Bial-Portela & C v. OHIM (Isdin), Case T-366/11, [2012], para 18, Globo Media v. EUIPO, Case T-262/16, [2017], para 20, Sports Division SR v. EUIPO, Case T-139/16, [2017], para 38, Claranet Europe v. EUIPO, Case T-129/16, [2017], para 22, Laboratorios Ern v. EUIPO II, Case T-700/16, [2017], para 24, RRTec v. EUIPO, Case T-912/16, [2017], para 31, Deutsche Post v. EUIPO, Case T-118/16, [2018], para 31, Kwang Yang Motor v. EUIPO, Case T-45/17, [2018], para 22. Tillotts Pharma v. EUIPO, Case T-362/16, [2018], para 20 and Deutsche Post v. EUIPO, Case T-537/15, [2018], para 34.

[18]Castellblanch v. OHIM, Case T-29/04, [2005] ECR II-5309, para 46, AMS Advanced Medical Services v. OHIM, Case T-425/03, para 51.

[19]CareAbout v. OHIM, Case T-356/14, [2015], para 24.

[20]TeleTech v. OHIM, Case T-288/03, [2005] ECR II-1767, paras 71 and 78.

[21]P.P.TV v. OHIM, Case T-118/07, [2011], para 24 and Messe Friedrichshafen v. EUIPO, Case T-224/16, [2017], para 37.

[22]Arctic Cat v. EUIPO, Case T-113/16, [2018], para 21.

other end, the court has found that the public may be the "average, non-specialist consumer,"[23] "general public,"[24] or the "public at large."[25]

The meaning of the terms "general public" and "public at large" by the General Court is unclear. Intuitively, the general public and the public at large is the population from which a sample—the average consumer—is derived. This is akin to terminology known from quantitative research where researchers "if they cannot collect data of all members of the population of interest (...) must invoke selection mechanisms" to select the relevant sample.[26] Sometimes, the General Court has used the general public and public at large interchangeably.[27] However, these terms are

---

[23]Vincenzo Fusco v. OHIM, Case T-185/03, [2005] ECR II-715, para 38.

[24]See for instance from decisions appealed to the Court of Justice on goods: Saiwa v. OHIM, Case T-344/03, [2006] ECR II-1097, para 29, Harman International Industries v. OHIM (Babara Becker), Case T-212/07, [2008] ECR II-3431, para 26, New Yorker SHK Jeans v. OHIM, Case T-415/09, [2011], para 87, WeserGold Getränkeindustrie, Case T-278/10, [2012], para 24, Bial-Portela & C v. OHIM (Isdin), Case T-366/11, [2012], para 18, Zoo Sport v. OHIM, Case T-455/12, [2013], para 30, Red Bull v. OHIM, Case T-78/13, [2015], para 24, Polo Club v. OHIM, Case T-581/13, [2015], para 34, Eugenia Mocek v. EUIPO, Case T-364/13, [2015], para 22, Pensa Pharma v. EUIPO, Joined cases T-544/12 and T-546/12, [2015], para 69, BH Stores v. EUIPO, Case T-657/13, [2015], para 50, Groupe Léa Nature v. EUIPO, Case T-341/13 RENV, [2017], para 34, BMB v. EUIPO, Case T-695/15, [2017], para 35 and Tetra Pharm (1997) v. EUIPO, Case T-441/16, [2017], paras 35-36. On both good and services or just services: Inex v. OHIM, Case T-153/03, [2006] ECR II-1677, para 49, MOL Magyar Olaj v. OHIM, Case T-367/12, [2014], para 31, Golden Balls v. OHIM (Intra-Presse), Case T-448/11, [2014], para 44, Cartoon Network v. OHIM, Case T-285/12, [2013], para 17, Argo Group v. OHIM, Case T-247/12, [2014], paras 26-27, Junited Autoglas v. OHIM, Case T-297/13, [2014], para 22, Pensa Pharma v. EUIPO, Joined cases T-544/12, Nanu-Nana v. EUIPO, Case, T-89/11, [2015], para 32 and Jordi Nogues v. EUIPO, Case T-350/13, [2017], para 19.

[25]Vimeo v. OHIM, Case T-96/14, [2015], para 26 Fetim v. OHIM, Case T-395/12, [2015], para 19, Skype v. OHIM, Case T-184/13, [2015], para 22, Globo Media v. EUIPO, Case T-262/16, [2017], para 24, Migros-Genossenschafts-Bund v. EUIPO, Case T-189/16, [2017], para 27, Freddo v. EUIPO, Case T-243/16, [2017], paras 26-28, Claranet Europe v. EUIPO, Case T-129/16, [2017], para 22, Laboratorios Ern v. EUIPO II, Case T-700/16, [2017], para 24, Sun Media v. EUIPO II, Case T-273/16, [2018], para 31, Bernhard Rintisch v. EUIPO, Case T-25/17, [2018], para 78, Şölen Çikolata Gıda Sanayi ve Ticaret v. EUIPO, Case T-648/16, [2018], para 27 and Gidon Anabi Blanga v. EUIPO, Case T-657/17, [2018], para 21.

[26]The chosen terminology is only made as a conceptual comparison to quantitative research, not to indicate that the average consumer as such has to be constructed through quantitative evidence. See Epstein, Lee, and Martin, Andrew D., 'Quantitative Approaches to Empirical Legal Research', in Cane, Peter and Kritzer, Herbert M. eds., The Oxford Handbook of Empirical Legal Research (1st edn, Oxford University Press, 2010), 901, p. 910. Jacoby has held that defining the "universe" (interchangeably with "population") is obviously of upmost importance. Jacoby, Jacob, 'Trademark Surveys Volume I: Designing, Implementing, and Evaluating Surveys', (1st edn, American Bar Association, 2013), p. 267. A too broad universe may be "likely to yield very few individuals (...) whose state of mind is relevant." *Ibid*, p. 338. The issue with a too narrow universe though, is "that representation can be skewed so the indication of likely confusion, secondary meaning, and so on is biased – sometimes severely in one direction or another." *Ibid*, 346.

[27]See Sun Media v. EUIPO II, Case T-273/16, [2018], para 31.

often used in contrast with professionals[28] and specialised consumers.[29] Also, the General Court has juxtaposed the average consumer with general public, finding "the general public, [to be] composed precisely of average consumers,"[30] "that the relevant public is made up of the average consumer, who is reasonably well informed and reasonably observant and circumspect, belonging to the general public"[31] and the relevant public being the "average members of the general public."[32] Considering these inconsistencies, not surprisingly, the EUIPO in their trademark guidelines seem to struggle when they try to set out some general principle on General Court's usage of the general public and public at large terminology.[33] As also pointed out by the EUIPO though, it is safe to say that the "relevant public" is used by the General Court as a collective term for whatever the public may be. However, in contrast with the finding by EUIPO, there is not enough consistency in General Court case law to claim that the average consumer is equally used as a collective term.

Country specific references have been made for example to the "general German consumer,"[34] the "German public,"[35] the "French public"[36] or the "English-speaking public and the non-English-speaking public."[37] Equally, that the relevant

---

[28]E.g. on the general public: Dimitrios Mitrakos v. EUIPO, Case T-15/17, [2018], paras 25-27, RP Technik GmbH Profilsysteme v. EUIPO, Case T-768/15, [2017], paras 22-28 and Stada Arzneimittel v. EUIPO, Case T-403/16, [2017], para 16. On the public at large: Bernhard Rintisch v. EUIPO, Case T-25/17, [2018], para 78 and Claranet Europe v. EUIPO, Case T-129/16, [2017], para 22.

[29]E.g. on the general public: Cotécnica v. EUIPO, Case T-136/17, [2018], para 25, Apax Partners UK v. EUIPO, Case T-209/16, [2017], para 25 and Messe Friedrichshafen v. EUIPO, Case T-224/16, [2017], para 37. On the public at large: Sun Media v. EUIPO I, Case T-204/16, [2018], para 30.

[30]Tulliallan Burlington v. EUIPO II, Case T-123/16, [2017], para 38 and Laboratorios Ern v. EUIPO II, Case T-700/16, [2017], paras 23-25. See similar finding on the public at large in Galletas Gullón v. EUIPO, Case T-456/16, [2017], para 86.

[31]Cofra Holding v. EUIPO, Case T-233/15, [2017], para 84.

[32]Deutsche Post v. EUIPO, Case T-537/15, [2018], para 34.

[33]"The term 'average consumer' is a legal concept that is used in the sense of the 'relevant consumer' or 'relevant public'. It should not be confused with the 'general public' or 'public at large', although the Courts sometimes use it in this sense. However, in the context of relative grounds, the term 'average consumer' must not be used as a synonym of 'general public' as it can refer to both, professional and general public. In this respect, in cases concerning the likelihood of confusion, the Court normally distinguishes between the general public (or public at large), and a professional or specialised public (or business customers), based on the goods and services in question." See the EUIPO TM Guidelines, Part C, Section 2, Opposition, 'Double Identity and Likelihood of Confusion, Chapter 3, Relevant Public and Degree of Attention', p. 4, and the chapter overall.

[34]Metropolis Inmobiliarias y Restauraciones v. OHIM, Case C-284/13 P, [2014], para 30, J & Joy v. EUIPO, Case T-389/15, [2017], para 21 and Frame v. EUIPO I, Case T-627/15, [2017], para 60.

[35]Deepak Rajani v. OHIM, Case T-100/06, [2008], para 58.

[36]Devinlec Développement Innovation v. OHIM, Case T-147/03, [2006] ECR II-11, paras 62-63.

[37]Red Bull v. OHIM, Case T-78/13, [2015], para 24. See Novartis v. EUIPO II, Case T-238/15, [2017], para 107 and Aldi v. EUIPO, Case T-736/15, [2017], paras 49-50.

average consumer may be "that of the European Union,"[38] "the average Community consumer,"[39] or the average "Danish or Finnish,"[40] "French,"[41] "German,"[42] "Italian,"[43] "Spanish,"[44] or "Swedish consumer,"[45] or the "average consumers in the United Kingdom."[46] Arguably, to indicate the average consumer as opposed to upstream purchasers it has been referred to as the *"end* consumer,"[47] *"end* users,"[48] *"final* consumer"[49] and "average Spanish *final* Consumer."[50] Many examples are found of casuistic moulding of the relevant public, such as "African immigrants in Europe,"[51] "adult consumers,"[52] "animal lovers,"[53] "average female consumers,"[54] "car owners,"[55] consumers using the relevant products as part of their "hobby,"[56] "do-it-yourself enthusiasts,"[57] "patients"[58] and "patients as end consumers."[59]

---

[38]Three-N-Products Private v. OHIM, Case T-313/10, [2011], para 27, Tayto Group v. EUIPO, Case T-816/14, [2016], para 47 and Altunis-Trading, Gestão e Serviços v. EUIPO, Case T-438/16, [2018].

[39]PJ Hungary Szolgáltató v. OHIM, Case T-580/08, [2011] ECR II-2423, para 71.

[40]Camper v. OHIM, Case T-43/05, [2006], para 54.

[41]Castellblanch v. OHIM, Case T-29/04, [2005] ECR II-5309, para 46.

[42]Athinaiki Oikogeniaki v. OHIM, Case T-35/04, [2006] ECR II-785, para 43.

[43]Icebreaker v. OHIM, Case T-112/09, [2010], para 22.

[44]Shaker v. OHIM, Case T-7/04, [2005] ECR II-2305, para 45.

[45]Hammarplast v. OHIM, Case T-499/04, [2006] ECR II-84, para 26.

[46]AMS Advanced Medical Services v. OHIM, Case T-425/03, para 51.

[47]Sunrider Corp. v. OHIM, Case T-203/02, [2004] ECR II-2811, para 65, Wellcome Foundation *et al* v. OHIM, Joined cases T-493/07, T-26/08 and T-27/08, [2009], para 50, Longevity Health Products v. OHIM, Case T-363/09, [2010], para 23, Skype v. OHIM, Case T-184/13, [2015], para 22, Opko Ireland v. EUIPO, Case T-88/16, [2017], paras 71 and 73, Novartis v. EUIPO II, Case T-238/15, [2017], para 53 and Azanta v. EUIPO, Case T-49/16, [2017], para 28 (italics added).

[48]Alcon v. OHIM, Case T-130/03, [2005] ECR II-3859, para 49 (italics added).

[49]Ruiz-Picasso v. OHIM, Case T-185/02, [2004] ECR II-1739, para 51, Three-N-Products Private v. OHIM, Case T-313/10, [2011], para 27 and Tillotts Pharma v. EUIPO, Case T-632/15, [2017] (italics added).

[50]Alecansan v. OHIM, Case T-202/03, [2006], para 36 (italics added).

[51]Preparados Alimenticios v. OHIM, Case T-377/10, [2013], para 28.

[52]PJ Hungary Szolgáltató v. OHIM, Case T-580/08, [2011] ECR II-2423, para 41.

[53]Continental Bulldog Club Deutschland v. OHIM, Case T-383/10, [2013], para 18.

[54]Sergio Rossi v. OHIM, Case T-169/03, [2006] ECR II-685, para 49.

[55]Apollo Tyres v. OHIM, Case T-109/11, [2013], para 56.

[56]Air Products and Chemicals v. OHIM, Joined Cases T-305/06 to T-307/06, para 34.

[57]Saint-Gobain Pam v. OHIM, Case T-364/05, [2007] ECR II-757, para 63 (refers to "DIY enthusiasts"), SFC Jardibric v. OHIM, Case T-417/12, [2013], para 51 and RP Technik GmbH Profilsysteme v. EUIPO, Case T-768/15, [2017], para 27.

[58]Wellcome Foundation *et al* v. OHIM, Joined cases T-493/07, T-26/08 and T-27/08, [2009], paras 49-50.

[59]Sanofi v. OHIM, Case T-493/12, [2014], para 18 and Tillotts Pharma v. EUIPO, Case T-362/16, [2018], para 20.

Based on the examples of the terminology used by the General Court of how to denote the relevant public, some relevant themes have been chosen to proceed with the contextualisation analysis. The themes are chosen to draw out some principles of how the contextualisation is conducted by the General Court and the national courts. The variables chosen for this chapter seek to capture the reality in which consumers purchase products bearing trademarks. Initially, it will be addressed how using the *average* consumer *per se* discounts the perception of consumers not within this consumer group. Following from this is an account of what are the overall criteria for assessing similarity between the products, and how they feed into the contextualisation of the average consumer. The assessment of the product market focuses on everyday consumer products and the assessment of the market place focuses on the internet decisions of the Court of Justice.

A key question is at what level of abstraction the average consumer has been contextualised to the facts. For instance with Diet Coca-Cola, is the average consumer contextualised at one extreme, at a high level of abstraction as part of a group of tangible, non-durable generic goods, or at a much lower level of abstraction as part of a series of branded diet colas?[60] In the appeal decision *Ruiz-Picasso v. OHIM*, the Court of Justice confirmed OHIM's finding that there are limits to how narrow contextualisation should be. The court found that the "authority" assessing "whether there is a likelihood of confusion *cannot reasonably be required to establish, for each category of goods*, the consumer's average amount of attention on the basis of the level of attention which he is capable of displaying in different situations."[61]

As clarified with the above examples from case law of the General Court, the relevant public may also be found among a professional population. A strain running through this chapter is not only positively contextualising the average consumer but also negatively, i.e. where to draw the line between at one end of the scale the professional population and at the other end the consumer population.

The Court of Justice contextualises the average consumer as part of distinctiveness in relation to certain non-traditional marks. This important caveat to the Court of Justice not going into the contextualisation of the average consumer is addressed under what may be called "*trademark* contextualisation." The chapter will finish with a summarising discussion.

---

[60] Jacoby, Jacob, 'Trademark Surveys Volume I: Designing, Implementing, and Evaluating Surveys', (1st edn, American Bar Association, 2013), p. 138-139.

[61] Ruiz-Picasso v. OHIM, Case C-361/04 P, [2006] ECR I-643, para 43 (italics added).

11.2 Discounting

11.2.1 Discounting the Homer Simpsons and Mr. Spocks?

The global appreciation test builds on certain assumptions of how consumers making purchasing decisions will process information manifested in trademarks.[62] It is assumed by judges that consumers make purchasing decisions based on a certain level of attentiveness. To be more exact, consumers do not entirely act on impulse, but somehow, they take in all or part of the factors of the purchasing scenario and the involved trademarks. An essential, and rather controversial aspect of the average consumer, is what is referred to as "discounting" in this book. Put differently, how judges through the average consumer *count* certain purchasing behavior as representative of the relevant public of the products. It is for the European judges to put themselves in the shoes of the relevant public. In 1936, Knopf stated that a judge "has to identify himself with matters encountering the trademark in life and mobilise his intuitive ability and insight into customer psychology to reach a correct and fair result." Knopf added sharply, though, that "many judges are too rigid and unimaginative to solve the task presented to them by trademark law."[63] The task faced by the judges has become more complex with the intense interstate trade in today's EU Internal Market, and not least with the advent of the internet.

The mechanical characteristics used by the Court of Justice in *Gut Springenheide* and *Lloyd* to describe the average consumer, indicate a fairly high confidence in the abilities of EU consumers to understand what happens in the marketplace and also a readiness to discount those sections of the public who do not understand this and thus count on those that do. That is to say that consumers "of the category of products concerned" *not* "deemed to be reasonably well-informed and reasonably observant and circumspect" are discounted by the Court of Justice.[64] The assumptions of the court in discounting some consumers in the moulding of the average consumer is an important factor in contextualising the average consumer to the market.

In *Marca Mode v. Adidas*, Advocate General Jacobs confirmed the view of Marca Mode (the junior owner) that "it can no longer be relevant that a minority of particularly inattentive consumers might possibly be confused." Put differently, it does not matter if a group of consumers being less attentive than average are likely to be confused. This means a group of consumers less than "reasonably well-informed

---

[62]See Weatherill, Stephen, 'Who is the 'Average Consumer'?', in Weatherill, Stephen and Bernitz, Ulf eds., The Regulation of the Unfair Commercial Practices Under EC Directive 2005/29 (1st edn, Oxford, Hart, 2007), 115, p. 123.

[63]In Norwegian: "Han må leve sig inn i all de forhold som møter varemerket i livet, og mobilisere all sin intuitive evne og innsikt i kundepsykologien for å komme til et riktig og rimelig resultat." and "mange dommere er for stivbente og fantasiløse til å løse den opgave som varemerkeretten stiller dem." Knoph, Ragnar, 'Åndsretten', (1st edn, Nationaltrykkeriet, 1936), p. 455-456.

[64]Lloyd Schuhfabrik Meyer v. Klijsen Handel BV, Case C-342/97, [1998] ECR I-3819, para 26 referring to Gut Springenheide and Tusky, Case C-210/96, [1998] ECR I-4657, para 31.

and reasonably observant and circumspect." Jacobs drew on an example from *CNL-SUCA v. HAG*, which he assessed in 1990. Referring to this opinion where he drew on a German court decision, he stated that "Community law had thankfully disempowered the consumer who confuses the mark 'LUCKY WHIP' with the mark 'Schöller-Nucki.'"[65] This German decision was according to Jacobs in *CNL-SUCA v. HAG*, "[a] decision that seems to postulate that a body of consumers afflicted with an acute form of dyslexia" would indicate that those consumers should be discounted.[66] As explained by Jacob LJ in *Reed Executive v. Reed Business Information* "[t]here must be allowance for defective recollection, which will of course vary with the goods in question (a fifty pence purchase in the station kiosk will involve different considerations from an once-in-a-lifetime expenditure of £50000)."[67] Comparing the confusion test in passing off and trademark law, Jacob LJ further held that "[i]t may be observed that both approaches *guard against too "nanny" a view of protection—to confuse only the careless or stupid is not enough.*"[68] As recently confirmed by Arnold J in *Enterprise v. Europcar*, "confusion on the part of those who are ill-informed or unobservant is *discounted.*"[69]

By discounting through a model of an average consumer, the Court of Justice seems to draw on two "cognitive systems" of human behaviour developed in psychology and now used in behavioural science.[70] The first system reflects a human, described by Sunstein, as a person that "works fast," "is often on automatic pilot" and is "controlled by emotions and intuitions."[71] Under this system, humans are "uncontrolled, effortless, associative, fast, unconscious and skilled."[72] The second system reflects humans that are "deliberative and reflective." A person under this system is in "self-control," "is a planner as well as a doer; it does what

---

[65]See Marca Mode v. Adidas, Case C-425/98, [2000] ECR I-4861, (opinion of AG Jacobs), para 30 (italics added) referring to his opinion in CNL-SUCA v. HAG, Case C-10/89, [1990] ECR I-3711, (opinion of AG Jacobs), para 36.

[66]CNL-SUCA v. HAG, Case C-10/89, [1990] ECR I-3711, (opinion of AG Jacobs), para 36.

[67]Reed Executive v. Reed Business Information, [2004] EWCA Civ 159, para 78.

[68]*Ibid*, para 82. The finding is also referred to by Lewison LJ in Interflora v. Marks & Spencer, [2012] EWCA Civ 1501, para 33.

[69]Enterprise v. Europcar, [2015] EWHC 17 (Ch), para 132 (italics added). This was first stated by Arnold J in Interflora v. Marks & Spencer, [2013] EWHC 1291 (Ch), para 209.

[70]According to Kahnemann, the system has been offered by the psychologists Keith Stanovich and Richard West. More broadly on the system, see Kahneman, Daniel, 'Thinking, Fast and Slow', (1st edn, Penguin, 2011), p. 19-24, Thaler, Richard H. and Sunstein, Cass R., 'Nudge: Improving Decisions about Health, Wealth, and Happiness', (1st edn, Yale University Press, 2008), p. 21-24 and Sunstein, Cass R., 'Why Nudge? The Politics of Libertarian Paternalism', (1st edn, Yale University Press, 2014), p. 26-34.

[71]Sunstein, Cass R., 'Why Nudge? The Politics of Libertarian Paternalism', (1st edn, Yale University Press, 2014), p. 26-27.

[72]Thaler, Richard H. and Sunstein, Cass R., 'Nudge: Improving Decisions about Health, Wealth, and Happiness', (1st edn, Yale University Press, 2008), p. 22.

is planned,"[73] is "effortful, deductive, slow, self-aware and rule-following."[74] Persons under the first system are humans and under the latter "Econs." Illustratively, Sunstein has held that examples of persons under system one are "Homer Simpson, James Dean from Rebel Without a Cause and Pippi Longstocking" and under system two the highly reflective Mr. Spock from Star Trek.[75] References to these characters are not farfetched in law. Hence, in a Canadian trademark infringement dispute based on confusion, in *Atomic Energy v. Areva*, it was held by Zinn J that "[i]n this industry [the nuclear power industry], the fact that *Homer Simpson* may be confused is insufficient to find confusion."[76] Reference to aspects of psychology as part of the conversation on the relevant public is not new. Beside the above quote by Knopf, Andreassen in 1948 also found that "the psychology of advertisement" may provide "certain modifications of the constructive *average norm.*"[77] More recently, Lassen has stated that predicting the reaction of the relevant public as part of assessing likelihood of confusion is "to a certain extent all about speculations on customer psychology."[78]

On what basis is the discounted minority in effect calculated? Are judges simply as found by Knopf putting themselves in the shoes of the average consumer, asking, "would I, or should I have been confused? From the outset, the Court of Justice by choosing the average consumer as the preferred relevant public seems to have placed itself in between the two cognitive systems, in between the Homer Simpsons and Mr. Spocks. Despite the average consumer often being used, the Court of Justice does not seem to have elaborated on what is meant by the characteristics one-by-one. In everyday language, the average consumer and its characteristics may be set out as: *"Someone who has or shows some knowledge about a wide range of subjects, or*

---

[73]Sunstein, Cass R., 'Why Nudge? The Politics of Libertarian Paternalism', (1st edn, Yale University Press, 2014), p. 26-27.

[74]Thaler, Richard H. and Sunstein, Cass R., 'Nudge: Improving Decisions about Health, Wealth, and Happiness', (1st edn, Yale University Press, 2008), p. 22.

[75]Sunstein, Cass R., 'Why Nudge? The Politics of Libertarian Paternalism', (1st edn, Yale University Press, 2014), p. 26. See also Thaler, Richard H. and Sunstein, Cass R., 'Nudge: Improving Decisions about Health, Wealth, and Happiness', (1st edn, Yale University Press, 2008), p. 24.

[76]Atomic Energy v. Areva, [2009] FC 980, para 28 (italics added). Corbin has elaborated on these cases in an article on the Canadian version of the average consumer. Corbin, Ruth M., 'The Moron in a Hurry – a Creature of Law Or Science?', in Archibald, Todd L. and Echlin, Randall Scott eds., Annual Review of Civil Litigation 2015 (1st edn, Carswell, 2015), 43, p. 43-46. See also Beebe, Barton, 'Trademark Law: An Open-Source Casebook', Trademark Infringement (V3 edn, 2016), p. 48.

[77]In Danish: "Reklamepsykologien" and "visse Modifikationer af den konstruktive *Gennemsnitsnorm*" (italics added). Andreasen, Hardy, 'Varemærkeretten i Konkurrenceretlig Belysning. En Retssammenlignende Analyse Af Varemærkerettens Grundbegreber Og En Fremstilling Af Ejendomstetten Til Varemærker', (1st edn, Ejnar Munksgaard, 1948), p. 298, and p. 298-301.

[78]In Norwegian: "Til en viss grad dreier det hele seg egentlig om gjetninger om kundepsykolgi." Lassen, Birger Stuevold, 'Oversikt Over Norsk Varemerkerett', (2nd edn, Universitetsforlaget, 1997), p. 265.

about one particular subject, is somewhat on guard, wary and unwilling to take risks."[79] Also in everyday language there seems to be good ground for simply denoting the "average consumer" the "ordinary consumer."[80] This is in line with Jacob LJ's finding in *Reed Executive v. Reed Business Information* that in effect, the average consumer is "the *ordinary consumer*, neither too careful nor too careless, but reasonably circumspect, well informed and observant."[81]

That the exercise of discounting serves a profound purpose in European trademark law may not come as a surprise since, essentially, it may have an acute impact on the result of a dispute on likelihood of confusion. Hence, Mellor *et al* have stated (with particular reference to the Interflora v. M&S infringement dispute) that "[a]s substantive principles of EU trademark law have become more settled, so litigants have sought to explore aspects of the "average consumer" to suit their arguments, often by bending the concepts."[82] What is more broadly at stake in this "bending" of the average consumer has been addressed by Kitchin LJ in *Interflora EWCA III*. Kitchin LJ thus found that the average consumer "has been created to strike the right balance between various competing interests including, on the one hand, the need to protect consumers and, on the other hand, the promotion of free trade in an openly competitive market, and also to provide a standard, defined in EU law, which national courts may then apply."[83]

11.2.2   Average as $\bar{x}$ or "Ordinary"?

Describing the average consumer as an "ordinary consumer" leaves out unfruitful discussion on whether "average" means a mathematical average or merely "ordinary" or "normal." Such discussions still emerge, though, in litigation and in scholarly literature. Mellor *et al*, among others, recently concluded, based on *Gut Springenheide,* that the term "average" does not mean a mathematical average and that the term found its way into EU law due to a (mis)translation of the German "Durchschnitt" into the English "average."[84] This is in line with the early

---

[79]The sentence is based on the explanations of the adjectives forming the characteristics of the average consumer as found in the Oxford University Press online English/English dictionary: "well-informed" is explained as "having or showing much knowledge about a wide range of subjects, or about one particular subject;" "observant" as for instance, "on guard;" "circumspect" as "wary and unwilling to take risks;" and "reasonably" as for instance, "somewhat."

[80]See Chap. 7, Sect. 7.4 and Chap. 8, Sect. 8.7.

[81]Reed Executive v. Reed Business Information, [2004] EWCA Civ 159, para 78 (italics added).

[82]Mellor, James, David Llewelyn, Moody-Stuart, Thomas, *et al*, 'Kerly's Law of Trade Marks and Trade Names', (16th edn, Sweet & Maxwell, 2018), p. 52.

[83]Interflora v. Marks & Spencer, [2014] EWCA Civ 1403, para 113.

[84]Mellor, James, David Llewelyn, Moody-Stuart, Thomas, *et al*, 'Kerly's Law of Trade Marks and Trade Names', (16th edn, Sweet & Maxwell, 2018), p. 59-62. See also Laustsen, Rasmus D., 'An Economic Analysis of EU Trademark Law; the Role of the Average Consumer in Trademark

development of the term pre *Sabel*.[85] To understand "average" in a mathematical sense requires some hard data from which to infer the average. Based on the role of evidence material supporting the assessment of the average consumer, the Court of Justice found in *Gut Springenheide* that a national court if it faces *"particular difficulty"* *"may have* recourse, under the conditions laid down by its own national law, to a consumer research poll or an expert's report *as guidance for its judgment*."[86] The understanding of this finding has recently been revisited by the court in *Shoe Branding v. Adidas* where it found that the argument "to the effect that evidence of a likelihood of confusion is necessary in order for a mark to be held to be 'misleading', is based on a misreading of that judgment [*Gut Springenheide*]."[87] Consequently, there is "no requirement that evidence of a likelihood of confusion on the part of a *significant number of consumers* be adduced in order for a mark or other forms of advertising to be held to be 'misleading'."[88] In *Interflora EWHC* Arnold J confirmed the finding of M&S that "the [average consumer] test is a "normative" one."[89] This is in line with the finding by the Court of Justice in *Gut Springenheide* as clarified further in *Shoe Branding v. Adidas* where it emerges that e.g. survey evidence, if a court is confronted with *particular difficulty, may serve* as *guidance*. As part of the Interflora v. M&S dispute there has been further grappling with the average consumer as something quantifiable. The flipside of the average consumer being normative is that it is not "mathematical" or "statistical."[90] The problems of understanding "average" in mathematical and statistical sense have also been highlighted in the Interflora v. M&S decisions. Intuitively, "average" would be understood as a simple mean,[91] which advocates that the average consumer is one "person," the *one* hypothetical *average* person. In a less strict sense, average could be understood as the range in which most consumers statistically would be found under the so-called "empirical rule."[92] These approaches have been rejected by the UK Court of Appeal in *Interflora EWCA III*.[93]

Infringement between Two Confusingly Similar Trademarks', in Lyngsie, Jacob, Mortensen, Bent O. G. and Østergaard, Kim eds., Rets- og Kontraktøkonomi: Law & Economics an Anthology (Djøf Publishing, 2016), 37, p. 56-57.

[85] See Chap. 8.

[86] Gut Springenheide and Tusky, Case C-210/96, [1998] ECR I-4657, para 37 (italics added). On the role of evidence, see also Chap. 1, Sect. 1.5.4.

[87] Shoe Branding v. Adidas, Case C-396/15 P, [2016], para 28.

[88] *Ibid*, para 30 (italics added).

[89] Interflora v. Marks & Spencer, [2013] EWHC 1291 (Ch), para 209. Later, this was confirmed by the UK Court of Appeal in Interflora v. Marks & Spencer, [2014] EWCA Civ 1403, para 124.

[90] Interflora v. Marks & Spencer, [2014] EWCA Civ 1403, respectively paras 124 and 128.

[91] Understood as "the sum of the measurements divided by the number of subjects." Agresti, Alan, and Barbara Finlay, 'Statistical Methods for the Social Sciences', (3rd edn, Upper Saddle River, N. J., Prentice Hall, 1999), p. 45.

[92] The "empirical rule" dictates that 68 % of all measurements on a bell-shaped distribution fall between -/+ one standard deviation from the sample mean. *Ibid*, p. 56-61.

[93] Interflora v. Marks & Spencer, [2014] EWCA Civ 1403, paras 128-129.

Lewison LJ found in *Interflora EWCA I* that "[s]uppose that a valid survey shows that in an election 49 per cent of the electorate support candidate A and 51 per cent support candidate B. It would be possible to say on the strength of such a survey that B will win the election. It would also be possible to say that a substantial proportion of the electorate will vote for candidate A."[94] As Mellor mentioned during a presentation on the average consumer, this finding could be seen as supporting a mathematical and statistical approach to the average consumer.[95] The UK Court of Appeal in *Interflora EWCA III* revisited this finding by Lewison LJ, specifying that this was not the case,[96] however, if "the court concludes that a significant proportion of the relevant public is likely to be confused such as to warrant the intervention of the court then we believe it may properly find infringement."[97]

Mellor *et al* have pointed out that it may vary to what extent national courts in the EU consider survey evidence, and if so, which proportion of likely confused consumer is enough for finding likelihood of confusion.[98]

Birss J in *Hearst v. AVELA* has firmly stated that "[t]he words[99] 'average' denotes that the person is typical. The term 'average' does not denote some form of *numerical mean, mode or median*."[100] Similarly, Wadlow has stated that since the average consumer in trademark law "is a legal construct rather than a real person, it

---

[94]The quote continues: "But what a survey does not, I think, tell you is: for whom will the average voter vote? In cases where acquired distinctiveness of a mark is in issue a survey may accurately identify that proportion of the relevant public which recognises the mark as a badge of trade origin. It will then be for the fact finding tribunal, with the aid of such a survey, to decide whether a significant proportion of the relevant public identify goods as originating from a particular undertaking because of the mark." Interflora v. Marks & Spencer, [2012] EWCA Civ 1501, para 35.

[95]As a curiosity, Mellor reasoned during the presentation that Lewison LJ's reference to election surveys might have reflected that the hearing in *Interflora EWCA I* took place 7 November 2012, one day after the election of Barack Obama in the US general election. If that is the reason for the reference to election surveys, it is doubtful that it would have been made, had the hearing taken place 8 November 2016, one day after Donald Trump was elected president in the US general election. To say the least, the 2016 US election exposed significant flaws in expert surveys. The presentation, where the author of this book was present, can be found at: Mellor, James, presentation under the heading 'The average consumer generally' as part of a conference under the heading 'The Average Consumer in Trade Mark Law and Passing Off' held at UCL in London 25 February 2015, at 3:50: https://www.youtube.com/watch?v=zqTC_-beZxk (last visited 26 May 2019), see from 8:30 onwards.

[96]Interflora v. Marks & Spencer, [2014] EWCA Civ 1403, para 128.

[97]*Ibid*, para 129.

[98]Mellor, James, David Llewelyn, Moody-Stuart, Thomas, *et al*, 'Kerly's Law of Trade Marks and Trade Names', (16th edn, Sweet & Maxwell, 2018), p. 65. When Mellor *et al* finish their chapter on the average consumer, they firmly stress that even if survey evidence could be of some relevance when establishing the average consumer, then "[u]ltimately, it is pointless to strive for precision where, once a court has directed itself as to the correct legal concept, the assessment is necessarily one of impression and is "broad brush"." *Ibid*, p. 65-66.

[99]That "word" is in plural must be a typo by the court.

[100]Hearst v. AVELA, [2014] EWHC 439 (Ch), para 60 (italics added). See also Arnold J referring to this in Supreme Petfoods v. Henry Bell, [2015] EWHC 256 (Ch), para 50.

follows that evidence from "real" average consumers is a contradiction in terms, so precluding (in most cases as a matter of principle) survey evidence and witness collection programmes."[101]

As it emerged in the foregoing chapter and in this section, the UK judges have been more outspoken on the broader role of the average consumer and, relevant here, the average consumer not as something mathematical and statistical. The NO Supreme Court has been more or less forced to address this issue as well. As it may be recalled from the foregoing chapter, the NO Supreme Court in *Klagenemnda v. W Pelz*, as later confirmed in *Søtt + Salt v. Pascal*,[102] found that for there to be a likelihood of confusion "it is required that one has to assume that a non-insubstantial part of the group of buyers will be misled."[103] This phrasing very much resembles the phrasing used in the Interflora v. M&S decisions and can be perceived as something quantifiable. In *Pangea v. Klagenemnda*, the NO Court of Appeal has clarified that this not the case.[104] As authority for finding that the average consumer was not quantifiable, the NO Court of Appeal inserted a quote from the leading Norwegian scholarly text on trademark law: "In this context, a non-insubstantial part has to be understood relatively: whether the absolute number of purchasers expected to be mistaken is high or low, normally is irrelevant. This does not apply without exceptions. It will not suffice that one purchaser can be expected to be mistaken, even if the goods are oil drilling rigs. If, on the other hand, it can be expected that thousands of purchasers may confuse the trademarks, this has to be sufficient to ascertain confusion, even if the product is e.g. toothpaste having a group of customers that must be counted in millions buying the product regularly."[105] The NO

---

[101]Wadlow, Christopher, 'The Law of Passing-Off: Unfair Competition by Misrepresentation', (5th edn, Sweet & Maxwell, 2016), p. 570. On this point, Wadlow sees a difference between the UK law of passing off and trademark law, since the former takes a broader approach to allowing the substantiation of consumer confusion e.g. through survey evidence. *Ibid.*

[102]Søtt + Salt v. Pascal, HR-2008-1686-A, [2008], NOSC.

[103]In Norwegian: "kreves at man må regne med at en ikke ubetydelig del av omsetningskretsen vil bli villedet." See further on the legislative requirement of the NO TM Act 1961 in Chap. 3, Sect. 3.3.2.3.

[104]Pangea v. Klagenemnda, LB-2014-52230, [2015], NOCA, p. 7.

[105]In Norwegian: "En ikke ubetydelig del må her oppfattes relativt: om det absolutte tall på kjøpere e.l. som man må regne med vil ta feil er stort eller lite, bør normalt ikke spille noen rolle. Helt ut kan dette likevel ikke gjelde. At man må regne med at én kjøper vil kunne ta feil, kan ikke være nok, selv om varen er boreplattformer. Hvis man på den annen side må regne med at tusener at kjøpere vil kunne forveksle varemerkene, må det være tilstrekkelig til å konstatere forvekselbarhet, selv om det dreier seg om en vare som f.eks. tannpasta, med en omsetningskrets som må regnes i millioner som alle foretar jevnlige kjøp." Pangea v. Klagenemnda, LB-2014-52230, [2015], NOCA, p. 7 referring to Lassen, Birger Stuevold, 'Oversikt Over Norsk Varemerkerett', (2nd edn, Universitetsforlaget, 1997), p. 267 (italics added). In an abbreviated version, this quotation has been repeated in the newer version of the book, see Lassen, Birger Stuevold and Stenvik, Are, 'Kjennetegnsrett', (3rd edn, Universitetsforlaget, 2011), p. 320.

Supreme Court in *Pangea v. Klagenemnda* did not assess this finding of the NO Court of Appeal.[106]

The Swedish judiciaries have not been so outspoken on the nature of the average consumer. However, in *Hela Pharma v. Cederroth* the SE Court of Appeal stated that the "question about risk of confusion is considered to be a question of normative character, i.e. a legal question. The consequence is that less importance is attached to proof of actual confusion but that proof in support of the finding of such confusion (e.g. confusion studies and other market surveys) may indicate it."[107]

In Danish case law, it has not been possible to find similar judicial statements. In the leading Danish textbook on intellectual property law, Schovsbo has stated that the average consumer is legal standard, "[h]owever, this is not to say that upon establishing the normal reaction of the relevant group of consumers, *market surveys* cannot be included," although "in such cases it is difficult to get a clear result" through surveys. "Partly for this reason (and due to the power of habit), the Danish judiciaries have probably traditionally been reluctant to attach weight to surveys, but this is maybe about to change."[108] Koktvedgaard has earlier expressed this traditional starting point, holding that the assessment has to be "based on case law and not on more or less in-depth market analyses."[109] The gist of this, Koktvedgaard continues, is that contextualising the "normal reaction of the relevant group of purchasers," judges "are confronted with matters that are normally not possible to

---

[106]The NO Supreme Court did not find sufficient similarity between the services and therefore, the court did not assess the perception of the relevant public. Pangea v. Klagenemnda, HR-2016-01993-A, [2016], NOSC, para 74. See also Chap. 10, Sect. 10.3.2.3.

[107]In Swedish: "Frågan om förväxlingsrisk anses vara en fråga av normativ karaktär, d.v.s. en rättsfråga. Följden därav blir att visad faktisk förväxling tillmäts mindre betydelse men att bevisning som syftar till att styrka sådan förväxling (t.ex. förväxlingsstudier eller andra marknadsundersökningar) kan verka indikativt i målet." Hela Pharma v. Cederroth, T 3341-09, [2010], SECA, p. 4-5 (italics added).

[108]In Danish: "Dermed er dog ikke sagt, at man ikke kan inddrage forbrugerkredsens antagelige normalreaktion og som led i vurderingen heri lægge vægt på *markedsundersøgelser*" and "[d]et kan i sådanne tilfælde være vanskeligt at få et klart resultat." "De danske domstole har nok til dels af denne grund (og på grund af vanens magt) traditionelt været tilbageholdende med at lægge vægt på undersøgelser, men dette er måske ved at ændre sig." Schovsbo, Jens, Rosenmeier, Morten and Petersen, Clement Salung, 'Immaterialret: Ophavsret, Patentret, Brugsmodelret, Designret, Varemærkeret', (5th edn, Jurist- og Økonomforbundets Forlag, 2018), p. 532, Interestingly, Schovsbo's reference to the average as a legal standard (or a "legal fiction" – a term he also uses) only appears in the 2018 edition of the book, where he also includes an elaborative section on the average consumer. Part of these amendments could be caused this book on the average consumer referred to be Schovsbo (in the PhD edition from 2017). See *ibid*, p. 475 and p. 532. Compare with Schovsbo's previous findings in the 2015 edition of the book. Schovsbo, Jens, Rosenmeier, Morten and Petersen, Clement Salung, 'Immaterialret: Ophavsret, Patentret, Brugsmodelret, Designret, Varemærkeret', (4th edn, Jurist- og Økonomforbundets Forlag, 2015), p. 612.

[109]In Danish: "*baseres på retspraksis, ikke på mere eller mindre dybtgående markedsanalyser.*" Koktvedgaard, Mogens, 'Konkurrenceprægede Immaterialretspositioner: Bidrag til Læren om de Lovbestemte Enerettigheder og Deres Forhold til den Almene Konkurrenceret', (1st edn, Juristforbundet, 1965), p. 178.

document in court," for which reason judges are left with "their own discretion."[110] Although, it is possible to find decisions where market surveys play a role, e.g. *PUMA v. Coop Danmark*,[111] there seems to be no doubt that in deciding the relevant public under Danish trademark law, the discretion is mainly based on normative considerations by the judges.

Relevant to all jurisdictions, it has also been stressed by the EU legislature in the recitals to the UCPD, that "[t]he average consumer test is not a statistical test" and that "[n]ational courts and authorities will have to exercise their own faculty of judgement, having regard to the case-law of the Court of Justice, to determine the typical reaction of the average consumer in a given case."[112]

11.3 Similarity of the Products

As part of assessing likelihood of confusion is an assessment of the "identity or similarity of the goods or services covered by the trade marks."[113] This involves a selection and comparison of the relevant products. It is not part of the analysis to map and analyse all the factors applied by the courts involved in this process. However, the selection of the relevant products clearly relates to the framing of the relevant public and hence the average consumer. Through various factors, the products to be compared are delimited by the courts, and it is within the consumers of this delimited group of products that the relevant public is found. As with the comparison of the marks, the difficult task is where there is merely a similarity between the products for which the junior trademark is applied for registration for or used for and those of the senior trade mark.

---

[110]In Danish: "normalreaktionen hos denne aftagerkreds," "står overfor forhold, der i almindelighed ikke lader sig dokumentere i retssalen" and "deres eget skøn." *Ibid*, p. 177.

[111]PUMA v. Coop Danmark, U.2011.3433, [2013], (DKSC). The decision was a "classical" Puma dispute where Coop had launched a shoe with a side application that somewhat resembled that of Puma's shoe. As opposed to *Sabel*, this decision was an infringement dispute. To decide likelihood of confusion two market surveys had been made, one with pre-made answers and the other without. *Ibid*, p. 3434. Puma claimed that there was likelihood of confusion, e.g. on the ground of the latter market survey showing that 10 % when shown Coop's shoe associated the shoe with Puma. As the DK MCH Court, the DK Supreme Court found there to be differences between the side applications of the shoes. The DK Supreme Court concluded that based on an "overall assessment and with support of the market surveys made, the court accepts that the application of the Coop shoe is so essentially different from Puma's application that there is no risk of confusion (. . .)." *Ibid*, p. 3438. In Danish: "Ud fra en helhedsvurdering og med støtte i de foretagne markedsundersøgelser tiltræder Højesteret, at applikationen på Coop-skoen adskiller sig så væsentligt fra Pumas form-strip, at der ikke er risiko for forveksling (. . .)."

[112]Recital 18 of the UCPD. See also Madsen, Palle Bo, 'Markedsret Del 2: Markedsføringsret og Konkurrenceværn', (6th edn, Jurist- og Økonomforbundets Forlag, 2015), p. 58-59.

[113]On this legislative requirement, see Chap. 9, Sect. 9.3.1.1.

As addressed earlier, the Nice Classification is the framework under European trademark law for categorising products as part of registration. The EU legislature in the most recent EU trademark legislation has set out that the Nice Classification in registration disputes must not be decisive for deciding similarity between the products. That said, the Nice Classification provides significant guidance when deciding this, in particular in registration disputes where the products of the conflicting marks are documented, for the senior trademark as part of the registration certificate, and for the junior mark as part of the application.[114] In infringement disputes, the EU trademark legislation stresses the influence of the products for which the senior trademark is *registered*.[115]

In *Lloyd*, the Court of Justice held that the varying attention of the average consumer depends on "the category of goods or services *in question*,"[116] and in *Sabel* that "the type of goods or services *in question* plays a decisive role in the global appreciation of the likelihood of confusion."[117] Although deciding what actually are the products "in question" is not part of the law, and hence mainly left for the General Court and relevant national courts, the Court of Justice in *Canon* laid down a non-exhaustive list of criteria to be considered. The court held that "[i]n assessing the similarity of the goods or services concerned, (. . .) all the relevant factors relating to those goods or services themselves should be taken into account. Those factors include, *inter alia*, their nature, their end users and their method of use and whether they are in competition with each other or are complementary."[118] In the appeal decision *Sunrider v. OHIM*, the Court of Justice added the "intended purpose" as an additional factor to be considered.[119] In this decision, the court also emphasised that the assessment of the similarity between the goods was an appraisal of the facts and hence left for the General Court.[120]

In the EUIPO TM Guidelines, the EUIPO describes in detail the factors applied by the CJEU (mainly the General Court) when comparing the products.[121] Although the Court of Justice in *Canon* merely referred to "end users," it also clearly showed that comparison of the products is a multifactor test of non-exhaustive factors. This allowed the General Court and national courts to also consider the relevant public

---

[114]On Nice Classification, see Chap. 3, Sect. 3.5.2.

[115]Hence, it is stipulated in the TM Regulation and TM Directive that "(. . .) the sign is identical with, or similar to, the trade mark and is used in relation to goods or services which are identical with, or similar to, the goods or services for which the trade mark is *registered*,". Cf. art. 9(2) of the TM Regulation and art. 10(2) of the TM Directive. (italics added).

[116]On this finding in *Lloyd* (italics added), see Chap. 1, Sect. 1.4.

[117]On this finding in *Sabel*, see Chap. 10, Sect. 10.2.2.

[118]Canon Kabushiki Kaisha v. Metro-Goldwyn-Mayer. Case C-39/97, [1998] ECR I-5507, para 23. See also the appeal decision Alcon v. OHIM, Case C-412/05 P, [2007] ECR I-3569, para 72.

[119]Sunrider v. OHIM, C-416/04 P, [2006] ECR I-4237, para 85.

[120]*Ibid*, paras 49-50 and 88.

[121]See the EUIPO TM Guidelines, Part C, Section 2, Opposition, 'Double Identity and Likelihood of Confusion, Chapter 2, Comparison of Goods and Services'. See also Bøggild, Frank, and Staunstrup, Kolja, 'EU-Varemærkeret', (1st edn, Karnov Group, 2015), p. 253-273.

more broadly (and not only end users) when comparing the products. Thus, in General Court case law, it is commonplace when the court compares products to find references to the relevant public, and whether the products are aimed at the same relevant public.[122] In the EUIPO TM Guidelines, the EUIPO also mentions the relevant public as a factor to be considered when comparing the products. However, the EUIPO categorises the relevant public as a less important factor in this context. This is especially so when dealing with products targeted for the general public, i.e. as exemplified in the following section, this means typically everyday consumer goods.[123] The reason behind this seems to be that the more homogenic the consumer group of products is (as for everyday consumer goods), the less it tells about the products to be compared and their similarity. This is in contrast with specialised goods where the relevant public potentially is significantly divergent.[124]

According to the EUIPO, a strong factor to consider when comparing the product, is "usual origin" of the products.[125] This means that "there is a strong indication of similarity when, in the mind of the relevant public, the goods/services have the same usual origin." However, according to the EUIPO, this factor is not to "be misinterpreted as turning the examination of likelihood of confusion and similarity of goods/services upside down." This is to say, that although the usual origin factor may be significant for deciding similarity of the product, it is not decisive for the overall assessment of likelihood of confusion.[126] Recently, the General Court has accepted the "usual origin" an independent factor for assessing the similarity between the products.[127] According to Tritton *et al*, this factor is important, and it

---

[122]Two recent examples of this are Novartis v. EUIPO I, Case T-214/15, [2017], para 55 and Kwang Yang Motor v. EUIPO, Case T-45/17, [2018], para 33.

[123]See the EUIPO TM Guidelines, Part C, Section 2, Opposition, 'Double Identity and Likelihood of Confusion, Chapter 2, Comparison of Goods and Services', p. 36. Here, the EUIPO has listed the following as "[g]enerally] strong factors" when comparing the products: their "[u]sual origin," "[p] urpose," "[n]ature," "[c]omplementarity," and if they are "[i]n competition." Besides the relevant public, the EUIPO also considers the following as less important factors: "[m]ethod of use," and "[d]istribution channels."

[124]A recent example of this is Novartis v. EUIPO I, Case T-214/15, [2017], para 55.

[125]Although not directly mentioned by the Court of Justice in *Canon*, the EUIPO finds some ground for the "usual origin" factor in *Canon*. See the EUIPO TM Guidelines, Part C, Section 2, Opposition, 'Double Identity and Likelihood of Confusion, Chapter 2, Comparison of Goods and Services', p. 32 and Canon Kabushiki Kaisha v. Metro-Goldwyn-Mayer. Case C-39/97, [1998] ECR I-5507, para 29.

[126]See the EUIPO TM Guidelines, Part C, Section 2, Opposition, 'Double Identity and Likelihood of Confusion, Chapter 2, Comparison of Goods and Services', p. 32. See also on this factor, Davis, Richard, St Quintin, Thomas and Tritton, Guy, 'Tritton on Intellectual Property in Europe', (5th edn, Sweet & Maxwell, 2018), p. 372-373.

[127]Emcur Gesundheitsmitte v. EUIPO, Case T-165/17, [2018], paras 55 and 61-63 (appeal to the Court of Justice in progress, see Case C-533/18 P) and Banca Monte and Wise Dialog Bank v. EUIPO, Case T-83/16, [2017], paras 62-64. Upon appeal, the Court of Justice refrained that the assessment of the similarity of the products is an appraisal left for the General Court, and hence did go further into this matter. Banca Monte and Wise Dialog Bank v. EUIPO, Case C-684/17 P, [2018], paras 21-25.

should manifest in a test where it is assumed "that the goods and services in issue are not marketed under a brand at all or alternatively under an unused brand of average distinctiveness."[128]

Overall, the products chosen for comparison delimits the population from which the relevant public is to be found. Thus, for instance in *Indo Internacional v. OHIM* related to certain optical/optician services in class 42 of the Nice Agreement, the General Court found that "[t]he relevant public for the assessment of the likelihood of confusion is composed of users likely to use both the goods or services covered by the earlier mark and those covered by the mark applied for."[129] Furthermore, that "when goods or services covered by one of the marks in issue are included in the larger designation covered by the other mark, the relevant public is defined by reference to the more specific wording."[130]

The above illustrates that in the *Canon* non-exhaustive multifactor test, the relevant public is an independent factor when assessing the similarity between the *products*. More important in this analysis of contextualisation, the overall process of choosing which products are to be compared has naturally a strong impact on how the relevant public is chosen and hence its contextualisation. As correctly summed up by the EUIPO, "the outcome of the comparison of goods/services plays an important role in defining the part of the public for whom likelihood of confusion is analysed because the relevant public is that of the goods/services found to be identical or similar."[131]

11.4   Different Product Markets

For goods there are different parameters according to which they may be divided. In contrast with services, goods fall into a category of tangible products. It is possible to divide goods into durables, such as cars, computers and cell-phones, and nondurables such as, foods, drinks, medical product, and clothes.[132] Essentially, nondurable

---

[128]Davis, Richard, St Quintin, Thomas and Tritton, Guy, 'Tritton on Intellectual Property in Europe', (5th edn, Sweet & Maxwell, 2018), p. 373. It is not possible to verify the source referred by Tritton *et al* as ground for this finding, *ibid*, footnote 367.

[129]Indo Internacional v. OHIM, Case T-260/08, [2012], para 23. The senior mark was registered for certain "optician's services" (*ibid*, para 6), and junior applied for registration of its mark for certain optical services (*ibid*, para 3). The General Court also referred to Apple Computer v. OHIM, Case T-328/05, [2008], para 23.

[130]Indo Internacional v. OHIM, Case T-260/08, [2012], para 24. Here the General Court referred to MeDiTA v. OHIM, Case T-270/09, [2010], para 28 that refer to Apple Computer v. OHIM, Case T-328/05, [2008], para 23.

[131]See the EUIPO TM Guidelines, Part C, Section 2, Opposition, 'Double Identity and Likelihood of Confusion, Chapter 2, Comparison of Goods and Services', p. 5.

[132]Bishop, Simon, and Mike Walker, 'The Economics of EC Competition Law: Concepts, Application and Measurement', (3rd edn, Sweet & Maxwell, 2010), p. 150 and Jacoby, Jacob, 'Trademark Surveys Volume I: Designing, Implementing, and Evaluating Surveys', (1st edn, American Bar Association, 2013), p. 137-138.

goods "are used up as they are consumed."[133] Probably the simplest and most repeated factual scenario involves consumers purchasing fast-moving consumer goods ("FMCG") in a retail setting, i.e. essentially everyday purchases of low-priced goods in supermarkets and shops. Those goods are sold B2C. The goods are typically bought after "a very brief decision-making moment at the time of purchase."[134] Besides the different product categories, the "brand"[135] of a product often is significant. That is to say, as per the earlier example, that a cola may not just be a soda, but a Diet Coca-Cola vis-à-vis other colas.[136]

On the backdrop of this understanding of products, the following is divided into an analysis of "everyday consumer goods" and "specialised goods," e.g. pharmaceutical goods. The term "everyday consumer goods" is used by the General Court in its factual assessment and seems to resonate with the understanding of FMCG. In its divide between law and fact, the Court of Justice has explicitly ruled that it will not contextualise the average consumer to the different product markets, be it in relation to "everyday consumer goods"[137] or more specialised goods, including pharmaceuticals.[138]

11.4.1 General Court Practice

11.4.1.1 Everyday Consumer Goods

As regards purchasing of everyday consumer goods, the General Court seems to operate a starting point that the relevant public is the average consumer "who is reasonably well informed and reasonably observant and circumspect, whose degree

---

[133]Jacoby, Jacob, 'Trademark Surveys Volume I: Designing, Implementing, and Evaluating Surveys', (1st edn, American Bar Association, 2013), p. 138.

[134]Jehoram, Tobias Cohen, van Nispen, Constant, and Huydecoper, Tony, 'European Trademark Law: Community Trademark Law and Harmonized National Trademark Law', (1st edn, Kluwer Law International, 2010), p. 288.

[135]A brand is something more than a merely the trademark as found by Advocate General Colomer in *Arsenal v. Reed*, stating "[t]he trade mark acquires a life of its own, making a statement, as I have suggested, about quality, reputation and even, in certain cases, a way of seeing life." Arsenal v. Reed, Case C-206/01, [2002] ECR I-10273, (opinion of AG Colomer), para 46. See also L'Oréal v. Bellure, Case C-487/07, [2009] ECR I-5185, (opinion of AG Mengozzi), para 52.

[136]Jacoby, Jacob, 'Trademark Surveys Volume I: Designing, Implementing, and Evaluating Surveys', (1st edn, American Bar Association, 2013), p. 138.

[137]Shoe Branding relating to sports shoes and clothing (Nice Agreement class 25). Shoe Branding v. Adidas, Case C-396/15 P, [2016], paras 13-16.

[138]Longevity Health Products v. OHIM relating to certain pharmaceuticals and other preparations for medical or veterinary purposes (Nice Agreement class 5). Longevity Health Products v. OHIM, Case C-81/11 P, [2012], paras 26-27.

of attention must be regarded as *average*."[139] Hence, the General Court operates an *average* consumer with an *average* level of attention. The court has recently negatively defined the average consumer vis-à-vis "a specialist public." The court has found that the relevant public is the average consumer when "the goods covered by the earlier mark and those covered by the mark applied for are everyday consumer goods, which are, accordingly, not intended for a specialist public."[140] It appears from General Court case law that attention of the average consumer purchasing "everyday consumer goods" may be low, high or average. Besides everyday consumer goods with the average consumer as the relevant public, sometimes, the relevant public is the average consumer, but the goods are not everyday consumer goods. Finally, sometimes, the relevant public is not the average consumer and the goods are specialised, i.e. marks within the B2B scenario. The first scenario is analysed in this section and the last two scenarios in the following section.

As explained by the EUIPO Board of Appeal, "everyday consumer goods" include "low-cost, mass-produced goods for everyday use"[141] where the average consumer is of an average level of attention, i.e. the starting point. In *Adidas v. OHIM (Shoe Branding)* the General Court found that "since sports shoes are everyday consumer goods, the relevant public is made of the average consumer, who is reasonably well informed and reasonably observant and circumspect, *whose degree of attention must be regarded as average when purchasing them*."[142] Referring to the finding of the EUIPO Board of Appeal, the General Court in *Yusuf Pempe v. EUIPO* has concluded that "as regards *normal mass circulation consumer goods*, goods attracting due consideration and goods that professionals might use, the

---

[139]Adidas v. OHIM, Case T-145/14, [2015], para 33 (italics added) (for the appeal decision, Shoe Branding v. Adidas, Case C-396/15 P, [2016], see e.g. Chap. 10, Sect. 10.2.3). See also Cofra Holding v. EUIPO, Case T-233/15, [2017], para 84, Enoitalia v. EUIPO, Case T-707/16, [2018], paras 22-26, Republic of Cyprus v. EUIPO II, Case T-847/16, [2018], para 24 and Republic of Cyprus v. EUIPO I, Case T-825/16, [2018], para 26.

[140]Specifically, the present case related to the average Polish consumer. LR Health & Beauty Systems v. OHIM, Case T-202/14, [2016], para 23. It has to be borne in mind though, that the General Court is occasionally much freer to consider in detail the facts of the initial dispute, and is never considering trademark infringement. Nonetheless, the commonly used "reasonably well-informed and reasonably observant and circumspect" phrase is adopted, and it is generally instructive in the discussion. See in more depths Chap. 11.

[141]This account of "everyday consumer goods" was not disputed by the General Court. LR Health & Beauty Systems v. OHIM, Case T-202/14, [2016], para 11. Although not using the term "every day consumer goods," the General Court has recently stated that "[a]lthough it does not take place on a daily basis, the purchase of household or kitchen utensils is nevertheless more commonplace, easier and cheaper than the purchase of items of furniture." By this statement, the General Court has indicated that the purchase frequency may affect the level of attention of the average consumer. The Cookware Company v. OHIM, Case T-535/14, [2016], para 29. See also the impact of brand loyalty below in footnote 183.

[142]Adidas v. OHIM (Shoe Branding), Case T-145/14, [2015], para 33 (italics added). In this paragraph, reference was made by the General Court to OHIM v. Shaker, Case C-334/05 P, [2007] ECR I-4529, para 35. As addressed in Chap. 9, *OHIM v. Shaker* on point of law of the average consumer added nothing new to the findings in *Sabel* and *Lloyd*. See Chap. 10, Sect. 10.2.3.

relevant public's level of attention would vary from average to high."[143] The General Court has also negatively defined the level of attention. In *Polo Club v. OHIM* the General Court defined it as "goods for everyday consumption and as directed at members of the general public, who are *not expected to pay a particularly high degree of attention to them.*"[144] As in this and other decisions, this is so even for certain fashion goods where "average consumers pay some attention to their appearance and are therefore capable of assessing the style, quality, finish and price of such goods when they purchase them" since "it is not apparent from the description of the goods in question that they are luxury goods or goods which are so sophisticated or expensive that the relevant public *would be likely to be particularly attentive with regard to them.*"[145] The level of attention may also be defined more neutrally as in *Ravensburger v. OHIM* as being "neither particularly high nor particularly low."[146] Sometimes the General Court is vaguer when setting out the level of attention of the average consumer. In *Lancôme v. OHIM I*, the court merely stated that "the relevant public's attention cannot be regarded as greater than it would be in relation to everyday consumer goods."[147] As regards certain durable goods, for instance loudspeakers, the General Court found in *Olive Line v. OHIM* that "the average consumer's level of attention is less than that paid to durable goods or, simply, goods of a higher value or for more exceptional use."[148] Similarly in *Migros-Genossenschafts-Bund v. EUIPO*, related to certain kitchen machines, including coffee machines, the General Court concluded that these goods "are durable

---

[143]Yusuf Pempe v. EUIPO, Case T-271/16, [2017], para 30 (italics added). "Mass circulation consumer goods" are assumed to be the same as everyday consumer goods.

[144]Polo Club v. OHIM, Case T-581/13, [2015], para 34 (italics added). See also N & C Franchise v. EUIPO, Case T-792/16, [2017], para 26.

[145]The Smiley Company v. OHIM, Case T-139/08, ECR II-3535, para 19 (italics added) referred to by the General Court in Polo Club v. OHIM, Case T-581/13, [2015], para 34. The former decision relates to lack of distinctive character, but the statement on the attention of the average consumer is generally applicable. See also more recently on likelihood of confusion N & C Franchise v. EUIPO, Case T-792/16, [2017], para 26.

[146]Ravensburger v. OHIM, Case T-243/08, [2010], para 24.

[147]Lancôme v. OHIM I, Case T-466/08, [2011] ECR II-1831, para 49. The General Court seemed to infer that it is given what the level of attention for everyday consumer goods is, if not high. The court itself has stated, though, that if not high, the level of attention for those goods may be average or low.

[148]Olive Line v. OHIM, Case T-273/10, [2012], para 40. In this paragraph, the General Court referred to Bang & Olufsen v. OHIM where the court stated that "[a]s regards everyday consumer goods, the average consumer's level of attention is less than that paid to durable goods or, simply, goods of a higher value or for more exceptional use." Bang & Olufsen v. OHIM, Case T-460/05, [2007] ECR II-4207, para 33. This decision is on the absolute ground for refusal of registration, but the finding generally applies. See also Tetra Pharm v. EUIPO, Case T-441/16, [2017], para 33.

goods, acquired on an occasional basis, they are purchased by attentive consumers –
both average consumers and professionals – who display a higher level of attention
than for the acquisition of everyday consumer goods."[149]

Examples of everyday consumer goods where the average consumer displays an
average level of attention are certain "staple food products for *daily* consumption"[150] or "*everyday* foodstuffs" (including, milk products,[151] meat, fish, poultry,
game,[152] rice, sugar,[153] flour and preparations made from cereals, bread, pastry and
confectionery[154]), certain drinks (including, coffee, tea,[155] alcoholic beverages,
including wine, spirits,[156] liqueur[157] and beer[158]), personal care products[159] (including, certain cleaning preparations and toilet preparations,[160] perfumery, air fresh-
eners,[161] cosmetics[162] and make-up preparations[163]) clothing, headgear[164] and
shoes[165] (including, sports shoes)[166] kitchen utensils,[167] games and play things.[168]
In *Tulliallan Burlington v. EUIPO*, the General Court stated that "[a]s regards *mass-
consumption goods*, such as soaps, toilet articles, leather articles and other similar

---

[149]Migros-Genossenschafts-Bund v. EUIPO, Case T-189/16, [2017], para 38. Reference was also
made to Dorma v. OHIM, Case T-500/10, [2011], para 64 that referred to *Bang & Olufsen v. OHIM*,
set out in the previous footnote.

[150]Saiwa v. OHIM, Case T-344/03, [2006] ECR II-1097, paras 29 (italics added).

[151]Organismos Kypriakis v. OHIM, Case T-534/10, para 22 (italics added). Here reference is made
to "everyday foodstuffs." The term "everyday food products" has also been used by the General
Court. See Oriental Kitchen v. OHIM, Case T-286/02, [2003] ECR II-4953, para 28.

[152]Meica Ammerländische Fleischwarenfabrik v. OHIM, Case T-247/14, [2016], para 79 (class
29 of the Nice Agreement) (appeal before the Court of Justice Case C-182/16 P).

[153]Athinaiki Oikogeniaki v. OHIM, Case T-35/04, [2006] ECR II-785, para 42.

[154]Saiwa v. OHIM, Case T-344/03, [2006] ECR II-1097, paras 29-30.

[155]Athinaiki Oikogeniaki v. OHIM, Case T-35/04, [2006] ECR II-785, para 42.

[156]Masottina v. OHIM, Case T-393/11, [2013], para 23.

[157]*Ibid* and Shaker v. OHIM, Case T-7/04 [2008] ECR II-2305, para 32.

[158]Bitburger Brauerei v. OHIM, Joined Cases T-350/04 to T-352/04, [2006] ECR II-4255, paras
43, 68 and 69.

[159]Tetra Pharm v. EUIPO, Case T-441/16, [2017], paras 33-35.

[160]Credentis v. OHIM, Case T-53/15, [2016], para 20 and LR Health & Beauty Systems v. OHIM,
Case T-202/14, [2016], para 23 (both class 3 of the Nice Agreement).

[161]L & D v. OHIM, Case T-168/04, [2006] ECR II-2699.

[162]Tetra Pharm (1997) v. EUIPO, Case T-441/16, [2017], paras 33-36.

[163]Lancôme v. OHIM I, Case T-466/08, [2011] ECR II-1831, para 49 and Lancôme v. OHIM II,
Case T-204/10, [2012], para 24 (class 3 of the Nice Agreement).

[164]J & Joy v. EUIPO, Case T-389/15, [2017], paras 22 and 29.

[165]Wolverine International v. OHIM, Case T-642/13, [2015], paras 45-46.

[166]Hence, "the Board of Appeal's finding that those differences will not pass unnoticed by the
consumer who pays attention to the details of sports shoes is, as the applicant claims, at odds with
the fact that the consumer of those products does not demonstrate a high degree of attention."
Adidas v. OHIM, Case T-145/14, [2015], para 32.

[167]The Cookware Company v. OHIM, Case T-535/14, [2016], para 29.

[168]Ravensburger v. OHIM, Case T-243/08, [2010], para 24.

articles, the relevant public in the present case *is the general public, composed precisely of average consumers.*"[169] The court seemed to impliedly set the level of attention of the relevant public as average by stating that the relevant public was "precisely" the average consumer.

Similar observations have been made by the General Court for "everyday services" directed at "the general public."[170]

Deviating from the starting point, the General Court has singled out certain "mass consumer goods"[171] and "everyday, rather low-priced consumer goods, [where] the relevant public pays them a rather low level of attention"[172] or "at most," an "*average* [level of attention] at the time of purchase."[173] For this type of goods, the General Court has stated that "the public must be considered to have a somewhat reduced level of attention when purchasing them."[174] Examples of such goods are socks,[175] chocolate, chocolate products, pastries and ice cream,[176] confectionery,[177] certain beverages, pasta,[178] bakery and pastry.[179] As it appears, in particular for foodstuffs and beverages, the General Court is inconsistent in its treatment of the level of attention, deviating between *average* and *low*.

Goods that from the outset are generic everyday consumer goods may deviate from this category of goods if the relevant sector comprises goods of a particular high price that causes "the consumer [to be] more attentive to the choice of mark."[180] It has been stated by the General Court on several occasions that price can cause a higher level of attention of the average consumer if the goods are "particular expensive." However, that "such an approach on the part of the consumer cannot

---

[169]Tulliallan Burlington v. EUIPO I, Case T-121/16, [2017], para 38 (italics added).

[170]This includes such services as the provision of hygienic care for humans (Credentis v. OHIM, Case T-53/15, [2016], para 20, (class 44 of the Nice Agreement.)) and of certain food and drink services in certain public outlets, where the relevant public's level of attention is average. Andrea Giuntoli v. OHIM, Case T-256/14, [2015], para 24 (class 43 of the Nice Agreement).

[171]Freddo v. EUIPO, Case T-243/16, [2017], para 26.

[172]X Technology Swiss, Case T-547/08, [2010], ECR II-2409, paras 43-45.

[173]Andrea Giuntoli v. OHIM, Case T-256/14, [2015], para 24.

[174]*Ibid.*

[175]X Technology Swiss, Case T-547/08, [2010], ECR II-2409, paras 43-45.

[176]August Storck v. OHIM, Case T-366/14, [2015], para 20. This decision is on the absolute grounds for refusal of registration, but the finding is generally applicable.

[177]Moscow Confectionery Factory v. EUIPO, Case T-795/16, [2018], paras 19-21.

[178]Mederer v. OHIM, Case T-210/14, [2016], para 28, referring to Bimbo v. OHIM, Case T-569/10, [2012], para 99. See also Andrea Giuntoli v. OHIM, Case T-256/14, [2015], para 24 (both Nice class 30).

[179]Bimbo v. OHIM, Case T-569/10, [2012], para 99.

[180]Wolverine International v. OHIM, Case T-642/13, [2015], paras 45-46. See also Masottina v. OHIM, Case T-393/11, [2013], para 23 and Nike v. OHIM, Case T-356/10, [2011], para 23.

be presumed without evidence with regard to all goods in that sector."[181] Other aspects with a similar effect are luxury goods,[182] goods invoking brand loyalty[183] and safety concerns.[184] If such evidence is not presented, it is the consumer group with the lowest level of attention that must be considered. For instance, in *Moscow Confectionery Factory v. EUIPO* on trademarks for confectionary, the General Court endorsed the finding by the EUIPO Board of Appeal "that the relevant public consisted of the public at large and that its level of attention varied from low, in the case of *low-priced confectionary designed for mass consumption*, to average, in the case of *luxury confectionary*."[185] However, here, the "assessment of the likelihood of confusion," should consider "the section of the public which has the lowest level of attention."[186]

The reasons for arguing a deviation from the starting point were illustrated in *Zoo Sport v. OHIM* on likelihood of confusion. The junior trademark owner (Zoo Sport) sought to register a figurative mark for certain goods and services, including clothing (maillots, footwear and sports shoes).[187] Essentially, Zoo Sport argued that the level of attention of the average consumer was higher than average whereas OHIM and the intervener (the senior trademark owner, K-2) supported the finding of the OHIM BOA that the level of attention was "average."[188] Before the General Court, Zoo Sport argued that its consumers, compared to the "average consumer," i) were doing sports more regularly,[189] ii) infrequently purchased its goods, and therefore sought more assistance and were more attentive when doing so, and iii) displayed a higher "sophistication" due to the "specific purpose" of its goods (e.g. "hiking, tennis or soccer").[190] As for the consumers of K-2, Zoo Sport argued i) that its goods were only sold a few places, ii) only for "athletes" (as opposed to "average consumers"), and iii) "are very expensive compared to goods from other manufacturers," and iv)

---

[181]New Look v. OHIM, Joined cases T-117/03 to T-119/03 and T-171/03, [2004] ECR II-3471, para 43. See also Phildar v. OHIM, Case T-99/06, [2009], para 84, Václav Hrbek v. OHIM, Case T-434/10, [2011], para 29 and Wolverine International v. OHIM, Case T-642/13, [2015], para 46.

[182]See by analogy, Polo Club v. OHIM, Case T-581/13, [2015], paras 34 and 79.

[183]In a registration case, the applicant claimed that consumers of household or kitchen utensils displayed a particular high degree of brand loyalty. Although this was rejected by the General Court as matter of fact, the court did not reject that the brand loyalty may affect the level of attention of the average consumer. As opposed to e.g. clothing and shoes, though, the General Court did not explicitly refer to household or kitchen utensils as everyday consumer goods. However, they have a similar effect on the level of attention of the relevant public as for everyday consumer goods, since the sale of these goods were partly "intended both for the general public — the level of attention of which is average." The Cookware Company v. OHIM, Case T-535/14, [2016], para 26. See also UAB Keturi kambariai v. EUIPO, Case T-202/16, [2017], paras 79 and 90.

[184]See on "food for babies" Hipp & Co. v. OHIM, Case T-221/06, [2009], para 40.

[185]Moscow Confectionery Factory v. EUIPO, Case T-795/16, [2018], para 19 (italics added).

[186]*Ibid*, para 21.

[187]Class 25 of the Nice Agreement.

[188]Zoo Sport v. OHIM, Case T-455/12, [2013], para 17.

[189]*Ibid*, para 31.

[190]*Ibid*, para 32.

that its consumers "have an in-depth knowledge of sports goods" (as opposed to "the public as a whole").[191] In sum, Zoo Sport argued that the level of attention of its and K-2's consumers was higher than for the average consumer and thus would "exclude all likelihood of confusion between the marks at issue."[192] The court disagreed with Zoo Sport finding that i) the higher level of attention of the relevant sector was factually unsupported,[193] ii) the goods were purchased both by consumers regularly doing sports and not doing sport,[194] iii) sports shoes were sold and used more broadly, and there was no factual ground for finding otherwise,[195] and iv) Zoo Sport's "claims concerning the specificity, the price and the method of distribution of the intervener's goods" "are not based on the list of goods covered by the earlier figurative mark."[196]

The ranges of goods covered by the General Court's "everyday consumer goods" category is rather broad, not least compared with the more narrow and well-defined group of FMCG. That the General Court may allow for a higher level of attention for certain everyday consumer goods may be seen as a necessary safety valve. This may be seen as indicating that these types of goods are outliers compared to core everyday consumer goods.[197] It should be borne in mind, though, that according to the court's practice there seems to be only a very limited scope for letting everyday consumer goods deviate from the starting point causing a higher level of attention. This was seen in *Zoo Sport v. OHIM*. From a legal perspective, this may be a reflection of the hierarchy of legal sources and as an indication that the General Court is following the precedents of the Court of Justice. The Court of Justice starting with *Lloyd* has shown that although allowing for variation, the court takes the average consumer with an average level of attention as the starting point.[198] An aspect of procedural matter, as also highlighted by *Zoo Sport v. OHIM*, is that the General Court is limiting lofty claims on deviating levels of attention not being factually supported. That said, the court has introduced a very strict requirement when it holds that for price to be an aspect affecting the level of attention of the average consumer it has to be proven as a relevant aspect for the whole sector. This requirement rules out the relevance of price for goods purchased with different frequencies and bought in different places. Potentially, this will come as an

---

[191] *Ibid*, para 33.

[192] *Ibid*, paras 32-33.

[193] *Ibid*, para 35.

[194] *Ibid*, para 36.

[195] *Ibid*, para 39.

[196] *Ibid*, para 40.

[197] Hence, in marketing literature it is also claimed that brands for sportswear and clothing "have been demonstrated to have important sign value for consumers regardless of age, gender or class." This citation confirms these goods to be outliers in the everyday consumer goods category. Hogg, Margaret K., Bruce, Margaret and Hill, Alexander J., 'Fashion Brand Preferences among Young Consumers', International Journal of Retail & Distribution Management, vol. 26/no. 8, (1998), pp. 293, p. 294.

[198] This follows from *Lloyd* onwards. See Chap. 10, Sect. 10.2.

advantage to the existing market players that in likelihood of confusion disputes in registration and infringement have an interest in supporting their confusion claims by arguing that highly attentive consumers should be discounted from the average consumer of everyday consumer goods. The flipside is that it leaves the new market entrants in a weaker position.

It is clear from the above analysis of General Court case law on everyday consumer goods that the court is not consistent in its way of setting out the level of attention of the average consumer, including deviations from starting point—i.e. the average level of attention. Part of the reasoning for the inconsistencies is of course also inconsistent terminology introduced by the parties involved in the dispute, the trademark owners, the EUIPO and the EUIPO Board of Appeal. In terms of terminology, it is often not self-explanatory and logical what is meant by the terms used by the court. For instance, what is meant by expressions set out above such as an average consumer that is "not expected to pay a particularly high degree of attention," and does not "display a higher level of attention than for the acquisition of everyday consumer goods" when the average consumer is not always deemed to display the same level of attention when buying everyday consumer goods?

Recently, in *Dimitrios Mitrakos v. EUIPO*, the applicant (Dimitrios Mitrakos) claimed that the EUIPO Board of Appeal had inconsistently stated that the "that consumers of alcoholic beverages are deemed to be *reasonably well informed and reasonably observant and circumspect and that they will have a reasonable level of attention*" and later in its decision "that *the level of attention of the average consumer is no higher than average*."[199] Contrary to the applicant's claim, the General Court clarified that "it must be noted that defining the level of attention of the relevant consumer as 'reasonable' or as 'no higher than average' can, in essence, be equated with stating that the level of attention of the relevant public is average."[200]

The above analysis and *Dimitrios Mitrakos v. EUIPO* show a need for the General Court to be more consistent in its terminology on the level of attention of the average consumer, and what is the level of attention average consumer for various kinds of everyday consumer goods.[201]

11.4.1.2 Specialised Goods

Outside of everyday consumer goods are specialised goods either sold B2C or B2B. If the goods are directed at specialised or professional purchasers, the "relevant public's attention will necessarily be greater than for everyday consumer goods."[202]

---

[199]Dimitrios Mitrakos v. EUIPO, Case T-15/17, [2018], para 26 (italics added).

[200]*Ibid*, para 27.

[201]For a similar finding on specialised good, see the below Sect. 11.4.1.2.

[202]"The relevant public" covers both young people (average consumer) interested in the relevant goods and professionals buying the relevant goods in a professional context. See also, Gigabyte

Aspects that may move goods outside the realm of everyday consumer goods may relate to how the goods are purchased and to the significance of the goods to the consumer. The influence of *how* the relevant goods are purchased has been shown from different angles. In *Inter-Ikea Systems v. OHIM* concerning furniture, IKEA (the senior owner) was interested in a relevant public with a lower level of attention to prevent registration of a junior mark. Hence, IKEA argued that its furniture was inexpensive and may be purchased quickly. The General Court found that although the "actual act of purchase may be completed quickly in the case of certain items of furniture, the process of comparison and reflection before the choice is made requires, by definition, a high level of attention." Increasing the level of attention was that "the average consumer does not regularly buy certain goods," including furniture.[203]

In *Václav Hrbek v. OHIM*, the General Court found as argued by the junior owner (Václav Hrbek) that "skiwear, ski footwear and headgear, as well as rucksacks" are "not everyday consumer items."[204] Decisive was not a particular high price of the goods, but aspects of "protection" and the attention paid to the "technical qualities" of the goods.[205] Arguably, buying a pair of ski boots normally only happens a few times and undergoes much scrutiny. This may also be the case for some skiwear, but it is not the case for the "whole sector" since some consumers when buying e.g. a skiing jacket do not pay the same attention when the jacket is for everyday use and not only for an annual skiing trip. This reasoning was also presented by the OHIM Board of Appeal in *Václav Hrbek v. OHIM*, not only for some goods but for all goods which for the reasons just given also seems to be a doubtful finding.[206] By comparison, the General Court found in *Hipp & Co. v. OHIM* on food for babies that this group of goods is of a wide range. Following from this, was "that while the group of average consumers for that category of goods, as identified, will also include careful parents, it will not in any way consist exclusively of such consumers" and therefore, the level of attention of the average consumer will not be higher.[207] It seems hard to reconcile *Václav Hrbek v. OHIM* and *Hipp & Co. v. OHIM*, including

---

Technology v. OHIM, Case T-451/11, [2013], para 38 related to certain specialised IT services referring to higher level of attention among specialised users. See also recently *Arctic Cat v. EUIPO*, where the applicant and EUIPO Board of Appeal found that "power sport vehicle-specific clothing" where "specialised goods", and that the "specialist consumers" involved in "power vehicle sports or, at the least, persons involved in such sports (...) have a higher than average level of attention". The General Court did not agree on the factual assessment based on this principle, but did not did dispute the principle as such principle. Arctic Cat v. EUIPO, Case T-113/16, [2018], paras 20-28.

[203]Inter-Ikea Systems v. OHIM, Case T-112/06, [2008], para 37. The court referred to Devinlec Développement Innovation v. OHIM, Case T-147/03, [2006] ECR II-11, para 63.

[204]Václav Hrbek v. OHIM, Case T-434/10, [2011], paras 26 and 31.

[205]*Ibid*, para 30.

[206]*Ibid*, para 28.

[207]Hipp & Co. v. OHIM, Case T-221/06, [2009], para 40.

the other decisions emphasising the importance of taking the sector as a whole into account.[208]

In several instances, the General Court has dealt with cases on a "mixed public," combined of consumers and professionals. For instance, in *Gauselmann v. OHIM* certain computer games, game machines and amusement apparatus were found by the court to be purchased by "the professional public [since] what are involved are goods sold in its area of specialization and second, by consumers belonging to the younger generation, who have a definite interest in goods such as the goods at issue of which they have specific expectations, for example, at the technological level."[209] In *Fetim v. OHIM* on certain goods and services related to construction and building activities, the General Court found that "first, the level of attention of professionals will be, in essence, higher than the average and, secondly, the level of attention of the public at large will, in the present case, also be high, since the goods and services at issue are relatively expensive and are not bought, in the case of the goods, or sought, in the case of the services, on a frequent basis."[210] There is also a higher level of attention for "do-it-yourself enthusiasts" of non-everyday consumer goods.[211] If the goods covered by the marks are to be used by both "the general public" and "professionals,"[212] "it is settled law that the public with the lowest attention level must be taken into consideration."[213]

Similar mechanisms are detected in General Court decisions on pharmaceuticals, based on the key assumption that consumers show a higher level of attention purchasing goods that affect their health. However, for pharmaceuticals, there has continuously been disputes on the divide between goods sold with or without prescription. If the pharmaceuticals are sold with prescription, the consumers of these goods have a very limited influence on which goods to choose, while for pharmaceuticals sold without prescription, the consumer are the one deciding which goods to buy.

In the appeal decision *Alcon v. OHIM*, the Court of Justice had to decide who was part of the relevant public, and its level of attention on "medicinal products requiring a doctor's prescription prior to their sale to end-users in pharmacies."[214] The court found contrary to the applicant (Alcon) that "the fact that intermediaries such as healthcare professionals are liable to influence or even to determine the choice made by the end-users is not, in itself, capable of excluding all likelihood of confusion on

---

[208]See above, Sect. 11.4.1.1.

[209]Gauselmann v. OHIM, Case T-106/09, [2010], para 20. See also Eliza Corporation v. OHIM, Case T-130/09, [2010], para 25.

[210]Fetim v. OHIM, Case T-395/12, [2015], para 21.

[211]See Saint-Gobain v. OHIM, Case T-364/05, [2007] ECR II-757, para 63 and SFC Jardibric v. OHIM, Case T-417/12, [2013], para 51.

[212]Argo Group, Case T-247/12, [2014], para 28.

[213]*Ibid*, para 29, The Cookware Company v. OHIM, Case T-535/14, [2016], para 27 and Ergo Versicherungsgruppe v. OHIM, Case T-220/09, [2011], paras 21-22.

[214]Alcon v. OHIM, Case C-412/05 P, [2007] ECR I-3569, para 52.

the part of those consumers as regards the origin of the goods at issue."[215] Further, the court confirmed the finding of the General Court that end-users had to be included in the relevant public since the goods were sold to these consumers in pharmacies. Thus, although "the choice of those products is influenced or determined by intermediaries, such a likelihood of confusion also exists for those consumers since they are likely to be faced with those products, even if that takes place during separate purchasing transactions for each of those individual products, at various times."[216] In addition, the Court of Justice confirmed the General Court's finding that end-users had to be taken into account since the marketing of the relevant pharmaceuticals was targeted at end-users, and though the goods were prescribed by professionals, "those professionals take into account their [the end-users'] perception of the trade marks at issue and, in particular, their requirements or preferences." The attention of the end-users was deemed to be high.[217] In several General Court decisions, similar conclusions have been reached by the court on pharmaceuticals, be they sold with or without prescription.[218] Comparable to the decisions on pharmaceuticals, the General Court found in *Novartis v. EUIPO II* that sanitary preparations " 'for medical use' have health implications for consumers, which justifies the view that their level of attention is high, in the same way as for pharmaceutical goods."[219] In this decision, the court also confirmed the EUIPO's finding that "the high level of attention of non-professional users of medicines is associated with the health implications of the medicines, and not with the intervention of a specialist."[220]

Despite the above precedence on pharmaceuticals, the Court of Justice has found that there may be instances where the pharmaceuticals are deemed to be targeted merely at health care professionals, since they will not reach the consumer (with or without prescription). Thus, in *Alcon v. OHIM/Robert Winzer Pharma*, the Court of

---

[215]*Ibid*, para 57.

[216]*Ibid*, para 58.

[217]*Ibid*, paras 59-61.

[218]Ferring v. OHIM, Case T-169/14, [2015], paras 30-31. See also Madaus v. OHIM, Case T-202/04, [2006] ECR II-01115, para 33, Mundipharma v. OHIM, Case T-256/04, [2007] ECR II-449, paras 44-47, Aventis Pharma and Nycomed GmbH, Case T-95/07 [2008], paras 27 and 29, Novartis v. OHIM, Case T-331/09, [2010] ECR II-5967, paras 28-29, Market Watch Franchise & Consulting v. OHIM, Case T-201/08, [2010], para 28, Azanta v. EUIPO, Case T-49/16, [2017], paras 23-28, Opko Ireland v. EUIPO, Case T-88/16, [2017], para 72, Tillotts Pharma v. EUIPO and Case T-632/15, [2017], paras 36-38.

[219]Novartis v. EUIPO II, Case T-238/15, [2017], paras 69-71.

[220]*Ibid*, para 66. Due to the findings by the court referred to in the foregoing footnote and the court's approach to goods affecting the health of the average consumer or someone close to it, this statement is generally applicable.

Justice confirmed the finding of General Court that the relevant public for ophthalmic pharmaceutical preparations was "ophthalmologists and ophthalmic surgeons."[221]

The General Court has also concluded that the average consumer has a higher level of attention not only where the products relate to the average consumer's health, but also where the products relate to the health of someone close to the average consumer. Hence the average consumer has a high level of attention for goods that concern "the health of (. . .) their domestic animals" and "the well-being and health of children."[222] As for medical and pharmaceutical goods, professionals "have a high degree of attentiveness, regardless of the therapeutic indications of the pharmaceutical products in question."[223]

It was established when dealing with everyday consumer goods that the inconsistencies in the terminology used in General Court decisions to frame the average consumer and its level of attention causes legal uncertainty.[224] Similar issues of inconsistency may be found when dealing with specialised goods. Thus, in *Novartis v. EUIPO II*, the applicant (Novartis) submitted "that the contested decision [of the EUIPO Board of Appeal] is not consistent, in so far as it states, on the one hand, that the level of attention displayed by the relevant public is *heightened* (. . .) and, on the other, that that *level is high*." However, the applicant accepted level of attention of the relevant public at times to be above average.[225] The General Court concluded that "from a grammatical point of view" and based on its previous decisions the EUIPO Board of Appeal had "referred to a level of attention which was 'heightened' in comparison with an average level of attention."[226]

The above analysis on specialised goods and *Novartis v. EUIPO II* together with the finding on everyday consumer goods reaffirm a need for the General Court to be more consistent in its terminology on the average consumer, including its level of attention.[227] It is reassuring though that the General Court has allowed for deviation from that starting point setting the attention of the average consumer slightly lower or higher. Yet this means it is more difficult to define what is the level of attention of the relevant public and, at the end, what constitutes likelihood of confusion. It is clear that the average consumer is the appropriate term for the relevant public when dealing with B2C where consumers may have "specific expectations" and have capricious tendencies. Contextualisation of the average consumer considering the

---

[221]Alcon v. OHIM/Robert Winzer Pharma, Case C-192/03 P, [2004] ECR I-8993, para 30. Although this decision turned on if a senior mark had become generic, the findings of the Court of Justice were referred by the Court of Justice in Alcon v. OHIM on likelihood of confusion. See Alcon v. OHIM, Case C-412/05 P, [2007] ECR I-3569, paras 48 and 66.

[222]Ferring v. OHIM, Case T-169/14, [2015], para 38.

[223]*Ibid*, para 35.

[224]See above Sect. 11.4.1.1.

[225]Novartis v. EUIPO II, Case T-238/15, [2017], para 55 (italics added).

[226]*Ibid*, paras 60-61.

[227]For a similar finding on specialised good, see the below Sect. 11.4.1.2.

level of specialisation of the goods is not to say that effects of confusion must be considered. It would be sensible to offer a greater protection against confusion, for instance for pharmaceuticals. If confusion of everyday consumer products is compared with for instance certain pharmaceuticals, it may be fatal for a consumer if he/she confuses pharmaceuticals.[228] However, the General Court has stated that the global appreciation test "must be carried out *objectively* and cannot be influenced by considerations that are unrelated to the commercial origin of the goods in question."[229] This *objectiveness* means disregarding "[a]ny harmful consequences linked to the incorrect use of a pharmaceutical product result[ing] from possible confusion on the part of the consumer as regards the identity or characteristics of the good at issue and not as regards their commercial origin."[230]

11.4.2 National Examples

In scrutinising national law, it is natural to take as a starting point how the different jurisdictions apply their versions of the average consumer to "everyday consumer goods." Based on the analysis of General Court case law, the vast majority of cases related to these goods are the key area for the average consumer in trademark law. Part of the national analysis is which goods are categorised as everyday consumer goods and what is the impact of this categorisation on the level of attention of the average consumer. If this basic categorisation is different across jurisdictions, then most likely the framing of the average consumer will not be.

11.4.2.1 UK

In *Interflora EWCA I*, Lewison LJ made some principle findings on applying the average consumer to "ordinary consumer goods and services." It was found by the judge that in cases related to those products "it is clear as a matter of domestic law that not only is the ultimate issue one for the judge, rather than the witnesses; but also

---

[228]For instance, a person died from a pharmacist dispensing the stronger PLENDIL (blood pressure medicine) instead of what the doctor had written ISORDIL (angina pain medicine). This example merely illustrates the danger of confusing pharmaceuticals. Arguably, there is some similarity between the names of the medicines, but the actual confusion was caused by the pharmacist misinterpreting the doctor's handwritten prescription. On this case, see Glabman, Maureen, 'Death by Handwriting', Trustee, vol. 59/9 (2005), pp. 29.

[229]Madaus v. OHIM, Case T-202/04, [2006] ECR II-1115, para 31 (italics added) and subsequently Astex Therapeutics v. OHIM, Case T-48/06, [2008], para 69.

[230]Madaus v. OHIM, Case T-202/04, [2006] ECR II-1115, para 32. On the objectiveness of the global appreciation test, see also Mellor, James, David Llewelyn, Moody-Stuart, Thomas, *et al*, 'Kerly's Law of Trade Marks and Trade Names', (16th edn, Sweet & Maxwell, 2018), p. 425-426.

that the judge can reach a conclusion in the absence of evidence from consumers."[231] The UK Court of Appeal has later referred to this finding.[232] Terminologically, "ordinary consumer goods" is identical with "everyday consumer goods" referred to by the General Court. It is clear from the finding that "ordinary consumer goods" feed into the framing of the average consumer. In three subsequent decisions the UK High Court could have assessed the level of attention of the average consumer purchasing everyday consumer goods (clothing and pet food), namely in *Jack Wills v. House of Fraser*, *Thomas Pink v. Viktoria's Secret* and *Supreme Petfoods v. Henry Bell*.[233] In the decisions, the respective senior owners claimed infringement of their UK and EU trademarks, *inter alia*, based on the likelihood of confusion, under the UK TM Act 1994 and the TM Regulation.

Jack Wills v. House of Fraser was an infringement dispute between the senior owner (Jack Wills) and the junior owner (House of Fraser). Jack Wills, a clothing retailer, sold casual clothing bearing its figurative logo. House of Fraser operating department stores introduced for sale in its stores its own line of competing clothing bearing a similar logo. The simplest version of the senior mark was registered as a UK national trademark and an EU trademark. It was found by Arnold J that "the average consumer in the present case is a consumer of men's clothing, and in particular casual clothing." As for the level of attention, it was found that "[t]he nature of the goods is such that he or she would exercise a *moderate* degree of attention" and that "clothing is primarily purchased on the basis of visual inspection."[234] It was concluded that a "significant proportion of consumers" is likely to be confused.[235]

In *Thomas Pink v. Viktoria's Secret*, Thomas Pink (the senior owner) claimed that Victoria's Secret (the junior owner) had infringed its senior figurative marks. The goods were mainly different clothing items. Birss J gave an in-depth account of the multitude of facets of the average consumer. It was found by the judge that among other aspects, the average consumer of clothing was i) tourists and locals, ii) shopping for themselves or others, iii) male and female, iv) making their purchases following from a targeted shopping or just browsing, and v) exercising "a moderate degree of attention to branding but will not scrutinise the fine print of swing tags and labels."[236] Due to the deviation of clothing, Viktoria's Secret "appeared to" have

---

[231]Interflora v. Marks & Spencer, [2012] EWCA Civ 1501, para 50.

[232]Interflora v. Marks & Spencer, [2014] EWCA Civ 1403, para 115, J.W. Spear v. Zynga, [2015] EWCA Civ 290, para 36(iii) and Comic Enterprises v. Twentieth Century Fox, [2016] EWCA Civ 41, para 34(iii).

[233]Jack Wills v. House of Fraser, [2014] EWHC 110 (Ch), Thomas Pink v. Viktoria's Secret, [2014] EWHC 2631 and Supreme Petfoods v. Henry Bell, [2015] EWHC 256 (Ch). Arnold J decided the first and last of the cases. Arnold J was also the one deciding the case in *Interflora EWHC* where he significantly contributed to interpreting the likelihood of confusion standard and the average consumer. See Interflora v. Marks & Spencer, [2013] EWHC 1291 (Ch), paras 194-224.

[234]Jack Wills v. House of Fraser, [2014] EWHC 110 (Ch), para 85 (italics added).

[235]*Ibid*, para 103.

[236]Thomas Pink v. Viktoria's Secret, [2014] EWHC 2631, para 117.

argued that its consumers were buying "low end clothing," whereas Thomas Pink's consumers were buying "luxury clothing." Inherent in this argument, the defendant seemed to hold that at least the consumers buying luxury goods would most likely not be confused since they would pay high attention to the trademarks when purchasing the clothing. Birss J rejected this argument finding that "[t]he average consumer represents consumers at all levels of the market."[237] The judge found there was likelihood of confusion for both marks.[238]

Supreme Petfoods v. Henry Bell related to the sale of foodstuffs for animals. The senior owner (Supreme Petfoods) claimed that the junior owner (Henry Bell) had infringed its trademarks. Intuitively, the Supreme Petfoods had an interest in a relevant public with as low attention as possible since this public would be more easily confused. Counterintuitively, though, Supreme Petfoods argued that the relevant public was not pet owners but also retailers, since some retailers removed the pet food from bigger bags into smaller containers, not always bearing the trademark, to be sold to consumers. It was found by Arnold J that "it is the perceptions of consumers (here, the pet owners) that matters, not the perceptions of intermediaries (here, wholesalers, retailers and veterinary practices). After all, members of the trade are less likely to be confused (or have their perceptions affected in other ways) than consumers, because they are more likely to be well informed and observant when it comes to trade marks for the goods in their sector."[239] Probably also puzzled by Petfood arguing a higher level of attention for part of the relevant public, Arnold J added that "[a]ccordingly, Supreme Petfoods' case is not disadvantaged by considering it from the perspective of pet owners."[240] Finally, Arnold J found that "[p]et owners are ordinary members of the public" and that "[p]et food is an every day product and consumers would only exercise a moderate degree of attention when purchasing it." It was concluded that there was no likelihood of confusion since there was "no distinctive resemblance between the sign and the [senior] Trade Marks."[241] One month before this decision, in *Enterprise v. Europcar*, Arnold J similarly found that the relevant public in vehicle rental services was a diverse group in terms of "level of attention" and "gender, age, social grouping, ethnicity and residence." The judge did not find that "it would make any difference to the outcome, however, if one posited an average consumer with a single, average level of attention, namely a medium level of attention."[242]

Recently, in *London Taxi v. Frazer-Nash* Arnold J of the UK High Court and LJ Floyd of the UK Court of Appeal disagreed on who should be included in the

---

[237] *Ibid*, para 117(iii).

[238] *Ibid*, paras 169 and 182.

[239] Supreme Petfoods v. Henry Bell, [2015] EWHC 256 (Ch), para 53.

[240] *Ibid*, para 54.

[241] *Ibid*, para 185.

[242] Enterprise v. Europcar, [2015] EWHC 17 (Ch), para 182.

average consumer.[243] Essentially, the claimant (London Taxi) claimed that the defendants (Frazer-Nash and Ecotive) by introduction of the Metrocab had infringed its senior UK and EU trademarks consisting of the shapes of the Fairway taxi, probably known by many as a "classical" London taxi.[244]

Among other goods in class 12, the EU trademark was registered for motor vehicles, and the UK trademark for taxis. In the appeal to the UK Court of Appeal, 26 grounds for the appeal were raised. Two of the grounds relevant to this analysis were addressed in both court instances were: "Is the average consumer in the present case (a) the taxi driver who purchases the cab or (b) the taxi driver who purchases the car together with members of the public who hire taxis?", and if the senior trademarks had been infringed due to likelihood confusion.[245]

For the first question on the average consumer, the claimant held "that there were two average consumers in the present case, namely (i) taxi drivers, and (ii) members of the public who hired taxis."[246] If the latter group would not be independently accounted for as part of the average consumer, the perception of hirers of taxis would be considered by taxi drivers.[247] Arnold J concluded that hirers of taxis should be included as part of the average consumer since they "are consumers of taxi services, and not of taxis. They are not end users of the goods, they are users of the service provided by the consumer of the goods."[248] However, Arnold J accepted that the perception of the hirers of taxis should be included as part of the perception of taxi drivers "since taxis are expensive and specialised vehicles, (. . .) are knowledgeable and careful purchasers, that is to say, their level of attention is fairly high."[249]

When assessing infringement, Arnold J gave what may interpreted as a subtle criticism of the claimant's counsel, since the claimant did not argue that there was a likelihood of confusion on taxi drivers, but on hirers of taxis. This was according to the judge a "fatal claim." To some extent this logically settled the matter for Arnold J since he had already concluded that hirers of taxi services were not independently

---

[243]London Taxi v. Frazer-Nash and Ecotive, [2016] EWHC 52 (Ch) and London Taxi v. Frazer-Nash and Ecotive, [2017] EWCA Civ 1729.

[244]It was the second defendant (Ecotive) that sought to introduce the Metrocab as such, whereas the first defendant (Frazer-Nash) were to supply parts Metrocab. See London Taxi v. Frazer-Nash and Ecotive, [2016] EWHC 52 (Ch), para 1.

[245]For an overview of the grounds, see London Taxi Company v Frazer-Nash and Ecotive, [2017] EWCA Civ 1729, para 19.

[246]London Taxi v. Frazer-Nash and Ecotive, [2016] EWHC 52 (Ch), para 160.

[247]*Ibid*, para 162. Although not considered when framing the average consumer, owners of taxi fleets could also have been considered when taxi drivers were not themselves owners of their taxis. See on this distinction, e.g. *ibid*, para 58. In this context it should be mentioned that even if drivers would not themselves own the taxis they would rent the taxis from the fleet owners, and this way affect the choice of the purchased taxi. Also, it would not change the level of attention of the average consumer decisively here, since taxi drivers are considered as having a high level of attention, and so would the fleet owners.

[248]*Ibid*, para 161. Further, Arnold J found no ground in Court of Justice and UK precedence for including taxi hirers as part of the average consumer.

[249]*Ibid*, para 163.

part of the average consumer. Although, if assumed that hirers were to be included, any confusion on taxi hirers would not change the conclusion that taxi drivers were not confused.[250] To avoid getting the conclusion wrong, Arnold J, despite his previous conclusion, assessed separately the likelihood of confusion of taxi hirers.[251] After globally assessing the likelihood of confusion, Arnold J concluded that although the low level of attention of taxi hirers was a factor "favouring a likelihood of confusion, the low distinctive character of the Trade Marks and the low degree of similarity between the new Metrocab and the Trade Marks outweigh those factors." I.e. there was no likelihood of confusion.[252]

In the UK Court of Appeal LJ Floyd (as agreed with by LJ Kitchin), in some detail went through the scarce Court of Justice and UK decisions that could be relevant for deciding the matter.[253] Arnold J did not go through the previous decisions though "since they are all clearly distinguishable from the present case."[254] LJ Floyd concluded that "[a]s with all issues in trade mark law, the answer to disputed questions is normally provided by considering the purpose of a trade mark which, broadly speaking, is to operate as a guarantee of origin to those who purchase or use the product." Therefore, "the term average consumer includes any class of consumer to whom the guarantee of origin is directed and who would be likely to rely on it, for example in making a decision to buy or use the goods. Against that background, I would not have thought it mattered whether a user was someone who took complete possession of the goods, or someone who merely hired the goods under the overall control of a third party." Conclusively, that "[t]he hirer is a person to whom the origin function of the vehicle trade mark might matter at the stage when he or she hires the taxi."[255] Further, LJ Floyd assumed that consumers of taxi services would address issues with the services with the supplier of the services, but if they would be dissatisfied due to reasons related to the taxi as such (and not the services), the hirers would be likely to blame the manufacturer of the taxi. Hence, taxi hirers are not "in principle" excluded from being part of the average consumer.[256] Floyd LJ agreed with Arnold J's conclusion on likelihood of confusion.[257]

---

[250]*Ibid*, para 247.

[251]*Ibid*, para 248.

[252]*Ibid*, para, 262.

[253]LJ Floyd referred to Björnekulla Fruktindustrier, Case C-371/02, [2004] ECR I-5791 and Kornspitz Company v. Pfahnl Backmittel, Case C-409/12, [2014], but concluded that the decisions did not clarify if the average consumer should include consumers (end users) "who does not take complete possession of the goods is a different question," London Taxi Company v Frazer-Nash and Ecotive, [2017] EWCA Civ 1729, paras 24-32. Here, LJ Floyd also addressed Schütz v. Delta Containers, [2011], EWHC 1712 (Ch) and GAP v. British American Group, [2016] EWHC 599 (Ch) that equally does not address a comparable situation.

[254]London Taxi v. Frazer-Nash and Ecotive, [2016] EWHC 52 (Ch), para 161.

[255]London Taxi Company v Frazer-Nash and Ecotive, [2017] EWCA Civ 1729, para 34.

[256]*Ibid*, para 35.

[257]*Ibid*, paras 83-85.

The decisions contain a fundamental question on the role of the average consumer when deciding likelihood of confusion. Although the disagreement between the court instances had no consequences on the conclusion reached by the courts on likelihood confusion, it may well have a significant impact in future decisions. By having to include a less attentive group of consumers as part of the average consumer will generally be to the advantage of the senior trademark owner and may thus affect the scope of the exclusivity of the senior and junior trademark owners and, to other market stakeholders.[258] Due to principle level of this question, it is regrettable that LJ Floyd did not take the opportunity to ask the Court of Justice for a preliminary ruling on this. It would be relevant to hear the Court of Justice's view on LJ Floyd's policy-based approach and what appears to be an expansive interpretation of "usual origin" principle.[259] LJ Floyd's approach causes a high degree of uncertainty on how the average consumer should be framed in comparable scenarios. Not least, since LJ Floyd bases part of his conclusion on the doubtful factual assumption that if a tax hirer experiences issues with the taxi vehicle as such, the hirer would "blame the manufacturer of the vehicle."[260] Arnold J took a narrower approach that seems better aligned with the current state of the law, until this has been further clarified by the Court of Justice.

11.4.2.2   Nordic Jurisdictions

In Sweden, the SE Court of Appeal in *Mast-Jägermeister v. Vin & Sprit* clearly stated referring to *Lloyd* that the level of attention of the average consumer may vary according to the relevant goods. Referring to older Swedish administrative practice the court found that the "group of purchasers for alcoholic beverages have a high degree of mark awareness."[261] Among different arguments, the court further found that "the high degree of awareness of buyers of alcoholic beverages also speaks against the risk of confusion."[262] As affirmed by the SE Supreme Court, the court found that there was likelihood of confusion.[263]

---

[258]This aspect feeds into the discussion on feedback loops in Chap. 12, Sect. 12.5.

[259]On the "usual origin" factor as a strong factor applied when comparing of the product, see above, Sect. 11.3.

[260]With all respect of the unique cultural connotations attached to the Fairway taxi, the author of this book would most likely remember the name of the taxi company (supplying the taxi services), if it for the third time in a row had issues with their vehicle causing delays in the transportation of the author from A to B. The author would primarily see this as a sign of poor maintenance of the taxi fleet, not issues caused by the manufacturer of the vehicle. For the next taxi ride, another taxi service provider (with a taxi fleet bearing another service provider's trademark) would be chosen.

[261]In Swedish: "har köparkretsen för alkoholhaltiga drycker tillskrivits en hög grad av märkesmedvetenhet." Mast-Jägermeister v. Vin & Sprit, T 799-99, [2001], p. 7.

[262]In Swedish: "Den höga medvetenheten hos köpare av starksprit talar också mot förväxlingsrisk." *Ibid*, p. 8.

[263]Mast-Jägermeister v. Vin & Sprit, T 2982-01, [2003], SESC, p. 5.

It was held by the SE District Court in *Kraft Foods v. Mars* that candy was "ordinary consumer goods" and that the "group of purchasers consists of the general public in Sweden."[264] In a more recent dispute between Mars and Kraft Foods, the SE Court of Appeal found when framing the average consumer that it had to be considered that candy as produced by the parties "consists of fast moving consumer goods being the target of impulse purchase."[265] The SE Court of Appeal did not relate these findings on the character of the goods specifically to the level of attention of the average consumer, but merely to the fact that candy is purchased after visual scrutiny.[266] However, it was found by the court in this more recent dispute that the character of the goods meant that they were exposed visually and according to how the marks were pronounced.[267]

In Denmark, in the two disputes on *inter alia* likelihood of confusion between Puma (the senior trademark owner) and Coop (the junior trademark owner) on their respective shoes heard by the DK MCH Court and the DK Supreme Court, either side sought to tailor the level of attention of the relevant public to their advantage. Generally, Coop had an interest in a more attentive public and Puma the opposite. In the first of the disputes from 2008, this tailoring of the relevant public was less pronounced. In this decision, there seemed to be a consensus between the parties that Puma's shoe was sold in sports goods shops and Coop's shoe in its supermarkets.[268] However, Puma argued before the DK MCH Court that "it is not uncommon that surplus stocks of the original [Puma] shoe are sold in supermarkets, for which reason the customers will not initially consider price and quality further, and when the shoe is bought and used, it is too late. Consequently, price is not relevant to the [overall] assessment [of confusion]."[269] The DK MCH Court found there to be a likelihood of confusion and the DK Supreme the opposite.

In the dispute from 2011, Coop argued before the DK MCH Court that "Puma's shoes are of excellent quality and are typically sold in lifestyle and sports goods stores where the buyer, typically a male aged 15–25 years, is guided by an assistant and pays between DKK 500–1000 for the shoe, which comes in a fancy red box. The

---

[264]In Swedish: "gängse konsumentvaror" "omsättningskretsen består av den breda allmänheten i Sverige." Kraft Foods v. Mars, T 14294-09 and T 7359-10, [2012], SEDC, p. 17.

[265]In Swedish: "utgörs av sådana dagligvaror som är föremål för spontanköp." Mars v. Kraft Foods, T 5406-15, [2016], SECA, p. 15.

[266]See respectively, Mars v. Kraft Foods, T 7141-12, [2013], SECA and Mars v. Kraft Foods, T 5406-15, [2016], SECA.

[267]Mars v. Kraft Foods, T 5406-15, [2016], SECA, p. 15.

[268]For instance, the CEO of Puma Denmark explained how the sports goods shops in Denmark paid attention to shoes with similar side applications sold in supermarkets. Coop Danmark v. Puma, U.2008.446H, [2007], (DKSC), p. 450. Coop argued before the DK MCH Court that it was when the Puma shoe was sold out in sports goods shops that the customer went to one of Coop's Kvickly supermarkets to buy the Coop shoe. *Ibid*, p. 451.

[269]In Danish: "Det er ikke ukendt, at restpartier af originale sko sælges i supermarkeder, hvorfor kunderne i første omgang ikke vil tænke nærmere over pris og kvalitet, og når skoen først er købt og anvendt, er det for sent. Prisen er derfor uden betydning for vurderingen." *Ibid*, p. 450.

Coop-shoe, on the other hand, is sold off-the-rack in Kvickly[270] to "Mr. and Mrs. Denmark"[271] who do not doubt that they are buying a cheap supermarket shoe."[272] Before the DK Supreme Court, Puma argued that "due to the similarity [between the marks and goods], and since both Puma's and Coop's shoes are sold off-the-rack in supermarkets and often at approximately the same prices, there is a risk of confusion."[273] The DK MCH Court and DK Supreme Court found for Coop. Although, in particular in the 2011 dispute, the framing of the relevant public and its level of attention was a theme among the parties, the courts did not explicitly address this.[274]

Recently, in *G-Star Raw v. Kings & Queens*, the claimant (G-Star) claimed that the defendant (Kings & Queens) by its use of among other trademarks RÅ and ЯÅ, had infringed various versions of the claimant's Danish and EU trademarks, including its RAW trademark registered for clothing and shoes. The relevant consumer group was a key theme in the decision. Thus, a country manager of the claimant explained that the "G-Star Raw customers are typically a male/female between 28–35 years old, price-conscious, quality-conscious, and they want to communicate that they use well-known brands."[275] Further, that there is risk of confusion.[276] The claimant held that "no Danish consumers will be in doubt that RÅ means RAW."[277] The defendant held that the "average consumer" would hardly link the disputed marks. This argument, the claimant found, was of no legal relevance, and it was not factually correct.[278]

---

[270]A supermarket chain owned by Coop.

[271]Essentially, meaning the "ordinary Dane."

[272]In Danish: "Pumas sko er af fremragende kvalitet og sælges typisk i lifestyle- og sportsforretninger, hvor køberen, der typisk er en sportsudøvende mand på 15-25 år, vejledes af en ekspedient og betaler 500-1.000 kr. for skoen, som leveres i en flot rød æske. Coop-skoen hænger derimod som stangvare i Kvickly og købes for omkring 100 kr. af "Hr. og Fru Danmark", som ikke er i tvivl om, at de har købt en billig supermarkedssko." Puma v. Coop Danmark, U.2011.3433, [2013], (DKSC), p. 3436.

[273]In Danish: "På grund af ligheden, og da både Pumas sko og Coops sko sælges som stangvarer i supermarkeder og ofte til priser, der ligger tæt på hinanden, er der en risiko for forveksling." *Ibid*, p. 3438.

[274]Similar arguments were presented by the parties in the declaratory action *OTCF v. Hummel* decided by DK MCH Court under the TM Regulation also related to e.g. likelihood of confusion between marks used for sports clothing. The defendant (OTCF) wanted the court to declare the it did not infringe the defendant's (Hummel) trademark right. The claimant advocated a level of attention of relevant public "higher than usual" (in Danish: "højere end sædvanligt") e.g. due to the price of the goods (OTCF v. Hummel, V-67-16, [2017], (DKMCHC), p. 18). The defendant advocated an "average level of attention" (in Danish: "gennemsnitligt opmærksom") of the relevant consumer (*ibid*, p. 22-23). Without further assessment of the average consumer, the court found for the defendant according to a global appreciation of likelihood of confusion (*ibid*, p. 27).

[275]In Danish: "G-Star Raw kunder er typisk en mand/kvinde mellem 28-35 år, som er prisbevidst og kvali-tetsbevidst, og som ønsker at kommunikere over for omverdenen, at de benytter velkendte brands." G-Star Raw v. Kings & Queens, A-35-17, [2018], (DKMCHC), p. 17.

[276]*Ibid*, p. 18.

[277]In Danish: "Ingen danske forbrugere vil være i tvivl om, at RAW betyder RÅ" *Ibid*, p. 28.

[278]*Ibid*, p. 29 and 33.

The manager of the defendant explained that the target group of the defendant's goods was the 15–25 year olds.[279] It was further explained that the consumer would not understand "RÅ" as "RAW," but as "cool" or "tough".[280]

It was established by the DK MCH Court that the likelihood of confusion had to be decided according to a global appreciation assessment, including the perception of the relevant public.[281] However, the court reached a dissenting decision. The two judges (including the specialist judge) giving the majority decision based their decision on the testimony given by the defendant's manager, i.e. emphasising the differences in meaning between RÅ and RAW. This, according to the judges, "corresponds to the average consumer's perception of mark's meaning and opinion content."[282] The specialist judge also found that "a substantial part of the customer group is assumed to be aware"[283] about the difference between the price and quality of the parties' goods (the claimant's goods being somewhat more expensive and of better quality than those of the defendant).[284] Thus, the judges found there to be no likelihood of confusion. The minority judge found there to be a likelihood of confusion mainly based on the meaning of the disputed marks.[285]

The decision is a clear example of the DK MCH Court applying the average consumer as a legal fiction. Essentially, the majority decision is based on the testimony given by a witness representing the defendant, but with no support of market evidence. The testimony of the claimant's representative advocates an attentive consumer and thus actually supports the majority decision. This was not addressed by the majority judges though. The decision also shows the disagreement between the judges on what may be expected of the average consumer. There seems to be no doubt that the decision is correct and in line with the EU average consumer. The opposite result would have significantly lowered the level of attention of the average consumer needed to prove likelihood of confusion.

In *Ankenævnet v. Chantelle*, a likelihood of confusion dispute in registration related to lingerie, Chantelle (the senior owner) argued before the DK MCH Court that "[t]he purchasers are mainly ordinary consumers, i.e. non-experts, for whom the principle of the imperfect recollection applies."[286] The DK IPO Board of Appeal argued that "women buying expensive French lingerie are fully aware which brands they want to buy. Since customers therefore are highly observant and brand

---

[279]*Ibid*, p. 18.

[280]Rå in Danish may be the same as raw in English, but it may also among others mean cool or tough.

[281]*Ibid*, p. 35-36.

[282]In Danish: "svare til gennemsnitsforbrugerens opfattelse af mærkets betydning og meningsindhold." *Ibid*, p. 37.

[283]In Danish: "en betydelig del af kundegruppen antages at være bevidste."

[284]*Ibid*.

[285]*Ibid*, p. 38.

[286]In Danish: "Køberkredsen er hovedsagelig almindelige forbrugere, dvs. ikke-eksperter, for hvem principet om det udviskede erindringsbillede er gældende." Ankenævnet v. Chantelle, U.2003.2366H, [2003], (DKSC), p. 2369.

conscious, a less strict assessment of likelihood of confusion has to be made."[287] The DK MMC found that many expensive lingerie goods are purchased as Christmas gifts by men who refer orally to the name of the goods.[288] The DK Supreme Court did not address the relevant consumers. The DK MCH Court found that there was likelihood of confusion and the DK Supreme Court the opposite.

In *Saint-Gobain v. Richter-System* on likelihood of confusion in registration between two wordmarks, the senior mark (ECOPHON) and the junior mark (EUROPHON) related to sound insulating materials and the level of attention of the relevant public played a prominent role. As affirmed by the DK Supreme Court, those "highly specialised products" are mainly purchased by "developers, contractors and self-employed carpenters, often based on advice from architects and according to professional considerations."[289] Besides identity between the goods, the courts found that there was no likelihood of confusion between the marks. The level of attention seemed to have an immediate impact on the assessment.

The state of the law in Norway is captured well by Lassen and Stenvik's textbook often referred to explicitly by the Norwegian courts stating that "[t]he cheaper and more insignificant the product is, and the more insignificant the quality of the product is to the buyer, the bigger the risk is that differences in the marks are overlooked." Therefore, marks for cheaper goods have to be further apart to avoid likelihood of confusion compared with expensive goods, and goods where quality is of particular importance to the buyer. The first category (cheaper goods) are for instance "light bulbs, salt, pins and matches," the second (expensive goods) "pianos, outboard motors and washing machines" and the third (quality goods), "pipe tobacco, perfume and mobile phones."[290] Obviously, there is a clear overlap between the second and third category of goods, since quality is often also a key feature for consumers of expensive goods. The NO District Court quoted the findings by Lassen and Stenvik in *NYX v. Laboratoire Nuxe* where the court as part of a registration dispute had to decide the likelihood of confusion between the figurative versions of Nuxe Paris (the senior mark) and Nyx (the junior mark) related to certain cosmetic goods. Initially, the court turned to the question on whether the relevant public was particularly "brand conscious."[291] The court found, building on

---

[287]In Danish: "Hertil kommer at de kvinder som køber dyrt fransk undertøj, fuldt ud er klar over hvilke mærker de ønsker at købe. Da kunderne således i høj grad er opmærksomme og mærkebevidste, må der anlægges en mindre streng forvekslingsbedømmelse." *Ibid*, p. 2369-2370.

[288]*Ibid*, p. 2370.

[289]In Danish: "højt specialiserede varer som fortrinsvis købes af bygherrer, entreprenører og tømrermestre, som oftest på grundlag af rådgivning der er givet af arkitekter efter nærmere faglige overvejelser." Saint-Gobain v. Richter-System, U.2006.1203H, [2006], (DKSC), p. 1208.

[290]The first quote in Norwegian: "Dess billigere og dess unselig varen er, og dess mindre roll dens kvalitet spiller for kjøperen, desto større er gjerne faren for at ulikheter i kjennetegnene overses." Lassen, Birger Stuevold and Stenvik, Are, 'Kjennetegnsrett', (3rd edn, Universitetsforlaget, 2011), p. 417.

[291]In Norwegian: "merkebevisst." NYX v. Laboratoire Nuxe, TOSLO-2014-79765, [2015], NODC, p. 7.

the NO Supreme Court decision *Klagenemnda v. W Pelz* that the assessment of confusion had to be made referring to the part of the public most likely to be confused.[292] It was acknowledged by the court that for certain parts of cosmetic goods, such as makeup and certain creams, "the average consumer may have a higher degree of brand consciousness."[293] Based on the finding by Lassen and Stenvik, the court found that "the average consumer has an average level of attention."[294] It was concluded by the court that there was no likelihood of confusion for the average consumer.[295] The finding in this decision is in line with the precedent of the NO Supreme Court in for instance, *Klagenemnda v. W Pelz*.[296]

As in Sweden, the Norwegian judiciary has assessed the level of attention of the average consumer when buying alcoholic beverages. Recently, in *Altia v. Arctic Beverage Group*, the NO District Court had to decide the validity of the junior mark CHILLIN against the senior registered mark CHILL OUT, both for wine and spirits.[297] A key question was whether there was likelihood of confusion between the two marks. The court found that the average consumer had to be found among the regular customers of Vinmonopolet.[298] The court noted that since none of the parties had produced sufficient evidence on the level of attention of the relevant public, the court had to make its own normative assessment of this matter.

Based on one of its previous decision from 2004, *Trading Scandinavia v. Patentstyret*, the court found that the level of attention of the average consumer is affected by "which kind of product is dealt with." Also, that "[w]e are in an area where it may be assumed that the public generally has a certain brand awareness." Furthermore, that this awareness "in recent years has been increased" since "[w]ine drinking has been become more widespread due to the welfare development, increased travelling, wine advertisement in newspapers and magazines, wine tastings etc." Adding to this, is the increased selection of wines and self-service in the stores of Vinmonopolet.[299]

---

[292]*Ibid* referring to Klagenemnda v. W Pelz, HR-1998-63-A, [1998], NOSC, p. 1992 and Lassen, Birger Stuevold and Stenvik, Are, 'Kjennetegnsrett', (3rd edn, Universitetsforlaget, 2011), p. 418.

[293]In Norwegian: "Retten antar at gjennomsnittsforbrukeren har en høyere merkebevissthet for sminke og ulike typer kremer." NYX v. Laboratoire Nuxe, TOSLO-2014-79765, [2015], NODC, p. 7. Reference was made by the court to Lancôme v. OHIM I, Case T-466/08, [2011] ECR II-1831, paras 48-49. On this latter decision, see above Sect. 11.4.1.1.

[294]In Norwegian: "gjennomsnittsforbrukeren har et middels oppmerksomhetsnivå". NYX v. Laboratoire Nuxe, TOSLO-2014-79765, [2015], NODC, p. 8.

[295]*Ibid*, p. 9.

[296]Klagenemnda v. W Pelz, HR-1998-63-A, [1998], NOSC, p. 1992-1993.

[297]Altia v. Arctic Beverage Group, TOSLO-2017-52797, [2018]. NODC.

[298]Vinmonopolet is a state-owned monopoly vendor of e.g. wine in Norway.

[299]Altia v. Arctic Beverage Group, TOSLO-2017-52797, [2018]. NODC, p. 7. In Norwegian: "hva slags vare det dreier seg om. Vi befinner oss på et område der man må anta at publikum generelt sett har en viss merkebevissthet. (. . .) de senere årene er blitt ytterligere skjerpet. Vindrikking er blitt mer utbredt som følge av velstandsutvikling, med økt reising, vinspalter i aviser og blader, vinsmakingskurs m.v." The quote is taken from the previous decision of the NO District Court Trading Scandinavia v. Patentstyret, TOSLO-2004-6764, [2004], NODC, p. 6.

11.5   Different Market Places

It is obvious that the internet has changed the shopping landscape compared to earlier. It is now possible for companies to "have both a "*brick and click*" presence" or only sell their goods on the internet.[300] Also, it is possible to use trademarks as part of Google AdWords. The case law cited so far relates mainly to the use of trademarks in the physical world. However, in seven decisions the Court of Justice has given preliminary rulings related to the use of trademarks in search engines,[301] one of which is *Interflora Court of Justice*, and one decision as well relating to the use of trademarks in the online auction site eBay.[302] These decisions are related to "double identity" issues, i.e. where the junior trademark owner's mark is identical to that of the senior trademark owner. In these decisions, though, some significant statements are made by the court on how to frame the average consumer and decide likelihood of confusion.

In the Google AdWords cases, the junior trademark owner had purchased AdWords identical to those of the senior trademark owner and used them to advertise links to websites offering identical products.[303] In these "double identity" cases there was, in accordance with the wording of the relevant provisions,[304] no requirement of finding confusion between the marks. Until the *Google France cases*,[305] confusion was presumed in comparable decisions.[306] However, in the *Google France cases*,[307] as upheld in subsequent decisions, the Court of Justice introduced a requirement of finding likelihood of confusion within the realm of the double identity cases. As set out by the Court of Justice, the use of AdWords may constitute trademark

---

[300]Jacoby, Jacob, 'Trademark Surveys Volume I: Designing, Implementing, and Evaluating Surveys', (1st edn, American Bar Association, 2013), p. 146 (italics added).

[301]Google France v. Louis Vuitton, Case C-236/08, [2010], Google France v. Viaticum, Case C-237/08, [2010], and Google France v CNRRH, Case C-238/08, [2010], (the cases C-236/08 – C-238/08 have been assessed jointly by the Court of Justice and will be referred to jointly as "Google France cases.") all published in [2010] ECR I-2417, Die BergSpechte Outdoor Reisen v. trekking.at Reisen, Case C-278/08, [2010] ECR I-2517, Eis.de v. BBY, Case C-91/09, [2010], Portakabin v. Primakabin, Case C-558/08, [2010] ECR I-6963, Interflora v. Marks & Spencer, Case C-323/09, [2011] ECR I-8625 (referred to in the main text as "Interflora Court of Justice"). The above decisions relate to using keyword tools (in Google terminology AdWords) consisting of trademarks.

[302]L'Oréal v. eBay International, Case C-324/09, [2011] ECR I-6011.

[303]For a further description of the factual and legal scenario, see e.g. *Google France cases*, Cases C-236/08 – C-238/08 [2010] ECR I-2417, paras 46-47.

[304]Now art. 9(2)(a) of the TM Regulation (art. 9(1)(a) of the TM Regulation 2009) and art. 10(2) (a) of the TM Directive (art. 5(1)(a) of the TM Directive 2008).

[305]*Google France cases*, Cases C-236/08 – C-238/08 [2010] ECR I-2417.

[306]See Bently, Lionel, Sherman, Brad, Gangjee, Dev and Johnson, Phillip 'Intellectual Property Law', (5th edn, Oxford University Press, 2018), p. 1118 and Cornish, William R., Llewelyn, David, and Alpin, Tanya, 'Intellectual Property: Patents, Copyright, Trademarks and Allied Rights', (8th edn, Sweet & Maxwell, 2013), p. 758.

[307]*Google France cases*, Cases C-236/08 – C-238/08, [2010] ECR I-2417.

infringement if "[t]he function of indicating the origin of the mark is adversely affected if the ad does not enable *normally informed and reasonably attentive internet users*, or enables them only with difficulty, to ascertain whether the goods or services referred to by the ad originate from the proprietor of the trade mark or an undertaking economically connected to it or, on the contrary, originate from a third party."[308] The court has upheld this stance in subsequent decisions related to the use of AdWords.[309] Also, the court stated that a similar approach applies to instances where the purchased AdWords are not identical to the trademark (i.e. outside the scope of double identity cases).[310] Besides inconsistently worded characteristics of the average consumer,[311] the Court of Justice in internet decisions consistently refers to the "*internet user*" and not only the "average consumer" as in physical world decisions.[312]

The decisions issued by the Court of Justice related to internet use of trademarks do not take different approaches according to the different products with which the trademarks are used.[313] The internet decisions related to instances where the trademark owner's trademarks are bought as keywords by others and used to prompt sponsored links to websites containing products identical with those of the trademark owner. These products have involved goods such as leather goods,[314] parts and building materials,[315] and perfumes, cosmetics and hair-care products,[316] and

[308] *Ibid*, para 84 (italics added).

[309] Die BergSpechte Outdoor Reisen v. trekking.at Reisen, Case C-278/08, [2010] ECR I-2517, paras 34-35, Portakabin v. Primakabin, Case C-558/08, [2010] ECR I-6963, paras 52-54, and L'Oréal v. eBay International, Case C-324/09, [2011] ECR I-6011, para 94. Not surprisingly, the Court of Justice in *Die BergSpechte Outdoor Reisen GmbH v. trekking.at* and *Portakabin BV v. Primakabin BV* confirmed its stance in the *Google France cases*. The cases are comparable to the facts, and the former decision was issued only two days after *Google France cases*, the latter four months after this decision.

[310] Die BergSpechte Outdoor Reisen v. trekking.at Reisen, Case C-278/08, [2010] ECR I-2517, paras 39-40, and Portakabin v. Primakabin, Case C-558/08, [2010] ECR I-6963, paras 52-53.

[311] In *L'Oréal v. eBay* and *Interflora Court of Justice* the Court of Justice stated that average internet users are "reasonably well-informed and reasonably observant." L'Oréal v. eBay International, Case C-324/09, [2011] ECR I-6011, para 94 and Interflora v. Marks & Spencer, Case C-323/09, [2011] ECR I-8625, paras 44 and 50. Consequently, on the face of it, there is a difference in wording between this definition of the average consumer and the above definition of the internet user as "normally informed and reasonably attentive internet users."

[312] See also Arnold J in Interflora v. Marks & Spencer [2013] EWHC 1291 (Ch), para 231.

[313] The Court of Justice might also be reluctant to do so in the future, since this would probably be perceived by the court as an assessment of the facts.

[314] Google France v. Louis Vuitton, Case C-236/08, [2010] ECR I-2417.

[315] Portakabin v. Primakabin, Case C-558/08, [2010] ECR I-6963.

[316] L'Oréal v. eBay International, Case C-324/09, [2011] ECR I-6011.

services such as travel-arrangement services,[317] matrimonial agency services,[318] and flower-delivery services.[319]

Although there is a difference between how the characteristics of the average consumer have been framed in the *Google France* decisions and the physical world decisions, the difference does not seem to have any material implications, partly because no explanation is given by the Court of Justice to the different wording of the characteristics, and partly because the different characteristics are not applied consistently to all internet decisions. As for the Court of Justice's consistent reference to the "average internet user" instead of the "average consumer" as in the physical world cases,[320] the Court of Justice seems to indicate that it has to be considered that the decisions related to the internet differ from the physical world decisions.[321]

From this brief review, it is also possible to detect a process of contextualisation, this time solely by the Court of Justice and confined to the criteria of the market place. Hence, when the average consumer is on the internet that is a specific market place different from the physical market place. When discounting is considered in the context of the internet, it seems uncontroversial that the Court of Justice has referred to *average internet users*. Not surprisingly, in the realm of the internet the ignorant and the highly attentive internet users are to be discounted. Arguably, it is the same as saying in the physical world that in decisions related to everyday consumer goods the relevant average consumer is the "average supermarket consumer."

So far, there have been no decisions of the General Court where it has referred to "*internet user*" as the relevant public. However, in *Novartis v. OHIM*, the General Court found that "the fact that an end consumer *could possibly obtain on the Internet* a medicinal product sold without prescription, without the advice of a pharmacist or

---

[317]Google France v. Viaticum, Case C-237/08, [2010] ECR I-2417 and Die BergSpechte Outdoor Reisen v. trekking.at Reisen, Case C-278/08, [2010] ECR I-2517.

[318]Google France v CNRRH, Case C-238/08, [2010] ECR I-2417.

[319]Interflora v. Marks & Spencer, Case C-323/09, [2011] ECR I-8625.

[320]See also Arnold J in Interflora v. Marks & Spencer [2013] EWHC 1291 (Ch), para 231.

[321]Dinwoodie and Gangjee have pointed out, based on Datacard Corporation v. Eagle, [2011] EWHC 244 (Pat), that "[i]t is too soon to know whether the elements of the consumer that the Court [of Justice] has devised in crafting the "average internet user" will give rise to more generally applicable evolutions in the construct of the consumer." Dinwoodie, Graeme, and Gangjee, Dev, 'The Image of the Consumer in EU Trade Mark Law', in Leczykiewicz, Dorota, and Weatherill, Stephen eds., The Images of the Consumer in EU Law: Legislation, Free Movement and Competition Law (1st edn, Hart, 2016), 339, p. 366, including footnote 140 of the text. Although tentatively, Davis has concluded that "[a] case in point is the courts' recognition of the average internet user as being somehow different from the average consumer." Davis, Jennifer, 'Revisiting the Average Consumer: An Uncertain Presence in European Trade Mark', Intellectual Property Quarterly, no. 1, (2015), pp. 15, p. 30. Based on case law, Wallberg has also seen the average internet user as rooted in the well established average consumer. Wallberg, Knud, 'Brug af Andres Varemærker i Digitale Medier: Et Bidrag til Afklaring af Varemærkerettens Indhold og Grænseflader', (1st edn, Jurist- og Økonomforbundets Forlag, 2015), p. 210-211.

physician, *is not such as to lower that consumer's degree of attentiveness when purchasing such goods.*"[322]

In the Nordic countries only a very limited number of cases has addressed the relevant public related to trademark use on the internet, including the cases on Google AdWords. More or less all of those decisions, though, refer to "internet users" as the relevant public.[323] In the UK, Arnold J in *Interflora EWHC* was outspoken on the connection between the "internet user" and the "average consumer:" "In Interflora (CJEU) the Court referred to "reasonably well-informed and reasonably observant internet users," which may just be a difference in translation. Regardless, it is clear that in these keyword advertising cases *"the "average consumer" and the "reasonably well-informed and reasonably observant internet user" are one and the same.*"[324]

11.6 Trademark Contextualisation

The Court of Justice has proved willing to contextualise the average consumer against the type of trademarks involved, here exemplified with specific attention paid to non-traditional trademarks and signs, such as sounds, shapes and smells. This shows that when the court refrains from assessing the average consumer's level of attention to certain goods and markets places, this does not apply unconditionally in the assessment of distinctive character.[325] As for general matters of assessing distinctive character, the Court of Justice has, as for products, referred to this assessment to be part of a factual assessment.[326] However, in several preliminary

---

[322]Besides this finding, the General Court made no principle remarks on the average consumer in the online environment. Novartis v. OHIM, Case T-331/09, [2010] ECR II-5967, para 28 (italics added). The court referred to this finding in in Novartis v. EUIPO II, Case T-238/15, [2017], paras 65-66. The latter decision is further dealt with in Sect. 11.4.1.2.

[323]See for instance, from Sweden: Elskling v. Kundkraft, [2012] MD 2012:15, para 99; Denmark: Billedbutikken v. Pixelpartner, U.2011.634S, [2010], (DKMCHC), p. 639 and STOK Emballage v. Fritex Emballage, V-3-14, [2015], (DKMCHC), p. 10. Differently, though, in Eico v. Multikøkkener where reference is merely made to "consumers." Eico v. Multikøkkener, SH2015.V-21-15S, [2015], (DKMCHC), p. 5. Norway: Although on unfair competition law, the NO Court of Appeal referred to "internet user" as the relevant public in Rørlegger Sentralen v. Rørleggervakta. Rørlegger Sentralen v. Rørleggervakta, [2014] LB-2012-118015 NOCA, p. 6.

[324]Interflora v. Marks & Spencer, [2013] EWHC 1291 (Ch), para 231 (italics added). See also Interflora v. Marks & Spencer, [2014] EWCA Civ 1403, para 112. See also the more recent *Victoria Plum v. Victorian Plumbing* where the formulations are used unchangeably, Victoria Plum v. Victorian Plumbing, [2016] EWHC 2911 (Ch), paras 17 and 62.

[325]On the relevance of the average consumer as part of assessing distinctive character, see Chap. 1, Sect. 1.5.1, including footnote 108.

[326]As mentioned in the introduction, the assessment of distinctive character of a mark is conducted referring to the perception of the average consumer. It has been ruled by the Court of Justice that this assessment is also a matter of fact to be assessed by "the competent authority." Henkel, Case C-218/01, [2004] ECR I-1725, paras 50 and 63 and also Koninklijke Philips Electronics v. Remington

rulings the Court of Justice has not refrained from more closely making assumptions on the actual perceptions of the average consumer—i.e. making closer assumptions of the perceptions of the average consumer in contrast with its known broader characteristics. Based on the wording of *OHIM v. Borco-Marken-Import* the Court of Justice in *August Storck* used the "empirical rule," that "[a]verage consumers are not *in the habit of making assumptions about the origin of products on the basis of their shape or the shape of their packaging in the absence of any graphic or word element.*"[327] This "empirical rule" seemingly derives from Advocate General Colomer in *Linde* where he assumed that "it is unlikely that the average consumer will perceive minor differences [between three-dimensional shapes] as an indication of the product's origin." Furthermore, "that such practical difficulties derive from the very nature of three-dimensional shapes and from the idiosyncrasies of consumers' habits rather than from what is alleged to be a stricter approach in the assessment of distinctive character."[328] The first time the Court of Justice appears to have applied this *empirical rule* was in *Libertel.*[329]

One can only speculate what is meant by an *empirical rule* since there seems to be no legal understanding of what it is. However, outside of law an "empirical rule" is well-known in statistics where it dictates deviations of measurements on a bell-shaped distribution. This understanding probably has to be rejected since it was concluded that average consumer is *normative* and not statistical.[330] Arguably, the

---

Consumer Products, Case C-299/99, [2002] ECR I-5475, paras 63 and 65. In the recent *August Storck v. EUIPO* appeal, the applicant, according to the Court of Justice, sought "to call into question the factual assessment made by the General Court" of descriptive character. The Court of Justice stated, that the applicant was seeking to have the Court of Justice conduct "a new assessment of the facts, without alleging in that regard any form of distortion of those facts by the General Court. However, since an appeal lies on points of law only, that argument must be rejected as manifestly inadmissible." August Storck v. EUIPO, Case C-636/15 P, [2016], para 36.

[327]OHIM v. BORCO, Case C-265/09 P, [2010] ECR I-8265, para 25 (the figurative sign 'α') and August Storck v. OHIM, Case C-24/05 P, [2006] ECR I-5677, para 25 (shape of a sweet). See also Henkel, Case C-218/01, [2004] ECR I-1725, para 52 (the shape of a bottle), Mag Instrument v. OHIM, Case C-136/02 P, [2004] ECR I-9165, para 30 (shape of a torch), Proctor Gamble, joined cases C-468/01 P to C-472/01 P, [2004] ECR I-5173, para 36 (the shape of tablets for washing machines), Libertel v. Benelux-Merkenbureau, Case C-104/01, [2003] ECR I-3793 (colour *per se*), para 65 and Linde *et al*, joined cases C-53/01 to C-55/01, [2003] ECR I-3161, para 48 (the shape of certain vehicles, a torch and a wrist watch).

[328]Linde *et al*, joined cases C-53/01 to C-55/01, [2003] ECR I-3161 (opinion of AG Colomer), para 12. See also recently Coca-Cola v. OHIM, Case T-411/14, [2016], para 37.

[329]Libertel v. Benelux-Merkenbureau, Case C-104/01, [2003] ECR I-3793, para 65. The empirical rule was not applied by the Court of Justice in *Linde*, although it was before this decision that Advocate General Colomer seemed to have laid the foundation for the empirical rule. The *Linde* decision was issued 3 April 2003 and *Libertel* 6 May 2003. Due to significant personal overlap between the judges composing the Court of Justice in the two decisions and the temporal proximity of the decisions, it does not seem farfetched to assume that Colomer's assumptions in *Linde* may have found their way into *Libertel*. With no explicit linking by the Court of Justice, though, this is mere speculation.

[330]The meaning of "empirical rule" in the statistical sense of standard deviation is addressed above in footnote 329, including the main text connected with it.

rule could be seen as a subsequent rationalisation by the Court of Justice. It could explain why the court, unlike for the average consumer as part of likelihood of confusion, is willing to move close to applying the average consumer to the factual circumstances as part of assessing distinctiveness for certain non-traditional marks. This sidestepping into this area of trademark law is relevant to the analysis in this book since it illustrates a willingness of the Court of Justice to steer development of trademark law by using the average consumer as proxy for trademark policy. The policy seems to be that certain shapes and colours should be kept free for others to use.[331] A less prominent reason could be the Court of Justice grasping at straws in *Libertel,* presumably referring to Colomer's seemingly unfounded assumption.[332]

11.7 Conclusion

Contextualising the average consumer in likelihood of confusion disputes is an immediate clash between this legal fiction and the market realities surrounding European trademark law. It was shown referring to *Adidas v. Shoe Branding* that the Court of Justice considers contextualisation to be part of the factual assessment. That said, the average consumer *per se* provides a steer for factual assessment by the General Court and national courts when the relevant public is the consumer public. To avoid this, the Court of Justice could have used a more neutral term such as the "ordinary purchaser," leaving it purely for the other courts to define this fiction. Probably, those courts would reach the result that the *ordinary purchaser* of for instance FMCG would be a consumer.

It was concluded that the General Court and national courts regard the average consumer as normative, and it was shown that in particular the UK High Court and Court of Appeal explicitly have addressed this in the Interflora v. M&S decisions. The characteristics of the average consumer, "reasonably well-informed and reasonably observant and circumspect," to a wide extent are left meaningless by the Court of Justice. However, they serve the important purpose of discounting from the average consumer the highly *inattentive* (the Homer Simpsons) and the highly

---

[331]See e.g. Libertel v. Benelux-Merkenbureau, Case C-104/01, [2003] ECR I-3793, para 66. This is also referred to as the "need to keep free" or the "principle of keeping free." For an analysis of these see Phillips, Jeremy, 'Trade Mark Law and the Need to Keep Free', International Review of Industrial Property and Competition Law, vol. 36/no. 4, (2005), pp. 389 and Laustsen, Rasmus D. 'The principle of keeping free within EU Trade Mark Law,' Rettid 2 (2010), pp. 1. available at: http://law.au.dk/fileadmin/Jura/dokumenter/forskning/rettid/2010/afh2-2010.pdf (last visited 26 May 2019). Recently, Pila has described *Libertel* and *Henkel* as examples where the Court of Justice makes both an "empirical" and "normative" assumption. Pila, Justine, 'The Subject Matter of Intellectual Property', (1st edn, Oxford University Press, 2017), p. 198-199.

[332]Jacob has stated that Colomer was "[k]nown for his flamboyant opinions." Jacob, Marc A., 'Precedents and Case-Based Reasoning in the European Court of Justice: Unfinished Business', (1st edn, Cambridge University Press, 2014), p. 209. Maybe not flamboyant, but Colomer's opinion in *Linde* is certainly notable.

attentive (the Mr. Spocks). On the face of it, the characteristics are superfluous since already the use of the neutral term "ordinary purchaser" or less so "ordinary consumer" indicates an inherent discounting. No one would sensibly perceive an ordinary consumer as highly attentive when doing grocery shopping for a regular household. The characteristics, however, could be seen as a way for the Court of Justice to stress the importance of discounting in particular towards the national courts. This view is also supported by the analysis of the early development of the average consumer by the Court of Justice where it clarified that consumers should not be regarded as gullible, inattentive Homer Simpsons.[333]

It was illustrated that the relevant public when assessing the similarity between the products is an independent factor in the *Canon* non-exhaustive multifactor test. At the same time, that the overall process of choosing which products are to be compared influences how the relevant public is chosen and hence its contextualisation.

Referring to General Court cases it was found that the court often refers to everyday consumer goods as somewhat resembling the more clearly defined FMCG. For everyday consumer goods, the average consumer is most often the relevant public. Tentatively, it was found that the average consumer as a starting point has an *average* level of attention, but that its attention may also be low or high for certain goods. In its reliance on the goods affecting the level of attention, the General Court creates inconsistency, in particular relating to certain foodstuffs and beverages, as the court is not clear on whether they cause a low or average degree of attention. Price was shown only to increase the level of attention if it was relevant to the sector as a whole. Finally, it was seen that the average consumer purchasing non-everyday consumer goods has a higher attention to goods where safety concerns are prominent, or goods purchased infrequently. In *Václav Hrbek v. OHIM* it was shown that when buying a skiing jacket, the average consumer would show a higher degree of attention since this does not share the characteristics of everyday consumer goods. This decision illustrates how tricky it is to apply the rather rigid "whole sector approach" of the General Court according to which an aspect of the goods has to apply to the whole sector of the goods to affect the level of attention of the average consumer. The relevant public may also be a more specialised group of consumers or professionals purchasing non-everyday consumer goods. The former is more attentive than the average consumer and the latter has the highest level of attention of any relevant public. It was established that the General Court uses inconsistent terminology for describing the relevant public and its level of attention. Thus, in the two recent General Court decisions *Dimitrios Mitrakos v. EUIPO* (on everyday consumer goods) and *Novartis v. EUIPO II* (on pharmaceuticals) the court had to conclude on the meaning of such inconsistent terminology. However, it was also established that part of the reason for the inconsistent terminology is such terminology introduced by the parties involved in the dispute.

---

[333]See Chap. 8, Sect. 8.6.

Focus of the analysis of national case law was how national judiciaries referring to everyday consumer goods see the level of attention of the average consumer. It was shown, as was also the case in the previous chapters, that the UK judiciaries have outspokenly followed the EU law approach. Although not obliged to follow the General Court precedents, the UK judiciaries seem to be very much in line with the practice of the General Court on everyday consumer goods. This was seen in *Interflora EWCA I* where the UK Court of Appeal referred to "ordinary consumer goods." It is clear from UK case law that the UK judiciaries also contextualise the average consumer. The disagreement between the UK High Court and Court of Appeal in the recent decisions in *London Taxi v. Frazer-Nash* clearly shows that it is not settled how the average consumer must be framed when deciding likelihood of confusion. Arnold J in the UK High Court concluded that hirers of taxis were not included in the average consumer, since the goods were the taxi vehicles as such. Floyd LJ in the UK Court of Appeal took a broader policy-based view and concluded that hirers were included since the relevant trademarks also served as guarantee of origin to the hirers. The disagreement between the courts had no implications for the outcome of the decisions though. However, since senior trademark owners have an interest in including less attentive consumers (and more easily confused consumers) as part of the average consumer, Floyd LJ's interpretation may prove advantageous to senior trademark owners in future comparable cases.

As the earlier analysis has shown, the contours of how the average consumer is applied fades when moving into the case law of the Nordic judiciaries. Overall, the Nordic judiciaries rarely conduct an explicit contextualisation. For instance, in the Danish dispute from 2011 between Puma and Coop contextualisation was shown to play a role among the parties who sought to mould the average consumer to their advantage. The parties' arguments gave the DK MCH Court and DK Supreme Court an opportunity in principle to address the level of attention of the average consumer, but they did not do so. In *G-Star Raw v. Kings & Queens*, the expectations of the DK MCH Court judges to the average consumer caused a dissenting decision. The majority judges rightly applied an average consumer aligned with EU practice, although this application was implicit.

Examples of tentative contextualisation by the Swedish and Norwegian courts were found. Different from General Court case law, the SE Court of Appeal in *Mast-Jägermeister v. Vin & Sprit* and the NO District Court in *Altia v. Arctic Beverage Group* found a higher degree of attention of the average consumer when purchasing alcoholic beverages. These examples together with the internal inconsistencies illustrates the difficulties in applying the average consumer to the market realities.

With the Google France cases and other decisions related to internet matters it was illustrated how the Court of Justice has introduced an "average internet user." At first glance, this is a contextualisation of the average consumer, but unless further clarified by the court, the two are to be regarded as substantially identical.

It was finally seen that the Court of Justice through an *empirical rule* has been willing to contextualise the average consumer by giving its view on how to assess the distinctiveness of certain untraditional marks. This can be regarded as the court feeding policy into European trademark law via the average consumer.

To contextualise the average consumer for everyday consumer goods it would be relevant for the courts to look closer at marketing literature regarding EU consumer markets, bearing in mind the above.[334] At the end, it is a matter of judicial choice to what extent knowledge of how consumers navigate the market place, for example as stated in marketing literature, plays into European trademark law through contextualisation of the average consumer—and how it *should do so*. As addressed in the introduction, this is a matter of how narrowly the average consumer should be contextualised.

---

[334]See e.g. the references to Underhill in Chap. 12, Sect. 12.7.

Part IV
Wrapping Up

Chapter 12
Putting the Average Consumer into Perspective

12.1 Lessons Learned

This book set out to test the proposition that European trademark law as part of the likelihood of confusion standard applies the average consumer incoherently and inconsistently. Testing the proposition was manifested in an overall divide between a horizontal and vertical analysis.

With its two legs, the horizontal analysis sought to analyse how the average consumer is one among other legal fictions. First, the average consumer was placed among other more or less distant "cousin" legal and non-legal fictions that share several features. The legal fictions were represented by the "informed user" in EU design law, the "person skilled in the art" in European patent law and the "reasonable person" in European tort law. Outside of law, insight was gained from looking into the "rational actor" model from economics. Second, an analysis was made of the average consumer under the UCPD, and its other consumer models.

The vertical analysis sought to analyse EU and national trademark legislation to expose how the UK (England and Wales), Sweden, Denmark and Norway lay out the likelihood of confusion standard as part of which the average consumer has been developed by the Court of Justice. A scrutiny was made of how the Court of Justice has developed the average consumer before and after Sabel, and how the General Court and the national judiciaries apply their version of the average consumer to different contexts, represented by different product markets and market places. A central aspect throughout the analyses was the average consumer as a legal fiction of normative and fictional elements.

Overall, the insight gained from the analyses is an overview of how fragmented and complex the average consumer is in European trademark law. Also, numerous specific elements are relevant to looking ahead. Immediately below, the lessons learned from the horizontal and vertical analyses are addressed. Following from this, it is addressed to what extent the average consumer, as it is applied under European

© Springer Nature Switzerland AG 2020
R. D. Laustsen, *The Average Consumer in Confusion-based Disputes in European Trademark Law and Similar Fictions*, https://doi.org/10.1007/978-3-030-26350-8_12

trademark law, complies with European trademark policy. Finally, this chapter gives an account of the purely normative angle of the analysis, i.e. how the average consumer should be applied from *de lege ferenda* and *de sententia ferenda* perspectives.[1] An example of how to provide a better steer for the average consumer is drawn from law and economics.

12.2 The Distant Cousins and the False Friends in European Law

In the first leg of the horizontal analysis, it was concluded that from a theoretical perspective the average consumer should be categorised as a *legal fiction* that resides within likelihood of confusion, which is a *legal standard*. As a legal fiction, the average consumer consists of normative and descriptive elements. These theoretical findings support the argument that emphasis should not be on the search for a "real" average consumer, since it does not exist. A key purpose of legal fictions is to suspend operative facts and to create a *workable* fiction *in law*. The analysis of this workability resides mainly in law, but account should also be taken of the real life assumptions forming the average consumer. As for the divide between the Court of Justice as the ultimate interpreter of EU law and other courts that apply the law to the factual circumstance, it was concluded that the more normative the average consumer is, the more it resides with the Court of Justice as the ultimate interpreter of EU law, and vice versa.[2]

When analysing the other legal fictions (the more or less distant cousins), it was seen that the average consumer resemblances the "informed user" from EU design law and the "person skilled in the art" from European patent law. The fictions are different; the average consumer having the lowest level of attention, the person skilled in the art the highest, and the informed user falling between the two. However, compared to their respective peers they all represent *average* or *ordinary* members of the group. Compared with the reasonable person in tort law, it was found that in developing the average consumer, inspiration could be found in the way the reasonable person is objectified when used to decide what is "acceptable" behaviour, for instance by bringing in the level of dangerousness and the protected interests involved. Referring to the rational actor model from economics, it was seen that the average consumer is more broadly a social science model that *per se* is not found in real life. Some resonance was seen between the average consumer and the rational actor due to the commonality of discounting some consumers from both models. However, the term "average consumer" is legal and does not translate directly into economics.

---

[1] On the understanding of these terms, see Chap. 2, Sects. 2.1 and 2.2.1.
[2] See Chap. 5, Sect. 5.3.2 and Chap. 11, Sect. 11.1. On the divide between the Court of Justice and other courts, see also Chap. 4.

Whereas the average consumer was less similar to the other fictions just mentioned it is closely related to the UCPD average consumer model under this directive. A key reason is that the UCPD uses the same wording and sets out the average consumer as known from Court of Justice practice. The directive has added though, that "social, cultural and linguistic factors, as interpreted by the Court of Justice" are to be considered. Two of the other consumer models under the UCPD, the "confident consumer" and "a particular group of consumers," illustrate the importance of contextualising the average consumer in ways not significantly different from the contextualisation of the average consumer in European trademark law. The last consumer model though under the directive, the "vulnerable consumers," was seen as markedly different from the average consumer in European trademark law. Children exemplified the vulnerable consumers. It was seen that case law of the General Court and the national courts on trademark law that involves children as the relevant public is scarce. The General Court and the national courts are hesitant to contextualise the average consumer to younger children. The General Court stated in one decision that if goods targeted at children are not actually purchased by them, but by adults, then the adult public will be the *relevant public*. It remains to be seen how the Court of Justice will position itself in an appeal decision or in a preliminary ruling where the actual target group of the relevant products is not present in the purchase situation, for instance, in the case of children's toys targeted at young children, but bought by parents.[3]

In terms of the functions that the other (different) legal fictions serve in their respective legal fields, it makes sense to say that the average consumer is somewhat harmonised functionally with them. They all serve to suspend certain operative facts and discount the least and most attentive and careless consumer. The level of harmonisation is naturally higher with the UCPD average consumer, with the significant rider that its average consumer is more narrowly contextualised in terms of the vulnerable consumers, represented by children. One reason for this is most likely that European trademark law and the UCPD serve different main purposes. The former directly protects the interests of senior trademark owners and their competitors, and the latter protects consumers and to a more limited extent businesses.

12.3 European Trademark Law: A Patchwork

It is clear from the analysis that European trademark law consists of different levels. Particularly, the interplay between the EU and the national levels were allocated as essential to developing the average consumer. Through an analysis of the dynamics of European trademark law, it was concluded that the likelihood of confusion standard in European trademark legislation has undergone maximum harmonisation.

---

[3]See Chap. 7, Sect. 7.5.2.

However, due to the vague legislative formulations of this standard it is ultimately for the Court of Justice and other European judiciaries to set the "floor and ceiling" of the relevant legislative provisions partly through the average consumer.[4] This interplay between the EU and national levels naturally involves the maximum harmonised legislative likelihood of confusion standard, but more important the dialogue between the Court of Justice and the national judiciaries.[5] In the comparative analysis of the national jurisdictions, it was presumed there is a functional similarity between the national trademark laws. This presumption was made bearing in mind though, that there is latitude for the national judiciaries to make a fact-based decision on what constitutes likelihood of confusion referring to the average consumer.[6] The overall finding was that the average consumer is harmonised under European trademark law, however, that this answer comes with a set of significant caveats that distort the level of harmonisation.

On many occasions, the Court of Justice has ruled on the average consumer. It was shown that the average consumer was developed in the early decisions of the Court of Justice pre *Sabel* related to consumer protection law and unfair competition law and this development was clarified. It was found, different from the finding of Advocate General Fennelly in *Estée Lauder*, that as far back as *Van Bennekom* from 1983 the Court of Justice referred to an "averagely well-informed consumer"[7] and that the average consumer was developed inconsistently. The Court of Justice was not always clear on how to address this consumer fiction and its characteristics. It was argued that part of the development could have been caused by a correlation between the judges in the Court of Justice in some of the decisions pre *Sabel*, in *Sabel, Gut Springenheide* and *Lloyd*.[8] In the early case law, the Court of Justice sent one clear message to the national judiciaries though; that consumers, represented by the early versions of the average consumer, were not gullible without critical sense. Also, a clear message was stated by the Court of Justice already in *Cassis de Dijon* that consumers needed "suitable information" to make their purchasing decisions.[9] Some inconsistency was detected in different language versions of the early decisions, and some of the versions provided some ground for arguing that the "*average consumer*" could be called the "*ordinary* consumer." These takeaways from the early case law of the Court of Justice are important since one of the most important characteristics of the average consumer in European trademark law is that some consumers are "discounted" from the fiction.

Through the legislative analysis of the likelihood of confusion standard in the TM Directive 1989 it was seen that this is a standard developed on the backdrop of established national standards, and not least on the backdrop of the confusion

---

[4]See Chap. 4, Sect. 4.2.1.

[5]*Ibid*, Sect. 4.3.1.

[6]See Chap. 2, Sect. 2.3.1.

[7]See Chap. 8, Sect. 8.5.

[8]See Chap. 10, Sect. 10.2.1.

[9]See Chap. 8, Sect. 8.3.

standard as addressed at the international level by the Paris Convention. In the UK, the standard is rooted in the law of passing off,[10] and in the Nordic jurisdictions, it can be traced back to early Nordic trademark collaborations, such as the Nordic TM Proposal 1882.[11] Although inevitably different national subtexts exist to these early standards, the standards indicate a somewhat common consistent legal frame present before introduction of the TM Directive 1989. Crucial to the analysis, the relevant provisions of the directive introduced "the relevant public." Further, the recitals of the directive stipulated that "numerous elements" should be considered in the assessment of likelihood of confusion. This was important to developing the global appreciation test. Obviously though, these legislative stipulations are vague and not as such vectors of consistency.

On a national level, there was an inconsistency between the UK and until 1 January 2019 all Nordic legislation, in that the latter legislation did not refer to a "relevant public." As per 1 January 2019 though, the Danish legislature introduced the "relevant public" as part of the likelihood of confusion standard in the DK TM Act 1991, whereas the Swedish legislature did not do this in their reform of the SE TM Act 2010. Despite the recent changes in the Danish legislation, the legislative intends of all the Nordic legislatures were and still are to follow the directive. Therefore, the current legislative inconsistency between the UK and Sweden/Norway should not be given too much weight.[12] As for Denmark, the author does not expect the recent Danish legislative changes to manifest in any changes to the judicial (lack of) application of the average consumer as part of the assessment of likelihood of confusion. The reasons for this assumption are that the legislative intends to follow the applicable trademark directives also underpinned the DK TM Act 1991 before the recent changes and the subtlety of the reasoning of the Danish judiciaries.

With the "trinity decisions," *Sabel*, *Lloyd* and *Gut Springenheide*, it was shown that they consolidated the average consumer as a matter of European trademark *law* as distinct from the *facts*. Whereas *Sabel* and *Lloyd* relate to trademark law, *Gut Springenheide* relates to unfair competition law, but all three decisions relate to consumers buying everyday goods. A key contribution of *Lloyd* was that the Court of Justice allowed for the attention of the average consumer to vary according to the relevant goods. Also, in a trademark law setting, *Lloyd* stated the now so mechanically referred to characteristics of the average consumer, i.e. *"reasonably well-informed and reasonably observant and circumspect."*[13] If the paths of precedents in Court of Justice case law are followed backwards, *Sabel* and *Lloyd* still stand as the key precedents of the average consumer in European trademark law. This indicates consistency, had it not been for the Court of Justice being often unclear in its references to precedents. In this respect, the General Court is even worse as it

---

[10]See Chap. 9, Sect. 9.3.2.1 and Chap. 10, Sect. 10.3.

[11]See Chap. 3, Sect. 3.3.2, Chap. 9, Sect. 9.3.2.2 and Chap. 10, Sect. 10.3.

[12]See Chap. 9, Sect. 9.3.2.2.

[13]See Chap. 10, Sects. 10.2.1–10.2.3.

often refers to its own precedents although the precedents ultimately refer to the precedents of the Court of Justice.[14]

In line with the legislative likelihood of confusion standard it was shown that, all national jurisdictions before the TM Directive 1989 have used comparable "multi-factor tests" to assess confusion.[15] The analyses of national case law solidified an issue caused by the difference between the UK Common Law Legal Family and the Nordic Legal Family. Overall, UK judiciaries are explicit in their ratios decidendi in contrast with the Nordic judiciaries, in particular the Danish, which are much more subtle in their reasoning. It is clear that the UK judiciaries implemented the average consumer as set out by the Court of Justice since they explicitly refer to precedents of the Court of Justice and use the terms well-known from EU law. The Nordic judiciaries are much more unclear in their reference to Court of Justice practice and the terminology used by the court. Especially, the Danish judiciaries rarely refer to EU practice in their rulings and rarely mention the relevant public. The DK Supreme Court has firmly taken a critical stance towards EU law with its recent *Ajos* ruling going against the *Ajos* preliminary ruling of the Court of Justice. In the decision, the DK Supreme Court found that there is no obligation to interpret a Danish provision *contra legem* in a dispute between two private parties, not even if this is dictated by an EU legal principle.[16]

It was established that the Court of Justice has emphasised that the average consumer and its characteristics is part of *the law* when assessing likelihood of confusion. A central question is how much legal guidance the Court of Justice actually adds by saying that the average consumer is *"reasonably well-informed and reasonably observant and circumspect"* and that its attention is likely to vary according to the goods? Besides some very important points relevant to contextualisation, not much. From that finding, it would thus be expected that the national courts address this as part of their legal qualification. Therefore, it is tempting to say that national judiciaries, including particularly the Danish, do not comply with EU law since they do not explicitly apply the EU average consumer and its characteristics in the assessment of likelihood of confusion. This would be incorrect for different reasons. First, it was shown that parties to the Nordic disputes now and then argue on how to frame the relevant public. Although the judges do not explicitly refer to these arguments in their ruling, the arguments naturally affect them. Second, to claim that decisions do not comply with EU law would somewhat require the outcome to be changed, had EU law been brought in. It has not been a task of this book to make this assessment of national case law, and essentially take on the mantle of the judge.

In contextualising the average consumer to the market realities, the Court of Justice has stated that this is for the General Court and the national judiciaries to do

---

[14] *Ibid*, Sect. 10.2.4.

[15] *Ibid*, Sect. 10.3.

[16] Ajos, Case 15/2014, [2016], (DKSC), p. 44-51. For further on the decision, see Chap. 3, Sect. 3.3.2.2.

so with the steers provided by the Court of Justice. As a natural consequence of the many disputes on the likelihood of confusion in registration that reach the General Court, this court has on many occasions contextualised the average consumer.[17] A key aspect in the contextualisation is the exercise of discounting the *inattentive* and highly *attentive* consumers, figuratively represented by respectively the Homer Simpsons and Mr. Spocks. Also from various aspects, it does not make sense to analyse an "average" in a quantitative sense due to the high number of variables vested in the average consumer and lacking ability to test them in real life.[18] Although quantitative evidence may play a role, there seems to be consensus among the judiciaries that the average consumer is a legal fiction and as such normative.[19]

When contextualising the average consumer to "everyday consumer goods," somewhat similar to fast moving consumer goods ("FMCG") known from e.g. marketing, its attention is *average*. For certain everyday consumer goods, the attention may be higher or lower. For instance, if price is relevant to the whole sector of the relevant goods, the attention may increase. It was found that the General Court is inconsistent in its categorisation of everyday consumer goods and that it has a rather broad understanding of this category of goods.[20] For certain specialised goods that are not everyday consumer goods, the level of attention of the average consumer may be increased, for instance, where health and safety are prominent factors. It was established that the General Court uses inconsistent terminology when describing the relevant public and its level of attention, but that such terminology may also be caused by terms introduced by the parties to a dispute. Further, it was shown that such inconsistencies may actually manifest in concrete claims from a party in disputes on likelihood of confusion.

It was clear that UK courts continuously and explicitly contextualise the average consumer to specific goods, but less clear with the Nordic judiciaries. In the London Taxi v. Frazer-Nash, the disagreement between the UK High Court and Court of Appeal shows that it is far from clear how the average consumer must be framed when assessing likelihood of confusion. The UK High Court took a narrow view in contrast with the broader policy-based view of the UK Court of Appeal where a group of less attentive consumers were included as part of the average consumer. Although not the case in *London Taxi v. Frazer-Nash*, this interpretation may be an advantage in future similar decisions for the senior trademark owners since they have an interest in a less attentive average consumer. The SE Court of Appeal in *Mast-Jägermeister v. Vin & Sprit* and the NO District Court in *Altia v. Arctic Beverage Group* found the average consumer to have a higher degree of attention when purchasing alcoholic beverages. This finding differs from the General Court's precedents on this. The Danish dispute from 2011 between Puma and Coop was an

---

[17]See Chap. 10, Sect. 10.2.4 and Chap. 11, Sect. 11.2.1.

[18]*Ibid*, Sect. 10.2 and Chap. 1, Sect. 1.2.

[19]See Chap. 1, Sect. 1.2 and Chap. 11, Sect. 11.2.2.

[20]See Chap. 11, Sect. 11.4.1.1.

example where the parties sought to contextualise the average consumer to their advantage, but where the DK MCH Court and the DK Supreme Court did not address this framing of the average consumer.

As part of contextualisation it was found that in the realm of the internet the average consumer is the "average internet user." It was concluded that this probably is not a "new" average consumer, but merely an obviously necessary contextualisation of the average consumer to trademark disputes related to the internet.

12.4   A Need for Concern?

The Court of Justice has created a legal fiction through its average consumer that based on the results of this book is harmonised to a certain level when it is applied by the General Court and the national courts. In line with the findings in fiction theory the focus should be on creating something *workable in law*. This means at EU level to create a fiction that will be workable by the Court of Justice when it interprets the law and as importantly by the General Court and national courts when they apply it to the facts. The solution has to be workable for the EUIPO and the national trademark offices. These stakeholder groups have not been addressed separately, but they are naturally imperative as an entrance point for the majority of non-disputed decisions on this, and for the disputes on likelihood of confusion decided by the boards of appeal of the offices but later litigated in court. Finding a workable solution involves two aspects. First, it begs a more detailed commenting on the inconsistencies vested in the average consumer. Second, it begs for an addressing of the normative side of the average consumer based on trademark policy. One thing is saying that the average consumer is a fiction consisting of normative and factual elements. The obvious follow-up question is then what *are* the normative elements and how *should* they be? This latter part of the query is addressed referring to trademark policy.[21]

On the face of it, the Court of Justice should never have started to use the term average consumer and the mechanically phrased and subsequently repeated characteristics "reasonably well-informed and reasonably observant and circumspect." In trademark law a more covering, neutral and simple term adding no characteristics would be the "ordinary purchaser."[22] *Ordinary* indicates that this is nothing numerical and hence, ends the unfruitful discussions of any numerical meanings *average* as part of the *average* consumer. Further, *ordinary* indicates a discounting of the most *inattentive* and *attentive* consumers (in the consumer scenario). It should be possible for courts to apply an "ordinary purchaser" to determine that the *purchaser* of for

---

[21]As laid out in Chap. 1, Sect. 1.3.

[22]This term was already found in the passing off decision from 1866 *Seixo v. Provezende*. See Chap. 9, Sect. 9.3.2.1.

example everyday consumer goods sold in supermarkets are consumers, and that the purchaser of chemicals in a B2B setting is a professional actor in that specific field. Currently though, there seems to be no chance that the term average consumer will be changed since the UCPD and certain *lex specialis* sectoral areas already have introduced this term[23] and due to the longstanding Court of Justice precedents in European trademark law where the term has been applied.

In relation to the horizontal aspects, it is preferable if the Court of Justice clarifies the substantial similarities and differences between the average consumer, the informed user from EU design law and the person skilled in the art (the sectoral expert) from patent law. In *PepsiCo v. Grupo Promer*, the court opened up the conversation, but merely stated the obvious, i.e. in an intuitive comparison that, the average consumer is the least attentive.[24] Especially, it would be valuable to have a clarification of the informed user vis-à-vis the average consumer since they reside in EU law. Such clarification would enlighten both trademark law and design law.

Most critically, there is a lack of clarification from the Court of Justice on how to distinguish between the average consumer under European trademark law and under the UCPD. An important lesson to be learned from the UCPD is the numerous factors included in the application of its average consumer, i.e. "social, cultural and linguistic factors." Although it has been seen that those factors are relevant to likelihood of confusion disputes in trademark law, it is unclear to what extent. Further, and more critically, it is unclear if there is a difference between how narrowly the average consumer should be contextualised under European trademark law and under the UCPD. It was indicated under the UCPD that the average consumer is contextualised more narrowly. This was exemplified by children as representatives of vulnerable consumers. It remains to be seen specifically how the Court of Justice in principle will define the role of young children when deciding on the likelihood of confusion for products targeted at them, but bought by their parents. In a broader perspective a clarification is needed of what impact the purposes of the two legislative regimes have on the application of the respective average consumers. Since consumers are the direct beneficiaries under the UCPD, it provides an argument for a closer contextualisation to ensure that consumers are actually protected.[25] When given the opportunity, the Court of Justice should clarify if the average *internet user* differs from the average *consumer*, although this is not presumed to be the case. A further clarification by the court of the understanding of the average consumer under the UCPD and the average internet user would provide a steer for the courts that based on the facts actually contextualise the average consumer.

The Court of Justice may play a more active role in shaping the average consumer by adjusting the law and policy underpinning the average consumer. As for the contextualisation of the average consumer though, the Court of Justice appears to have a more limited role to play in laying out more detailed principles since

---

[23]See Chap. 1, Sect. 1.5.5.
[24]See Chap. 6, Sects. 6.2 and 6.4.
[25]See Chap. 7, Sects. 7.2, 7.5.2 and 7.6.

contextualisation is purely for the General Court and national courts. This is in line with the finding in *Shoe Branding v. Adidas*.[26] However, as shown in the realm of deciding distinctive character of non-traditional marks, the Court of Justice made the "empirical rule" that "[a]verage consumers are not *in the habit of making assumptions about the origin of products on the basis of their shape or the shape of their packaging in the absence of any graphic or word element*."[27] The Court seems to imply that if the interests at stake are serious enough then it will make the balancing exercise of how the average consumer should be framed and make overall presumptions about how the average consumer behave. It was found that Advocate General Colomer in *Linde* without further ground introduced this "empirical rule."[28] The grounds for the presumptions of Colomer cannot be tested.[29] However, at least, the Advocates General could make explicit presumptions on how consumers behave in certain situations as also addressed below.

12.5 Bringing in Trademark Policy

Besides the detailed improvements of the law, one question remains in the analysis, namely how the average consumer as portrayed in this book complies with trademark policy.[30] This question is narrowly related to the normative side of the average consumer. Dinwoodie has posed the central question if trademark law should be *proactive* or *reactive*. More precisely, "should trademark law be structured *reactively* to protect whatever consumer understandings or producer goodwill develops, or should it *proactively* seek to shape the ways in which consumers shop and producers sell or seek to acquire rights, thus shaping how the economy functions?"[31] The suggested improvements support a more proactive role for the Court of Justice. This stance is supported below with reference to trademark policy. If more trademark policy was brought into the framing of the average consumer this fiction would be better rooted in the reason for being of European trademark law, including the functions of trademarks and the European trademark system as such. As importantly, by clarifying these policy interests, the Court of Justice could provide some objective elements and remove the average consumer away from the operational facts of each decision by the General Court and the national courts on likelihood of confusion and

---

[26]See Chap. 11, Sect. 11.1.

[27]OHIM v. BORCO, Case C-265/09 P, [2010] ECR I-8265, para 25. See Chap. 11, Sect. 11.1.

[28]See Chap. 11, Sect. 11.6.

[29]Anecdotally, the author of this book has heard from an employee at the EUIPO that this presumption has its origin in a presentation made by an expert on consumer behaviour. Several members of the CJEU allegedly attended the presentation.

[30]See Chap. 1, Sect. 1.3.

[31]Dinwoodie, Graeme B., 'Trademarks and Territory: Detaching Trademark Law from the Nation-State', Houston Law Review, vol. 41/no. 3, (2004), pp. 885, p. 889-890 (italics added).

increase the coherence and consistency. As it may be recalled, Kitchin LJ found in *Interflora EWCA III* that vested in the average consumer is a balancing "between various competing interests including, on the one hand, the need to protect consumers and, on the other hand, the promotion of free trade in an openly competitive market, and also to provide a standard, defined in EU law, which national courts may then apply."[32] Through trademark policy, the Court of Justice may proactively steer this balancing exercise of the various interest vested in the average consumer providing a better steer not only for the average consumer, but for European trademark law.

As seen throughout the analyses it potentially matters a great deal to the outcome of a dispute on likelihood of confusion how the average consumer is framed.[33] The potential proactive impact on European trademark law of the average consumer can be illustrated by a "feedback loop" that builds on a line of thought developed in intellectual property law by Gibson.[34] If the feedback loop is adapted to the average consumer in European trademark law, the law affects reality that at the end affects/ feedbacks into the law. Applied to the average consumer, the first part of the loop is the relationship between the Court of Justice and the General Court and the national courts. The General Court and national courts apply the principles of the Court of Justice when they adjudicate the specific dispute at hand on likelihood of confusion. According to the adjudicated result of the dispute, the parties to the dispute navigate in the marketplace. Presumably, competitors of the parties will do the same, and more broadly, market players in other markets will also navigate according to the legal principles derived from the dispute. The last link of the loop consists of consumers. Although they are not parties to the likelihood of confusion dispute, they will be immediately affected by the outcome of the dispute. For example, in a "classical" Puma dispute a junior competitor that introduces a shoe with a similar trademark (the side application) has to remove its shoe from the market, if the average consumer is likely to be confused. Potentially, this may cause other competitors to be reluctant to introduce shoes with some similarity to Puma's trademark. This effect may ripple into other markets. When the type of products in the markets has changed; will the perception of the average consumer change accordingly over

---

[32]Interflora v. Marks & Spencer, [2014] EWCA Civ 1403, para 113. See Chap. 11, Sects. 11.2.1 and 11.4.2.

[33]See e.g. Chap. 11, Sect. 11.4.1.1.

[34]The focus of Gibson's article is how the grey areas of intellectual property law, including trademark law, will expand licensing markets of senior right owners due to risk aversion among competitors. In sum, the feedback loop in trademark law is described as: First, that if a trademark is unlicensed by the senior trademark owner, "use is likely to cause confusion among consumers as to whether the mark owner produced, sponsored, or approved of the goods." Second, to be on the safe side, junior users of trademarks will seek a license from the senior owner, even if unnecessary. Third, as a "norm," consumers will become used to seeing an expanding practice of licensed trademarks. "And what consumers view as the norm becomes the norm because consumer perception is trademark law's touchstone." Gibson, James, 'Risk Aversion and Rights Accretion in Intellectual Property Law', the Yale Law Journal, vol. 116 (2007), pp. 882, p. 907-908. Generally, on trademark law, *ibid*, p. 907-927.

time? If consumers get used to seeing fewer shoes with certain similarity to Puma's shoe bearing somewhat similar trademarks it might make the average consumer more likely to be confused, and vice versa had the court found that there was no likelihood of confusion. Ending the loop; how does the "changed" average consumer feedback into the law, if at all?

The feedback loop mechanism was recently addressed by the NO District Court in the mentioned *Altia v. Arctic Beverage Group*. Here, the court had to decide if there was a likelihood of confusion between two trademarks both for wine and spirits. Part of the court's findings was an increase of wine consumption, the selection of wine and the wine offered as the self-service in shops.[35] Comparable to the above feedback loop, the court then speculated on the consequences of its precedence to the marketplace. Two of its previous similar decisions had not been appealed by the Norwegian Industrial Property Office being a party to these decisions. According to the court, this essentially meant that the Norwegian state had accepted a marketplace for wine, where the stakeholders (the businesses and the relevant public) had to accept a fairly high degree of similarity between marks used for competing products, and that this would influence the brand building of the businesses.[36]

How could ultimately the Court of Justice proactively steer the above feedback loop, and what about the General Court and the national courts? To fully give an answer to those questions and address all the complex variables vested in this feedback loop structure is outside the scope of this finalising analysis. One important point though is that the Court of Justice should be clearer and more proactive on trademark policy, specifically, how the policy feeds into average consumer. Trademark policy would be a way for the Court of Justice to proactively control the feedback loop. It would be a way for the court to control the ripple effects of the feedback loop from specific case results into the same market and other markets before it potentially affects the law from the bottom up through the average consumer.

To use trademark policy in balancing interests necessitates a clarification of what the policy is. With the current EU trademark legislation, the EU legislature still leaves a significant leeway for the Court of Justice to decide what European trademark policy is. The inconsistencies between the trademark laws at national level potentially affect the traditional role of the European trademark system in creating undistorted competition in the EU.[37] Particularly, the Court of Justice should clarify the divide between the average consumer under European trademark law and the UCPD, including the vulnerable consumers. It would also invite the court to give an account on what role if any consumer protection should play. As indicated, consumer protection in EU trademark law is somewhat emerging with

---

[35] Altia v. Arctic Beverage Group, TOSLO-2017-52797, [2018]. NODC. For further on the decision, see Chap. 11, Sect. 11.4.2.2.

[36] Altia v. Arctic Beverage Group, TOSLO-2017-52797, [2018]. NODC, p. 7.

[37] On this role of the trademark system, see Chap. 1, Sect. 1.3.3.

reference to consumer protection in the EU Charter and in the EESC TM Opinion 2013.

A clarification is particularly needed by the Court of Justice of the functions of trademarks other than the origin function, i.e. the quality, communication, investment and advertising functions.[38] Especially, the overlap and the difference between the origin and the quality functions are relevant, since the origin function was allocated as underpinning the likelihood of confusion assessment. As for the legal origin function of trademarks, it is clear that the average consumer is where this function is tested, i.e. if the origin function of the senior mark is affected by the use of the junior mark.[39]

Throughout the book it has been stated that the characteristics of the average consumer are used in a rather mechanical way, chiefly, by the Court of Justice, the General Court and the UK courts, and what is even worse they rarely are used by the Nordic courts. In a broader perspective, it has been claimed by Fhima that courts tend to decide if the origin function is affected when assessing likelihood of confusion with the factors of the global appreciation test "in a weird sort of algebra, treating the confusion finding as an inevitable outcome of finding similarity on each of those factors, thus losing sight of how real consumers might behave."[40] Based on recent case law on distinctiveness Fhima has argued that "reality" should be brought in to ensure a clearer picture on "how trade marks function in the marketplace."[41] It is not the stance of this book that more evidence case-by-case should be presented on the average consumer to make probable that the origin function is affected. Due to the many factual scenarios to which trademark law has to be applied, this would leave the average consumer more fragmented and less workable than today. Not least, the litigation costs would most probably increase. In essence, it is the stance that too much focus should not be attached to finding consumer confusion case-by-case.

Grynberg has argued that in US trademark infringement disputes on confusion, not only the interests of the senior trademark owner are in danger of being harmed, also consumer interests may be harmed, not least the interests of the consumer group relying on the mark used by the junior trademark owner.[42] Moreover, Grynberg has argued that "[t]reating trademark litigation as consumer conflict corrects some of the traditional narrative's shortcomings by more accurately representing the range of interests at stake."[43] Likewise, Gibson has argued on US trademark law that trademark owners "vindicate the consumer interest in avoiding fraud" creating "an

---

[38] *Ibid*, Sect. 1.3.1.

[39] See Chap. 9, Sect. 9.3.1.1. Broadly, on the origin function see Chap. 1, Sect. 1.3.1.

[40] Fhima, Ilanah, 'Introducing Reality into Trade Mark Law', Journal of Intellectual Property Law & Practice, vol. 9/no. 8, (2014), pp. 1, p. 3.

[41] *Ibid*, p. 4.

[42] See Grynberg, Michael, 'Trademark Litigation as Consumer Conflict', New York University Law Review, vol. 83/no. 1, (2008), pp. 60, p. 83.

[43] See *ibid*, p. 87.

agency relationship, with the producer as the agent, acting in the interests of the principal, the consumer."[44] These findings provide an argument for introducing an objectified requirement for the confusion to have a certain level of "seriousness," not only referring to the average consumer, but consumers more broadly. At the legislative level, it may be recalled that the EU legislature rejected to insert a requirement in the TM Directive 1989 that the likelihood of confusion had to be "serious".[45] However, a certain *seriousness* could be introduced judicially by paying more attention to the non-confused consumers. For instance, some consumers may gain value from being reminded of the Puma shoe when buying a similar shoe with a similar trademark produced by a supermarket chain, as long as they are not likely to be confused when they buy the shoe. It may be valuable for those consumers that they through the resemblances with Puma shoes get connotations to known shoes, with known features and trademark.

A way forward would be for the Advocates General to include more trademark policy into their opinions. They have a much more leeway than the Court of Justice to build their opinions on broader policy arguments and have already proved willing to do so. For instance, they have referred to the economic function of trademarks as lowering consumer search costs,[46] a function also advocated by the EESC in the EESC TM Opinion 2013.[47] Should the Court of Justice assume that rest on opinions of the Advocates General who based them on explicit policy reasoning, it would be clearer on which scientific ground the assumptions are based. In terms of means of interpretation, the Court of Justice also has a room for including policy into its decisions through its related *purposive interpretation* and interpreting through *argument for intention*.[48] Below it is laid out how the average consumer could be contextualised more precisely referring to the economic function of trademarks as lowering consumer search costs.[49]

12.6 Law and Economics: A Search Cost Analysis

Elsewhere, the author of this book by way of neoclassical economic theory has illustrated how it would be possible to set a benchmark against which the average consumer may be evaluated and contextualised more precisely. The benchmark builds on the connection between the essential *legal* function of trademarks, the origin function, and their *economic* function as lowering consumer search costs and

---

[44]Gibson, James, 'Trademark Law as an Agency Problem', (2015 (an unpublished draft is with the author of this book)), p. 1.

[45]See Chap. 9, Sect. 9.3.1.2.

[46]See Chap. 4, Sect. 4.3.5, including footnote 158.

[47]See Chap. 1, Sect. 1.3.2 and Chap. 4, Sect. 4.3.4.

[48]On those means of interpretation, see Chap. 4, Sect. 4.3.4.

[49]See Chap. 1, Sect. 1.3.2.

solving an information asymmetry between sellers and consumers. Legal protection of the origin function is, a prerequisite for lowering consumer search costs. This connection was established in Chap. 1.[50] Economic theory could offer a better way to contextualise the average consumer based on the search costs function of trademarks referring to different categories of goods, and to the market places in which the goods are sold. This is essentially the divide between *product market* and *market place* (the physical and the online markets), a divide equally followed in the legal analysis in the foregoing chapter.[51]

A central theme in the previous chapter was how goods in case law of the General Court, and to some extent the national courts, have been divided into everyday consumer goods and more specialised goods. Economic theory has a different and more distinct taxonomy of dividing different kinds of goods, namely the division into experience goods, search goods and credence goods. It is appropriate to regard this classification of goods as a sliding scale with search goods at one end (with the lowest consumer search costs) and credence goods at the other end (with the highest consumer search costs) and experience goods falling between the two.[52] In terms of experience goods, consumers are assumed to know about the price before making a purchase, but consumers cannot decide if there is a positive relationship between the price and quality of the goods until they have made their purchase. Hence, "in the absence of any other information, the consumer would not know if he were better off experimenting with low- or high-priced brands."[53] Search goods are goods infrequently purchased by consumers and where the quality of the goods to a higher degree may be assessed before making a purchase.[54] Finally, credence goods may also be goods infrequently purchased but where the quality of the goods cannot be assessed by examining or handling the item before and after having placed the purchase.[55]

---

[50]See Chap. 1, Sects. 1.3.1 and 1.3.2.

[51]See Laustsen, Rasmus D., 'An Economic Analysis of EU Trademark Law; the Role of the Average Consumer in Trademark Infringement between Two Confusingly Similar Trademarks', in Lyngsie, Jacob, Mortensen, Bent O. G. and Østergaard, Kim eds., Rets- og Kontraktøkonomi: Law & Economics an Anthology (Djøf Publishing, 2016), 37, in particular p. 47-53.

[52]Laband, David N., 'An Objective Measure of Search Versus Experience Goods', Economic Inquiry, vol. 29/no. 3, (1991), pp. 497, p. 498. Laband has presented a similar view in terms of classifying search and experience goods in two extreme categories. However, Laband's classification does not consider that credence goods are logically further away from search goods since even higher search costs are incurred on credence goods than on experience goods by consumers when obtaining information on the goods.

[53]Darby, Michael R., and Karni, Edi, 'Free Competition and the Optimal Amount of Fraud', Journal of Law and Economics, vol. 16/no. 1, (1973), pp. 67, p. 311-312, p. 313.

[54]Economides, Nicolas, 'The Economics of Trade Marks', Trademark Reporter, vol. 78 (1987), pp. 523, p. 531. Examples of such products are washing machines, refrigerators, television sets and HiFi equipment.

[55]Darby, Michael R., and Karni, Edi, 'Free Competition and the Optimal Amount of Fraud', Journal of Law and Economics, vol. 16/no. 1, (1973), pp. 67, p. 68-69, Redmond, William, 'Three Modes of Competition in the Marketplace', American Journal of Economics and Sociology, vol.

Economic theory illustrates that it is possible yet complex to analyse the size of consumer search costs in different product markets. This categorisation of goods based on economic theory might be more realistic, yet generalizable—and workable. There may also be variations between how the different goods and their level of search costs manifest themselves in different market places.[56] In this context, further research would be needed on how trademarks used as part of keywords in search engines (in Google terminology AdWords) affect the level of consumer search costs. Equally, research is needed on the effect on the level of consumer search costs when trademarks are used in online platforms and websites to facilitate consumer searches for product information.[57]

12.7   Future Research

Besides the search costs theory, reference was made to neoclassical theory by way of the rational actor model. This model from economics was used to better understand the average consumer, including to test the scholarly comparisons made between these two models.[58] It does not suffice though to merely look for improvements of the average consumer in neoclassical economic theory through search cost theory and the rational actor model. It has been indicated that by bringing in the "behavioral man"[59] from behavioural science a more realistic view on the average consumer could be created. This was earlier mentioned referring to Thaler and Sunstein. Posner's critique of the behavioural man is that it is an unclear model.[60] Further, Posner has argued that in behavioural economics there is a "loss of predictive power" and that the answer to rational choice economist on what the ""rational man" would do in a given situation," is normally fairly certain "and it can be compared with

---

72/no. 2, (2013), pp. 423, p. 429 and Posner, Richard A., 'Economic Analysis of Law', (9th edn, Aspen, 2014), p. 121. Redmond refers to certain services of a technical nature as credence goods, including certain legal, medical and repair services. Posner refers to cars as examples of credence goods. According to Darby and Karni, the purchaser of credence goods will not have a different experience after having purchased the goods. The quality of credence goods may not be assessed until after a longer post sale time has passed.

[56]See particularly, Laustsen, Rasmus D., 'An Economic Analysis of EU Trademark Law; the Role of the Average Consumer in Trademark Infringement between Two Confusingly Similar Trademarks', in Lyngsie, Jacob, Mortensen, Bent O. G. and Østergaard, Kim eds., Rets- og Kontraktøkonomi: Law & Economics an Anthology (Djøf Publishing, 2016), 37, p. 51-53.

[57]Examples of well-known e-commerce platforms are eBay and Amazon.com. Examples of the use of trademarks for online information search are search engines (like Google), user generated content (such as TripAdvisor, Trustpilot and PriceRunner).

[58]On the rational actor model, see Chap. 6, Sects. 6.6.1–6.6.2.

[59]Posner, Richard A., 'Rational Choice, Behavioral Economics, and the Law', Stanford Law Review, vol. 50 (1997-1998), pp. 1551, p. 1559.

[60]Ibid. On the behavioural man, see Chap. 6, Sect. 6.6.3 and the summarising discussion in Sect. 6.6.4.

actual behaviour to see whether the prediction is confirmed."[61] Towfigh and Petersen have recently held that "in the absence of an equally conclusive alternative behavioural model, it [the rational actor model] is still the prevalent concept in economics, and therefore also in the economic analysis of law."[62]

By bringing in other areas of social science, it is not an aim as such to reach one grant theory that supports a one-size-fits-all average consumer. The focus has been to illustrate how non-legal social science theory may also contribute to creating a more workable average consumer model and designate areas where future research could be done. Other scholars have recently suggested to bring in insights from other social science areas to strengthen the average consumer fiction in law.

Corbin, who has analysed the average consumer from a Canadian perspective, has suggested the introduction of a so-called "social science test" to measure the behaviour of the "notional" average consumer.[63] This test consists of three main criteria: First, *reliability*—that "the scientific findings [are] generalizable, universal." Second, *validity*—questioning, "if the right things have been measured the right way." Third, relevance—do "the results address the evidentiary burden" of the court?[64]

Weatherall has suggested to improve and make more practical the empirical tests of the average consumer. One way of doing this, according to Weatherall, could be a further focus on how cognitive psychologists perceive consumer decision making processes. In practice, this end could be reached through "smaller scale 'quick and dirty' survey or experimental work" or "seeking *convergent* evidence from a series of different questions or tests."[65] Besides substantial advantages, these methods of generating evidence would also be "effective methods for overcoming costs."[66]

From marketing literature Underhill has drawn attention to studies indicating that "[s]ometimes people just don't remember every little thing they saw or did in a store – they weren't shopping with the thought that they'd had to recall it later." For instance, a consumer survey showed that someone remembered seeing a Marlboro

---

[61]Posner, Richard A., 'Rational Choice, Behavioral Economics, and the Law', Stanford Law Review, vol. 50 (1997-1998), pp. 1551, p. 1559.

[62]Towfigh, Emanuel V. and Petersen, Niels, 'Economic Methods for Lawyers', (1st edn, Edward Elgar, 2015), p. 18.

[63]Corbin, Ruth M., 'The Moron in a Hurry – a Creature of Law Or Science?', in Archibald, Todd L. and Echlin, Randall Scott eds., Annual Review of Civil Litigation 2015 (1st edn, Carswell, 2015), 43, p. 56.

[64]*Ibid*, p. 58-61.

[65]Weatherall, Kimberlee, 'The Consumer as the Empirical Measure of Trade Mark Law', Modern Law Review, vol. 80/no. 1, (2017), pp. 57, p. 85-86. Weatherall seems to respond to Dinwoodie and Gangjee who also refer to similar "quick and dirty" approaches that could "have limited predictive value in the real world." Dinwoodie, Graeme, and Gangjee, Dev, 'The Image of the Consumer in EU Trade Mark Law', in Leczykiewicz, Dorota, and Weatherill, Stephen eds., The Images of the Consumer in EU Law: Legislation, Free Movement and Competition Law (1st edn, Hart, 2016), 339, p. 365.

[66]Weatherall, Kimberlee, 'The Consumer as the Empirical Measure of Trade Mark Law', Modern Law Review, vol. 80/no. 1, (2017), pp. 57, p. 85.

brand although no Marlboro branded goods were found in the store where the survey was made. Also, Underhill has claimed that "we are dangerously over-retailed" and that "we are generating stores a lot faster than we are producing new shoppers."[67] Furthermore, that "[t]he level of impulse purchasing is going through the roof – in supermarkets and everywhere else"[68] "for both sexes."[69] These findings are in line with Thaler who from a behavioural science viewpoint has found that the average consumer who shops groceries is not "dumb, but rather (. . .) he does not spend all of his time thinking about how to make decisions. A grocery shopper (. . .) spends a couple of hours a week shopping and devotes a rational amount of (scarce) mental energy."[70] Does this insight from marketing and behavioural science literature actually indicate that the query in trademark law on "likelihood of confusion" is outdated in a modern retail setting? Do consumers actually reach a stage of confusion at all when shopping, or is it more a question of interpreting how consumers behave in a retail setting.[71]

A subtle critique of the likelihood of confusion query was already aired by Koktvedgaard in 1965 where he criticised the principle of imperfect recollection crucial to deciding this query in court.[72] Koktvedgaard found that this principle "almost results in smile of the judge who has the marks in front of him in respectively appendix A and appendix B and naturally will not refrain from having them side-by-side. If he has done so in merely the split second it will take to perceive the marks, then significant parts of the litigating attorneys' arguments on the similarity and difference between the marks will have no effect on him."[73] The judicial principle of imperfect recollection seems even more detached from reality today

---

[67]Paco Underhill, Why We Buy: The Science of Shopping: Updated and Revised for the Internet, the Global Consumer and Beyond (1st ed. 2009), p. 24.

[68]*Ibid*, p. 25.

[69]In 2009 Underhill stated that grocery studies had shown that 60-70 % of all grocery purchases in supermarkets were unplanned. *Ibid*, p. 105.

[70]Thaler, Richard, 'Toward a Positive Theory and Consumer Choice', in Kahneman, Daniel and Tversky, Amos eds., Choices, Values, and Frames (1st edn, Cambridge University Press, 2000), 269, p. 269 (italics added). See Chap. 6, Sect. 6.6.3.

[71]Besides the findings by Underhill, inspiration for this observation came, when the author of this book had an enlightening talk with marketing professor Lisa R. Szykman on this book project. Confronted with the trademark law's focus on consumer confusion, Szykman intuitively responded that consumers in a retail setting do not reach the stage where they are confused (or likely to be) in the cognitive sense of the word. See also Chap. 6, Sect. 6.6.4.

[72]On the principle, see Chap. 11, Sect. 11.1.

[73]In Danish: "appellerer vel nærmest til smilet hos den dommer, der har varemærkerne liggende som henholdsvis bilag A og bilag B, og som naturligvis ikke kan undlade at lægge dem ved siden af hinanden. Har han imidlertid gjort det blot i den brøkdel af et sekund, som det tager at opfatte mærkerne, vil store dele af de procederende advokaters argumentation om ligheden eller forskelligheden mellem mærkerne prelle af på ham." Koktvedgaard, Mogens, 'Konkurrenceprægede Immaterialretspositioner: Bidrag til Læren om de Lovbestemte Enerettigheder og Deres Forhold til den Almene Konkurrenceret', (1st edn, Juristforbundet, 1965), p. 179.

where the retail setting is more complex than in 1965, and we as consumers, according to Underhill, are "over-retailed."

This book has pointed out incoherence and inconsistency in European trademark law. There is room for legal improvement, and the Court of Justice should open up for bringing in more trademark policy into the framing of the average consumer. This policy builds on the legal functions, mainly the origin function, but also opens up for bringing in other areas of social science. One obvious area is economics theory, since it was mentioned in the preparatory works of the TM Directive, another area is behavioural science. The average consumer begs further legal analyses that involve more jurisdictions across a broader area of the trademark law infrastructure, but these analyses should also include insights from other areas of social science. It would be if non-legal researchers made projects reverse to this book, mainly focusing on their respective area of social science to analyse certain key legal presumptions of the average consumer in European trademark law.

Table of Legislation, Preparatory Works Etc.

International and European

Treaties and Conventions

Paris Convention for the Protection of Industrial Property of March 20 1883, as most recently amended on 28 September 1979 (the "*Paris Convention*")

Protocol on the Interpretation of Article 69 EPC of 5 October 1973 as revised by the Act revising the EPC of 29 November 2001 (the "*EPC Protocol*")

Agreement establishing the World Trade Organisation of 15 April 1994 (the "*WTO Agreement*")

Agreement on the European Economic Area Final Act of 3 March 1994, [1994], OJ L 1 (the "*EEA Agreement*")

Agreement on Trade-Related Aspects of Intellectual Property Rights of 15 April 1994 (the "*TRIPS Agreement*")

European Patent Convention 16th edition of June 2016 (the "*EPC*")

Nice Agreement Concerning the International Classification of Goods and Services for the Purposes of the Registration of Marks 11th edition, version 2019 entering into force 1 January 2019 (the "*Nice Agreement*")

Preparatory Works Etc.

WIPO Joint Recommendation Concerning Provisions on the Protection of Well-Known Marks adopted by the Assembly of the Paris Union for the Protection of Industrial Property and the General Assembly of WIPO at the Thirty-Fourth Series of Meetings of the Assemblies of the Member States of WIPO September 20 to 29 1999 (the "*WIPO Recommendations*")

© Springer Nature Switzerland AG 2020
R. D. Laustsen, *The Average Consumer in Confusion-based Disputes in European Trademark Law and Similar Fictions*, https://doi.org/10.1007/978-3-030-26350-8

European Group on Tort Law, Principles of European Tort Law of May 2005, available at: http://civil.udg.edu/php/biblioteca/items/283/PETL.pdf (last visited 26 May 2019) (the "*PETL*")

von Bar, Christian *et al* eds., 'Principles, Definitions and Model Rules of European Private Law – Draft Common Frame of Reference (DCFR) Outline Edition', (1st edn, Sellier European Law Publishers, 2009) (the "*DCFR*")

European Intellectual Property Office Annual Report 2017, available at: https://euipo.europa.eu/tunnel-web/secure/webdav/guest/document_library/contentPdfs/about_euipo/annual_report/annual_report_2017_en.pdf (last visited 26 May 2019)

Guidelines for Examination in the European Patent Office of November 2017 (the "*EPO Guidelines*"), available at: https://www.epo.org/law-practice/legal-texts/guidelines/archive/guidelines-2017.html (last visited 26 May 2019)

Case Law of the Boards of Appeal of the European Patent Office 8th Edition of July 2016 (the "*EPO Case Law*"), available at: https://www.epo.org/law-practice/case-law-appeals/case-law.html (last visited 26 May 2019)

Supplement to the EPO Case Law published in Supplementary publication 3, Official Journal EPO 2018 (the "*EPO Case Law Supplement*"), available at: http://www.epo.org/law-practice/legal-texts/official-journal/2018/etc/se3/2018-se3.pdf (last visited 26 May 2019)

European Union

Primary Law

Treaties

Treaty of Rome of 25 March 1957 establishing the European Economic Community (the "*EEC Treaty*")

Single European Act, of 28 February 1987, [1987] OJ L 169/1 (the "*Single European Act*")

Treaty of Maastricht signed on 7 February 1992, [1992], OJ C191 /01

Treaty of Amsterdam, [1997], OJ C340/01 (the "*Amsterdam Treaty*")

Treaty of Nice, [2002] OJ C 325/01 (the "*Nice Treaty*")

Treaty on the European Union (consolidated version), [2006] OJ C 321 E/5 (the "*TEU Pre-Lisbon*")

Treaty Establishing the European Community (consolidated version), [2006] OJ C 321 E/37 (the "*TFEU Pre-Lisbon*")

Treaty of Lisbon amending the Treaty on European Union and the Treaty Establishing the European Community of 13 December 2007, [2007] OJ C 306/01 (the "*Lisbon Treaty*")

Treaty of European Union (consolidated version), [2012] OJ C 326/13 (the "*TEU*")

TEU Protocol (No 3) on the Statute of the Court of Justice of the European Union (the *"Statute of the CJEU"*)

Treaty on the Functioning of the European Union (consolidated version), [2012] OJ C 326/47 (the *"TFEU"*)

Charter of Fundamental Rights of the European Union

Charter of Fundamental Rights of the European Union, [2012] OJ C 326/391 (the *"EU Charter"*)

Secondary Legislation

Regulations

Council Regulation (EEC) No 1907/90 of 26 June 1990 on certain marketing standards for eggs, [1990] OJ L173 (the *"Egg Regulation"*)

Council Regulation (EC) No 40/94 of 20 December 1993 on the Community trade Mark, [1994] OJ L 11/1 (the *"TM Regulation 1994"*)

Council Regulation (EC) No 6/2002 of 12 December 2001 on Community designs, [2002] OJ L 3/1 (the *"Design Regulation"*)

Council Regulation (EC) No 1028/2006 of 19 June 2006 on marketing standards for eggs, [2006] OJ L186/1

EP and Council directive (EC) No 2006/123 of 12 December 2006 on services of the Internal Market (the *"Service Directive"*)

EP and Council Regulation (EC) No 1924/2006 of 20 December 2006 on nutrition and health claims made on foods, [2006] OJ L 404/9

Commission Regulation (EC) No 557/2007 of 23 May 2007 laying down detailed rules for implementing Council Regulation (EC) No 1028/2006 on marketing standards for eggs, [2007] OJ L132/5

Council Regulation (EC) No 207/2009 of 26 February 2009 on the Community trade mark (codified version), [2009] OJ L 78/1 (the *"TM Regulation 2009"*)

EP and Council Regulation (EC) No 1223/2009 of 30 November 2009 on cosmetic products, [2009] OJ L342/59

EP and Council Regulation (EU) No 1169/2011 of 25 October 2011 on the provision of food information to consumers, amending Regulations (EC) No 1924/2006 and (EC) No 1925/2006 of the European Parliament and of the Council, and repealing Commission Directive 87/250/EEC, Council Directive 90/496/EEC, Commission Directive 1999/10/EC, Directive 2000/13/EC of the European Parliament and of the Council, Commission Directives 2002/67/EC and 2008/5/EC and Commission Regulation (EC) No 608/2004, [2011] OJ L 304/18

EP and Council Regulation (EU) No 1257/2012 of 17 December 2012 implementing enhanced cooperation in the area of the creation of unitary patent protection, [2012] OJ L361/1 (the *"Unitary Patent Regulation"*)

Council Regulation (EU) No 1260/2012 of 17 December 2012 implementing enhanced cooperation in the area of the creation of unitary patent protection with regard to the applicable translation arrangements, [2012] OJ L361/89 (the *"Patent Translations Regulation"*)

Commission Regulation (EU) No 609/2013 of 12 June 2013 on food intended for infants and young children, food for special medical purposes, and total diet replacement for weight control, [2013] OJ L 181/35

Commission Regulation (EU) No 907/2013 of 20 September 2013 setting the rules for applications concerning the use of generic descriptors (denominations), [2013] OJ L 251/7

EP and Council Regulation (EU) 2015/2424 of 16 December 2015 amending Council Regulation (EC) No 207/2009 on the Community trade mark and Commission Regulation (EC) No 2868/95 implementing Council Regulation (EC) No 40/94 on the Community trade mark, and repealing Commission Regulation (EC) No 2869/95 on the fees payable to the Office for Harmonization in the Internal Market (Trade Marks and Designs), [2015] OJ L 341/21 (the *"TM Amendment Regulation"*)

European Parliament and Council Regulation (EU) 2017/1001 of 14 June 2017 on the European Union trade mark (codification), OJ L 154/3 (the *"TM Regulation"*)

European Parliament and Council Regulation (EU) 2017/1369 of 4 July 2017 setting a framework for energy labelling and repealing Directive 2010/30/EU [2017] OJ L 198/1

Directives

Council Directive of 26 January 1965 on the approximation of provisions laid down by law, regulation or administrative action relating to proprietary medicinal products (65/65/EEC), [1965] OJ 369/65 (the *"Medical Product Directive 1965"*)

Council Directive of 27 July 1976 on the approximation of the laws of the Member States relating to cosmetic products (76/768/EEC), [1976] OJ L262/169

Council Directive of 10 September 1984 relating to the approximation of the laws, regulations and administrative provisions of the Member States concerning misleading advertising, [1984] OJ L250/17

Council Directive 85/374/EEC of 25 July 1985 on the approximation of the laws, regulations and administrative provisions of the Member States concerning liability for defective products, [1985] OJ L 210/29

First Council Directive of 21 December 1988 to approximate the laws of the Member States relating to trade marks (89/104/EEC), [1989] OJ L 40/1 (the *"TM Directive 1989"*)

Council Directive of 24 September 1990 on nutrition labelling for foodstuffs (90/496/EEC), [1990] OJ L 276/40

EP and Council Directive 98/71/EC of 13 October 1998 on the legal protection of designs, [1998] OJ L 289/28 (the "*Design Directive*")

EP and Council Directive 2001/83/EC of 6 November 2001 on the Community code relating to medicinal products for human use, [2001] OJ L311/67

EP and Council Directive 2005/29/EC of 11 May 2005 concerning unfair business-to-consumer commercial practices in the internal market and amending Council Directive 84/450/EEC, Directives 97/7/EC, 98/27/EC and 2002/65/EC of the European Parliament and of the Council and Regulation (EC) No 2006/2004 of the European Parliament and of the Council (Unfair Commercial Practices Directive), [2005] OJ L 149/22 (the "*UCPD*")

Commission Directive 2007/29/EC of 30 May 2007 amending Directive 96/8/EC as regards labelling, advertising or presenting foods intended for use in energy-restricted diets for weight reduction, [2007] OJ L 139/22

EP and Council Directive 2008/95/EC of 22 October 2008 to approximate the laws of the Member States relating to trade marks (Codified version), [2008] OJ L 299/25 (the "*TM Directive 2008*")

EP and Council Directive (EU) No 2015/2436 of 16 December 2015 to approximate the laws of the Member States relating to trade marks (Recast), [2015] OJ L 336/1 (the "*TM Directive*")

Preparatory Works Etc.

Commission Memorandum on the creation of an EEC trade mark adopted by the Commission on 6 July 1976, [1976] Bulletin of the European Communities Supplement 8/76 (the "*TM Memorandum 1976*")

Commission Proposal for a first Council Directive to approximate the laws of the Member States relating to trade marks of 31 December 1980, [1980] OJ C 351/1 (the "*TM Directive Proposal 1980*")

EESC opinion on the proposal for a first Council Directive to approximate the laws of the Member States relating to trade marks and the proposal for a Council Regulation on Community trade marks of 30 November 1981, [1981] OJ C 310/22

Commission Green Paper on the legal protection of industrial design No 111/51311/91 of June 1991 (the "*Design Green Paper*")

Commission Proposal for a European Parliament and Council Regulation on the Community Design COM(93) 342 final-COD 463 of 3 December 1993, (the "*Design Regulation Proposal*")

Commission Notice on the definition of relevant market for the purposes of Community competition law of 9 December 1997, [1997] OJ C372/03

Commission Staff Working Paper Extended Impact Assessment on the EP and Council Directive concerning unfair business-to-consumer commercial practices in the Internal Market and amending directives 84/450/EEC, 97/7/EC and 98/27/

EC (the Unfair Commercial Practices Directive) of 18 June 2003, COM(2003) 356 final (the "*UCPD Working Paper 2003*")

European Parliament legislative resolution on the proposal for a European Parliament and Council directive concerning unfair business-to-consumer commercial practices in the Internal Market and amending Directives 84/450/EEC, 97/7/EC and 98/27/EC (the Unfair Commercial Practices Directive) (COM(2003) 356 – C5-0288/2003 – 2003/0134(COD)) (Codecision procedure: first reading), P5_TA (2004)0298

Treaty Establishing a Constitution for Europe [2004] (the "EU Constitutional Treaty")

Guidelines Concerning Proceedings Before the Office for Harmonization in the Internal Market (Trade Marks and Designs), Part B Examination, Final version April 2008, available at: https://euipo.europa.eu/tunnel-web/secure/webdav/guest/document_library/contentPdfs/law_and_practice/guidelines/ctm/examination_en.pdf (last visited 26 May 2019)

Opinion of the European Economic and Social Committee on the 'Proposal for a Directive of the European Parliament and of the Council to approximate the laws of the Member States relating to trade marks' of 12 November 2013, COM(2013) 162 final — 2013/0089 (COD), [2013] OJ C 327/09 (the "*EESC TM Opinion 2013*")

EP and Council Proposal for a Directive to approximate the laws of the Member States relating to trade marks of 27 March 2013, COM(2013) 162 final 2013/89 (COD)

Study on the Overall Functioning of the European Trade Mark System presented by Max Planck Institute for Intellectual Property and Competition Law Munich 15 February 2011 (the "*Max Planck TM Report*")

Council Agreement on a Unified Patent Court (2013/C 175/01) of 20 June 2013, [2013] OJ C 175/1 (the "*Agreement on the Patent Court*")

Commission, Free movement of goods: Guide to the Application of Treaty Provisions Governing the Free Movement of Goods, of 18 December 2013

Publication of the lists of Community trade mark courts and Community design courts in accordance with Article 95(4) of Council Regulation (EC) No 207/2009 on the Community trade mark and Article 80(4) of Regulation (EC) No 6/2002 of 24 September 2014 on Community designs [2014] C 332/06

Commission Staff Working Document Guidance on the Implementation/Application of Directive 2005/29/EC on Unfair Commercial Practices Accompanying the document Communication From the Commission to the European Parliament, the Council, the European Economic and Social Committee and the Regions – A comprehensive approach to stimulating cross-border e-Commerce for Europe's citizens and businesses (COM(2016) 320 final) of 25 May 2016 SWD(2016) 163 final (the "*UCPD Working Paper 2016*")

Commission, EP, Council, EESC and the Committee of the Regions Communication on a Standardisation package. European Standards for the 21st Century of 1 June 2016, COM(2016) 358 final

EUIPO Guidelines for Examination of European Union Trade Marks, Final Version 1.0 of 1 October 2017 (the "*EUIPO TM Guidelines*"), available at: https://euipo.europa.eu/ohimportal/en/trade-mark-guidelines (last visited 26 May 2019)

Guidelines for Examination of Registered Community Designs EUIPO on the Examination of Design Invalidity Applications, Draft Version 1.0 of 1 October 2018 are available at: https://euipo.europa.eu/ohimportal/da/draft-design-guidelines-2018 (last visited 26 May 2019)

National Jurisdictions

United Kingdom (England and Wales)

Legislation

Trade Marks Act 1938 (C. 22) (the "*UK TM Act 1938*")
Trade Marks Act 1994 Commencement Order, [1994] (No. 2550 C. 52)
Trade Marks Act 1994 (consolidated version) (C.26) (the "*UK TM Act 1994*")
Consumer Protection from Unfair Trading Regulations 2008, No. 1277 of 8 May 2008
Trade Marks Regulations 2018, no. 825

Preparatory Works Etc.

Reform of Trade Marks Law, [1990] (Cm 1203) (the "*UK TM White Paper*")
Explanatory Memorandum to the Trade Marks Regulations 2018, No. 825

Nordic

Motiver til det af de Svensk-Norsk-Dansk kommitterede Forslag til Lov om beskyttelse af Varemærker of 12 August 1882 (the "*Nordic TM Proposal 1882*")

Sweden

Legislation

Rättegångsbalk, 1942:740 of 18 July 1942 (as changed 15 November 2016)
Varumärkeslagen, No 644 of 2 December 1960 (the "*SE TM Act 1960*")

Varumärkeslagen, SFS 2010:1877 of 9 December 2010 (the "*SE TM Act 2010*")
Lag om ändring i varumärkeslagen (2010:1877), SFS 2018:1652 of 15 November
    2018

Preparatory works etc.

Regeringens proposition 2009/10:225 Ny varumärkeslag och ändringar i firmalagen,
    of 3 June 2010 (the "*SE TM Prop. 2009/10:225*")
Karnov Commentary for the SE TM Act 2010 as updated 25 May 2018
Regeringens proposition 2017/18:267 Modernare regler om varumärken och en ny
    lag om företagsnamn, of 7 June 2018 (the "*SE TM Prop. 2018/18:267*")

Denmark

Legislation

Varemærkeloven, Act. No 52 of 17 April 1890 (the "*DK TM Act 1890*")
Varemærkelov, Act. No 211 of 11 June 1959 (the "*DK TM Act 1959*")
Varemærkelov, Act No 341 of 6 June 1991 (the "*DK TM Act 1991*")
Bekendtgørelse af markedsføringsloven, Act No 1216 of 25 September 2013
Bekendtgørelse af varemærkeloven, Consolidated Act No 192 of 1 March 2016
Bekendtgørelse af retsplejeloven, Consolidated Act No 1257 of 13 October 2016
Lov om ændring af varemærkeloven og forskellige andre love og om ophævelse af
    fællesmærkeloven, Consolidated Act No 1533 of 18 December 2018

Preparatory Works etc.

Betænkning vedrørende en ny dansk varemærkelov, No 199 of 18 April 1958 (the
    "*DK TM Bet. 199/1958*")
Forslag til varemærkelov, No 1990/2 LSF 83 of 10 June 1991 (the "*DK TM Prop.
    1990/2*")
Karnov Commentary for the DK TM Act 1991 as updated 1 July 2017
Erhvervs-, Vækst- og Eksportudvalget 2017-18, ERU Alm.del Bilag 261, Udkast til
    Forslag til Lov om ændring af varemærkeloven, fællesmærkeloven, designloven
    og gassikkerhedsloven, of 25 June 2018 (the "*DK TM Prop. 261/2017-18*")

Norway

Legislation

Varemerkeloven, Act No 4 of 3 March 1961 (the "*NO TM Act 1961*")
Lov om mekling og rettergang i sivile tvister (tvisteloven), No 90 of 17 June 2005 (as changed 22 April 2016)
Markedsføringsloven, Act No 2 of 9 January 2009, as most recently amended 1 July 2016
Varemerkeloven, Act No 8 of 26 March 2010, as most recently changed by Act No 65 of 19 June 2015 (the "*NO TM Act 2010*")

Preparatory Works etc.

Om samtykke til ratifikasion av Avtale om Det europeiske økonomiske samarbeidsområde (EØS), undertegnet i Oporto 2. mai 1992, St.prp. nr. 100 (1991-1992), of 15 May 1992 (the "*NO Prop. 100 (1991-1992)*")
Om lov om beskyttelse av varemerker (varemerkeloven), Ot.prp. nr. 98 (2008–2009), of 15 May 2009 (the "*NO Prop. 98/200809*")

Table of Cases

© Springer Nature Switzerland AG 2020
R. D. Laustsen, *The Average Consumer in Confusion-based Disputes in European Trademark Law and Similar Fictions*, https://doi.org/10.1007/978-3-030-26350-8

2014 February 6: Blomqvist v. Rolex, Case C-98/13, [2014]
2014 March 6: Kornspitz Company v. Pfahnl Backmittel, Case C-409/12, [2014]
2014 June 19: Karen Millen v. Dunnes Stores, Case C-345/13, [2014]
2015 April 16: Nemzeti v. Magyarország, Case C-388/13, [2015]
2015 September 16: Nestlé v. Cadbury, Case C-215/14, [2015]
2015 October 22: BGW Beratungs-Gesellschaft v. Bodo Scholz, Case C-20/14, [2015]
2016 March 3: Daimler v. Együd Garage, Case C-179/15, [2016]
2016 April 16: Ajos, Case C-441/14, [2016] (Grand Chamber)
2016 May 11: August Storck v. EUIPO, Case C-636/15 P, [2016]
2016 July 7: Citroën Commerce v. ZLW, Case C-476/14, [2016]
2016 October 26: Canal Digital Danmark, Case C-611/14, [2016]
2017 July 20: Ornua v. Tindale & Stanton, Case C-93/16, [2017]
2017 September 21: Easy Sanitary Solutions v. Group Nivelles, Joined Cases C-361/15 P and C-405/15 P, [2017]
2017 October 19: Europamur Alimentación v. Dirección General de Comercio y Protección del Consumidor, Case C-295/16, [2017]
2017 December 20: Schweppes v. Red Paralela, Case C-291/16, [2017]
2018 March 8: DOCERAM v. CeramTec, Case C-395/16, [2018]
2018 April 17: Egenberger v. Evangelisches Werk für Diakonie und Entwicklung, Case C-414/16, [2018] (Grand Chamber)
2018 July 25: Mitsubishi v. Duma Forklifts, Case C-129/17, [2018]

Appeals from the General Court

2004 April 28: Matratzen Concord v. OHIM I, Case C-3/03 P, [2004] ECR I-3657
2004 April 29: Procter & Gamble v. OHIM, Joined cases C-473/01 P and C-474/01 P, [2004] ECR I-5173
2004 September 16: SAT.1 v. OHIM, Case C-329/02 P, [2004] ECR I-8317
2004 October 12: Vedial v. OHIM, Case C-106/03 P, [2004] ECR I-9573
2006 January 26: Ruiz-Picasso v. OHIM, Case C-361/04 P, [2006] ECR I-643
2006 March 23: Mülhens v. OHIM, Case C-206/04 P, [2006] ECR I-2717
2006 May 11: Sunrider v. OHIM, C-416/04 P, [2006] ECR I-4237
2007 March 9: Alecansan v. OHIM, Case C-196/06 P, [2007]
2007 April 24: Castellblanch v. OHIM, Case C-131/06 P, [2007]
2007 April 26: Alcon v. OHIM, Case C-412/05 P, [2007] ECR I-3569
2008 July 17: OHIM v. Shaker, Case C-334/05 P, [2007] ECR I-4529
2008 December 18: Albert René v. OHIM, Case C-16/06 P, [2008] ECR I-10053
2009 July 16: American Clothing v. OHIM, Joined Cases C-202/08 P and C-208/08 P, [2009]
2009 September 3: Aceites del Sur-Coosur v. Koipe Corporación, Case C-498/07 P, [2009] ECR I-7371
2010 March 4: Kaul v. OHIM, Case C-193/09 P, [2010] ECR I-2

Opinions of Advocates General

Preliminary References

Appeals from the General Court

General Court

Tried by the Court of Justice

Not Tried by the Court of Justice

EUIPO Board of Appeal

EFTA Court

UK

UK Supreme Court ("UKSC")

UK Court of Appeal ("EWCA")

UK High Court ("EWHC")

Tried by EWCA

1865 Novmber 14: Seixo v. Provezende, (1865-66) LR 1, Ch App 192
2002 December 12: Arsenal v. Reed [2002] EWHC 2695 (Ch) # III
2006 March 23: O2 v. Hutchison, [2006] EWHC 534 (Ch)
2013 May 21: Interflora v. Marks & Spencer, [2013] EWHC 1291 (Ch), ("*Interflora EWHC*")
2014 February 7: Comic Enterprises v. Twentieth Century Fox, [2014] EWHC 185 (Ch)
2016 January 20: London Taxi v. Frazer-Nash and Ecotive, [2016] EWHC 52 (Ch)
2017 October 26: Generics trading, Synthon v. Yeda Research and Development and Teva Pharmaceuticals, [2017] EWHC 2629 (Pat)

Not Tried by EWCA

1978 October 18: Morning Star v. Express Newspapers, [1979] FSR 113, (EWHC)
1996 May 23: British Sugar v. Robertson, [1996] RPC 281, (EWHC)
2010 October 20: Och-Ziff v. Och Capital, [2010] EWHC 2599 (Ch)
2011 February 14: Datacard v. Eagle Technologies, [2011] EWHC 244 (Pat)
2011 July 5: Schütz v. Delta Containers, [2011], EWHC 1712 (Ch)
2014 January 31: Jack Wills v. House of Fraser, [2014] EWHC 110 (Ch)
2014 February 25: Hearst v. AVELA, [2014] EWHC 439 (Ch)
2014 July 31: Thomas Pink v. Viktoria's Secret, [2014] EWHC 2631 (Ch)
2015 January 13: Enterprise v. Europcar, [2015] EWHC 17 (Ch)
2015 February 12: Supreme Petfoods v. Henry Bell, [2015] EWHC 256 (Ch)
2016 March 15: GAP v. British American Group, [2016] EWHC 599 (Ch)
2016 November 18: Victoria Plum v. Victorian Plumbing, [2016] EWHC 2911 (Ch)
2018 June 28: Walton International, Giordano v. Verweij Fashion, [2018] EWHC 1608 (Ch)

Sweden

SE Supreme Court ("SESC")

2003 May 9: Mast-Jägermeister v. Vin & Sprit, T 2982-01, [2003], SESC
2003 November 27: IFX v. PN, T 2228-00, [2003], SESC
2017 November 22: Länsförsäkringar v. Matek, T 3403-14, [2017], SESC

SE Court of Appeal ("SECA")

2000 May 8: Nihlmark v. IFX Infoforex Scandinavia, T 900-96, [2000], SECA
2001 July 6: Mast-Jägermeister v. Vin & Sprit, T 799-99, [2001], SECA
2010 February 26: Hela Pharma v. Cederroth, T 3341-09, [2010], SECA
2013 June 24: Mars v. Kraft Foods, T 7141-12, [2013], SECA
2014 April 8: Folksam v. Folkia, T 289-13, [2014], SECA
2014 June 3: Matek v. Länsförsäkringar, T 3270-13, [2014], SECA
2015 January 23: Swedish Match v. V2 Distribution, T 768-14, [2015], SECA
2016 June 2: Mars v. Kraft Foods, T 5406-15, [2016], SECA

SE District Court ("SEDC")

Tried by SECA

2009 June 25: Konfektyrfabriken v. Concorp, T 9619-09, [2009], SEDC
2012 July 4: Kraft Foods v. Mars, T 14294-09 and T 7359-10, [2012], SEDC
2012 December 7: Folksam v. Folkia, T12057-11, [2012], SEDC
2013 December 20: Swedish Match v. V2 Distribution, T 13352-1 and T 5357-12, [2013], SEDC
2015 May 13: Kraft Foods v. Mars, T 14298-09, [2015], SEDC

Not Tried by SECA

2012 December 11: Elskling v. Kundkraft, [2012] MD 2012:15

Denmark

DK Supreme Court ("DKSC")[1]

1999 December 2: Lube v. Dansk Droge, U.2000.506H, [1999], (DKSC)
2003 August 19: Ankenævnet v. Chantelle, U.2003.2366H, [2003], (DKSC)
2006 January 24: Saint-Gobain v. Richter-System, U.2006.1203H, [2006], (DKSC)
2007 March 6: B-Young v. Mind Companies, U.2007.1477H, [2007], (DKSC)
2007 November 20: Coop Danmark v. Puma, U.2008.446H, [2007], (DKSC)

---

[1]The decisions appealed to the DK Supreme Court appear in the published versions of the DK Supreme Court decisions.

2008 December 17: Ankenævnet v. Nestlé (prev. Novartis), U.2009.754, [2008], (DKSC)

2010 April 15: TBL Trailer v. TLT, U.2010.1908H, [2006], (DKSC)

2011 September 14: PUMA v. Coop Danmark, U.2011.3433, [2013], (DKSC)

2011 October 3: VN Legetøj v. Hasbro Europe, U.2012.107H, [2011], (DKSC)

2012 August 24: Elite Licensing v. Elite NYC, U.2012.3383H, [2012], (DKSC)

2013 November 19: Hedegaard v. Hardi, U.2014.488H, [2013], (DKSC)

2013 December 18: Grundfos v. CO-industri, U.2014.914H, [2013], (DKSC)

2014 September 19: Jensens Bøfhus v. Sæby Fiskehal, U.2014.3658H, [2014], (DKSC)

2016 December 6: Ajos, Case 15/2014, [2016], (DKSC) (unofficial English translation) available here: http://www.supremecourt.dk/supremecourt/nyheder/pressemeddelelser/Documents/Judgment%2015-2014.pdf (last visited 26 May 2019)

2016 December 6: Ajos, Sag 15/2014, [2016], (DKSC) (official Danish version)

DK Court of Appeal ("DKCA")

2015 October 19: VMR Products v V2H, U.2016.679Ø [2015], (DKCA)

DK Maritime and Commercial High Court ("DK MCH Court/ DKMCHC")

Tried by DKSC

2010 November 17: Billedbutikken v. Pixelpartner, U.2011.634S, [2010], (DKMCHC)

2015 December 16: Eico v. Multikøkkener, SH2015.V-21-15S, [2015], (DKMCHC)

Not Tried by DKSC or DKCA

2015 May 6: STOK Emballage v. Fritex Emballage, V-3-14, [2015], (DKMCHC)

2017 November 8: OTCF v. Hummel, V-67-16, [2017], (DKMCHC)

2018 February 28: G-Star Raw v. Kings & Queens, A-35-17, [2018], (DKMCHC)

Norway

NO Supreme Court ("NOSC")

1995 December 14: Mozell, HR-1995-167-B, [1995], NOSC
1998 November 24: Budejovicky Budvar v. Anheuser-Busch, HR-1998-55-A, [1998], NOSC
1998 December 18: Klagenemnda v. W Pelz, HR-1998-63-A, [1998], NOSC
1999 April 30: Fetter Klovn v. TOP-TOY, HR-1999-34-A, [1999], NOSC
2002 April 11: Klagenemnda v. Jo-Bolaget Fruktprodukter, HR-2001-1049, [2002], NOSC
2006 November 23: Vesta Forsikring v. Trygg-Hansa, Rt 2006 1473, [2006], NOSC
2008 October 2: Søtt + Salt v. Pascal Drift, HR-2008-1686-A, [2008], NOSC
2009 September 2: Eisai v. Krka, HR-2009-1735-A, [2009], NOSC
2016 September 22: Pangea v. Klagenemnda, HR-2016-01993-A, [2016], NOSC

NO Court of Appeal ("NOCA")

Tried by NOSC

1998 January 28: Pelz v. Klagenemnda, LB-1997-2383, [1998], NOCA
1998 May 28: Fetter Klovn v. TOP-TOY, LB-1997-3336, [1998], NOCA
2015 December 11: Pangea v. Klagenemnda, LB-2014-52230, [2015], NOCA

Not Tried by NOSC

2010 June 28: Esthetique Norge v. Parfyme Handlernes Innkjøpssamarbeid, LB-2010-94902, NOCA
2014 February 28: Ranstad Holding v. Top Temp Holding, LB-2012-154945, [2014], NOCA
2014 January 22: Rørlegger Sentralen v. Rørleggervakta, [2014] LB-2012-118015 NOCA

NO District Court ("NODC")

Tried by NOSC and NOCA

2006 October 27: Søtt + Salt v. Pascal, TOSLO-2006-86520, [2006], NODC

Not Tried by NOCA

2004 November 5: Trading Scandinavia v. Patentstyret, TOSLO-2004-6764, [2004], NODC
2015 February 26: NYX v. Laboratoire Nuxe, TOSLO-2014-79765, [2015], NODC
2018 January 19: Altia v. Arctic Beverage Group, TOSLO-2017-52797, [2018]. NODC

EPO Boards of Appeal

1982 March 5: Fives-Cail Babcock v. Fontanié, T 32/81, [1982]
1987 September 22: Gerber Scientific Instrument v. Rudolf Hell, T 222/86, [1987]
1996 February 6: Suimitomo Rubber v. Michelin, T 676/94, [1996]
1996 February 14: Allied Colloids v. SNF Floerger, T 39/93, [1996]
2001 August 9: Sequis v. Inex, T 4/98, [2001] OJ 496813
2002 April 30: Alza v. Elf, T 26/98, [2002]
2007 October 23: Lucent Technologies, T 1364/05, [2007]
2013 March 20: Bayer Pharma v. Leon Farma, T 637/09, [2013]
2016 November 26: CardinalCommerce Corporation, T 1463/11, [2016]

Other Decisions

Canada

2009 September 30: Atomic Energy v. Areva, [2009] FC 980

The USA

2000 June 22: Mindgames v. Western Publishing, 218 F.3d 652 (7th Cir.), [2000]

Bibliography

Books, Journal Articles Etc.

Abbamonte, Guiseppe B., 'The Unfair Commercial Practices Directive and its General Prohibition', in Weatherill, Stephen and Ulf Bernitz eds., The Regulation of the Unfair Commercial Practices Under EC Directive 2005/29 (1st edn, Hart, 2007), 11

Achinstein, Peter, 'Theoretical Models', The British Journal for the Philosophy of Science, vol. 16/no. 62, (1965), pp. 102

Adams, Maurice, 'Doing what Doesn't Come Naturally on the Distinctiveness of Comparative Law', in van Hoecke, Mark ed., Methodologies of Legal Research: What Kind of Method for what Kind of Discipline? (1st edn, Hart, 2011), 229

Addis, Michela, and Stefano Podestà, 'Long Life to Marketing Research: A Postmodern View', European Journal of Marketing, vol. 39/no. 3/4, (2005), pp. 386

Agresti, Alan, and Barbara Finlay, 'Statistical Methods for the Social Sciences', (3rd edn, Upper Saddle River, N.J., Prentice Hall, 1999)

Akerlof, George A., 'The Market for "Lemons": Quality Uncertainty and the Market Mechanism', the Quarterly Journal of Economics, vol. 84/no. 3, (1970), pp. 488

Alexander, Gregory S, 'Comparing the Two Legal Realisms-American and Scandinavian', the American Journal of Comparative Law, vol. 50/no. 1, (2002), pp. 131

Alvisi, Chiara, 'The Reasonable Consumer Under European and Italian Regulations on Unfair Business-to-Consumer Commercial Practices', in Bongiovanni, Giorgio, Giovanni Sartor and Chiara Valentini eds., Reasonableness and Law (1st edn, Springer, 2009), 283

Andreasen, Hardy, 'Varemærkeretten i Konkurrenceretlig Belysning. En Retssammenlignende Analyse Af Varemærkerettens Grundbegreber Og En Fremstilling Af Ejendomstetten Til Varemærker', (1st edn, Ejnar Munksgaard, 1948)

Ariely, Dan, 'The Upside of Irrationality: The Unexpected Benefits of Defying Logic at Work and at Home', (1st edn, Harper Perennial, 2010)

Armstrong, Kenneth, 'Governing Goods: Content and Context', in Arnull, Anthony and Damian Chalmers eds., The Oxford Handbook of European Union Law (1st edn, Oxford University Press, 2015), 508

Arnold, Sir Richard, 'An Overview of European Harmonization Measures in Intellectual Property Law', in Ohly, Ansgar and Justine Pila eds., The Europeanization of Intellectual Property Law: Towards a European Legal Methodology (1st edn, Oxford University Press, 2013), 25

Arnull, Anthony, 'Arsenal Football Club Plc v. Matthew Reed, High Court, Chancery Division, Judgment of 6 April 2001, [2001] 2 CMLR 23; Case C-206/01, Arsenal Football Club Plc

v. Matthew Reed, Court of Justice of the European Communities (Full Court), Judgment of 12 November 2002, [2003] 1 CMLR 12; Arsenal Football Club Plc v. Matthew Reed, High Court, Chancery Division, Judgment of 12 December 2002, [2003] 1 CMLR 13', Common Market Law Review, vol. 40/no. 3, (2003), pp. 753

Arnull, Anthony, 'Judicial Review in the European Union', in Arnull, Anthony and Damian Chalmers eds., The Oxford Handbook of European Union Law (1st edn, Oxford University Press, 2015), 376

Arnull, Anthony, 'The European Union and its Court of Justice', (2nd edn, Oxford University Press, 2006)

Austin, Graeme W., 'Trademarks and the Burdened Imagination', Brooklyn Law Review, vol. 69/no. 3, (2004), pp. 827

Azoulai, Loïc, 'The Complex Weave of Harmonization', in Arnull, Anthony and Damian Chalmers eds., The Oxford Handbook of European Union Law (1st edn, Oxford University Press, 2015), 589

Azoulai, Loïc, 'The Europeanisation of Legal Concepts', in Neergaard, Ulla and Ruth Nielsen eds., European Legal Method in a Multi-Level EU Legal Order (1st edn, Djøf Publishing, 2012), 165

Bar, Christian von, and Clive, Eric, 'Principles, Definitions and Model Rules of European Private Law Draft Common Frame of Reference (DCFR)', (1st edn, Oxford University Press, 2010)

Barnard, Catherine, 'The Substantive Law of the EU: The Four Freedoms', (5th edn, Oxford University Press, 2016)

Beck, Gunnar, 'The Legal Reasoning of the Court of Justice of the EU', (1st edn, Hart, 2012)

Beebe, Barton, 'An Empirical Study of the Multifactor Tests for Trademark Infringement', California Law Review, vol. 94 (2006), pp. 1581

Beebe, Barton, 'Trademark Law: An Open-Source Casebook', (V3 edn, 2016)

Beebe, Barton, Thomas F. Cotter, Mark A. Lemley, *et al*, 'Trademarks, Unfair Competition, and Business Torts', (1st edn, Aspen, 2011)

Bengoetxea, Joxerramon, 'The Legal Reasoning of the European Court of Justice: Towards a European Jurisprudence', (1st edn, Clarendon Press, 1993)

Bently, Lionel, 'From communication to thing: historical aspects of the conceptualisation of trade marks as property', in Dinwoodie, Graeme B., and Janis, Mark D. eds., Trademark Law and Theory: A Handbook of Contemporary Research (1st edn, Edward Elgar, 2008), 41

Bently, Lionel, Sherman, Brad, Gangjee, Dev and Johnson, Phillip 'Intellectual Property Law', (5th edn, Oxford University Press, 2018),

Bernitz, Ulf, 'The Unfair Commercial Practices Directive: Its Scope, Ambitions and Relation to the Law of Unfair Competition', in Weatherill, Stephen and Bernitz, Ulf eds., The Regulation of Unfair Commercial Practices Under EC Directive 2005/29 (1st edn, Oxford, Hart, 2007), 33

Bernitz, Ulf, Karnell, Gunnar, Lars Pherson, *et al*, 'Immaterialrätt Och Otillbörlig Konkurrens', (14th edn, Jure Bokhandel, 2017)

Bishop, Simon, and Mike Walker, 'The Economics of EC Competition Law: Concepts, Application and Measurement', (3rd edn, Sweet & Maxwell, 2010)

Björkwall, Pia, 'The Unified Patent Court and the Inventive Step', in Ballardini, Rosa Maria, Norrgård, Marcus and Bruun, Niklas eds., Transitions in European Patent Law: Influences of the Unitary Patent Package (1st edn, Wolters Kluwer, 2015), 85

Bleken, Håkon, 'Ekvivalens i Norsk Patentrett', NIR, vol. 2 (2010), pp. 108

Blythe, Alice, 'In Search of Mr. Average: Attempting to Identify the Average Consumer and His Role within Trade Mark Law', European Intellectual Property Review, vol. 37/no. 11, (2015), pp. 709

Bobek, Michal, 'The Court of Justice of the European Union', in Arnull, Anthony and Chalmers, Damian eds., The Oxford Handbook of European Union Law (1st edn, Oxford University Press, 2015), 153

Bodenhausen, Georg, 'Guide to the Application of the Paris Convention for the Protection of Industrial Property as Revised at Stockholm in 1967', (1st edn, World Intellectual Property Organization, 1968)

Bøggild, Frank, and Staunstrup, Kolja, 'EU-Varemærkeret', (1st edn, Karnov Group, 2015)

Böhler, Christian, 'A Thin Line between the Rationalization of Consumer Choices and Overburdening Market Participants. Are the Courts Able to Keep the Balance?', European Food and Feed Law Review, vol. 10/no. 1, (2015), pp. 34

Bradley, Kieran St Clair, 'Powers and Procedures in the EU Constitution: Legal Bases and the Court', in Craig, Paul and Búrca, Gráinne de eds., The Evolution of EU Law (1st edn, Oxford University Press, 2011), 85

Bridge, John, 'National Legal Tradition and Community Law: Legislative Drafting and Judicial Interpretation in England and the European Community', Journal of Common Market Studies, vol. XIX/no. 4, (1981), pp. 351

Brückner-Hofmann, Johanna, 'Article 6: Individual Character', in Hasselblatt, Gordian N. ed., Community Design Law: A Commentary (1st edn, Beck/Hart, 2015), 78

Burk, Dan L. 'Law and Economics of Intellectual Property: In Search of First Principles', Annual Review of Law and Social Science, vol. 8/(2012), pp. 397

Burk, Dan L., and Mark A. Lemley, 'Fence Posts or Sign Posts? Rethinking Patent Claim Construction', University of Pennsylvania Law Review, vol. 157 (2009), pp. 1743

Burrell, Robert, and Handler, Michael, 'Making Sense of Trade Mark Law', Intellectual Property Quarterly, no. 4, (2003), pp. 388

Burrows, Noreen, and Greaves, Rosa, 'The Advocate General and EC Law', (1st edn, Oxford University Press, 2007)

Bussani, Mauro, and Infantino, Marta, 'The Many Cultures of Tort Liability', in Bussani, Mauro and Sebok, Anthony J. eds., Comparative Tort Law: Global Perspectives (1st edn, Edward Elgar, 2015), 11

Calabresi, Guido, 'Ideals, Beliefs, Attitudes, and the Law: Private Law Perspectives on a Public Law Problem', (1st edn, Syracuse University Press, 1985)

Calboli, Irene, 'The Role of Comparative Legal Analysis in Intellectual Property: From Good to Great?', in Dinwoodie, Graeme B. ed., Methods and Perspectives in Intellectual Property (1st edn, Edward Elgar, 2013), 3

Campinos, António, 'Foreword', in Hasselblatt, Gordian N. ed., Community Trade Mark Regulation (EC) no 207/2009: A Commentary (1st edn, Beck/Hart, 2015)

Cane, Peter, 'The Anatomy of Tort Law', (1st edn, Hart, 1997)

Carboni, Anna. 'Confusion Surveys and Confused Judges', Jiplp, vol. 10/no. 1, (2015), pp. 1

Carlsen, Rigmor, 'Varemærker: Registreringspraksis', (1st edn, Direktoratet for Patent- og Varemærkevæsenet, 1980)

Christiansen, Claus Barrett, 'Denmark', in Hasselblatt, Gordian N. ed., Community Trade Mark Regulation (EC) no 207/2009: A Commentary (1st edn, Beck/Hart, 2015), 1292

Cohen, Tobias J., Nispen, Constantant van, and Huydecoper, Tony, 'European Trademark Law: Community Trademark Law and Harmonized National Trademark Law', (1st edn, Wolters Kluwer, 2010)

Confirmation Hearing on the Nomination of John G. Roberts, Jr. to be Chief Justice of the United States. Committee on the Judiciary United States Senate, 109th Congress 1st session September 12-15, 2005, Serial No. J–109–37

Conley, James G., Bican, Peter M., and Ernst, Holger, 'Value Articulation: A Framework for the Strategic Management of Intellectual Property', California Management Review, vol. 55/no. 4, (2013), pp. 102

Conway, Gerard, 'The Limits of Legal Reasoning and the European Court of Justice', (1st edn, Cambridge University Press, 2012)

Cooter, Robert, and Ulen, Thomas, 'Law and Economics', (6th edn, Pearson, 2014)

Corbin, Ruth M., 'The Moron in a Hurry – a Creature of Law Or Science?', in Archibald, Todd L. and Echlin, Randall Scott eds., Annual Review of Civil Litigation 2015 (1st edn, Carswell, 2015), 43

Cornish, William R., 'Intellectual Property: Patents, Copyright, Trade Marks, Allied Rights', (1st edn, Sweet & Maxwell, 1981)

Cornish, William R., Llewelyn, David, and Alpin, Tanya, 'Intellectual Property: Patents, Copyright, Trademarks and Allied Rights', (8th edn, Sweet & Maxwell, 2013)

Cornish, William, and Phillips, Jennifer, 'The Economic Function of Trade Marks: An Analysis with Special Reference to Developing Countries', IIC, vol. 13/1, (1982), pp. 41

Correa, Carlos M., 'Trade Related Aspects of Intellectual Property Rights: A Commentary on the TRIPS Agreement', (1st edn, Oxford University Press, 2007)

Craig, Paul, 'Accountability', in Arnull, Anthony and Damian Chalmers eds., The Oxford Handbook of European Union Law (1st edn, Oxford University Press, 2015a), 431

Craig, Paul, 'Report on the United Kingdom', in Slaughter, Anne-Marie, Stone, Alec and Weiler, Joseph H. eds., The European Court and National Courts: Doctrine & Jurisprudence: Legal Change in its Social Context (1st edn, Hart, 1998), 195

Craig, Paul P., 'The Lisbon Treaty: Law, Politics, and Treaty Reform', (1st edn, Oxford University Press, 2010)

Craig, Paul, and Búrca, Gráinne de, 'EU Law: Text, Cases, and Materials', (6th edn, Oxford University Press, 2015b)

Cross, Frank, Jacobi, Tanja and Tiller, Emerson, 'A Positive Political Theory of Rules and Standards', University of Illinois Law Review, no. 1, (2012), pp. 1

Cross, Rupert, and Harris, J. W., 'Precedent in English Law', (4th edn, Oxford University Press, 1991)

Crotty, Michael, 'The Foundations of Social Research: Meaning and Perspective in the Research Process', (1st edn, Sage, 1998)

Curtin, Deirdre, and Manucharyan, Tatevik, 'Legal Acts and Hierarchy of Norms in EU Law', in Arnull, Anthony and Chalmers, Damian eds., The Oxford Handbook of European Union Law (1st edn, Oxford University Press, 2015), 103

Curtis, Lee, and Somers, Lauren, 'What a Brexit would Mean for UK and EU Trademark Law', World Trademark Review, vol. October/November (2015)

Dahlman, Magnus, 'Sweden', in Hasselblatt, Gordian N. ed., Community Trade Mark Regulation (EC) no 207/2009: A Commentary (1st edn, Beck/Hart, 2015), 1438

Dalberg-Larsen, Jørgen, 'Perspektiver på ret & retsvidenskab – Retssociologiske og retsteoretiske artikler', (1st edn, Jurist- og Økonomforbundets Forlag, 2009)

Dam, Cees van, 'European Tort Law', (2nd edn, Oxford University Press, 2013)

Danielsen, Jens Hartig, 'Parallelhandel og Varernes Frie Bevægelighed', (1st edn, Jurist- og Økonomforbundets Forlag, 2005)

Darby, Michael R., and Karni, Edi, 'Free Competition and the Optimal Amount of Fraud', Journal of Law and Economics, vol. 16/no. 1, (1973), pp. 67

Dashwood, Alan, 'Wyatt and Dashwood's European Union Law', (6th edn, Hart, 2011)

David, René, and Brierley, John EC, 'Major Legal Systems in the World Today', (3rd edn, Free Press, 1985)

Davies, Gareth, 'Consumer Protection as an Obstacle to the Free Movement of Goods', ERA Forum, vol. 4/no. 3, (2003), pp. 55

Davies, Gareth, 'Internal Market Adjudication and the Quality of Life in Europe', Columbia Journal of European Union Law, vol. 21/no. 2, (2014-2015), pp. 289

Davis, Jennifer, 'Locating the Average Consumer: His Judicial Origins, Intellectual Influences and Current Role in European Trade Mark Law', Intellectual Property Quarterly, no. 2, (2005), pp. 183

Davis, Jennifer, 'Promoting the Public Interest and the European Trade Mark Directive: A Contradictory Approach', ERA Forum, vol. 14/no. 1, (2013), pp. 117

Davis, Jennifer, 'Revisiting the Average Consumer: An Uncertain Presence in European Trade Mark', Intellectual Property Quarterly, no. 1, (2015), pp. 15

Davis, Richard, Longstaff, Ben, et al, 'Tritton on Intellectual Property in Europe', (4th edn, Sweet & Maxwell, 2014)

Davis, Richard, St Quintin, Thomas and Tritton, Guy, 'Tritton on Intellectual Property in Europe', (5th edn, Sweet & Maxwell, 2018)

Del Mar, Maksymilian, 'Legal Fictions and Legal Change', International Journal of Law in Context, Vol. 9/no. 4, (2013), pp. 442

Del Mar, Maksymilian, 'Legal Fictions and Legal Change in the Common Law Tradition', in Del Mar, Maksymilian and Twining, William eds., Legal Fictions in Theory and Practice (1st edn, Springer, 2015), 225

Dent, Chris, 'Confusion in a Legal Regime Built on Deception: The Case of Trade Marks', Queen Mary Journal of Intellectual Property, vol. 5/no. 1, (2015), pp. 2

Deutsch, Erwin, 'Allgemeines Haftungsrecht', (2nd edn, Heymanns, 1996)

Devlin, Allan, 'Fundamental Principles of Law and Economics', (1st edn, Routledge, 2014)

Dimopoulos, Angelos, 'An Institutional Perspective II: The Role of the CJEU in the Unitary (EU) Patent System', in Pila, Justine and Wadlow, Christopher eds., The Unitary EU Patent System (1st edn, Hart, 2015), 57

Dinwoodie, Graeme B., 'Introduction', in Dinwoodie, Graeme B. ed., Intellectual Property and General Legal Principles: Is IP a Lex Specialis? (1st edn, Edward Elgar, 2015), 1

Dinwoodie, Graeme B, 'The Europeanization of Trade Mark Law', in Ohly, Ansgar and Pila, Justine eds., The Europeanization of Intellectual Property Law: Towards a European Legal Methodology (1st edn, Oxford University Press, 2013), 72

Dinwoodie, Graeme B., 'Trademarks and Territory: Detaching Trademark Law from the Nation-State', Houston Law Review, vol. 41/no. 3, (2004), pp. 885

Dinwoodie, Graeme B., 'What Linguistics can do for Trademark Law', in Bently, Lionel, Davis, Jennifer and Ginsburg, Jane C. eds., Trade Marks and Brands: An Interdisciplinary Critique (1st edn, Cambridge University Press, 2008), 140

Dinwoodie, Graeme, and Gangjee, Dev, 'The Image of the Consumer in European Trade Mark Law', Social Science Research Network (SSRN), (draft of 3 November 2014), pp. 1

Dinwoodie, Graeme, and Gangjee, Dev, 'The Image of the Consumer in EU Trade Mark Law', in Leczykiewicz, Dorota, and Weatherill, Stephen eds., The Images of the Consumer in EU Law: Legislation, Free Movement and Competition Law (1st edn, Hart, 2016), 339

Diver, Colin S., The Optimal Precision of Administrative Rules, The Yale Law Journal, vol. 93/no. 1 (1983), pp. 65

Djurovic, Mateja, 'European Law on Unfair Commercial Practices and Contract Law', (1st edn, Hart, 2016)

Dogan, Stacey L., and Lemley, Mark A., 'Trademarks and Consumer Search Costs on the Internet', Houston Law Review, vol. 41/no. 3, (2004), pp. 777

Dratler, Jay, and McJohn, Stephen M., 'Intellectual Property Law: Commercial, Creative and Industrial Property: Volume One', (, Law Journal Press, 2016)

Duivenvoorde, Bram B., 'The Consumer Benchmarks in the Unfair Commercial Practices Directive', (1st edn, Springer, 2015)

Durovic, Mateja, 'European Law on Unfair Commercial Practices and Contract Law', (1st edn, Hart, 2016)

Economides, Nicolas, 'The Economics of Trade Marks', Trademark Reporter, vol. 78 (1987), pp. 523

Ehrlich, Isaac, and Posner, Richard A., 'An Economic Analysis of Legal Rulemaking', the Journal of Legal Studies, vol. 3/no. 1, (1974), pp. 257

Elsmore, Matthew J., 'Intangible Assets for Intangible Deliverables: Trade Marks at Your Service', Journal of Intellectual Property Law & Practice, vol. 3/no. 9, (2008), pp. 580

Elster, Jon, 'Reason and Rationality', (1st edn, Princeton University Press, 2009)

Engelbrekt, Antonina Bakardjieva, 'Fair Trading Law in Flux? National Legacies, Institutional Choice and the Process of Europeanisation', (1st edn, Stockholm University, 2003)

Engelbrekt, Antonina Bakardjieva, 'The Scandinavian Model of Unfair Competition Law', in Hilty, Reto M. and Henning-Bodewig, Frauke eds., Law Against Unfair Competition: Towards a New Paradigm in Europe? (1st edn, Springer, 2007), 161

Epstein, Lee, and Martin, Andrew D., 'Quantitative Approaches to Empirical Legal Research', in Cane, Peter and Kritzer, Herbert M. eds., The Oxford Handbook of Empirical Legal Research (1st edn, Oxford University Press, 2010), 901

Evald, Jens, 'Juridisk Teori, Metode og Videnskab', (1st edn, Jurist- og Økonomforbundets Forlag, 2016)

Eyben, Bo von, and Isager, Helle, 'Lærebog i Erstatningsret', (8th edn, Jurist- og Økonomforbundets Forlag, 2015)

Farnsworth, **Ward** and Grady, Mark F., 'Torts: Cases and Questions', (2nd edn, Aspen, 2009)

Fhima, Ilanah, 'Introducing Reality into Trade Mark Law', Journal of Intellectual Property Law & Practice, vol. 9/no. 8, (2014), pp. 1

Fhima, Ilanah S., 'Initial Interest Confusion', Journal of Intellectual Property Law & Practice, vol. 8/no. 4, (2013), pp. 311

Fhima, Ilanah, and Denvir, Catrina, 'An Empirical Analysis of the Likelihood of Confusion Factors in European Trade Mark Law', IIC, vol. 46/no. 3, (2015), pp. 310

Fhima, Ilanah S., and Gangjee, Dev S., 'The Confusion Test in European Trade Mark Law', (1st edn, Oxford University Press, 2019 (forthcoming))

Finkelstein, Claire, 'Legal Theory and the Rational Actor', in Mele, Alfred R. and Rawling, Piers eds., The Oxford Handbook of Rationality (1st edn, Oxford University Press, 2004), 399

Firth, Alison, Lea, Gary R. and Cornford, Peter, 'Trade Marks: Law and Practice', (4th edn, Jordans, 2016)

Frändberg, Åke, 'An Essay on Legal Concept Formation', in Jaap C., Hage and von der Pfordten, Dietmar eds., Concepts in Law (1st edn, Springer, 2009), 1

Friant-Perrot, Marine, 'The Vulnerable Consumer in the UCPD and Other Provisions of EU Law', in van Boom, Willem, Garde, Amandine and Akseli, Orkun eds., The European Unfair Commercial Practices Directive: Impact, Enforcement Strategies and National Legal Systems (1st edn, Farnham, Ashgate, 2014), 89

Friedmann, Danny, 'EU opens door for sound marks: will scent marks follow?', Journal of Intellectual Property Law & Practice, vol. 10/no. 12, (2015), pp. 931

Friedman, Lawrence M. 'Law, Economics and Society', Hofstra Law Review, vol. 39 (2010-2011), pp. 487

Fromer, Jeanne C., and Lemley, Mark A., 'The Audience in Intellectual Property Infringement', Michigan Law Review, vol. 112/no. 7, (2014), pp. 1251

Fuller, Lon L., 'Legal Fictions', (1st edn, Stanford University Press, 1967)

Gallagher, William E., and Goodstein, Ronald C., 'Inference Versus Speculation in Trademark Infringement Litigation: Abandoning the Fiction of the Vulcan Mind Meld', Trademark Reporter, vol. 94/no. 6, (2004), pp. 1229

Gangjee, Dev S., 'Property in brands. The commodification of conversation', in Howe, Helena and Griffiths, Jonathan ed., Concepts of Property in Intellectual Property Law (1st edn, Cambridge University Press, 2013), 29

Garde, Amandine, 'Can the UCP Directive Really Be a Vector of Legal Certainty?' in van Boom, Willem, Garde, Amandine and Akseli, Orkun eds., The European Unfair Commercial Practices Directive: Impact, Enforcement Strategies and National Legal Systems (1st edn, Farnham, Ashgate, 2014), 109

Geiger, Christophe, 'The Construction of Intellectual Property in the European Union: Searching for Coherence', in Geiger, Christophe ed., Constructing European Intellectual Property: Achievements and New Perspectives (1st edn, Edward Elgar, 2013), 5

Gerring, John, 'What Makes a Concept Good? A Criterial Framework for Understanding Concept Formation in the Social Sciences', Polity, vol. 31/no. 3, (1999), pp. 357

Gervais, Daniel, 'The TRIPS Agreement: Drafting History and Analysis', (4th edn, Sweet & Maxwell, 2012)

Gestel, Rob Van, and Micklitz, Hans-W, 'Revitalising Doctrinal Legal Research in Europe: What about Methodology?', in Neergaard, Ulla, Nielsen, Ruth and Roseberry, Lynn M. eds., European Legal Method-Paradoxes and Revitalisation (1st edn, Djøf Publishing, 2011), 25

Gestel, Rob Van, Micklitz, Hans-W and Maduro, Miguel Poiares, 'Methodology in the New Legal World', EUI Working Papers, (2012/13), pp. 1

Gibson, James, 'Risk Aversion and Rights Accretion in Intellectual Property Law', the Yale Law Journal, vol. 116 (2007), pp. 882

Gibson, James, 'Trademark Law as an Agency Problem', (2015 (an unpublished draft is with the author of this book))

Gielen, Charles, 'Harmonisation of trade mark law in Europe: the first trade mark harmonisation Directive of the European Council', European Intellectual Property Review, vol. 14/no. 8, (1992), pp. 262

Glabman, Maureen, 'Death by Handwriting', Trustee, vol. 59/9 (2005), pp. 29

Glazer, Daniel C., and Dhamija, Dev R., 'Revisiting Initial Interest Confusion on the Internet', Trademark Reporter, vol. 95/no. 5, (2005), pp. 952

Glinski, Carola, and Joerges, Christian, 'European Unity in Diversity?! A Conflicts-Law: Re-Construction of Controversial Current Developments', in Purnhagen, Kai, Rott, Peter and Micklitz, Hans-W eds., Varieties of European Economic Law and Regulation: Liber Amicorum for Hans-W Micklitz (1st edn, Springer, 2014), 285

Golecki, Mariusz J., 'Homo Economicus Versus Homo Iuridicus Two Views on the Coase Theorem and the Integrity of Discourse Within the Law and Economics Scholarship', in Mathis, Klaus ed., Law and Economics in Europe: Foundations and Applications (1st edn, Springer, 2014), 69

Griffiths, Andrew, 'An Economic Perspective on Trade Mark Law', (1st edn, Edward Elgar, 2011)

Griffiths, Andrew, 'Brands, Business and Social Responsibility', in Faure, Michael and Stephen, Frank ed., Essays in the Law and Economics of Regulation in Honour of Anthony Ogus (1st edn, Intersentia, 2008), pp. 193

Griller, Stefan, 'Is this a Constitution? Remarks on a Contested Concept', in Griller, Stefan and Ziller, Jacques eds., the Lisbon Treaty: EU Constitutionalism without a Constitutional Treaty? (1st edn, Springer, 2008), 21

Groves, Peter, 'A Dictionary of Intellectual Property Law', (1st edn, Edward Elgar, 2011)

Grundén, Örjan, 'En Ny Nordisk Känneteckensrätt Inför 2000-Talet?', NIR, vol. 4 (1994), pp. 542

Grynberg, Michael, 'The Judicial Role in Trademark Law', Boston College Law Review, vol. 52, (2011), pp. 1283

Grynberg, Michael, 'Trademark Litigation as Consumer Conflict', New York University Law Review, vol. 83/no. 1, (2008), pp. 60

Gummesson, Evert, 'Qualitative Research in Marketing: Road-Map for a Wilderness of Complexity and Unpredictability', European Journal of Marketing, vol. 39/no. 3/4, (2005), pp. 309

Gundersen, Aase, 'Norsk Varemerkerett i Lys Av EU-Utviklingen', NIR, vol. 1 (2005), pp. 106

Gundersen, Aase, 'Fra Norsk Rettspraksis', NIR, vol. 6/(2007), pp. 578

Hamilton, K. Scott, 'Prolegomenon to Myth and Fiction in Legal Reasoning, Common Law Adjudication and Critical Legal Studies', the Wayne Law Review, vol. 35 (1988-1989), pp. 1449

Hannerstig, Niclas, 'The Average Consumer – Legal Fiction or Reality? A Comparative Study between European and American Trademark Law', LUP Student Papers (2011)

Hasselblatt, Gordian N., 'Article 1: Community Trade Marks', in Hasselblatt, Gordian N. ed., Community Trade Mark Regulation (EC) no 207/2009: A Commentary (1st edn, Beck/Hart, 2015a), 4

Hasselblatt, Gordian N., 'Article 5: Novelty', in Hasselblatt, Gordian N. ed., Community Design Law: A Commentary (1st edn, Beck/Hart, 2015b), 67

Hasselblatt, Gordian N., 'Community Trade Mark Regulation (EC) no 207/2009: A Commentary', (1st edn, Community trade mark regulation (EC) no 207/2009: A commentary, Beck/Hart, 2015c)

Heath, Guy *et al*, 'Annual Review of EU Trademark Law: 2013 in Review', Trademark Reporter, vol. 104/no. 2, (2014)

Heath, Guy *et al*, 'Annual Review of EU Trademark Law: 2015 in Review', Trademark Reporter, vol. 106/no. 2, (2016)

Heiding, Sture, 'Om Registrerade Varumärken Och Inarbetade Kännetecken', (1st edn, Almqvist & Wiksells, 1946)

Heiding, Sture, 'Svensk Varumärkes Rätt', (3rd edn, Affärsekonomi, 1966)

Herbert, A. P., 'Uncommon Law – being Sixty-Six Cases Revised and Collected in One Volume, Including Ten Cases Not Published before', (6th edn, Methuen & Co. Ltd, 1948)

Hesselink, Martijn W., 'A European Legal Method?: On European Private Law and Scientific Method', European Law Journal, vol. 15/no. 1, (2009), pp. 20

Heymann, Laura A., 'The Reasonable Person in Trademark Law', Saint Louis University Law Journal, vol. 52/no. 3, (2008), pp. 781

Hillion, Christophe, 'Tous Pour Un, Un Pour Tous! Coherence in the External Relations of the European Union', in Cremona, Marise ed., Developments in EU External Relations Law (1st edn, Oxford University Press, 2008), 10

Hoffer, George E. and Michael D. Pratt, 'Used Vehicles, Lemons Markets, and used Car Rules: Some Empirical Evidence', Journal of Consumer Policy, vol. 10/no. 4, (1987), pp. 409

Hogg, Margaret K., Bruce, Margaret and Hill, Alexander J., 'Fashion Brand Preferences among Young Consumers', International Journal of Retail & Distribution Management, vol. 26/no. 8, (1998), pp. 293

Horsey, Kirsty, and Erika Rackley, 'Tort Law', (4th edn, Oxford University Press, 2015)

Horspool, Margot, Humphreys, Matthew, and Wells-Greco, Michael, 'European Union Law', (10th edn, Oxford University Press, 2018)

Howells, Geraint G., 'Europe's (Lack of) Vision on Consumer Protection: A Case of Rhetoric Hiding Substance?', in Leczykiewicz, Dorota, and Weatherill, Stephen eds., The Images of the Consumer in EU Law: Legislation, Free Movement and Competition Law (1st edn, Hart, 2016), 431

Howells, Geraint G., 'Unfair Commercial Practices Directive – A Missed Opportunity?', in Weatherill, Stephen and Bernitz, Ulf eds., The Regulation of the Unfair Commercial Practices Under EC Directive 2005/29 (1st edn, Oxford, Hart, 2007), 103

Howells, Geraint G., Micklitz, Hans-W, and Wilhelmsson, Thomas, 'European Fair Trading Law the Unfair Commercial Practices Directive', (1st edn, Ashgate, 2006)

Howells, Geraint, Twigg-Flesner, Christian and Wilhelmsson, Thomas, 'Rethinking EU Consumer Law', (1st edn, Routledge, 2018)

Howells, Geraint G., and Weatherill, Stephen, 'Consumer Protection Law', (2nd edn, Routledge, 2005)

Howells, Geraint, and Wilhelmsson, Thomas, 'EC Consumer Law: Has it Come of Age?', European Law Review, vol. 28/no. 3, (2003), pp. 370

Hude, Harry, and Olsen, Julie, 'Haandbog i Varemærkeret: Kommenteret Udgave Af Lov Om Varemærker Af 7. April 1936', (1st edn, Reitzel, 1945)

Husa, Jaakko, Nuotio, Kimmo and Pihlajamäki, Heikki, 'Nordic Law – between Tradition and Dynamism', in Jaakko, Husa, Nuotio, Kimmo and Pihlajamäki, Heikki eds., Nordic Law – between Tradition and Dynamism (1st edn, Intersentia, 2007), pp. 1

Husa, Jaakko, and Tapani, Jussi, 'Germanic and Nordic Fraud – A Comparative Look Under the Surface of Commonalities', Global Jurist Advances, vol. 5/no. 2, (2005), pp. 1

Hyllinge, Claus. 'Sammanfattning Av Diskussionen Rörande En Ny Nordisk Känneteckenrätt Inför 2000-Talet', NIR, vol. 4/(1994), pp. 545

Incardona, Rossella, and Poncibò, Cristina, 'The Average Consumer, the Unfair Commercial Practices Directive, and the Cognitive Revolution', Journal of Consumer Policy, vol. 30/no. 1, (2007), pp. 21

Jääskinen, Niilo, 'Back to the Begriffshimmel? A Plea for an Analytical Perspective in European Law', in Prechal, Sacha and van Roermund, G. eds., The Coherence of EU Law: The Search for Unity in Divergent Concepts (1st edn, Oxford University Press, 2008), 451

Jääskinen, Niilo, 'The Future of European Intellectual Property Law Courts: Intellectual Property and the European Judicial Architecture', in Ohly, Ansgar and Pila, Justine eds., The

Europeanization of Intellectual Property Law: Towards a European Legal Methodology (1st edn, Oxford University Press, 2013), 217

Jacob, Robin, 'IP and Other Things: A Collection of Essays and Speeches', (1st edn, Hart, 2015)

Jacob, Robin, 'The Relationship between European and National Courts in Intellectual Property Law', in Ohly, Ansgar and Pila, Justine eds., The Europeanization of Intellectual Property Law: Towards a European Legal Methodology (1st edn, Oxford University Press, 2013), 185

Jacob, Marc A., 'Precedents and Case-Based Reasoning in the European Court of Justice: Unfinished Business', (1st edn, Cambridge University Press, 2014)

Jacoby, Jacob, 'Is it Rational to Assume Consumer Rationality? Some Consumer Psychological Perspectives on Rational Choice Theory', Roger Williams University Law Review, vol. 6 (2000-2001), pp. 81

Jacoby, Jacob, 'Trademark Surveys Volume I: Designing, Implementing, and Evaluating Surveys', (1st edn, American Bar Association, 2013)

Jadeja, Nicole *et al*, 'Cast back into the sea of uncertainty – A doctrine of equivalents in UK law? The Supreme Court ruling in Actavis v Eli Lilly', Journal of Intellectual Property Law & Practice, vol. 13/no. 7, (2018), pp. 564

Jaeger-Lenz, Andrea, 'Article 8: Relative Grounds for Refusal', in Hasselblatt, Gordian N. ed., Community Trade Mark Regulation (EC) no 207/2009: A Commentary (1st edn, Beck/Hart, 2015), 198

Jaffey, Peter, 'The New European Trade Marks Regime', International Review of Industrial Property and Competition Law, vol. 28/no. 2, (1997), pp. 153

Jehoram, Tobias Cohen, van Nispen, Constant, and Huydecoper, Tony, 'European Trademark Law: Community Trademark Law and Harmonized National Trademark Law', (1st edn, Kluwer Law International, 2010)

Jolls, Christine, Sunstein, Cass R. and Thaler, Richard, 'A Behavioral Approach to Law and Economics', Stanford Law Review, vol. 50/no. 5, (1998), pp. 1471

Kähler, Lorenz, 'The Influence of Normative Reasons on the Formation of Legal Concepts', in Hage, Jaap C. and von der Pfordten, Dietmar eds., Concepts in Law (1st edn, Springer, 2009), 81

Kahneman, Daniel, 'Thinking, Fast and Slow', (1st edn, Penguin, 2011)

Kaplow, Louis 'Rules Versus Standards: An Economic Analysis', Duke Law Journal, vol. 42 (1992), pp. 557

Keirsbilck, Bert, 'The New European Law of Unfair Commercial Practices and Competition Law', (1st edn, Hart, 2011)

Kelman, Mark, 'A Guide to Critical Legal Studies', (1st edn, Harvard University Press, 1987)

Kelsen, Hans, 'General Theory of Norms', (Clarendon Press, 1991)

Kelsen, Hans, 'On the Theory of Juridic Fictions with Special Consideration of Vaihinger's Philosophy of the as-if', in Del Mar, Maksymilian and Twining, William eds., Legal Fictions in Theory and Practice (1st edn, Springer, 2015), 3

Kemppinen, Hikki, Kemppinen, Jukka and Kemppinen, Seppa, 'The Doctrine of Equivalents and the Interpretation of the Extent of Protection Conferred by a Patent', in Ballardini, Rosa Maria, Marcus, Norrgård and Bruun, Niklas eds., Transitions in European Patent Law: Influences of the Unitary Patent Package (1st edn, Wolters Kluwer, 2015), 167

Kenyon, George N., and Sen, Kabir C., 'The Perception of Quality: Mapping Product and Service Quality to Consumer Perceptions', (1st edn, Springer, 2015)

Kiikeri, Markku, 'Comparative Legal Reasoning and European Law', (1st edn, Springer, 2001)

Kirkpatrick, Richard L., 'Likelihood of Confusion in Trademark Law', (1st edn, Practising Law Institute, 1995)

Kitch, Edmund W., 'The Nature and Function of the Patent System', the Journal of Law & Economics, vol. 20/no. 2, (1977), pp. 265

Klein, David M., and Glazer, Daniel C., 'Reconsidering Initial Interest Confusion on the Internet', Trademark Reporter, vol. 93/no. 5, (2003), pp. 1035

Klerman, Daniel, 'Trademark Dilution, Search Costs, and Naked Licensing', Fordham Law Review, vol. 74/no. 4, (2006), pp. 1759

Knoph, Ragnar, 'Åndsretten', (1st edn, Nationaltrykkeriet, 1936)

Kobbernagel, Jan, 'Konkurrencens Retlige Regulering II: Mærkeretten', (1st edn, Nyt Nordisk Forlag, 1967)

Koktvedgaard, Mogens, 'Konkurrenceprægede Immaterialretspositioner: Bidrag til Læren om de Lovbestemte Enerettigheder og Deres Forhold til den Almene Konkurrenceret', (1st edn, Juristforbundet, 1965)

Koktvedgaard, Mogens, 'Lærebog i Immaterialret: Ophavsret, Fotoret, Patentret, Mønsterret, Varemærkeret', (1st edn, Jurist- og Økonomforbundets Forlag, 1988)

Koktvedgaard, Mogens, 'Lærebog i Immaterialret: Ophavsret, Patentret, Brugsmodelret, Mønsterret, Varemærkeret', (5th edn, Jurist- og Økonomforbundets Forlag, 1999)

Koktvedgaard, Mogens, and Wallberg, Knud, 'Varemærkeloven af 6. Juni 1991 og Fællesmærkeloven af 6. Juni 1991 med Indledning og Kommentarer', (1st edn, Jurist- og Økonomforbundets Forlag, 1994)

Komárek, Jan, 'Legal Reasoning in EU Law', in Arnull, Anthony and Chalmers, Damian eds., The Oxford Handbook of European Union Law (1st edn, Oxford University Press, 2015), 28

Koopmans, Thijmen, 'Stare Decisis in European Law', in O'Keeffe, David and Schermers, Henry G. eds., Essays in European Law and Integration: To Mark the Silver Jubilee of the Europa Institute, Leiden, 1957-1982 (1st edn, Kluwer Law International, 1982), 11

Koziol, Helmut, 'Liability Based on Fault: Subjective or Objective Yardstick?', the Maastricht Journal of European and Comparative Law, vol. 5 (1998), pp. 111

Kransell, Arne, 'The Average Expert', NIR, vol. 2 (1982), pp. 196

Kroher, Jürgen, 'Article 56: Inventive Step', in Singer, Margarete and Stauder, Dieter eds., European Patent Convention: A Commentary: Volume 1 (1st edn, Sweet & Maxwell, 2003), 141

Kur, Annette, 'Well-Known Marks, Highly Renowened Marks and Marks Having a (High) Reputation – What's It All About', IIC, vol. 23/no. 2, (1992), pp. 28

Kur, Annette and Senftleben, Martin, 'European Trade Mark Law: A Commentary', (1st edn, Oxford University Press, 2017)

Laband, David N., 'An Objective Measure of Search Versus Experience Goods', Economic Inquiry, vol. 29/no. 3, (1991), pp. 497

Landes, William M., and Posner, Richard A., 'The Economic Structure of Intellectual Property Law', (1st edn, Harvard University Press, 2003)

Lando, Ole, 'Kort Indføring i Komparativ Ret', (3rd edn, Jurist- og Økonomforbundets Forlag, 2009)

Lassen, Birger Stuevold, 'Oversikt Over Norsk Varemerkerett', (2nd edn, Universitetsforlaget, 1997)

Lassen, Birger Stuevold and Stenvik, Are, 'Kjennetegnsrett', (3rd edn, Universitetsforlaget, 2011)

Lasser, Michel de, 'Judicial Deliberations: A Comparative Analysis of Transparency and Legitimacy', (1st, Oxford University Press, 2004)

Laustsen, Rasmus D., 'An Economic Analysis of EU Trademark Law; the Role of the Average Consumer in Trademark Infringement between Two Confusingly Similar Trademarks', in Lyngsie, Jacob, Mortensen, Bent O. G. and Østergaard, Kim eds., Rets- og Kontraktøkonomi: Law & Economics an Anthology (Djøf Publishing, 2016), 37

Laustsen, Rasmus D. 'The principle of keeping free within EU Trade Mark Law,' Rettid 2 (2010), pp. 1, available at: http://law.au.dk/fileadmin/Jura/dokumenter/forskning/rettid/2010/afh2-2010.pdf (last visited 26 May 2019)

Leczykiewicz, Dorota and Weatherill, Stephen, 'The Images of the Consumer in EU Law', in Leczykiewicz, Dorota and Weatherill, Stephen eds., The Images of the Consumer in EU Law: Legislation, Free Movement and Competition Law (1st edn, Hart, 2016), 1

Legrand, Pierre, 'European Legal Systems are Not Converging', ICLQ, vol. 45 no. 1, (1996), pp. 52

Levin, Marianne, 'Lärobok i Immaterialrätt: Upphovsrätt, Patenträtt, Mönsterrätt, Känneteckensrätt i Sverige, EU och Internationellt', (11th, Norstedts Juridik, 2017)

Levitsky, Jonathan E., 'The Europeanization of the British Legal Style', Am. J. Comp. L., vol. 42/no. 2, (1994), pp. 347

Lince, Tim. 'Trademarks in a Post-Brexit World: An Infographic', World Trademark Review, 2016

Lind, Douglas, 'The Pragmatic Value of Legal Fictions', in Del Mar, Maksymilian and Twining, William eds., Legal Fictions in Theory and Practice (1st edn, Springer, 2015), 83

Lindgreen, Nicolai, Schovsbo, Jens and Thorsen, Jesper, 'Patentloven med Kommentarer', (2nd edn, Jurist- og Økonomforbundets Forlag, 2018)

Little, Trevor, '"Don't Panic": Call for Calm as Brexit Vote Creates Uncertainty Over Future Scope of Trademark Protection', World Trademark Review, 2016

Luginbuehl, Stefan, 'An Institutional Perspective I: The Role of the EPO in the Unitary (EU) Patent System', in Pila, Justine and Wadlow, Christopher eds., The Unitary EU Patent System (1st edn, Hart, 2015), 45

Lundmark, Thomas, 'Charting the Divide between Common and Civil Law', (1st edn, Oxford University Press, 2012)

Lunell, Erika, 'Okonventionella Varumärken: Form, Färg, Doft, Ljud', (1st edn, Stockholm, 2007)

MacCormick, Neil, 'Legal Reasoning and Legal Theory', (1st edn, Oxford University Press, 1978)

MacCormick, Neil, and Summers, Robert D., 'Interpretation and Justification', in MacCormick, Neil and Summers, Robert D. eds., Interpreting Statutes (1st edn, Routledge, 1991), 511

Madsen, Palle Bo, 'Markedsret Del 2: Markedsføringsret og Konkurrenceværn', (6th edn, Jurist- og Økonomforbundets Forlag, 2015)

Maduro, Miguel Poiares, 'Interpreting European Law: Judicial Adjudication in a Context of Constitutional Pluralism', European Journal of Legal Studies, vol. 1/no. 2, (2007), pp. 1

Maduro, Miguel Poiares, 'Interpreting European Law – on Why and how Law and Policy Meet at the European Court of Justice', in Koch, Henning *et al* eds., Europe: The New Legal Realism: Essays in Honour of Hjalte Rasmussen (1st edn, Djøf Publishing, 2010), 457

Maeyaert, Paul, and Muyldermans, Jeroen, 'Likelihood of Confusion in Trademark Law: A Practical Guide Based on the Case Law in Community Trade Mark Oppositions from 2002 to 2012', Trademark Reporter, vol. 103/no. 5, (2013), pp. 1032

Mak, Vanessa, 'Standards of Protection: In Search of the 'Average Consumer' of EU Law in the Proposal for a Consumer Rights Directive', European Review of Private Law, vol. 19/no. 1, (2011), pp. 25

Mak, Vanessa, 'The Consumer in European Regulatory Private Law', in Leczykiewicz, Dorota, and Weatherill, Stephen eds., The Images of the Consumer in EU Law: Legislation, Free Movement and Competition Law (1st edn, Hart, 2016), 381

Malbon, Justin, Lawson, Charles and Davison, Mark, 'The WTO Agreement on Trade-Related Aspects of Intellectual Property Rights: A Commentary', (1st edn, Edward Elgar, 2014)

Manea, Ruxandra, 'Article 2: Office', in Hasselblatt, Gordian N. ed., Community Trade Mark Regulation (EC) no 207/2009: A Commentary (1st edn, Beck/Hart, 2015), 35

Maniatis, Spyros M., 'Competition and the Economics of Trade Marks', in Sterling, Adrian ed., Intellectual Property and Market Freedom, (1st edn, Sweet & Maxwell, 1997), 63

Mar, Maksymilian del, 'Legal Fictions and Legal Change', International Journal of Law in Context, vol. 9/no. 4, (2013), pp. 442

Mare, Thomas de la, and Donnelly, Catherine, 'Preliminary Rulings and EU Legal Integration: Evolution and Stasis', in Craig, Paul and Búrca, Gráinne de eds., The Evolution of EU Law (1st edn, Oxford University Press, 2011), 363

Markesinis, Basil S., 'Foreign Law and Comparative Methodology: A Subject and a Thesis', (1st edn, Hart, 1997)

Mathis, Klaus, 'Efficiency Instead of Justice – Searching for the Philosophical Foundations of the Economic Analysis of Law', (1st edn, Springer, 2009)

Mathis, Klaus ed., European Perspectives on Behavioural Law and Economics. Foundations and Applications (1st edn, Springer, 2015), foreword

Matuszewski, Kenneth A. 'Casting out Confusion: How Exclusive Appellate Jurisdiction in the Federal Circuit would Clarify Trademark Law', INTA Papers (2016), pp. 1

McEvoy, Sebastian. , 'Descriptive and Purposive Categories of Comparative Law', in Monateri, P. G. ed., Methods of Comparative Law (1st edn, Edward Elgar, 2012), 144

McGinley, Ann C., 'Reasonable Men?', Connecticut Law Review, vol. 45/no. 1, (2012), pp. 1

McKenna, Mark P., 'A Consumer Decision-Making Theory of Trade Mark Law', Virginia Law Review, vol. 98 (2012), pp. 67

Mellor, James, Llewelyn, David, Moody-Stuart, Thomas *et al*, 'Kerly's Law of Trade Marks and Trade Names. 1st Supplement', (1st edn, Sweet & Maxwell, 2014)

Mellor, James, David Llewelyn, Moody-Stuart, Thomas, *et al*, 'Kerly's Law of Trade Marks and Trade Names', (16th edn, Sweet & Maxwell, 2018)

Merryman, John Henry, 'The Civil Law Tradition: An Introduction to the Legal Systems of Western Europe and Latin America', (1st edn, Stanford University Press, 1985)

Micklitz, Hans-W., 'The Consumer: Marketised, Fragmentised, Constitutionalised', in Leczykiewicz, Dorota, and Weatherill, Stephen eds., The Images of the Consumer in EU Law: Legislation, Free Movement and Competition Law (1st edn, Hart, 2016), 21

Micklitz, Hans-W., 'Unfair Commercial Practices and Misleading Advertising', in Micklitz, Hans-W, Reich, Norbert and Rott, Peter eds., Understanding EU Consumer Law (1st edn, Intersentia, 2009), 61

Missiroli, Antonio, 'European Security Policy: The Challenge of Coherence', European Foreign Affairs Review, vol. 6/(2001), pp. 177

Moran, Mayo, 'Rethinking the Reasonable Person: An Egalitarian Reconstruction of the Objective Standard', (1st edn, Oxford University Press, 2003)

Moscona, Ron, 'Reforms to European Union Trade Mark Law', Intellectual Property & Technology Law Journal, vol. 28/no. 5, (2016), pp. 20

Mühlendahl, Alexander von, Dimitris Botis, Spyros M. Maniatis, *et al*, 'Trade Mark Law in Europe: A Practical Jurisprudence', (3rd edn, Oxford University Press, 2016)

Murphy, Gregory L., 'The Big Book of Concepts', (1st edn, Bradford Books, 2004)

Musker, David C., 'Community Design Regulation, Art. 6', in Gielen, Charles and von Bomhard, Verena eds., Concise European Trade Mark and Design Law (2nd edn, Kluwer Law International, 2017), 640

Nelson, Phillip, 'Information and Consumer Behavior', Journal of Political Economy, vol. 78/no. 2, (1970), pp. 311

Nielsen, Ruth, 'Legal Realism and EU Law', in Koch, Henning *et al* eds., Europe: The New Legal Realism: Essays in Honour of Hjalte Rasmussen (1st edn, Djøf Publishing, 2010), 545

Nielsen, Ruth, 'New European Legal Realism – New Problems, New Solutions?', in Neergaard, Ulla and Nielsen, Ruth eds., European Legal Method: Towards a New European Legal Realism? (1st edn, Djøf Publishing, 2013), 75

Ohly, Ansgar, 'Concluding Remarks: Postmodernism and Beyond', in Ohly, Ansgar and Pila, Justine eds., The Europeanization of Intellectual Property Law: Towards a European Legal Methodology (1st edn, Oxford University Press, 2013), 255

Ohly, Ansgar, 'Introduction: The Quest for Common Principles of European Intellectual Property Law – Useful, Futile, Dangerous?', in Ohly, Ansgar ed., Common Principles of European Intellectual Property Law (1st edn, Mohr Siebeck, 2012), 3

Olsen, Henrik Palmer, 'Nyere Nordisk Retsfilosofi', in Hammerslev, Ole and Olsen, Henrik Palmer eds., Retsfilosofi: Centrale Tekster og Temaer (1st edn, Hans Reitzels Forlag, 2011), 571

Ozga, S. A., 'Imperfect Markets through Lack of Knowledge', the Quarterly Journal of Economics, vol. 74/no. 1, (1960), pp. 29

Pagenberg, Jochen, 'the Evaluation of the "Inventive Step" in the European Patent System – More Objective Standards Needed: Part One', International Review of Industrial Property and Competition Law, vol. 9/no. 1, (1978a), pp. 1

Pagenberg, Jochen, 'the Evaluation of the "Inventive Step" in the European Patent System – More Objective Standards Needed: Part Two', International Review of Industrial Property and Competition Law, vol. 9/no. 2, (1978b), pp. 121

Parisi, Francesco, 'The Language of Law and Economics. A Dictionary', (1st edn, Cambridge University Press, 2013)

Parisi, Francesco and Fon, Vincy, 'The Economics of Lawmaking', (1edn, Oxford University Press, 2009)

Paride, Bertozzi, 'Dizionario dei brocardi e dei latinismi giuridici', (6th edn, IPSOA, 2009)

Pattaro, Enrico, A Treatise of Legal Philosophy and General Jurisprudence: Volume 4: Scientia Juris, Legal Doctrine as Knowledge of Law, (1st edn, Springer, 2005)

Peczenik, Aleksander, 'Atheoryoflegaldoctrine', Ratio Juris, vol. 14/no. 14, (2001), pp. 75

Petty, Ross D., 'Initial Interest Confusion Versus Consumer Sovereignty: A Consumer Protection Perspective on Trademark Infringement', Trademark Reporter, vol. 98/no. 3, (2008), pp. 757

Pfordten, Dietmar von der, 'About Concepts in Law', in Hage, Jaap C. and Dietmar von der Pfordten eds., Concepts in Law (1st edn, Springer, 2009), 1

Pherson, Lars, 'Varumärken från Konsumentsynpunkt: En Rättsvetenskaplig Studie', (1st edn, Liber Förlag, 1981)

Phillips, Jeremy, 'Trade Mark Law and the Need to Keep Free', International Review of Industrial Property and Competition Law, vol. 36/no. 4, (2005), pp. 389

Phillips, Jeremy, 'Trade Mark Law a Practical Anatomy', (1st edn, Oxford University Press, 2003)

Pila, Justine, 'A Constitutionalized Doctrine of Precedent and the Marleasing Principle as Bases for a European Legal Methodology', in Ohly, Ansgar and Pila, Justine eds., The Europeanization of Intellectual Property Law: Towards a European Legal Methodology (1st edn, Oxford University Press, 2013a), 227

Pila, Justine, 'An Historical Perspective I: The Unitary Patent Package', in Pila, Justine and Wadlow, Christopher eds., The Unitary EU Patent System (1st edn, Hart, 2015), 9

Pila, Justine, 'Intellectual Property as a Case Study in Europeanization: Methodological Themes and Context', in Ohly, Ansgar and Pila, Justine eds., The Europeanization of Intellectual Property Law: Towards a European Legal Methodology (1st edn, Oxford University Press, 2013b), 3

Pila, Justine, 'The Subject Matter of Intellectual Property', (1st edn, Oxford University Press, 2017)

Pindyck, Robert and Rubinfeld, Daniel, 'Microeconomics', (9th edn, Pearson, 2018)

Plesner, Peter-Ulrik et al, 'Den Europæiske Patentdomstol: Retsplejen ved den Fælles Patentdomstol', (1st edn, Jurist- og Økonomforbundets Forlag, 2018)

Posner, Richard A., 'Economic Analysis of Law', (9th edn, Aspen, 2014)

Posner, Richard A., 'How Judges Think', (1st edn, Harvard University Press, 2008)

Posner, Richard A., 'Intellectual Property: The Law and Economics Approach', the Journal of Economic Perspectives, vol. 19/no. 2, (2005), pp. 57

Posner, Richard A., 'Rational Choice, Behavioral Economics, and the Law', Stanford Law Review, vol. 50 (1997-1998), pp. 1551

Posner, Richard A., 'The Problems of Jurisprudence', (1st edn, Harvard University Press, 1990)

Prechal, Sacha, 'Binding Unity in EU Legal Order: An Introduction', in Prechal, Sacha and Roermund, G. van eds., The Coherence of EU Law: The Search for Unity in Divergent Concepts (1st edn, Oxford University Press, 2008), 1

Rakowski, Eric, 'Book Review of Schauer, Frederick. Playing by the Rules: A Philosophical Examination of Rules-Based Decision Making in Law and in Life', Ethics, vol. 103/no. 1, (1993), pp. 828

Ramsay, Iain, 'Consumer Law and Policy: Text and Materials on Regulating Consumer Markets', (3rd edn, Hart, 2012)

Ramsay, Iain, 'Rationales for Intervention in the Consumer Marketplace', (1st edn, Office of Fair Trading, 1984)

Rasmussen, Hjalte, 'On Law and Policy in the European Court of Justice: A Comparative Study in Judicial Policymaking', (1st edn, Martinus Nijhoff, 1986)

Redmond, William, 'Three Modes of Competition in the Marketplace', American Journal of Economics and Sociology, vol. 72/no. 2, (2013), pp. 423

Reich, Norbert, ' Vulnerable Consumers in EU Law', in Leczykiewicz, Dorota and Weatherill, Stephen eds., The Images of the Consumer in EU Law: Legislation, Free Movement and Competition Law (1st edn, Hart, 2016), 139

Reich, Norbert, Micklitz, Hans-W., and Rott, Peter, 'European Consumer Law', (2nd edn, Intersentia, 2014)

Ricketson, Sam, 'The Paris Convention for the Protection of Industrial Property: A Commentary', (1st edn, Oxford University Press, 2015)

Riis, Thomas and Trzaskowski, Jan, 'Det markedsretlige persongalleri', in Dahl, Børge, Riis, Thomas and Trzaskowski, Jan eds., Liber Amicorum: Peter Møgelvang-hansen (1st edn, Ex Tuto Publishing, 2016), pp. 439

Ripstein, Arthur, 'Reasonable Persons in Private Law', in Bongiovanni, Giorgio, Sartor, Giovanni and Valentini, Chiara eds., Reasonableness and Law (1st edn, Springer, 2009), 255

Rognstad, Ole-Andreas, 'Intellectual Property Law', in Baudenbacher, Carl ed., The Handbook of EEA Law (1st edn, Springer, 2016), 703

Rognstad, Ole-Andreas, Stenvik, Are and Lassen, Birger Stuevold, 'Fra norsk rettspraksis', NIR, vol. 3 (2002), p. 310

Rosati, Eleonora, 'Luxembourg, we have a Problem: Where have the Advocates General Gone?', Journal of Intellectual Property Law & Practice, vol. 9/no. 8, (2014), pp. 619

Rose, Carol M., 'Introduction: A Real Property Lawyer Cautiously Inspects the Edges of Intellectual Property', in Dreyfuss, Rochelle Cooper and Ginsburg, Jane C. eds., Intellectual Property at the Edge: The Contested Contours of IP (1st edn, Cambridge University Press, 2014), 1

Ross, Alf, 'Directives and Norms', (1st edn, Clark, 1968)

Ross, Alf, 'Legal Fictions', in Hughes, Graham ed., Law, Reason, and Justice: Essays in Legal Philosophy, (1st edn, Springer, 1969), 217

Ross, Alf, 'On Law and Justice', (1st edn, University of California Press, 1959)

Rothman, Jennifer E., 'Initial Interest Confusion: Standing at the Crossroads of Trademark Law', Cardozo Law Review, vol. 27/no. 1, (2005), pp. 105

Samuel, Geoffrey, 'An Introduction to Comparative Law – Theory and Method', (1st edn, Hart, 2014)

Samuel, Geoffrey, 'Does One Need an Understanding of Methodology in Law before One can Understand Methodology in Comparative Law?', in van Hoecke, Mark ed., Methodologies of Legal Research: What Kind of Method for what Kind of Discipline? (1st edn, Hart, 2011), 177

Samuel, Geoffrey, 'Is Law a Fiction?', in Del Mar, Maksymilian and Twining, William eds., Legal Fictions in Theory and Practice (1st edn, Springer, 2015), 31

Sanders, Anselm Kamperman and Maniatis, Spyros M., 'A Consumer Trade Mark: Protection Based on Origin and Quality', European Intellectual Property Review, vol. 15/no. 11, (1993), pp. 406

Schauer, Frederick, 'Legal Fictions Revisited', in Del Mar, Maksymilian and Twining, William eds., Legal Fictions in Theory and Practice (1st edn, Springer, 2015), 113

Schauer, Frederick, 'Playing by the Rules – A Philosophical Examination of Rule-Based Decision-Making in Law and in Life', (1st edn, Clarendon, 1992)

Schennen, Detlef, 'Chapter II: Revocation and Prior Rights', in Singer, Margarete and Stauder, Dieter eds., European Patent Convention: A Commentary: Volume 2 (1st edn, Sweet & Maxwell, 2003), 560

Schlag, Pierre, 'Essay and Responses – Spam Jurisprudence, Air Law, and the Rank Anxiety of Nothing Happening (A Report on the State of the Art)', Geo. L.J., vol. 97/no. 3, (2009), pp. 803

Schlag, Pierre, 'Rules and Standards', UCLA Law Review, vol. 33 (1985-1986), pp. 379

Scholes, Annette Nordhausen, 'Behavioural Economics and the Autonomous Consumer', Cambridge Yearbook of European Legal Studies, vol. 14/no. 1, (2011), pp. 297

Schovsbo, Jens, 'Forord', in Schovsbo, Jens ed., Netværksmødet 2003: Immaterialrettens Afbalancering (1st edn, Jurist- og Økonomforbundets Forlag, 2003), 7

Schovsbo, Jens, 'Lærebog i Immaterialret: Ophavsret, Patentret, Brugsmodelret, Designret, Varemærkeret', (7th edn, Jurist- og Økonomforbundets Forlag, 2005)

Schovsbo, Jens, Rosenmeier, Morten and Petersen, Clement Salung, 'Immaterialret: Ophavsret, Patentret, Brugsmodelret, Designret, Varemærkeret', (4th edn, Jurist- og Økonomforbundets Forlag, 2015)

Schovsbo, Jens, Rosenmeier, Morten and Petersen, Clement Salung, 'Immaterialret: Ophavsret, Patentret, Brugsmodelret, Designret, Varemærkeret', (5th edn, Jurist- og Økonomforbundets Forlag, 2018)

Schovsbo, Jens, and Svendsen, Niels Holm, 'Designret: Designloven Med Kommentarer', (2nd edn, Jurist- og Økonomforbundets Forlag, 2013)

Schuhmacher, Wolfgang, 'The Unfair Commercial Practices Directive', in Hilty, Reto M. and Henning-Bodewig, Frauke eds., Law Against Unfair Competition: Towards a New Paradigm in Europe? (1st edn, Springer, 2007), 127

Scourfield, Tom, 'United Kingdom', in Hasselblatt, Gordian N. ed., Community Trade Mark Regulation (EC) no 207/2009: A Commentary (1st edn, Beck/Hart, 2015), 1443

Segal, Jeffrey A., 'Judicial Behaviour', in Goodin, Robert E. ed., The Oxford Handbook of Political Science (1st, Oxford University Press, 2011), 275

Senftleben, Martin, 'Trade Mark Protection – A Black Hole in the Intellectual Property Galaxy?', IIC, vol. 42/no. 4, (2011), pp. 383

Senftleben, Martin, 'Vigeland and the Status of Cultural Concerns in Trade Mark Law – The EFTA Court Develops More Effective Tools for the Preservation of the Public Domain', IIC, vol. 48/no. 6, (2017) pp. 683

Seville, Catherine, 'EU Intellectual Property Law and Policy', (2nd edn, Edward Elgar, 2016)

Shavell, Steven. 'Law Versus Morality as Regulators of Conduct', American Law and Economics Review, vol. 4/no. 2, (2002), pp. 227

Sherry, Suzanna. 'Foundational Facts and Doctrinal Change', University of Illinois Law Review, vol. 2011/no. 1, (2011), pp. 145

Sibony, Anne-Lise, 'Can EU Consumer Law Benefit from Behavioural Insights? An Analysis of the Unfair Practices Directive', in Mathis, Klaus ed., European Perspectives on Behavioural Law and Economics. Foundations and Applications (1st edn, Springer, 2015), 71

Sibony, Anne-Lise, and Helleringer, Geneviève, 'EU Consumer Protection and Behavioural Sciences: Revolution Or Reform?', in Alemanno, Alberto and Sibony, Anne-Lise eds., Nudge and the Law: A European Perspective (1st edn, Hart, 2016), 209

Siems, Mathias, 'Comparative Law', (1st edn, Cambridge University Press, 2014)

Siems, Mathias M., 'A World Without Law Professors', in van Hoecke, Mark ed., Methodologies of Legal Research: What Kind of Method for what Kind of Discipline? (1st edn, Hart, 2011), 71

Simon, Ilanah, 'How Does "Essential Function" Doctrine Drive European Trade Mark Law?', IIC, vol. 36/4, (2005), pp. 401

Sjåfjell, Beate, 'Towards a Sustainable European Company Law: A Normative Analysis of the Objectives of EU Law, with the Takeover Directive as a Test Case', (1st edn, Kluwer Law International, 2009)

Skouris, Vassilios, 'Preface', in Peers, Steve, et al eds., The EU Charter of Fundamental Rights: A Commentary (1st edn, Hart, 2014), i

Skrzydło-Tefelska, Ewa, and Żuk, Mateusz, 'Article 9: Rights Conferred by a Community Trade Mark', in Hasselblatt, Gordian N. ed., Community Trade Mark Regulation (EC) no 207/2009: A Commentary (1st edn, Beck/Hart, 2015), 295

Smiths, Jan M., 'Nordic Law in a European Context: Some Comparative Observations', in Husa, Jaakko, Nuotio, Kimmo and Pihlajamäki, Heikki eds., Nordic Law – between Tradition and Dynamism (1st edn, Intersentia, 2007), 55

Sørensen, Karsten Engsig, Nielsen, Poul Runge and Danielsen, Jens Hartig, 'EU-Retten', (6th edn, Jurist- og Økonomforbundets Forlag, 2014)

Spaak, Torben, 'Guidance and Constraint: The Action-Guiding Capacity of Neil MacCormick's Theory of Legal Reasoning', Law and Philosophy, vol. 26 (2007), pp. 343

Stauder, Dieter, 'Article 64: Extent of Protection', in Singer, Margarete and Stauder, Dieter eds., European Patent Convention: A Commentary: Volume 1 (1st edn, Sweet & Maxwell, 2003), 236

Stavropoulos, Nicos, 'Objectivity in Law', (1st edn, Clarendon Press, 1996)

Stenvik, Are, 'Patentrett', (3rd edn, Cappelen Damm, 2013)

Stenvik, Are, 'Protection for Equivalents Under Patent Law – Theories and Practice', IIC, vol. 32/no. 1, (2001), pp. 1

Stigler, George J., 'Economists and Public Policy', AEI Journal on Government and Society, vol. May/June (1982), pp. 13

Stone, David, 'European Union Design Law. A Practitioners' Guide.', (2nd edn, Oxford University Press, 2016)

Stone, David, 'European Union Design Law – Highlights of Recent Case Law from the Court of Justice', IP Litigator, vol. January/February (2013), pp. 32

Stuyck, Jules, 'Consumer Concepts in EU Secondary Law', Working Paper (2014), pp. 1

Stuyck, Jules, 'Setting the Scene', in Micklitz, Hans-W. *et al* eds., Cases, Materials and Text on Consumer Law (1st edn, Ius Commune, 2010), 1

Sullivan, Kathleen M., 'The Justices of Rules and Standards', Harvard Law Review, vol. 106/no. 1, (1992), pp. 22

Sunstein, Cass R., 'Why Nudge? The Politics of Libertarian Paternalism', (1st edn, Yale University Press, 2014)

Tamm, Ditlev, 'The Danes and their Legal Heritage', in Dahl, Børge *et al* eds., Danish Law in a European Perspective (1st edn, Thomson – GadJura, 1996), 33

Thaler, Richard, 'Toward a Positive Theory and Consumer Choice', in Kahneman, Daniel and Tversky, Amos eds., Choices, Values, and Frames (1st edn, Cambridge University Press, 2000), 269

Thaler, Richard H. and Sunstein, Cass R., 'Nudge: Improving Decisions about Health, Wealth, and Happiness', (1st edn, Yale University Press, 2008)

Thommessen, Ø., 'Lovene om Varemerker og Fellesmerker av 3. Mars 1961', (1st edn, Gyldendal Norsk Forlag, 1961)

Thorning, Louise Christina, and Finnanger, Solvår Winnie, 'Trademark Protection in the European Union with a Scandinavian View', (1st edn, Thomson Reuters, 2010)

Towfigh, Emanuel V. and Petersen, Niels, 'Economic Methods for Lawyers', (1st edn, Edward Elgar, 2015)

Tridimas, Takis, 'Bifurcated Justice: The Dual Character of Judicial Protection in EU Law', in Rosas, Allan, Levits, Egils and Bot, Yves eds., The Court of Justice and the Construction of Europe: Analyses and Perspectives on Sixty Years of Case-Law – La Cour de Justice et la Construction de l'Europe: Analyses et Perspectives de Soixante Ans de Jurisprudence (1st edn, T.M.C. Asser Press, 2013), 367

Tridimas, Takis, 'Dialogue with National Courts: Dialogue, Cooperation and Instability', in Arnull, Anthony and Chalmers, Damian eds., The Oxford Handbook of European Union Law (1st edn, Oxford University Press, 2015), 403

Tridimas, Takis, 'Knocking on Heaven's Door. Fragmentation, Efficiency and Defiance in the Preliminary Reference Procedure', Common Market Law Review, vol. 40, (2003), pp. 9

Tridimas, Takis, 'The General Principles of EU Law', (2nd, Oxford University Press, 2006)

Tridimas, Takis, 'the Role of the Advocate General in the Development of Community Law: Some Reflections', Common Market Law Review, vol. 34/no. 6, (1997), pp. 1349

Trzaskowski, Jan, 'Behavioural Economics, Neuroscience, and the Unfair Commercial Practises Directive', Journal of Consumer Policy, vol. 34/no. 3, (2011), pp. 377

Trzaskowski, Jan, 'The Unfair Commercial Practices Directive and Vulnerable Consumers', Conference Paper, (2013), pp. 1

Tuori, Kaarlo, 'Can we Still Speak of the Coherence of Law?', in Modéer, Kjell Å ed., Aleksander Peczenik Memorial Seminar: Pufendorf Seminar, Lund, March 10, 2006a (1st edn, Corpus Iuris, 2007), pp. 56

Tuori, Kaarlo, 'Critical Legal Positivism', (1st edn, Ashgate, 2002)

Tuori, Kaarlo, 'Law and Beyond the Nation-State', in Modéer, Kjell Å and Diestelkamp, Bernhard eds., Liber Amicorum Kjell Å Modéer (1st edn, Juristförlaget, 2007), 691

Tuori, Kaarlo, 'Ratio and Voluntas: the Tension between Reason and Will in Law', (1st edn, Ashgate, 2010)

Tuori, Kaarlo, 'Self-Description and External Description of the Law', NoFo vol. 2 (2006b), pp. 27

Tvarnø, Christina D., and Nielsen, Ruth, 'Retskilder Og Retsteorier', (5th edn, Jurist- og Økonomforbundets Forlag, 2017)

Twigg-Flesner, Christian, 'The Importance of Law and Harmonisation', in Leczykiewicz, Dorota and Weatherill, Stephen eds., The Images of the Consumer in EU Law: Legislation, Free Movement and Competition Law (1st edn, Hart, 2016), 183

Underhill, Paco, 'Why we Buy: The Science of Shopping: Updated and Revised for the Internet, the Global Consumer and Beyond', (1st edn, Simon & Schuster, 2009)

Vaihinger, Hans, 'The Philosophy of 'as if': A System of the Theoretical, Practical and Religious Fictions of Mankind', (1st edn, Harcourt Brace, 1924)

van Hoecke, Mark, 'Legal Doctrine: Which Method(s) for what Kind of Discipline?', in van Hoecke, Mark ed., Methodologies of Legal Research: What Kind of Method for what Kind of Discipline? (1st edn, Hart, 2011), 1

van Hoecke, Mark, 'Preface', in van Hoecke, Mark ed., Methodologies of Legal Research: What Kind of Method for what Kind of Discipline? (1st edn, Hart, 2011)

van Hoecke, Mark, and Ost, Francois, 'Legal Doctrine in Crisis: Towards a European Legal Science', Legal Studies, vol. 18 (1998), pp. 197

Vaquero, Álvaro Núñez, 'Five Models of Legal Science', Revus, vol. 19 (2013), pp. 53

Viken, Monica, 'Legal Aspects regarding the use of Market Surveys as Evidence', NIR, vol. 3/(2012), pp. 220

Viken, Monica, 'Markedsundersøkelser som Bevis i Varemerke- og Markedsføringsrett', (1st edn, Oslo, Gyldendal, 2011)

Visser, Derk, 'The Annotated European Patent Convention', (23rd edn, H.Tel., 2015)

Vranken, Jan, 'Methodology of Legal Doctrinal Research: A Comment on Westerman', in van Hoecke, Mark ed., Methodologies of Legal Research: What Kind of Method for what Kind of Discipline? (1st edn, Hart, 2011), 111

Vries, Sybe Alexander de, 'The Court of Justice's 'Paradigm Consumer" in EU Free Movement Law', in Leczykiewicz, Dorota, and Weatherill, Stephen eds., The Images of the Consumer in EU Law: Legislation, Free Movement and Competition Law (1st edn, Hart, 2016), 401

Wadlow, Christopher, 'An Historical Perspective II: The Unified Patent Court', in Pila, Justine and Wadlow, Christopher eds., The Unitary EU Patent System (1st edn, Hart, 2015), 33

Wadlow, Christopher, 'The Impact of General EU Law on Industrial Property Law', in Ohly, Ansgar and Pila, Justine eds., The Europeanization of Intellectual Property Law: Towards a European Legal Methodology (1st edn, Oxford University Press, 2013), 103

Wadlow, Christopher, 'The Law of Passing-Off: Unfair Competition by Misrepresentation', (5th edn, Sweet & Maxwell, 2016)

Waelde, Charlotte, Brown, Abbe, Kheria, Smita *et al*, 'Contemporary Intellectual Property: Law and Policy', (4th edn, Oxford University Press, 2016)

Wager, Hannu, and Jayashree, Watal, 'Introduction to the TRIPS Agreement', in Taubman, Antony, Hannu, Wager and Jayashree, Watal eds., A Handbook on the WTO TRIPS Agreement (1st edn, Cambridge University Press, 2012), 1

Wallberg, Knud, 'Brug af Andres Varemærker i Digitale Medier: Et Bidrag til Afklaring af Varemærkerettens Indhold og Grænseflader', (1st edn, Jurist- og Økonomforbundets Forlag, 2015a)

Wallberg, Knud, 'Varemærket: Varemærkeloven og Fællesmærkeloven Med Kommentarer: EF-Varemærket, Madrid-Protokollen', (4th edn, Jurist- og Økonomforbundets Forlag, 2008)

Wallberg, Knud, 'The European Trademark Reform. An Overview from a Danish Perspective', NIR, vol. 1 (2015b), pp. 107

Wallberg, Knud and Ravn, Michael Francke, 'Varemærkeret: Varemærkeloven og Fællesmærkeloven Med Kommentarer', (5th edn, Jurist- og Økonomforbundets Forlag, 2017)

Watkins, Dawn, and Mandy Burton, 'Introduction', in Watkins, Dawn and Mandy Burton eds., Research Methods in Law (1st edn, Routledge, 2013), 1

Weatherall, Kimberlee, 'The Consumer as the Empirical Measure of Trade Mark Law', Modern Law Review, vol. 80/no. 1, (2017), pp. 57

Weatherill, Stephen, 'Art. 38 – Consumer Protection', in Peers, Steve *et al* eds., The EU Charter of Fundamental Rights: A Commentary (1st edn, Hart, 2014), 1005

Weatherill, Stephen, 'Consumer Policy', in Craig, Paul and Búrca, GrÁinne De eds., The Evolution of EU Law (2nd edn, Oxford University Press, 2011), 837

Weatherill, Stephen, 'Empowerment is Not the Only Fruit', in Leczykiewicz, Dorota and Weatherill, Stephen eds., The Images of the Consumer in EU Law: Legislation, Free Movement and Competition Law (1st edn, Hart, 2016a), 203

Weatherill, Stephen, 'EU Consumer Law and Policy', (2nd edn, Edward Elgar, 2013)

Weatherill, Stephen, 'From Economic Rights to Fundamental Rights', in Vries, Sybe Alexander de, Bernitz, Ulf and Weatherill, Stephen eds., The Protection of Fundamental Rights in the EU After Lisbon (1st edn, Hart, 2013), 11

Weatherill, Stephen, 'Law and Values in the European Union', (1st edn, Oxford University Press, 2016b)

Weatherill, Stephen, 'Who is the 'Average Consumer'?', in Weatherill, Stephen and Bernitz, Ulf eds., The Regulation of the Unfair Commercial Practices Under EC Directive 2005/29 (1st edn, Oxford, Hart, 2007), 115

Weatherill, Stephen, and Beaumont, Paul, 'EU Law: The Essential Guide to the Legal Workings of the European Union', (3rd edn, Penguin, 1999)

Wessman, Richard, 'Varumärkeslagen: En Kommentar', (1st edn, Wolters Kluwer, 2014)

Westerman, Pauline C., 'Open or Autonomous? The Debate on Legal Methodology as a Reflection of the Debate on Law', in van Hoecke, Mark ed., Methodologies of Legal Research: What Kind of Method for what Kind of Discipline? (1st edn, Hart, 2011), 87

White, T. A. Blanco, and Robin, Jacob, 'Kerly's Law of Trade Marks and Trade Names', (10th edn, Sweet & Maxwell, 1972)

Widera, Philipp, 'Has Pemetrexed revived the Doctrine of Equivalence?', Journal of Intellectual Property Law & Practice, vol. 13/no. 3, (2018), pp. 238

Widmer, Pierre, 'Liability Based on Fault: Introduction', in European Group on Tort Law ed., European Group on Tort Law: Principles of European Tort Law: Text and Commentary (1st edn, Springer, 2005), 64

Wiebe, Andreas, 'How Much Nature for the Consumer? Misleading Advertising, Trademark Law and the European Average Consumer Standard in the Food Sector', Corporate Governance eJournal, no. 32, 2015, (2015), pp. 1

Wilhelmsson, Thomas, 'The Abuse of the "Confident Consumer" as a Justification for EC Consumer Law', Journal of Consumer Policy, vol. 27 (2004), pp. 317

Wilhelmsson, Thomas, 'The Average European Consumer: A Legal Fiction?', in Wilhelmsson, Thomas, Paunio, Elina and Pohjolainen, Annika eds., Private Law and the Many Cultures of Europe (1st edn, Kluwer Law International, 2007a), 243

Wilhelmsson, Thomas, 'the Informed Consumer v the Vulnerable Consumer in European Unfair Commercial Practices Law – A Comment', in Howells, Geraint *et al*, The Yearbook on Consumer Law 2007 (1st edn, Ashgate, 2007b), 211

Willett, Chris, and Morgan-Taylor, Martin, 'Recognising the Limits of Transparency in EU Consumer Law', in Devenney, James and Kenny, Mel eds., European Consumer Protection: Theory and Practice (1st edn, Cambridge University Press, 2012), 143

Witte, and Bruno de, 'Direct Effect, Primacy and the Nature of the Legal Order', in Craig, Paul and Búrca, Gráinne de eds., The Evolution of EU Law (1st edn, Oxford University Press, 2011), 323

Zahle, Henrik, 'At Forske Ret – Essays Om Juridisk Forskningspraksis', (1st edn, Gyldendal, 2007)

Zweigert, Konrad, and Kötz, Hein, 'Introduction to Comparative Law', (3rd edn, Oxford University Press, 1998)

Ørstavik, Inger Berg, 'Ekvivalenslærens Innhold som Rettsnorm i Norsk Patentrett', NIR, vol. 2 (2010), pp. 134

Internet Sources

Annual Report 2017 Judicial Activity. Synopsis of the judicial activity of the Court of Justice, the General Court and the Civil Service Tribunal, available at: https://curia.europa.eu/jcms/upload/docs/application/pdf/2018-04/_ra_2017_en.pdf (last visited 26 May 2019)

Arnold, Richard, presentation under the heading 'The average consumer in passing off' as part of a conference under the heading 'The Average Consumer in Trade Mark Law and Passing Off' held at UCL in London 25 February 2015, at 17:50: https://www.youtube.com/watch?v=zqTC_-beZxk (last visited 26 May 2019)

EFTA, 'This is EFTA 2015', (booklet on EFTA), available at: http://www.efta.int/publications/this-is-efta-2015 (last visited 26 May 2019)

Mellor, James, presentation under the heading 'The average consumer generally' as part of a conference under the heading 'The Average Consumer in Trade Mark Law and Passing Off' held at UCL in London 25 February 2015, at 3:50: https://www.youtube.com/watch?v=zqTC_-beZxk (last visited 26 May 2019)

Phillips, Jeremy (responsible for the post), 'A Nerd By Any Other Name', The IP Kat (28 October 2004): http://ipkitten.blogspot.dk/2004/10/nerd-by-any-other-name.html (last visited 26 May 2019)

Phillips, Jeremy (responsible for the post), 'The Consumer Protection Function of Trade Marks: Just so?', The IP Kat (21 November 2014): http://ipkitten.blogspot.dk/2014/11/the-consumer-protection-function-of.html (last visited 26 May 2019)

Stanford Philosophy Encyclopedia section 1. Available at: https://plato.stanford.edu/entries/abduction/ (last visited 26 May 2019)

Printed by Printforce, the Netherlands